Dimensions of Human Behavior

Person and Environment

Dimensions of Human Behavior

Person and Environment

Elizabeth D. Hutchison

Virginia Commonwealth University

Visual Essays edited by Shelley Kowalski
University of Oregon

738-0905

Pine Forge Press

Thousand Oaks, California • London • New Delhi

For information, address:

Pine Forge Press
A Sage Publications Company
2455 Teller Road
Thousand Oaks, California 91320
(805) 499-4224
E-mail: sales@pfp.sagepub.com

Sage Publications Ltd.
6 Bonhill Street
London EC2A 4PU
United Kingdom

Sage Publications India Pvt. Ltd.
M-32 Market
Greater Kailash I
New Delhi 110 048 India

Production Management: Scratchgravel Publishing Services
Copy Editor: Margaret C. Tropp
Typesetter: Scratchgravel Publishing Services
Visual Essays Design: Lisa Mirski Devenish
Cover Designer: Deborah Davis and Greg Draus
Production Coordinator: Windy Just

Printed in the United States of America
99 00 01 02 03 10 9 8 7 6 5 4 3 2

Library of Congress Cataloging-in-Publication Data

Dimensions of human behavior. Person and environment / [edited] by
    Elizabeth Hutchison.
        p.   cm.
    Includes bibliographical references (p.   ) and index.
    ISBN 0-8039-9032-4 (pbk.)
    1. Social psychology.   2. Human behavior.   3. Social structure.
4. Social service.   I. Hutchison, Elizabeth.   II. Title: Person and
environment.
    HM251.D55   1999
    302—dc21   98-31533
                                                                        CIP

ABOUT THE AUTHOR

Elizabeth D. Hutchison, M.S.W., Ph.D., is an Associate Professor in the School of Social Work at Virginia Commonwealth University. She has practiced in health, mental health, and child welfare. Her major areas of interest are child welfare, social work practice with nonvoluntary clients, and the human behavior curriculum. She teaches human behavior courses at the B.S.W., M.S.W., and doctoral levels.

ABOUT THE PUBLISHER

Pine Forge Press is a new educational publisher, dedicated to publishing innovative books and software throughout the social sciences. On this and any other of our publications, we welcome your comments. Please call or write us at:

Pine Forge Press
A Sage Publications Company
2455 Teller Road
Thousand Oaks, CA 91320
(805) 499-4224
E-mail: sales@pfp.sagepub.com

Visit our new World Wide Web site, your direct link to a multitude of online resources:
http://www.pineforge.com

To Hutch, who provides constancy and change,
and whose encouragement and technical expertise
made this book possible.

BRIEF CONTENTS

CONTENTS

REFLECTION   *A Day in the Life of a School Social Worker:*
One Person's Multifaceted Social Work Practice / 64

PART II   The Multiple Dimensions of Person

VISUAL ESSAY   *Understanding the Whole Person / 70*

CHAPTER 3   The Biological Person / 81

by Stephen French Gilson

CHAPTER 4   The Psychological Person: Cognition, Emotion, and Self / 109

by Joseph Walsh

CHAPTER 5

The Psychological Person: Stress, Coping, and Adaptation / 133

by Joseph Walsh

CHAPTER 6 ## The Spiritual Person / 157

by Michael J. Sheridan

REFLECTION *An Interview with John: Social Work Practice That Integrates Biological, Psychological, and Spiritual Person / 189*

by Martin Schwartz

PART III ## The Multiple Dimensions of Environment

VISUAL ESSAY *Being in the World / 194*

CHAPTER 7 ## The Physical Environment / 203

CHAPTER 8   **Social Institutions and Social Structure / 231**

CHAPTER 9   **Culture / 265**

by Linwood Cousins

CHAPTER 10 Formal Organizations / 297

CHAPTER 11 Communities / 327

CHAPTER 12 **Social Movements / 353**

CHAPTER 13 **Small Groups / 379**

by Elizabeth P. Cramer

BRIEF CONTENTS:
THE CHANGING LIFE COURSE

PREFACE

I have always been intrigued with human behavior. I didn't know any social workers when I was growing up—or even know there was a social work profession—but I felt an immediate connection to social work and social workers during my junior year in college when I enrolled in an elective course entitled Introduction to Social Work and Social Welfare. What attracted me most was the approach social workers take to understanding human behavior. I was a sociology major, minoring in psychology, and it seemed that each of these disciplines — as well as disciplines such as economics, political science, and ethics—added pieces to the puzzle of human behavior; that is, they each provided new ways to think about the complexities of human behavior. Unfortunately, it wasn't until several years later when I was a hospital social worker that I began to wish I had been a bit more attentive to my course work in biology, because that discipline holds other pieces to the puzzle of human behavior. But when I sat in that Introduction to Social Work and Social Welfare course, it seemed that the pieces of the puzzle were coming together. I was inspired by the optimism about creating a more humane world, and I was impressed by an approach to human behavior that clearly cut across disciplinary lines.

Just out of college, amid the tumultuous societal changes of the late 1960s, I became an M.S.W. student. I began to recognize the challenge of developing the holistic understanding of human behavior that has been the enduring signature of social work. I also was introduced to the tensions in social work education, contrasting breadth of knowledge versus depth of knowledge. I found that I was unprepared for the intensity of the struggle to apply what I was learning about general patterns of human behavior to the complex, unique situations that I encountered in the field. I was surprised to find that being a social worker meant learning to understand my own behavior as well as the behavior of others.

Since completing my M.S.W., I have provided services in a variety of social work settings, including hospitals, nursing homes, state mental health and mental retardation institutions, community mental health centers, a school-based program, public child welfare, and a city jail. Sometimes the target of change was an individual, and other times the focus was on bringing about changes in dyadic or family relationships, communities, organizations, or social institutions. I have also performed a variety of social work roles, including case manager, therapist, teacher, advocate, group facilitator, consultant, collaborator, program planner, administrator, and researcher. I love the diversity of social work settings and the multiple roles of practice. My varied experiences have strengthened my commitment to the pursuit of social justice, enhanced my fascination with human behavior, and reinforced my belief in the need to understand human behavior holistically.

For almost twenty years, I have been teaching courses in Human Behavior in the Social Environment to undergraduate students, M.S.W. students, and doctoral students. The students and I struggle with the same challenges that I encountered as a social work student in the late 1960s: the daunting task of developing a holistic understanding of human behavior, the issue of breadth versus depth of knowledge, and discovering how to use general knowledge about human behavior in unique practice situations. My experiences as student and teacher of human behavior led me to write this book.

Holistic Understanding of Human Behavior

Social work has historically used the idea of person-in-environment to develop a holistic understanding of human behavior. This idea has also become popular with most social and behavioral science disciplines. Recently, we have recognized the need to add the aspect of time to the person-environment construct, to capture the dynamic, changing nature of person-in-environment.

The purpose of this book is to help you breathe life into the abstract idea of person-in-environment. I identify relevant dimensions of person and relevant dimensions of environment, and my colleagues and I present up-to-date reports on theory and research about each of these dimensions. All the while, we encourage you to link the micro world of personal experience with the macro world of social trends—to recognize the unity of person and environment. We help you make this connection by showing how several of the same theories have been used to understand dimensions of both person and environment. A companion volume to this book, *The Changing Life Course,* builds on the multiple dimensions of person and environment analyzed in this book and demonstrates how they work together with dimensions of time to produce patterns in unique life course journeys.

Breadth versus Depth

The most difficult challenge I face as a student and teacher of human behavior is to develop a broad, multidimensional approach to human behavior without unacceptable sacrifice of depth. It is indeed a formidable task to build a knowledge base both wide and deep. After years of struggle, I have reluctantly concluded that although both breadth and depth are necessary, it is better for social workers to err on the side of breadth. Let me tell you why.

Social workers are doers; we use what we know to tell us what to do. If we have a narrow band of knowledge, no matter how impressive its depth, we will "understand" the practice situations we encounter only from this perspective. This will lead us to use the same solutions for all situations, rather than to tailor solutions to the unique situations we encounter. The emerging risk and resilience literature suggests that human behavior is influenced by the multiple risk factors and protective factors inherent in contemporary social arrangements. What we need is a multidimensional knowledge base that allows us to scan widely for and think critically about risk factors and protective factors and to craft multipronged intervention programs to reduce risks and to strengthen protective factors.

To reflect recent developments in the social and behavioral sciences, this book introduces dimensions of human behavior that are not covered in similar texts. Chapters on the biological and spiritual dimensions of person, the physical environment, social institutions, and social movements provide important insights into human behavior not usually covered in social work texts. In addition, we provide up-to-date information on the typically identified dimensions of human behavior.

General Knowledge and Unique Situations

The purpose of the social and behavioral sciences is to help us understand *general patterns* in person-environment transactions. The purpose of social work assessment is to understand *unique configurations* of person and environment dimensions. Those who practice social work must weave what they know about unique situations with general knowledge. To assist you in this process, we begin each chapter with a story or stories, which we then intertwine with contemporary theory and research. We also call attention to the successes and failures of theory and research to accommodate human diversity related to gender, race and ethnicity, culture, sexual orientation, and disability.

Features of This Book

The task of developing a solid knowledge base for doing social work can seem overwhelming. For me it is an exciting journey, because I am learning about my own behavior as well as the behavior of others. What I learn enriches my personal life as well as my professional life. My colleagues and I wanted to write a book that provides a state-of-the-art knowledge base, but we also want you to find pleasure in your learning. We have tried to write as we teach, with enthusiasm for the content and a desire to connect with your process of learning. We have developed some special features that we hope will aid your learning process:

- *Visual Essays.* Each part of the book is introduced with a visual essay that makes use of photographs and other graphic materials to help you "see" the dimensions of person and environment and to imagine how they work together.

- *Reflections.* Each part of the book ends with a reflection on social work practice that chronicles the activities of one social worker and provides questions for you to consider how this social worker's practice reflects the content of the preceding chapters.

- *Exhibits.* Much information in every chapter has been helpfully summarized in graphical or tabular form to help you understand and retain ideas.

- *Case Studies.* Each chapter in the book begins with one or more narratives so that you can put human faces on theory and research; these case studies help you weave unique, real-life situations with general knowledge.

- *Margin Notes.* Margin notes are used in Chapters 3–14 as reminders of the ideas from the theoretical perspectives discussed in Chapter 2. The margin notes can help you become more comfortable with the multitheoretical knowledge base of human behavior presented in the book.

- *Implications for Social Work Practice.* Each chapter ends with a set of practice principles that will guide your use of general knowledge in social work practice.

One Last Word

I imagine that you, like me, are intrigued by human behavior. That is probably a part of what attracts you to social work. I hope that reading this book reinforces your fascination with human behavior. I also hope that when you finish this book, and in the years to come, you will have new ideas about the possibilities for social work action.

You can help me in my learning process by letting me know what you liked or didn't like about the book. Write to me at the following address, and describe your reactions to the book. You can also fill out and return the form at the end of the book. Enjoy a life full of learning about human behavior!

Elizabeth D. Hutchison
School of Social Work
Virginia Commonwealth University
Richmond, Virginia 23284-2027
E-mail: ehutch@atlas.vcu.edu

ACKNOWLEDGMENTS

This book and its companion volume have taken far longer to write than I had planned or others had counted on. It has often been a lonely journey, and yet I am indebted to so many people who have helped in so many ways to make the books a reality.

In the beginning, and through the entire journey, Steve Rutter, publisher and president of Pine Forge Press, was a constant presence. He has a vision of a new generation of social work textbooks, strong in both content and pedagogy and affordable to students. He has forgiven delays and missed deadlines, pushed me to exhaustion and anger, encouraged me when I was discouraged, left me alone when I was cranky and testy, and provided the ideas for the best features of the books.

Jeff Edleson and Richard Tolman got me involved in this project and gave important feedback and encouragement at the various stages of development. Jim Forte provided helpful insights in the early stages of conceptualization.

I am eternally grateful to the contributing authors, who came on board after the project was conceptualized, reinvigorated me with their enthusiasm, and reminded me of the synergy of collaborative efforts. They have responded in good humor to tight deadlines, requests for special features, and multiple reviews and requests for revisions.

In the later stages of this project, a whole host of people connected to Pine Forge Press became part of my life and helped me with the many processes and procedures that are involved in getting a project like this into print. Becky Smith amazed me! She took our early drafts, rough as they were and written in multiple voices, and helped us polish and bring coherence to them. She was demanding yet gentle-hearted in her feedback. She is really good at what she does! Peggy Tropp competently provided further editorial refinement. Anne Draus of Scratchgravel Publishing Services guided the production of the books. Anne kept me on track with gentle prompts, and she has taken the glitches and complications of this complex project in stride. First Sherith Pankratz and later Windy Just helped with the many details that were a mystery to me. Shelley Kowalski edited the visual essays.

Helpful comments and contributions were provided by the social work educators who reviewed drafts of the manuscript. They are:

Susan Fineran, Boston University
James Forte, Christopher Newport University
Maureen Connelly, Frostburg State University
Lois Cowles, Idaho State University
Kathryn Skinner, Marywood College
Cynthia Bishop, Meredith College
Anita Sharma, Northeast Louisiana University
Wayne Busby, Pittsburgh State University
Martin Bloom, University of Connecticut
Nancy Kropf, University of Georgia

James Taylor, University of Kansas
Michael Spencer, University of Michigan
David Lawson Burton, University of Michigan
David Pugh, Youngstown State University
James Wolk, Georgia State University
Alice Chornesky, New Mexico State University
William D. Eldridge, Ohio State University
William R. Downs, University of Northern Iowa
Carol H. Meyer, Columbia University
Nadine Medlin, Creighton University
Margaret Fontanesi, University of Arkansas, Fayetteville

Several students in the VCU School of Social Work have made contributions to the project at different stages. Susan Cummings and Sheila Crowley provided research assistance in the early conceptual phase of the project. Dan Arnold developed the web site resources.

I am also grateful to Dean Frank Baskind and my colleagues at the School of Social Work at VCU. They have tolerated my preoccupation, my whining, and my absences. They filled in for me while I was on scholarly leave to begin work on the book during the fall of 1994. They have given me support and encouragement and reined in their incredulity that this project was taking so long. I am particularly grateful for the support and insights of Stephen Gilson, Marcia Harrigan, Michael Sheridan, and Joe Walsh.

Special gratitude goes to my students, who have also been my teachers. They have added fun to my learning as well as to my teaching. Their contributions are embedded in the fabric of this book.

My deepest gratitude goes to my family, Hutch, Brad, and Abby. They have given me space to work, taken an interest in my project, supported me through the times of discouragement, and showered me with love. Each has added something to the project. Brad prodded me to include material on the physical environment. Abby helped me appreciate the journalistic style of using narratives to develop ideas and provided editorial assistance with the first draft. Hutch patiently assisted with my computer emergencies, helped us turn words into graphics, and brought order to the chaos of computer files created over time by multiple authors and multiple software systems.

■   ■   ■

Grateful acknowledgments are made to reprint the following:

Chapter 2: Reprinted by permission. Hutchison, E., and L. Charlesworth. 1998. "Human Behavior in the Social Environment: The Role of Gender in the Expansion of Practice Knowledge." In *The Role of Gender in Practice Knowledge*, ed. J. Figueirra-McDonough, F. E. Netting, and A. Nichols-Casebolt. Pp. 41–92. New York: Garland.

Exhibit 6.1: Reprinted by permission of the Society for Spirituality and Social Work. O'Brien, P. 1992. "Social Work and Spirituality: Clarifying the Concept for Practice." *Spirituality and Social Work Journal.* 3 (1), 13–18.

Exhibit 6.4: Reprinted by permission of the Society for Spirituality and Social Work. Titone, A. M. 1991. "Spirituality and Psychotherapy in Social Work Practice." *Spirituality and Social Work Communicator,* 2 (1), 7–9.

Chapter 7, "A Place of Her Own for Cheryl": Lifchez, R., and C. Davis. 1987. "Living Upstairs, Leaving Home, and at the Moscow Circus." In *With Wings: An Anthology of Literature By and About Women with Disabilities,* ed. M. Saxton and F. Howe. Springer Publishing Company, Inc., New York 10012. Used by permission.

Exhibit 8.2: Reprinted by permission. Farley, R. 1996. *The American Reality: Who We Are, How We Got Here, Where We Are Going.* Figure 4.4, p. 118. New York: Russell Sage Foundation.

Exhibit 10.1: A. Farazmand, *Modern Organizations: Administrative Theory in Contemporary Society.* Copyright © 1994 by Praeger Publishers. Reproduced with permission of Greenwood Publishing Group, Inc., Westport, CT.

Exhibit 10.8: Reprinted with permission of the publisher. From *Cultural Diversity in Organizations,* copyright © 1993 by T. Cox Jr., Berrett-Koehler Publishers, Inc., San Francisco, CA. All rights reserved.

Exhibit 10.11: R. Golembiewski, *Modern Organizations.* Copyright © 1994 by Praeger Publishers. Reproduced with permission of Greenwood Publishing Group, Inc., Westport, CT.

Chapter 11, Ann and Evan Maxwell Story: From *Edge City* by Joel Garreau. Copyright 1991 by Joel Garreau. Used by permission of Doubleday, a division of Bantam Doubleday Dell Publishing Group, Inc.

Exhibit 13.3: From K. E. Reid. 1997. *Social Work Practice with Groups: A Clinical Perspective* (2nd ed.). Pacific Grove, CA: Brooks/Cole.

Additional acknowledgments are made to reprint the following photographs:

pages 6, 64, *Learning Spanish Grammer* © Joe Rodrigeuz/Black Star; page 6, *Domestic Violence* © Corbis Bettman; page 7, *Grace Thomas and Her Children* © Marc Pesetsky/Reuters Corbis-Bettman; page 7, *Brownie Troop Ceremony* © Emily Niebrand; page 8, *Line Up for Pork* © AP/Wide World Photos; page 9, *No Money* © AP/Wide World Photos; page 9, *Blind Man in Wheelchair* © Emily Niebrand; page 9, *Tired Diabetic* © Stacey Kowalski.

page 70, *Lolita Just, 8 months pregnant* © Michael Just; page 70, *Diabetes Treatment* © Corbis-Bettman; page 70, *Diabetic Girl 1* © Emily Niebrand; page 70, *Diabetic Girl 2* © Emily Niebrand; page 71, *Strong Arm* © Emily Niebrand; page 71, *Manicurist* © Stacey Kowalski; page 72, *Poor Children with Doll* © Gordon Parks/Library of Congress; page 72, *Woman Office Cleaner* © Stacey Kowalski; page 72, *Brick Washer* © Emily Niebrand; page 73, *Navigation Games at Museum* © Reuter/Corbis-Bettman; page 73, *Beny Alagen* at Packard Bell © Reuter/Corbis-Bettman; page 74, *Stressed Executive* © Emily Niebrand; page 74, *Angry Phone Call* © Emily Niebrand; pages 75, 189, *Crashed Out* © Stacey Kowalski; page 76, *Couple in Park* © Stacey Kowalski; page 77, *Joggers* © Stacey Kowalski; page 77, *Bus Lift* © Stacey Kowalski; page 78,

Angled Crucifix © Stacey Kowalski; page 78, *Hindu Wedding* © Corbis-Bettman; page 78, *Altruism* © Emily Niebrand; page 79, *Meditation* © Emily Niebrand; page 79, *Japanese Gardens* © Stacey Kowalski.

page 194, *Peaceful Bedroom* © Stacey Kowalski; page 194, *Crowded Women's Refuge* © Reuter/Corbis-Bettman; page 195, *Desks and Desks* © Reuter/Corbis-Bettman; page 195, *Children Take a Nap* © Reuter/Corbis-Bettman; page 196, *Ellis Island* © AP/Wide World Photos; page 197, *MCWC Worker* © Stacey Kowalski; page 197, *Earthquake* © Rick Bowmer/AP; page 198, *New Mexican Children's Parade* © Annie Popkins; page 198, *Chess Players in Park* © AP/Wide World Photos; page 199, *Stop Destroying Children* © Gabe Kirchehheimer/Black Star; page 199, *Lolita Demonstration* © P.F. Bentley/Black Star; pages 200, 428, *Women on Stairs* © Annie Popkins; page 201, *Happy Female Family* © Emily Niebrand; page 201, *Summer Camp Friends* © Thom O'Connor/Black Star; page 201, *Father Feeding Christian* © Reuter/Corbis-Bettman.

CONTRIBUTING AUTHORS

Leanne W. Charlesworth, M.S.W., Ph.D., is a project director with the University of Maryland School of Social Work's welfare research group. She has held various child welfare positions. Her areas of interest include social welfare policy and poverty issues. She has taught human behavior and research at the School of Social Work at Virginia Commonwealth University.

Linwood Cousins, M.S.W., M.A., Ph.D., holds a joint appointment as an Assistant Professor of Social Work and Anthropology at Western Michigan University. He has practiced in child welfare and family services, and his current research, teaching, and practice interests include the socio-cultural manifestations of race, ethnicity, and class in the lives and schooling of African American youths and their families.

Elizabeth P. Cramer, M.S.W., Ph.D., L.C.S.W., A.C.S.W., is an Assistant Professor in the School of Social Work at Virginia Commonwealth University. Her primary research and service areas are domestic violence, lesbian and gay male issues, and group work. She teaches in the areas of foundation and clinical practice, social justice, and lesbian and bisexual women. She lives with her partner, their adoptive daughter, and four lovely pets.

Stephen French Gilson, M.S.W., Ph.D. in Medical Sciences, is an Assistant Professor in the School of Social Work at Virginia Commonwealth University. Following receipt of his doctoral degree, he was awarded an Intramural Research Training Award Fellowship at the Addiction Research Center, Neuroscience Branch, Neuroimaging and Drug Action Section, National Institute on Drug Abuse. His research interests include the development of disability identity and the politics of the disability community; disability theory; and self determination, choice, and empowerment by disabled people. He teaches courses in human behavior, health issues in social work practice, and behavioral science theory. Dr. Gilson identifies as a disabled person and is actively involved in disability advocacy.

Martin Schwartz, M.S.W., Ed.D., L.C.S.W., B.C.D., is a Professor in the School of Social Work at Virginia Commonwealth University. He previously taught at Columbia University School of Social Work and Yale University Department of Psychiatry. His major areas of interest are HIV/AIDS and the gay male identity process. He teaches human behavior, clinical practice, and social work with AIDS patients. He maintains a varied clinical practice and was elected as a member of the Social Work Practice Academy.

Michael J. Sheridan, M.S.W., Ph.D., is an Associate Professor in the School of Social Work at Virginia Commonwealth University. Her practice experience includes work in health, mental health, corrections, and youth and family services. Her major areas of interest are spirituality and social work, families and substance abuse, and the needs of incarcerated persons. She teaches social justice and research at the B.S.W, M.S.W., and doctoral levels.

Nancy R. Vosler, M.S.W., Ph.D., is an Associate Professor in the George Warren Brown School of Social Work, Washington University in St. Louis. Her research interests include the impact of unemployment and poverty on families, welfare reform, and nonmarital co-parenting. She recently published a book entitled *New Approaches to Family Practice: Confronting Economic Stress* (Sage, 1996). She teaches social policy and family practice courses and is Coordinator of the School's Family Therapy Specialization. She serves on the Board of Fathers' Support Center, St. Louis, a new agency addressing the service needs of unmarried fathers and their children.

Joseph Walsh, M.S.W., Ph.D., L.C.S.W., is an Associate Professor in the School of Social Work at Virginia Commonwealth University. He was educated at Ohio State University and has worked for 25 years in community mental health settings. His major areas of interest are clinical social work, serious mental illness, and psychopharmacology. Dr. Walsh teaches courses in social work practice and research while maintaining a small clinical practice.

Dimensions of Human Behavior

Person and Environment

PART I

A Multidimensional Approach for Multifaceted Social Work

Consider the following people:

- Caroline O'Malley is knocking at the door of a family reported to her agency for child abuse.
- Sylvia Smith and other members of her team at the rehabilitation hospital are meeting with the family of an 18-year-old man who is recovering from head injuries sustained in a motorcycle accident.
- Mark Adams is on the way to the county jail to assess the suicide risk of an inmate.
- Helen Moore is preparing a report for a legislative committee.
- Juanita Alvarez is talking with a homeless man about taking his psychotropic medications.
- Stan Weslowski is meeting with a couple who would like to adopt a child.
- Andrea Thomas is analyzing the results of a needs assessment recently conducted at the service center for older adults where she works.
- Anthony Pacino is wrapping up a meeting of a cancer support group.
- Sam Belick is writing a social history for tomorrow's team meeting at the high school where he works.
- Sarah Sahair has just begun a meeting of a recreational group of 9- and 10-year-old girls.
- Jane Kerr is facilitating the monthly meeting of an interagency coalition of service providers for substance-abusing women and their children.
- Ann Noles is planning a fund-raising project for the local Boys and Girls Clubs.
- Meg Hart is wrapping up her fourth counseling session with a lesbian couple.
- Chien Liu is meeting with a community group concerned about youth gang behavior in their neighborhood.
- Mary Wells is talking with one of her clients at a rape crisis center.

What do these people have in common? You have probably guessed that they are all social workers. They work in a variety of settings, and they are involved in a variety of activities, but they all are doing social work. Social work is, indeed, a multifaceted profession. And because it is multifaceted, social workers need a multidimensional understanding of human behavior. This book provides such an understanding.

The purpose of the two chapters in Part I is to introduce you to a multidimensional way of thinking about human behavior and to set the stage for subsequent discussion. In Chapter 1, you will be introduced to the multiple dimensions of person, environment, and time that will serve as the framework for the book. You will be given some tools to help you think critically about the multiple theories and varieties of research that make up our general knowledge of these dimensions of human behavior. And you will learn about the organization of the book. In Chapter 2, you will encounter eight theoretical perspectives that contribute to multidimensional understanding. You will learn about their central ideas and their scientific merits. Most important, you will consider the usefulness of these eight theoretical perspectives for social work. The reflection at the end of Part I illustrates the multifaceted nature of a day in the life of one social worker.

Looking at a Complex World

Consider a line.

It is a single-dimensional representation of reality but still is useful.

It can give direction, like an arrow.

It can make connections between two items to show a relationship.

But a single-dimensional line is limited in what it can tell us about the real world. The real world is multidimensional. It has spatial and temporal dimensions. And within these dimensions, people live out very complex and dynamic lives.

Now consider a cube.

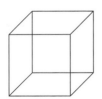

It too is useful for describing and analyzing aspects of the world. It shows not only direction and relationship, as a line does, but also depth. But a cube too is limited in what it can tell us about the real world.

Consider how your image of the cube might change if you looked at it interacting with many other elements, as in a kaleidoscope. So it is with the world in which social workers function. This book urges you to look at the world as you might look at the ever-changing pattern in a kaleidoscope, appreciating its many elements and its complexity.

The multiple aspects of human behavior—person, environment, and time—will be explored throughout these pages. As you read, you will need to hold various dimensions of person, environment, and time in mind in order to develop a more complete picture of the world and of social work.

Furthermore, you will need to develop the ability to look at situations from as many different perspectives as possible. As a social worker, you will need to be able to look at each individual and situation from a variety of angles and positions.

Imagine that you have been called on to help a youngster having trouble adjusting to school. Naturally, you should look at the educational environment to understand the forces influencing the child.

But you can't stop there. You also need to look at the home environment. In this case, you might learn that the family is headed by a single mother who is overcoming domestic abuse and who has recently moved with her family into subsidized housing.

In looking for ways to assist the troubled child and her family, you might consult with social service agencies that have helped other children and families through difficult periods.

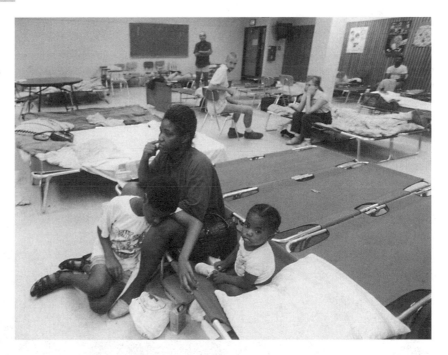

You might also need to help link the child and her family with other organizations outside the school setting, such as this Brownie troop, so she has positive interactions with other children and adults while trying to overcome her school difficulties.

Social workers generally encounter a great many other situations and settings. However, every case can be approached, as this one has been, from multiple perspectives.

As a social worker, you should also have a good grasp of general knowledge about human behavior and at the same time be able to apply that knowledge flexibly. General knowledge, which comes from both theory and research, helps social workers put their clients' lives into larger perspective. At the same time, all social workers must recognize that each individual responds to events in a unique way.

This line of people wrapping around the block is composed of people on welfare waiting for handouts of meat. Theory and research about social conditions and trends can give us a general perspective on the lives of these people.

However, only by discovering the unique details of their lives can we understand what brings individuals like these to us for help. Yes, they are part of a large group of poor people who share many traits. But each one has also experienced life in a unique way that no other person has experienced.

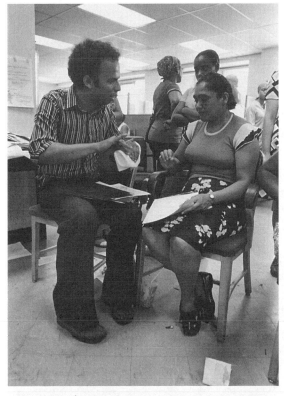

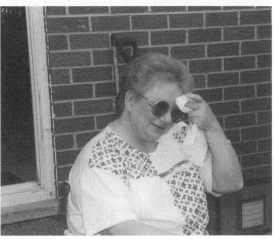

General knowledge about human behavior and a good understanding of individuals' lives are the basic tools we need to do social work.

CHAPTER 1

Aspects of Human Behavior: Person, Environment, Time

SINA'S DETERMINATION TO SURVIVE

Sina is an attractive, soft-spoken, and gracious Cambodian-American woman who looks younger than her 44 years. She lives in the suburbs of a small Eastern city with her husband and four of her five children. If you speak with Sina, you will need to be very attentive and enunciate clearly, because Sina still struggles with the English language. You will be impressed with the sincerity of her efforts, however. If Sina gets to know you well, she may tell you some of her story, and you most likely will be struck by the matter-of-fact manner in which she recounts a story that to you probably seems quite remarkable.

Sina grew up in a suburb of Phnom Penh, Cambodia. Because there were so many children in the family into which she was born, Sina and her two younger sisters were sent to be raised by relatives who lived nearby and who could not have children of their own. Sina had a happy childhood with these relatives and thinks of them as her parents (therefore, I will refer to them as her parents). Sina's parents were merchants, and she worked in the store with them. Her marriage at the age of 16 was arranged. Both Sina and her husband completed the equivalent of our high school education and were considered, in Cambodia, to be quite well educated. Sina's husband worked as a mechanic until they left the Phnom Penh area.

When the Khmer Rouge soldiers came to the outskirts of Phnom Penh in April 1975, Sina had no idea that her pleasant life was about to be so radically changed. The soldiers spread the word that the Americans were planning to bomb Phnom Penh and that everyone had to leave the area for a little while. The whole city was quickly evacuated. Sina, who was pregnant, headed for the countryside with her husband, 4-year-old daughter, and very large extended families from both sides. In the countryside, people were instructed to build houses, which most of them did not know how to do. Very soon, it became apparent that all was not well. The soldiers became very dictatorial and were particularly harsh with people who appeared educated and otherwise demonstrated "Western ways." Sina and her family started trying to hide their "Western ways." They got rid of eyeglasses and books, changed their linguistic style to appear less educated, and tried to fake farming skills.

Things got worse. People, particularly men, began disappearing in the night, and gunshots were heard. Stories spread about terrible things happening. Rice began to disappear, and there was not enough to eat. The evacuees were forced to go to political meetings that lasted for hours. Fear was continual, but nighttime was the worst. That was when people disappeared and the gunshots were heard. The realization that they were prisoners came slowly. But the atrocities intensified, and soon it was not uncommon to witness people, even family members, being shot in front of you. People had to work in the rice fields all day, but they were not allowed to eat the rice. Many people were starving to death. Malaria and dysentery were common. Members of Sina's extended family held up as well as could be expected, but her husband's brothers disappeared and were believed to be dead, and his sisters became ill and died. Sina's baby was underweight and sick at delivery, and Sina was relieved to have enough milk to feed her. Starvation and fear were constant companions.

Sina and her family stayed in the camp for about three years. She became pregnant again. Her husband's parents died of starvation. One night, Sina said to her husband, "We have to escape." Her husband said, "No, I am afraid." Sina insisted that they were going, that she could take no more, and she knew that there had to be a better life for her children. Sina rounded up her parents and her sisters and told them that they were going. They too were afraid and tried to dissuade her. But Sina was resolved to go, and they left in the middle of the night—pregnant Sina, her husband and two daughters, her parents, and her two sisters. Some of them were without shoes. They were very anxious about the possibility of being apprehended by the soldiers as they fled, and there were land mines everywhere.

Leaving camp, they entered the jungle. They ate whatever they could find— Sina is very vague when she talks about what they ate—and were constantly afraid of being apprehended by soldiers or stepping on a land mine. Night was still the most frightening time. Sina's husband was always near tears. After a few days, they could only travel a few miles per day, because they were too weak to walk and some were sick with malaria and dysentery. Sina is not sure how long it took them to get to Thailand, but she estimates four or five months. They just kept moving, with no clear idea where they were headed. In Thailand, they stayed in a United Nations camp for about two years. It was months before they could take solid food, and it took them a long time to recover from the aftermath of starvation and trauma. Sina gave birth to her third child soon after reaching the camp, and a fourth child before they left the camp to come to the United States.

Sina and her family were sponsored as immigrants by a refugee resettlement organization. With the help of a sponsor and an agency social worker, they were settled into an apartment when they first arrived, and Sina and her husband soon found jobs. The social worker also helped the family to understand and navigate the school system and the health care system and to make sense of their new world. Over the years, Sina has made episodic contact with agency social workers to seek information about community organizations or to discuss challenges the family was facing. Recently, she came to the agency to talk about her husband's constant sadness.

Sina's husband is still employed by the same construction company that hired him as a newly arrived refugee. At first, Sina worked as a hotel maid, but she now has a job as a case aide with a social service organization. When money is tight, she still works part-time as a maid. A fifth child was born after arriving in the United States, and all of the children have made good adjustments to their new environment. Sina and her husband put a high value on education, and the children have done well in school. The family's sponsor helped them to buy a house in the suburbs a few years ago.

Sina and members of her extended family report that they still have trouble being in the dark, and they get very anxious if the food supply runs low. Sina's husband seems very sad all the time, and he sometimes suggests that he should have stayed and died. Sina, however, thinks they had no choice but to leave, for the sake of the children, and she is matter-of-fact about their struggles. Sina is always motivated to learn something new. She has become a U.S. citizen and is putting great efforts into learning English. She has converted from Buddhism to Catholicism, but her husband has not. Sina and her husband sometimes have a great deal of tension between them because he thinks she is more assertive than women should be. Sina is not sure if this problem would have arisen between them if they had been able to continue with their lives in Cambodia. Sina is more comfortable in her current environment than her husband is, but she sometimes wonders why Americans are so brash, so loud, so direct, so demanding, and so lacking in humility.

The Complexity of Human Behavior

As eventful as it has been, Sina's story is still unfolding. As a social worker, you will become a part of many unfolding life stories, and you will want to have a way of thinking about them. The purpose of this book is to provide a way for you to think about the nature and complexities of the people and situations that are at the center of social work practice. Three major aspects of this approach to human behavior are the person, the environment, and time.

If we focus on the *person*, we observe that Sina must have been blessed with a healthy biological constitution initially and must have been nurtured well in her youth. She was able to carry babies to term through starvation, illness, and a journey through a jungle. She was able to recover in the hospital camp when many others died of damaged bodies and/or broken spirits. She has emotional resilience and a belief in her own capabilities. Sina and her husband have both survived physically, but she has survived spiritually as well, with a zest for life and hope for the future that he lacks.

If we focus on the *environment*, we see many influences on Sina's story. Consider first the physical environment: Sina moved from a comfortable suburban environment into a very primitive rural prison camp. From there, she wandered in the jungle, with tigers and snakes as her fellow travelers and torrential rains, imagined soldiers, and land mines as foes. Her next stop was a hospital camp and, finally, an American city.

Sina's story has also been powerfully influenced by the geopolitical unrest of her early adulthood. Her relationships with social institutions have changed over time, and she has had to learn new rules based on her changing place in the social structure. Prior to evacuation, as an educated urban woman, she enjoyed high status and the respect that comes with it. In the prison camp, she had to learn to conceal that status and encountered greater powerlessness than she could have previously imagined. In the United States, she has often experienced the loss of status that comes from language barrier, regardless of one's educational background.

Culture, too, has been a powerful influence in Sina's story. She faced no stigma for being given to relatives at birth, because that was not an unusual custom in Cambodia where there was no birth control and extended families were close. Culture recommended what may appear to the reader to be an early marriage and that her partner would be chosen for her. Culture also held that women lack power and influence, and yet Sina assumed a powerful role in her family's escape from the prison camp. Culture accorded a high value to humility, indirect communication, and saving face. The suburban, modernized lifestyle in which Sina was reared contributed a value on education that was not shared with Cambodians who lived in rural areas. And now, Sina lives biculturally. She assists the social workers at her agency to understand the communication patterns of Cambodian clients, and yet she is often baffled by the communication patterns of her native-born American neighbors and coworkers. She is influenced by changing gender roles but is unhappy with the tension that such changes have produced in her marital relationship.

The momentous changes Sina encountered in the physical environment are paralleled by changes in community and organizational environments over time. Sina moved from a suburban community, where she was surrounded by extended family and long-term friends, to a prison camp, where fear was the driving force of relationships and loss of loved ones a common occurrence. Next she moved to a hospital camp, where recovery and taking note of losses took all the available energy. Finally, she moved to a city in the United States, where many people were willing to help but everything seemed strange and the language barrier was a serious impediment. Sina has found several organizations particularly helpful in mediating her struggles with resettlement: the refugee resettlement program that sponsored her family, the social service organization for which she works, the Catholic church of which she is a member, and the schools her children attend. Sina has drawn strength and courage from her associations with these organizations, and she differs from her husband in this regard.

A final dimension of the environment, family, is paramount to Sina. She was lucky that she did not have to leave many family members behind or see them die in the prison camp. Her husband was not so lucky. Sina's children are central to her life, and she suggests that they have motivated her to survive and reach beyond survival with hope. Sina and her husband are devoted to each other, but she is sorry about the tension in their relationship and her husband's enormous sadness. She is grateful, however, that her husband has not self-medicated his grief with alcohol as she has seen other Cambodian-American men do in her work.

If we now focus on the influence of *time*, we see that war and atrocity, escape, and resettlement have been powerful life events for Sina and her family. These events have left many trace effects in their current life. Experiences with past environments have left them with fear of the dark, panic regarding food shortages, and a preference for suburban environments. Both Sina and her husband have minor chronic medical problems from their years of hardship. Sina's husband has no surviving member of his family of origin, and his grief, and perhaps survivor's guilt, over the massive losses is severe. Language barrier is the most persistent reminder that this is not home. Luckily, Sina has managed to smuggle some personal documents and photographs out of Cambodia, and she uses these to invite fond memories of past joyful events, including her traditional Cambodian wedding. These memories give her pleasure, but Sina lives mostly in the present, while anticipating the future with confidence. To her husband, however, the past holds more positive meaning than either the present or future does.

Person, environment, and time interact dynamically. Relationships are reconfigured as the multiple influences on human behavior ebb and flow. The actions of one person can only be understood in relation to the actions of other people and in relation to ever-changing situations. Person and environment depend on each other for their definition; the same person in a different environment, or the same environment with a different person, most likely will yield different behaviors. In reality, of course, any configuration or situation involves multiple persons and multiple environments. We will be referring, at points, to this approach as a **transactional approach**, because that is the name used by other scholars who focus on changing relationships among inseparable aspects of a unity (Altman & Rogoff, 1987; Dewey & Bentley, 1949).

Sina's story provides a good illustration of the inseparability of person, environment, and time. What made her decide to attempt to escape from the prison camp? Was it something within her, something about her physical and social environment, or something about that time of her life? Or a combination of all three? What leads her, now, to reach out for help for her husband? It is impossible to focus on person, environment, and time independently; they are inseparable.

A Multidimensional Approach

Thinking about human behavior as changing configurations of person and environment over time is a multidimensional approach. Such an approach is not new. Social work has historically recognized human behavior as an interaction of person with environment. The earliest social work practice book, *Social Diagnosis,* written by Mary Richmond in 1917, identified the social situation and the personality of the client as the dual focus of social work assessment. In the late 1960s, general systems theory and other related formulations were incorporated into the way social work scholars think about human behavior (Anderson & Carter, 1974; Bloom, 1984; Germain, 1973; Hartman, 1970; Hearn, 1958, 1969; Meyer, 1976; Pincus & Minahan, 1973; Siporin, 1975). These approaches—which have been called systems, ecological, ecosystem, and configural approaches—have helped social workers to understand the "pattern and flow" (Altman & Rogoff, 1987) of the processes and activities involved in the relationships between person and environment.

We need, of course, to move beyond general statements about the inseparability of person and environment and about changing configurations to bring these ideas alive in our day-to-day experiences as social workers and to understand how to talk with Sina about her concerns. A vast multidisciplinary literature, of both theory and research, is available to help us. The good news is that the multifaceted nature of this literature provides a broad knowledge base for the varied settings and roles involved in social work practice. The bad news is that this literature is highly fragmented. What we need is a structure for organizing our thinking about this multifaceted, fragmented literature.

The multidimensional approach provided in this book should help. This approach is built on the three major aspects of human behavior: person, environment, and time. Although in this book and in the companion volume we will focus on each of these aspects separately, keep in mind that no single aspect can be entirely understood without attention to the other aspects.

We can get a clearer picture of these three aspects if we think about the important dimensions of each—about what it is that we should study about person, about environment, and about time. Exhibit 1.1 provides a graphic overview of the dimensions of person, environment, and time discussed in this book.

Keep in mind that **dimension** refers to a feature that can be focused on separately but that cannot be understood without also considering other features. The dimensions identified in this book are usually studied as detached or semidetached realities, with one dimension characterized as causing or leading to another. However, I do not see dimensions as detached realities, and I am not presenting a causal model. I want instead to show how these dimensions work together, how they are embedded with each other, and how many possibilities are opened for social work

EXHIBIT 1.1

Person, Environment, and Time Dimensions

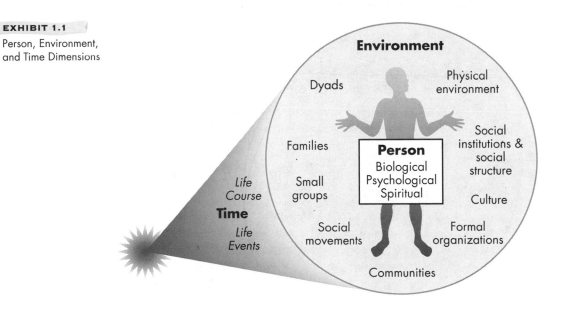

practice when we think about human behavior this way. I do think, however, that focusing on specific dimensions one at a time can clarify general, abstract statements about changing configurations of person and environment.

Personal Dimensions

Any story could be told from the perspective of any person in the story. I have told a story from Sina's perspective, but this story could have been told from the perspectives of a variety of other persons: a Khmer Rouge soldier, Sina's husband, her mother, one of her children, a member of the sponsoring family, the social worker. You will want to recognize the multiple perspectives held by different persons involved in the stories of which you become a part in your social work activities.

You also will want tools for thinking about the various dimensions of the persons involved in these stories. Until recent years, social work scholars described the approach of social work as *psychosocial,* giving primacy to psychological dimensions of the person. Personality, ego states, emotion, and cognition are the important features of the person in this approach. Currently, however, the social work literature, like contemporary scholarship in other disciplines (for example, Johnson et al.,1990; Kaplan, Sadock, & Grebb, 1994; Longres, 1995; Saleeby, 1992), takes a **biopsychosocial approach**. In this approach, psychology cannot be separated from biology. Emotions and cognitions affect the health of the body, and are affected by it.

In recent years, social work scholars, as well as psychology scholars, have been debating whether spirituality should also be considered a personal dimension. Recent developments in neuroscience have delivered a near-fatal blow to the Cartesian dualism of mind/body and have generated new explorations of the unity of the biological, psychological, and spiritual dimensions of the person. For example, recent research has focused on the ways that emotions and thoughts, as well as spiritual states, influence the immune system (Maier, Watkins, & Fleshner, 1994; Moyers, 1993). Thus this book gives substantial coverage to all three of these dimensions.

Environmental Dimensions

Social workers have always thought about the environment as multidimensional. As early as 1901, Mary Richmond presented a model of case coordination that took into account not only personal dimensions but also family, neighborhood, civic organizations, private charitable organizations, and public relief organizations (see Exhibit 1.2). Like contemporary social workers, Richmond saw the environment as multidimensional. Although social work scholars have continually revised their understanding of the multidimensional environment, Richmond's model is a forerunner of contemporary models.

Several models for classifying dimensions of the environment have been proposed more recently, six of which are summarized in Exhibit 1.3. Among social work scholars, Anderson and Carter (1974) made a historic contribution to systemic thinking about human behavior with the first edition of their *Human Behavior in the Social Evnironment: A Social Systems Approach,* one of the earliest textbooks on human behavior authored by social workers. Their classification of

EXHIBIT 1.2

Mary Richmond's 1901 Model of Case Coordination

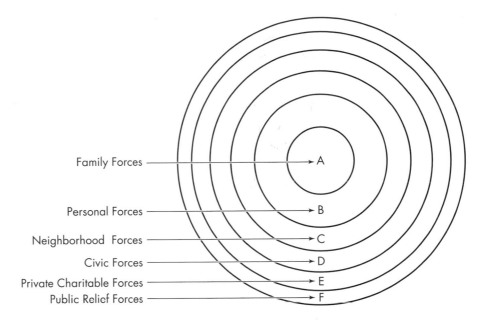

Family Forces ——————→ A

Personal Forces ——————→ B

Neighborhood Forces ——————→ C

Civic Forces ——————→ D

Private Charitable Forces ——————→ E

Public Relief Forces ——————→ F

A. *Family Forces.*
   Capacity of each member for
   Affection.
   Training.
   Endeavor.
   Social development.

B. *Personal Forces.*
   Kindred.
   Friends.

C. *Neighborhood Forces.*
   Neighbors, landlords, tradesmen.
   Former and present employers.
   Clergymen, Sunday-school teachers,
     fellow church members.
   Doctors.
   Trade-unions, fraternal and benefit
     societies, social clubs,
     fellow-workmen.
   Libraries, educational clubs, classes,
     settlements, etc.
   Thrift agencies, savings-banks,
     stamp-savings, building and loan
     associations.

D. *Civic Forces.*
   School-teachers, truant officers.
   Police, police magistrates, probation
     officers, reformatories.

Health department, sanitary
   inspectors, factory inspectors.
Postmen.
Parks, baths, etc.

E. *Private Charitable Forces.*
   Charity organization society.
   Church of denomination to which
     family belongs.
   Benevolent individuals.
   National, special, and general relief
     societies.
   Charitable employment agencies and
     work-rooms.
   Fresh-air society, children's aid
     society, society for protection of
     children, children's homes, etc.
   District nurses, sick-diet kitchens,
     dispensaries, hospitals, etc.
   Society for suppression of vice,
     prisoner's aid society, etc.

F. *Public Relief Forces.*
   Almshouses.
   Outdoor poor department.
   Public hospitals and dispensaries.

Source: Richmond, 1901.

EXHIBIT 1.3
Models of
Environmental
Dimensions

Field/Author	Proposed Dimensions	Definition of Dimension
Psychology Bronfenbrenner (1989)	Microsystem	Face-to-face settings
	Mesosystem	Linkages between microsystems containing the focal person
	Exosystem	Linkages between two settings, one of which does not contain the focal person but influences her or him
	Macrosystem	Culture, subculture, or other broad social context
Ford & Lerner (1992)	Natural environments	Products of nature (rain, land, gravity, plants)
	Designed environments	Physical aspects constructed by humans
	Human environments	Personal interactions
	Sociocultural environments	Humanly created means for maintaining coherent, large social groups
Social Work Anderson & Carter (1990)	Culture & society	Culture as way of life; society as group of people who have learned to live and work together
	Communities	Population whose members consciously identify with one another
	Organizations	Social system with purpose of achieving specific goals
	Groups	Patterns of association in which persons engage most of their "selves" from day to day
	Families	Social unit with primary responsibility for socialization
Bloom (1990)	Primary groups	Two or more persons with relatively persisting face-to-face communications
	Secondary groups	Larger organizations with specialized claim on certain parts of individual's interests and activities
	Sociocultural contexts	Ethnic heritage and societal order
	Physical environment & time	Natural and built environment, personal time and historical time

(continued)

EXHIBIT 1.3

Models of
Environmental
Dimensions
(continued)

Field/Author	Proposed Dimensions	Definition of Dimension
Carter & McGoldrick (1988b)	Nuclear family	Parents and children living together
	Extended family	Multigenerational family
	Community, work, friends	Sources of support and stress for families
	Social, cultural, political, economic	Gender, religion, ethnicity, social class
Schriver (1995)	Families	The intimate units where we carry out most of our lives
	Groups	Two or more individuals with shared purpose and common interaction
	Organizations	Collectivities of people working together to accomplish a goal or goals
	Communities	Collectivities of people with shared interests, regular interaction, and mutual identification

environmental dimensions has had a significant impact on the way social workers think about the environment. Anderson and Carter divide the environment into five dimensions: culture and society, communities, organizations, groups, and families. Some recent models have added the physical environment (natural and designed environments) as a separate dimension. Failure to include the physical environment has most notably hampered social work's ability to respond to persons with disabilities.

In 1958, Herman Stein and Richard Cloward published an edited reader, *Social Perspectives on Behavior: A Reader in Social Science for Social Work and Related Professions.* In the preface, they commented that social work had failed, in the midst of its fascination with dynamic psychology, to keep abreast of developments in sociology, cultural anthropology, and social psychology. Unfortunately, social work continues to fall behind in its incorporation of the "social" in social work. To have an up-to-date understanding of the multidimensional environment, social workers need knowledge about the eight dimensions of environment presented as chapters in this book: the physical environment, social institutions and social structure, culture, formal organizations, communities, social movements, small groups, and families. We also need knowledge about dyadic relationships—relationships between two people, the most basic social relationships. Dyadic relationships receive attention throughout the book, and are the focus of the reflection at the end of Part II. Simultaneous consideration of multiple environmental dimensions provides new possibilities for action, perhaps even new or revised approaches to social work practice.

These dimensions are neither mutually exclusive nor hierarchically ordered. For example, family is sometimes referred to as a social institution; families can also be considered small groups or dyads; and family theorists write about family culture. Remember, dimensions are useful ways of thinking about person/environment configurations, but you should not think of them as detached realities.

Time Dimensions

When I was a doctoral student in a social work practice course, Professor Max Siporin began his discussion about social work assessment with the comment "The date is the most important information on a written social work assessment." This was Siporin's way of acknowledging the importance of time in human behavior, of recognizing that person/environment transactions are ever-changing, dynamic, and flowing.

Carol Werner, Irwin Altman, and Diana Oxley's (1985) thinking about time is particularly useful for social workers. They suggest that we should think in terms of both linear time and cyclical time. **Linear time** is past, present, and future. People, environments, and the relationships between them have histories and futures, as well as a present, as seen in Sina's story. Some person/environment configurations put greater emphasis on the past, some on the present, and some on the future. Sometimes, the pace of change is more rapid than at other times; it is easy to imagine that the three years spent in the prison camps seemed much longer to Sina and her family than the preceding three years in their suburban home. Keep in mind, too, that social workers become part of changing, dynamic situations. In your transactions, remember that you as well as those with whom you interact bring the effects of the past to current transactions, and that the future for all of you will be affected by your current transactions. You should also remember that ways of thinking about human behavior are constantly changing because they are developing in changing configurations of person and environment. For this reason, this book will often tell you about the history of ideas as well as suggest some future possibilities.

Werner et al. (1985) also alert us to the effects of **cyclical time,** which is repetitive, recurring, spiraling. Cycles of behavior can recur in different patterns: daily, weekly, monthly, seasonally, annually, or in some other regular or partially regular pattern. As I work on this book in mid-July, I am cognizant that summer "vacation" is more than half over, and soon my time will be spent preparing lectures, grading papers, and making visits to field agencies, all activities that I do not engage in during the summer. I am also remembering the rhythm of the school semester: the intense activity to get the semester "up and rolling"; the "settling in time" when I think "I can handle this"; the accelerated pace beginning around mid-semester when I am determinedly focused on time management; and the hectic last weeks when, in spite of my best intentions, my health maintenance program is seriously compromised and I find myself wondering "How did I let this happen again?" This cycle has been repeating for almost twenty years, but it is never exactly the same. Stability, as well as change, comes with cyclical time.

There is also a temporal scope, or duration, to changing configurations. In linear time, the scope of some events is brief, such as a birthday party, an accident, loss of a job, winning the lottery, or a natural disaster. Werner et al. (1985) refer to these brief events as *incidents;* in this book, they will be called **life events.** Although life events are brief in scope, they may produce serious and long-lasting effects. Sina's remarkable story includes several of these transformational events, such as evacuation, escape, and resettlement.

Other events are long and complex transactions of people and environments. Werner et al. (1985) refer to these longer events as *stages;* it is the dimension of time that has been incorporated into life stage theories of human behavior. This book, however, uses a life course rather than life stage perspective. As explained in Chapter 2, life stage theories have been criticized for their overstatement of the consistency of the sequence of stages and of the timing of human behavior. In contrast, a **life course perspective** assumes that each person's life has a unique **trajectory**—a long-term pattern of stability and change—based on his/her own unique person/ environment configurations over time, but that shared social and historical contexts produce some commonalities (George, 1993). A life course perspective is stagelike because it proposes that each person experiences a number of **transitions,** or changes in roles and statuses that represent a distinct departure from prior roles and statuses. These transitions may be unique, may be shared with a particular group of persons, or may be widely shared. A life course perspective also recognizes **life course markers** that are widely shared by particular **cohorts**—groups of persons who are of the same age group at the time of a particular social change within a given culture. But it also recognizes the influence of unexpected life events. Sina and her husband share much in common with other parents of adolescent and young adult offspring, but they have also experienced some life events that few of us share. In fact, even though they passed together through these events, it cannot be said that Sina and her husband have shared exactly the same life course.

The General and the Unique

Let's assume that your field instructor has asked you to meet with Sina regarding her concerns about her husband. How will you know how to talk with her and what to talk with her about? What questions will you have before you get started? What do you want to know more about? Most likely, you want to know something about Sina's unique life story, and you must decide how much of that to learn from agency records and your field instructor and how much to wait and hear from Sina herself. But you will probably want to know some other, more general types of information that will not be in the agency record, and that you know your field instructor expects you to take some personal responsibility for learning. This general information might include aspects of Cambodian culture, family functioning, Buddhism and Catholicism, grief reactions, post–traumatic stress reactions, clinical depression, and cross-cultural communication.

Carol Meyer (1993) suggests that effective social work practice involves balancing an individualized (unique) assessment of the specific person(s) in a specific situation with general knowledge about human behavior:

> Practitioners of a profession must draw upon general knowledge about the class of clients of which the particular client may be a representative, and about the general nature of problems indicated in the case. The reliance upon general knowledge to help explain a unique case situation is one of the distinguishing features of a professionally educated vs. a volunteer or agency-trained social worker. (Meyer, 1993, p. 10)

Professional social workers weave idiosyncratic details of a client's story with general knowledge about patterns of relationships between persons and situations. Although Meyer writes about work with one particular client, her suggestions about general knowledge and unique situations could apply equally well to work with families, small groups, neighborhoods, and so on. You might want, for example, to form a mutual aid group of Cambodian men or develop an outreach program in a Cambodian neighborhood.

I want to emphasize two ideas about the relationship between general and unique knowledge: (1) It was Sina's unique story that suggested which general knowledge content was needed. (2) The general knowledge will suggest **hypotheses** to be explored and tested, not facts to be applied, in transactions with Sina (Schutt, 1996, p. 45). For example, your examination of general knowledge may lead you to hypothesize that Sina's husband understands the tenets of Buddhism to direct him to hold himself personally responsible for his own suffering. You may hypothesize that, like many Southeast Asians, he would find it disgraceful to engage in direct conversation about his emotions. You may have learned that although seeking help for physical problems was acceptable in Cambodia, there were no special professions for addressing emotional problems. This understanding may lead you to hypothesize that Sina's husband would be more comfortable talking about his situation in terms of its biological aspects instead of its emotional aspects. Some hypotheses will not be supported in this unique situation, but many hypotheses will prove to be useful. Ultimately, of course, you want to understand how Cambodian culture, family functioning, Buddhism and Catholicism, grief reactions, post–traumatic stress reactions, clinical depression, cross-cultural communication, and all the rest come together to form a whole in Sina's unfolding life story. That is a lot to think about, but such complexity is what makes social work such a demanding and exciting profession.

Today, the need to focus on "'diverse person(s) in diverse environments'" is more important than ever (Germain, 1994, p. 88). We are developing a heightened consciousness of human differences—gender differences, racial and ethnic differences, cultural differences, religious differences, differences in sexual orientation, differences in family forms, and so on—and the need to consider how they affect individuals. These differences among people are not new but simply newly recognized. Because of the globalization of cultures and economies, we are becoming a more diverse society all the time. We are experiencing a new tension to navigate the line between cultural sensitivity and stereotypical thinking about individuals. It is the intent of this book to capture the diversity of human experience in a manner that is respectful of all groups and conveys a positive value of human diversity. However, one of the challenges of diversity is the reality that power arrangements provide different opportunities for different groups. Maximizing the options for members of nondominant groups is part of social work's traditional mission, and it is important for social workers to understand power relations and processes of oppression.

Professional social workers must also struggle continuously with the tension between the general and the unique. The transactional, multidimensional approach presented in this book is well suited to this struggle. As suggested earlier, transactional approaches are interested both in unique events and in patterns across similar events (Altman & Rogoff, 1987). A multidimensional approach allows examination of an idiosyncratic event from several perspectives and opens the possibilities for considering the variety of factors that contribute to a particular transaction. Both the transactional and multidimensional approaches facilitate social work's emphasis on human diversity.

To assist you in moving between general knowledge and unique stories, each chapter in this book will begin, as this one did, with a story or stories. Each of these unique stories will suggest which general knowledge is needed. Then, throughout the chapter, the stories will be woven together with the relevant general knowledge. Keep in mind as you read that general knowledge is necessary, but you will not be an effective practitioner unless you take the time to learn about the unique life course of each person or collectivity you serve.

General Knowledge: Theory and Research

General knowledge has recently come under attack for failure to recognize the uniqueness of persons and situations. Some would suggest that there can be no "general" knowledge because all situations are unique. I think you can see, however, that the details of Sina's unique story are inadequate for guiding you in thinking about how to talk with her and what to talk about. You also need some general knowledge about human behavior, which you can draw from two sources: theory and research.

Social workers use **theory** to help organize and make sense of the situations we encounter. Reid and Smith (1989, p. 45) suggest:

> Scratch any social worker and you will find a theoretician. Her own theoretical perspectives about people and practice may be informed by theories in print (or formal theories) but are put together in her own way with many modifications and additions growing out of her own professional and personal experience.

Thus, theory gives us a framework for interpreting person/environment transactions and planning interventions.

If you are to make good use of theory, you should know something about how it is constructed. **Concepts** are the building blocks of theory. They are symbols that allow us to communicate about the phenomena of interest. Culture, family functioning, Buddhism, grief reaction, post–traumatic stress disorder, clinical depression, and cross-cultural communication are all concepts relevant to Sina's story.

Theoretical concepts are put together to form **propositions** or assertions. For example, attachment theory asserts that loss of an attachment figure leads to a grief reaction. This proposition, which asserts a particular relationship among the concepts of loss, attachment figure, and grief, may help us understand the behavior of Sina's husband.

Social and behavioral science theories are based on **assumptions** about the nature of human social life. These theoretical assumptions have raised a number of controversies, three of which are worth introducing at this point (Burrell & Morgan, 1979; Martin & O'Connor, 1989; Monte, 1995):

- Do the dimensions of human behavior have an **objective reality** that exists outside of a person's consciousness, or is all reality based on personal perception (**subjective reality**)?

- Is human behavior determined by forces beyond the control of the person (**determinism**), or are persons free and proactive agents in the creation of their behavior (**voluntarism**)?

- Are the patterned interactions among people characterized by harmony, unity, and social cohesion or by conflict, domination, coercion, and exploitation?

The nature of these controversies will become more apparent to you in Chapter 2. The contributing authors and I will be taking a middle ground on all of them: We assume that reality has both objective and subjective aspects, that human behavior is partially constrained and partially free, and that social life is marked by both cohesion and conflict.

Theory is one source of general knowledge about human behavior. Research is the other. Rubin and Babbie (1993, p. xxv) remind us that "the practitioner who just conforms to ongoing practices without keeping abreast of the latest research in his or her field is not doing all possible to see that his or her clients get the best possible service." **Research** is typically viewed, in simple terms, as a problem-solving process, or a method of seeking answers to questions. The research process includes a careful, purposeful observation of events with the intent to note and record them in terms of their attributes and to look for patterns in those events.

Just as there are controversies about theoretical assumptions, there are also controversies about what constitutes appropriate research methods for understanding human behavior. Modern science is based on several assumptions, generally recognized as a **positivist perspective:** Findings of one study should be applicable to other groups; complex phenomena can be studied by reducing them to some component part; scientific methods are value-free. **Quantitative methods of research** are the preferred methods from the perspective of modern science. These methods use quantifiable measures of concepts, standardize the collection of data, attend only to preselected variables, and use statistical methods to look for patterns and associations. However, critics of these methods argue that quantitative methods cannot possibly capture the complex nature of social life. These critics suggest a need to replace existing methods with **qualitative methods of research,** providing "a firsthand, holistic understanding of phenomena of interest by means of a flexible strategy of problem formulation and data collection shaped as the investigation proceeds" (Reid & Smith, 1989, p. 87). Researchers using qualitative methods are more likely to present their findings in words than in numbers, and to attempt to capture the settings of behavior. They are likely to report the transactions of researcher and participant, as well as the values of the researcher, because they assume that value-free research is impossible. In this controversy, it is my position that there is no single research method that can adequately capture the whole, the complexity, of human behavior. Both quantitative and qualitative research methods have a place in a multidimensional approach.

Critical Use of Theory and Research

Theories of and research about human behavior are nearly boundless and constantly growing. This book presents an up-to-date account of the current state of knowledge about human behavior, but quite possibly some of this knowledge will eventually be found mistaken. Thus, you are encouraged to be an active reader—reading with a sense of inquiry and curiosity, but also with a healthy skepticism. Eileen Gambrill (1990, p. 75) suggests that the active reader should

EXHIBIT 1.4

Questions Asked by
the Active Reader

1. What is the evidence for this statement?
2. Is this true for all people (for me, for my client, for other people I know)?
3. How can I use this information in my practice?
4. Is there anything left out of this argument?
5. What is the main point of this section?
6. Can I summarize the argument?
7. How does this relate to other evidence about this topic?

Source: Based on Gambrill, 1990, p. 75.

think about the questions listed in Exhibit 1.4. I hope that you will incorporate these questions into your reading of this book.

As you read this book and other sources of general knowledge, you will also want to begin to think critically about the theory and research that they present. Social and behavioral science scholars disagree about the criteria for evaluating theory and research. However, I recommend the criteria presented in Exhibit 1.5 because they are consistent with the transactional, multidimensional approach of this book.

The five criteria for evaluating a theory presented in Exhibit 1.5 are used in Chapter 2 to evaluate eight theoretical perspectives relevant to social work. Judging theory on the basis of coherence and conceptual clarity, testability, and compatibility raises little or no controversy in the social and behavioral science literature. However, the criterion of comprehensiveness is specifically related to the multidimensional approach of this book and would be challenged by many social scientists and social workers. And the criterion of significance for social work practice—relevant only to students of human behavior who are social workers—examines the utility of the theory for a profession that highly values social justice.

Exhibit 1.5 also presents six questions to ask when reading a research report. These criteria can be applied to either quantitative or qualitative research. Many research reports would be strengthened if their authors were to attend to these criteria.

Theory and Research in a Multidimensional Approach

As you travel the journey on which this book takes you, you should have a clear understanding of the assumptions the contributing authors and I make about the role of theory and research in understanding human behavior. That understanding will assist you to be a critical reader of the book. I have written about some of these assumptions earlier in the chapter, but I summarize them for you here for emphasis.

Our assumptions about theory are as follows:

■ Changing configurations of persons and environments may involve unique, unrepeatable events, but they also may involve consistencies and patterns of similar events. Therefore, general statements and theories are possible, but should not be expected to fit all situations or all aspects of a given situation.

EXHIBIT 1.5

Criteria for
Evaluating Theory
and Research

Criteria for Evaluating Theory

Coherence and conceptual clarity. Are the concepts clearly defined and consistently used? Is the theory free of logical inconsistencies? Is it stated in the simplest possible way, without oversimplifying?

Comprehensiveness. Does the theory include multiple dimensions of persons, environments, and time? Does it account for things that other theories have overlooked or been unable to account for?

Testability. Can the concepts and propositions be expressed in language that makes them observable and accessible to corroboration or refutation by persons other than the theoretician?

Compatibility with existing theory and research. With which existing theories is this theory compatible? Incompatible? Is it incompatible with any theories that have received significant empirical validation?

Significance of theory for social work practice. Does the theory assist in the understanding of person and environment transactions over time? Can it accommodate uniqueness and diversity? Does it assist in understanding power arrangements and systems of oppression? Does it value human relationships and recognize the mutual dependence and obligation of persons and communities? Does it promote social justice? Does the theory suggest principles of action?

Criteria for Evaluating Research

Multidimensionality. Does the research include multiple dimensions of persons, environments, and time? If not, do the researchers acknowledge the omissions, connect the research to larger programs of research that include omitted dimensions, and/or recommend further research to include omitted dimensions?

Acknowledgment of the influence of setting. Does the researcher specify attributes of the setting of the research, acknowledge the possible contribution of the setting to research outcomes, and present the findings of similar research across a range of settings?

Acknowledgment of differences in meaning. Does the researcher specify the meanings of the research process to the research participants, and the contributions of these meanings to the research outcomes?

Acknowledgment of the influence of the researcher. Does the researcher specify the attributes of the researcher and the role of the researcher in the observed person/ environment configurations? Does the researcher specify the possible contributions of the researcher to research outcomes?

Specification of inferences. Does the researcher specify how inferences are made, based on the data?

Suitability of measures. Does the researcher use measures that seem suited to, and sensitive to, the situation being researched?

- Each situation allows examination from several perspectives, and using a variety of theoretical perspectives brings more dimensions of the situation into view. Different situations call for different combinations of theoretical concepts and propositions.

- Theories, like situations, are unfolding and should be viewed as tentative statements. Theoretical propositions serve as hypotheses to be tested, not as factual statements about the situation under examination.

- Given the complexity of human behavior, a given transaction is probably not predictable, but we do not rule out the possibility of prediction.

- Our goal as social workers should be to develop maximum understanding of situations in terms of whatever theoretical concepts and propositions apply. Multiple theoretical perspectives are necessary when taking a multidimensional approach to human behavior. This point will be the focus of Chapter 2.

- Social life is fraught with contradictions as well as consistencies, so it is acceptable to use multiple theoretical approaches that introduce contradictions. You will discover some contradictions in the theories discussed in Chapter 2.

Our assumptions about research include the following:

- Any setting is an acceptable research setting, but studying a variety of settings enhances the knowledge-building process.

- The researcher should always consider the contribution of the setting to the research findings.

- The characteristics, biases, and role of the researcher constitute aspects of the phenomenon under study and should be considered in interpretation of data. The meanings of the research activities to the participants are also important dimensions of the research situation and should also be considered in interpreting the data.

- Standardized measures should be used only when they are suited to the situation under study.

- Understanding of human behavior may be advanced by both traditional and nontraditional methods of research.

- Research projects that exclude person, environment, or time dimensions may advance understanding of human behavior, but the researcher should recognize the omissions in interpretation of the data.

Organization of the Book

This book covers two of the three aspects of human behavior: person and environment. The third aspect, time, is covered in a companion volume titled *Dimensions of Human Behavior: The Changing Life Course.*

In this book, Part I includes two stage-setting chapters that introduce the framework for the book and provide a foundation for thinking critically about the discussions of theory and research presented in Parts II and III. A reflection at the end of Part I demonstrates the multifaceted nature of social work. Part II comprises four chapters that analyze the multiple dimensions of persons and environments—one chapter each on the biological person and the spiritual person, and two chapters on the psychological person. A reflection at the end of Part II emphasizes the importance of attending to all three dimensions of the person in social work practice. The eight chapters of Part III discuss the environmental dimensions: the physical environment, social institutions and social structure, culture, formal organizations, communities, social movements, small groups, and families. At the end of Part III, a reflection demonstrates how one social worker focuses on several dimensions of environment.

Presenting personal and environmental dimensions separately is a risky approach. I do not wish to reinforce any tendency to think about human behavior in a way that camouflages the inseparability of person and environment. We have taken this approach, however, for two reasons. First, the personal and environmental dimensions, for the most part, have been studied separately, often by different disciplines, and usually as detached or semidetached entities. Second, I want to introduce some dimensions of persons and environments not typically covered in social work textbooks and provide updated knowledge about all of the dimensions. However, it is important to remember that no single dimension of human behavior can be understood without attention to other dimensions. Thus, frequent references to other dimensions throughout Parts II and III should help develop an understanding of the unity of persons, environments, and time.

IMPLICATIONS FOR SOCIAL WORK PRACTICE

The multidimensional approach outlined in this chapter suggests several principles for social work assessment and intervention, for both prevention and remediation services:

- In the assessment process, collect information about all of the critical dimensions of the changing configuration of person and environment.

- In the assessment process, attempt to see the situation from a variety of perspectives. Use multiple data sources, including the person(s), significant others, and direct observations.

- Allow people to tell their own stories, and pay attention to how they describe the pattern and flow of their person/environment configurations.

- Use the multidimensional data base to develop a dynamic picture of the person-environment configuration.

- Link intervention strategies to the dimensions of the assessment.

- In general, expect more effective outcomes from interventions that are multidimensional, because the situation itself is multidimensional.

- Allow the unique stories of people and situations to direct the choice of theory and research to be used.

- Use general knowledge to suggest tentative hypotheses to be explored in the unique situation.
- Think of social work practice as a continuous, dialectical movement between unique knowledge and general knowledge.

MAIN POINTS

1. This book provides a way of thinking about human behavior in terms of changing configurations of persons and environments. Its approach is transactional and multidimensional.

2. Although person, environment, and time are inseparable, we can focus on them separately by thinking about the relevant dimensions of each.

3. A dimension is a feature of person, environment, or time that can be focused on separately, but that cannot be understood without also considering other relevant features.

4. Relevant personal dimensions include the biological, the psychological, and the spiritual.

5. Nine dimensions of environment that have relevance for social work are the physical environment, social institutions and social structure, culture, formal organizations, communities, social movements, small groups, families, and dyads. These dimensions have been studied separately, but they are neither mutually exclusive nor hierarchically ordered.

6. Two dimensions of time, based on temporal scope, are life events and life course.

7. The transactional approach presented in this book is interested in both unique events and patterns across similar events. Such an approach facilitates social work's emphasis on human diversity.

8. Special attention should be paid to power relations and processes of oppression.

9. General knowledge, as well as knowledge about the unique situation, is necessary for effective social work practice.

10. General knowledge about human behavior comes from two sources: theory and research.

11. Theory can be evaluated according to the following five criteria: coherence and conceptual clarity, comprehensiveness, testability, compatibility with existing theory and research, and significance for social work practice.

12. The transactional approach suggests that research should be evaluated according to the following criteria: inclusion of multiple dimensions of persons, environments,

and time; specification of the attributes of the research setting; specification of the meaning of the research to participants; specification of the attributes and role of the researcher; specification of how inferences are made; and suitability of the measures to the situation.

13. Contemporary social and behavioral science is marked by controversies about theoretical assumptions and research methods: objective versus subjective reality, determinism versus voluntarism, cohesion versus conflict. The multidimensional perspective presented in this book takes a middle ground on these controversies.

14. A multidimensional approach to human behavior requires multiple theoretical perspectives.

KEY TERMS

assumptions

biopsychosocial approach

cohorts

concepts

cyclical time

determinism

dimension

hypotheses

life course markers

life course perspective

life events

linear time

objective reality

positivist perspective

propositions

qualitative methods of research

quantitative methods of research

research

subjective reality

theory

trajectory

transactional approach

transitions

voluntarism

WORLD WIDE WEB RESOURCES

Each chapter of this textbook will contain a list of Internet resources and Web sites that may be useful to the reader in his or her search for further information. Each site listing will include the address and a brief description of the contents of the site. The reader should be aware that the information contained in Web sites may not be truthful or reliable and should be confirmed before being used as a reference. The reader should also be aware that Internet addresses, or URLs, are constantly changing; therefore, the addresses listed may no longer be active or accurate. Many of the Internet sites listed in each chapter contain links to other Internet sites containing more information on the topic. The reader may use these links for further investigation.

Information not included in the WWW Resources sections of each chapter can be found by using one of the many Internet search engines provided free of charge on the Internet. These search engines enable you to search using keywords or phrases, or you can use the search engines' topical listings. You should use several search engines when researching a topic, as each will retrieve different Internet sites.

YAHOO
http:// www.yahoo.com
EXCITE
http:// www.excite.com
HOTBOT
http:// www.hotbot.com
LYCOS
http:// www.lycos.com

Many Internet sites provide statistical data that are very useful for research. The majority are government sites; therefore, the addresses will be more reliable, and the information provided can be deemed more trustworthy.

U.S. Census Bureau Official Statistics
http:// www.census.gov/
Provides statistics on a wide variety of topics, including age, college enrollment, disabilities, migration, race, and voter registration.

Social Statistics Briefing Room
http:// www.whitehouse.gov/fsbr/ssbr.html
White House site contains current federal statistics on crime, demographics, health, education, and economics.

National Center for Health Statistics
http:// cdc.gov/nchswww/default.htm
Health statistics from the Centers for Disease Control on topics such as life expectancy, the uninsured population, and disabilities.

Statistical Resources on the Web
http:// www.lib.umich.edu/libhome/Documents.center/stats.html
Hosted by the University of Michigan, this site provides links to various statistical information on the Internet, including such topics as housing, demographics, and sociology.

World Wide Web Resources for Social Workers
http://pages.nyu.edu/~gh5/gh-w3-f.htm
Written and maintained by Professor Gary Holden of New York University's School of Social Work, this site contains links to many federal and state Internet sites as well as journals, assessment and measurement tools, and sites pertaining to client issues.

CHAPTER 2

Theoretical Perspectives on Human Behavior

Elizabeth D. Hutchison, Virginia Commonwealth University, and Leanne Wood Charlesworth, University of Maryland

INTERGENERATIONAL STRESSES IN THE CLARK FAMILY

You have been asked to investigate the possibility that Martha Clark's family caregivers are emotionally and physically abusing her, as well as neglecting her. Martha Clark is an 81-year-old widow who has lived with her 58-year-old son, Al, and his wife, Betty, since moving from her one-story apartment in a senior housing project when her husband died. Mrs. Clark never held a job outside the home, and her current income consists of the $400 per month she receives from Social Security. She has no savings. Mrs. Clark has arthritis that limits her mobility, making it difficult for her to walk the stairs from the main floor of Al and Betty's home to her bedroom, and the only bathroom, on the second floor. Mrs. Clark also has heart disease and diabetes. She has been challenged by periodic episodes of depression throughout adulthood, and she has been despondent since her husband died two years ago.

Nine months ago, Al Clark was laid off from the plant where he had worked for the past 15 years. He had a massive heart attack six months ago, and he remains very fearful of having a second heart attack. Betty Clark works an 8:30-to-4:30 shift at the factory where she has worked on and off for 30 years. Currently, there is a rumor that the company is planning to relocate the factory outside the United States. Al and Betty Clark have two young adult children, both of whom live out of town. Their son, father of two children, was recently divorced; their daughter is pregnant with her third child. Both children are struggling financially, and their son often turns to Al and Betty with his grief about the divorce.

Before she leaves for work every morning, Betty prepares breakfast for Al and Martha. Most mornings, Martha does not come down until it's almost time for Betty to leave for work, and then Martha only picks at her food. Al has become concerned that Martha usually eats no lunch, and he admits that on several occasions he has lost his temper, screamed at his mother, and even hit her a few times. He feels angry, frustrated, and a failure for losing his temper, but he doesn't know how to get his mother to eat. He also discovered recently that she has not been taking her medication for depression. When he discovered that, he berated Martha, screaming that she is "just a useless old woman."

Since Al's heart attack, money has been tight. The family car needed an expensive repair, and the hot water heater had to be replaced. Martha's medications are not covered by Medicare, and for the past two weeks Al and Betty have not renewed some of her prescriptions, hoping each week that the money situation will be better next week. Al and Betty often have harsh words about the money problems.

Martha Clark reports that Al and Betty are doing a good job caring for her. She says that she has lived too long anyway, and that Al is right: she is a useless old woman. The doctor tells her that walking would be good for both her arthritis and her heart disease, but she spends most of her time sitting in a chair in her bedroom. She says she does not eat because she has no appetite.

Multiple Perspectives for a Multidimensional Approach

The unfolding story of Martha Clark, her son, and her daughter-in-law is certainly unique in the way particular persons and environments are interacting over time. As a social worker, you need to understand these details about the situation of the Clark family. However, if you are to be helpful in improving the situation, you also need some general knowledge that will assist you in thinking about its unique elements. As suggested in Chapter 1, the range of general knowledge offered by a multitheoretical approach is necessary when taking a multidimensional approach to human behavior. The purpose of this chapter is to introduce you to eight theoretical perspectives that are particularly useful for thinking about changing configurations of persons and environments: systems perspective, conflict perspective, rational choice perspective, social constructionist perspective, psychodynamic perspective, developmental perspective, social behavioral perspective, and humanistic perspective.

As Exhibit 2.1 demonstrates, you will find these eight perspectives threaded throughout the discussions in Parts II and III of this book and in the companion volume, *Dimensions of Human Behavior: The Changing Life Course*. In this volume, margin notes are used to help you recognize ideas from specific perspectives. The margin notes in *The Changing Life Course* are questions intended to help you think critically about the implications of the dimensions in the practice of social work. Our purpose in this chapter is to introduce the central ideas of the eight perspectives and to analyze their scientific merit, as well as their significance for social work practice. The five criteria for critical understanding of theory, identified in Chapter 1, provide the framework for the discussion of perspectives: coherence and conceptual clarity, comprehensiveness, testability, compatibility with existing theory and research, and significance for social work practice.

Four of the perspectives introduced in this chapter are based in sociology, four are based in psychology, and several have interdisciplinary roots. Carel Germain (1994), in her historical overview, suggests that social work professionals began with a preference for sociological knowledge, moved over time to a preference for psychological knowledge, and have recently come to seek knowledge of both environmental and personal factors. This recent trend is consistent with the multidimensional, transactional approach of this book. Overall, however, the eight perspectives described here do not adequately embrace the biological and spiritual dimensions, and you will find few traces of them in the chapters on the biological person and the spiritual person.

As noted in Chapter 1, diversity is a major theme of this book. In earlier versions of the eight perspectives, few, if any, met Germain's criterion for attention to diverse persons in diverse environments. Each of the perspectives has continued to evolve, however, and the current trend is to reconstruct the perspectives to better accommodate diversity. Recent theorizing also suggests that the boundaries between perspectives are blurring, consistent with George Ritzer's

EXHIBIT 2.1
Chapters Drawing on Each Theoretical Perspective

Theoretical Perspective	Chapters in *Dimensions of Human Behavior: Person and Environment*	Chapters in *Dimensions of Human Behavior: The Changing Life Course*
Sociology-Based Perspectives		
Systems Perspective	3 The Biological Person 5 The Psychological Person: Stress, Coping, and Adaptation 6 The Spiritual Person 7 The Physical Environment 8 Social Institutions and Social Structure 9 Culture 10 Formal Organizations 11 Communities 13 Small Groups 14 Families	3 Conception, Pregnancy, and Birth 4 Infancy and Early Childhood 5 Middle Childhood 6 Adolescence 7 Adulthood 8 Late Adulthood
Conflict Perspective	3 The Biological Person 5 The Psychological Person: Stress, Coping, and Adaptation 6 The Spiritual Person 7 The Physical Environment 8 Social Institutions and Social Structure 9 Culture 10 Formal Organizations 11 Communities 12 Social Movements 14 Families	3 Conception, Pregnancy, and Birth 4 Infancy and Early Childhood 5 Middle Childhood 6 Adolescence 7 Adulthood
Rational Choice Perspective	8 Social Institutions and Social Structure 10 Formal Organizations 12 Social Movements 13 Small Groups	3 Conception, Pregnancy, and Birth 4 Infancy and Early Childhood 5 Middle Childhood 6 Adolescence 7 Adulthood 8 Late Adulthood
Social Constructionist Perspective	3 The Biological Person 4 The Psychological Person: Cognition, Emotion, and Self 5 The Psychological Person: Stress, Coping, and Adaptation 7 The Physical Environment 8 Social Institutions and Social Structure 9 Culture 10 Formal Organizations 11 Communities 12 Social Movements 13 Small Groups 14 Families	3 Conception, Pregnancy, and Birth 4 Infancy and Early Childhood 5 Middle Childhood 6 Adolescence 7 Adulthood 8 Late Adulthood

(continued)

EXHIBIT 2.1

Chapters Drawing on Each Theoretical Perspective *(continued)*

Theoretical Perspective	Chapters in *Dimensions of Human Behavior: Person and Environment*		Chapters in *Dimensions of Human Behavior: The Changing Life Course*	
Psychology-Based Perspectives				
Psychodynamic Perspective	4	The Psychological Person: Cognition, Emotion, and Self	3	Conception, Pregnancy, and Birth
	5	The Psychological Person: Stress, Coping, and Adaptation	4	Infancy and Early Childhood
	6	The Spiritual Person	5	Middle Childhood
	7	The Physical Environment	6	Adolescence
	9	Culture	7	Adulthood
	12	Social Movements	8	Late Adulthood
	13	Small Groups		
	14	Families		
Developmental Perspective	3	The Biological Person	3	Conception, Pregnancy, and Birth
	4	The Psychological Person: Cognition, Emotion, and Self	4	Infancy and Early Childhood
	5	The Psychological Person: Stress, Coping, and Adaptation	5	Middle Childhood
	6	The Spiritual Person	6	Adolescence
	7	The Physical Environment	7	Adulthood
	12	Social Movements	8	Late Adulthood
	13	Small Groups		
	14	Families		
Social Behavioral Perspective	4	The Psychological Person: Cognition, Emotion, and Self	3	Conception, Pregnancy, and Birth
	6	The Spiritual Person	4	Infancy and Early Childhood
	7	The Physical Environment	5	Middle Childhood
	8	Social Institutions and Social Structure	6	Adolescence
	9	Culture	7	Adulthood
	13	Small Groups	8	Late Adulthood
	14	Families		
Humanistic Perspective	3	The Biological Person	4	Infancy and Early Childhood
	4	The Psychological Person: Cognition, Emotion, and Self	5	Middle Childhood
	6	The Spiritual Person	6	Adolescence
	8	Social Institutions and Social Structure	7	Adulthood
	9	Culture	8	Late Adulthood
	10	Formal Organizations		
	13	Small Groups		
	14	Families		

(1992) prediction that the 1990s would be an era of theoretical synthesizing. As you read about each of the perspectives, think not only about how it can be applied in social work practice but also how well it represents all the complexities of human behavior.

The Systems Perspective

When you read the story at the beginning of this chapter, you probably first thought of it as a story about a family system—a story about Martha Clark, her son Al, and her daughter-in-law Betty—rather than "Martha Clark's story." You probably noted how Martha's, Al's, and Betty's lives are interrelated, how they influence one another's behavior, and what impact each of them has on the overall well-being of the family. You may be thinking that Al's treatment of Martha contributes to her despondence, and that her despondent behaviors are feeding his sense of failure and frustration. You also may note that this family, like other families, has a **boundary** indicating who is in and who is out, and you may be wondering if the boundary around this family is as closed as it appears, with minimal input from friends, extended family, neighborhood, church, and so on. You may also have noted the influence of larger systems on this family: the insecurity of the labor market, the limitations of the health care delivery system, historical gender roles that influenced Martha to confine her work history to the home.

You can see, in Exhibit 2.2, how these observations about Martha, Al, and Betty fit with the central ideas of the **systems perspective**. The systems perspective sees human behavior as the outcome of reciprocal interactions of persons operating within organized and integrated social systems. Its roots are very interdisciplinary. During the 1940s and 1950s, a variety of disciplines—including mathematics, physics, engineering, biology, psychology, cultural anthropology, economics, and sociology—began looking at phenomena as the outcome of interactions within and among systems. Mathematicians and engineers used the new ideas about system **feedback mechanisms**—the processes by which information about past behaviors in a system are fed back into the system in a circular manner—to develop military technology for World War II; scientists at the Bell Laboratories used the same ideas to develop transistors and other communication technology (Becvar & Becvar, 1996). Later, George Engel (1977) used the same ideas to develop a biopsychosocial model of disease.

Social workers were attracted to the systems perspective in the 1960s, as they shifted from a psychiatric model to a model more inclusive of environment. Social work has drawn most heavily on the work of sociologists Talcott Parsons and Robert Merton, psychologists Kurt Lewin and Uri Bronfenbrenner, and biologist Ludwig von Bertalanffy. With the possible exception of the developmental perspective, the systems perspective thus has the greatest potential of the perspectives discussed in this chapter to accommodate the biological person. In addition, systems theorists recognize—even if they do not always make clear—the social, cultural, eco-

EXHIBIT 2.2

Central Ideas of the
Systems Perspective

- Systems are made up of interrelated members (parts) that constitute an ordered whole.
- Each part of the system impacts all other parts, and the system as a whole.
- All systems are subsystems of other larger systems.
- Systems maintain boundaries that give them their identities.
- Systems tend toward homeostasis, or equilibrium.

nomic, and political environments of human behavior. They acknowledge the role of external influences and demands in creating and maintaining patterns of interaction within the system.

Thus, the systems perspective is much like the transactional approach of this book. However, early systems theory saw persons and environments as separate but interrelated, whereas a transactional approach emphasizes the inseparability of persons and environments. Nor did early theorizing in the systems perspective deal with the time dimension—the focus was always on the present. But recent formulations have attempted to add a time dimension to accommodate both past and future influences on human behavior (see Bronfenbrenner, 1989; Ford & Lerner, 1992; Hannerz, 1992; Wachs, 1992).

The social workers who first adopted the systems perspective were heavily influenced by **functionalist sociology,** which was the dominant sociological theory during the 1940s and 1950s. In functionalism, social systems are thought to remain in a relatively stable state. Each part of the system serves an essential function in maintaining the system, and the functions of the various parts are coordinated to produce a well-functioning whole. The biggest problem with this perspective is that it tends to assume that interactions take place within a **closed system,** isolated from exchanges with other systems and thus unable to receive needed resources. An **open system,** as Exhibit 2.3 illustrates, is more likely to receive resources from external systems. Actually, there is no such thing as a totally closed system, because it could not survive without some external resources, but much of social science research is based on a closed-system model and does not account for intersystem exchanges.

Functionalist sociology also assumes that social systems are held together by social consensus and shared values. The focus is on maintenance of the "normal" or "healthy" state of affairs, known as homeostasis or equilibrium, a state that all members work hard to maintain and restore. What is good for the system is considered good for each of the parts, and conflict and change are seen as threats to be overcome (Wallace & Wolf, 1995). This emphasis on system equilibrium and on the necessity of traditional roles to hold systems together has led many to

EXHIBIT 2.3
Closed and Open
Systems

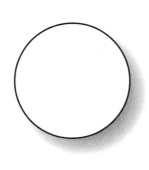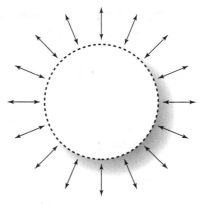

Closed System:
No Exchange with
External Systems

Open System:
Exchange of Resources
with External Systems

criticize the systems perspective in the functionalist tradition as socially conservative (Cohen, 1968; Gouldner, 1970). Contemporary systems theory, however, has begun to recognize power and oppression, and recent social work textbooks written from the systems perspective recognize both conflict and cooperation, stability and change, as inherent in system interactions (see Longres, 1995; Martin & O'Connor, 1989).

Now let's look at how the systems perspective can help us analyze the problems in the Clark family. Consider the roles played by each person and the stresses the family has faced as a result of role transitions over the past two years. **Role** refers to the usual behaviors of persons occupying a particular social position. Martha Clark went from being wife and co-manager of her own home to a less well defined role in the home of Al and Betty. Al has seen his relationship with his mother change toward a caregiver role, has lost his role as worker, and has taken on a "sick" role. We might anticipate that Betty is experiencing role overload as she becomes the only wage earner, maintains the role of primary housekeeper, and takes on new caregiver roles with both her mother-in-law and her husband.

In the systems perspective, the structure of roles is an important mechanism for maintaining system balance. You can understand why this might be if you think for a moment about the sometimes rocky transitions in roles across the life course—from infancy, through childhood, adolescence, adulthood, and late adulthood. At each passage, the individual has to redefine her or his relationships with others in the environment.

The conceptualization of role incorporates several key concepts (Davis, 1986; Germain, 1994; Longres, 1995):

- **Expected role.** The set of behaviors that others expect of persons in a particular social position. Much of the stress in the Clark family stems from changing abilities to fulfill expected roles. Al, for example, feels the pressure of expectations that he will fill the breadwinner role.

- **Enacted role.** The way in which a specific person in a particular position actually behaves. Al is struggling with the caregiver role, and the community questions how well he is performing, or enacting, that role.

- **Role overload.** A set of roles that, taken together, are too demanding. As suggested earlier, we can well imagine that Betty may be currently experiencing role overload. This is a hypothesis that you will want to explore.

- **Role ambiguity.** Unclear expectations for successful performance of a given role. You will want to explore the possibility that both Martha and Al are facing some role ambiguity. Martha may not be clear what her role should be in Al and Betty's house, and Al may have lots of questions about the role of heart patient.

- **Role conflict.** Incompatible expectations for the various roles a person holds, or competing expectations for performance in a particular role. Betty, like many employed caregivers, may be experiencing conflict between work and family roles.

Although popular, the systems perspective is often criticized as vague and somewhat ambiguous. Early theorists rarely applied their work to the empirical world, and many concepts were not clearly defined for research or practice purposes. However, this aspect of the systems perspective has been strengthened in recent years; systems concepts have been applied in research on social support and on the relationship between socioeconomic stressors and social and individual problems (see Garbarino, 1976, 1977; Garbarino & Sherman, 1980; Gelles, 1992; Zuravin, 1986, 1989). We agree with Germain (1994) that the systems perspective is more useful for understanding human behavior than for directing social work interventions, but several social work practice textbooks were based on the systems perspective in the 1970s and 1980s (see Germain & Gitterman, 1980; Meyer, 1983; Pincus & Minahan, 1973; Siporin, 1975). Its value is that, like the transactional approach in this book, the systems perspective suggests that we should widen the scope of assessment and intervention (Allen-Meares & Lane, 1987) and expect better outcomes from multidimensional interventions (Ford & Lerner, 1992).

The Conflict Perspective

In your case assessment with the Clark family, you have probably observed that Martha Clark is highly dependent on Al and Betty. Thus, another way of looking at her situation is to suggest that her lack of power in the family contributes to her problems. In a larger sense, Martha is a member of a class of people—old, poor, frail, single women—who hold little power in society. You may also note that Al and Betty, while holding more power in the family than Martha, hold little power in the labor market; they are vulnerable to the economic interests of other, more dominant, groups. You could be thinking in a new way about recent political debates about health care funding now that you have recognized the financial strain this family faces and its inability to pay for Martha Clark's medications. You may also note the authority associated with your role as protective investigator, and you wonder how Martha, Al, and Betty will react to your power. Compare these observations with the central ideas of the conflict perspective, presented in Exhibit 2.4.

The **conflict perspective** has emerged over and over again in history, drawing attention to conflict, dominance, and oppression in social life (Collins, 1994). The conflict perspective typically looks for sources of conflict, and causes of human behavior, in the economic and political arenas. In sociology, the conflict perspective has two traditions: a utopian tradition that foresees a society in which there is no longer a basis for social conflict, and a second tradition that sees conflict as inevitable in social life (Wallace & Wolf, 1995).

EXHIBIT 2.4

Central Ideas of the
Conflict Perspective

- Groups and individuals try to advance their own interests over the interests of others.
- Power is unequally divided, and some social groups dominate others.
- Social order is based on the manipulation and control of nondominant groups by dominant groups.
- Lack of open conflict is a sign of exploitation.
- Social change is driven by conflict, with periods of change interrupting long periods of stability.

The roots of contemporary conflict theory are usually traced to the works of Karl Marx and his collaborator Friedrich Engels, and to the works of Max Weber. Marx (1887/1967) and Engels (1884/1970) focused on economic structures, but Weber (1904–1905/1958) criticized this singular emphasis in favor of a multidimensional perspective on social class. Contemporary conflict theory tends to favor Weber's multidimensional perspective, calling attention to a confluence of social, economic, and political structures in the creation of inequality (Collins, 1994; Ritzer, 1992; Wallace & Wolf, 1995). As you have probably noted, Weber's perspective is also more consistent with the multidimensional approach of this book.

Power relationships are the focus of the conflict perspective. Some theorists in the conflict tradition limit their focus to the large-scale structure of power relationships, but many theorists also look at the reactions and adaptations of individual members of nondominant groups. Habermas (1984, 1987) and other **critical theorists** are interested in the connections between culture, social structure, and personality, paying particular attention to the role of individual perception. Coser (1956) proposes a **pluralistic theory of social conflict,** which recognizes that more than one social conflict is going on at all times, and that individuals hold cross-cutting and overlapping memberships in status groups. Thus, it seeks to understand life experience by looking at simultaneous memberships—for example, a white, Italian-American, Protestant, heterosexual, male semiskilled worker, or a black, African-American, Catholic, lesbian, female professional worker. Social conflict exists between economic groups, racial groups, ethnic groups, religious groups, age groups, and gender groups.

Conflict theory has developed, in the main, through attempts to codify persistent themes in history (Collins, 1990). The preferred research method is empirical historical research that looks at large-scale patterns of history (see Mann, 1986; McCarthy & Zald, 1977; Skocpol, 1979; Wallerstein, 1974–1989). As with other methods of research, critics have attacked some interpretations of historical data from the conflict perspective, but the historical analyses of Mann, Skocpol, and Wallerstein are some of the most influential works in contemporary sociology. In addition to historical analysis, conflict theorists have used experimental methods to study reactions to coercive power (see Willer, 1987) and naturalistic inquiry to study social ranking through interaction rituals (Collins, 1981). Contemporary conflict theorists are also drawing on network analysis, which plots the relationships among a group of people, and are finding support for their propositions about power and domination (see Burt, 1983).

Concepts of power and social conflict came into social work in the 1960s (Germain, 1994). These concepts have great value for understanding community, group, and family relationships, as well as the power differential between social worker and client. The conflict perspective, as it currently exists, however, is weak in suggesting principles of action beyond assessment. Randall Collins, a conflict theorist, suggests that "where conflict theory is weak is in explaining what will happen after the revolution, or after a successful movement has won some power" (Collins, 1994, p. 178). The conflict perspective is nonetheless crucial to social work because it shines a spotlight on how domination and oppression might be affecting human behavior, because it illuminates processes by which people become estranged and discouraged, and because it encourages social workers to consider the meaning of their power relationships with clients, particularly nonvoluntary clients (Cingolani, 1984). Social movement theories (see Chapter 12), which are based in the conflict perspective, have some implications for mobilization of oppressed groups, but the conflict perspective, in general, provides little in the way of policy direction. It is stronger in helping us to understand how the Clark family came to be discouraged than in guiding policies that might prevent or alleviate such situations.

The Rational Choice Perspective

Another way to think about the Clark family is to focus on the costs and benefits that each of them derives from interacting with the others. You might suggest that Martha Clark receives the benefit of having most of her basic needs met, but endures the cost of feeling that she has nothing to offer in exchange, as well as the blows to body and spirit delivered by her son. She seems to think that the care she is receiving is as good as she deserves, and probably sees no better alternative. Al Clark benefits from the household management that Betty provides but has recently endured the cost of feeling that his contributions, economic and otherwise, are not equal to hers, as well as the cost of feeling inadequate in his ability to meet his mother's needs. Now he must endure the embarrassment of an adult protective investigation. By virtue of the greater resources she brings to exchanges, Betty Clark holds a power position in the family, but she endures the cost of inadequate support from her husband and mother-in-law. Exhibit 2.5 reveals a fit between these observations about the Clark family and the central ideas of the rational choice perspective.

The **rational choice perspective** sees human behavior as based on self-interest and rational choices about effective ways to accomplish goals. The perspective is interdisciplinary, with strong roots in utilitarian philosophy, economics, and social behaviorism. Social workers are most familiar with social exchange theory in sociology, rational choice models of organizations, public choice theory in political science, and the emerging social network theory. As Collins (1994) notes, the rational choice perspective is a very old tradition in social thought, but the roots of contemporary sociological theories of rational choice are generally traced to Claude Levi-Strauss, George Homans, and Peter Blau. Other theorists making major contributions include John Thibaut and Harold Kelley, James March and Herbert Simon, Michael Hechter, James Coleman, James Buchanan, Richard Emerson, and Karen Cook.

Social exchange theory starts with the premise that social behavior is based on the desire to maximize benefits and minimize costs. In the early development of social exchange theory, Homans (1958) insisted that behavior can be understood at the psychological level, denying the

EXHIBIT 2.5

Central Ideas of the
Rational Choice
Perspective

- People are rational and goal-directed.
- Social exchange is based on self-interest, with actors trying to maximize rewards and minimize costs.
- Reciprocity of exchange is essential to social life.
- Power comes from unequal resources in an exchange.

relevance of the cultural and social environments. Homans was particularly forceful in attacking the Parsonian view that individuals are influenced in their behavior by role expectations that emanate from sociocultural systems. History, to Homans, was important only because the history of rewards for past behavior informs an actor about what is in his or her best interest. More recent formulations of social exchange theory have moved from this position toward a greater emphasis on the social, economic, political, and historical contexts of social exchanges (see Levi, Cook, O'Brien, & Faye, 1990). These formulations would emphasize how the Clark family conflicts are influenced by the structure of the labor market and political decisions about health care. Beginning with the work of Peter Blau (1964), social exchange theorists and researchers have taken a strong interest in how power is negotiated at all levels, from interactions between two people to Realpolitik among nations. Particularly noteworthy in this regard is Emerson's (1972a, 1972b) power-dependency theory and Karen Cook's (1987) exchange network theory.

Some feminists have criticized exchange theory on the grounds that its emphasis on rational calculation of personal advantage is a male attitude and does not represent the female perspective (Collins, 1994). This criticism might be shared by ethnic groups who are more collectivist, and less individualist, than white Anglo-Saxon Protestant Americans. In fact, Homans developed his American version of exchange theory partially in reaction to Levi-Strauss's French collectivist version, which argued that social exchange is driven by collective, cultural, symbolic forces and not based simply on self-interest (Ekeh, 1974). Recently, Karen Cook and her colleagues (Cook, O'Brien, & Kollock, 1990) have undertaken a synthesis of social exchange and symbolic interaction theories (see the discussion of the social constructionist perspective), recognizing the possibility that different people hold different definitions of positive outcomes in social exchange.

Thibaut and Kelley's (Kelley & Thibaut, 1978; Thibaut & Kelley, 1959) concepts of comparison level and comparison level alternatives are also useful in accommodating diversity of experience. **Comparison level,** a standard for evaluating the rewards and costs of a given relationship, is based on what the evaluator feels he or she deserves. Martha Clark's suggestion that she is receiving good care may well be based on such a standard; she may well believe that a woman in her situation deserves no better care. **Comparison level alternative** is the lowest level of outcomes a person will accept in light of alternative opportunities. Martha Clark might find her current situation less acceptable if she had another son or daughter who was in a position to provide a better quality of life.

As the rational choice perspective has developed, two conceptual puzzles have emerged, one at the individual level and one at the collective level. At the individual level, the individual's capacity to process information and make rational decisions is limited. At the collective level, how is collective action possible if each actor maximizes rewards and minimizes costs? To their credit, recent theorists have embraced these puzzles. Recent developments in the rational choice perspective emphasize the limits to rational choice in social life (see Cook et al., 1990; Levi et al., 1990; March & Simon, 1958). James Coleman (1990) is particularly noted for his attempts to employ rational choice theory to activate collective action for the purpose of social justice.

The rational choice perspective has stimulated empirical research at several levels of analysis, with mixed results. Cognitive psychologists Daniel Kahneman and Amos Tversky (1982,

1984) dealt a blow to the rational choice perspective in the 1980s. They reported research findings that individual choices and decisions are often inconsistent with assumed rationality and that, indeed, situations are often too complicated for individuals to ascertain what is the most rational choice. On the other hand, more than modest support for the perspective has been found in research on dyads, families, and labor markets (see Adams & Jacobsen, 1964; Becker, 1981; Blood & Wolfe, 1960; Burgess & Nielsen, 1974; Carter & Glick, 1976). Collins (1988) suggests that a serious problem for the rational choice perspective is the lack of a common metric for calculating the costs and benefits derived from social exchange. Contemporary theorists acknowledge the inherent imprecision of this metric and suggest that the rational choice perspective must find a way to incorporate both what people value and the context of social exchange (see Cook et al., 1990).

Some versions of rational choice theory serve as little more than a defense of the rationality of the marketplace of social exchange, suggesting a noninterventionist approach. In other words, if all social exchanges are based on rational choices, then who are we to interfere with this process? This stance, of course, is inconsistent with the purposes of social work.

Other versions of rational choice theory emphasize the ways in which patterns of exchange lead to social inequalities and social injustices. Some theorists in this tradition have begun to propose solutions for creating social solidarity while recognizing the self-interestedness that is characteristic of Western, industrialized societies. These attempts have led Collins (1994) to suggest that, out of all current social theories, contemporary rational choice theories have the greatest chance of informing social policy. One of the most promising approaches is that of Coleman (1990), who explores possible incentives to encourage actors to behave in ways more beneficial to others. For example, Coleman has recommended financial incentives for providing nurturant care to children and adolescents at risk of becoming an economic drain on society—incentives that increase with the potential hazard to society. He has also proposed lifting the legal immunity of members of corporate boards to encourage them to act in a more prosocial manner.

Theorists in the rational choice tradition are also advancing **social network theory,** which actually has intellectual roots in the systems perspective. Still in the early stages of development, social network theory already provides useful tools for person/environment assessments and holds great promise for the future (Specht, 1986). Social workers make use of social network theory at the micro level, to assess and enhance the social support networks of individual clients and families (see Collins & Pancoast, 1976; Tracy & Whittaker, 1990). Social work administrators and planners use social network theory to understand and enhance the exchange of resources in networks of social service providers (see Streeter & Gillespie, 1992).

Social networks are typically presented visually as **sociograms,** which illustrate the relations among network members (see Hartman, 1978, 1995; Meyer, 1993). Members of the network—individuals, groups, or organizations—are represented as points, and lines are drawn between pairs of points to demonstrate a relationship between them. Arrows are often used to show the flow of exchanges in a relationship. These graphic displays illuminate such issues as network size, density of relationships, strength of relationships, reciprocity of relationships, and access to power and influence. Sociograms are usually called **ecomaps** in the social work literature. An ecomap of the Clark family is presented in Exhibit 2.6.

EXHIBIT 2.6

Ecomap of the Clark
Family

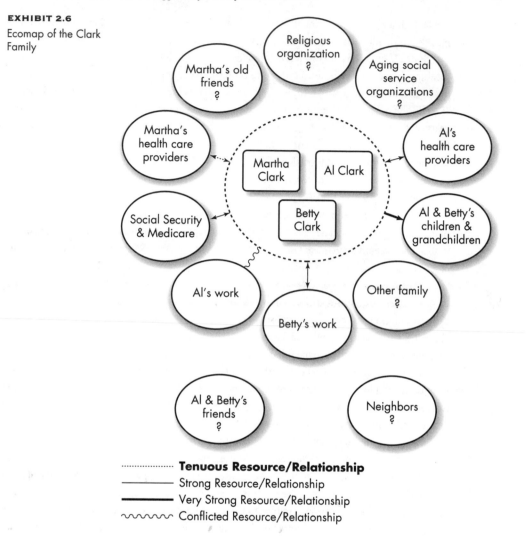

·················· **Tenuous Resource/Relationship**
———————— Strong Resource/Relationship
▬▬▬▬▬▬ Very Strong Resource/Relationship
∿∿∿∿∿∿ Conflicted Resource/Relationship

The Social Constructionist Perspective

Both Martha Clark and her son sometimes think of her as a "useless old woman." You may be thinking that this idea could be contributing to Martha's growing despondency and passive approach to life, and to her son's impatient treatment of her. Their current interactions help to reinforce this idea. It is likely, however, that both Martha and her son entered the current situation with a shared understanding about "useless old women." This is an understanding that may have been developed and sustained across generations in their family, but it also clearly reflects traditional images of old women in the popular culture. You may also be wondering what kinds of ideas Martha, Al, and Betty have about gender roles and about heart disease, and how their cur-

EXHIBIT 2.7
Central Ideas
of the Social
Constructionist
Perspective

- Actors are free, active, and creative.
- Social reality is created when actors, in social interaction, develop a common understanding of their world.
- Social interaction is grounded in language customs, as well as cultural and historical contexts.
- People can modify meanings in the process of interaction.
- Society consists of social processes, not social structures.

rent interactions are affected by these ideas. By considering these issues, you have begun to explore the central ideas of the social constructionist perspective (see Exhibit 2.7).

To understand human behavior, the **social constructionist perspective** focuses on "actors, the way in which they construct social reality, and the action that results from such construction" (Ritzer, 1992, p. 176). The intellectual roots of the social constructionist perspective are usually traced to the German philosopher Edmund Husserl, as well as to the philosophical pragmatism of John Dewey and early theorists in the symbolic interaction tradition including Charles Horton Cooley, W. I. Thomas, and George Herbert Mead. More recent theorists include Herbert Blumer, Erving Goffman, Alfred Schutz, Harold Garfinkel, Peter Berger, and Thomas Luckmann. Collins (1994) suggests that social constructionist theorizing is the type of sociology that American sociologists do best.

To the social constructionist, there is no singular objective reality, only the shared subjective realities that are created as people interact. Constructionists emphasize the existence of multiple social and cultural realities, developed in changing configurations of persons and environments. The sociopolitical environment and history of any situation play an important role in understanding human behavior, particularly if these are significant to the individual. However, social constructionists disagree about how constraining the environment is. The dominant position is probably the one represented by Schutz's (1932/1967) **phenomenological sociology**. While arguing that people shape social reality, Schutz also suggests that individuals and groups are constrained by the preexisting social and cultural structures created by their predecessors. Schutz does not provide theoretical tools for understanding social institutions and their links to individual constructions of reality, however.

In his 1975 presidential address to the American Sociological Association, Lewis Coser attacked ethnomethodology, another theory in the social constructionist tradition, for ignoring "institutional factors in general, and the centrality of power in social interaction in particular" (Coser, 1975, p. 696). In a similar vein, Wallace and Wolf (1995) and Ritzer (1992) have suggested that symbolic interactionism, ethnomethodology, and phenomenological sociology all lack the theoretical tools necessary for the analysis of power relationships. Middleton (1989) has suggested that many contemporary postmodern versions of social constructionism, by ignoring power while focusing on multiple voices and multiple meanings in the construction of reality, reduce oppression to difference. These critics suggest that some actors have greater power than others to privilege their own constructions of reality and to disadvantage the constructions of other actors.

This criticism cannot be leveled at all versions of social constructionism, however. Social work scholars have been particularly attracted to those versions of the social constructionist perspective that have incorporated pieces of the conflict tradition (Laird, 1994; Saleeby, 1994; Witkin & Gottschalk, 1988), particularly to the early work of Michel Foucault (1969) on the relationship between power and knowledge. They propose that in contemporary society, minority or "local" knowledges are denied credibility in majority-dominated social arenas and suggest that social work practitioners can bring credibility to minority viewpoints by allowing oppressed individuals and groups to tell their own stories.

Social constructionism, particularly the original phenomenological and symbolic interactional concepts, is criticized at times as vague and difficult to operationalize for empirical research. However, many social constructionist proponents have challenged this criticism and offered alternative criteria for evaluating theory (see Witkin & Gottschalk, 1988), as well as an alternative research methodology, **constructivist research** (Lincoln & Guba, 1985), that is sensitive to the context of the research, seeks the views of key parties, and takes into account the interactions involved in the research process (Sherman & Reid, 1994). Sociologists in the conflict and rational choice traditions have begun to incorporate social constructionist ideas and now use a mix of qualitative and quantitative research methodologies to accommodate both objective and subjective reality (see Collins, 1990; Cook et al., 1990).

Cynthia Franklin (1995) suggests that the emphasis on social context is the reason that social constructionism is often pointed to as an important theory for social work practice (see Imre, 1984; Rodwell, 1987; Saleeby, 1994; Weick, 1994). Social constructionism gives new meaning to the old social work adage "Begin where the client is." The social work relationship begins with developing an understanding of how the client views the situation and what the client would like to have happen. The current interest in narrative and storytelling therapies is based on the social constructionist perspective. In addition to this attention to the client's construction of reality, the social worker should engage the client in thinking about the social, cultural, and historical environments in which this version of reality was constructed. As Laird (1994) and Saleeby (1994) suggest, such conversations with members of oppressed groups may lead to empowerment through restorying. In your work with the Clark family, you might want to test this hypothesis by inviting Martha Clark to tell her story about how she came to see herself as "just a useless old woman." In the process, she might realize that another interpretation of her status is possible. At the level of groups and organizations, the social constructionist perspective recommends getting discordant groups to engage in sincere discussion of their disparate constructions of reality and to negotiate lines of actions acceptable to all (Fox & Miller, 1995) (see Chapter 10 for further discussion).

The Psychodynamic Perspective

Martha Clark's despondence, her loss of confidence and hope are apparent—and easy to understand. Think about the losses she has recently experienced: loss of husband, loss of home, loss of privacy, loss of income, and loss of health. You may begin to wonder, given her long-term struggle with depression, about the possibility of early experiences with loss, deprivation, or

EXHIBIT 2.8

Central Ideas of the
Psychodynamic
Perspective

- Emotions have a central place in human behavior.

- Unconscious, as well as conscious, mental activity serves as the motivating force in human behavior.

- Early childhood experiences are central in the patterning of an individual's emotions, and therefore, central to problems of living throughout life.

- Individuals may become overwhelmed by internal and/or external demands.

- Individuals frequently use ego defense mechanisms to avoid becoming overwhelmed by internal and/or external demands.

trauma. You may also note her son's anger and frustration. Think about the losses he too has recently experienced: loss of father, loss of job, loss of income, loss of privacy, and loss of health. You also may wonder if he has a residue of anger toward his mother, perhaps related to childhood deprivation that he experienced during her episodes of depression. Is it possible that his label of "useless old woman" is a projection of his own sense of uselessness? As you explore the Clark family's situation from the psychodynamic perspective (see Exhibit 2.8), these and other possibilities emerge.

The **psychodynamic perspective** is concerned with how internal processes such as needs, drives, and emotions motivate human behavior. The perspective has evolved over the years, moving from the classical psychodynamic emphasis on innate drives and unconscious processes toward greater emphasis on the adaptive capacities of individuals and their interactions with the environment. The origins of all psychodynamic theories are in the work of Sigmund Freud; other prominent theorists in the evolving psychodynamic perspective include Anna Freud, Melanie Klein, Margaret Mahler, Karen Horney, Heinz Hartmann, Robert W. White, Donald Winnicott, Otto Kernberg, Heinz Kohut, and Erik Erikson. More recent formulations of the perspective include ego psychology and object relations theories. You will read more about the psychodynamic perspective in Chapter 4.

In general, the psychodynamic perspective takes account of the environments of behavior only in the sense that these environments are conceptualized as presenting conflicts with which the individual must struggle. Recent formulations put greater emphasis on human behavior as a response to challenges in the environment than was found in classical theory, but theoretical propositions about internal processes continue to predominate. When environmental forces are considered, they include only passing mention of social forces beyond the family. Social, economic, political, and historical environments of human behavior are probably implied in ego psychology, but they are not explicated. This failure to expand the view of social beyond the family has led to accusations that psychodynamic theories are "mother blaming" and "family blaming" (Luepnitz, 1988).

Theorists in the psychodynamic tradition search for universal laws of behavior and their applicability to unique individuals. Thus, diversity of experience at the group level has been quite neglected in this tradition. Moreover, in the main, "universal" laws have been developed through analysis of heterosexual men of white, Anglo-Saxon, middle-class culture.

Feminists, as well as members of racial and ethnic minority groups, have criticized the psychodynamic bias toward thinking of people as autonomous individuals (Berzoff, 1989; Bricker-Jenkins, Hooyman, & Gottlieb, 1991; Gilligan, 1982; Ho, 1992; Sue & Sue, 1990). These critics suggest that viewing this standard as "normal" makes the connectedness found among many women and members of racial and ethnic minority groups seem pathological. Overemphasis on autonomy may also lead us to think of Martha Clark's growing dependence in pathological terms.

Psychodynamic theories are strong in their recognition of power dynamics in parent/child relationships, and in exploration of the life worlds of children. They are weak in looking at power issues in other relationships, however, including gender relationships. Early on, Freud recognized gender differences, even gender inequality, but attributed them to moral deficits within women.

Erik Erikson's theory, which has been widely used in social work curricula, has a somewhat greater emphasis on social forces. However, Erikson's work has been criticized for its lack of attention to the life worlds of women, racial minorities, and sexual minorities (Berzoff, 1989; Chestang, 1972; Kravetz, 1982; Kropf & Greene, 1994; Schwartz, 1973; Wesley, 1975). Chestang (1972) has asserted that Erikson's theory does not take into account the persistently hostile environments in which minority group members interact, or the extraordinary coping strategies needed to negotiate those environments.

Criticisms that the psychodynamic perspective lacks logical consistency and empirical support are directed primarily at Freud's original concepts and propositions, which were not measurable and not entirely consistent. Ego psychology and object relations theorists strengthened the logical consistency of the psychodynamic perspective by expanding and clarifying definitions of major concepts, and later psychodynamic theorists translated Freud's ideas into more measurable terms. Consequently, much empirical work has been based on the psychodynamic perspective. Contradictions in the research findings may be due in large part to the use of different definitions and measures. Some concepts, such as mastery or competence, have strong empirical support, but this support has been generated primarily by other schools of thought, such as developmental psychology and Albert Bandura's social behaviorism.

Most versions of the psychodynamic perspective have included clinical theory as well as human behavior theory. Differences of opinion about principles of practice reflect the theoretical evolution that has occurred. Practice principles common to all versions of the psychodynamic perspective include the centrality of the professional/client relationship, the curative value of expressing emotional conflicts and understanding past events, and the goals of self-awareness and self-control. Thus, you would be interested in having both Martha and Al discuss their past, as well as present, emotional conflicts. In contrast to the classical psychodynamic approach, recent formulations include directive as well as nondirective intervention, short-term as well as long-term intervention, and environmental manipulations—such as locating a day-care program for Martha—as well as intrapsychic manipulations such as emotional catharsis. Ego psychology has also been used to develop principles for prevention activities in addition to principles of remediation (Goldstein, 1984, 1986). In general, however, the psychodynamic perspective does not suggest practice principles at the level of communities, organizations, and social institutions. Thus, it would not help you to think about how to influence public policy to secure coverage for Martha Clark's medications.

The Developmental Perspective

Another way to think about the story of the Clark family is to view their situation in terms of the developmental tasks they face. You might note that Martha Clark is entering late old age and struggling with the chronic illnesses and losses that people in this life stage frequently experience. She must make peace with the life that she has lived and find purpose to continue to live. You might also note that Al and Betty are part of the "sandwich generation," which must take on caregiving responsibilities for the older generation while also continuing to provide support to the generation behind them. They may be plagued with fears about their own vulnerability to the aging process. These observations are consistent with the central ideas of the developmental perspective, summarized in Exhibit 2.9.

The focus of the **developmental perspective** is on how human behavior changes and stays the same across the life cycle. The study of life cycle development is rooted in Freud's (1905/1953) theory of psychosexual stages of childhood development, but Erikson (1963) has been the most influential developmental theorist to date because his model of development includes adult, as well as child, stages of development. Other early developmental theorists include Margaret Mahler, Harry Stack Sullivan, and Jean Piaget. More recent developmental theorists include Daniel Levinson, George Vaillant, Roger Gould, Lawrence Kohlberg, Robert Havighurst, Barbara Newman, and Philip Newman. Bernice Neugarten (1979) was one of the first developmental theorists to study women as well as men. In the past several decades, sociologists have applied the developmental perspective to the study of family life stages (Carter & McGoldrick, 1988a; Duvall, 1962).

A frequent criticism of the developmental perspective is that it fails to take account of the social, economic, political, and historical environments of human behavior. Although some theorists conceptualize stages of development as biopsychosocial phenomena and recognize the way social forces affect individual development, most, including Erikson, see the stages as universal. All traditional developmental theorists ignore economic and political forces. The failure of developmental theories to deal with historical time has prompted researchers of adult behavior to point out the cohort effects on human behavior that arise when groups of persons born in the same historical time share cultural influences and historical events at the same period in their lives.

These criticisms have helped to stimulate development of the life course perspective in sociology. This perspective conceptualizes the life course as a social, rather than psychological, phenomenon that is nonetheless unique for each individual, with some common life course markers,

EXHIBIT 2.9

Central Ideas of the Developmental Perspective

- Human development occurs in clearly defined stages.
- Each stage of life is qualitatively different from all other stages.
- Stages of development are sequential, with each stage building on earlier stages.
- Stages of development are universal.
- All environments provide the support necessary for development.

or transitions, related to shared social and historical contexts (George, 1993). The life course perspective would suggest that Martha Clark's beliefs about what it means to be "old" or to be female have been influenced by the historical time in which she has lived and are probably shared by many other women her age. The evolving life course model respects the idea of role transition that is so central to the developmental perspective, but it also recognizes the multiplicity of interacting factors that contribute to diversity in the timing and experience of these transitions. As you may recall, the life course perspective is the conceptual framework for the companion volume to this book.

The traditional developmental perspective does not take account of power relationships, with the possible exception of power dynamics in the parent/child relationship. Moreover, traditional developmental models are based on the average white, middle-class, heterosexual, Anglo-Saxon male and ignore the life worlds of members of nondominant groups. In response to these limitations, several women have developed life cycle models for women (Gilligan, 1982; Jordan, 1992; Weenolsen, 1988). Daniel Levinson's (1996) recent study of women's lives, which includes a sample of women diversified by race and social class, acknowledges the impact of gender power differentials. Proponents of the family life cycle perspective have begun to respond with discussion of gender in the family life cycle. They are also presenting models of the family life cycle for gay and lesbian couples and for poor and minority families (Colon, 1980; Falicov & Karrer, 1980; Fulmer, 1988; Hines, 1988; McGoldrick, 1988; McWhirter & Mattison, 1984; Slater, 1995). Some of these discussions give explicit consideration to the impact of oppression, but others do not.

Classical developmental theory's notion of life stages is internally consistent, and many of Erikson's ideas have been employed and verified in empirical research. One example is Marcia's (1993) study of identity development, which supports Erikson's propositions about the development of identity in adolescence. As noted previously, however, much of developmental research has been based on white, heterosexual, middle-class males. Another concern is that by defining normal as average, developmental research fails to capture the life worlds of groups who deviate even moderately from the average, or even to capture the broad range of behavior considered normal. Thus, the consistency of and empirical support for the developmental perspective are based to some extent on statistical masking of diversity.

Through some lenses, the developmental perspective can be viewed as optimistic. Most people face life crises and challenges at some point, and many people have been reassured to hear that their struggle is "typical." Because the developmental perspective sees individuals as having the possibility to rework their inner experiences, as well as their family relationships, clients may be assisted in finding new strategies for getting their lives back "on course." For example, Al Clark could explore new roles that would make him feel more productive.

Erikson's model has often been used for assessment purposes in social work practice, and in a positive sense, the model can aid indirectly in the identification of potential personal and social developmental resources. Traditional developmental theories should be applied, however, only with recognition of the ethnocentrism expressed in them. They suggest, for example, that there is one right way to raise a child, one "appropriate" type of relationship with the family of origin, and one "healthy" way to develop intimate relationships in adulthood. Although it is harder to extrapolate practice principles from the more complex, emerging life course perspective, it seems more promising for understanding diverse persons in diverse environments. It suggests that individuals must always be assessed within familial, cultural, and historical contexts.

The Social Behavioral Perspective

In your assessment of Martha Clark, you may think that she has developed feelings of incompetence, which may have some relationship to her episodes of depression. Perhaps Martha's prior experiences reinforced a sense of incompetence rather than competence. Perhaps certain aspects of her current environment further reinforce this belief. For example, when she moved from a one-story apartment in senior housing to the two-story home of Al and Betty, certain aspects of the new physical environment, such as stairs, complicated her ability to do things for herself. You may also want to learn more about her son's aggressive behavior. When did it begin? How often does it happen? In which kinds of situations and environments? Is he imitating behavior that he saw modeled in his parents' home? Viewing the Clark family's situation from the social behavioral perspective (see Exhibit 2.10) leads you to pursue such questions in your assessment.

As you probably recall from a course in psychology, theories in the **social behavioral perspective** suggest that human behavior is learned as individuals interact with their environments. But behaviorists disagree among themselves about the processes by which behavior is learned. This book presents a very inclusive view of behaviorism, including both the "hard" behaviorism of classical and operant conditioning and the "soft" behaviorism of cognitive social learning theory. **Classical conditioning theory,** which sees behavior as the result of associating a conditioned stimulus with an unconditioned stimulus, can be traced to the Russian physiologist Ivan Pavlov. **Operant conditioning theory**, which sees behavior as the result of reinforcement, is built on the work of two American psychologists, John B. Watson and B. F. Skinner. **Cognitive social learning theory**, with Albert Bandura as its chief contemporary proponent, suggests that behavior is also learned by imitation and through cognitive processes.

Although contemporary proponents of the social behavioral perspective generally recognize that cognition exists, a major split has developed over the role of cognition in human behavior.

EXHIBIT 2.10
Central Ideas of the Social Behavioral Perspective

- Human behavior is learned when individuals interact with the environment.
- Similar learning processes taking place in different environments produce differences in human behavior.
- Human behavior is learned by association of environmental stimuli.
- Human behavior is learned by reinforcement.
- Human behavior is learned by imitation.
- Human behavior is influenced by personal expectations and meanings.

The central question is whether thoughts are antecedents or results of behavior—the indepen-dent or dependent variable. "Hard" behaviorism, when it recognizes cognition at all, sees it as a result, not a cause, of behavior; "soft" behaviorism, however, sees cognition as both result and cause of behavior. In short, "hard" behaviorism sees human behavior as totally determined by environment; "soft" behaviorism sees human behavior as resulting from the reciprocal interac-tion of person and environment.

Differences in behavior, in the social behavioral perspective, occur when the same learning processes occur in different environments. The theory does not allow for variations in learning processes based on biology. Typically, the social behavioral perspective searches for the *one* envi-ronmental factor, or contingency, that has reinforced *one* specific behavior. Thus, a proponent of this perspective might attribute Martha Clark's current depression to her son's abusive behavior and ignore both her previous episodes and the multiple losses that she has faced since her husband's death. The identified contingency is usually in the micro system (such as the family), or sometimes in the meso system (for example, a school classroom), but these systems are not typically put in social, economic, political, or historical contexts. One exception is Albert Bandura's cognitive social learning theory, which acknowledges broad systemic influences on the development of gender roles. Social work scholars applying behavioral principles have also made notable efforts in recent years to incorporate a broader view of the environments of hu-man behavior (Berlin, 1983; Gambrill, 1987; Reid, 1985).

Bruce Thyer (1994) suggests that "behavior social work practice is embedded in traditional social work values of respect for individuals, maximizing client autonomy, and working toward the elimination of racism, discrimination, and social injustice" (p. 136). "Hard" behaviorism pro-vides few theoretical tools for understanding or changing power relationships, however. Operant behavioral theory recommends rewards over punishment, but it does not account for the coer-cion and oppression inherent in power relationships at every system level. It is quite possible, therefore, for the professional behavior modifier to be in service to oppressive forces.

In contrast, Bandura (1986) writes specifically about power as related to gender roles. He also presents the concepts of **self-efficacy**, by which he means a sense of personal competence, and **efficacy expectation**, by which he means an expectation that one can personally accom-plish a goal (Bandura, 1977a, 1986). Persons in nondominant positions are seen as particularly vulnerable to **learned helplessness** (see Mikulincer, 1994; Seligman, 1992), in which a person's prior experience with environmental forces has led to low self-efficacy and efficacy expectation. You may find the concepts of self-efficacy and learned helplessness particularly useful in think-ing about both Martha's and Al's situations. Both have experienced some defeats and changes in their physical functioning that may be leading them to expect less of themselves and to resist measures that might improve their functioning.

Social behavioral concepts are easily measured for empirical investigation because theoriz-ing has been based, in very large part, on laboratory research. This characteristic is also a draw-back of the social behavioral perspective, however, because laboratory experiments by design eliminate much of the complexity of person/environment configurations. Overall, the social be-havioral perspective sacrifices multidimensional understanding to gain logical consistency. Christopher Monte (1995) suggests that all versions of the social behavioral perspective have had their "share of confirmations and disconfirmations" (p. 769). In general, however, it seems fair to say that there is a relatively high degree of empirical support for the propositions of both "hard" and "soft" behaviorism (see Thyer, 1991).

A major strength of the social behavioral perspective is the ease with which principles of behavior modification can be extrapolated, and it is probably a rare person who has not used social behavioral principles of action at some point. Social workers and psychologists, primarily, have used social behavioral methods to modify atypical behavior of individuals. But these methods have not been used effectively to produce social reform. Richard Stuart (1989) reminds us that behavior modification was once a "social movement" that appealed to young social reformers who were more interested in changing social conditions that produce atypical behaviors than in changing systems for managing atypical behavior. Skinner's *Walden Two* was the impetus for attempts by these young reformers to build nonpunitive communities, which represented significant modification of social conditions (see Kinkade, 1973; Wheeler, 1973).

The Humanistic Perspective

In a sense, Martha Clark has shown a lot of strength to persevere through all of the losses she has experienced over the past two years, even though many of her attempts to cope are not working well for her. You could reason that biology and social circumstances constrain her behavioral choices to some degree but that Martha is making choices and is capable of rethinking those choices. However, your reflections about her situation may be very different from her own, and thus your overarching concern is to get a chance to meet with Martha and hear more about how she sees her situation. Similarly, you applaud Al and Betty's commitment to their mother's care, even though some of their attempts to cope are not currently working well for them. You reason that social circumstances serve as constraints to Al's behavior, but you also think that he has made conscious choices and is capable of reworking those choices. The same can be said for Betty. You are eager to hear how both Al and Betty see their current situation. Your thoughts and planned course of action at this point reflect the humanistic perspective, summarized in Exhibit 2.11.

The humanistic perspective is often called the third force of psychology, because it was developed in reaction to the determinism found in early versions of both the psychodynamic and behavioral perspectives (Monte, 1995). We are using the term **humanistic perspective** to

EXHIBIT 2.11

Central Ideas of the Humanistic Perspective

- Humans are "spiritual, rational, purposeful, and autonomous" (Monte, 1995, p. 665).
- Human behavior can be understood only from the vantage point of the phenomenol self—from the internal frame of reference of the individual.
- People make psychologically destructive demands on each other, and attempts to meet those demands produce anxiety.
- Human behavior is driven by a desire for growth and competence, and by a need for love and acceptance.

include humanistic psychology and existential psychology, both of which emphasize the individual's freedom of action. The term also includes the existential sociology tradition, which counters the structural determinism found in some sociological theories and presents as a dominant theme the idea that people are simultaneously free and constrained, both active and passive agents.

Like social constructionism, the humanistic perspective is often traced to the German phenomenological philosopher Edmund Husserl (Krill, 1986). It is also influenced by a host of existential philosophers, beginning with Soren Kierkegaard and including Freidrich Nietzche, Martin Heidegger, Jean-Paul Sartre, Albert Camus, Simone de Beauvoir, Martin Buber, and Paul Tillich. Other early contributors to existential psychology include Viktor Frankl, Rollo May, Carl Jung, R. D. Laing, Karen Horney, and Erich Fromm. Perhaps the most influential contributions to humanistic psychology were made by Carl Rogers (1951) and Abraham Maslow (1962). Carl Rogers began his professional career at the Rochester Child Guidance Center, where he worked with social workers who had been trained at the Philadelphia School of Social Work. He has acknowledged the influence of Otto Rank, Jessie Taft, and the social workers at the Rochester agency on his thinking about the importance of responding to client feelings (Hart, 1970).

The internal life of the individual is the focus of the humanistic perspective and, as might be expected, most theorists in the tradition give limited attention to the environments of human behavior. Taking the lead from existential philosophers, R. D. Laing sees humans as interrelated with their worlds and frowns on the word *environment* because it implies a fragmented person. In discussions of human behavior, however, Laing (1967, 1969) emphasizes the insane situations in which human behavior is enacted. Erich Fromm was heavily influenced by Karl Marx and is much more inclusive of environment than other theorists in the humanistic perspective, emphasizing industrialization, Protestant reformation, capitalism, and technological revolution as alienating contexts against which humans search for meaning (Fromm, 1941). Although existential sociologists emphasize the importance of feelings and emotions, they also focus on the problematic nature of social life under modernization (see Fontana, 1984). A dehumanizing world is implicit in the works of Maslow and Rogers, but neither theorist focuses on the environments of human behavior, nor do they acknowledge that some environments are more dehumanizing than others.

The humanistic perspective, with its almost singular consideration of an internal frame of reference, devotes more attention to individual differences than to differences between groups. The works of Fromm and Horney are striking exceptions to this statement. Karen Horney identified culturally based gender differences at a time when psychology either ignored gender or took a "biology as destiny" approach. She also lost favor among other psychodynamic theorists by reworking Freud's conceptualization of the Oedipus conflict and of feminine psychology to produce a more gender-sensitive perspective (Horney, 1939, 1967).

The humanistic perspective, with its emphasis on search for meaning, is the only perspective presented in this chapter to explicitly recognize the role of spirituality in human behavior. Other theories of spirituality are discussed in Chapter 6.

In general, far too little attention is given in the humanistic tradition to the processes by which institutional oppression influences the **phenomenal self**—the individual's subjectively felt and interpreted experience of "who I am." Like the social constructionist perspective, however, the humanistic perspective is sometimes quite strong in giving voice to experiences of members of nondominant groups. With the emphasis on the phenomenal self, members of nondominant groups are more likely to have preferential input into the telling of their own stories. Your intention to hear and honor the stories of Martha, Al, and Betty may be a novel experience for each of them, and you may, indeed, hear very different stories than you expect to hear. Fromm and Maccoby (1970) illustrate this emphasis in their identification of the different life worlds of members of groups of different socioeconomic statuses in a Mexican village. Most significantly, Rogers developed his respect for the personal self, and consequently his client-centered approach to therapy, when he realized that his perception of the life worlds of his low-income clients in the Child Guidance Clinic were very different from their own perceptions (Hart, 1970).

Theories in the humanistic perspective are often criticized for being vague and highly abstract, with concepts such as "being" and "phenomenal self." Indeed, theorists in the humanistic perspective, in general, have not been afraid to sacrifice coherence to gain what they see as a more complete understanding of human behavior. As might be expected, empirically minded scholars have not been attracted to the humanistic perspective, and consequently there is little empirical literature to support the perspective. A notable exception is the clinical side of Rogers's theory. Rogers began a rigorous program of empirical investigation of the therapeutic process, and such research has provided strong empirical support for his conceptualization of the necessary conditions for the therapeutic relationship: warmth, empathy, and genuineness (Monte, 1995).

If the social constructionist perspective gives new meaning to the old social work adage "Begin where the client is," it is social work's historical involvement in the development of the humanistic perspective that gave original meaning to the adage. The humanistic perspective suggests that social workers begin by developing an understanding of how the client views the situation and, with its emphasis on the individual drive for growth and competence, recommends a "strengths" rather than "pathology" approach to practice. From this perspective, then, you might note the strong commitment to helping one another displayed by the Clark family, which might be the basis for successful intervention. At the organizational level, the humanistic perspective has been used by organizational theorists, such as Douglas McGregor (1960), to prescribe administrative actions that focus on employee well-being as the best route to organizational efficiency and effectiveness. Conflict theorists have criticized the organizational humanists, however, for their failure to take account of the ways in which organizations are instruments of domination (Hearn & Parkin, 1993).

The Merits of Multiple Perspectives

You can see that each of these perspectives puts a different lens on the unfolding story of the Clark family. But do these different ways of thinking make you more effective when you meet with clients like the Clarks? We think so. It was suggested in Chapter 1 that each situation can be examined from several perspectives, and that using a variety of perspectives brings more dimensions of the situation into view. Eileen Gambrill (1990) has suggested that all of us, whether new or experienced social workers, have biases that predispose us to do too little thinking, rather than too much, about the practice situations we confront. We are, she suggests, particularly proned to ignore information that is contrary to our hypotheses about situations. Consequently, we tend to end our search for understanding prematurely. One step we can take to prevent this premature closure is to think about practice situations from multiple theoretical perspectives.

The fields of psychology and sociology offer a variety of patterned ways of thinking about changing person/environment configurations, ways that have been worked out over time to assist in understanding human behavior. They are tools that can help us make sense of the situations we encounter. We do not mean to suggest that all eight of the perspectives discussed in this chapter will be equally useful, or even useful at all, in all situations. But each of these perspectives will be useful in some situations that you encounter as a social worker, and therefore should be in your general knowledge base. We hope that over time you will begin to use these multiple perspectives in an integrated fashion so that you can see the many dimensions, the contradictions as well as the consistencies, in stories like the Clark family's. We remind you, again, however, to use general knowledge only to generate hypotheses to be tested in specific situations.

IMPLICATIONS FOR SOCIAL WORK PRACTICE

The eight perspectives on human behavior discussed in this chapter suggest a variety of principles for social work assessment and intervention:

- In assessment, consider any recent role transitions, as well as role ambiguity, role overload, and role conflict. Assist families and groups to renegotiate unsatisfactory role structures. Develop networks of support for persons experiencing challenging role transitions.

- In assessment, consider power arrangements and forces of oppression, and the alienation that emanates from them. Assist in the development of advocacy efforts to challenge patterns of dominance, when possible. Be aware of the power dynamics in your relationships with clients; when working with nonvoluntary clients, speak directly about the limits and uses of your power.

- In assessment, consider the patterns of exchange in the social support networks of individual clients, families, and organizations, using sociograms (ecomaps) for network mapping when useful. Assist individuals, families, and organizations to renegotiate unsatisfactory patterns of exchange, when possible. Consider how social policy can increase the rewards for prosocial behavior.

- Begin your work by understanding how clients view their situations. Engage clients in thinking about the environments in which these constructions of situations have developed. When working in situations characterized by differences in belief systems, assist members to engage in sincere discussions and to negotiate lines of actions.

- Assist clients to express emotional conflicts and to understand how these are related to past events, when appropriate. Assist clients to develop self-awareness and self-control, where needed. Assist clients to locate and use needed environmental resources.

- In assessment, consider the familial, cultural, and historical contexts in the timing and experience of developmental transitions.

- In assessment, consider the variety of learning processes by which behavior is learned. Be sensitive to the possibility of learned helplessness when clients lack motivation for change. Consider issues of social justice and fairness before engaging in behavior modification.

- Be aware of the potential for significant differences between your assessment of the situation and the client's own assessment. Focus on strengths rather than pathology.

MAIN POINTS

1. Both sociological and psychological theories are needed for considering changing configurations of persons and environments.

2. Four sociological perspectives (systems, conflict, rational choice, and social constructionist) and four psychological perspectives (psychodynamic, developmental, social behavioral, and humanistic) can help social workers bring different dimensions of person/environment configurations into view.

3. The systems perspective sees human behavior as the outcome of reciprocal interactions of persons operating within organized and integrated social systems.

4. The conflict perspective draws attention to conflict, dominance, and oppression in social life.

5. The rational choice perspective sees human behavior as based on self-interest and rational choices about effective goal accomplishment.

6. The social constructionist perspective recognizes no objective reality, only the shared subjective realities that are created as people interact. The social constructionist thus sees multiple social and cultural realities.

7. The psychodynamic perspective is concerned with how internal processes such as needs, drives, and emotions motivate human behavior.

8. The developmental perspective focuses on how behavior changes and stays the same across the life cycle.

9. Theories in the social behavioral perspective suggest that human behavior is learned as individuals interact with their environments.

10. The humanistic perspective emphasizes freedom of action, while recognizing that people are both free and constrained. It focuses on strengths rather than pathologies.

11. Using multiple perspectives for thinking about changing person/environment configurations can help us avoid a premature end to our search for understanding.

KEY TERMS

boundary	open system
classical conditioning theory	operant conditioning theory
closed system	phenomenal self
cognitive social learning theory	phenomenological sociology
comparison level	pluralistic theory of social conflict
comparison level alternative	psychodynamic perspective
conflict perspective	rational choice perspective
constructivist research	role
critical theorists	role ambiguity
developmental perspective	role conflict
ecomaps	role overload
efficacy expectation	self-efficacy
enacted role	social behavioral perspective
expected role	social constructionist perspective
feedback mechanisms	social exchange theory
functionalist sociology	social network theory
humanistic perspective	sociograms
learned helplessness	systems perspective

WORLD WIDE WEB RESOURCES

Humanistic Psychology
http://www.ahpweb.org/aboutahp/whatis.html
Web site maintained by the Association of Humanistic Psychology containing the history of humanistic psychology, information on Carl Rogers, the humanistic view of human behavior, methods of inquiry, and humanistic psychotherapies.

Types of Theories
http://www.grohol.com/therapy.htm
Site run by Dr. John Grohol, Psy.D., listing four major schools of theory and therapy: psychodynamic, cognitive-behavioral, humanistic, and eclectic.

William Alanson White Institute
http://wawhite.org/
The William Alanson White Institute of Psychiatry, Psychoanalysis, and Psychology was co-founded by Harry Stack Sullivan and Erich Fromm. This site contains contemporary psychoanalysis journal articles, definition and description of psychoanalysis, issues of transference/countertransference, and links to other psychoanalytic sites.

Randall Collins – Conflict Theory
http://www.runet.edu/~Iridener/courses/COLLINR1.HTML
Site maintained by Larry Ridener, professor of sociology at Radford University. Contains an excerpt from Randall Collins, *Conflict of Sociology* (New York: Academic Press, 1974), pp. 56–61. Discussion of the basics of conflict theory.

APA Online
http://www.psych.org/
The American Psychiatric Association site contains information on policy advocacy, clinical resources, research resources, current news, and education.

A Day in the Life of a School Social Worker: One Person's Multifaceted Social Work Practice

Mary Gay Hutcherson has worked in a variety of social work settings, including a state psychiatric hospital, protective services, hospitals, and the Red Cross. Currently, she works in the Social Work Department of a suburban school system. She loves this position because of the variety of roles she gets to play in the course of a day. Mary Gay provides social work services to three schools—two elementary schools and one high school. We are going to follow her through a typical day's work at the high school.

Early morning. Mary Gay arrives at the high school, as usual, at about 7:00 A.M. She feeds the fish in her office and goes immediately to meet with one of the special education teachers, to touch base about a student with whom they have both been working.

Earlier in the week, the student had reported to the teacher that his mother had been behaving very strangely for a few weeks—laughing to herself all day, not paying bills, and quitting her job. There was no food in the house, and his mother was not providing care to his younger siblings. The teacher had called Mary Gay to discuss this situation, because she knew that Mary Gay had met with the mother. Mary Gay was concerned and thought that she should go to the home to assess the situation. Because the student knew the teacher well and trusted her, Mary Gay asked the teacher to join her on the home visit.

When they arrived at the home, they found the situation very much as the student had described it. After assessing the situation, Mary Gay returned to her office and called the crisis unit at the county mental health center. She also placed a call to child protective services because of her concern about the care of the children. The crisis worker agreed to see the client if she could be brought to the crisis center. Mary Gay contacted the police department to request assistance in transporting the mother to the crisis center; she met them at the home and persuaded the mother to go for the assessment. The crisis worker recommended that the mother needed to be hospitalized. Mary Gay consulted with the child protection agency to discuss arrangements for the care of the children, and called relatives in another state to let them know what was happening with the family.

This morning, Mary Gay is checking with the teacher to get a report on how the student is coping with this family crisis. She learns that the student and his siblings are being well cared for and seem to be coping adequately with the situation.

Mary Gay goes back to her office and checks her phone messages. She has a message to call Ms. C at home. Mary Gay is well acquainted with Ms. C, because she has been working with her and her daughter, Jan, for several weeks. Jan, a ninth-grader, has a seizure disorder and severe migraine headaches. She has been refusing to come to school because she does not want the other students to see her while she is having a seizure. She gets very anxious in the mornings when it is about time for the school bus, and anxiety exacerbates both the seizure disorder and the migraines.

Mary Gay has been working with Jan to help her learn to use relaxation exercises before getting on the school bus. She has been working with Ms. C about making firmer demands that Jan get on the school bus in the mornings. She has been collaborating with teachers and other school personnel to help them be more supportive of Jan's efforts to be in school. She has asked some of Jan's teachers to reach out to her. She has also been trying to get Jan involved in the after-school Bible Study Group, where she might make connections with other students with similar interests. She has referred Jan to the school psychologist to have the necessary testing completed to qualify Jan for special education services.

This morning, Ms. C is distressed. Jan was scheduled to meet with the psychologist this morning, but she did not want to come to school. She was afraid that the meeting with the psychologist would upset her and precipitate a seizure. Ms. C also reports that her employer has given her a warning that she must become more consistent in arriving at work punctually. She is "at her wit's end" with trying to get Jan on the school bus in the mornings. Mary Gay and Ms. C problem-solve how Ms. C can talk with her employer about her situation. They agree that a top priority is to get Jan tested, so that she will be eligible to have a special education plan developed. Mary Gay tells Ms. C that she will see what she can do to facilitate that.

Mary Gay goes to the office of the school psychologist and discusses Jan's situation. She requests that the psychologist go to Jan's home to do the testing. The psychologist, who has never done testing away from the office and is reluctant to do so now, gets called away to a meeting. Mary Gay resolves to take this issue up later.

Midmorning. Mary Gay leaves the school and drives to the nearby shopping mall, where she and prevention staff from the county mental health center are presenting a two-hour parent training program, "Love and Logic." Attendance is good today—15 parents present—and the parents are receptive.

Early afternoon. When Mary Gay arrives back at school, she has a few minutes to finish writing a social history report for tomorrow's meeting of the Special Education Eligibility Team. Then she goes across the hall to attend today's meeting to review three applications. After this meeting, Mary Gay has a few minutes to talk with the psychologist about Jan's evaluation and to return phone calls.

Then she moves on to a meeting with the Student Assistance Team. This team reviews referrals from teachers and parents that involve a variety of student problems. Recently it seems that most of the situations are drug-related, and Mary Gay suggests that the Student

Assistance Team invite a substance abuse consultant from the county mental health center to meet with them. Other team members like this idea, and Mary Gay volunteers to make the call.

Midafternoon. A teacher from one of the elementary schools calls to consult with Mary Gay about a potential child abuse situation. Mary Gay concludes that the situation needs to be reported and calls a social worker at protective services because the teacher is uncomfortable about making the call herself.

Mary Gay meets for a few minutes with the social work student for whom she is serving as field instructor, to review the social history report that the student will be presenting at tomorrow's Special Education Eligibility Team meeting. Mary Gay is pleased with the progress the student is making and tells her so.

Late afternoon. Mary Gay makes two home visits to meet with families of students who have been referred for special education eligibility screening. Both students are thought to have undiagnosed learning disabilities. Mary Gay sees these meetings with families as the core of her job as a school social worker. In addition to obtaining social history data, her goal is to get the family "on board" as active members of the team. She wants to understand how the family feels about learning disabilities, and she wants to make sure that they understand the process of eligibility screening, what to expect at the team meeting, and the criteria used for diagnosing a learning disability. She prefers to have these conversations in the families' homes—on their turf—to get a better understanding of the family's needs and strengths and to allow the family the opportunity to be interviewed in the comfort of familiar surroundings.

In her second visit today, Mary Gay learns that the single mother is facing severe financial problems. As she problem-solves with the mother, she realizes that this family does not qualify for the free lunch program because the mother is employed. She reminds herself to check with the school principal about the possibility of waiving this policy, which is detrimental to families like this one.

Evening. After a quick dinner, Mary Gay is off to the weekly meeting of the Organization for Sexual Minority Youth. Mary Gay was instrumental in forming this group a few years ago when she became aware that these youth were frequent targets of hate crimes. The purpose of the group is twofold: to be supportive to gay and lesbian youth, and to work with the community to develop better understanding of issues facing these youth. Although this is not an official part of Mary Gay's work as a school social worker, she sees it as a part of her professional obligation to actively promote social justice.

Something to Think About

I continue to be impressed with the multifaceted nature of social work practice and challenged by the demands of such work. In the beginning, of course, the demands seemed overwhelming—just as they did when I was first learning to play the piano and to play basketball. The following questions should help you think about your own process of learning to do social work:

- How does this day in the life of Mary Gay Hutcherson fit with the understanding you had about what social work is when you decided you wanted to be a social worker? How is it similar, and how is it different?

- What about the way your family and friends understand social work? Which of Mary Gay's activities fit with their picture of social work? Given this day in Mary Gay's life, how would you answer when Aunt Louise asks "What is social work, anyway?"

- How does this day fit with your experiences, to date, as a social work student? How is it similar, and how is it different?

- As you follow Mary Gay through the day, think about what general information she needs for each of the activities in which she engages. What have you learned already—from experience and education—in each of these knowledge areas? What else do you need to learn to be able to step into Mary Gay's shoes?

- What dimensions of person and environment seem to be important to Mary Gay's work on this particular day? Do the same dimensions seem important across the different activities of the day, or do you find yourself thinking more about specific dimensions during specific episodes?

- How might you draw on specific theoretical perspectives to assist in any of the social work roles played by Mary Gay on this day?

PART II

The Multiple Dimensions of Person

The multiple dimensions of person, environment, and time have unity; they are inseparable and embedded. That is the way I think about them, and the way I am encouraging you to think about them. However, you will be better able to think about the unity of the three aspects of human behavior when you have developed a clearer understanding of the different dimensions encompassed by each one. A review of theory and research about the different dimensions will help you to sharpen your thinking about what is involved in the changing configurations of persons and environments.

The purpose of the four chapters in Part II is to provide you with an up-to-date understanding of theory and research about the dimensions of person. It begins with a chapter on the biological dimension and ends with one on the spiritual dimension. Because so much has been written about the psychological dimension, it is divided into two chapters: the first one about the basic elements of a person's psychology, and the second one about the processes a person uses to maintain psychological balance in a changing environment. The reflection at the end of Part II illustrates the integration of the biological, psychological, and spiritual dimensions in social work practice.

With a state-of-the-art knowledge base about the multiple dimensions of persons, you will be prepared to consider the interactions among persons and environments—the subject of Part III. And then you will be able to think more comprehensively and more clearly about the ways configurations of persons and environments change across the life course. The discussion of the life course in the companion volume to this book will attempt to put the dimensions of persons and environments back together and help you think about their embeddedness.

Understanding the Whole Person

What does it mean to be a person? At root, a human being is a biological mass of living tissue: blood, bones, organs, glands, nerves. Beyond the tissue are psychological and spiritual dimensions to consider.

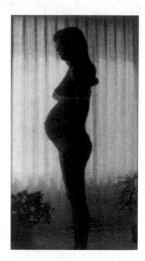

But let's begin by looking at the biological person. Social workers often help people adjust or adapt to biological changes, including diseases like diabetes. Although diabetes can easily be detected, many people go years before diagnosis and treatment, which leads to pervasive physical problems involving several biological systems. By helping to make sure that testing is available, even for children, social workers can greatly improve people's lives.

Genes can predispose us to diabetes, but lifestyle also plays a large role. As social workers, we need to understand how people can be more active in their own health management. Even children with diabetes can learn what to eat and how to administer insulin to lessen the impact the disease has on their everyday lives.

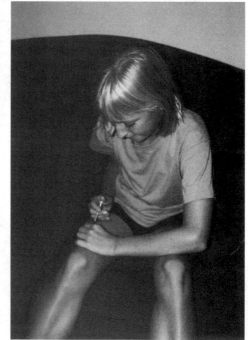

Disease isn't the only aspect of the biological person that is relevant to social workers. We can also help people understand that exercise and conditioning of the bones and muscles that nature gave us can result in improvements to the biological system. Advocating good nutrition, immunizations, and safety precautions like seat belts and protected sex is another way we can influence clients' physical health.

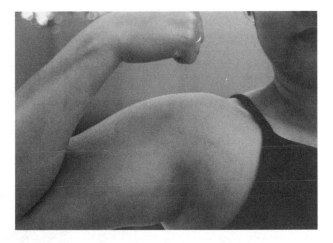

We also need to acknowledge that the environment people live in can negatively impact their bodies. Living in a polluted area, being exposed to high levels of stress, and working with carcinogens all have the potential to do damage. The person who makes other people's hands and nails beautiful by giving manicures risks getting cancer from breathing in the toxic chemicals that are used.

Social workers view biological health as not only an individual experience but also as a community issue. They seek to promote healthy communities and open access to health care as well as to educate individuals about healthy lifestyles.

The biological person is closely related to the psycho-logical person. Our physical makeup and health plays an important role in the way our brains function. And our cognitive abilities affect how we think about problems and situations as well as how we synthesize and apply information.

Through play, children refine the cognitive skills they need to perform the complex tasks associated with well-paying jobs. Poor children often don't get the stimulus they need to compete in a high-tech world.

As adults, they may be limited to manual labor.

But for youngsters fortunate enough to have sufficient time and resources to play, the world is enlarged. This young boy plays games at a museum, simultaneously increasing his imagination and his sense of history.

That sort of mind expansion is just what it takes to develop the cognitive skills needed to prosper in the information age. Beny Alagen, for instance, has used his well-developed cognitive skills to create a computer firm. To give all children the opportunity for such success, social workers need to be concerned about children's opportunities for play and learning.

Another dimension of the psychological person that concerns social workers is emotion. Social workers must be able to accurately recognize emotions, both in themselves and in their clients. They must also be able to help clients recognize and deal with their own emotions. The difficulty is that people respond differently to the events in their lives.

For example, can you determine which of the two people below is most stressed? The more demonstrative person is not always the one being most affected by stress. Cultural factors play a large part in the expression of emotions. In our society, men have traditionally been more stoic than women are, but that does not mean men feel less stress.

We all experience some level of stress from time to time. But sometimes that stress becomes overwhelming.

In the case of crisis, we may be unable to solve problems in the usual way. A person who is not able to cope may feel immobilized and on the brink of complete collapse. In these situations, we need to rely on something or someone outside ourselves.

Social support is the most common method of
coping with stress. Usually people get support by
talking with others—friends, family, or a social
worker or therapist.

Another effective way to cope with the stresses of life is to exercise. By "working out" physically, we can often work out our psychological problems. And if we work out in a group, we not only exercise our bodies and promote an overall sense of well-being; we also benefit from socializing with others.

Sometimes, however, the only way to really relieve stress is to change the environment. For instance, society can support people with disabilities in their efforts to cope with life by making more of the physical environment wheelchair accessible. Public transportation that has been adapted offers a way for people with disabilities to get around and thus simultaneously reduces their stress levels and expands their opportunities.

In addition to considering the biological person and the psychological person, social workers should take into account the spiritual aspects of being human.

Spirituality is often equated with religious practice. However, religion is more narrow than spirituality.

Nevertheless, social workers need to recognize that religious elements may be part of their clients' culture and background, influencing how they behave even when they claim to be "not religious." For example, this couple from India (below, left) are engaging in a traditional Hindu wedding more for their relatives' sake than out of their own personal convictions. Yet the couple is not immune from the gender hierarchy traditionally found in Hindu cultures.

Beyond religion, spirituality may be expressed as altruism. An act like helping a person in a wheelchair navigate a busy street (below, right) gives us a deeper and more profound connection to other people, which is one of the initial steps in expanding spiritual awareness. Indeed, many social workers choose the profession because it offers spiritual connection.

Others seek to expand spiritual awareness through practices like meditation and prayer.

The contemplation of nature is another way to seek connection with forces beyond ourselves.

Whatever the focus—the well-being of other people, the inner self, or some larger force, such as nature, the universe, or the ultimate reality—spirituality can be taken to mean the search for connection. Thus it helps to link all the dimensions of person with the environment and the passage of time.

CHAPTER 3

The Biological Person

Stephen French Gilson, Virginia Commonwealth University

The author wishes to thank Andrew S. Levitas, MD, Michael Godschalk, MD, and June M. Stapleton, PhD, for their helpful comments, insights, and suggestions for this chapter.

CHANGING BODIES: MAGGIE, BESS, MELISSA, THOMAS, AND MAX

When you, as a social worker, sit down with a client, you face a multifaceted person. You will perhaps be most likely to focus on the client's psychosocial realities. But sometimes the biological dimension is the first and most germane piece of the puzzle, as it was for these five clients.

■ ■ ■ ■ ■

Maggie was in love with Sam. That is the only plausible explanation that her family could come up with for why she was riding on the back of Sam's brand-new motorcycle not wearing a helmet. Late one night, the police called her parents and informed them that Maggie had been thrown 20 feet from the rear of the motorcycle that Sam was driving. He had swerved onto the shoulder of the road to avoid running into a car. Sam was not hurt, but Maggie sustained multiple fractures and a severe closed head injury. She was in a coma for three weeks. Miraculously, over a six-month period, all of Maggie's external bodily injuries, including the fractures, healed, and she was able to walk and talk with no apparent residual impairments. Cognitively, Maggie was not so lucky. She was able to read, but could not retain what she had just read a minute ago. She lost all of her previous knowledge of math and could not do the simplest addition and subtraction problems. Copying her name from a piece of paper to another page would take her at least five minutes. Sometimes she would astound and even hurt her friends with blunt, tactless remarks, and she would occasionally become irritated out of all proportion to the stimulus. Maggie had just finished her junior year in college when the accident occurred, and everyone expected that she would return to school, finish her degree, marry Sam, and live happily ever after. But two years after the accident, Maggie's family knows, in their hearts, that she is not going to finish her last year of college. Sam is about to get engaged to another woman, but Maggie thinks she is still dating Sam and that he is just waiting for her to finish college before they get married. Everyone who knew Maggie before the accident cannot understand why her personality has changed so markedly, saying, "She's a completely different person!" Helping her will require that you understand what has happened to Maggie's body and how it affects her behavior.

■ ■ ■ ■ ■

Bess at the age of 52 was enjoying her "empty nest" just before you met her. The youngest of her three children had married six months ago, and although she was proud of what she had accomplished as a single mother, she was now ready to get on with her life. Her first order of business was to get her body back into shape, so she started on a high-carbohydrate, low-fat diet she had read about in a magazine. Drinking the recommended eight glasses of water or more each day was easy, because it seemed that she was always thirsty. But

CASE STUDY

Bess was losing more weight than she thought possible on a diet, and she was always cheating! Bess had thought that she would have to get more exercise to lose weight, but even walking to and from her car at the grocery store tired her out. One morning, Bess did not show up at the convenience store where she worked. Since it was very unusual for her not to call, nor to answer her phone, a coworker went over to her apartment. When there was no response to the knocking and pounding on the door, a neighbor, who had a key, opened the door to Bess's apartment. The coworker and neighbor found Bess sitting on her couch, still in her nightclothes, which were drenched with perspiration. Bess was very confused, unable to answer simple questions correctly. Paramedics transported Bess to the hospital. In the emergency room, after some blood work, a doctor diagnosed diabetes mellitus. Bess has recently begun to attend a psychoeducational group for persons with diabetes, which you lead.

■ ■ ■ ■ ■

Melissa's "perfect life" has just fallen apart. She went to her physician for a routine annual physical exam two months before her wedding. As she does with all of her patients, the doctor asked if Melissa had ever been tested for HIV. Melissa said no, and gave her permission for an AIDS test to be run with all of the other routine blood work. One week after her physical, the doctor's office called and asked Melissa to return for more blood work, because of what was thought to be an inaccuracy in the report. Another week passed, but Melissa did not think again about the tests because she had been told that she would not hear anything if everything was normal. Melissa's physician called her at home at 8:00 in the morning and asked her to come to her office after work that day. Because she was distracted by the wedding plans and a busy schedule at work, Melissa did not think anything of the doctor's request. When Melissa arrived at the doctor's office that afternoon, she was immediately taken to the doctor's private office. The doctor came in, sat down, and told Melissa that two separate blood tests had confirmed that she was HIV positive. Melissa spent more than three hours with her physician that evening, and soon thereafter she began to attend your HIV support group. Melissa has never used illicit drugs, and she has had only two sexual partners. She and her fiancé had decided not to have intercourse until they married, so he was not a prime suspect for passing along the infection. Melissa has remembered that the man with whom she was involved prior to meeting her fiancé would not talk about his past. He once mentioned having gone to a methadone clinic for a while, but he never used drugs in her presence, and she never even considered the fact that he was, or had been, addicted to drugs. Melissa has not seen this former lover for the past three years, ever since she moved away from Ohio.

CASE STUDY

■ ■ ■ ■ ■

Thomas is 30 years of age and lives with his parents. Both of his parents are very overweight, as are his two older sisters. Thomas loves his mom's cooking, but sometime ago realized that its high fat and high sodium content were contributing to his parents' obesity and high blood pressure. In contrast, Thomas takes pride in watching his diet (when he isn't eating at home) and is pretty smug about being the only one in the family who is underweight. Being called "the thin man" is, to Thomas, a compliment. He also boasts about being in great physical shape, and exercises to the point of being dizzy. After one of his dizziness episodes, a friend told him that he should get his blood pressure checked. Although Thomas knew of the high incidence of heart disease among African Americans, he never considered that he would have a problem. After all, he is young and in good physical shape. Out of curiosity, the next time Thomas stopped at his local drugstore, he decided to use one of those self-monitoring blood pressure machines. To his astonishment, the reading came back 200/105. Thomas will need your help to adopt some major lifestyle changes.

■ ■ ■ ■ ■

Max is a polio survivor. He contracted the disease when he was 2 years old, and it affected only his legs. He never had any breathing difficulties, nor any involvement in his arms. In fact, after six months in the hospital and another six months of therapy when he returned home, Max appeared to be "cured." Afterward, as he was growing up, no one would ever guess that there had been anything wrong with him. He could keep up with his friends except that he could never run very long distances. Now, 43 years later, Max has developed the symptoms of post-polio syndrome. He has noticed increasing weakness in his legs, unusual fatigue, and a lot of pain all over his body. A recent evaluation at a university clinic confirmed the diagnosis of post-polio syndrome, and the clinicians who saw him recommended that he consider getting the type of brace that is inserted in his shoes to support both ankles and that he use forearm crutches for walking long distances. Max has earned his living all his life as a housepainter. He needs your help figuring out how to cope with these new developments and how to support his two young children.

The Social Work Perspective on Biology

During your social work education you have probably discussed the bio-psycho-social-spiritual model in both human behavior and practice courses. It is a theoretical model that explains behavior from an interdependent systems, or transactional, perspective. But have you ever won-

dered why the biological dimension comes first? Is it because the biological ʔ
to be examined prior to the psychological, or social, or spiritual aspects of humu.
ten physical changes are indeed the basis of an array of psychological, social, and sр..
challenges.

Gaining full understanding of how the physical body operates may not be possible for most
social workers; after all, medical professionals spend many years in pursuit of that knowledge.
Nevertheless, social workers need a working knowledge of the body's systems and the ways in
which they transact with other dimensions of human behavior (Johnson et al., 1990; Saleebey,
1985, 1992; Weick, 1986).

There is strong conceptual, theoretical, and empirical evidence of relationships among
physical health, psychological health, and social experiences (House, Landis, & Umberson, 1988;
Levine, Coe, & Wiener, 1989; Weitz, 1996). For example, Holmberg and Kane (1995) provide.
clear evidence that persons with persistent and long-term psychiatric disorders exhibit a high
rate of physical health problems. These medical conditions, which occur concurrently with behavioral and psychological symptoms, "may contribute significantly to psychiatric
symptomology or be the sole cause of psychiatric symptoms" (Holmberg & Kane, 1995, p. 291).
Thus, psychotherapy or psychosocial support may not be the intervention most needed by the
individual.

Systems perspective   Although social workers do not need to be able to diagnose medical conditions, our assessments of individuals should help us determine whether referrals to biomedical professionals are
needed. And in our ongoing work, we should be able to assess what type of advocacy may be
needed to better assure that biological needs and issues are addressed. For example, the social
work administrator who is developing or operating a shelter, a food kitchen, or an advocacy center may need to integrate medical and mental health services with employment, housing, financial, and companionship services (Gelberg & Linn, 1988). Even the social worker who is primarily involved in the health care field may need to branch out and consider community and public
health issues. The social health model proposed by Lowe (1997) calls for us to view health not
only as an individual experience, but within the context of the community, group, and organization. Lowe recommends a model of social work practice that seeks to promote healthy communities as well as empowering individuals, families, and groups to advocate for their own health
needs. The delivery of broad-based social health services may occur in places such as schools,
workplaces, community centers, and places of faith, in addition to hospitals and medical clinics.

Humanistic perspective   Although social workers need to take physical health into account, we must avoid the temptation to view the social problems of individuals within a disease framework. Efficiency is an
advantage of a disease framework, because "any disease theory brings together a body of knowledge about symptoms, course, etiology and treatments and provides direction on how to proceed once a diagnosis is selected" (Mechanic, 1995, p. 1209). However, focusing on disease may
mask the strengths of individuals who have biological problems and may thus limit our ability
to intervene successfully.

Social constructionist perspective   The experience of a physical disability, such as paralysis or low vision, receives much of its
meaning from political, social, cultural, and economic contexts (Gilson, Tusler, & Gill, 1997;
Hahn, 1993; Thomson, 1996; Wang, 1992; Zola, 1993). Thus, the functional limitations associated with a disability depend on the physical, social, and attitudinal environment; the characteristics of the task; personal attitude; and available supports such as assistive technology,

personal assistance services, accessible transportation, and community living options (Mechanic, 1995).

Discussions in social work journals of the role that biology plays in human behavior have commonly been associated with just a few issues:

- Human immunodeficiency virus (HIV) and acquired immune deficiency (AIDS) (Littrell, 1996; Safyer & Spies-Karotkin, 1988; Wiener, Moss, Davidson, & Fair, 1992)

- Mental health and mental illness (Bentley & Walsh, 1996; Cohen, 1989; Farmer & Pandurangi, 1997; Farmer, Walsh, & Bentley, 1998; Johnson, 1989; Taylor, 1989; Walsh, 1998)

- Violence (Johnson, 1996)

- Alcohol and other drugs (Wallace, 1989)

These discussions make considerable contributions to our overall understanding of human behavior, but they tend to be indirect examinations of medical conditions and their impact on psychosocial functioning (Barber, 1994; Begun, 1993; Berkman, Millar, Holmes, & Bonander, 1991; Subramanian & Ell, 1989). They do not provide an overview of biological systems and their interaction. When more in-depth discussion is presented, it is usually limited to a review of the central nervous system and its role in mental illness, divorcing the functioning of the central nervous system from the other human biological systems. The social work profession also tends to develop a fascination with conjecture in the popular press about "new findings" and "advancements," which often overstates the significance of these developments.

To their credit, social workers have demonstrated an interest in understanding connections between social and emotional supports and physical health and wellness, and in understanding mind/body interactions (Hiratuska, 1994; Nee, 1995). One recent area of interest has been psychoneuroimmunology—the study of the relationships among psychological well-being, the immune system, and overall health. Foss (1994) suggests that "changes in the immune and neuroimmune measures correlate with changes in psychological states. . . . The implication is that patients, by refocusing their consciousness, altering their mental or emotional 'programs,' can actively participate in the healing process" (p. 39). Further, Nee (1995) presents convincing evidence of the "effects of psychosocial interactions at the cellular level" (p. 259).

In a review of several studies that investigated the relationship between psychosocial factors and longevity, Nee (1995) reports that involvement in the gay community increases the survival time of gay men with acquired immune deficiency syndrome (Caumartin, Joseph, & Chmiel, cited in Nee, 1995); men and women with a high level of social contacts with family and friends have prolonged longevity (Berkman & Syme, cited in Nee, 1995); lack of social interaction has a similar effect on mortality as do health risks such as high serum cholesterol, smoking, and high blood pressure (House, Landis, & Umberson, cited in Nee, 1995); and some individuals in great distress show poorer DNA repair of certain blood cells after X-irradiation than do others in less distress, suggesting a possible link between the incidence of cancer and distress (Kiecolt-Glaser, Stephen, Lipetz, Speicher, & Glaser, cited in Nee, 1995).

Conflict perspective

This mind/body connection, however, although the basis for many important discoveries about health and illness, may also unintentionally lead us to reduce biological issues to a simple faith in "mind over matter." The danger is that we will fail to consider the full range of environmental influences on health, and blame individuals for their illnesses or diagnoses. We cannot forget that health and illness are also influenced by social, political, cultural, and economic experiences (Saleebey, 1994). For example, the lack of access to health care, not of psychological well-being, is what places many children at risk for disease and poor health. Social forces (sexism, racism, classism) and access to power also influence the coping process (Banyard & Graham-Bermann, 1993).

Systems perspective
Developmental perspective

Social workers can profitably explore the links between human biology and human behavior in a variety of ways. Some promising lines of inquiry include brain plasticity and functional recovery following brain injury (Horn, 1991; Selzer, 1995), intellectual growth spurts in adolescence (Andrich & Styles, 1994), impact of stressors on mental health (Nicholson, 1997), developmental factors during childhood that influence the capability of an individual to attend to stimuli and information (Gilson, 1991), use of neuroimaging techniques to evaluate the effects of drug abuse and treatment (Walsh et al., 1994), treatment of AIDS dementia complex (Villemagne et al., 1996), and cardiovascular effects of drugs such as nicotine (Soria et al., 1996). However, only five biological systems are discussed in this chapter: the nervous system, the endocrine system, the immune system, the cardiovascular system, and the muscloskeletal system. All the other biological systems (including digestive, respiratory, urinary, and reproductive systems) also warrant our attention, but the five described here are commonly involved in many of the biologically based problems that social workers encounter, and they can serve as a model for our thinking about other systems.

Before we begin to look at these five systems individually, I want to emphasize their connectedness with one another. Just as human behavior is a complex transaction of person and environment, biological functioning is the result of complex transactions among all biological systems (Ader, Felten, & Cohen, 1990). No one system operates in isolation from other systems.

Nervous System

At the beginning of the chapter you met Maggie, who is like the more than half a million Americans hospitalized each year with a **brain injury (BI).** Brain injuries include head injuries that result from falls, automobile accidents, infections and viruses, insufficient oxygen, and poisoning.

Each type of BI may present specific issues and problems for the individual. However, brain injury in general can affect cognitive, physical, and psychological skills. Cognitive problems may present as difficulties with language and communication, information processing, memory, and perception. Maggie's difficulty in writing her name is an example of such problems, as well as a reflection of fine motor skill deficits. Physical limitations often present as difficulty with ambulation (walking), balance and coordination, strength, and endurance. Psychological problems may come from two different sources. They may be *primary,* or directly related to the BI, often seen as irritability and judgment errors. Or they may be *reactive* to the adjustments required to live with the BI and its consequences, typically seen as depression and changes in self-esteem. Maggie's difficulty in recognizing that Sam is not going to marry her and her misjudgments in other social situations are symptoms of the psychological consequences of her BI.

The nervous system is divided into three major subsystems:

- **Central nervous system (CNS)**—the brain and the spinal cord.
- **Peripheral nervous system (PNS)**—spinal and cranial nerves.
- **Autonomic nervous system (ANS)**—nerves controlling cardiovascular, gastrointestinal, genitourinary, and respiratory systems.

The brain sends signals to the spinal cord, which in turn relays the message to specific parts of the body by way of the PNS. Messages from the PNS to the brain travel back by way of a similar pathway (Carey, 1990). Note that Maggie's brain injury affects only a part of her nervous system—in fact, only part of the CNS. Damage to other parts of the nervous system can have devastating effects, but I will focus on her brain injury because it is so closely linked with behavioral issues.

The human brain, which constitutes only about 2 percent of total body weight, may contain as many as 10 million neurons. Its three major internal regions are referred to as the forebrain, midbrain, and hindbrain. Viewed from the side (Exhibit 3.1), the largest structure visible is the cerebral cortex, part of the forebrain. The **cerebral cortex** is the seat of higher mental functions, including thinking, planning, and problem solving.

The cerebral cortex is more highly developed in humans than in any other animal. It is divided into two hemispheres—left and right—that are interconnected by nerve fibers. The hemispheres are thought to be specialized—one side for language and the other for processing of spatial information, such as maps and pictures. Each hemisphere primarily controls the opposite side of the body, so that damage to one side of the brain may cause numbness or paralysis of the opposite arm and leg.

EXHIBT 3.1
Selected Areas of the Brain

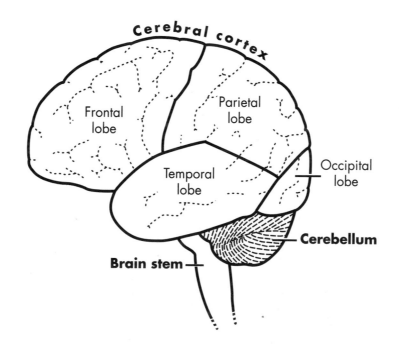

The cerebral cortex has four lobes, depicted in Exhibit 3.1. As Exhibit 3.2 explains, functions such as vision, hearing, and speech are distributed in selected regions, with some lobes being associated with more than one function. The frontal lobe is the largest, making up nearly one-third of the surface of the cerebral cortex. Lesions of any one of the lobes can have a dramatic impact on the functions of that lobe (Carpenter, 1991; Earle, 1987).

Other forebrain structures process information from the sensory organs and send it to the cortex, or receive orders from cortical centers and relay them on down. Also in the forebrain are centers for memory and emotion, as well as control of essential functions such as hunger, thirst, and sex drive.

The midbrain is a small area, but it contains important centers for sleep and pain, as well as relay centers for sensory information and control of movement.

Exhibit 3.1 also shows part of the hindbrain, including the cerebellum. The **cerebellum** controls complex motor programming, including maintaining muscle tone and posture. Other hindbrain structures are essential to the regulation of vegetative functions, including breathing, heart rate, and blood pressure. The brain stem connects the cerebral cortex to the spinal cord.

The basic working unit of all the nervous systems is the **neuron,** or nerve cell. The human body has a great diversity of neuronal types, but all consist of a cell body with a nucleus and a conduction fiber, or **axon**. Extending from the cell body are dendrites, which conduct impulses to the neurons from the axons of other nerve cells. Exhibit 3.3 shows how neurons are linked by axons and dendrites.

The connection between each axon and dendrite is actually a gap called a **synapse.** Synapses utilize chemical and electrical **neurotransmitters** to communicate. As the inset box in Exhibit 3.3 shows, nerve impulses travel from the cell body to the ends of the axons, where they trigger the release of neurotransmitters. The adjacent dendrite of another neuron has receptors

EXHIBIT 3.2

Regions of the Cerebral Cortex

Brain Region	Function
Frontal lobe	Motor behavior
	Expressive language
	Social functioning
	Concentration and ability to attend
	Reasoning and thinking
	Orientation to time, place, and person
Temporal lobe	Language
	Memory
	Emotions
Parietal lobe	Intellectual processing
	Integration of sensory information
Left parietal lobe	Verbal processing
Right parietal lobe	Visual/spatial processing
Occipital lobe	Vision

EXHIBIT 3.3

Features of a
Typical Neuron

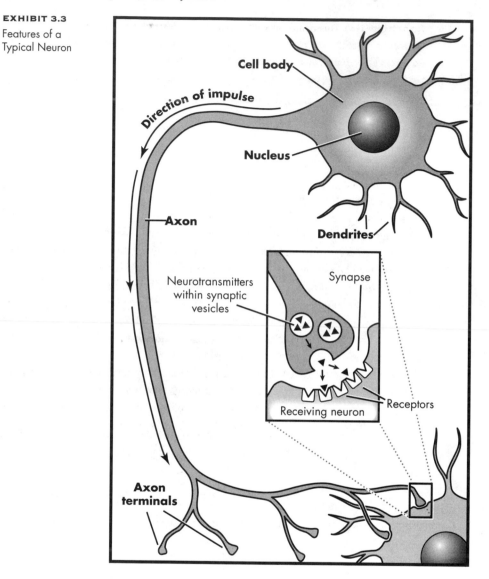

distinctively shaped to fit particular types of neurotransmitters. When the neurotransmitter fits into a slot, the message is passed along.

Although neurotransmitters are the focus of much current research, scientists are not exactly sure about all that neurotransmitters do. Essentially, they either excite or inhibit nervous system responses. But we know very little about many of the neurotransmitters, and we may not yet have discovered them all. Here are a few of the known types:

- **Acetylcholine (ACh).** The first neurotransmitter identified (nearly 70 years ago) is an excitatory neurotransmitter active in both the CNS and the PNS. Acetylcholine may be critical for intellectual activities such as memory.

- **Dopamine (DA).** This neurotransmitter, which is widely present in the CNS and PNS, is implicated in regulation of the endocrine system. Dopamine is thought to play a role in influencing emotional behavior, cognition, and motor activity.

- **Norepinephrine (NE).** Like dopamine, norepinephrine appears in many parts of the body. It may play a role in learning and memory and is also secreted by the adrenal gland in response to stress or events that produce arousal. Norepinephrine connects the brain stem with the cerebral cortex (Bentley & Walsh, 1996).

- **Serotonin.** Present in blood platelets, the lining of the digestive tract, and in a tract from the midbrain to all brain regions, this neurotransmitter is thought to be a factor in many body functions. Serotonin plays a role in sensory processes, muscular activity, thinking, states of consciousness, mood, depression, and anxiety (Bentley & Walsh, 1996).

- **Amino acids.** Some types of the unit molecules found in proteins are distributed throughout the brain and other body tissues. One of these amino acids, **gamma aminobutyric acid** (GABA), is thought to play a critical role in inhibiting the firing of impulses of some cells. Thus, GABA is believed to play an important role in many functions of the CNS, such as locomotor activity, cardiovascular reactions, pituitary function, and anxiety (Bentley & Walsh, 1996).

- **Peptides.** Amino acids that are joined together as peptides have only recently been studied as neurotransmitters. **Opioids,** many of which are peptides, play an important role in activities ranging from moderating pain to causing sleepiness. **Endorphins** are neuropeptides that help to minimize pain and enhance adaptive behavior (Carey, 1990; Kaplan, Sadock, & Grebb, 1994).

Not only the levels of a neurotransmitter but also the balance between two or more neurotransmitters affect behavior. Thus, psychotrophic medications affect behaviors and symptoms associated with mental illness by changing the level of specific neurotransmitters and altering the balance among neurotransmitters. Knowledge about the effects of neurotransmitters on human behavior can help social workers to make decisions about referring individuals for medications evaluation and to follow up on compliance with medication treatment regimens (Long, 1996).

For Maggie, as for many survivors of brain injury, her skills, abilities, and deficits will be affected by a variety of circumstances, including which part of the brain was injured, her achievements prior to injury, her social and psychological supports, and the training and education that she is offered following her accident. Tremendous advances are being made in rehabilitation following brain injuries (Horn, 1991). The better the social worker understands brain functions and brain plasticity, the more helpful the intervention will be. We may be able to help with adjustment or adaptation to changes as well as the recovery of functions. Maggie could benefit from cognitive retraining, support in finding and maintaining employment, family counseling, and individual counseling that will help her end her relationship with Sam. A key to recovery for many individuals who have experienced similar trauma is an opportunity to interact with peers and other survivors. Such peer networks provide the individual with access to new skills, and a key link to psychological and social support. A social worker working with someone like Maggie may need to adopt several roles: case manager, advocate, counselor, resource coordinator, and/or referral source.

Endocrine System

Remember Bess, the middle-aged woman diagnosed with diabetes mellitus? If you had first met her in a nonhospital setting, you might have interpreted her behaviors quite differently. Her dieting and trying to lose weight seem commonplace, and initially you might have been quite pleased with her success. If Bess had told you that she was tired, you might have suggested that she slow down and get more rest, or perhaps that she include vitamins in her diet. Sitting in her nightclothes on her couch all morning and missing work might suggest alcohol or other drug use. Confusion and inability to answer simple questions could signal stroke, dementia, or a mental illness such as schizophrenia. But only a thorough medical assessment revealed the true cause of Bess's behaviors: a physical health condition traceable to a malfunction in the endocrine system.

The **endocrine system** plays a crucial role in growth, metabolism, development, learning, and memory. It is made up of **glands** that secrete hormones into the blood system. Those hormones bind to receptors in target organs, much as neurotransmitters do, and affect the metabolism or function of those organs (Besser & Thorner, 1994; Kapit, Macey, & Meisami, 1987; Mader, 1998; Rosenzweig & Leiman, 1982). Distinguishing differences between hormones and neurotransmitters are often the distance of travel from the point of release to the target, as well as the route of travel. Hormones travel long distances through the blood stream; neurotransmitters travel shorter distances from cell to cell, across the snyaptic cleft.

Endocrine glands include the pineal, pituitary, thyroid, parathyroid, pancreas, and adrenal. Endocrine cells are also found in some organs whose function is primarily nonendocrine: the hypothalamus, liver, thymus, heart, kidney, stomach, duodenum, testes, and ovaries. Exhibit 3.4 lists some of the better-known glands and organs, the hormones they produce, and their effects on other body structures.

The most basic form of hormonal communication is from an endocrine cell through the blood system to a target cell. A more complex form of hormonal communication is directly from an endocrine gland to a target endocrine gland. The endocrine system regulates the secretion of hormones through a **feedback control mechanism**. Output consists of hormones released from an endocrine gland; input consists of hormones taken into a target tissue or organ. The system is self-regulating. Similar to neurotransmitters, hormones have specific receptors, so that the hormone released from one gland has a specific target tissue or organ (Mader, 1998).

A good example of a feedback loop is presented in Exhibit 3.5. The hypothalamus secretes gonadotropin releasing hormone (GnRH), which binds to receptors in the anterior pituitary and stimulates the secretion of leutinizing hormone (LH). LH binds to receptors in the ovaries to stimulate the production of estrogen. Estrogen has a negative effect on the secretion of LH and GnRH at both the pituitary and hypothalamus, thus completing the loop. Loops like this one allow the body to finely control the secretion of hormones.

Another good way to understand the feedback control mechanism is to observe the results when it malfunctions. Consider what has happened to Bess, who has been diagnosed with the most common illness caused by hormonal imbalance: **diabetes mellitus**. Insulin deficiency or resistance to insulin's effects are the bases of diabetes mellitus. Insulin and glucagon are released by the pancreas. They regulate the metabolism of carbohydrates, the source of cell energy, which

EXHIBIT 3.4

Selected Endocrine Glands and Their Effects

Gland	Hormone	Effect
Hypothalamus	Releasing and release-inhibiting factors	■ Targets pituitary gland, which affects many hormonal activities
Pituitary	Adrenocorticotropic (ACTH)	■ Stimulates adrenal cortex
	Growth (GH, somatotropic)	■ Stimulates cell division, protein synthesis, and bone growth
	Vasopressin	■ Stimulates water reabsorption by kidneys
	Prolactin	■ Stimulates milk production in mammary glands
Testes	Androgens (testosterone)	■ Stimulates development of sex organs, skin, muscles, bones, and sperm ■ Stimulates development and maintenance of secondary male sex characteristics
Ovaries	Estrogen and progesterone	■ Stimulates development of sex organs, skin, muscles, bones, and uterine lining ■ Stimulates development and maintenance of secondary female sex characteristics
Adrenal	Epinephrine	■ Stimulates fight-or-flight reactions in heart and other muscles ■ Raises blood glucose levels
	Adrenal cortical steroids	■ Stimulates sex characteristics
Pancreas	Insulin	■ Targets liver, muscles, adipose tissues
	Glucogon	■ Lowers blood glucose levels ■ Promotes formation of glycogen, proteins, and fats
Thymus	Thymosins	■ Triggers development of T lymphocytes, which orchestrate immune system response
Pineal	Melatonin	■ Maintains circadian rhythms (daily cycles of activity)
Thyroid	Thyroxin	■ Plays role in growth and development ■ Stimulates metabolic rate of all organs

are essential for the maintenance of blood glucose levels (blood sugar). High blood glucose levels stimulate the release of insulin, which in turn helps to decrease blood sugar by promoting the uptake of glucose by tissues. Low blood sugar stimulates the release of glucagon, which in turn stimulates the liver to release glucose, raising blood sugar. In individuals with insulin deficiency, muscle cells are deprived of glucose. As an alternative, those muscle cells tap fat and protein

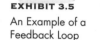

EXHIBIT 3.5

An Example of a
Feedback Loop

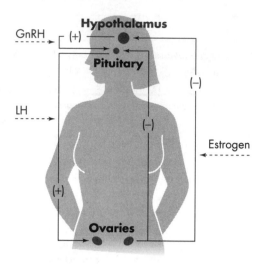

reserves in muscle tissue as energy resources. The results include wasting of muscles, weakness, weight loss, and **metabolic acidosis**, a chemical imbalance in the blood. The increase in blood acidity suppresses higher nervous system functions, leading to coma. Continued suppression of the respiratory centers in the brain leads to death (Kapit et al., 1987).

Nearly 5 percent of the population of the United States has diabetes mellitus. Juvenile-onset diabetes (Type I) is found in children and young adults; maturity-onset diabetes (Type II) most commonly arises in individuals over the age of 40 who are also obese. Type I diabetes may be an autoimmune disease and does not appear to have genetic or familial traits. Type II diabetes shows a strong familial association.

For Bess, as for many individuals with symptoms indicating the presence of a medical condition, the crucial role of the social worker is to supply information and knowledge about the symptoms and the diagnosed condition. Social workers can also help "translate" this information so clients will understand what is happening to them. This should not be construed to imply that clients like Bess are not capable of understanding medical terms. Rather, as in any specialized field, becoming comfortable with the terminology often takes time. The social worker must also help Bess begin to examine the lifestyle changes that may be called for with this diagnosis. What might it mean in terms of diet, exercise, home and work responsibilities, and so forth? Bess may need assistance in working with her insurance company to plan how her care will be paid for. She may also need counseling as she works to adjust to her life with this new condition.

Immune System

Melissa, whom you met earlier, is far from alone in testing positive for HIV. About 1 million Americans—nearly 1 out of every 250—are infected with **human immunodeficiency virus (HIV),** the virus that causes **acquired immunodeficiency syndrome (AIDS).** The United

States currently has 513,000 cases of AIDS, of which 85 percent are male and 15 percent are female—47 percent of European, 35 percent of African, and 17 percent of Hispanic ancestry (Commonwealth of Virginia, 1996). AIDS is the leading cause of death among men and women 15 to 44 years old in the United States (Novello, 1993). According to the Centers for Disease Control and Prevention, the fastest growing groups of persons reported with AIDS have been men and women who acquire HIV through heterosexual contact, a group to which Melissa now belongs. Although HIV is more easily transmitted from men to women, it can be transmitted from women to men. Heterosexual transmission has occurred mainly through vaginal intercourse.

Once a person is infected with HIV, the disease-fighting immune system gradually weakens. This weakened immune system lets other diseases begin to attack the body. Over the next few years, Melissa will learn a great deal about how her body protects itself against disease and infection. Hopefully, she will also adopt behaviors that will lessen the impact of specific illnesses and help her live longer.

The **immune system** is made up of organs and cells that work together to defend the body against disease (Kennedy, Kiecolt-Glaser, & Glaser, 1988; Sarafino, 1990). When operating in an optimal manner, the immune system is able to distinguish our own cells and organs from foreign elements (Sarafino, 1990). When the body recognizes something as foreign, the immune system mobilizes body resources and attacks. The foreign substance that can trigger an immune response may be a tissue or organ transplant or, more commonly, an antigen. **Antigens** include bacteria, fungi, protozoa, and viruses.

Sometimes, however, the immune system is mistakenly directed at parts of the body it was designed to protect, resulting in **autoimmune diseases**. Examples include rheumatoid arthritis, rheumatic fever, and lupus erythematosus. With rheumatoid arthritis, the immune system is directed against tissues and bones at the joints. In rheumatic fever, the immune system targets the muscles of the heart. With lupus erythematosus, the immune system affects various parts of the body including the skin and kidneys (Sarafino, 1990).

Organs of the immune system are located throughout the body. They have primary involvement in the development of **lymphocytes**, or white blood cells (Sarafino, 1990). The main lymphatic organs include the following:

- **Bone marrow.** The largest organ in the body, bone marrow is the soft tissue in the core of bones. There are two types of bone marrow, red and yellow. Yellow bone marrow is inactive. In adults, red bone marrow is found in the sternum, ribs, vertebrae, skull, and long bones. The bone marrow produces both red (erythrocytes) and white (leukocytes and lymphocytes) blood cells.

- **Lymph nodes.** Small oval or round spongy masses distributed throughout the body (Sarafino, 1990), lymph nodes are connected by a network of lymphatic vessels that contain a clear fluid called lymph. As the lymph passes through a lymph node, it is purified of infectious organisms. These vessels ultimately empty into the blood stream.

- **Spleen.** An organ in the upper left quadrant of the abdomen, the spleen functions much like a very large lymph node, except that instead of lymph, blood passes through it. The spleen filters out antigens and removes ineffective or worn-out red blood cells from the body (Sarafino, 1990). An injured spleen can be removed, but the individual becomes more susceptible to certain infections (Mader, 1998).

■ **Thymus.** Located along the trachea in the chest behind the sternum, the thymus secretes thymosins, hormones believed to trigger the development of T cells. **T cells**—white blood cells that mature in the thymus—slow down, fight, and attack antigens (Mader, 1998).

The immune system's response to antigens occurs in both specific and nonspecific ways (Safyer & Spies-Karotkin, 1988). **Nonspecific immunity** is more general. "Scavenger" cells, or phagocytes, which circulate in the blood and lymph, are attracted by biochemical signals to congregate at the site of a wound and ingest antigens (Safyer & Spies-Karotkin, 1988; Sarafino, 1990). This process, known as **phagocytosis,** is quite effective but has a couple of limitations. First, certain bacteria and most viruses can survive after they have been engulfed. Second, since our bodies are under constant "attack" and our phagocytes are constantly busy, a major assault on the immune system can easily overwhelm the nonspecific response. Thus, specific immunity is essential (Safyer & Spies-Karotkin, 1988).

Specific immunity, or acquired immunity, involves the lymphocytes. They not only respond to an infection, but develop a memory of that infection and allow the body to raise a rapid defense against it in subsequent exposure. Certain lympohcytes produce **antibodies**—protein molecules designed to attach to the surface of specific invaders. The antibodies recruit other protein substances that puncture the membrane of invading microorganisms, causing the invaders to explode. The antibodies are assisted in this battle by T cells, which destroy foreign cells directly and orchestrate the immune response. Following the "primary response," the antibodies remain in the circulatory system at significant levels until they are no longer needed. With re-exposure to the same antigen, a "secondary immune response" occurs, characterized by a more rapid rise in antibody levels—a period of hours rather than days. This rapid response is possible because the initial exposure to the antigen stimulated the production of memory cells. **Memory T cells** store the information needed to produce specific antibodies. Memory T cells also have very long lives (Safyer & Spies-Karotkin, 1988).

Developmental perspective

The immune system becomes increasingly effective throughout childhood and declines in effectiveness in older adulthood. Infants are born with relatively little immune defense, but their immune system develops in efficiency and complexity. As the child develops, the incidence of serious illness declines. During adolescence and most of adulthood, the immune system, for most individuals, functions at a high level of effectiveness. As we age, although the numbers of lymphocytes and antibodies circulating in the lymph and blood do not decrease, their potency diminishes.

The functioning of the immune system can be hampered by a diet low in vitamins A, E, and C and high in fats and cholesterol, and by excess weight (Sarafino, 1990). But there are far more serious problems with the immune system, such as HIV, that are life threatening. HIV, like other viruses, infects "normal" cells and "hijacks" their genetic machinery. These infected cells in essence become factories that make copies of the HIV, which then go on to infect other cells. The "hijacked" cells are destroyed. Favorite targets of HIV are the T cells that tell other cells when to start fighting off infections. HIV thus weakens the immune system and makes it increasingly difficult for the body to fight off other diseases and infections. Most of us host organisms such as fungi, viruses, and parasites that live inside us without causing disease. However, for people with HIV, because of the low T cell count, these same organisms can cause serious infection.

When such a disease occurs, or when the individual's number of T cells drops below a certain level, the person with HIV is considered to have AIDS (Markowitz, 1997).

Melissa's life will undergo significant changes as symptoms of HIV infection begin to emerge. Like other women with HIV, Melissa will be at increased risk of repeated serious yeast infections of the vagina, and she may also be at increased risk for cancer of the cervix and pelvic inflammatory disease. Both men and women are vulnerable to opportunistic diseases and infections such as Kaposi's sarcoma, cytomeglo virus (CMV), AIDS retinopathy, pneumocystis carinii pneumonia (PCP), mycobacterium tuberculosis, and Candida albicans (thrush); cognitive conditions and illnesses such as AIDS dementia, loss of memory, loss of judgment, and depression; and other symptoms such as gastrointestinal dysfunction/distress, joint pain, anemia, and low platelet counts. The social worker can help to educate Melissa about these increased risks. Melissa will need to take precautions to protect her health and the health of others. She can be supported in staying well by getting early treatment, adopting a healthy lifestyle, and remaining hopeful and informed about new treatments (Novello, 1993).

The social worker may also have a role to play in working with Melissa as she tells her family and fiancé about her diagnosis. Melissa and her fiancé will need advice about how to practice safe sex. Because at present HIV cannot be eradicated and the long-term outlook for people with AIDS is uncertain, the social worker should also be available to work with Melissa, her fiancé, and her family as they adjust to her diagnosis, and the inevitable grief.

Because of the tremendous costs for medications, particularly new medications, the social worker will need to link Melissa to sources of financial support. This aid will become increasingly critical as her income declines and her medical expenses increase. Medications such as **protease inhibitors**—drugs that slow down the spread of HIV—are not a cure, but they allow the individual with HIV to fight off other infections and live longer (Markowitz, 1997). Side effects of some of the drugs are just as debilitating as the effects of AIDS.

In addition to providing Melissa with information about her immune system, HIV, AIDS, and other physical health issues, the social worker should advise her of the protections under the Americans with Disabilities Act of 1990. Melissa has joined an HIV support group, but the social worker may also need to offer to provide her with or refer her to counseling. The social worker may also have a role to play on behalf of all the "Melissas," working to address the issues of social injustice and social intolerance—in part by providing HIV/AIDS education to business groups, schools, civic and volunteer associations, and neighborhood groups.

Cardiovascular System

According to current estimates, 57 million Americans, or more than one in five, have one or more types of **cardiovascular disease**, the most common cause of death in this country. An estimated 50 million Americans aged 6 and over have high blood pressure, 14 million have a history of coronary heart disease ("heart attack"), and 4 million have a history of having had a stroke (American Heart Association, 1997b).

Thomas's cardiovascular problem is **high blood pressure (hypertension),** defined as a blood pressure reading equal to or greater than 140/90 (his was 200/105). African Americans,

Puerto Ricans, Cubans, and Mexican Americans are all more likely to suffer from high blood pressure than are European-Americans. In 1993, the death rates related to high blood pressure were 6.5 per 100,000 population for white males and 4.8 for white females, versus 30 for black males and 22.6 for black females. High blood pressure also tends to be more common in people with lower education and income levels (American Heart Association, 1997a).

The cost of cardiovascular diseases and strokes in 1997 was estimated at $259.1 billion. This figure includes direct health expenditures (cost of physicians and other health professionals, hospital and nursing home services, medications, home health care, and other medical durables) and indirect costs (lost productivity associated with morbidity and mortality) (American Heart Association, 1997b).

To better understand cardiovascular disease, it is important to understand the functioning of the **cardiovascular system,** which is made up of the heart and the blood circulatory system (Kapit et al., 1987; Mader, 1998). The heart's walls are made of specialized muscle. As muscle contractions shorten and squeeze the hollow cavities of the heart, blood is forced in the directions permitted by the opening or closing of valves. Blood vessels continually carry blood from the heart to the rest of the body's tissues and then return the blood to the heart. Exhibit 3.6 shows the direction of the blood's flow through the heart.

There are three types of blood vessels:

- **Arteries** have thick walls that contain elastic and muscular tissues. The elastic tissues allow the arteries to expand and accommodate the increase in blood volume that occurs after each heart beat. **Arterioles** are small arteries that branch into smaller vessels called capillaries.

- **Capillaries** allow the exchange of nutrients and waste material with the body's cells. Oxygen and nutrients transfer out of a capillary into the tissue fluid surrounding cells, and the capillary absorbs carbon dioxide and other wastes from the cells.

- **Veins** take blood from the capillaries and return it to the heart. Some of the major veins in the arms and legs have valves that allow the blood to flow only toward the heart when they are open and block any backward flow when they are closed (Kapit et al., 1987; Mader, 1998).

The heart has two sides (right and left) separated by the septum. Each side is divided into an upper and a lower chamber. The two upper, thin-walled chambers are called **atria** (singular **atrium**). The atria are smaller than the two lower, thick-walled chambers, called **ventricles**. Valves within the heart direct the flow of blood from chamber to chamber, and when closed prevent its backward flow (Kapit et al., 1987; Mader, 1998).

As Exhibit 3.6 shows, the right side of the heart pumps blood to the lungs, and the left side of the heart pumps blood to the tissues of the body. Blood from body tissues that is low in oxygen and high in carbon dioxide (deoxygenated blood) enters the right atrium. The right atrium then sends blood through a valve to the right ventricle. The right ventricle then sends the blood through another valve and the pulmonary arteries into the lungs. In the lungs, the blood gives up carbon dioxide and takes in oxygen. Pulmonary veins then carry blood that is high in oxygen (oxygenated blood) from the lungs to the left atrium. From the left atrium, blood is sent through a valve to the left ventricle. The blood is then sent through a valve into the aorta for distribution around the body (Kapit et al., 1987; Mader, 1998).

EXHIBIT 3.6

The Direction of
Blood Flow through
the Heart

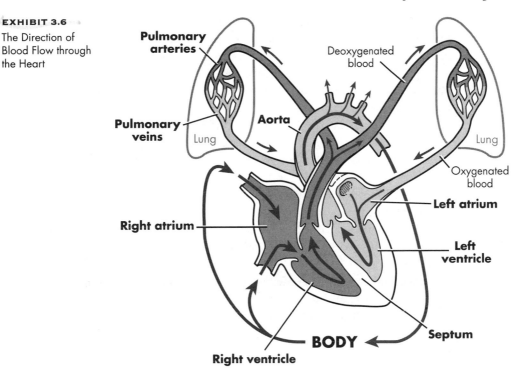

Contraction and relaxation of the heart moves the blood from the ventricles to the lungs and to the body. The right and left sides of the heart contract together—first the two atria, then the two ventricles. The heart contracts ("beats") about 70 times per minute. The contraction and relaxation cycle is called the cardiac cycle. The sound of the heartbeat, as heard through a stethoscope, is caused by the opening and closing of the heart valves.

Although the heart will beat independent of any nervous system stimulation, regulation of the heart is primarily the responsibility of the ANS. **Parasympathetic activities** of the nervous system, which tend to be thought of as normal or routine activities, slow the heart rate. **Sympathetic activities,** associated with stress, increase the heart rate.

As blood is pumped from the aorta into the arteries, their elastic walls swell, followed by an immediate recoiling. The alternating expansion and recoiling of the arterial wall is the pulse. The pulse rate is normally about 70 times per minute, the rate of the heartbeat.

Blood pressure is a measure of the pressure of the blood against the wall of a blood vessel. A sphygmomanometer is used to measure blood pressure. The cuff of the sphygmomanometer is placed around the upper arm over an artery. A pressure gauge is used to measure the **systolic blood pressure**, the highest arterial pressure, which results from ejection of blood from the aorta. **Diastolic blood pressure,** the lowest arterial pressure, occurs while the ventricles of the heart are relaxing. Normal blood pressure for a young adult is 120 mm of mercury (Hg) systole over 80 mm Hg of mercury dystole, or 120/80 (Kapit et al., 1987; Mader, 1998).

While blood pressure accounts for the movement of blood from the heart to the body by way of arteries and arterioles, skeletal muscle contractions move the blood through the venous system. As skeletal muscles contract, they push against the thin or weak walls of the veins, causing the blood to move past valves. Once past the valve, the blood cannot return, forcing it to move toward the heart.

High blood pressure has been called the silent killer, because many people like Thomas have it without noticeable symptoms. It is the leading cause of strokes and is a major risk factor for heart attacks and kidney failure.

Anyone like Thomas, suddenly faced with startling information, such as a dramatic change in what was believed to be good health, should be expected to experience denial, questioning, self-reflection, self-critique, and even anger. The social worker can play many critical roles with such a person. For someone like Thomas, social circumstances complicate the picture. Perceptions of racial discrimination, daily hassles, and stressful life events (Gary, 1995) place him at increased risk for having a stroke or dying as a result of his high blood pressure. Social workers are uniquely positioned to see the links between sociocultural issues—such as vocational and educational opportunities, economics and income, housing, and criminal victimization—and health issues.

On a micro level, it is critical that Thomas seek medical examination and treatment. The social worker can supplement the doctor's care by helping Thomas learn the essential elements of effective health practice, including knowledge of what it means to have high blood pressure, its causes, and strategies for decreasing the health risks. If medication is prescribed, the social worker can help to assure compliance with the medication regimen.

The social worker should also be able to help Thomas develop a strategy for making lifestyle changes that will help lower his blood pressure. He may need to examine his sources of stress and patterns of coping. He may need help in evaluating what he eats, how much exercise he gets on a regular basis, and his social and economic supports.

Because high blood pressure appears to affect other family members, the social worker can also help Thomas's family understand lifestyle factors that might contribute to high blood pressure, such as exposure to stress, cigarette/tobacco use, a diet high in cholesterol, physical inactivity, and excess weight.

Because African Americans and some other minorities are at increased risk for high blood pressure, the social worker may need to work on a macro level with community organizations, community centers, and religious organizations to put in place an education and prevention program as well as a physician and health care provider referral program. Because these health issues are also often tied to experiences of discrimination and prejudice, the social worker will also need to attend to the sociocultural issues of unemployment and underemployment, differential earnings and low incomes, housing availability, safety, family relationships and supports, and criminal as well as social victimization.

Musculoskeletal System

Today polio, a viral infection of the nerves that control muscles, has been nearly eradicated in industrialized countries. But mid-century, the disease was much more common, and it temporarily or permanently paralyzed both children and adults. Of the 300,000 polio survivors now living in the United States, about 25 percent may be affected by **post-poliomyelitis syndrome (PPS),** progressive atrophy of muscles in those who once had polio (National Institute of Neurological Disorders and Stroke, 1997). At the beginning of the chapter you met Max, who has PPS.

PPS has many causes. Some of the symptoms may be the result of the natural aging of muscles and joints damaged by polio or by overuse of unaffected muscles. Unrelated medical conditions may lead to new symptoms in polio survivors and a progression of earlier weaknesses. Unexplained new muscle atrophy and weakness may also develop. The overuse or repetitive use of weakened muscle fibers and tissues leads to musculoskeletal pain, which in turn leads to an increased need for rest, further atrophy, and possibly an increasing level of impairment (Maynard, 1998).

For Max, as for many survivors of polio, this onset of new symptoms is completely unexpected. It may signal increasing physical impairment, which will require new adjustments and adaptations. A social worker who wishes to help someone like Max must first acquire a knowledge base and then work to develop the client's rehabilitation and socioemotional resources.

At the center of PPS is dysfunction in the **musculoskeletal system**. The contraction and relaxation of muscles attached to the skeleton is the basis for all voluntary movements. More than 600 skeletal muscles in the body account for about 40 percent of our body weight.

When a muscle contracts, it shortens; it can only pull, not push. Therefore, to enable us to extend and to flex a joint, muscles work in "antagonistic pairs." As an example, when the hamstring group in the back of the leg contracts, the quadriceps in the front relax, which allows the leg to bend at the knee. When the quadriceps contract, the hamstring relaxes allowing the leg to extend.

The contraction of a muscle occurs in response to an electrical impulse passed to the muscle by a controlling nerve that releases acetylcholine. When a muscle receives a single stimulus, it responds with a "twitch," a contraction lasting only a fraction of a second. But when repeated stimulations occur close together, the muscle cannot fully relax between impulses. As a result, each contraction benefits from the previous one, giving a combined contraction greater than an individual twitch. When stimulation is sufficiently rapid, the twitches cease to be jerky and fuse into a smooth contraction/movement called tetanus. However, tetanus that continues eventually produces muscle fatigue due to depletion of energy reserves.

Skeletal muscles exhibit tone when some muscles are always contracted. Tone is critical if we are to maintain body posture. If all the muscle fibers in the neck, trunk, and legs were to relax, our bodies would collapse.

Nerve fibers embedded in the muscles emit nerve impulses that communicate the state of particular muscles to the central nervous system (CNS). This communication allows the CNS to coordinate the contraction of muscles (Kapit et al., 1987; Mader, 1998).

In its entirety, the musculosketal system both supports the body and allows it to move. The skeleton, particularly the large heavy bones of the legs, supports the body against the pull of gravity and protects soft body parts. Most essentially, the skull protects the brain, the rib cage protects the heart and lungs, and the vertebrae protect and support the spinal cord.

Bones serve as sites for the attachment of muscles. It may not seem so, but bone is a very active tissue, supplied with nerves and blood vessels. Throughout life, bone cells repair, remold, and rejuvenate in response to stresses, strains, and fractures (Kapit et al., 1987).

A typical long bone, such as those found in the legs, has a cavity surrounded by a dense area. The dense area contains compact bone. The cavernous area contains blood vessels and nerves surrounded by spongy bone. Far from being weak, spongy bone is designed for strength. It is the site of red marrow, the specialized tissue that produces red and white blood cells. The cavity of a long bone also contains yellow marrow, which is a fat-storage tissue (Mader, 1998; Kapit et al., 1987).

Developmental perspective

Most bones begin as cartilage. In long bones, such as those of the arms and legs, growth and calcification (hardening) begin in early childhood and continue through adolescence. Growth hormones and thyroid hormones stimulate bone growth during childhood. Androgens, which are responsible for the adolescent growth spurt, stimulate bone growth during puberty. In late adolescence, androgens terminate bone growth.

Bones are joined together at joints. Long bones and their corresponding joints are what permit flexible body movement (Mader, 1998). Joints are classified according to the amount of movement they permit. Bones of the cranium, which are sutured together, are examples of immovable joints. Joints between the vertebrae are slightly movable. Freely movable joints, which connect two bones separated by a cavity, are called **synovial joints**. Synovial joints may be hinge joints (knee and elbow) or ball-and-socket joints (attachment of the femur to the hipbone). Exhibit 3.7 shows the structure of the knee joint. Synovial joints are prone to arthritis because the bones gradually lose their protective covering and grate against each other as they move (Mader, 1998).

The bones in a joint are held together by **ligaments; tendons** connect muscle to bone. The ends of the bones are capped by cartilage, which gives added strength and support to the joint.

EXHIBIT 3.7
Structure of the Knee Joint

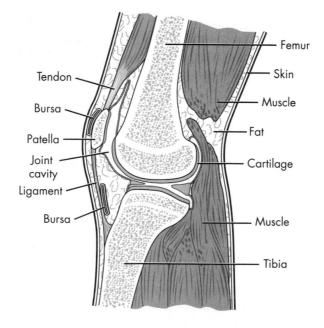

Friction between tendons and ligaments and between tendons and bones is eased by fluid-filled sacs called bursae. Inflammation of the bursae is called bursitis.

Although overuse is damaging to the musculoskeletal system, underuse is too. Without a certain amount of use, muscles atrophy, and bone density declines. Thus, the advice given to many polio survivors has been "Use it or lose it." Unfortunately, this advice may have inadvertently contributed to Max's post-polio symptoms.

Social workers and other health care professionals have generally believed that the greater the degree of independence the better. Therefore, they have often discouraged a person with a disability from depending on environmental modifications, such as ramps, elevators, and electrically operated doors, or on assistive devices. **Assistive devices** are those that enable a person with a disability to communicate, see, hear, or maneuver. Examples include manual wheelchairs, motorized wheelchairs, motorized scooters, and other aids that enhance mobility; hearing aids, telephone communication devices for the Deaf (TTD/TTY), assistive listening devices, visual and audible signal systems, and other aids that enhance an individual's ability to hear; and voice-synthesized computer modules, optical scanners, talking software, Braille printers, and other devices that enhance the ability of an individual with a sight impairment to communicate.

Those who believed that working to overcome challenges was a helpful approach in adjusting to or working with disability were well-meaning. But hidden within this belief system was the impression that having a disability made the individual less than whole, less than competent, and less than capable. Having attended school before the Rehabilitation Act of 1973, the Individual Education Act of 1975, and the Americans with Disabilities Act of 1990, Max spent his early years in a world with little understanding or acceptance of disability. For Max, as for many people with disabilities, the pressure was and is to "overcome" or to succeed "in spite of" a disability. Unfortunately, that pressure may have contributed to Max's current problem. For Max and many other people with disabilities, "Conserve it to preserve it" is a far better adage than "Use it or lose it."

The social worker has many options for working with Max. First, however, Max needs to receive a thorough examination by a physician knowledgeable about polio and PPS. The social worker should then be able to serve as a resource and referral agent. She or he may need to work with rehabilitation professionals, such as physical therapists and occupational therapists, in identifying needed adaptations in Max's home and work environment. The social worker can provide counseling, but should also refer Max to a PPS peer support group. Because Max may need to acquire new assistive technology, the social worker may also need to intervene with insurance companies reluctant to purchase expensive equipment.

Biology, Human Behavior, and Social Work

Human behavior is often the cause of biological system dysfunction. Not wearing a helmet when riding a motorcycle may lead to brain injury. Adults who have poor nutrition and low levels of regular exercise are at risk for obesity, which contributes to the development of diabetes. Unprotected sex increases the risk of HIV infection. But it is not our behavior alone that makes us vulnerable to illness. For some people, the combination of heredity and high levels of exposure to stress could increase the possibility of, among other things, high blood pressure and heart disease. The lack of access to preventive health care or immunizations could increase the risk of infections from viruses such as poliomyelitis.

Just as behavior affects our bodily functions, the state of our biological system affects our behavior. It is truly a dialectic relationship. Our state of health has an influence not only on our cognitive performance, but also on our emotional comfort and well-being—and vice versa. For example, values and beliefs may be "tested" by our experiences of poor health. But values and beliefs have also been shown to influence our experience of, and response to, illness. For example, some individuals who believe in spiritually based healing or miracles recover even when given no reason for hope by medical professionals. Another example would be the work that has shown a direct relationship between longevity once diagnosed with a fatal disorder, such as cancer or AIDS, and social and peer support.

Our health also has a direct impact on our social status and social integration; that is, it can affect the behavior of others. For example, when people develop AIDS-related illnesses, they usually cannot hide their health status because of the level of care they need and the effect of the illness on their appearance. People with AIDS are often seen as outsiders and ostracized to a certain extent from their communities and pre-AIDS support systems. Lack of understanding and fear that "it could happen to me" create behaviors within the general public that isolate individuals with AIDS.

We also must not forget that economic status plays a role in access to health care, and that treatment and care can have an impact on our continued economic viability. People with good medical insurance coverage, or who are very wealthy, can buy the services and equipment they need to create a good quality of life for themselves even when their biological systems break down. They are still thought of as "contributing" members of society. However, catastrophic and chronic illness can deplete financial resources to the point that both quality of life and ability to contribute to the economy are affected. In fact, a status of "second-class citizenship" is often imposed on chronically ill individuals, whom many consider a drain on society.

What does this interconnectedness mean for us as social workers? We must serve as clinicians, educators, case managers, service coordinators, and prevention specialists, as well as advocates. For example, we cannot address an individual's depression in response to post-polio syndrome without also being a case manager and finding resources that will assist in better management of the symptoms. We cannot provide counseling about adjustment and grief in relation to the course of AIDS without also assuming the role of educator. A service coordinator, another social work role, can help a clinician find the resources for assisting an individual to deal with an acquired illness or condition.

Social workers must continuously strive to learn about biological systems and their impact on human behavior. Such knowledge is necessary to deal with anxiety and misconceptions—our personal anxiety and misconceptions as well as those within the community. Becoming more knowledgeable about biological systems helps us to be more equal and valuable partners with other health care professionals. The knowledge that we acquire in this area helps us explain to individuals, families, couples, groups, and communities information which, at times, may seem mysterious to them, thereby allowing them to become more active in their own health management. As we become more knowledgeable, we become more effective advocates, whether we are working on behalf of one individual or an entire community.

IMPLICATIONS FOR SOCIAL WORK PRACTICE

This discussion of the biological person suggests several principles for social work assessment and intervention:

- Develop a working knowledge of the body's systems, their interconnectedness, and the ways they transact with other dimensions of human behavior.

- In assessments and interventions, recognize that experiences of health and illness are influenced by the social, political, cultural, and economic context.

- Recognize that the meanings attached to health and illness influence not only the somatic experience, but also the values and socioemotional response assigned to health and illness.

- In assessment and intervention activities, look for the ways that behavior affects biological functions, and the ways biological systems affect behaviors.

- In assessment and interventions, evaluate the influence of health status on cognitive performance, emotional comfort, and overall well-being.

- In assessment and intervention, consider the ways in which one person's health status is affecting other people, particularly other family members.

- Where appropriate, incorporate multiple roles into practice related to the health of the biological system, including the roles of clinician, educator, case manager, service coordinator, prevention specialist, and advocate.

MAIN POINTS

1. There is strong evidence of relationships among physical health, psychological health, and social experiences.

2. Biological functioning is the result of complex transactions among all biological systems. No biological system operates in isolation from others.

3. We should be cautious that focusing on disease does not mask the strengths of individuals with biological problems.

4. The experience of physical disability gets much of its meaning from political, social, cultural, and economic contexts.

5. Brain injury can affect cognitive, physical, and psychological skills.

6. The nervous system is divided into three major subsystems: central nervous system,

peripheral nervous system, and autonomic nervous system. The brain sends signals to the spinal cord, which relays message to specific parts of the body. The basic working unit of the nervous system is the neuron (nerve cell). Neurotransmitters excite or inhibit nervous system responses.

7. The endocrine system plays a crucial role in growth, metabolism, development, learning, and memory.

8. Insulin deficiency or resistance to insulin's effects is the basis of diabetes mellitus, the most common illness caused by hormonal imbalance.

9. AIDS is the leading cause of death among men and women ages 15 to 44 in the United States.

10. The immune system is made up of organs and cells that work together to defend the body against disease. Autoimmune diseases occur when the immune system mistakenly targets parts of the body. Nonspecific immunity is general engulfment of foreign substances. In specific immunity, memory cells are created to respond to specific foreign substances if encountered again.

11. Cardiovascular disease is the most common cause of death in the United States.

12. The cardiovascular system is made up of the heart and the blood circulatory system. The cardiac cycle consists of contraction and relaxation of the heart. Blood pressure is the measure of the pressure of the blood against the wall of a blood vessel. Exposure to stress, cigarette/tobacco use, a diet high in cholesterol, physical inactivity, and excess weight are lifestyle factors that increase the risk of high blood pressure.

13. Post-poliomyelitis syndrome is a progressive atrophy of muscles in those who once had polio.

14. The contraction and relaxation of muscles attached to the skeleton is the basis for all voluntary movements. Both overuse and underuse damage the musculoskeletal system.

15. Human behavior can cause biological system dysfunction, and the state of our biological system affects our behavior.

16. To help people cope with biological problems, social workers can work as clinicians, educators, case managers, service coordinators, and prevention specialists.

KEY TERMS

acetylcholine (ACh)
acquired immunodeficiency syndrome (AIDS)
amino acids

antibodies
antigens
arteries

arterioles
assistive devices
atria (singular atrium)
autoimmune diseases
autonomic nervous system (ANS)
axon
blood pressure
bone marrow
brain injury (BI)
capillaries
cardiovascular disease
cardiovascular system
central nervous system (CNS)
cerebellum
cerebral cortex
diabetes mellitus
diastolic blood pressure
dopamine (DA)
endocrine system
endorphins
feedback control mechanism
gamma aminobutyric acid (GABA)
glands
high blood pressure (hypertension)
human immunodeficiency virus (HIV)
immune system
ligaments
lymph nodes

lymphocytes
memory T cells
metabolic acidosis
musculoskeletal system
neuron
neurotransmitters
nonspecific immunity
norepinephrine (NE)
opioids
parasympathetic activities
peptides
peripheral nervous system (PNS)
phagocytosis
post-poliomyelitis syndrome (PPS)
protease inhibitors
serotonin
specific immunity
spleen
sympathetic activities
synapse
synovial joints
systolic blood pressure
T cells
tendons
thymus
veins
ventricles

WORLD WIDE WEB RESOURCES

MedWeb
http://www.gen.emory.edu/MEDWEB/keyword.html
Emory University Health Sciences Center Library site contains links to many health-related topics, including AIDS, developmental disabilities, internal medicine, oncology, preventive medicine, PTSD, and substance abuse.

Human Anatomy On-Line
http://www.innerbody.com/indexbody.html
Interactive anatomy lesson. Point and click on body parts and internal organs to receive information. Demo version of product by Informative Graphics. Must have Java enabled on Internet browser.

UA Physiology

http://www.physiol.arizona.edu/CELL/InstructionalMaterial.html

Site maintained by the University of Arizona Department of Physiology contains instructional information on human anatomy and physiology, cellular physiology, cardiovascular, endocrine, gastrointestinal, muscular, neuro, renal, and respiratory systems.

CHAPTER 4

The Psychological Person: Cognition, Emotion, and Self

Joseph Walsh, Virginia Commonwealth University

SHEILA'S DIFFICULT TRANSITION TO UNIVERSITY LIFE

Sheila, age 22 and in her first semester at the state university, experienced a crisis during the seventh week of classes. It was the midpoint of the semester, when instructors were required to give "interim" grades so that students would clearly understand their academic status before the final date for course drops passed. Sheila knew that she was having trouble in all four of her courses, but was shocked to receive two Cs and two Ds. She realized that she was at risk of failing two courses! Her chronic sense of sadness became worse; she had the occasional thoughts of suicide that she had experienced in the past. Sheila knew that she needed to study that weekend, but instead she made the five-hour drive to her parents' home, feeling a need to be around familiar faces. She had no close friends at school. Distraught, Sheila considered dropping out, but her parents convinced her to talk to her academic adviser first.

Sheila had been quiet during her only previous meeting with the adviser, but this time she vented much emotion. Her adviser learned that Sheila had been a troubled young woman for quite some time. In fact, Sheila said that she had felt depressed and inferior to her peers since childhood. The patterns of negative thinking and feeling that influenced Sheila's current crisis had been in place for 10 years. At this moment, Sheila believed that she simply did not have the intelligence to succeed in college. She did, in fact, have a diagnosed learning disability, a type of dyslexia that made it difficult for her to read and write. A special university adviser was helping her manage this problem within her course load, although not all of the professors seemed sympathetic to her situation. Neither did Sheila believe that she had the social competence to make friends, male or female, or the strength of will to overcome her negative moods and outlook. She believed her depression was a basic part of her personality. After all, she couldn't recall ever feeling differently.

Sheila's family included her parents and an older sister (by two years), Amy. During the previous two years, Sheila had commuted from her family home to a nearby community college. She had stayed home and worked for one year after high school graduation, without the motivation or direction to continue with schooling. Amy was, in contrast, the "star" child, who attended a major university to pursue a career in commercial art after winning academic awards throughout her high school years. Sheila had watched Amy, so polished and popular, make her way easily and independently into the world. Sheila, by comparison, knew that she could not function so well. Eventually, she decided to enroll in the community college for general education studies. She felt awkward around the other students, as usual, but liked the small size of the school. It was peaceful and kept Sheila near her parents.

When Sheila completed her studies at the community college, she applied for admission to the state university. She decided to major in art preservation,

CASE STUDY

an area of study similar to Amy's. Sheila's adjustment to the state university had been difficult from the beginning. She was intimidated by the grand scale of the institution: the size of the classes, the more distant, formal manner of her professors, the large numbers of students she saw on the campus streets, and the crowds in the student union. The university seemed cold, and the students unfriendly. Sheila believed that the other students saw her as a misfit. She didn't dress well, was not interesting or sophisticated, and was not intelligent enough to stand out in her classes. Even as she sat in the back of her classrooms, she believed that others were thinking of her, in her own words, as a "geek." Sheila even felt out of place in her off-campus living quarters. A cousin had found her a basement apartment in a house in which a married couple resided. The walls were thin, and Sheila felt that she lacked privacy.

Many students experience a difficult transition to college. Sheila's academic adviser, however, was struck by several family themes that seemed to contribute to Sheila's low self-esteem. Sheila's paternal grandmother, a powerful matriarch, had always lived near the family. She disapproved of much of her grandchildren's behavior, and was frequently critical of them to the point of cruelty. She had good social graces, and thus was particularly unhappy with Sheila's lack of social competence. Sheila's mother was always reluctant to disagree with her mother-in-law or defend her children. This passivity made Sheila angry at her mother, as did the fact that her mother argued with her father quite often, and was known to have had several affairs.

Sheila was closer to her father, who was also fond of her, but he maintained a strict work ethic and believed that productive people should have no time for play. He felt that his children showed disrespect to him when they "wasted time" with recreation. Amy seemed able to take her father's admonitions in stride, and was closer in spirit and personality to her exuberant mother. Sheila, however, felt guilty when violating her father's wishes. They did have a special relationship, and her father tended to confide in Sheila, but he sometimes did so inappropriately. He told her on several occasions that he was thinking of divorcing his wife, and that in fact Sheila might have been fathered by one of his wife's boyfriends.

Thus, during her transition to the university, Sheila was faced with the task of making her way with a learning disability, a work ethic that did not permit her to enjoy college life and young adulthood, a personal history of being criticized with little balancing support, and even a lack of identity. Now, in her seventh week, Sheila was depressed and vaguely suicidal—an outsider among her peers, without acknowledged strengths, and feeling all alone.

Cognition and Emotion

Sheila's difficult transition to college life reflects her personal **psychology,** which can be defined as her mind and her mental processes. Her story illustrates the impact on social functioning of a person's particular patterns of cognition and emotion. **Cognition** can be defined as a person's conscious thinking processes—the mental activities of which the individual is fully aware. Cognition includes taking in relevant information from the environment, synthesizing that information, and formulating a plan of action based on that synthesis (Beck & Weishaar, 1995). **Beliefs** are ideas that we hold to be true and are key elements of our cognition. Our assessment of any idea as true or false is based on the synthesis of information. Erroneous beliefs, which may result from misinterpretations of perceptions or from conclusions based on insufficient evidence, are frequently behind social dysfunction.

Emotion can be understood as a feeling state characterized by the person's appraisal of a stimulus, by changes in bodily sensations, and by displays of expressive gestures (Thoits, 1989). The term *emotion* is often used interchangeably with the term **affect**, but the latter term refers only to the physiological manifestations of feelings. Affect may be the result of **drives** (innate compulsions to gratify basic needs). It generates both conscious and **unconscious** feelings (those of which we are not aware but which influence our behavior). In contrast, emotion is always consciously experienced. Nor is emotion the same as **mood**, a feeling disposition that is more chronic than emotion, less intense, and less tied to a specific situation.

The evolution of psychological thought in this century has consisted largely of a debate about the origins of cognition and emotion, the nature of their influence on behavior, and their influence on each other. The only point of agreement seems to be that cognition and emotion are complex and interactive.

Theories of Cognition

Theories of cognition, which emerged in the 1950s, assume that conscious thinking is the basis for almost all behavior and emotions. Emotions are defined within these theories as the physiological responses that follow our cognitive evaluations of input—that is, thoughts produce emotions.

Cognitive Theory

Developmental perspective

Jean Piaget's **cognitive theory** is the most influential theory of cognition in social work and psychology (Maier, 1978). In his system, our capacity for reasoning develops in stages, from infancy through adolescence and early adulthood. Piaget sees the four stages as sequential and interdependent, evolving from activity without thought to thought with less emphasis on activity—from doing, to doing knowingly, and finally to conceptualizing. He sees physical and neurological development as necessary for cognitive development.

A central concept in Piaget's theory is **schema** (plural **schemata**), defined as an internalized representation of the world or a systematic pattern of thought, action, and problem solving. Our schemata develop through **social learning** (watching and absorbing the experiences of

Stage	Description
Sensorimotor stage (birth to 2 years)	The infant is egocentric; he or she gradually learns to coordinate sensory and motor activities and develops a beginning sense of objects existing apart from the self.
Preoperational stage (2 to 7 years)	The child remains primarily egocentric but discovers rules (regularities) that can be applied to new incoming information. The child tends to overgeneralize rules, however, and thus makes many cognitive errors.
Concrete operations stage (7 to 11 years)	The child can solve concrete problems through the application of logical problem-solving strategies.
Formal operations stage (11 to adulthood)	The person becomes able to solve real and hypothetical problems using abstract concepts.

others) or direct learning (our own experiences). Both of these processes may involve **assimilation** (responding to experiences based on existing schemata) or **accommodation** (changing schemata when new situations cannot be incorporated within an existing one). As children, we are motivated to develop schemata as a means of maintaining psychological **equilibrium**, or balance. Any experience that we cannot assimilate creates anxiety, but if our schemata are adjusted to accommodate the new experience, the desired state of equilibrium will be restored. From this perspective, you might interpret Sheila's difficulties in college as an inability to achieve equilibrium by accommodating new experience within her existing schemata. As a shy person, Sheila was accustomed to making friends very slowly in environments where she interacted with relatively small numbers of peers. She could not easily adjust to the challenge of initiating friendships quickly in a much larger and more transient student population.

Another of Piaget's central ideas is that cognitive development unfolds sequentially. Infants are unable to differentiate between "self" and the external world; the primary task in early cognitive development is the gradual reduction of such **egocentricity**, or self-centeredness. The child gradually learns to perform **cognitive operations**—to use abstract thoughts and ideas that are not tied to sensory and motor information. Piaget's four stages of normal cognitive development are summarized in Exhibit 4.1.

Information Processing Theory

Cognitive theory has been very influential but, as you might guess, leaves many aspects of cognitive functioning unexplained. Whereas Piaget sought to explain how cognition develops, **information processing theory** offers details about how our cognitive processes are organized (Granvold, 1994). This theory maintains that there is a clear distinction between the thinker and the external environment; each is an independent, objective entity in the processing of inputs and outputs. We receive stimulation from the outside and code it with sensory receptors in the nervous system. The information is first represented in some set of brain activities and then integrated (by accommodation or assimilation) and stored for purposes of present and future adaptation to the environment. All of us develop increasingly sophisticated problem-solving processes through the evolution of our cognitive patterns, which enable us to draw attention to particular inputs as significant.

Information processing is a **sensory theory** in that it depicts information as flowing passively from the external world inward through the senses to the mind. It views the mind as having distinct parts—including the sensory register, short-term memory, and long-term memory—that make unique contributions to thinking in a specific sequence. In contrast, a **motor theory** such as Piaget's sees the mind as playing an active role in processing—not merely recording but actually constructing the nature of the input it receives. In Sheila's case, information processing theory would say that she simply has not experienced a situation like her current one and thus lacks the schemata to adapt. Cognitive theory would suggest that faulty processing somewhere in Sheila's past is making her adjustment difficult.

Social Learning Theory

Social behavioral perspective

According to **social learning theory,** we are motivated by nature to experience pleasure and avoid pain. Social learning theorists acknowledge that thoughts and emotions exist, but understand them as behaviors in need of explaining rather than as primary motivating factors.

Social learning theory relies to a great extent on social behavioral principles of conditioning, which assert that behavior is shaped by its reinforcing or punishing consequences (operant conditioning) and antecedents (classical conditioning). Albert Bandura (1977) added the principle of vicarious learning, or **modeling,** which asserts that behavior is also acquired by witnessing how the actions of others are reinforced. Social learning theorists, unlike other social behavioral theorists, do assert that thinking takes place between the occurrence of a stimulus and our response. They call this thought process **cognitive mediation.** The unique patterns we learn for evaluating environmental stimuli explain why each of us may adopt very different behaviors in response to the same stimulus—for example, why Sheila's reaction to the crowds in the student union is very different from the reactions of some of her peers. Bandura (1977b, 1986) takes this idea a step further and asserts that we engage in self-observations and make self-judgments about our competence and mastery. We then act on the basis of these self-judgments. It is clear that Sheila made very negative self-judgments about her competence as she began her studies at the university.

Theories of Moral Reasoning

Developmental perspective

Morality is our sensitivity to, and knowledge of, what is right and wrong. It develops from our acquired principles of justice and ways of caring for others. Theories of moral reasoning are similar to those of cognitive development in that a sequential process is involved. Familiarity with these theories can help social workers understand how clients make decisions and develop

EXHIBIT 4.2

Kohlberg's Stages of Moral Development

Stage	Description
Preconventional	
1. Heteronomous morality	Accepting what the world says is right
2. Instrumental purpose	Defining the good as whatever is agreeable to the self and those in the immediate environment
Conventional	
3. Interpersonal experiences	Seeking conformity and consistency in moral action with significant others
4. The societal point of view	Seeking conformity and consistency with what one perceives to be the opinions of the larger community
Postconventional	
5. Ethics	Observing individual and group (societal) rights
6. Conscience and logic	Seeking to apply universal principles of right and wrong

preferences for action in various situations. Both of these issues are important in our efforts to develop goals with clients. The best-known theories of moral reasoning are those of Kohlberg and Gilligan.

Kohlberg (1969) formulated six stages of moral development, beginning in childhood and unfolding through adolescence and young adulthood (see Exhibit 4.2). The first two stages represent **preconventional morality,** in which the child's primary motivation is to avoid immediate punishment and receive immediate rewards. **Conventional morality** emphasizes adherence to social rules. A person at this level of morality might be very troubled, as Sheila is, by circumstances that make her or him different from other people. Many people never move beyond this level to **postconventional morality,** which is characterized by a concern with moral principles transcending those of their own society.

One limitation of Kohlberg's theory is that it does not take into account gender differences (his subjects were all male). In fact, he claims that women do not advance through all six stages as often as men. Addressing this issue, Gilligan (1982) notes that boys tend to emphasize independence, autonomy, and the rights of others in their moral thinking, whereas girls develop an ethic of care that grows out of a concern for the needs of others rather than the value of independence. Research indicates that boys do tend to emphasize ethical principles while girls emphasize caring, but these differences are not great (Papalia & Olds, 1995). Such small differences may be due not so much to gender as to the typical dilemmas men and women face in their lives. The care orientation may reflect women's lack of power, and thus their desire to curry favor with those who are more powerful, or their assignment to the caregiving role. You will see in Chapter 5 that Sheila frequently baby-sat for a friend of hers, and that this was one of few activities that made her feel good about herself. Galotti (1989) asked a sample of men and women to respond to a set of hypothetical scenarios in which all respondents needed to assume positions

EXHIBIT 4.3

Gilligan's Three
Stages of Moral
Development

Stage	Description
Survival orientation	Egocentric concerns of emotional and physical survival are primary.
Conventional care	The person defines as right those actions that please significant others.
Integrated care	A person's right actions take into account the needs of others as well as the self.

of limited power and were required to assume caregiving roles. Under these conditions, he found that the moral responses of men and women were similar.

Both Kohlberg's and Gilligan's stages of moral reasoning, like Piaget's cognitive theory, are characterized by an increasing ability to think abstractly as the person progresses through adolescence. But Gilligan articulates three stages of moral development, listed in Exhibit 4.3, that place greater emphasis than Kohlberg does on the ethic of care.

Theories of Cognition in Social Work Practice

When theories of cognition first emerged, they were mainly a reaction against psychodynamic theories, which focused on the influence of unconscious thought. Many practitioners had come to believe that although some mental processes may be categorized as unconscious, they have only a minor influence on behavior. Rather, conscious thinking is the basis for almost all behavior and emotions (Lantz, 1996).

Piaget's cognitive theory postulates that we develop mental schemata, or general information-processing rules that become enduring concepts, from past experiences. Schemata are the basis for the way individuals screen, discriminate, and code stimuli; categorize and evaluate experiences; and make judgments. Cognition is viewed as active: our minds do not merely receive and process external stimuli but are active in constructing the reality they seek to apprehend. We are "rational" to the extent that our schemata, the basis for our perceptions, accommodate available environmental evidence and our decisions do not rely solely on preconceived notions of the external world.

So long as a person's cognitive style helps to achieve his or her goals, it is considered healthy. However, a person's thinking patterns can become distorted, featuring patterns of bias that dismiss relevant environmental information from judgment, which can lead in turn to the maladaptive emotional responses described in Exhibit 4.4. These **cognitive errors** are habits of thought that lead people to distort input from the environment and experience psychological distress (Granvold, 1994).

As a social worker, you could use cognitive theory to surmise that Sheila feels depressed because she subjectively assesses her life situations in a distorted manner. For example, arbitrary inference may lead her to conclude that because the university students do not approach her in the crowded student union, they are not friendly. Because she mistakenly concludes that they are

EXHIBIT 4.4

Common Cognitive
Distortions

Cognitive Error	Description
Absolute thinking	Viewing experiences as all good or all bad, and failing to understand that experiences can be a mixture of both
Overgeneralization	Assuming that deficiencies in one area of life necessarily imply deficiencies in other areas
Selective abstraction	Focusing only on the negative aspects of a situation, and consequently overlooking its positive aspects
Arbitrary inference	Reaching a negative conclusion about a situation with insufficient evidence
Magnification	Creating large problems out of small ones
Minimization	Making large problems small, and thus not dealing adequately with them
Personalization	Accepting blame for negative events without sufficient evidence

not friendly, she may also conclude that she will continue to be lonely at the university, and this thought produces her emotional response of sadness.

To adjust her emotions and mood, Sheila needs to learn to evaluate her external environment differently. She needs to change some of the beliefs, expectations, and meanings she attaches to events, because they are not objectively true. She might conclude, for example, that the union is simply not an appropriate place to meet people, because it is crowded and students tend to be hurrying through lunch and off to classes. Sheila can either change her perceptions or change the troubling environments by seeking out new situations. In either case, cognitive theorists would make Sheila's thinking the primary target of change activity, assuming that cognitive change will in turn produce changes in her emotional states.

Cognitive theory is a highly rational approach to human behavior. Even though the theory assumes that many of a person's beliefs are irrational and distorted, it also assumes that human beings have great potential to correct these beliefs in light of contradictory evidence. In clinical assessment, the social worker must assess the client's schemata, identify any faulty thinking patterns, and consider the evidence supporting a client's beliefs. During intervention, the social worker helps the client adjust his or her cognitive process to better facilitate goal attainment. As a result, the client will also experience more positive emotions. Sheila's belief that other students in the busy union have critical thoughts about her as she passes by is an arbitrary inference, based on her own inclination to think poorly of herself. To help her overcome this cognitive error, the social worker could review the available evidence, helping Sheila to understand that the other students probably did not notice her at all.

Social learning theory takes the tendency in cognitive theory to deemphasize innate drives and unconscious thinking even further. Some practitioners in the social learning tradition make no attempt to understand internal processes at all and avoid making any inferences about them. Social workers who practice from the behavioral approach conceptualize thoughts and emotions

EXHIBIT 4.5

Four Behavioral
Change Strategies

Strategy	Description
Desensitization	Confronting a difficult challenge through a step-by-step process of approach and anxiety control
Shaping	Differentially reinforcing approximations of a desired but difficult behavior so as to help the person eventually master the behavior
Behavioral rehearsal	Role-playing a desired behavior after seeing it modeled appropriately, and then applying the skill to real-life situations
Extinction	Eliminating a behavior by reinforcing alternative behaviors

as behaviors subject to **reinforcement contingencies** (Gambrill, 1994). Thus, behaviors can be modified through the application of specific action-oriented methods, such as those listed in Exhibit 4.5. If Sheila is depressed, the social worker would help to identify the things that reinforce her depressed behavior and adjust them so that her emotional states (as revealed in behaviors) will change in response. Through desensitization and behavioral rehearsal, for example, Sheila could learn step by step to approach a small group of students at a lunch table and ask to join them. Her positive reinforcers might include success in these measured experiences, a new sense of efficacy, reduced anxiety, and the affirmation of her social worker.

Theories of Emotion

Emotion is physiologically programmed into the human brain (see Chapter 3). Its expression is primarily mediated by the hypothalamus, while the experience of emotion is a limbic function. But emotion also involves a cognitive labeling of these programmed feelings, which is at least partially a learned process. That is, some emotional experience is an interpretation, and not merely given by our physiological state. For example, two students might feel anxious walking into the classroom on the first day of a semester. The anxiety would be a normal reaction to entering a new and unfamiliar situation. However, one student might interpret the anxiety as a heightened alertness that will serve her well in adjusting to the new students and professor, whereas the other student might interpret the same emotion as evidence that she is not prepared to manage the course material. The first student may become excited, while the second student becomes distressed.

Many theorists distinguish between primary and secondary emotions (Thoits, 1989; Turner, 1996). The **primary emotions** may have evolved as specific reactions with survival value for the human species. They mobilize us, focus our attention, and signal our state of mind to others. There is no consensus on what the primary emotions are, but they are usually limited to anger, fear, sadness, joy, and anticipation (Panksepp, 1991). The **secondary emotions** are more variable among people and are socially acquired. They evolved as humans developed more sophisticated means of learning, controlling, and managing emotions to promote flexible cohesion in social groups. The secondary emotions may result from combinations of the primary emotions (Plutchik, 1991), and their greater numbers also imply that our cognitive processes are significant in labeling them. These emotions include (but are not limited to) envy, jealousy, anxiety, guilt, shame, relief, hope, depression, pride, love, gratitude, and compassion (Lazarus & Lazarus, 1994).

The autonomic nervous system is central to our processing of emotion. This system consists of nerve tracts running from the base of the brain, through the spinal cord, and into the internal organs of the body. It is concerned with maintaining the body's physical homeostasis. Tracts from one branch of this system, the sympathetic division, produce physiological changes that help make us more alert and active. These changes are sustained by the release of hormones from the endocrine glands into the bloodstream. As part of the feedback control mechanism, parasympathetic system nerve tracts produce opposite, or calming, effects in the body. The two systems work together to maintain an appropriate level of physical arousal.

Still, psychologists have debated for more than a century about the sources of emotion. Theories range from those that emphasize physiology to those that emphasize the purely social context, and they give variable weight to the role of cognition.

Physiological Theories of Emotion

The James/Lange theory (James, 1890), developed a century ago, speculated that our bodies produce automatic physiological reactions to any stimulus. We notice these reactions after the fact and then attempt through cognition to make sense of them. This "making sense" involves labeling the emotion. Thus, emotion follows cognition, which itself follows the physiological reaction to a stimulus. James believed that a distinct emotion arises from each physiological reaction.

A few decades later, Cannon (1924) argued that physiological arousal and the experience of emotion are unrelated. He stated (unlike James) that our physiological responses to a stimulus are nonspecific and only prepare us for a general fight-or-flight response (to confront or avoid the stimulus). This response in itself has nothing to do with the experience of emotion, because any particular physiological activity may give rise to different emotional states, and may not even involve our emotions at all. Thus, a separate cognitive process produces our feeling of emotion. Emotion derives from the associations we make based on prior attempts to understand the sensation of arousal.

Physiology-based theories of emotion lost favor in the mid-20th century, but recent brain research is once again suggesting a strong link between physiological processes and emotion. Magai (1996) asserts that emotions originate in our neurophysiology and that our personalities are organized around "affective biases." All of us possess five primary human emotions: happiness, sadness, fear, anger, and interest/excitement. These emotions are instinctual, "hard-wired" into our brains, and are the source of our motivations. When our emotions are activated, they have a pervasive influence on our cognition and behavior. A key theme in this theory is that emotions influence cognition, a principle opposite to that stressed in cognitive theory.

For example, an affective bias toward sadness may be activated by a personal or material loss. The sadness has a temporary physical response: a slowing down and a decrease in general effort. It also leads us to withdraw in situations where our efforts to recover the loss would likely be ineffective. The sadness thus allows us time to reevaluate our needs and regain energy for more focused attempts to reach more achievable goals. It is also a signal within our social networks for others to provide us with support. The sadness of others promotes our own empathic responses. In contrast, anger tends to increase our energy and motivate behavior that is intended to overcome frustration. Further, it is a signal to others to respond to us with avoidance, compliance, or submission so that we may resolve the problem confronting us.

Psychological Theories of Emotion

Perhaps the most contentious debates about the role of cognition in emotion have taken place among psychological theorists. As Exhibit 4.6 shows, some have considered emotion as primary, and others have considered cognition as primary. Theories in the social behavioral perspective, somewhat like physiology-based theories, assume an automatic, programmed response that is then interpreted as emotion.

Psychodynamic perspective

Psychoanalytic Theory.   Freud's landmark work *The Interpretation of Dreams,* first published in 1899, signaled the arrival of **psychoanalytic theory.** Freud's theories became prominent in the United States by the early 1900s, immediately influencing the young profession of social work, and were a dominant force through the 1950s. Psychoanalytic thinking continues to be influential in social work today, through the theories of ego psychology and self psychology.

At the basis of psychoanalytic theory is the primacy of internal drives and unconscious mental activity in human behavior. Sexual and aggressive drives are not "feelings" in themselves, but they motivate behavior that will presumably gratify our impulses. We experience positive emotions when our drives are gratified, and negative emotions when they are frustrated.

Our conscious mental functioning takes place within the **ego,** that part of the personality responsible for negotiating between internal drives and the outside world. It is here that cognition occurs, but it is driven by those unconscious thoughts that are focused on drive satisfaction.

In psychoanalytic thought, then, conscious thinking is a product of the drives, from which our emotions also spring. By nature, we are pleasure seekers and "feelers," not thinkers.

EXHIBIT 4.6

Psychological Views
of the Source of
Emotion

Emotion as Primary

Stimulus ⟶ Emotion ⟶ Interpretation

Cognition as Primary

Stimulus ⟶ Interpretation ⟶ Emotion

Behavior as Primary

Stimulus ⟶ Behavior ⟶ Interpretation ⟶ Emotion

Source: Adapted from Ellsworth, 1991.

Thoughts are our means of deciding how to gratify our drives. Defense mechanisms result from our need to indirectly manage drives when we become frustrated, as we frequently do in the social world, where we must negotiate acceptable behaviors with others. The need to manage drives also contributes to the development of our unconscious mental processes. According to psychoanalytic theory, personal growth cannot be achieved by attending only to conscious processes. We need to explore all of our thoughts and feelings to understand our essential drives. Change requires that we uncover unconscious material and the accompanying feelings that are repressed, or kept out of consciousness.

Ego Psychology. **Ego psychology**, which emerged in the 1930s (Goldstein, 1995), shifted to a more balanced perspective on the influences of cognition and emotion in social functioning. As an adaptation of psychoanalytic theory, it signaled a reaction against Freud's heavy emphasis on drives and highlighted the ego's role in promoting healthy social functioning. Ego psychology represents an effort to build a holistic psychology of normal development.

> **Psychodynamic perspective**

In ego psychology, the ego is conceived of as present from birth, and not as derived from the need to reconcile drives within the constraints of social living, as psychoanalytic theory would say. The ego is the source of our attention, concentration, learning, memory, will, and perception. Both past and present experiences are relevant in influencing social functioning. The influence of the drives on emotions and thoughts is not dismissed, but the autonomy of the ego, and thus conscious thought processes, receives greater emphasis than in psychoanalytic theory. The ego moderates internal conflicts, which may relate to drive frustration, but it also mediates the interactions of a healthy person with stressful environmental conditions. If we experience sadness, then, it is possible that we are having conflicts related to drive frustration that are internal in origin. However, it is also possible that we are experiencing person/environment conflicts in which our coping efforts are not effective; the negative emotion may result from a frustration of our ability to manage an environmental stressor and thus arise from cognitive activities. Sheila may be experiencing both types of conflict. Her anger at the lack of adequate nurturance in her early family history may have been turned inward to produce a depression that has persisted in all of her environments. At the same time, the mismatch between her personal needs for mastery and the demands of this particular academic environment may be contributing to her frustration and depression.

Attribution Theory. Attribution theory was the first of the psychological theories of emotion to give clear primacy to cognition as a producer of emotions (Schacter & Singer, 1962). **Attribution theory** holds that our experience of emotion is based on conscious evaluations we make about physiological sensations in particular social settings. We respond to situations as we understand them cognitively, which leads directly to our experience of a particular emotion. For example, Sheila has often experienced anxiety, but she interprets it differently in dealing with her strict father (who makes her feel guilty about enjoying life) and her fellow students (who make her feel ashamed of who she is). Attribution theory also notes that the social setting determines the type of emotion experienced; the physiological response determines the strength of the reaction. In other words, the nature of the social setting is key to the process of emotional experience.

> **Social behavioral perspective**

Weiner (1985) has further refined attribution theory, stating that our initial reactions to any stimulus are limited to the sense of whether it will have positive or negative consequences for us. Afterward, we consider what has caused the event, which leads to modification of the emotion we feel. The less we understand about the physiological nature of a sensation, the less likely we are to perceive it as physiological, and the more likely it is that we will be influenced by external cues in determining its cause and labeling the emotion. Thus, our perceptions of internal versus external cause determine in part the type of emotion that we experience. For example, if we experience frustration, the emotion of shame may emerge if we decide that it is due to our own behavior. However, we may experience anger if we decide that the frustration is due to the actions of someone else.

Lazarus (1980) has proposed a three-part psychological theory of emotion based on appraisals of situations. He suggests that emotion develops when we assess a situation as somehow relevant to a personal value or life concern. First, we make an unconscious appraisal of whether a situation constitutes a threat. This appraisal is followed by coping responses, which may be cognitive, physiological, or both, and may be conscious or unconscious. Once these coping mechanisms are in place, we reappraise the situation and label our associated emotion. This process implies that our feelings originate with an automatic evaluative judgment. We decide whether there is a threat, take immediate coping action to deal with it, and then take a closer look to see exactly what was involved in the situation. At the end of this process, we experience a specific emotion.

Social Theories of Emotion

Social theories of emotion also take the view that cognition precedes emotion. But they emphasize the purpose of emotion, which is to sustain shared interpersonal norms and social cohesion. Two social theories are considered here.

Social constructionist perspective

Averill's (1980) theory states that emotions can be understood as socially constructed, transitory roles. They can be considered socially constructed because they originate in our appraisals of situations. They are transitory in that they are time limited. Finally, emotions are roles because they include a range of socially acceptable actions that may be performed in a certain social context. We organize and interpret our physiological reactions to stimuli with regard to the social norms involved in the particular situations where these reactions occur. Emotions permit us, in response to these stimuli, to step out of the conventional social roles to which people not experiencing the emotion are held. For example, in our culture, we generally would not say that we wish to harm someone unless we were feeling anger. We would generally not lash out verbally at a friend or spouse unless we felt frustrated. We would generally not withdraw from certain personal responsibilities and ask others for comfort unless we felt sad. Because of the social function of emotions, we often experience them as passions, or feelings not under our control. Experiencing passion permits unconventional behavior because we assume that we are somehow not "ourselves," not able to control what we do at that moment. Our society has adopted this mode of thinking about emotions because it allows us to distance ourselves from some of our actions. Emotions are thus legitimized social roles, or permissible behaviors for persons when in particular emotional states.

Social constructionist
perspective Mead, the originator of symbolic interaction theory, took a somewhat different view. He suggested that emotions develop as symbols for communication (Franks, 1991). He also believed that humans are by nature more sensitive to visual than to verbal cues. Emotional expressions are thus particularly powerful in that they are apprehended visually rather than verbally. Our emotional expression is a signal about how we are inclined to act in a situation, and others can adjust their own behavior in response to our perceived inclinations. Sheila's lack of eye contact, tendency to look down, and physical distancing from others are manifestations of her sadness. Other persons, in response, may choose either to offer her support or, more likely in a classroom setting, to avoid her if they interpret her expressions as a desire for distance.

Theories of Emotion in Social Work Practice

The preceding theories are useful in assessment and intervention with clients because they enhance the social worker's understanding of the origins of emotional experiences and how negative emotional states may emerge and influence behavior. The social worker can help the client develop more positive emotional response sets by providing insight or corrective experiences. What follows, however, is a theory that is even more precise in identifying the processes of emotional experience.

Greenberg (1996) has offered an emotion-focused practice theory, similar to psychoanalytic theory, that promises to help in social work interventions. Greenberg asserts that all primary emotions—those that originate as biologically based rapid responses—are adaptive. Every primary emotion we experience has the purpose of helping us adjust our relationship with an environmental situation to enhance coping. Secondary emotions emerge from these primary emotions as a result of cognitive mediation. Problems in social functioning may occur in one of four scenarios, summarized in Exhibit 4.7.

From this perspective, it is the **preconscious** (mental activity that is out of awareness but can be brought into awareness with prompting) appraisal of situations in relation to our needs that creates emotions. Further, as Mead (1934) pointed out, we experience our emotions as images, not as verbal thoughts. Emotions are difficult to apprehend cognitively, and in our attempts to do so we may mistake their essence. The bad feelings that trouble us come not from those primary emotional responses, which, if experienced directly, would tend to dissipate, but

EXHIBIT 4.7
Four Sources of
Emotion-Based
Problems in Social
Functioning

1. A primary emotion may not achieve its aim of changing our relationship with the environment to facilitate adaptation.
2. We may, prior to awareness of a primary emotion, deny, distort, avoid, or repress it, and thus become unable to constructively address our person/environment challenge.
3. We may develop cognitive distortions, or irrational "meaning construction" processes, that produce negative secondary emotions.
4. We may regulate our appropriate emotional experiences poorly, by either minimizing or not maintaining control over them.

from cognitive distortions of those responses. We tend to appraise situations accurately with our primary emotions, but our frustration in achieving affective goals can produce cognitive distortions. Thus, in contrast to the assumptions of cognitive theory, distortions of thought may be the result of emotional phenomena rather than their cause.

Consider Sheila's depression as an example. Perhaps she is interpersonally sensitive by nature and accurately perceives aloofness in others. Her affective goals of closeness are threatened by this appraisal, and the intensity of her reaction to this frustration becomes problematic. Her emotional patterns evoke tendencies to withdraw temporarily and to become less active in response to discouragement or sadness. To this point, the process may be adaptive, as she may be able to rest and regain energy during her temporary withdrawal. This particular feeling state, however, may become a cue for negative thoughts about herself, which then prevent her from actively addressing her frustrations.

Personal reality, then, may be as much a product of emotion as cognition. In any situation, the meaning we construct may automatically determine our conscious cognitive responses. It is when we directly experience primary emotions that we are functioning in an adaptive manner.

In emotion-focused practice, the social worker would attempt to activate the person's primary emotional reactions, making them more available to awareness within the safety of the social worker/client relationship and making secondary emotional reactions amenable to change when necessary. Emotional reactions, cognitive appraisals, and action tendencies may then be identified more clearly by the client. Affective needs can be identified, the sequencing of the emotional/cognitive process can be clarified, and a new sense of self may emerge along with an improved capacity for self-direction.

From this perspective, a social worker could help Sheila understand that she carries much anger at her family because of their long-term lack of adequate support for her emotional development. Sheila could be encouraged within the safety of the social worker/client relationship to experience and ventilate that anger. Once Sheila can consciously identify and experience that negative emotion, she may be less incapacitated by the depression, which is a secondary emotion resulting from her suppression of anger. She would then have more energy to devote to her own social and academic goals.

Cognitive/Emotional "Disorders"

As social workers, we are reluctant to label people as having cognitive or emotional "disorders." Instead, we conceptualize problems in social functioning as mismatches in the fit between person and environment. Still, in our study of the psychological person, we can consider how problems are manifested in the client's cognitive and emotional patterns. Many social workers are employed in mental health agencies and use the *Diagnostic and Statistical Manual of Mental Disorders* (DSM) (American Psychiatric Association, 1994) to make diagnoses as part of a comprehensive client assessment. Four examples of disorders selected from the DSM can illustrate how either cognitive or emotional characteristics may predominate in a client's symptom profile, even though both aspects of the psychological person are always present.

Two disorders that feature cognitive symptoms are obsessive-compulsive disorder and anorexia nervosa. Obsessive-compulsive disorder is an anxiety disorder that, when featuring obsessions, is characterized by persistent thoughts that are experienced as intrusive, inappropriate, unwelcome, and distressful. The thoughts are more than excessive worries about real problems, and the person is unable to ignore or suppress them. In anorexia nervosa, an eating disorder, the person becomes obsessional about food, thinking about it almost constantly. The person refuses to maintain a reasonable body weight because of distorted beliefs about physical appearance and the effects of food on the body.

Two disorders that feature emotional symptoms are dysthymia and agoraphobia. Dysthymia, a mood disorder, is characterized by a lengthy period of depression. It features the emotion of sadness, which persists regardless of external events. Agoraphobia is an anxiety disorder characterized by fear. The person is afraid to be in situations (such as crowds) or places (such as large open areas) from which escape might be difficult or embarrassing. The person must restrict his or her range of social mobility out of fear of having a panic attack (being overwhelmed by anxiety) for reasons that are not consciously clear.

As a social worker, you might note that Sheila is depressed and also has a mild form of agoraphobia. She feels uncomfortable and insecure on the large, crowded campus and developed fears of having panic attacks when in the student union. This building includes several large open areas that are highly congested at certain times of the day. Sheila is concerned that people there look at her critically. You might conclude that Sheila's problems are primarily emotional. However, Sheila's cognitive patterns have contributed to the development of her negative emotions. Her overall self-assessment sustains her depression, and her distorted beliefs about the attitudes of others contribute to her fears of being in the crowded union. It is rarely the case that only cognitive factors or only emotional factors are behind a client's problems.

The Self

It remains for us to integrate cognition and emotion into a cohesive notion of the self. This is a difficult task—one that may, in fact, be impossible to achieve. All of us possess a sense of self, but it is difficult to articulate. How would you define self? Most of us tend to think of it as incorporating an essence that is more or less enduring. But beyond that, what would you say? Thinkers from the fields of philosophy, theology, sociology, psychology, and social work have struggled to identify the essence of the self, and they offer us a range of perspectives: self as a soul, as an organizing activity, as a cognitive structure, as a verbal activity, as an experience of cohesion, or as a flow of experience (Levin, 1992). See Exhibit 4.8 for a summary of these perspectives.

The Self as Soul

Understanding the self as a soul appeals to those who see their essence as constant throughout life and perhaps transcending their physical lives. The soul may be identical with the conscious self; or the soul may be separate from (but intimately connected with) the self. This idea is based

EXHIBIT 4.8

Six Concepts of the
Sense of Self

Concept	Definition
The self as:	
Soul	A constant, unchanging self, existing apart from its material environment and material body, perhaps transcending the life of the physical body
Organizing activity	The initiator of activity, organizer of drives, and mediator of both internal and person/environment conflicts; an evolving entity in the synthesizing of experiences
Cognitive structure	The thinker and definer of reality through conscious activities that support the primacy of thought
Verbal activity	The product of internal monologues (self-talk) and shared conversation with others; the product of what we tell ourselves about who we are
Experience of cohesion	The sense of cohesion achieved through action and reflection; the three-part self (grandiose, idealized, and twinship components)
Flow of experience	The self-in-process, the changing self

on certain spiritual traditions (see Chapter 6), and though widely shared, it does not easily lend itself to examination in terms of changing configurations of person and environment. If the self as soul is constant, that is, it may not be substantively influenced by transactional processes. This self can be conceived as existing apart from its material environment.

The Self as Organizing Activity

The notion of self as an organizing activity incorporates the notions of action, initiative, and organization. We certainly experience ourselves as capable of initiating action, and the sense of organization emerges in our synthesizing activities and experiences.

Psychoanalytic theory and ego psychology are consistent with these ideas, as they conceptualize the ego as the organizer of drives and mediator of internal and external conflicts. In both theories, the ego organizes the drives in response to external restrictions on their satisfaction. The ego is neither thought nor emotion, but a coordinator of both processes. In ego psychology, this self is present from birth and includes a drive to mastery and competence. In traditional psychoanalytic theory, the ego is not present from birth and must develop, and the drives thought to motivate human behavior do not include mastery and competence. In both theories, the ego is responsible for defensive functions, judgment, rational thinking, and reality awareness.

Psychodynamic
perspective

The ego is largely, although not entirely, conscious, while the other portions of the mind—including the id (the source of drives) and the superego (our sense of ideal behavior)—remain outside awareness and thus cannot be apprehended as part of our sense of self. Healthy human behavior is enhanced by bringing unconscious mental activity into conscious awareness, so we can have more choices and solve problems more rationally.

The Self as Cognitive Structure

The self as a cognitive structure is accepted as at least a part of most accounts of the self. All of us are in touch (although to varying degrees) with our conscious thinking processes and may come to accept them as representing our essence. This cognitive structure includes self-representations that develop within our schemata. The self as thinker implies that action and emotion originate in thought.

Humanistic perspective

Social behavioral perspective

This self may be consistent with the view of reality as a human construction. As thinkers, our sense of self evolves as we actively participate in processing stimuli and define our realities in accordance with our perceptions. The cognitive self is thus interactional and dynamic, not static.

The Self as Verbal Activity: Symbolic Interactionism

Social constructionist perspective

The self can be understood as the product of the stories we tell ourselves about who we are, who we were, and how we became who we are. We change by changing the stories we tell ourselves, according to the theory of symbolic interactionism.

Symbolic interactionism seeks a resolution to the idea that person and environment are separate and opposite (Blumer, 1969; Gergen & Davis, 1985; Mead, 1934). It stresses that we develop a sense of meaning in the world though interaction with our physical and social environments, which include other people but also all manifestations of cultural life. The mind represents our capacity to respond subjectively to external stimuli through conceptualizing, defining, symbolizing, valuing, and reflecting. This activity is not mechanical, but a creative and selective construction. Through social interaction, interpretation of symbols (objects and ideas with shared cultural meanings), and the filtering processes of the mind, we acquire meaning about ourselves and the world. The sense of self develops from our perceptions of how others perceive us. It is a role-taking process at odds with the psychoanlytic view that self involves internal drives. Symbolic interactionism suggests that we define ourselves through the attitudes and behavior of others toward us, and ultimately from the standards of our society. Our sense of self changes with the changing expectations of others about how we should behave, think, and feel.

The medium through which these processes occur is language. Words are symbols, and language is a product of the shared understandings of people within a culture. Thus, social interaction involves an ongoing negotiation of the meanings of words among persons. Consciousness and the sense of self become possible through language as we learn to talk to ourselves, or think, using these symbols (Wood & Wardell, 1983).

Communicators must share an understanding of the cultural norms and rules governing conduct for their interaction to proceed coherently. Symbolic interactionism suggests that socialization is a highly dynamic process that continues throughout life and consists of the creation of new meanings, understandings, and definitions of situations through social interaction (Mortimer & Simmons, 1978). We change as we bring structure to ambiguous social situations to solve problems.

The concept of self includes both the *I* and the *me* (Lane, 1984). The *I* is the conscious self—what we are aware of in self-reflection and what actively processes information and solves problems. This self emerges as we become objects of our own thoughts. It develops through the influence of **significant others**—persons who have immediate influence on our self-definitions. The *me,* on the other hand, incorporates the thoughts, feelings, and attitudes that we have internalized over time and that are beneath the level of ready awareness. The *me* is influenced by **generalized others**—the types of people whose expectations have come to guide our behavior over time.

Significant others can shape our sense of self (the *I*), even if other acquaintances (family and friends) have already made their mark on us. Sheila's sense of herself as unattractive, unintelligent, and socially incompetent may have originated in critical messages she received from her family, neighbors, teachers, and peers early in life. They may have acted toward her in ways that encouraged her to assume dependent and subservient roles. But interacting with other people who have more positive expectations for Sheila might influence her to enact different behaviors and lead eventually to greater social competence. If these alternative social actions became prevalent in her life, Sheila's *me* would experience change as well. She might come to think of herself as more independent and attractive. By guidance and example, an individual may become involved in a community of supportive individuals whose role expectations strengthen the self-concept. The sense of self as competent in specific situations may improve, and the sense of having a substantial role as a member of a social group may develop.

The Self as the Experience of Cohesion: Self Psychology

Psychodynamic perspective

Self psychology, which derives from psychoanalytic theory, conceives of the self as experienced cohesion through action and reflection (Flanagan, 1996). Essentially, the self is the self-image, or what each of us perceives when we look into the mirror. It is not fundamentally cognitive or affective, but a mixture of both elements of the psychological self.

Self psychology proposes that the self has three parts, and our sense of cohesion results from their mutual development:

- *Grandiose self* arises from the positive affirmations we internalize from others; it gives rise to our ambitions and enthusiasm.

- *Idealized parent image* represents guidance from others, which results in our ability to be self-directed and to set goals.

- *Twinship* represents our natural social propensities to connect with others and, through this process, to develop our individual talents and skills.

Significant others are essential parts of the self in this view. They provide us with emotional stability, energy, and an internal sense of cohesion. We all require the affirmation and support of others to feel competent and internally cohesive. We always try to achieve higher levels of coherence, improve our capacity to regulate self-esteem, and integrate new relationships with our older ones. Our psychological growth occurs primarily through empathic understanding from others.

Persons who experience problems in functioning may be experiencing situational stress or "disorders" of the self. Such problematic self-states may be characterized by understimulation or overstimulation in transactions with the environment, excessive external stress, or fragmentation (a feeling of incompleteness due to insufficient affirmation, idealization, or twinship experiences). Change is contingent on restoring self-esteem through corrective interpersonal experiences.

Consider Sheila's case. She is depressed and has a poor self-image. Perhaps she did not receive adequate affirmations from her family while she was growing up, did not receive sufficient direction from other adults and mentors to develop mature self-direction, or did not develop the social skills required to form and maintain the relationships that would help her mature in age-appropriate ways. Her self may thus be incomplete, or fragmented, which would be the source of her negative affect. Corrective experience in any of these three areas—perhaps through supportive relationships with her academic adviser (affirmation), teachers and employers (idealized parent image), and student peers on campus (twinship)   might enhance her sense of self.

The Self as a Flow of Experience

Humanistic
perspective

The concept of self as an ongoing process of experience may be closer to what we actually live than any of the other concepts. The sense that the flow is the actuality is incorporated in the philosophy and practice theory of **existentialism** (Krill, 1996). Persons who assume the existential viewpoint hold that there is no standard or "correct" human nature; we are all unique, alone, and unable to be categorized. What we are is a subjective and ever-changing notion. The self is never any "thing" at a single point in time, because we are defined by the process of becoming, a process to which there is no end point. The self is always in process. Our essence is defined by our freedom to make choices and our need to discover or create meaning (sometimes called *will* or *drive*) for ourselves. The self unfolds as we make commitments to ideals outside ourselves (Frankl, 1988).

Existential philosophy is often seen as a pessimistic view of reality because it emphasizes human loneliness, but it does remind us of our uniqueness and the idea that we can always make choices about the directions our lives will take. However negatively Sheila sees herself, for example, she need not necessarily maintain that self-image. She can and will always make choices that will make her a different person—that is, a different self. If Sheila can be helped to recognize her free will, she can perhaps make those choices that will enable her to define herself differently.

IMPLICATIONS FOR SOCIAL WORK PRACTICE

The study of the psychological person as a thinking and feeling being and as a self has many implications for social work practice:

- Be alert to the possibility that practice interventions may need to focus on any of several systems, including family, small groups, organizations, and communities. The person's transactions with all of these systems affects psychological functioning.

- Where appropriate, help individual clients to develop a stronger sense of competence through both ego-supportive and ego-modifying interventions.

- Where appropriate, help individual clients to enhance problem-solving skills through techniques directed at both cognitive reorganization and behavioral change.

- Where appropriate, help individual clients strengthen the sense of self by bringing balance to emotional and cognitive experiences.

- Where appropriate, encourage clients to become involved in small group experiences that assist them to understand and change their thoughts, emotions, and behaviors.

- Help clients assess their transactions with formal organizations and the effects of these transactions on their psychological functioning.

- Help clients assess and make necessary changes in their transactions with the community. A person's perspective on his or her community may be influenced by its spatial organization, the conflicts among different groups, the relative harmony of the overall social system, the potential for bonding and meeting spiritual needs, and the community's networks of organizations.

MAIN POINTS

1. Cognition and emotion are different but interrelated internal processes. The nature of their relationship has long been debated.

2. Cognition includes the conscious thinking processes of taking in relevant information from the environment, synthesizing that information, and formulating a plan of action based on that synthesis.

3. Cognitive processes develop sequentially from childhood through adolescence, beginning as concrete thought and evolving through abstract thought.

4. Moral development is related to cognitive development, as it proceeds from stages of egocentrism through assimilation of abstract principles of justice and caring. There is some evidence that, at higher levels of moral reasoning, women tend to prioritize caring while men are more sensitive to abstract principles of justice.

5. Cognitive theory in social work practice asserts that thinking, not emotion, should be the focus of intervention. Many problems in human functioning develop from misperceptions of stimuli or erroneous habits of thought.

6. Cognitive theory maintains that emotions are the products of cognitive evaluations of situations. Adjusting a person's thought patterns will result in improved problem-solving skills and more positive emotions.

7. Emotions can be understood as feeling states characterized by appraisals of a stimulus, changes in bodily sensations, and displays of expressive gestures.

8. Theories of emotion emphasize that the physiological activities associated with emotion occur automatically in response to environmental events.

9. Emotions may be predispositional, forming the core of personality and shaping cognitive functioning. Or they may be the result of cognitive efforts to understand and label the coping response.

10. Psychoanalytic theories assert that satisfaction and frustration of innate drives are the basis of emotional experience.

11. Ego psychology seeks a more balanced view of the origins and relative effects of cognition and emotion on human behavior.

12. Social learning theory asserts that all behavior (thoughts, actions, and emotions) is the product of the reinforcement contingencies that people experience.

13. The symptoms of psychological problems may be primarily cognitive or emotional, but both aspects of the person influence the development of problems.

14. All persons have a sense of self, but this self is difficult to articulate and is not the same for all persons. The concept of self tends to be similar to that of self-image, although some viewpoints extend it to include properties outside of immediate awareness.

15. The self may be conceptualized as soul, organizing activity, cognitive structure, verbal activity, experience of cohesion, or flow of experience.

KEY TERMS

accommodation
affect
assimilation
attribution theory
beliefs
cognition
cognitive errors
cognitive mediation
cognitive operations

cognitive theory
conventional morality
drives
ego
egocentricity
ego psychology
emotion
equilibrium
existentialism

generalized others
information processing theory
modeling
mood
morality
motor theory
postconventional morality
preconscious
preconventional morality
primary emotions
psychoanalytic theory

psychology
reinforcement contingencies
schema (schemata)
secondary emotions
self psychology
sensory theory
significant others
social learning
social learning theory
unconscious

WORLD WIDE WEB RESOURCES

The Emotion Home Page
http://emotion.salk.edu/emotion.html
Site presented by the Salk Institute contains information on emotion research from the psychological, neuroscience, and computational perspectives. Provides an historical perspective on emotion and links to other Internet resources on emotion.

Personality and Consciousness
http://www.wynja.com/personality/theorists.html
Site maintained by Eric Pettifor discusses the major theorists of personality psychology, including Alfred Adler, Sigmund Freud, Carl Jung, George Kelly, Abraham Maslow, Carl Rogers, and B. F. Skinner. Contains information on both the theory and the philosophy of the theorists' therapy. Also contains links and other Internet resources.

Self Psychology Page
http://www.selfpsychology.org/
Site maintained by David Wolf contains definition of self psychology, bibliography, papers, and discussion groups on self psychology, and links to other Internet sites.

CHAPTER 5

The Psychological Person: Stress, Coping, and Adaptation

Joseph Walsh, Virginia Commonwealth University

SHEILA'S COPING STRATEGIES FOR COLLEGE

Midway through her first semester at the state university, Sheila (whom you met in Chapter 4) had reached a crisis point. It was bad enough that she was having trouble academically. But even worse, she was feeling isolated from her fellow students and thinking of herself as hopelessly incompetent at making friends. She was depressed and expected no better for the foreseeable future.

Fortunately, Sheila's parents convinced her to talk with her academic adviser. The adviser immediately became more involved in helping Sheila manage her dyslexia. Sheila learned to become more assertive with her instructors so that they understood her special challenges with the course work.

The academic adviser also encouraged Sheila to begin seeing a counselor. Over several months, the counselor, Paul, helped Sheila focus her thoughts and feelings in ways that were productive for her problem solving. First, Sheila found an apartment that afforded her some privacy and personal space. Then, she got a part-time job at a shop on the campus perimeter to help keep busy and involved with people. With Paul's encouragement, Sheila also joined some small university clubs focused on academic topics as a way for her to feel more comfortable on campus and begin interacting with other students. She made a couple of good friends whose attention helped her believe that she was a person of worth. Sheila's counselor also helped her learn not to bury her emotions by escaping to her apartment, into her work, or back to her parents' home; rather, Sheila learned to experience her emotions as valid indicators that she was feeling threatened. This new way of coping was frightening to Sheila, but Paul's support helped her develop a greater sense of competence to manage stress.

By the end of her first year at the university, Sheila was still mildly depressed but feeling significantly better than she had been a few months before. She felt more sure of herself, had more friends, and was looking forward to her second year at the university.

The Concept of Stress

We all think and feel, as you learned in Chapter 4, and those processes interact to influence our social functioning. In this chapter, we will focus specifically on how the psychological person manages challenges to social functioning, particularly stress.

Stress can be defined as any event in which environmental and/or internal demands tax or exceed the adaptive resources of an individual. Stress may be biological (a disturbance in bodily systems), psychological (cognitive and emotional factors involved in the evaluation of a threat), and even social (the disruption of a social unit). Sheila experienced psychological stress, of course, as evidenced by her troublesome thoughts and feelings of depression, but she also experienced other types of stress. She experienced biological stress because, in an effort to attend classes, study, and work, she did not give her body adequate rest. As a result, she was susceptible to colds and the flu, which kept her in bed for several days each month and compounded her worries about managing coursework. Sheila also experienced social stress, because she had left the slow-paced, interpersonally comfortable environments of her home and community college to attend the university.

Three Categories of Psychological Stress

Psychological stress, about which we are primarily concerned in this chapter, can be broken down into three categories (Lazarus & Lazarus, 1994):

1. **Harm** refers to a damaging event that has already occurred. Sheila avoided interaction with her classmates during much of the first semester, which may have led them to decide that she is aloof and that they should not try to approach her socially. Sheila has to accept that this rejection happened and that some harm has been done to her as a result, although she can learn from the experience and try to change in the future.

2. **Threat** is probably the most common form of psychological stress. We perceive a potential for harm that has not yet happened. We feel stress because we are apprehensive about the possibility of the negative event. Sheila felt threatened when she walked into a classroom during the first semester, because she anticipated rejection from her classmates. We can be proactive in managing threats to ensure that they do not in fact occur and result in harm to us.

3. **Challenge** consists of events we appraise as opportunities rather than occasions for alarm. We are mobilized to struggle against the obstacle, as with a threat, but our attitude is quite different. Faced with a threat, we are likely to act defensively to protect ourselves. Our defensiveness sends a negative message to the environment: We don't want to change; we want to be left alone. In a state of challenge, however, we are excited, expansive, and confident about the task to be undertaken. The challenge may be an exciting and productive experience for us. In her second year at the university, Sheila may feel more excited than before about entering a classroom full of strangers at the beginning of a semester. She may look forward with more confidence to meeting some persons who may become friends.

Stress has been measured in several ways (Aldwin, 1994; Lazarus & Lazarus, 1994). One of the earliest attempts to measure stress consisted of a list of life events, uncommon events that bring about some change in our lives—death of a loved one, marriage, becoming a parent, and so forth. The use of life events to measure stress is based on the assumption that major changes are stressful because they involve losses and disrupt our behavioral patterns. More recently, stress has also been measured as **daily hassles**, common occurrences that are taxing—standing in line waiting, misplacing or losing things, dealing with troublesome coworkers, worrying about money, and many more. It is thought that an accumulation of daily hassles takes a greater toll on our coping capacities than do relatively rare life events. Sociologists and community psychologists study stress by measuring **role strain**—problems experienced in the performance of specific roles such as romantic partner, caregiver, or worker. Research on caregiver burden is one example of measuring stress as role strain (Aldwin, 1994).

Stress and Crisis

A **crisis** is a major upset in our psychological equilibrium due to some harm, threat, or challenge with which we cannot cope (Hepworth, Rooney, & Larsen, 1997). The crisis poses an obstacle to achieving a personal goal, but we cannot overcome the obstacle through our usual methods of problem solving. We temporarily lack either the necessary knowledge for coping or the ability to focus on the problem because we feel overwhelmed. A crisis episode often results when we face a serious stressor with which we have had no prior experience. It may be biological (major illness), interpersonal (the sudden loss of a loved one), or environmental (unemployment or a natural disaster such as flood or fire).

Crisis episodes occur in three stages:

1. Our level of tension increases sharply.

2. We try and fail to cope with the stress, which further increases our tension and contributes to our sense of being overwhelmed. We are particularly receptive to receiving help from others at this time.

3. The crisis episode ends, either negatively (unhealthy coping) or positively (successful management of the crisis).

According to Lazarus (1993), we can regard anxiety, guilt, shame, sadness, envy, jealousy, and disgust as stress emotions. They are the emotions most likely to emerge in a person experiencing crisis.

Sheila's poor midterm grades during her first semester illustrate some of these points. First, she was overwhelmed by the negative emotions of shame and sadness. Then, she retreated to her parents' home, where she received much needed support from her family. With their encouragement, she sought additional support from her academic adviser and a counselor. Finally, as the crisis situation stabilized, Sheila concluded that she could take some actions to relieve her feelings of loneliness and incompetence (a positive outcome).

Traumatic Stress

Although a single event may pose a crisis for one person but not another, some stressors are so severe that they are almost universally experienced as crisis. The stress is so overwhelming that almost anyone would be affected. The term **traumatic stress** is used to refer to events that involve actual or threatened severe injury or death, of oneself or significant others (American Psychiatric Association, 1994). Three types of traumatic stress have been identified: natural (such as flood, tornado, earthquake) and technological (such as nuclear) disasters; war and related problems, such as concentration camps; and individual trauma, such as being raped, assaulted, or tortured (Aldwin, 1994). People respond to traumatic stress with helplessness, terror, and horror (American Psychiatric Association, 1994).

Some occupations—particularly those of emergency workers such as police officers, firefighters, and disaster relief workers—involve regular exposure to traumatic events that most people do not experience in a lifetime. The literature about the stress faced by emergency workers refers to these traumatic events as **critical incidents (CIs)** and the reaction to them as **critical incident stress** (Prichard, 1996). Emergency workers, particularly police officers and firefighters, may experience threats to their own lives and the lives of their colleagues, as well as encountering "mass casualties of a gory and grotesque nature" (Prichard, 1996, p. 19). Figley (1995) suggests that emergency workers may experience **compassion stress**, which he defines as a "feeling of deep sympathy and sorrow for another who is stricken by suffering or misfortune, accompanied by a strong desire to alleviate the pain or remove its cause" (p. 299). Figley further suggests that any professionals who work regularly with trauma survivors are susceptible to compassion stress. Many social workers fall into this category.

Vulnerability to Stress

Our experience of stress is in part related to our individual biological constitutions and our previous experiences with stress. Research from the field of mental illness underscores this point. In an attempt to understand the causes of schizophrenia and other disorders, several researchers have postulated "stress/diathesis" models of mental illness (Gottesman, 1991). These models are based on empirical data indicating that schizophrenia develops from the interaction of environmental stresses and a **diathesis,** or vulnerability, to schizophrenia. The diathesis may be biological (a genetic or biochemical predisposition), environmental (history of severe stressors), or both (Kaplan & Sadock, 1998). Most models, however, emphasize biological factors.

Stress/diathesis models suggest that all persons do not have an equal chance of developing schizophrenia, because it depends in part on one's chemical makeup. A person at risk may have an innate inability to manage high levels of stimulation from the outside world. One model postulates that the onset of schizophrenia is 70 percent related to innate predisposition and 30 percent related to external stress (Gottesman, 1991).

The stress/diathesis view highlights a probable interaction between constitutional and environmental factors in our experience and tolerance of stress. It suggests that a single event may pose a crisis for one person but not another. In its broadest versions, it also suggests that vulnerability to stress is related to one's position in the social structure, with some social positions exposed to a greater number of adverse situations—such as poverty, racism, and blocked opportunities—than others (Aldwin, 1994).

Coping and Adaptation

Coping can be defined as our efforts to master the demands of stress, and includes the thoughts, feelings, and actions that constitute these efforts. **Adaptation** may involve adjustments in our biological responses, in our perceptions, or in our lifestyle.

Biological Coping

The biological view of stress and coping emphasizes the body's attempts to maintain physical equilibrium, or **homeostasis,** which is a steady state of functioning (Seyle, 1991). Stress is considered the result of any demand on the body (specifically, the nervous and hormonal systems) during perceived emergencies to prepare for fight (confrontation) or flight (escape). A stressor may be any biological process, emotion, or thought.

The body's response to a stressor is called the **general adaptation syndrome.** It occurs in three stages:

1. *Alarm.* The body first becomes aware of a threat.

2. *Resistance.* The body attempts to restore homeostasis.

3. *Exhaustion.* The body terminates coping efforts because of its inability to physically sustain the state of disequilibrium.

Exhibit 5.1 explains how the body responds to stress.

EXHIBIT 5.1

The General Adaptation Syndrome

Alarm	Resistance		Exhaustion

Transmission of signals about some threat via nervous and vascular (blood) systems	First mediator effects:
	■ Hormone discharge
	■ Stimulation of lymphatic organs
	■ Enlargement of adrenal glands
	■ Feelings of fatigue
		■ Activation of hypothalamus (link between brain and endocrine system)
		■ Production of corticotropin releasing factor (CRF)
		■ Activation of pituitary gland by CRF
		■ Release of adrenocorticotropic hormone (ACTH) by pituitary gland
		■ ACTH impact on adrenal cortex
		■ Secretion of cortoids for:
		  – Energy and adaptation
		  – Enzymatic activation of connective tissue inflammatory potential (which protects all organ systems)
		
		■ Hormonal secretions
		■ Adrenalin (for energy)
		  – Increases pulse rate
		  – Increases blood pressure
		  – Increases blood circulation
		  – Stimulates central nervous system activity
			Gradual reversal of all processes
			
			Cumulative wear and tear on the body's resources

In this context, resistance has a different meaning than is generally used in social work: an active, positive response of the body in which endorphins and specialized cells of the immune system fight off stress and infection. Our immune systems are constructed for adaptation to stress, but cumulative wear and tear of multiple stress episodes can gradually deplete our body's resources. Common outcomes of chronic stress include stomach and intestinal disorders, high blood pressure, heart problems, and emotional problems. If only to preserve healthy physical functioning, we must combat and prevent stress.

Psychological Coping

Psychodynamic perspective

The psychological aspect of managing stress can be viewed in two different ways. Some theorists consider coping ability to be a stable personality characteristic, or **trait;** others see it instead as a transient **state**—a process that changes over time depending on the context (Lazarus, 1993).

Those who consider coping to be a *trait* see it as an acquired defensive style. **Defense mechanisms** are unconscious, automatic responses that enable us to minimize perceived threats or keep them out of our awareness entirely. Exhibit 5.2 lists the common defense mechanisms identified by ego psychology (discussed in Chapter 4). Some defense mechanisms are considered healthier, or more adaptive, than others. Sheila's denial of her need for intimacy, for example, did not help her meet her goal of developing relationships with peers. But through the defense of sublimation (channeling the need for intimacy into alternative and socially acceptable outlets), she has become an excellent caregiver to a friend's child.

EXHIBIT 5.2

Common Defense Mechanisms

Defense Mechanism	Definition	Example
Denial	Negating an important aspect of reality that one may actually perceive.	A woman with anorexia acknowledges her actual weight and strict dieting practices, but firmly believes that she is maintaining good self-care by dieting.
Displacement	Shifting feelings about one person or situation onto another.	A student's anger at her professor, who is threatening as an authority figure, is transposed into anger at her boyfriend, a safer target.
Intellectualization	Avoiding unacceptable emotions by thinking or talking about them rather than experiencing them directly.	A person talks to her counselor about the fact that she is sad but shows no emotional evidence of sadness, which makes it harder for her to understand its effects on her life.
Introjection	Taking characteristics of another person into the self in order to avoid a direct expression of emotions. The emotions originally felt about the other person are now felt toward the self.	An abused woman feels angry with herself rather than her abusing partner, because she has taken on his belief that she is an inadequate caregiver. Believing otherwise would make her more fearful that the desired relationship might end.

(continued on next page)

EXHIBIT 5.2

Common Defense Mechanisms *(continued)*

Defense Mechanism	Definition	Example
Isolation of affect	Consciously experiencing an emotion in a "safe" context rather than the threatening context in which it was first unconsciously experienced.	A person does not experience sadness at the funeral of a family member, but the following week weeps uncontrollably at the death of a pet hamster.
Projection	Attributing unacceptable thoughts and feelings to others.	A man does not want to be angry at his girlfriend, so when he is upset with her he avoids owning that emotion by assuming that she is angry at him.
Rationalization	Using convincing reasons to justify ideas, feelings, or actions so as to avoid recognizing true motives.	A student copes with the guilt normally associated with cheating on an exam by reasoning that he was too ill the previous week to prepare as well as he wanted.
Reaction formation	Replacing an unwanted unconscious impulse with its opposite in conscious behavior.	A person cannot bear to be angry with his boss, so after a conflict he convinces himself that the boss is worthy of loyalty and demonstrates this by volunteering to work overtime.
Regression	Resuming behaviors associated with an earlier developmental stage or level of functioning in order to avoid present anxiety. The behavior may or may not help to resolve the anxiety.	A young man throws a temper tantrum as a means of discharging his frustration when he cannot master a task on his computer. The startled computer technician, who had been reluctant to attend to the situation, now comes forth to provide assistance.
Repression	Keeping unwanted thoughts and feelings entirely out of awareness.	A son may begin to generate an impulse of hatred for his father, but because the impulse would be consciously unacceptable, he represses the hatred and does not become aware of it.
Somatization	Converting intolerable impulses into somatic symptoms.	A person who is unable to express his negative emotions develops frequent stomachaches as a result.
Sublimation	Converting an impulse from a socially unacceptable aim to a socially acceptable one.	An angry, aggressive young man becomes a star on his school's debate team.
Undoing	Nullifying an undesired impulse with an act of reparation.	A man who feels guilty about having lustful thoughts about a coworker tries to make amends to his wife by purchasing a special gift for her.

Source: Adapted from Goldstein, 1995.

Those who see coping as a *state*, or process, observe that our coping strategies change in different situations. After all, our perceptions of threats, and what we focus on in a situation, change. The context also has an impact on our perceived and actual abilities to apply effective coping mechanisms. From this perspective, Sheila's use of denial would be adaptive at some times and maladaptive at others. Perhaps her denial of loneliness during the first academic semester helped her focus on her studies, which would help her achieve her goal of receiving an education. During the summer, however, when classes are out of session, she might become aware that her avoidance of relationships has prevented her from attaining interpersonal goals. Her efforts to cope with loneliness might also change when she can afford more energy to confront the issue.

Systems perspective   The trait and state approaches can usefully be combined. We can think of coping as a general pattern of managing stress that incorporates some flexibility across diverse contexts. This summary perspective is consistent with the development of cognitive schemata through the dual processes of assimilation and accommodation, described in Chapter 4.

Coping Styles

Another way to look at coping is by the way the person responds to crisis. Coping efforts may be problem-focused or emotion-focused. The function of **problem-focused coping** is to change the situation by acting on the environment. This method tends to dominate whenever we view situations as controllable by action. For example, Sheila was concerned about her professors' insensitivity to her learning disability. When she took action to educate them about it and explain more clearly how she learns best in a classroom setting, she was using problem-focused coping. In contrast, the function of **emotion-focused coping** is to change either the way the stressful situation is attended to (by vigilance or avoidance) or the meaning to oneself of what is happening. The external situation does not change, but our behaviors or attitudes change with respect to it, and we may thus effectively manage the stressor. When we view stressful conditions as unchangeable, emotion-focused coping may dominate. If Sheila learns that one of her professors has no empathy for students with learning disabilities, she might avoid taking that professor's courses in the future, or decide that getting a good grade in that course is not as important as being exposed to the course material.

Conflict perspective   American culture tends to venerate problem-focused coping and the independently functioning self, and to distrust emotion-focused coping and what may be called **relational coping**. Relational coping takes into account actions that maximize the survival of others—such as our families, children, and friends—as well as ourselves (Banyard & Graham-Bermann, 1993). Feminist theorists propose that women are more likely than men to employ the relational coping strategies of negotiation and forbearance. As social workers, we must be careful not to assume that one type of coping is superior to the other. Banyard and Graham-Bermann (1993) emphasize the need to consider how power imbalances and social forces such as racism and sexism affect the coping strategies of individuals. Such considerations will help us give clients credit for the extraordinary coping efforts they need to make in hostile environments.

Lazarus (1993) has identified some particular behaviors typical of each coping style.

- *Problem-focused coping:* confrontation, problem solving.
- *Emotion-focused coping:* distancing, escape or avoidance, positive reappraisal.
- *Problem or emotion-focused coping (depending on context):* self-control, search for social support, acceptance of responsibility.

Lazarus emphasizes that all of us use any or several of these mechanisms at different times. None of them is any person's sole means of managing stress.

Using Lazarus's model, we might note that Sheila did not initially employ many problem-focused coping strategies to manage stressors at the university and overused emotion-focused methods. For example, Sheila accepted responsibility (that is, blamed herself) for her difficulties at first and tried without success to control her moods through force of will. Later, she distanced herself from her emotions and avoided stressors by spending more time away from campus working, and she was in fact quite skilled at this job. When she began seeking social support, she became more problem-focused.

I probably don't need to tell you that college students face many predictable stressors when attending to the demands of academic work. A few years ago, I wanted to learn more about how students use both problem- and emotion-focused coping strategies in response to stress. I surveyed social work students in two Human Behavior in the Social Environment courses at a large urban university at the beginning of an academic year about their anticipated stressors and the ways they might cope with them. The results of this informal survey are outlined in Exhibit 5.3. The students chose problem- and emotion-focused coping strategies almost equally—a healthy mix.

Coping with Traumatic Stress

People exhibit some similarities between the way they cope with traumatic stress and the way they cope with everyday stress. For both types of stress, they use "problem-focused action, social support, negotiation skills, humor, altruism, and prayer" (Aldwin, 1994, p. 188). However, Aldwin (1994, pp. 188–190) reports several ways in which coping with traumatic stress differs from coping with everyday stress:

- Because people tend to have much less control in traumatic situations, their primary emotion-focused coping strategy is emotional numbing, or the constriction of emotional expression. They also make greater use of the defense mechanism of denial.
- Confiding in others takes on greater importance.
- The process of coping tends to take a much longer time. Reactions can be delayed, for months or even years.
- Search for meaning takes on greater importance, and transformation in personal identity is more common.

Although there is evidence of long-term negative consequences of traumatic stress, trauma survivors sometimes report positive outcomes as well. Studies have found that 34 percent of Holocaust survivors and 50 percent of rape survivors report positive personal changes following their experiences with traumatic stress (Burt & Katz, 1987; Kahana, 1992).

EXHIBIT 5.3

Coping Styles among Social Work Students

Problem-Focused Coping

Confrontation
- Learn to say no.

Problem Solving
- Exercise.
- Work with other students.
- Talk with professors.
- Go to the beach (for relaxation).
- Manage time.
- Undertake self-care.
- Reserve time for oneself.
- Stay ahead.
- Use relaxation techniques.
- Walk.
- Clean the house.
- Carry own lunch (save money).
- Aim for good nutrition.
- Take breaks.
- Look for "free" social activities.
- Pursue art interest.
- Organize tasks.
- Carefully budget finances.
- Plan for a job search.

Self-Control
- Bear down and "gut it out."
- Take on a job.

Search for Social Support
- Talk.
- Network with others.
- Demand support from others.
- Reserve time with family.

Emotion-Focused Coping

Distancing
- Deny that problem exists.
- Procrastinate.

Escape or Avoidance
- Drink.
- Smoke.
- Drink too much caffeine.
- Overeat, undereat.
- Give up.
- Vent on others.
- Curse other drivers.
- Neglect others.
- Watch too much television.
- Neglect other important concerns.
- Use charge cards.

Positive Reappraisal
- Think of money produced by job.
- Maintain perpective.
- Maintain flexibility.
- Reframe frustrations as growth opportunities.

Self-Control
- Push too hard.
- Study all night.

Search for Social Support
- Seek intimacy.
- Engage in sex.
- Participate in therapy.

Acceptance of Responsibility
- Cry.

However, many trauma survivors experience a set of symptoms known as **post–traumatic stress disorder** (American Psychiatric Association, 1994). These symptoms include:

- *Persistent reliving of the traumatic event.* Intrusive distressing recollections of the event; distressing dreams of the event; a sense of reliving the event; intense distress when exposed to cues of the event.

- *Persistent avoidance of stimuli associated with the traumatic event.* Avoidance of thoughts or feelings connected to the event; avoidance of places, activities, and people connected to the event; inability to recall aspects of the trauma; loss of interest in activities; feeling detached from others; emotional numbing; no sense of a future.

- *Persistent high state of arousal.* Difficulty sleeping; irritability; difficulty concentrating; excessive attention to stimuli; exaggerated startle response.

Symptoms of post–traumatic stress disorder have been noted as soon as one week following the traumatic event, or as long as 30 years after (Kaplan & Sadock, 1998). Kaplan and Sadock (1998) report that complete recovery from symptoms occurs in 30 percent of the cases, mild symptoms continue over time in 40 percent, moderate symptoms continue in 20 percent, and symptoms persist or get worse in about 10 percent. Children and older adults have the most trouble coping with traumatic events. A strong system of social support helps to prevent or to foster recovery from post–traumatic stress disorder. Besides providing support, we may be helpful by encouraging the person to discuss the traumatic event and by providing education about a variety of coping mechanisms (Kaplan & Sadock, 1998).

Social Support

In coping with the demands of daily life, our social supports—the people we rely on to enrich our lives—can be invaluable. **Social support** can be formally defined as the interpersonal interactions and relationships that provide us with assistance or feelings of attachment to persons we perceive as caring (Hobfoll, Freedy, Lane, & Geller, 1990). Three types of social support resources are available (Walsh & Connelly, 1996):

- *Material support*—food, clothing, shelter, and other concrete items.
- *Emotional support*—interpersonal support.
- *Instrumental support*—services provided by casual contacts, such as grocers, hairstylists, and landlords.

Our **social network** includes not just our social support but all the people with whom we regularly interact and the patterns of interaction that result from exchanging resources with them (Specht, 1986). Network relationships often occur in **clusters** (distinct categories such as nuclear family, extended family, friends, neighbors, community relations, school, work, church, recreational groups, professional associations). Network relationships are not synonymous with support; they may be negative or positive. But the scope of the network does tend to indicate our potential social support (Vaux, 1990). Having supportive others in a variety of clusters indicates that we are supported in many areas of our lives, rather than being limited to relatively few

EXHIBIT 5.4

Sheila's Social Network

Network Cluster	Network Member*	Type of Support
Family of origin	Mother*	Material and emotional
	Father*	Material and emotional
	Sister*	Emotional
Extended family	Grandmother*	Emotional
Intimate friends	Christine*	Emotional
	Tiffany*	Emotional
	Ben*	Emotional
Neighborhood	Landlord	Instrumental
Informal community relations	None	
School	Barbara	Instrumental
	Terri	Instrumental
	Academic adviser	Instrumental
	Instructor	Instrumental
	Paul* (counselor)	Emotional
Work	Kim	Instrumental
	Thomas	Instrumental
	Laura	Instrumental
Church/religion	None	
Recreation	None	
Associations	None	

*The asterisk indicates that Sheila considers this person to be a personal network member.

sources. Our **personal network** includes those from the social network who, in our view, provide us with our most essential supports.

Exhibit 5.4 displays Sheila's social network. She now has two close friends at the university with whom she spends much time. She met both Christine and Ben in her classes. Christine has a young child, Tiffany, for whom Sheila frequently baby-sits. Sheila feels a special closeness to the infant, who makes her feel unconditionally accepted and worthwhile. Ironically, Sheila finds herself doing much advice-giving and caregiving for these friends while wanting (but lacking) nurturing for herself. Still, Sheila feels good about the nature of these relationships, because she does not want to confide too much in her friends. She is concerned that they might reject her if they get to know her too well. Sheila feels some instrumental connection with several coworkers because they represent consistency in her life and affirm her competence as a worker. She is also supported emotionally as well as materially by her family members, with whom she keeps in regular contact. Sheila particularly looks to her sister for understanding and emotional support, and uses her sister as a model in many ways. She has always enjoyed seeing her parents and, ironically, even the grandmother who can be so critical of her. They make her feel more "whole" and reinforce her sense of identity, even though, like many young adults working toward independence, she has mixed feelings about spending more than a few days at a time with them. At school, Sheila has casual relationships with two classmates, her adviser, and a couple of faculty members, although she does not identify them as significant. They qualify as instrumental resources for her.

Systems perspective
Psychodynamic perspective

In total, Sheila has 17 persons in her social support system, representing six of a possible ten clusters. She identifies 8 of these people as personal, or primary, supports. It is noteworthy that more than half of her network members (9) provide only instrumental support, which is an important type but the most limited. Because persons in the general population tend to identify about 25 network members (Vaux, 1988), we can see that Sheila's support system, on which she relies to cope with stress, is still probably not adequate for her needs at this time in her life.

How Social Support Aids Coping

The experience of stress creates a physiological state of emotional arousal, which reduces the efficiency of cognitive functions (Caplan, 1990). When we experience stress, we become less effective at focusing our attention and scanning the environment for relevant information. We cannot access the memories that normally bring meaning to our perceptions, judgment, planning, and integration of feedback from others. These memory impairments reduce our ability to maintain a consistent sense of identity.

Social support helps in these situations by acting as an "auxiliary ego." Our social support, particularly our personal network, compensates for our perceptual deficits, reminds us of our sense of self, and monitors the adequacy of our functioning. Caplan (1990) has identified ten characteristics of effective support:

- Nurtures and promotes an ordered worldview
- Promotes hope
- Promotes timely withdrawal and initiative
- Provides guidance
- Provides a communication channel with the social world
- Affirms one's personal identity
- Provides material help
- Contains distress through reassurance and affirmation
- Ensures adequate rest
- Mobilizes other personal supports

Systems perspective

Caplan recognizes *formal* support systems (service organizations) and *informal* support systems (such as friends and neighbors) and also stresses the distinct support role of religion, which attends to the spiritual realm. This topic is explored in Chapter 6.

Two schools of thought have emerged around the question of how we internalize social support (Cohen & Wills, 1985): the main effect model and the buffering model.

Systems perspective
Social constructionist perspective

In the **main effect model,** support is seen as related to our overall sense of well-being. Social networks provide us with regular positive experiences, and within the network a set of stable roles (expectations for our behavior) enables us to enjoy stability of mood, predictability in life situations, and recognition of self-worth. We simply don't experience many potential stressors as such, because with our built-in sense of support we do not perceive situations as threats.

In the **buffering model,** support is seen as a factor that intervenes between a stressful event and our reaction. Recognizing our supports helps us to diminish or prevent a stress response. We recognize a potential stressor, but our perception that we have resources available redefines the potential for harm or reduces the stress reaction by influencing our cognitive, emotional, and physiological processes.

Most research on social support focuses on its buffering effects, in part because these effects are more accessible to measurement. Social support as a main effect is difficult to isolate, because it is influenced by, and may be an outcome of, our psychological development and ability to form attachments. The main effect model has its roots in sociology, particularly symbolic interaction theory, in which our sense of self is said to be shaped by behavioral expectations acquired through our interactions with others. The buffering model, more a product of ego psychology, conceptualizes social support as an external source of emotional, informational, and instrumental aid (Auslander & Litwin, 1987).

How Social Workers Evaluate Social Support

There is no consensus about how social workers can evaluate a client's level of social support. The simplest procedure is to ask for the client's subjective perceptions of support from family and friends (Procidano & Heller, 1983). One of the most complex procedures uses eight indicators of social support: available listening, task appreciation, task challenge, emotional support, emotional challenge, reality confirmation, tangible assistance, and personal assistance (Richman, Rosenfeld, & Hardy, 1993). One particularly useful model includes three social support indicators (Vaux, 1988):

- *Listing of social network resources.* The client lists all the people with whom he or she regularly interacts.

- *Accounts of supportive behavior.* The client identifies specific episodes of receiving support from others in the recent past.

- *Perceptions of support.* The client subjectively assesses the adequacy of the support received from various sources.

In assessing a client's social supports from this perspective, the social worker first asks the client to list all persons with whom he or she has interacted in the past one or two weeks. Next, the social worker asks the client to draw from that list the persons he or she perceives to be supportive in significant ways (significance is intended to be open to the client's interpretation). The client is asked to describe specific recent acts of support provided by those significant others. Finally, the social worker asks the client to evaluate the adequacy of the support received from specific sources, and in general. Based on this assessment, the social worker can identify both subjective and objective support indicators with the client and target underutilized clusters for support development.

Shiela's support network is outlined in Exhibit 5.4. From a full assessment of her social supports, a social worker might conclude that her personal network is rather small, consisting only of her sister, counselor, and three friends. Sheila might report to the social worker that she does not perceive many of her interactions to be supportive. The social worker might explore with Sheila her school, neighborhood, and work clusters for the possibility of developing new supports.

Normal and Abnormal Coping

Most people readily assess the coping behaviors they observe in others as "normal" or "abnormal." But what does "normal" mean? We all apply different criteria. The standards we use to classify coping thoughts and feelings as normal or abnormal are important, however, because they have implications for how we view ourselves and how we behave toward those different from us. For example, Sheila was concerned that she was perceived as abnormal by other students at the university because of her social isolation and her inadequacy. Most likely, other students did not notice her at all. It is interesting that, in Sheila's view, her physical appearance and her demeanor revealed her as abnormal. However, her appearance did not stand out, and her feelings were not as evident to others as she thought.

Social workers struggle just as much to define *normal* and *abnormal* as anybody else. And their definitions may have greater consequences. Misidentifying someone as normal may forestall needed interventions; misidentifying someone as abnormal may create a stigma or become a self-fulfilling prophecy. To avoid such problems, social workers may profitably consider how four different disciplines define *normal*.

The Medical (Psychiatric) Perspective

One definition from psychiatry, a branch of medicine, states that we are normal when we are in harmony with ourselves and our environment. Normality is characterized by conformity with our community and culture. We can be deviant from some social norms, so long as our deviance does not impair our reasoning, judgment, intellectual capacity, and ability to make personal and social adaptations (Campbell, 1996).

The current definition of **mental disorder** used by the American Psychiatric Association (1994), which is intended to help psychiatrists and many other professionals distinguish between normality and abnormality, is a "significant behavioral or psychological syndrome or pattern that occurs in an individual and that is associated with present distress (e.g., a painful symptom) or disability (i. e., impairment in one or more important areas of functioning) or with significantly increased risk of suffering death, pain, disability, or an important loss of freedom" (p. xxiii). The syndrome or pattern "must not be an expectable and culturally sanctioned response to a particular event" (p. xxiii). Whatever its cause, "it must currently be considered a manifestation of behavioral, psychological, or biological dysfunction in the individual" (p. xxiii). Neither deviant behavior nor conflicts between an individual and society are to be considered mental disorders unless they are symptomatic of problems within the individual.

Axis I	Clinical or mental disorders	
	Other conditions that may be a focus of clinical attention	
Axis II	Personality disorders	
	Mental retardation	
Axis III	General medical conditions	
Axis IV	Psychosocial and environmental problems	
	Primary support group	Economic
	Social environment	Access to health care services
	Educational	Interaction with the legal system
	Occupational	Other psychosocial and
	Housing	environmental problems
Axis V	Global assessment of functioning (based on the clinician's judgment):	
	90–100	Superior functioning in a wide range of activities
	0–10	Persistent danger of severely hurting self or others, persistent inability to maintain personal hygiene, or serious suicidal acts with clear expectation of death

Source: Adapted from American Psychiatric Association, 1994.

In summary, the medical model of abnormality focuses on underlying disturbances within the person. An assessment of the disturbance results in a diagnosis based on a cluster of observable symptoms. This is sometimes referred to as the disease model of abnormality. Interventions, or treatments, focus on changing the individual. The abnormal person must experience changes within him/herself (rather than induce environmental change) in order to be considered normal again. Exhibit 5.5 summarizes the format for diagnosing mental disorders as developed by American psychiatry and published in the *Diagnostic and Statistical Manual of Mental Disorders* (4th ed.), generally referred to as DSM-IV. Many people in the helping professions follow this format, including social workers in some service settings.

Psychological Perspectives

Developmental
perspective

One major difference between psychiatry and psychology is that psychiatry tends to emphasize biological and somatic interventions to return the person to a state of normalcy, whereas psychology emphasizes various cognitive, behavioral, or reflective interventions. The field of psychological theory is quite broad, but some theories are distinctive in that they postulate that people normally progress through a sequence of life stages. The time context thus becomes important. Each new stage of personality development builds on previous stages, and any unsuccessful transitions can result in abnormal behavior—that is, a deviant pattern of coping with

EXHIBIT 5.6
Erikson's Stages of
Psychosocial
Development

Life Stage	Psychosocial Challenge	Significant Others
Infancy	Trust versus mistrust	Maternal person
Early childhood	Autonomy versus shame and doubt	Parental persons
Play age	Initiative versus guilt	Family
School age	Industry versus inferiority	Neighborhood
Adolescence	Identity versus identity diffusion	Peers
Young adulthood	Intimacy versus isolation	Partners
Adulthood	Generativity versus self-absorption	Household
Mature age	Integrity versus disgust and despair	Humanity

threats and challenges. An unsuccessful struggle through one stage implies that the person will experience difficulties in mastering subsequent stages.

One life-stage view of normality very well known in social work is that of Erik Erikson (1968), who proposed eight stages of normal **psychosocial development** (see Exhibit 5.6). Sheila, although 22 years old, is still struggling with the two developmental stages of adolescence (in which the issue is identity versus identity diffusion) and young adulthood (in which the issue is intimacy versus isolation). Common challenges in adolescence include developing a sense of one's potential and place in society by negotiating issues of self-certainty versus apathy, role experimentation versus negative identity, and anticipation of achievement versus work paralysis. Challenges in young adulthood include developing a capacity for interpersonal intimacy as opposed to feeling socially empty or isolated within the family unit. According to Erikson's theory, Sheila's difficulties are related to her lack of success in negotiating one or more of the four preceding developmental phases.

From this perspective, Sheila's experience of stress would not be seen as abnormal but her inability to make coping choices that promote positive personal adaptation would signal psychological abnormality. For example, in her first semester at the university, Sheila was having difficulty with role experimentation (identity versus identity diffusion). She lacked the necessary sense of competence and self-efficacy to allow herself to try out various social roles. She avoided social situations such as study groups, recreational activities, and university organizations in which she might learn more about the kinds of people she liked, what her main social interests were, and what range of careers she might enjoy. Instead, she was "stuck" with a negative identity, or self-image, and could not readily advance in her social development. From a stage theory perspective, her means of coping with the challenge of identity development would be seen as maladaptive, or abnormal.

The Sociological Approach: Deviance

Social contructionist
perspective

The field of sociology offers a variety of approaches to the study of abnormality, or deviance. These approaches derive from theoretical perspectives as diverse as functionalist sociology, social disorganization theory, control theory, and feminist theory (Traub & Little, 1994). As an example, consider one sociological perspective on deviance derived from symbolic interactionism.

It states that those who cannot constrain their behaviors within role limitations acceptable to others become labeled as deviant. Thus, **deviance** is a negative labeling that is assigned when one is considered by a majority of significant others to be in violation of the prescribed social order (Hewitt, 1994). Put more simply, we are unable to grasp the perspective from which the deviant person thinks and acts; the person's behavior does not make sense to us. We conclude that our inability to understand the other person's perspective is due to that person's shortcomings rather than to our own rigidity, and we label the behavior as deviant. The deviance label may be mitigated if the individual accepts that he or she should think or behave otherwise and tries to conform to the social order (Anderson, 1994).

From this viewpoint, Sheila would be perceived as abnormal, or deviant, only by those who had sufficient knowledge of her thoughts and feelings to form an opinion about her allegiance to their ideas of appropriate social behavior. Those who knew Sheila well might understand the basis for her negative thoughts and emotions, and in that context continue to view her as normal in her coping efforts. However, it is significant that Sheila continues to avoid intimacy with her university classmates and work peers so that she will not become well known to them. Because she still views herself as somewhat deviant, she wants to avoid being seen as deviant (or abnormal) by others, which in her view would lead to their rejection of her. This circular reasoning poorly serves Sheila's efforts to cope with stress in ways that promote her personal goals.

The Social Work Perspective: Social Functioning

The profession of social work is characterized by the consideration of systems and the reciprocal impact of persons and their environments (the bio-psycho-social-spiritual perspective) on human behavior. Social workers tend not to classify individuals as abnormal. Instead, they consider the person-in-environment as an ongoing transactional process that facilitates or blocks one's ability to experience satisfactory social functioning. In fact, in clinical social work, the term **normalization** refers to helping clients realize that their thoughts and feelings are shared by many other individuals in similar circumstances (Hepworth et al., 1997).

Germain and Gitterman (1996) identify three types of situations most likely to produce problems in social functioning: stressful life transitions, relationship difficulties, and environmental unresponsiveness. Note that all three are transactional, and do not rely on evaluating the client as normal or abnormal.

Social work's **person-in-environment (PIE) classification system** formally organizes the assessment of individuals around the four factors shown in Exhibit 5.7 (Karls & Wandrei, 1994): social functioning problems, environmental problems, mental health problems, and physical health problems. Such a broad classification scheme helps ensure that Sheila's range of needs will be addressed. The authors of the PIE system state that it "underlines the importance of conceptualizing a person in an interactive context" and that "pathological and psychological limitations are accounted for but are not accorded extraordinary attention" (p. x). Thus, the system avoids labeling a client as abnormal. At the same time, however, it offers no way to assess the client's strengths and resources.

With the exception of its neglect of strengths and resources, the PIE assessment system is appropriate for social work because it was specifically developed to promote a holistic biopsychosocial perspective on human behavior. For example, at a mental health center that subscribed to

EXHIBIT 5.7

The Person-in-Environment (PIE) Classification System

Factor I: Social Functioning Problems

A. Social role in which each problem is identified
1. Family (parent, spouse, child, sibling, other, significant other)
2. Other interpersonal (lover, friend, neighbor, member, other)
3. Occupational (worker/paid, worker/home, worker/volunteer, student, other)

B. Type of problem in social role
1. Power   4. Dependency   7. Victimization
2. Ambivalence   5. Loss   8. Mixed
3. Responsibility   6. Isolation   9. Other

C. Severity of problem
1. No problem   4. High severity
2. Low severity   5. Very high severity
3. Moderate severity   6. Catastrophic

D. Duration of problem
1. More than five years   4. Two to four weeks
2. One to five years   5. Two weeks or less
3. Six months to one year

E. Ability of client to cope with problem
1. Outstanding coping skills   4. Somewhat inadequate
2. Above average   5. Inadequate
3. Adequate   6. No coping skills

Factor II: Environmental Problems

A. Social system where each problem is identified
1. Economic/basic need   4. Health, safety, social services
2. Education/training   5. Voluntary association
3. Judicial/legal   6. Affectional support

B. Specific type of problem within each social system

C. Severity of problem

D. Duration of problem

Factor III: Mental Health Problems

A. Clinical syndromes (Axis I of DSM)

B. Personality and developmental disorders (Axis II of DSM)

Factor IV: Physical Health Problems

A. Disease diagnosed by a physician

B. Other health problems reported by client and others

psychiatry's DSM-IV classification system, Sheila might be given an Axis I diagnosis of adjustment disorder or dysthymic disorder, and her dyslexia might be diagnosed on Axis III. In addition, some clinicians might use Axis IV to note that Sheila has some school adjustment problems. With the PIE, the social worker would, in addition to her mental and physical health concerns, assess Sheila's overall social and occupational functioning, as well as any specific environmental problems. For example, her problems with the student role might be highlighted on Factor 1, including her ambivalence and isolation, the high severity of her impairment, its six months to one year's duration, and the inadequacy of her coping skills. Her environmental stressors on Factor II might include a deficiency in affectional support, of high severity, with a duration of six months to one year. Assessment with PIE provides Sheila and the social worker with more avenues for intervention, which might include personal interventions, interpersonal interventions, and environmental interventions.

IMPLICATIONS FOR SOCIAL WORK PRACTICE

Psychological functioning is facilitated or impeded by the person's ability to effectively manage stress. Social work practice may be productively focused on helping clients acquire stress management skills in the following ways:

- Help clients identify their sources of stress and patterns of coping.

- In the assessment process, recognize the possibility of particular vulnerabilities to stress.

- Help clients assess the effectiveness of particular coping strategies for specific situations.

- Where appropriate, help clients develop a stronger sense of competence in problem solving and coping. Identify specific problems and related skill-building needs, teach and rehearse skills, and implement graduated applications to real-life situations.

- Where appropriate, use case management activities focused on developing a client's social supports through linkages with potentially supportive others in a variety of social network clusters.

- Recognize families as possible sources of stress as well as support.

- Recognize the benefits that psychoeducational groups, therapy groups, and mutual aid groups may have for helping clients cope with stress.

- Where appropriate, take the roles of mediator and advocate to attempt to influence organizations to be more responsive to the needs of staff and clients. When appropriate, take the roles of planner and administrator to introduce flexibility into organizational policies and procedures so that agency/environment transactions become mutually responsive.

- Think of the community as a network of organizations when assessing a client's community support resources.

- Link clients who experience stress related to inadequate community ties to an array of formal and informal organizations that provide them with a greater sense of belonging in their communities.

- When working with persons in crisis, attempt to alleviate distress and facilitate a return to the previous level of functioning.

- Assess with clients the meaning of hazardous events, the precipitating factors, and potential and actual support systems. When working with persons in crisis, use a here-and-now orientation, and use tasks to enhance support systems. Help clients connect current stress with patterns of past functioning and to initiate improved coping methods. As the crisis phase terminates, review tasks accomplished, including new coping skills and social supports developed.

MAIN POINTS

1. Stress may be biological, psychological, or social in origin. All stressors are experienced by the body systemically through a general adaptation response.

2. Three types of stress are harm, threat, and challenge.

3. A crisis is a type of stress in which the person is unable to overcome a major obstacle through usual methods of problem solving and, as a result, feels immobilized.

4. Traumatic stress refers to events that are so overwhelming that almost anyone would be affected—events such as natural and technological disasters, war, and physical assault.

5. Stress/diathesis theories, as applied to serious mental illness, postulate that coping is a combination of learned skills and personality characteristics innate to one's biological constitution.

6. Coping may be conceptualized as a stable personality characteristic, a process unique to each situation, or a combination of both.

7. Coping efforts may be problem-focused or emotion-focused.

8. There are both similarities and differences between the ways people cope with everyday stress and the ways they cope with traumatic stress.

9. All people rely on social supports as means of dealing with stress. Caplan's ten characteristics of social support summarize how these work.

10. Social support may be conceptualized as providing a main effect (an overall sense of well-being) or a stress buffer (a variable that intervenes between the occurrence of a stressor and one's evaluation of the stress).

11. Classification of human behavior as normal or abnormal differs among the helping professions. Psychiatry focuses on personal inadequacy in goal attainment and in social presentation, from a context of disease or disorder. Psychology focuses on personal inadequacy in a developmental context and often deemphasizes the idea of disease. Sociology considers abnormality, or deviance, as an inability to fulfill a significant social role within a range of accepted behaviors as assessed by significant others in the community.

12. Social work is reluctant to label persons as abnormal, because all behavior is conceptualized as transactional and related to the nature of the social context.

KEY TERMS

adaptation

buffering model

challenge

clusters

compassion stress

coping

crisis

critical incident stress

critical incidents (CIs)

daily hassles

defense mechanisms

deviance

diathesis

emotion-focused coping

general adaptation syndrome

harm

homeostasis

main effect model

mental disorder

normalization

personal network

person-in-environment (PIE) classification
    system

post–traumatic stress disorder

problem-focused coping

psychosocial development

relational coping

role strain

social network

social support

state

stress

stress/diathesis models

threat

trait

traumatic stress

WORLD WIDE WEB RESOURCES

Stress Management

http://www.pp.okstate.edu/ehs/links/stress.htm

Oklahoma State University site contains links to stress management sites on the medical basis of stress and basic guidelines for coping.

Stress Management: A Review of Principles

http://www.unl.edu/stress/mgmt/

University of Nebraska–Lincoln site discusses stressors and stress responses, the psychophysiology of stress, physiology of stress, and stress-related disorders.

CHAPTER 6

The Spiritual Person

Michael J. Sheridan, Virginia Commonwealth University

SEAN'S SEARCH FOR MEANING AND CONNECTION

Sean was born into a large Irish-American, Catholic family on a cold day in February 1950. His birth was followed within a span of 10 years by the births of his two sisters and two brothers. Sean's parents, Joseph and Mary Cassidy, lived in Boston, Massachusetts, where their families had first immigrated during the late 1800s. The Cassidy clan consisted of numerous aunts, uncles, and cousins, plus Mary's mother and father; Joseph's parents were both deceased.

Joseph and his brothers, Sam and Elliot, ran a small trucking business, which specialized in carrying produce to various markets in New England. Joseph was the head of the company, but he still took his turn hauling produce. Although the business had struggled in the beginning, it eventually grew into a fairly stable source of income for the three brothers' families. Mary was a full-time homemaker who spent her days caring for her growing family.

The Catholic religion was an important facet of the Cassidy household. All of the children were enrolled in Catholic schools, and weekends were dedicated to church activities. Mary was particularly active in their church and made sure that the children were involved either as acolytes or as members of the choir. Although Joseph accompanied Mary to church, his personal connection to the Catholic faith was not as strong as hers—a difference that sometimes caused difficulties between them.

Sean remembers his early childhood with fondness—especially the strong sense of belonging that came from his large extended family, his school, and the church. He felt close to his mother and nurtured by her. He was in awe of his father, who would swoop into the house after being gone for several days and entertain them with colorful stories of his trips on the road.

The tenor of the household changed dramatically in Sean's 10th year, however, when his Uncle Elliot was killed in a trucking accident on his way home from a trip to Maine. The entire Cassidy clan was devastated, but Sean's father was particularly hard hit. While most of the family found solace in the teachings and rituals of their faith, Joseph became increasingly morose and seemed to find comfort only in the company of a whiskey bottle—a practice he had previously avoided because of his own father's alcoholism. He felt responsible for his brother's family following Elliot's death and worried about how he could support both families financially. He became more and more withdrawn and tense, and Mary and the children learned to tip-toe around him when he was at home so not to "upset him."

The situation went from bad to worse. Sean's parents argued more and more as his father's drinking increased and he began to miss work. The children were fearful and felt that things were out of control. Several of them, including Sean, started to have problems in school with falling grades and fights

CASE STUDY

with other kids. Sean's feelings about his father began to change. Where once he was proud of him, now he was both frightened and ashamed of him. He no longer felt close to his mother, who seemed constantly preoccupied with either arguing with his father or praying to God to save her husband.

The family tension ended when Sean's father was killed in a trucking accident similar to the one that had taken the life of his brother. Joseph had been drinking on a late night run and lost control of the truck, which went off the road, smashed into a tree, and caught fire. Sean went with his Uncle Sam to identify his father's charred remains—an experience that haunted him for many years. The family quietly buried Joseph and never voiced their fears that his death had perhaps not been "accidental." Sean was 15 years old at the time.

The remainder of Sean's growing up years were spent trying to help his mother keep the family together, while growing increasingly distant and angry with her and the rest of his life. He found himself rebelling against everything—his family, school, the church—and all that they stood for. When he graduated from high school in 1968, the world around him was in turmoil, and so was he.

Although he was able to go off to college, thanks to a small college fund, financial aid, and money saved from part-time jobs, Sean found it difficult to concentrate on his studies. There was too much else going on. Civil rights, the Vietnam war, free love, and the drug culture were vastly more interesting than his courses in English literature, and he was exposed to ideas that were radically different from the perspectives he had been taught at home. He found himself particularly enjoying long discussions with other students about the hypocrisy of religion and mainstream politics and the need to break away from all of the values of the "establishment." He felt a sense of belonging and connection in his group of counterculture friends that he had not experienced since early childhood.

One of these friends was a free spirit named Molly, who was different from any girl he had known in Boston. She taught him the art of smoking dope and dropping acid and the pleasures of lovemaking while stoned out of his mind. On a whim one weekend, they decided to drop out of college and go join a commune in the country where they could live their lives free from the "shackles of society." Initially, Sean felt at home in this new environment and believed that he had finally found his true purpose in life. However, as time went by, Sean's drug and alcohol use grew more intense, until finally even Molly was complaining to him about it. One morning, after a particularly upsetting fight with Molly, Sean went off to his favorite place in the woods to be alone and think about things. He recognized how desperately unhappy and alone he felt and how scared he was about his substance use, which he knew was out of

CASE STUDY

control. He wondered whether his father's death had been a suicide and realized that he felt somewhat suicidal himself. He missed his family and felt guilty about his distance from them. A sense of panic grew inside him, and he began to do something he had not done in a very long time—he began to pray. As he prayed, tears started to stream down his face as he allowed himself to feel the pain of his father's death and despair about the changes in his family—feelings he had kept bottled up inside for years. His tears turned to deep sob, and he thought he was going to drown in the depths of his sorrow. Suddenly, he felt a warm presence, as if someone had his arms around him, and he heard his father's voice say quietly in his ear, "It will be all right, son, it will be all right." The power and comfort of this experience was incredibly intense, although Sean began to doubt it as quickly as he experienced it. It seemed so bizarre to him, and yet so real and natural, to feel his father's presence and to hear his voice at the very moment that he finally let himself grieve for him.

This experience was a turning point for Sean, although he still struggled to make sense of it and told no one about it. He went home to his family and had long talks with his mother about his father and the family. He stopped his use of alcohol and drugs, started attending AA and NA meetings, and got some counseling. Eventually, Sean re-enrolled in college and at the age of 27 completed his degree in English, with a focus on journalism. He then found work with an environmental group writing brochures and advocacy materials, which fit with his sense of social consciousness. He had made peace with his mother, was reunited with his family, and felt like he was on track again.

On his 28th birthday he met Nancy, a young woman who came to a birthday celebration his friends threw for him. He was immediately taken by her and, after a year of dating, they married and settled in the Boston area. Nancy was a social worker who worked in a youth program in the inner city and was very committed to her work. She had also had family difficulties—her mother was an alcoholic—and Sean found it easy to talk with her about his own life. He finally told her of his experience in the woods when it seemed that his father had come to comfort him. He told her that he still did not know whether it had really happened or was a "figment of my imagination," but that it clearly had helped him make an important decision in his life.

Nancy and Sean began to talk more and more about their early experiences with religion, both positive and negative, and about their current beliefs. Sean shared with his wife the concepts of a "higher power" that he had gained from AA and NA and his growing sense that there was "something more" to life than the everyday reality. They began to read books on different faith traditions and began to practice meditation and study Celtic shamanism together. They

CASE STUDY

talked about the core themes of love and compassion that seemed to be central to many of the religions they were studying. Although neither had a desire to return to the faiths of their childhood, both Sean and Nancy recognized that they would like to be a part of some spiritual community.

But the decision to actually join a church did not come until after the birth of their first child, when they joined a Unitarian Universalist congregation. Over the years, Sean and Nancy have felt that this community has provided a good spiritual foundation for both themselves and their two boys. They have found personal meaning in the worship services and a sense of social responsibility and connectedness in the church's outreach programs. They have been members for 15 years.

Sean still reads a lot of different religious writings and feels that there is a good fit between the practices of meditation and shamanism and the teachings of his adopted faith. He sees his involvement in the Unitarian church and his personal practices as different but equally important expressions of his spiritual life, and he is becoming more and more aware of the "sacred in everyday life." He is very conscious of trying to transmit this sense of spirituality to his sons as they move into adolescence and young adulthood. Both personal faith and a spiritual community are especially important to both Sean and Nancy these days, as they have just learned that Nancy has advanced-stage breast cancer.

The Spiritual Dimension

Systems perspective

Sean's story could be viewed through many different lenses. The biopsychosocial framework currently utilized by social work would be helpful in understanding many facets of his life. Knowledge of the biological influences on behavior would be useful in understanding the intergenerational pattern of substance abuse and biochemical depression in the Cassidy family. Psychological perspectives would shed light on Sean's struggles during adolescence and young adulthood, as well as help us understand the crisis that he and his wife currently face. Social theories on family dynamics, ethnicity and culture, social movements, socioeconomic class, and social institutions would provide invaluable information about the various interacting systems in which Sean's life is embedded. This use of multiple perspectives to understand human behavior is consistent with social work's focus on changing configurations of person and environment.

However, the biopsychosocial framework omits an important dimension of human existence: spirituality. Some writers see this omission as antithetical to social work's commitment to holistic practice (Canda, 1988; Joseph, 1987, 1988; Loewenberg, 1988; Marty, 1980; Ortiz, 1991;

Sermabeikian, 1994; Siporin, 1985; Spencer, 1961). What would be gained if we added a spiritual lens to our attempt to understand Sean's life? And how would this perspective help you as a social worker in working with Sean and his wife in their current life situation?

The Meaning of Spirituality

The concept of spirituality is one that is often confused with religion. But recent social work literature includes a number of attempts to delineate these terms and distinguish them from one another (Carroll, 1998; Dudley & Helfgott, 1990; Joseph, 1987, 1988; Sheridan, Bullis, Adcock, Berlin, & Miller, 1992; Sheridan, Wilmer, & Atcheson, 1994; Siporin, 1985). Canda (1997b) has analyzed the major themes in these various writings and proposes the following definitions:

Spirituality "relates to the person's search for a sense of meaning and morally fulfilling relationships between oneself, other people, the encompassing universe, and the . . . ground of existence, whether a person understands this in terms that are theistic, atheistic, nontheistic, or any combination of these" (p. 302). **Religion** "involves the patterning of spiritual beliefs and practices into social institutions, with community support and traditions maintained over time" (p. 303). Thus spirituality is a broader concept than religion, and spiritual expression may or may not involve a particular religious faith or religious institution. As we can see in Sean's story, his involvement in both the Catholic and Unitarian churches is only part of a larger spiritual journey that has included many different experiences and influences.

Regardless of the precise words that are used to capture the meaning of spirituality, it brings to mind many related themes. Exhibit 6.1 lists 20 symbolic themes of spirituality identified by Patrick O'Brien (1992). He describes these themes as the "bridges that allow the essence [of spirituality] to cross into experience" (p. 3). Sean's life story reveals a number of these themes, or bridges to spiritual understanding: the nature and meaning of self and the intention and purpose of human existence; mystical, altered states of consciousness; prayer, meditation, and quiet contemplation; and answers to pain, suffering, and death.

The Role of Spirituality in Human Development

The idea that spirituality is an important dimension of human behavior is not a new one in social work or in the other helping professions. Although Freud (1928) asserted that all religious and spiritual beliefs were either illusions or projections of unconscious wishes, many other early behavioral science theorists viewed the role of spirituality differently.

Psychodynamic perspective

Developmental perspective

Notably, Carl Jung, a student of Freud's, differed with his former teacher and mentor in regard to the topic of spirituality. Jung's (1933) theory of personality includes physical, mental, and spiritual selves, which all strive for unity and wholeness within each person. An important archetype in Jung's view is the Spirit, which is "universally present in the preconscious makeup of the human psyche" (1959, p. 214). Jung further proposed that the evolution of consciousness and the struggle to find a spiritual outlook on life were the primary developmental tasks in midlife. If successfully accomplished, the result was *individuation*, which he defined as "the moment when the finite mind realizes it is rooted in the infinite" (Keutzer, 1982, p. 76).

EXHIBIT 6.1

Symbolic Themes
of Spirituality

1. Morality, ethics, justice, and right effort.
2. The nature and meaning of self and the intention and purpose of human existence.
3. Interconnection, wholeness, alignment, and integration of persons, place, time, and events.
4. Creativity, inspiration, and intuition.
5. Altruistic service for the benefit of others.
6. The mystery and wonder that are woven into nature, the universe, and the unknown.
7. Socio-cultural-historical traditions, rituals, and myths.
8. Virtues (such as compassion, universal love, peace, patience, forgiveness, hope, honesty, trust, faith).
9. Mystical, altered states of consciousness.
10. Sexuality.
11. Openness, willingness, surrender, and receptivity.
12. The power of choice, freedom, and responsibility.
13. Special wisdom or revealed knowledge.
14. Prayer, meditation, and quiet contemplation.
15. Answers to pain, suffering, and death.
16. Identity and relation to the metaphysical ground of existence, ultimate reality, and life force.
17. The relationship of cause and effect regarding prosperity or poverty.
18. Beliefs or experiences related to noncorporeal reality or the unobstructed universe.
19. The path to enlightenment or salvation.
20. Sensitive awareness of the earth and the nonhuman world.

Source: Adapted from Patrick J. O'Brien, 1992.

**Psychodynamic
perspective**

    Robert Assagioli (1965, 1973), in an approach known as psychosynthesis, also emphasized the spiritual dimension. His view of the human psyche includes the constructs of "higher unconscious" or "superconscious" as the source of creativity and spirituality. In Assagioli's view, some psychological disturbances are best understood as crises of spiritual awakening rather than symptoms of psychopathology. In such cases, the responsibility of the therapist is to facilitate the client's exploration of spiritual possibilities while dealing with the difficulties that such awakenings can engender. As Assagioli defined it, " 'spiritual' refers not only to experiences traditionally considered religious but to *all* the states of awareness, all the human functions and activities which have as their common denominator the possession of *values* higher than average" (1989, p. 30).

**Humanistic
perspective**

    A third major contributor to early formulations on spirituality and human behavior was Abraham Maslow, founding father of humanistic psychology. Maslow described spirituality as innate and "part of the human essence . . . a defining characteristic of human nature" (1971, p. 325). In his study of optimally functioning people, he characterized people at the top of his hierarchy as "transcendent self-actualizers" and described them as having (among other traits) a more holistic view of life; a natural tendency toward cooperative action; a tendency to be motivated by truth, goodness, and unity; a greater appreciation for peak experiences; an ability to go beyond their ego self to higher levels of identity; and more awareness of the sacredness of every person and of every living thing. Maslow later came to believe that even this definition was not adequate to explain the highest levels of human potential. Near the end of his life, he predicted the emergence of a more expansive understanding of human behavior, "a still 'higher' Fourth psychology, transpersonal, trans-human, centered in the cosmos, rather than in human needs and interests, going beyond humanness, identity, self-actualization, and the like" (Wittine, 1987, p. 53).

Describing this evolution as a "Fourth Force" psychology, Cowley (1993, 1996) states that four major therapeutic approaches have emerged over the past century, each developed in response to our understanding of human behavior and human needs at the time:

Psychodynamic perspective

- *First Force therapies* are based on dynamic theories of human behavior. The prime concern of these therapies is dealing with repression and resolving instinctual conflicts by developing insight.

Social behavioral perspective

- *Second Force therapies* evolved from behavioral theories. These therapies focus on learned habits and seek to remove symptoms through various processes of direct learning.

Humanistic perspective

- *Third Force therapies* are rooted in experiential/humanistic/existential theories. These therapies center on dealing with existential despair and seek the actualization of the person's potential through techniques grounded in immediate experiencing.

- *Fourth Force therapies* are based on transpersonal theories. These therapies specifically target the spiritual dimension. They focus on helping the person let go of ego attachments—external identifications with the mind/body—and develop self-transcendence through various spiritually based practices (Cowley, 1996).

The Fourth Force builds upon the previous three forces, and thus incorporates existing knowledge concerning human behavior within its framework. What differentiates the Fourth Force—the **transpersonal approach**—from other theoretical orientations is the premise that some states of human consciousness and potential go beyond our traditional views of health and normality. These states explicitly address the spiritual dimension of human existence (Cowley & Derezotes, 1994).

Transpersonal Theories of Human Development

The term *transpersonal* literally means "beyond" or "through" the "persona" or "mask" (Wittine, 1987). When applied to theories of human behavior, *transpersonal* means going beyond identity rooted in the individual body or ego to include spiritual experience or higher levels of consciousness. A major objective of transpersonal theories is to integrate spirituality within a larger framework of human behavior.

Developmental
perspective

Two theorists who have developed comprehensive perspectives on spiritual development are James Fowler and Ken Wilber. Although these two theorists are certainly not the only writers in this area, they have produced two of the best-known and most widely used models of spiritual development in the field today. The following sections provide an overview of these two transpersonal theories of human behavior and a consideration of Sean's search for connection and meaning from each perspective.

Stages of Faith Development

James Fowler's (1981) theory of faith development grew out of 359 in-depth interviews conducted between 1972 and 1981 in Boston, Chicago, and Toronto. The sample was overwhelmingly white (97.8%), largely Christian (over 85%), evenly divided by gender, and widely distributed in terms of age (3.5 to 84 years). Each semi-structured interview consisted of a life review of more than 30 questions about life-shaping experiences and relationships, present values and commitments, and religion. After the responses were analyzed, interviewees were placed in one of six **faith stages**. Fowler found a generally positive relationship between age and stage development; as age increased, so did the tendency for persons to be in higher stages. However, only a minority of persons revealed characteristics of stages 5 or 6, regardless of age.

To Fowler, **faith** is broader than religious faith, creed, or belief. It can, in fact, be expressed even by people who do not believe in God. Instead, faith is a universal aspect of human existence, "an integral, centering process, underlying the formation of beliefs, values, and meanings that (1) gives coherence and direction to people's lives, (2) links them in shared trusts and loyalties with others, (3) grounds their personal stances and communal loyalties in a sense of relatedness to a larger frame of reference, and (4) enables them to face and deal with the limited conditions of life, relying upon that which has the quality of ultimacy in their lives" (Fowler, 1996, p. 56). Faith as defined by Fowler is similar to the definition of spirituality given at the beginning of this chapter and is clearly distinguished from more particular notions of belief or religion.

Another important concept in Fowler's theory is the **ultimate environment**—the highest level of reality. Faith is not only your internal image of the ultimate environment, but also your relationship with that image; it is *relational,* not merely cognitive. Your view of the ultimate environment—as personal or impersonal, trustworthy or not dependable, capable of dialogue or silent, purposeful or based on chance—and your relationship with it is an evolving, dynamic process that is strongly influenced by your experiences throughout the life course.

Fowler's stages of faith development should not be viewed as goals to be achieved or as steps necessary for "salvation." Rather, they help us understand a person's values, beliefs, and sense of meaning and help us better appreciate the tasks, tensions, and challenges at various points in life.

Now let us turn to a brief description of each of Fowler's faith stages (which number seven if you count the pre-stage of infancy), based on both his early research and later theoretical refinements. As you read through these descriptions, refer to Exhibit 6.2, which summarizes some of the features of each faith stage and correlates Fowlers's stages with Piaget's stages of cognitive development and Kohlberg's stages of moral development (both described in Chapter 4).

EXHIBIT 6.2
Fowler's Faith Stages

Faith Stage	Life Stage	Emerging Strength	Potential Danger	Form of Logic (Piaget)	Form of Moral Judgment (Kohlberg)
Pre-stage: Primal faith	Infancy	A fund of basic trust and relational experience of mutuality.	Either excessive narcissism, which distorts dynamics of mutuality, or isolation and failed mutuality stemming from abuse, neglect, or inconsistent caregiving.		
Stage 1: Intuitive projective faith	Early childhood	Birth of imagination and the ability to unify and grasp the experience-world in powerful images.	Possible "possession" of imagination by images of terror and destructiveness (via stories of hell and the devil) or from exploitation of child's imagination through heavy indoctrination.	Preoperational	Punishment/reward
Stage 2: Mythic-literal faith	Middle childhood and beyond	The power of narrative and emergence of story, drama, and myth as ways to give meaning to experience.	Development of highly controlling, stilted perfectionism, or abiding sense of "badness" due to mistreatment, neglect, or disfavor of significant others.	Concrete operational	Instrumental hedonism (reciprocal fairness)
Stage 3: Synthetic-conventional faith	Adolescence and beyond	Formation of a personal myth of one's own becoming in identity in faith, which incorporates both the past and anticipated future within images of the ultimate.	Overinternalization of external expectations and evaluations of others impairing autonomy of judgment and action, or nihilistic despair about or false intimacy in one's relationship with the ultimate reality.	Early formal operations	Interpersonal expectations and concordance
Stage 4: Individual-reflective faith	Young adulthood and beyond	The capacity to reflect critically on both self and outlook.	Excessive confidence in the conscious mind and critical thought, resulting in a kind of narcissism and overassimilation of perspectives of others into one's worldview.	Formal operations (dichotomizing)	Societal perspective: Reflective relativism or class-biased universalism

EXHIBIT 6.2

Fowler's Faith Stages *(continued)*

Faith Stage	Life Stage	Emerging Strength	Potential Danger	Form of Logic (Piaget)	Form of Moral Judgment (Kohlberg)
Stage 5: Conjunctive faith	Midlife and beyond	"Ironic imagination," or the capacity to see and be in one's group (and one's group's most powerful meanings), while simultaneously recognizing that they are relative, partial, and distorted understandings of transcendent reality.	Possibility of paralyzing passivity or inaction, resulting in complacency or cynical withdrawal, stemming from one's paradoxical understanding of truth.	Formal operations (dialectical)	Prior to society: Principled higher law (universal and critical)
Stage 6: Universalizing faith	Midlife and beyond	Actualizers of the spirit ir an inclusive and fulfilled human community; capacity to serve as lures for others relative to spiritual development.	None identified.	Formal operations (synthetic)	Loyalty to being

Source: James W. Fowler, 1980, 1981.

Pre-Stage: Primal Faith. Fowler observes, "We all begin the pilgrimage of faith as infants" (1981, p. 119). At a time in life when we first learn to trust (or not trust) our immediate environment and develop a sense of object permanence ("mother or caregiver will return to me"), our first pre-images of the ultimate environment also develop. If nurturance by caregivers is consistent, the infant develops a sense of trust and safety about the universe and the divine—or feels "at home" in his or her life space. Conversely, negative experiences can produce images of the ultimate as untrustworthy, punitive, or arbitrary.

Early experiences in this phase form the foundation for all that comes later in faith development. The transition to stage 1 begins with the integration of thought and language, which facilitates the use of symbols in speech and ritual play.

It is probably safe to assume that Sean was able to develop at least a "good enough" fund of basic trust and an adequate relational experience for later development of a relationship with the ultimate, given what we know about his family at the time of his birth. According to Fowler, this early experience set the stage for Sean's later faith development.

Stage 1: Intuitive-Projective Faith. This stage generally emerges in children aged 2 to 7, who have the new tools of speech and symbolic representation to help them organize experience in a meaningful way. However, their thought patterns are generally fluid and magical and are considered to be "preoperational" (in Piaget's terms). Ways of knowing are largely based in intuition and imagination. Awareness of self is generally egocentric, and children at this age have only a rudimentary ability to take the perspective of others. It is at this time that children also have their first awareness of death and sex and learn the strong familial and cultural taboos surrounding these aspects of life. Thus, faith at this stage is fantasy-filled and imitative and can be powerfully and permanently influenced by the examples, modes, actions, and stories of significant adults and forces in the child's life. Because faith images at this stage can be powerful and long-lasting, it is important to honor the child's own process of faith development. Although this stage normally ends at about age 6 or 7, it may be found in adolescents or adults who are experiencing psychological difficulties or in members of cults that rely heavily on dreams and vision imagery.

Two excerpts from Fowler's interviews with young children illustrate the strong influence of family and culture on faith development at this stage. Six-year-old Freddy, reared in a Catholic family, declares that God knows when you do something bad because "He spreads all around the world in one day." Four-and-a-half-year-old Sally, whose parents have intentionally avoided exposing her to religious symbols, states that sometimes she believes in God because he shows up in shows like "Leave It to Beaver." When asked what God looks like, she replies, "He doesn't look like anything. He's all around you." Both of these children's images and their relationships with the ultimate environment stem from the messages that surround them, filtered through their own imagination and abilities to make meaning of these messages.

The major factors facilitating a transition to Fowler's next stage are the emergence of concrete operational thinking (in Piaget's terms) and the resolution of Oedipal issues about attraction to the parent of the opposite sex and competition with the parent of the same sex (in Freud's terms). What is most critical during this transition is that the child be allowed to clarify for him/herself the distinctions between what is real and what only seems to be real.

Sean's story does not tell us much about development of his early images of the ultimate environment. However, we can speculate that many of these images were drawn from his family's Catholic faith. In working with Sean, we would want to understand how this process of image making was handled by his family and others in his life and how much support he was given for his own intuition and imagination during this time.

Stage 2: Mythic-Literal Faith.   During this stage, generally beginning between ages 7 and 8, the child begins to take on the stories, beliefs, and practices that symbolize belonging to his or her community. There is a high level of conformity to the beliefs and practices of the community, and symbols are seen as one-dimensional and literal in meaning. For example, someone in this faith stage may view the wine used in Christian communion as the actual blood of Jesus Christ. Authority and tradition are very powerful influences, as the child incorporates the moral rules and attitudes of those around him or her. The ability to engage in concrete operations allows the child to sort out fantasy and reality, which reorders the imaginative picture of the world as conceived in stage 1. Especially important during stage 2 is the role of narrative and story, which become the major way of providing coherence and meaning to experience. Thus, persons at stage 2 can be deeply affected by symbolic and dramatic presentations concerning the ultimate reality, such as the wearing of special garments and the circling of the Ka'ba seven times during Muslims' annual pilgrimage to Mekkah. There is also an increased capacity to take the perspective of others, and ideas concerning reciprocity and fairness become central. Because of the emphasis on order, rules, and literal meaning, a person at this stage does not need an intense personal relationship with the ultimate environment. Although the majority of persons demonstrating stage 2 characteristics in Fowler's study were in their elementary school years, he found some adolescents and a few adults who displayed the qualities of this faith stage.

The transition to stage 3 occurs with the breakdown of literalism, disillusionment with previous teachers, and clashes or conflicts between accounts by various authority figures (such as the creation story versus the theory of evolution). Movement into Piaget's formal operational thought and development of the capacity for mutual perspective taking allow for deeper reflection and create the need for a more personal relationship with the ultimate environment.

If Fowler had interviewed Sean at age 10 before his uncle's death, Sean more than likely would have reflected Mythic-Literal faith. As you remember from Sean's story, the Catholic church was a central force in both his family and his community. Sean had learned much about the world and his place in it from the rich narratives and symbols of the Catholic religion, and they helped create a sense of order and meaning in his life. He felt a strong sense of guidance and belonging in this faith community. It would be useful to know what meaning Sean made of the deaths of both his uncle and father, based on the narratives and practices he was exposed to in his faith community. These early losses, and his family's responses to them, were undoubtedly major factors in Sean's continuing faith development as he moved into adolescence.

Stage 3: Synthetic-Conventional Faith.   Adolescence brings the capacity for abstract thinking and the manipulation of concepts, which strongly affects the process by which a person forms an identity. This is also a time when a person's environments broaden, as adolescents become increasingly influenced by peers, by school or work, and by the media and popular culture.

All of these environments "mirror" back different images of the self and the ultimate reality, which must be drawn together in forming both identity and faith. Values, commitments, and relationships are oriented to obtaining approval and affirmation from significant others, making this a stage of conformity and conventionalism. Authority is perceived as external and may be found in traditional authority figures, such as parents and teachers, or in the consensus of a valued group, such as one's peers.

Faith at stage 3 must provide a coherent orientation in the middle of a complex and diverse world. It must also help the person synthesize a host of information and provide a basis for personal identity and outlook. Images of the ultimate reality reflect qualities experienced in personal relationships, such as the compassion exhibited by an admired parent or teacher. Beliefs and values are often deeply felt at stage 3, but they are primarily tacit rather than critically examined. A person has an **ideology**, or outlook, but has not objectified it for systematic reflection and is largely unaware of having it. Differences in outlook between people are understood as differences in "kinds" of people. Finally, although symbols are not perceived as literally as they are in stage 2, symbols that evoke deep meaning and loyalty are not seen as separate from what they symbolize. For example, a Jewish person in this faith stage experiences the salt water and bitter herbs used in the Passover supper as direct representations of the tears and bitterness of slavery. Although this faith stage is most evident in adolescence, Fowler reports that a considerable number of adults also fall within this stage, and it can become a long-lasting or permanent structure of faith and identity for these individuals.

Factors leading to the transition to stage 4 may include serious clashes or contradictions between authority figures; changes by officially sanctioned leaders in practices or policies that were previously deemed sacred (such as changing the language of Mass from Latin to the vernacular); and experiences that lead to critical reflection about one's own beliefs and values. Frequently the experience of "leaving home"—physically or emotionally—can precipitate the kind of examination that leads to a transition from stage 3 to stage 4.

Conflict perspective

The events that occurred in Sean's life during his adolescence had a profound effect on his faith development. Not only did he lose his uncle and his father, but these losses strongly impacted his family system for some time. It is easy to imagine that Sean experienced this period as a series of betrayals—betrayed by his father for leaving him (emotionally after Uncle Elliott's death and then physically by dying himself); betrayed by his mother for becoming so engrossed in her own concerns that she grew distant with her son; betrayed by the church and its teachings for not being able to bring real comfort to his family during these crises; and even betrayed by God, with whom he could not seem to connect during this time. This sense of betrayal at many levels probably led him to reject his earlier faith conceptualizations somewhat prematurely and created difficulties for him as he moved into young adulthood.

Stage 4: Individuative-Reflective Faith. The transition to late adolescence and early adulthood brings with it an increased responsibility for one's own commitments, lifestyle, beliefs, and attitudes. The person is no longer defined by the composite of his or her roles and meanings to others. One begins to construct an individualized self (identity) and outlook (ideology) from the previously held conventional faith. This process requires struggling with a series of unavoidable tensions: individuality versus being defined by one's group or group membership; subjectivity and one's strongly felt but unexamined feelings versus objectivity and critical reflection; self-fulfillment and self-actualization versus service to and being for others; commitment to the relative versus struggle with the possibility of an absolute. As a result of this process, previously held creeds, symbols, and stories are demythologized through critical analysis. The ultimate environment becomes an explicit meaning system, and symbols are reshaped into new and more powerful conceptualizations. For example, the sage and rituals used during "smudging" by some First Nations people may take on deeper and wider meanings related to cleansing beyond their roles in sacred ceremonies. The goal is to create a rational, workable, and personal worldview.

Fowler states that an ideal time for movement into stage 4 is the early to mid-20s; for many adults, however, this transition (if it comes at all) occurs during the 30s or 40s. This process represents an upheaval in one's life at any point and can last for five to seven years or even longer. Readiness for movement to the next stage may come in the form of a growing awareness of the paradoxes and complexities of life—all of which may threaten the clear distinctions and boundaries that have been carefully formed during stage 4. The transition to stage 5 often occurs when one begins to pay attention to inner voices and images that have previously been submerged or set aside.

If we look at Sean's life during his late adolescence and early 20s, we see a young man in turmoil. Having rejected the faith structures of his childhood, he is drawn to the worldview of the people he meets at college and the new and unorthodox ideas circulating during the late '60s and early '70s. He sets his heart on resistance to the old structures, and he buries his pain in mind-altering substances. He finds passion and purpose in politics and in personal relationships. He is indeed critical of the values, beliefs, and symbols of his past, but is this really a process of critical examination? He is certainly trying to express his individuality, but is he really developing a personal self (identity) and outlook (ideology)?

Using Fowler's framework as a guide, it could be argued that Sean does not truly move into stage 4 until after his experience in the woods, when he feels his father's presence and decides to go home and work things out with his family. It is only after he deals with the pain and unresolved losses of his childhood and his own self-destructive behaviors that he truly begins to critically examine his past beliefs and construct his own worldview. He is assisted in this process by his relationship with his wife, who also appears to be engaged in her own evolving faith identity. As they both move into their 30s, they take on the serious responsibility of defining their own commitments, lifestyle, values, and beliefs.

Stage 5: Conjunctive Faith.   Most people do not reach stage 5; only about one out of every six interviewees in Fowler's sample over the age of 31 fit the characteristics of this stage. Fowler did not find anyone at this faith stage prior to midlife. Conjunctive faith involves the integration of much that was suppressed or went unrecognized during the rational certainty of stage 4. During stage 5, therefore, the person must rework and reclaim his or her past and become open to the voices of the "deeper self." Symbolic power is also reunited with conceptual meanings at a deeper level. For example, a person in this stage may view the cross displayed during religious services as both a symbol of the crucifixion of Christ and a representation of sacrifice or death and rebirth. As a result of this process, polarities in life are no longer seen as problems to be solved, but rather as realities to be accepted. "Either/or" debates become "both/and" resolutions. For example, both determinism and free will may be considered to play a role in life; God may be experienced as both personal and abstract; humanity may be understood to be both good and evil. In stage 5, the person strives to unify opposites in mind and in experience.

Closely related to this new tolerance for paradox is an increased vulnerability to the truths of those who are "other." Importantly, this vulnerability includes a critical examination of one's social unconscious—the myths, ideal images, and prejudices that are deeply internalized as a result of membership within a certain social class, religious tradition, ethnic group, and so on. The definition of "community" expands beyond one's immediate environment or one's personal faith community to encompass all human beings. A person at stage 5 also becomes aware that one's personal faith, however defined, is of supreme value and that commitments based on this faith must be carried out regardless of the consequences. Finally, a person in stage 5 is ready to spend his or her energies in the service of generating identity and meaning within the lives of others. Transition to stage 6—which very few individuals experience—comes when the person can no longer live within the paradoxical and divided world of stage 5 and is willing to make the sacrifices necessary to move into Universalizing faith.

We see glimpses of emerging Conjunctive faith in Sean's story as he moves into midlife. We know that with his wife, Nancy, Sean purposefully studied different religious and spiritual traditions and was able to identify and appreciate common truths from various paths. Sean has also integrated different spiritual practices into his daily life as part of his spiritual journey. Both Sean and Nancy have developed a broad social consciousness and embrace a sense of community that is larger than their own immediate network. There are also signs of commitment to faith generativity, not only with their own sons but with a wider circle of persons as well. Further clarity about how far Sean has moved into Conjunctive faith would be helpful in order to understand how well he will be able to deal with the paradox of both crisis and opportunity inherent in his wife's current illness. An understanding of faith stage development would also be useful in helping both Sean and Nancy garner the supports that they will need in the weeks and months ahead.

Conflict perspective
    Stage 6: Universalizing Faith.   In order to clearly understand the unique qualities of persons in stage 6, we need to emphasize the dilemmas faced by persons in stage 5, or Conjunctive faith. A person at this previous level has a heightened understanding of the possibilities of human existence because of his or her ability to embrace paradox. For example, injustice is seen more clearly because there is an enlarged awareness of the demands of justice and their implications. Partial truths, and their limitations, are recognized because there is a sense of a more expanded vision of truth. Symbols, myths, and rituals are appreciated and cherished at a deeper level, because there is knowledge of the depth of reality that symbols, myths, and rituals reflect. Divisions within the human family are felt with vivid pain because the possibility of an inclusive commonwealth of all being is recognized. Persons at stage 5 remain divided, however, because the self is caught between these universalizing understandings and the need to preserve one's own well-being. Or, even if willing to move beyond personal well-being, the person believes that the alternatives to the existing socioeconomic system are more unjust or destructive than the

status quo. Thus, the person remains loyal to the present order and to its institutions, groups, and compromises.

Movement into stage 6 (Universalizing faith) requires that the person be able to act regardless of the threats to self, to primary groups, and to the institutional arrangements of the present order. Thus, the person at this stage becomes a disciplined, activist embodiment of the imperatives of absolute love and justice of which stage 5 persons have partial comprehension. Persons at stage 6 live sacrificial lives aimed at the transformation of humankind. As Fowler (1981, pp. 200–201) describes them, persons at the Universalizing stage of faith development

> have generated faith compositions in which their felt sense of an ultimate environment is inclusive of all being. They have become incarnators and actualizers of the spirit of an inclusive and fulfilled human community ... they create zones of liberation from social, political, economic and ideological shackles. ... Living with a sense of felt participation in a power that unifies and transforms the world, Universalizers are often experienced as subversive of the structures (including religious structures) by which we sustain our individual and corporate survival, security, and significance. ... The rare persons who may be described by this stage have a special grace that makes them seem more lucid, more simple, and yet somehow more fully human than the rest of us. ... Life is both loved and held too loosely. Such persons are ready for fellowship with persons at any of the other stages and from any other faith tradition.

Given this description, it is not surprising that very few persons are ever considered to be at this stage of faith development. Fowler identifies Gandhi, Mother Teresa, and Martin Luther King, Jr., during the last years of his life as Universalizers.

Fowler hastens to add that just because a person embodies the qualities of Universalizing faith does not mean that he or she is perfect in a moral, psychological, or leadership sense—a point he illustrates with a story about Gandhi's less than perfect treatment of his wife and sons while reaching out to the Untouchables of India. Although not perfect, Universalizers shake up our notions of normalcy and call into question the compromise arrangements that the rest of us accept based on our conventional understandings of justice. As such, Universalizers "lean into the future of God for all being" (Fowler, 1981, p. 211).

As we reflect on Sean's story, it is clear that he is not at the Universalizing stage of faith development. Given the rarity of such persons, it is unlikely that he will develop into this stage. Sean is probably best characterized as in transition from stage 4 (Individuative-Reflective faith) to stage 5 (Conjunctive faith).

Full-Spectrum Model of Consciousness

Ken Wilber first published his transpersonal theory of development in *The Spectrum of Consciousness* in 1977, but continues to develop and refine the model in numerous writings. His work reflects a unique integration of biology, history, psychology, sociology, philosophy, and religion. It is rooted in both conventional Western approaches and Eastern contemplative traditions. Wilber's overall model is comprehensive and complex, addressing development at both the individual and collective (or social) levels. Wilber's most recent ideas about individual develop-ment (see Wilber, 1995, 1996, 1997; Wilber, Engler, & Brown, 1986) are summarized here.

Wilber's full-spectrum model of consciousness has three major components:

1. **Basic structures** are those deep and inherent levels of consciousness that, once they emerge during development, tend to remain in existence throughout the life of the indi-vidual. Wilber posits 10 major structures or levels of consciousness, all of which are poten-tially present at the onset of development, but each of which emerges sequentially, one level at a time. Levels cannot be skipped over, and each level incorporates the capacities of earlier levels. This process of incorporation is rooted in the concept of *holons* or "that which, being a *whole* in one context, is simultaneously a *part* in another" (Wilber, 1995, p. 18). Thus, Wilber refers to his spectrum of consciousness as a *holarchy* (rather than a hierarchy), be-cause it reflects an ordering of holons (or increasing levels of complexity and wholeness) throughout the developmental process.

2. **Transitional structures** are temporary or stage-specific perspectives or worldviews. In de-scribing how human beings move through the basic structures or levels of consciousness, Wilber uses the metaphor of a ladder. The basic structures themselves he likens to the rungs of the ladder. When a person moves from one rung to the next, he or she temporarily gains a different perspective or worldview, including a different *self-identity*, a different *self-need*, and a different *moral stance*. New perspectives eventually replace these transitional struc-tures, but the actual rungs (or basic structures) remain in existence and are an enduring part of the person. To illustrate the distinction between basic and transitional structures, Wilber points to the differences between Piaget's stages of cognitive development and Kohl-berg's stages of moral development. In cognition, when a person moves to level 4 (formal operations), the cognitive structures of earlier stages (sensorimotor, preoperational, con-crete operational) are not lost, but are still accessible to the person; they remain as basic structures. In moral development, however, higher stages replace lower stages, in that a per-son does not simultaneously act from stage 1 (preconventional) and stage 5 (postconven-tional) morality; thus, these stages are transitional structures.

3. **Self system** refers to the person climbing the ladder of spiritual development. The self sys-tem (or self) mediates between the basic structures and the transitional stages. It is also the locus of several crucial capacities and operations: *identification,* or the locus of self-identity; *organization,* or that which gives cohesiveness to the psyche; *will,* or the locus of choice within the constraints of the present developmental level; *defense,* or the locus of phase-spe-cific and phase-appropriate defense mechanisms; *metabolism,* or the ability to metabolize or "digest" experience; and *navigation,* or the capacity to make developmental choices by moving up or down the developmental ladder or staying at a particular level.

As a person negotiates each unfolding basic structure, he or she moves from a narrower to a wider self-identity. At each point, the self goes though a **fulcrum,** or switch point, in its develop-ment. Specifically, each time the self steps up to a new rung on the developmental ladder, it goes through a three-step process. First, the self becomes comfortable and eventually identifies with the basic functioning of that level. Second, new experiences begin to challenge the way of being at this level, and the self begins to differentiate or "disidentify" with it. Third, the self begins to move toward and identify with the next level while integrating the functioning of the previous basic structure into the new organization. If the person is able to negotiate these fulcrum points successfully, development is largely nonproblematic. However, disturbances at the different fulcrum points produce various pathologies. Although Wilber lists specific types of pathology at each level, he also states that we must take into account "the standard cautions and qualifications ... [of] no pure cases, the influence of cultural influences, genetic predispositions, genetic and traumatic arrests, and blended cases" (1996, p. 107).

Wilber has an additional caveat: Although the process of development in his model is hierarchical (or "holarchical"), it is not strictly linear. Rather, it involves "all sorts of regressions, spirals, temporary leaps forward, peak experiences, and so on" (Wilber, 1996, p. 148). A person does not have to master all of the competencies of one level to move into the next; in fact, the self at any given level will often respond about 50% from one level, 25% from the level above, and 25% from the level below. Furthermore, people can have a spiritual or peak experience at any level, but they will have to make sense of this experience within their current stage and may have to grow and develop further to really accommodate the full depth or meaning of that experience. As Wilber puts it, "They still have to go from acorn to oak if they are going to become one with the forest" (1996, p. 152).

Exhibit 6.3 depicts Wilber's 10 basic structures or stages of consciousness, along with their corresponding fulcrums, pathologies, and treatment modalities. His model is rooted in the "perennial philosophy," which he states is evident across all cultures and across all ages. Also referred to as the Great Chain of Being, this philosophy proposes that reality or consciousness moves from matter to body to mind to soul to spirit. This spectrum of consciousness can be further categorized into the three phases of development described here.

The Prepersonal or Pre-egoic Phase. At the point of birth, the self leaves the *Primary Matrix* (stage 0), a state of early fusion that serves as the foundation from which all differentiation will occur during subsequent development. It then enters the Prepersonal phase, which has three primary structures or stages.

Stage 1 (ages 0–2), the *Sensoriphysical stage,* is characterized by a primary orientation to the material or physical world. At first, the self is identified with this world, in that the physical self and the physical environment are experienced as the same thing—there is no difference between "inside" and "outside." Eventually the infant begins to differentiate between physical sensations in its body and those in the environment. This differentiation produces the birth of the physical self, or the development of clear physical boundaries. During this stage, bodily needs and urges largely drive behavior, but simple sensorimotor skills and the capacity for early mental imaging also begin to develop.

Stage 2 (ages 2–4), the *Phantasmic-Emotional stage,* is characterized by the development of realistic boundaries around the emotional self. Initially, the infant is fused emotionally with its caregivers and treats the world as an extension of itself. This narcissism is normal. The infant is not "selfish"; it is simply incapable of thinking about itself as separate from the world. Thus, what it is feeling, the world is feeling. The task at this stage is to learn to distinguish one's own

EXHIBIT 6.3
Wilber's Full Spectrum of Consciousness

Phase of Development	Stage	Basic Structures of Consciousness	Corresponding Fulcrums	Characteristic Pathologies	Treatment Modalities
				Nondual	
Transpersonal or Trans-egoic	9	Causal	F-9	Causal pathology	Formless mysticism
	8	Subtle	F-8	Subtle pathology	Deity mysticism
	7	Psychic	F-7	Psychic disorders	Nature mysticism
Personal or Egoic	6	Centauric or Vision-Logic	F-6	Existential pathology	Existential therapy
	5	Formal-Reflexive Mind (formal operations)	F-5	Identity neuroses	Introspection
	4	Rule/Role Mind (concrete operations)	F-4	Script pathology (problems with roles or rules)	Script analysis
Prepersonal or Pre-egoic	3	Representational-Mind	F-3	Psychoneuroses	Uncovering techniques
	2	Phantasmic-Emotional	F-2	Narcissistic-borderline	Structuring/building techniques
	1	Sensoriphysical	F-1	Psychoses	Physiological/pacification techniques
	0	Primary Matrix	F-0	Perinatal pathology	Intense regressive therapies
				Nondual	

Sources: Ken Wilber, 1996; Robbins, Chatterjee, & Canda, 1998.

emotions from the emotions found in the environment. This stage corresponds to Piaget's early preoperational period, when cognitive ability moves from simple images to the use of symbols and language expands rapidly.

Stage 3 (ages 4–7), the *Representational-Mind stage,* brings the birth of the cognitive or mental self. At this point, the child is able to move beyond images and symbols to formulate concepts and more sophisticated mental representations of things. This stage corresponds to Piaget's later preoperational period, which sees emerging skills in the areas of numbers, classifications, and interrelationships. These new cognitive abilities permit the child to have a deepened sense of self as a separate ego, and thus move from the Pre-egoic to the Egoic phase of development. The worldview at this last stage of the Prepersonal (or Pre-egoic) phase is still *egocentric,* however, in that the child has little capacity to assume the roles of others.

Given the information that we have about Sean's early life, it is safe to assume that he negotiated the various fulcrum points of the Prepersonal or Pre-egoic phase relatively well. It is apparent that he had incorporated the basic structures of this phase and was able to continue his development in the Personal or Egoic level.

The Personal or Egoic Phase. This phase of development consists of three more stages.

Stage 4 (ages 7–11), the *Rule/Role Mind stage,* is ushered in by the capacity for concrete operational thought—the ability to form mental rules and take mental roles. A major focus of development at this point is learning how to perform various roles and to fit in with one's primary groups. This stage is crucial because it allows the child to finally learn to take the perspective of others. It is the first movement away from a worldview that is egocentric to one that is *sociocentric*—toward care and concern about others beyond the self. However, this expanding worldview is limited to one's familial and sociocultural memberships; assessment of those who are different (not of *my* group, *my* tribe, *my* ideology) is largely ethnocentric. Furthermore, cognitive ability is still primarily concrete in nature.

Stage 5 (adolescence and beyond), the *Formal-Reflexive Mind stage,* brings the capacity for formal operational thinking, which includes the ability to think abstractly and analytically and to make hypotheses and inferences. At this point, the person is able to critically judge the roles and rules that, at the previous stage, were simply learned and accepted. In critically examining the norms of one's own social group, one can also begin to understand and appreciate the different personal and cultural perspectives of others. Worldview again shifts, from sociocentric to *worldcentric,* and the person gains the ability to grasp the common humanity that underlies social and cultural differences.

Stage 6, the *Centauric or Vision-Logic stage,* brings a deepening and maturation of the worldcentric view. Although formal operational thought permitted synthesis and integration of abstract concepts in the previous stage, it tended to be dichotomous in nature (either/or thinking). The Vision-Logic stage is characterized by the capacity for a more holistic, integrated, dialectic (both/and) type of thinking, which allows the person to more deeply understand networks of interactions. The person grasps both the integration of mind and body (hence, the name Centauric) and the interconnection of oneself with other beings, both human and nonhuman. This realization produces an autonomous self that is not isolated or egocentric, but is instead highly involved in its networks of responsibility and service.

At the end of the Personal (or Egoic) phase of development, the person has developed a capacity for a truly global perspective that is able to transcend the personal ego and any particular sociocultural perspective. According to Wilber, Vision-Logic is the cutting edge of human development to date, not attained by most people. Although it is the highest stage of development recognized by most conventional theorists, for Wilber it is only the doorway to transpersonal levels of consciousness.

In terms of Wilber's model, it is clear that Sean's current development is within the upper stages of the Personal or Egoic realm, as evidenced by his ability for critical reflection and his developing worldcentric perspective. He is possibly moving into the Centauric/Vision-Logic level of consciousness. This level is roughly analogous to Fowler's Conjunctive faith stage, as both stages are characterized by the ability to have an integrative and dialectical view of life and the capacity to grasp the interconnectedness of things.

Thus, according to Exhibit 6.3, existential therapies may be the most appropriate therapeutic approach to use with Sean at this time. Some of the issues that Wilber lists at the Vision-Logic level include seeking an overall meaning in life, grappling with personal mortality and finitude, and finding the "courage to be" in the face of a lonely and unexpected death. It is clear that Sean could be struggling with any or all of these issues as he moves into midlife while simultaneously dealing with his wife's potentially life-threatening illness.

The Transpersonal or Trans-egoic Phase.   The integration of mind and body at the level of Vision-Logic means that the observing self becomes aware of both the mind and the body as *experiences* and thus has the capacity to *transcend* ego-based reality. Thus, the person can move beyond egocentrism and ethnocentrism to embrace a worldcentric awareness of the complete interdependence of all things in the cosmos. The person retains all the capacities developed during previous levels, but is able to incorporate these functions into new levels of consciousness.

Stage 7, the *Psychic stage,* is characterized by a continuing evolution of consciousness as the observing self develops more and more depth. Wilber refers to this evolving inner sense as the Witness because it represents an awareness that moves beyond ordinary reality (sensorimotor, rational, existential) into the transpersonal (beyond ego) levels. A distinguishing spiritual experience at this stage is a strong interconnectedness of self with nature. For example, a person may temporarily "become one" with a mountain or bird or tree. This type of experience is not psychotic fusion—the person is still very clear about his or her own personal boundaries—but it is a strong awareness of communion with the natural world. At this point, one's higher self becomes a World Soul and experiences *nature mysticism.* Because of this powerful experience of connection and identification, there is a natural deepening of compassion for all living things, including nature itself.

Stage 8, the *Subtle stage,* is characterized by an awareness of more subtle processes than are commonly experienced in gross, ordinary states of waking consciousness. Examples of such processes are interior light and sounds, awareness of transpersonal archetypes, and extreme states of bliss, love, and compassion. At this point, even nature is transcended, yet understood as a manifest expression of the ultimate. One's sense of connection and identification is extended to communion with the Deity, or union with God, by whatever name. Thus, consciousness at this level is not just nature mysticism—union with the natural world—but gives way to *deity mysti-*

cism. This level of consciousness can be experienced in many forms, often rooted in the person's personal or cultural history. For example, a Christian may feel union with Christ, while a Buddhist might experience connection with the Buddha.

Stage 9, the *Causal stage,* transcends all distinctions between subject and object (even self and God). The Witness is experienced as pure consciousness, pure awareness, and prior to the manifestation of anything. Thus, this state is said to be timeless, spaceless, and objectless. As Wilber describes it, "Space, time, objects—all of those merely parade by. But you are the Witness, the pure Seer that is itself pure Emptiness, pure Freedom, pure Openness, the great Emptiness through which the entire parade passes, never touching you, never tempting you, never hurting you, never consoling you" (1996, p. 224). This state is pure *formless mysticism,* in that all objects, even God as a perceived form, vanish into pure consciousness. This stage of consciousness is sometimes referred to as the "full Enlightenment, ultimate release, pure nirvana" (1996, p. 226). But it is still not the final story.

Stage 10, *Nondual,* is characterized by disidentification with even the Witness. The interior sense of *being* a Witness disappears, and the Witness turns out to be everything that *is* witnessed. In the causal stage, Emptiness is a level of awareness at that particular state (awareness of pure consciousness without form). At the Nondual stage, Emptiness *becomes* pure Consciousness itself. There is no sense of "two," there is only "one" (hence the name Nondual). Essentially, the person's awareness has moved beyond nature, deity, and formless mysticism to *nondual mysticism.* Furthermore, it is not really a stage among other stages, but is rather the condition or reality of *all* stages. It is simultaneously the source, the process, and the realization of consciousness. Wilber describes it as "the Ground or Suchness or Isness of *all* stages, at all times, in all dimensions: the Being of all beings, the Condition of all conditions, the Nature of all Natures" (1995, p. 301). Wilber does not depict the Nondual as a separate stage in his illustration of the structures of consciousness, because it represents the ground or origin of all the other stages—the paper on which the figure is drawn.

Prepersonal and Personal phases of consciousness should sound familiar to students of conventional approaches to human development. In contrast, the stages of the Transpersonal phase (and the language used to describe them) are most likely unfamiliar to those who are not well versed in contemplative Eastern ideas about human development. However, it is this synthesis of both conventional and contemplative approaches and the inclusion of "higher-order" levels of development that is Wilber's primary contribution to our attempts to understand human behavior. He is proposing that the personal level of development, with its achievement of strong ego development and self-actualization, is not the highest potential of human existence. Rather, the ultimate goal of human development is the "spirit" level—beyond ego or self to self-transcendence and unity with the ultimate reality. The capacity for attaining the highest levels of consciousness is innate within each human being, although Wilber acknowledges that very few people reach the higher transpersonal levels. He describes these individuals as "a rather small pool of daring men and women—both yesterday and today—who have bucked the system, fought the average and the normal, and struck out toward the new and higher spheres of awareness" (Wilber, 1996, p. 198).

As for the characteristic pathologies, or problems in development at each stage, all of the disorders or conditions listed in Exhibit 6.3 for the lower phases of development are well recognized within conventional diagnostic approaches (albeit with different labels). It is again at the Transpersonal level that Wilber strikes new ground, by including what he calls psychic disorders and subtle or causal pathologies. Examples of such problems in living include unsought spiritual awakenings, psychic inflation, split life-goals, integration/identification failure, pseudo-nirvana, and failure to differentiate or integrate. Wilber states that although these conditions are not well known, because most people do not reach these higher levels of development, they must be understood in order to be treated properly when they do occur.

Again, the treatment modalities listed in Exhibit 6.3 at the Prepersonal and Personal levels are well known to most social workers. However, the approaches that Wilber proposes for Transpersonal level disorders—nature mysticism, deity mysticism, and formless mysticism—are largely unknown (and sound a bit strange) to the majority of helping professionals. But they have been used in non-Western cultures for centuries. Furthermore, they are becoming more widely accepted in this country as effective, alternative treatment approaches (as in meditation/yoga, visualization, dreamwork, disidentification techniques, body work, acupuncture, journaling, intuition techniques, and the like). Wilber stresses that practitioners should be able to correctly identify the level of development in order to provide the most appropriate treatment. If not, a problem at the Transpersonal level (such as a spiritual awakening) may be treated as if it were a Prepersonal or Personal disorder (a psychotic episode or existential crisis), or vice versa.

How do Wilber's ideas about the Transpersonal or Trans-egoic phase help us work with someone like Sean, who may be at a fulcrum point? We would have to talk with Sean more about his contemplative practices (meditation and shamanism) to see if he has begun to develop any of the capacities at the Psychic level other than the one "inner vision" that he experienced when he was younger. It is quite possible that this early event represented a "peak experience" or "peek" into transpersonal consciousness for Sean, although he was clearly not in a transpersonal level of development at the time. Thus, he had to interpret this experience initially within his existing developmental stage (probably the beginning phase of the Formal-Reflexive Mind) and continue to revisit and "make meaning" of the experience as he moved into higher stages of consciousness. It is unlikely that Sean will move significantly into the Transpersonal phase of Wilber's developmental spectrum unless he makes deliberate and consistent efforts to engage in the extensive practices required to reach these higher stages of consciousness. Thus, we could support Sean's spiritual practices during this time, while watching for signs of possible difficulties at the Transpersonal level.

A Critique of Fowler's and Wilber's Theories

Both Fowler's and Wilber's models of spiritual development reflect Fourth Force theory in that they incorporate the first three forces (dynamic, behavior, and experiential/ humanistic/existential theories). In fact, both Fowler and Wilber use many of the same theorists as foundations for their own work (for example, Piaget, Kohlberg, Maslow). And both are clearly proposing higher and more transcendent levels of human development than have been previously proposed by conventional theorists.

Conflict perspective

As developmental models, both Fowler's and Wilber's models are open to the criticisms launched at all developmental perspectives: Such perspectives do not pay enough attention to social, economic, political, and historical factors and the role of power dynamics and oppression in human development. Developmental perspectives are also said to convey the idea that there is only one "right" way to proceed down the developmental path, and thus display an ethnocentrism often rooted in middle-class, heterosexual, Anglo-Saxon male life experience.

Both Fowler and Wilber might counter by pointing out that familial, cultural, and historical contexts are considered in their models. Wilber, in particular, would highlight the extensive use of cross-cultural knowledge in the development of his theory and point to the cessation of ethnocentrism as a major characteristic of his later stages of consciousness. Both would also support the notion of "many paths" in spiritual development, although they would say that these many paths have common features in their evolution.

Although Fowler's model was developed through an inductive research process and Wilber's formulations are grounded in multiple areas of research, there has been little attempt at empirical verification of either model. However, limited empirical exploration of Fowler's faith stages has provided partial support for his framework (Das & Harries, 1996; Furushima, 1983; Mischey, 1981; Swenson, Fuller, & Clements, 1993). The paucity of research is somewhat understandable given the difficulties of empirical investigation in such an abstract realm. It is difficult enough to operationalize and measure such concepts as formal operational cognition or self-esteem; the challenge of investigating transcendence or a World Soul is even more daunting! Nonetheless, strategies from both positivist and constructivist research approaches are currently available to study interior states and subjective experiences of meaning, as well as biophysical manifestations of different states of consciousness. (See Chapters 1 and 2 for a review of positivist and constructivist research approaches.) As is true for all theories of human behavior, transpersonal models such as Fowler's and Wilber's need to be specifically tested and refined through the research process. Furthermore, this research must be replicated with different groups (defined by gender, age, race, ethnicity, socioeconomic status, geopolitical membership, and the like) in order to explore the degree of universality in the models.

The most obvious difference between the two models is that Wilber provides more substance and specification than Fowler does about what transpersonal levels of development look like and how they evolve. Wilber also provides much more detailed descriptions of the potential pitfalls of spiritual development than Fowler. Fowler provides only a general overview of the possible dangers or deficits of development at each of his faith stages. However, Fowler provides more specification about the content and process of spiritual development at the prepersonal and personal levels. In terms of their utility for social work practice, we could say that Fowler's model is more descriptive, while Wilber's is more prescriptive.

Although only formulations concerning individual development have been presented here, Wilber has also developed stages of consciousness for larger systems. These macro or sociocultural stages parallel the first six individual stages of consciousness and are referred to as Archaic, Magical, Mythic, Mythic-Rational, Rational, and Vision-Logic or Centauric (Wilber, 1995, 1996). These stages reflect changes in human evolution over time, including shifts in such areas as technological/economic production, gender roles, family and social organization, worldviews, and conceptualizations of religion and spirituality. Each era has a typical mode of consciousness, although some individuals are always at the cutting edge of spiritual development, helping to move humanity forward. Wilber states that we have moved as a human species to the beginning phases of the Vision-Logic or Centauric stage, as evidenced by an increase in global awareness and the beginnings of a transrational, transcultural, and worldcentric vision.

Although Fowler does not explicitly include macro or sociocultural stages in his theory, his most recent writings also address the application of faith stages to larger systems (1996). He describes our current political and social landscape as a standoff between those with "orthodox" and "progressive" worldviews, each with their own different assessments of social, political, and economic reality. The orthodox worldview reflects the Synthetic-Conventional stage of faith development; the progressive perspective is grounded in the Individuative-Reflective stage. Because of the standoff, Fowler states that we are locked in the either/or thinking of the "culture wars." He proposes that until we move as a society beyond orthodox and progressive paradigms to the Conjunctive faith stage (with its capacity for integrated, dialectic, both/and thinking), we will not be able to effectively address the serious problems of our times. Such movement will require a different level of dialogue and debate about the role of spirituality in both our private and public lives. Although the level of specificity regarding spiritual development at the macro level is very different for Fowler and Wilbur, both theorists are making connections between the micro and macro levels of spiritual development.

In conclusion, both Fowler and Wilber provide perspectives beyond our traditional biopsychosocial framework that allow us to better understand people like Sean and suggest a direction for working with them in their life crises. However, we still need viable practice theories that explicitly address the spiritual dimension. An example of such a practice theory is Elizabeth Smith's "Trans-egoic Model" of intervention, originally developed for work with cancer patients and later expanded to apply to other issues of loss, such as divorce (Smith, 1995; Smith & Gray, 1995). This model outlines four therapeutic stages and specific techniques that could be quite useful in working with Sean and his family. However, it too must be tested and revised to determine its utility and applicability to a wide range of client situations.

The Role of Spirituality in Social Work

Interest in spirituality within the social work profession seems to have come full circle. Social work originated in religious institutions and the practice of charity (Fauri, 1988; Leiby, 1977, 1985; Marty, 1980; Niebuhr, 1932; Popple & Leighninger, 1990). During the early 1900s, however, social work began to distance itself from its early sectarian roots during a period of increased professionalization. This movement mirrored a shift within the larger society, which began to replace moral explanations of human problems with a scientific, rational understanding. The social work profession increasingly relied on empiricism, secular humanism, and libertarian morality as the major foundation for its values, ethics, and practice approaches (Imre, 1984; Siporin, 1986). As Russel (1998) describes this stage: "Religion and spirituality were increasingly viewed, at best, as unnecessary and irrelevant, and, at worst, as illogical and pathological" (p. 17).

A resurgence of interest in spirituality within the profession began in the late 1970s and gained momentum during the 1980s (Canda, 1997b; Russel, 1998). Indicators of this new phase within the profession include growing numbers of publications and presentations on the topic, the development of a national Society for Spirituality and Social Work, and the reintroduction of references to religious and spiritual diversity in the Council on Social Work Education's Curriculum Policy Statement after an absence of more than 20 years. The appropriate role of spirituality within the profession, however, remains the subject of ongoing debate (Amato–von Hemert, 1994; Canda, 1997a; Canda & Chambers, 1994; Clark, 1994; Sullivan, 1994; Weisman, 1997). Again, this trend toward reexamination and reintegration of spirituality within the profession reflects similar developments within the larger culture (Gallup & Castelli, 1989; Roof, 1993).

Perhaps one of the most significant developments is the growing body of literature on religion and spirituality and social work practice. One area of this scholarship focuses on the significance of the spiritual realm to various special populations. Examples of this literature include writings on the importance of spirituality to First Nations peoples (Yellow Bird, 1995), persons with disabilities (Gourgey, 1994), sexual minorities (Wagner, Serafini, Rabkin, Remien, & Williams, 1994), women (Nathanson, 1995), African American families (Logan, Freeman, & McRoy, 1990), Appalachian cultures (Carter, 1984), Southeast Asian refugees (Canda & Phaobtong, 1992), persons who are incarcerated (Sheridan, 1995), the elderly (Moberg, 1990), Hispanic communities (Delgado & Humm-Delgado, 1982), and religious families (Nakhaima & Dicks, 1995). Still another body of scholarship explores the need to consider the spiritual dimension when working with clients who are facing various personal challenges or problems in living, including practice with persons with mental illness (Walsh, 1995), substance abuse and other addictions (Morell, 1996), death and dying issues (Millison & Dudley, 1990), divorce (Smith & Gray, 1995), health concerns (Musick, 1996), trauma (Brende & Goldsmith, 1991), and caregiving responsibilities (Burton & Richardson, 1996). Still others address the relevance of religion and spirituality to macro-level social work and policy formulation (Breton, 1989; Canda & Chambers, 1994; Johnson, 1990; Netting, 1984; Ressler, 1998).

During this same period, a series of empirical studies has investigated the attitudes and behaviors of social work professionals. Several studies of social work practitioners have shown generally favorable attitudes toward the role of spirituality in practice and an understanding of the importance of spirituality in the lives of clients (Canda, 1988; Derezotes, 1995; Derezotes & Evans, 1995; Joseph, 1988; Sheridan & Bullis, 1991; Sheridan et al., 1992). A few studies report that the majority of social work educators and students favor inclusion of content on religion and spirituality in the social work curriculum either through electives, required courses, or infusion of material into existing courses (Dudley & Helfgott, 1990; Sheridan et al., 1994; Sheridan & Amato–von Hemert, in press). Moreover, students are already using several religiously oriented or spiritually sensitive intervention techniques with clients in their field placements or work settings (such as gathering information on clients' religious or spiritual backgrounds, using religious or spiritual language and concepts, recommending religious or spiritual programs, and praying privately for clients) (Sheridan & Amato–von Hemert, in press).

These results contrast with consistent findings that practitioners, faculty, and students receive very little content on religious or spiritual matters during their social work studies. Specifically, from 73% to more than 88% of respondents report "little or no" exposure to such material (Derezotes, 1995; Joseph, 1988; Sheridan & Amato–von Hemert, in press; Sheridan et al., 1992; Sheridan et al., 1994). These findings raise concerns about how well social workers can address spiritual issues with clients without benefit of education and training in this area.

Increased knowledge and attention concerning spirituality and social work have implications for theory, goals of practice, the nature of the helping relationship, assessment, and intervention strategies. In the realm of *theory,* this chapter has described two major transpersonal theories and noted some practice theory. Other spirituality-related theories exist as well. They all provide a more comprehensive view of human behavior by explicitly addressing spiritual evolution as an essential part of overall development. However, none of these theories has yet been adequately tested.

The *goals of practice* can also be affected by inclusion of a spiritual focus. A focus on spirituality opens up a wider range of possible supports and resources for the client and offers a different vantage point from which to make meaning of life challenges. Spirituality and a transpersonal perspective also enhance well-being through their expanded view of human potential. In Sean's case, for example, the goals for practice could incorporate both his personal spirituality and his religious connections within the community to deal with the problem at hand (such as development of a "care circle" among Sean's church community), while facilitating his own continued growth and development (through support for ongoing spiritual reflection and exploration).

Deliberate attention to the spiritual dimension also influences *the nature of the helping relationship* between client and social worker. When clients share their religious or spiritual lives, social workers must accept these offerings with respect, openness, and a willingness to learn. Social workers must be able to critically examine their own biases and prejudices with regard to religion and spirituality, just as they are expected to do with regard to other areas of difference (gender, race, age, sexual orientation, and so on). They must also feel comfortable being in the student role at times. In Sean's case, the social worker must be willing to learn about Sean's religious and spiritual beliefs *from Sean*, rather than be the "expert" in this area. Furthermore, social workers need to be actively engaged with issues of purpose, meaning, and connection in their own lives through continual self-reflection and disciplined efforts toward personal growth. It would be extremely difficult (if not impossible) for someone without a similar interest in such issues to help Sean work through his current struggle with meaning and connection. All of these dynamics tend to create a more egalitarian partnership between social worker and client, with the social worker acting in the role of guide, midwife, or cocreator rather than interpreter, director, or adviser (Cowley, 1996).

Assessment is another area affected by attention to spirituality. Gathering a client's religious or spiritual history is as important as learning about biopsychosocial factors. This assessment needs to go beyond the surface features of faith affiliation (such as Protestant, Catholic, Jewish, or Muslim) to include deeper facets of a person's spiritual life. Anita Titone (1991) has developed a set of questions that she offers as a useful tool for both assessment and relationship building (see Exhibit 6.4). Social workers also need to assess both the positive and negative aspects of clients' religious or spiritual beliefs and practices (Joseph, 1987, 1988; Sheridan & Bullis, 1991). For example, Sean's understanding of the meaning of suffering or the issue of guilt might be either helpful or harmful in dealing with his wife's illness and his own midlife experiences.

Assessment must also be able to distinguish between a religious/spiritual problem and a mental disorder. Recent changes to the *Diagnostic and Statistical Manual of Mental Disorders* (DMS-IV) provide guidance in this area. "Religious or spiritual problem" is now included as a

EXHIBIT 6.4

Questions for
Spiritual Assessment

1. What nourishes you spiritually? For example: music, nature, intimacy, witnessing heroism, meditation, creative expression, sharing another's joy?

2. What is the difference between shame and guilt? What is healthy and unhealthy shame and guilt?

3. Do you believe there is a Supreme Being?

4. If yes, what is that Being like? What does he/she look like?

5. What were some of the important faith or religious issues in your family background?

6. What do you mean when you say your spirits are low? Is that different from being sad or depressed?

7. What are the areas of compatibility and conflict between you and your spouse (or other significant persons) regarding spirituality?

8. What is an incident in your life that precipitated a change in your belief about the meaning of life?

9. What helps you maintain a sense of hope when there is no immediate apparent basis for it?

10. How and when have you prayed or meditated? What is the difference?

11. What does God think about your feeling angry, inadequate, guilty?

12. Do you need forgiveness from yourself or someone else?

13. How long do you think God wants you to feel guilty?

14. How is your spirituality a rebellion against your parents; a conformity to your parents (or one of them)?

15. Which is the most sensitive subject between you and your spouse (or other significant persons): money, sex, spirituality, children's discipline?

16. What is most frightening to you about death? What do you think would help you have a peaceful death?

17. What is your opinion about the meaning of suffering?

18. Do you have rituals in your family? Have they diminished or stabilized or increased recently?

Source: Anita M. Titone, 1991.

condition (*not* a mental disorder) that is appropriate for clinical attention. Types of religious problems under this new category include difficulties resulting from a change in one's denomination or conversion to a new religion, intensified adherence to beliefs or practices, loss or questioning of faith, guilt, or cult involvement. Spiritual problems may include distress due to mystical experiences, near-death experiences, spiritual emergence/emergency, meditation, or separation from a spiritual teacher (Turner, Lukoff, Barnhouse, & Lu, 1995). This framework would be helpful in understanding Sean's mystical experience as a young adult. Accurate assessment of such an occurrence can help determine whether the experience needs to be integrated and used as a stimulus for personal growth, or whether it should be recognized as a sign of mental instability.

Emerging interest in spirituality also suggests a number of religiously or spiritually-oriented helping techniques that can be used as social work *interventions.* These techniques may include guided relaxation, meditation, dreamwork, visualization or guided imagery, self-reflective journaling, breathing techniques, use of ritual, mind/body work, reading spiritually-oriented materials, and use of prayer (Achterberg, 1985; Canda, 1990; Cowley, 1996; Grof, 1988; Hendricks & Weinhold, 1982; Hutton, 1994; Keefe, 1996; Laird, 1984; Muff, 1996). In conjunction with conventional therapeutic approaches, spiritually based interventions hold much promise. However, they also hold the potential for harm if used by untrained practitioners. Thus, social workers must develop the necessary knowledge and skills required for effective use of such interventions. Furthermore, application of spiritually based interventions must be grounded within an ethical framework. Unfortunately, little in the social work literature provides direction in this area. An exception is Canda's (1990) detailed discussion of the ethical use of holistic prayer in practice, which includes a range of options and the necessary conditions for ethical use of this technique with clients. More of this kind of discussion is needed as we develop ethical guidelines for the use of spiritually based interventions in practice.

IMPLICATIONS FOR SOCIAL WORK PRACTICE

Given our current understanding and knowledge of spirituality and human behavior, the following practice principles can be offered only as preliminary guidelines for spiritually sensitive practice:

- Be respectful of different religious or spiritual paths and willing to learn about the role and meaning of various beliefs, practices, and experiences for various client systems (individuals, groups, communities).

- Critically examine your own values, beliefs, and biases concerning religion and spirituality, and be willing to work through any unresolved or negative feelings or experiences in this area that may adversely affect your work with clients.

- Develop a working knowledge of the beliefs and practices frequently encountered in your work with clients, especially those of newly arriving immigrants/refugees or nondominant groups (for example, Buddhist beliefs of Southeast Asian refugees; spiritual traditions of First Nations peoples).

- Engage in ongoing self-reflection about what brings purpose, meaning, and connection in your own life, and make disciplined efforts toward your own spiritual development, however you define this process.

- Conduct comprehensive spiritual assessments with clients at all levels, and use this information in service planning and delivery.

- Acquire the knowledge and skills necessary to employ spiritually based intervention techniques appropriately and effectively.

■ Seek information about the various religious and spiritual organizations/services/leaders pertinent to your practice, and develop good working relationships with these resources for purposes of referral and collaboration.

MAIN POINTS

1. Spirituality is a universal and fundamental aspect of human existence.

2. Spirituality is a broad concept that includes a search for purpose, meaning, and connection among oneself, other people, the universe, and the ultimate reality, which can be experienced within either a religious or nonreligious framework.

3. Religion refers to a set of beliefs, practices, and traditions experienced within a specific social institution over time. As such, it is a narrower and more particularized concept than spirituality.

4. Our understanding of human behavior at all levels can be expanded and enriched by inclusion of the spiritual dimension.

5. Spiritual development can be conceptualized as moving through a series of stages—each with its own particular characteristics—similar to physical, cognitive, or psychosocial development.

6. Fowler's theory of stages of faith development enumerates seven stages. The ultimate stage, called Universaling faith, is attained by only a few people at midlife or beyond.

7. Wilber's full-spectrum model of consciousness delineates 10 stages of consciousness, grouped into Prepersonal, Personal, and Transpersonal phases. Like Fowler, Wilber sees very few persons evolving to the higher levels of consciousness, at least at this point in time.

8. Both Fowler's and Wilber's models envision an endpoint in human development that is beyond a mature ego and self-actualization, allowing human beings to transcend the body and the ego and to experience a wider and deeper connection with all beings and the universe. Thus, these theories can be considered Fourth Force therapies, within the transpersonal perspective of human behavior.

9. Developmental models of spiritual development, like Fowler's and Wilber's, contribute to our understanding of human capacities for growth and development and offer a different perspective for social work practice at both the micro and macro levels.

10. Theories of spiritual development need to be tested and refined to determine their applicability across various groups, cultures, and contexts.

11. Social work's relationship to religion and spirituality has changed over time—beginning with strong religious or moral foundations, then moving to increased professionalization and secularization, and currently experiencing a resurgence of interest and attention. The appropriate role of spirituality within the profession is presently a topic of debate.

12. A growing body of literature explores the relevance of spirituality to various client populations and life situations and the role of spirituality in both micro and macro practice.

13. Integration of spirituality into social work practice has implications for theory, goals of practice, the nature of the helping relationship, assessment, and intervention. Dialogue and development are needed within the profession in all of these areas.

KEY TERMS

basic structures
faith
faith stages
fulcrum
ideology
religion

self system
spirituality
transitional structures
transpersonal approach
ultimate environment

WORLD WIDE WEB RESOURCES

Adult Faith Development: Current Thinking
http://www.hope.edu/academic/psychology/335/webrep/faithdev.html
Site maintained by Hope College outlines James Fowlet's theory of development, including implications, medical findings, disagreements, and references.

Spirituality and Religion: Gay Life Net Links
http://gaylife.miningco.com/msub12.htm
Resource site developed by General Internet, Inc., provides links and information pertaining to gay spiritiuality and religion.

Yahoo! Religious Faiths and Practices
http://www.yahoo.com/Society_and_Culture/Religion/Faiths_and_Practices/
Comprehensive listing of links to Internet sites concerning many world religions, from African religions to Zoroastrianism.

An Interview with John:
Social Work Practice That Integrates
Biological, Psychological, and Spiritual Person

Martin Schwartz, Virginia Commonwealth University

John is a 35-year-old white gay male who sought therapy when his relationship of 10 years ended because of his partner's infidelities. John grew up in an intact blue-collar family in the American Midwest. He described his family as cold, rigid, and very religious. John secured affection and adulation through church activities that began at an early age when he became a child preacher. He did well in school and was able to secure a full scholarship at a local religious college. Although aware of his homosexual yearnings, which were totally unacceptable to his religion, John married a woman when he was 21. The marriage ended three years later when John was able to discuss his homosexuality with his wife.

Following the dissolution of the marriage, John moved to the South and lived openly as a gay male. Although he had been able to come out to himself and enter a gay relationship, he maintained an internal homophobia fueled by his devout religious attitude about homosexuality. John just about severed any relationship with his family, and this estrangement caused a great deal of emotional pain when his mother died suddenly. Following her death, he maintained a rather superficial contact with his father and brother. The ending of his gay relationship reawakened earlier doubts of adequacy as well as guilt and shame about acting on his sexual orientation.

During therapy, John was diagnosed with AIDS after a sudden hospitalization for meningitis. Within a few months, John had quickly moved to the terminal stage of AIDS, manifested by numerous opportunistic diseases and frequent hospitalizations. At the time of this interview, he was totally isolated because he had little strength to venture outside his apartment except for visits to his physicians. His conversations about his illness and impending death often focused on not having his religion to help him through this painful journey. John was clinically depressed and could not find the inner resources to cope with his situation.

As I entered the apartment, I immediately noticed that the lights were on and the venetian blinds were open to allow the sunlight into the apartment. John was sitting in the living room listening to a recording of a Beethoven symphony.

J. Marty, do you hear how beautiful it is? God, I haven't listened to this recording for months. I've missed my music.

M. Yes, it is beautiful. More than that, it's beautiful to hear you talk about your music.

J. I got so much to talk to you about. Sit down and listen—don't say anything. I haven't figured it all out—but something happened to me that has changed—I'm going to cry—but Marty, it's not like the other times. Inside I feel good—no—I feel at rest—shit—I just know I'm different from last week.

M. Okay, okay—slow—I'm here and I'm listening. Just talk—let it out.

J. After our session last week, Mike called me. Remember him? 20-year-old kid I met at our group 4–5 months ago. You know he was pretty sick—worse than me. Well, he was alone, and it sounded like he was in bad shape. So, I called my cab driver and he came up to the apartment and drove me over to Mike's place. Mike was in bed—crap and urine all over him. I don't know how, but I washed him, changed his clothes. I knew he was going—told him that he needed to be in the hospital. He pleaded with me not to call anybody—he wanted to end in his own bed. Marty—I was scared shitless—I didn't know what to do. Christ, I was just about able to stand—but all I could hear was his crying not to leave him. So, I stayed with him all day and all night. (Tears are running down John's face—I give him some tissues.) I held him; I talked to him; and Marty, this is going to blow you out of the water, I prayed with him. (Lots of tears; lots of tissues. This time John really let go. I got up from my chair and I held him in my arms—saying nothing—saying a lot till he was able to go on.) I told Mike that it was okay to go—he had had enough pain—and he died in my arms.

M. John, are you okay? Sounds like a difficult experience—you really were a friend. But yet it sounds like something else happened to you.

J. Yeah, that's what I'm talking about. It was, I know this sounds crazy, but it was beautiful. Mike was so calm at the end—and I felt something inside that I haven't felt in years. I was at peace. There was something about my helping Mike that helped me. When I was saying the prayer, I was back home again—not home—back. Marty, I know I'm going to die soon, but I'm okay about it. I'm going to spend the time I have left to enjoy whatever I have—my music—but Marty, I can hear every note now. I'm going to smell every rose now—I'm okay with who I am—and I know now that God loves me. (More tears, more tissue, more holding.) Does it make sense? You must think I'm crazy.

M. No—no. Far from it. Maybe we don't have to understand everything. What is important is that you've turned a corner—and you are feeling—what did you say—more at peace? That's what is important. I'm happy for you and your feelings.

J. Marty, I'm exhausted.

M. I can understand. Why don't we just sit here and listen to the music. Any special CD?

J. No—they're all special. (John smiles.)

John died four weeks later in the hospital, with his father and his brother by his bed; he asked me to be there too. John also asked me to say some words at the cemetery—he had chosen a sonnet by Shakespeare.

Something to Think About

This interview is one event in Marty's social work practice with John. I think you can see how important it is for Marty to be responsive to John as a biological person, a psychological person, and a spiritual person. These questions will help you think about how you might use what you have been learning to be helpful to someone like John:

- What have you learned about the immune system, T cells, HIV, and AIDS that might be helpful to you in your work with John? How might you use this information? What else would you want to know about the biology of AIDS—or about John's biological system?

- What do you know about John's cognitive and emotional life? Do any psychological theories seem particularly useful in understanding John's situation? What could you say about John's sense of self?

- Do you think of the stress in John's life as biological, psychological, or social in nature? Describe the nature of this stress. What coping methods do you see John using? What types of social support does he need? How does this change as he moves into the terminal stage of AIDS?

- What influence—both negative and positive—did religion and spirituality have on John's adjustment to AIDS? Which of Patrick O'Brien's themes of spirituality seem the most pertinent to John's life, and why? John's assistance to Mike while he was dying seemed to be transformative for John. What about this episode seemed so powerful?

- How do you think about John's depression? Is it biological? Is it psychological (cognitive? emotional?)? Is it spiritual? Is it some interplay of biology, psychology, and spirit?

PART III

The Multiple Dimensions of Environment

Social workers have always recognized the important role the environment plays in human behavior and, equally important, have always understood the environment as multidimensional. The social work literature has not been consistent in identifying the important dimensions of environment, however. Although all dimensions of environment are intertwined and inseparable, social scientists have developed specialized literature on several specific dimensions. Both the environment, and the study of it, become more complex with each new era of technological development—making our efforts to understand the environment ever more challenging.

The purpose of the eight chapters in Part III is to provide you with an up-to-date understanding of the multidisciplinary theory and research about dimensions of environment. It begins with a chapter (Chapter 7) on an important dimension that is often overlooked in the social work literature, the physical environment. Next comes a chapter (Chapter 8) on contemporary trends in social institutions and social structure. Chapter 9 then reviews our historical attempts to understand culture and presents a contemporary framework to help us become more competent social workers in a multicultural world. Chapters 10–12 cover the large-scale configurations of formal organizations, communities, and social movements. Part III ends with two chapters (Chapters 13 and 14) on the smaller-scale configurations of small groups and families. The reflection to Part III illustrates one social worker's activities within a multidimensional environment.

In Part II, you learned about the multiple dimensions of persons. When you put that knowledge together with the knowledge gained about multiple dimensions of environments, you will be better prepared to understand the situations you encounter in social work practice. This multidimensional approach prepares you well to think about the changing configurations of persons and environments across the life course—the subject of the companion volume to this book.

Being in the World

Think for a moment of the environment in which you are reading this book. Did you think immediately of the room you're in? Or did you think of the building, the social institution, or the culture? Maybe you thought of all these and more. Environment has many dimensions.

The physical environment, which is one such dimension, has a significant effect on the people within that environment. Consider the quiet serenity of this sunlit bedroom. This is a physical environment that provides positive stimulation and allows for relaxation.

Not all environments are so conducive to well-being, however. Physical environments like this overcrowded women's shelter keep inhabitants on edge and make it more difficult for them to gain control over their lives.

This office environment reflects the bureaucratic nature of the formal organization housed within it. Not only do the pathways created by desks and partitions channel people's physical movements; they also create invisible hallways for people's actions and responses.

Despite the inadequacies of some settings, people can often inhabit them comfortably if other aspects of environment are positive. These children find rest in the stark but nurturing environment of their low-income day care center.

When we think of environment, we readily notice buildings and landscapes and even organizations. Less readily do we think of the social institutions with which we interact: the education system, the government, and so on. Institutions are less visible to us than the physical environment and formal organizations, although they may affect our lives more profoundly.

Institutions have both a physical aspect and an ethos, or a way of being within the institution, which are closely linked. At Ellis Island, for instance, new immigrants immediately encountered some of the symbols and structures of the U.S. government. The immigrants' socialization into the American way of life thus started almost immediately on their arrival.

Institutions are also the source of the numerous policies that influence who gets what kind of help and where they get it. Whether people convicted of drug use are given help with their addictions or merely sentenced to work crews is determined by institutional programs and policies. Without access to greater social resources, this woman may have trouble overcoming her drug problems and becoming re-integrated into society.

Social policy and the physical environment often intersect. People can easily be displaced from their homes and customary way of life through natural disaster, and many live "one paycheck away from poverty." During crises like these, social workers may be called on to deal not only with the emotional distress of individuals but also with the logistics of housing and caring for an entire community.

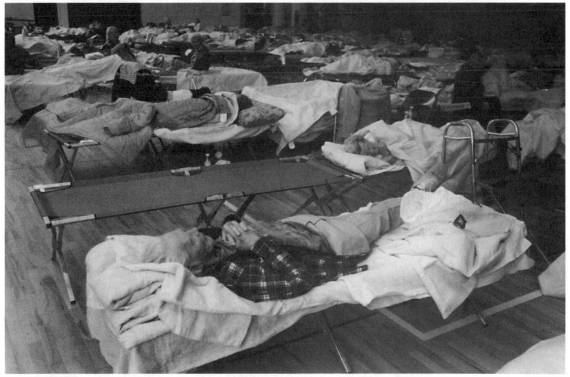

The culture we live in influences our behavior in ways even less direct and more pervasive than the ways institutions influence us. As you can see in this procession of New Mexico children, Latino and Catholic values, norms, and beliefs can have a great effect on dress, behavior, social relationships, and other aspects of culture. In the physical closeness and camaraderie between the children, you can also see community.

Community appears in various guises. Looking on these chess matches in the park, we can focus on camaraderie or competition or perhaps some other aspect of community.

Sometimes the competition for resources and recognition results in social movements. Many social movements are focused on the very same issues that are important to social workers. Here a fathers' rights demonstrator points up a possible consequence of arbitrary child custody arrangements.

Here the women of a small neighborhood band together. Their concern is a remake of the movie *Lolita*, which they see as promoting the sexual exploitation of youth. Their collective action is part of a larger social movement against child pornography.

Just as social workers need to pay attention to the societal and physical aspects of clients' environments, so they need to understand with whom clients interact in these various environments. Many clients are part of a small informal group that provides social support, like this group of neighborhood women. Social workers may also establish therapy groups that serve the same purpose.

Families can also be considered small groups. But social workers need to recognize that families vary widely in form. There is no single way to form a family.

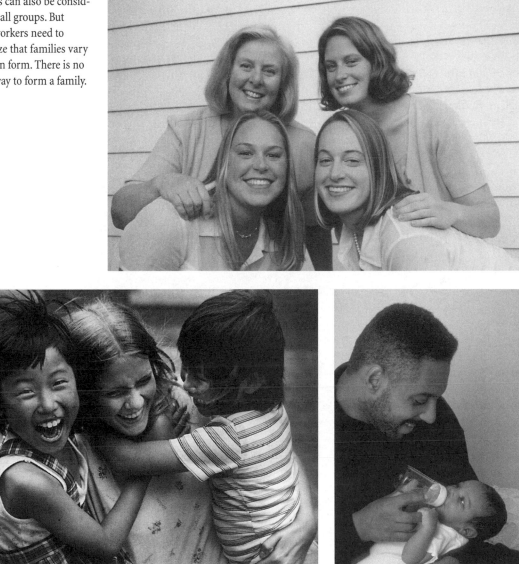

Only by taking account of these multiple dimensions of environment, and the myriad forms these dimensions may take, can we recognize the uniqueness of the situations we encounter in practice.

CHAPTER 7

The Physical Environment

A PLACE OF HER OWN FOR CHERYL

I left home when I was twenty-two years old. I would like to say that my reasons for leaving were the same as anyone of my age, but it wouldn't be true. "I want my independence," everyone says when moving out on their own, but what it meant for me as a disabled person was not quite what it meant for an able-bodied woman. It was not merely that I wanted to be closer to my job, or that my parents were putting a damper on their daughter's sexual activity (the absence of which was then so total that I regarded myself as nearly neutered). I left because I envisioned myself living with aging parents possibly for the rest of my life, simply because I feared to find out whether or not I could take care of myself.

I lived and quarreled with my parents in an inaccessible home, unable to get in and out unaided. I couldn't afford a car: Father was always reminding me how expensive "under-25" insurance was and expressing doubts that I could get a wheelchair in and out of a car myself, despite my telling him that I had, in fact, done it. (It never occurred to anyone to equip the family car with hand controls.) Taxis were financially disastrous alternatives, and obviously, I couldn't get a wheelchair on a bus. I went places if and when my parents were willing to drive me; they drove me everywhere I wanted, as long as I wanted what they wanted.

My mother believed that I couldn't minister to my own bowel care needs without her; she had convinced me, too, for a long time, but I was beginning to question this. The idea that she might be mistaken was intensely disturbing. It seemed as if she needed to feel needed so badly that my independence would be sacrificed. I was coming to resent her participation in my care as a gross and humiliating intrusion on my body, as an assault to my spirit. In the most basic physical sense, I had no privacy and I felt as if I were being repeatedly violated.

Suffice it to say we did not get along. Our household was perpetually engaged in an undeclared civil war. The only way to break the Gordian knot of our conflict was for someone to leave or die. Until I convinced myself that I might be able to live on my own, the only way out I could see was suicide. I was beginning to think of it continually, and it terrified me. When I realized that anything had to be better than this, I finally found the courage to plan the move.

Eventually, my parents realized that I was right; I had to go. My relatives were astonished that they would "let me go," as if it were their duty to compel me to stay. In reminding them that I was a reasonably intelligent adult, my mother reminded herself. Before too long, my parents (with who knows what internal conflicts) were helping me to look for an apartment.

CASE STUDY

As a low-income wheelchair user (salary of a junior secretary), my require-ments for a dwelling were quite specific. The rent had to be $125 or less. The place had to be within a few blocks of Boston University, where I worked, since I was determined to push to the office, except in bad weather, when I would have to pay for a cab. (Incidentally, cabs were very hard to get for such short runs, since the drivers thought the effort of getting my wheelchair in and out was not adequately offset by the low fare. In winter, I would wait for up to an hour.) I had to be able to enter the apartment unaided and be able to maneu-ver in the kitchen and bathroom. Realtors told us only the size, the location, and the rent; therefore, we had to run around to all prospective apartments, a colossal waste of time.

This was 1967, and most of the buildings in Boston's Back Bay were hope-less. None of them had accessible front entrances. Most landlords refused to rent to me, saying, "What the hell do you think I'm running, a nursing home?" Finally, Mr. Greenblatt rented me a basement studio near Kenmore Square and let my parents pay to have the back door ramped, "conditional upon the ap-proval of the other tenants." Success! Let me describe this palatial abode.

To get to the rear entry, I had to push down an alley running between a nightclub-disco-bar and a movie theater. The alley, which had about a one-in-eight gradient, culminated in an expanse of fractured blacktop and loose dirt, which was deeply rutted and pocked by water-filled holes. I would never lose my fear of falling into them. I wasn't afraid of getting wet; I was petrified of being unable to get back into my chair in such a lonely spot, since the place was alive with rats. These weren't just any rats; they were Back Bay rats, enor-mous, sleek, and fearless. In daylight they stood in your path and watched you approach, as if appraising your edibility. The route disgusted me, but it led to the only semi-affordable, partially accessible place I could find in the area; therefore, in the absence of choice, I suspended judgment.

Inside, the studio was wood-paneled and dim. Some of the darkness was caused by the filth on the windows, the outside of which were uncleanable, because the burglar screens bolted onto the frames. A front burner on the stove didn't work and, since I couldn't reach the rear burners, it necessitated my cooking one-dish meals until I bought a hotplate (Mr. Greenblatt never did repair the stove). Although the bathroom door was wide enough, I had to re-move it, since it blocked access to the tub; this was all right for me, but I thought it would disconcert any company I might have.

My parents let me take several pieces of furniture, some dishes and glass-ware, and their apprehensive blessings for the new venture. They moved the furniture in for me, cleaned the place up, and got a carpenter to build a ramp, under which the rats subsequently made a fine home of their own. I could see that my parents were far from pleased with the place. I wondered if they thought I liked it or hated it. This, my first apartment, was small, dark, roach-infested, hard to get around in, and surrounded by an army of vermin, but I loved it. It was mine. The door had a dead-bolt lock, and I could have all the privacy I wanted.

That first night, as my parents left me at my apartment, they assured me that I could call them any time of day or night; I had only to say the word and I could come home. I thought they were hoping my independence would be temporary, but I realize now how anxious they must have been. I've seen the same pattern when disabled friends leave home. . . .

The next morning was Sunday. I awoke at nine and lay there in bed, blissfully surveying my books, clothes, couch, walls, floor, ceiling, and door, luxuriating in my splendid squalor. I could let people in or not. I could buy the food I wanted, eat when I wanted to, go to bed or stay up when I wanted, go out when I wanted . . . I would choose. I didn't have to come home early because my parents didn't like to stay up late. I didn't have to ask my father to drive me anywhere. I could experience whatever presented itself, without asking my parents if it was all right with them. That was real independence. I thought of all that freedom and the new life I had begun. As I threw back the covers—I remember as if it were this morning—an incredibly wide grin stole across my face. (Lifchez & Davis, 1987, pp. 68–71)

The Relationship between the Physical Environment and Human Behavior

This powerful story of human strength and triumph is told by Cheryl Davis and her coauthor, Raymond Lifchez. As with most stories we hear as social workers, Cheryl's story provides multidimensional information about changing configurations of person and environment. It presents issues of life course development, family conflict, physical disability, and a struggle for emotional well-being. And, of course, a supremely important dimension of this unfolding story is the physical environment.

Perhaps the most obvious aspect of Cheryl's relationship with her physical environment is **accessibility**—the ease with which Cheryl can act in her environment. But accessibility is only one relevant aspect. Gerald Weisman (1981) has identified 11 key concepts that unify the multidisciplinary study of the relationship between human behavior and the physical environment. A slightly revised version of these concepts appears in Exhibit 7.1. Cheryl's story addresses another 7 of Weismans's 11 concepts: **adaptability** (a ramp added, a door removed); **comfort**

EXHIBIT 7.1

Key Concepts for Understanding Physical Environment–Behavior Relationships

Concept	Definition
Accessibility	Ease in movement through and use of an environment.
Activity	Perceived intensity of ongoing behavior within an environment.
Adaptability	Extent to which an environment and its components can be reorganized to accommodate new or different patterns of behavior.
Comfort	Extent to which an environment provides sensory and mobility "fit" and facilitates task performance.
Control	Extent to which an environment facilitates personalization and conveys territorial claims to space.
Crowding	Unpleasant experience of being spatially cramped.
Legibility	Ease with which people can conceptualize key elements and spatial relationships within an environment and effectively find their way.
Meaning	Extent to which an environment holds individual or cultural meaning(s) for people (e.g. attachment, challenge, beauty).
Privacy	Selective control of access to the self or to one's group.
Sensory stimulation	Quality and intensity of stimulation as experienced by the various sensory modalities.
Sociality	Degree to which an environment facilitates or inhibits social interaction among people.

Source: Adapted from Weisman, 1981. Reproduced with permission of the author.

("small, dark, roach-infested, hard to get around in, and surrounded by an army of vermin"); **control** ("It was *mine*"); **crowding** (Can friends be entertained without feeling crowded?); **privacy** ("The door had a dead-bolt lock, and I could have all the privacy I wanted"); and **sensory stimulation** (lack of sunlight). We are also aware that the physical environment of the new apartment may hold very different **meanings** for the storyteller, for her parents, and for friends who visit. Three other concepts—activity, legibility, and sociality—will be introduced later in the chapter.

When we as social workers make person-in-environment assessments, we ought to pay attention to the physical environment, which has an inescapable influence on human behavior. Unfortunately, the social work literature includes only scant coverage of the physical environment. A handful of social work scholars (Germain, 1978, 1981; Gutheil, 1991, 1992; Resnick & Jaffee, 1982; Seabury, 1971) have provided most of the existing analyses of the implications for social work of recent theory and research. The relationship between human behavior and the physical environment is a multidisciplinary study that includes contributions from the social sciences of psychology, sociology, geography, and anthropology as well as from the design disciplines of architecture, landscape architecture, interior design, and urban and regional planning.

The empirical research on these issues is often contradictory, as you might expect in a multidisciplinary field at such an early stage of analysis. This chapter will give you some ways of thinking about the relationship between human behavior and the physical environment as you begin to consider the role it plays in the stories of the people you encounter in practice.

Most theorists start from an assumption that person and physical environment are separate entities and emphasize the ways in which the physical environment influences behavior. Some theorists, however, start from an assumption of person/environment unity and propose interlocking and ongoing processes of coexistence between people and physical environments—people shape their environment just as the physical environment influences them—an approach called transactionalism (see Minami & Tanaka, 1995; Wapner, 1995). As noted in Chapter 1, this book takes a transactional approach, which is consistent with the assumption of person/environment unity.

Three broad categories of theory about human behavior and the physical environment are introduced in this chapter: stimulation theories, control theories, and behavior settings theories. The first two categories, stimulation theories and control theories, originated in the theoretical approach that assumes separation of person and physical environment, but they have increasingly recognized the interrelatedness of person and physical environment. Behavior settings theories have always been based in transactionalism. Each of these categories of theory, and the research they have stimulated, provide useful possibilities for social workers to consider as they participate in person/environment assessments, although stimulation theories and control theories have been more widely used than behavior settings theories. Exhibit 7.2 presents the key ideas and important concepts of these three types of theory.

EXHIBIT 7.2

Three Categories of Theories about the Relationship between the Physical Environment and Human Behavior

Theories	Key Ideas	Important Concepts
Stimulation Theories	The physical environment is a source of sensory information essential for human well-being. Patterns of stimulation influence thinking, emotions, social interaction, and health.	Stimulus overload Stimulus deprivation
Control Theories	Humans desire control over their physical environments. Some person/environment configurations provide more control over the physical environment than others.	Personal space Territoriality Crowding Privacy
Behavior Settings Theories	Consistent, uniform patterns of behavior occur in particular settings. Behaviors of different persons in the same setting are more similar than the behaviors of the same person in different settings.	Behavior settings Programs Staffing

Stimulation Theories

Have you thought about how you would react to the lack of light in Cheryl's new apartment? That concern is consistent with stimulation theories. **Stimulation theories** focus on the physical environment as a source of sensory information that is essential for human well-being. The stimulation may be light, color, heat, texture, or scent, or it may be buildings, streets, and parks. Stimulation theorists propose that patterns of stimulation influence thinking, feelings, social interaction, and health.

Stimulation varies by amount—intensity, frequency, duration, number of sources—as well as by type. Stimulation theories that are based on theories of psychophysiological arousal assume that moderate levels of stimulation are optimum for human behavior (Sundstrom, Bell, Busby, & Asmus, 1996). Thus, both **stimulus overload** (too much stimulation) and **stimulus deprivation** (too little stimulation), have a negative effect on human behavior. Theorists interested in the behavioral and health effects of stimulus overload have built on Hans Selye's work regarding stress (see Chapter 5).

Social behavioral perspective
Social constructionist perspective

Some stimulation theories focus on the direct, concrete effect of stimulation on behavior; others focus on the meanings people construct regarding particular stimuli. In fact, as Gutheil (1992) suggests, "people respond to both concrete and symbolic aspects of their physical settings" (p. 391). A doorway too narrow to accommodate a wheelchair has a concrete effect on the behavior of a person in a wheelchair; it will also have a symbolic effect, contributing to the person's feelings of exclusion and stigma. You probably will have a very different emotional reaction to a loud bang if it occurs during a street riot or at a New Year's Eve party; your understanding of the meaning of the noise has a strong influence on your reactions. In this case, your response is primarily symbolic. Stimulation theories alert social workers to consider the quality and intensity of sensory stimulation in the environments where their clients live and work.

Control Theories

Psychodynamic perspective
Social behavioral perspective

The ability to gain control over her physical environment is the central theme of Cheryl's story. In that way, the story is a powerful demonstration of the ideas found in control theories. **Control theories** focus on the issue of how much control we have over our physical environments and the attempts we make to gain control (Gifford, 1987). Four concepts are central to the work of control theorists: personal space, territoriality, crowding, and privacy. Personal space and territoriality are **boundary regulating mechanisms** that we use to gain greater control over our physical environments. (See Chapter 13 for discussion of personal space, territoriality, density, and crowding in relation to small groups.)

Social constructionist perspective
Developmental perspective

Personal space is the physical distance we choose to maintain in interpersonal relationships. Sommer (1969, p. 26) has defined it as "an area with invisible boundaries surrounding a person's body into which intruders may not come." More recent formulations (Gifford, 1987) emphasize that personal space is not stable, but contracts and expands with changing interpersonal circumstances and with variations in physical settings. The distance you desire when talking with your best friend is likely to be different from the distance you prefer when talking with a stranger, or even with a known authority figure like your social work professor. The desired distance for any of these interpersonal situations is likely to expand in small spaces (Sinha &

Mukherjee, 1996). We will want to recognize our own personal space requirements in different work situations and be sensitive to the personal space requirements of our coworkers and clients. Variations in personal space are also thought to be related to age, gender, and culture, but the research findings are somewhat contradictory. Personal space increases with age until about age 12 (Evans & Howard, 1973; Hayduk, 1983; Sinha, Nayyar, & Mukherjee, 1995). Males have generally been found to require greater personal space than females, but research indicates that the largest interpersonal distances are kept in male/male pairs, followed by female/female pairs, with the smallest interpersonal distances kept in male/female pairs (Akande, 1997; Kilbury, Bordieri, & Wong, 1996). The empirical literature contains some contradictions regarding cultural variations in personal space, but Gifford (1987) suggests that the evidence points toward a continuum that ranges from close interpersonal distances for Arabs and Latin Americans to distant interpersonal distances for Britons and Germans.

Previous research (Langer, Fiske, Taylor, & Chanowitz, 1976; Stephens & Clark, 1987) found that people maintain larger interpersonal distances when interacting with people with disabilities. However, one group of researchers recently found that research participants sat closer to a research assistant in a wheelchair than to one without a visible disability (Kilbury et al.,1996). These researchers conjectured that these contradictory findings may indicate that recent legislation is reducing the stigma of disability. Some of this legislation will be discussed later in this chapter.

Personal space is a concept about individual behavior and about the use of space to control the interpersonal environment. **Territoriality** refers primarily to the behavior of small groups, or individuals in those groups, as they seek control over physical as well as interpersonal space (Taylor, 1988). Territoriality is "a pattern of behavior and attitudes held by an individual or group that is based on perceived, attempted, or actual control of a definable physical space" (Gifford, 1987, p. 137). Territoriality leads us to mark, or personalize, our territory to signify our "ownership," and to engage in a variety of behaviors to protect it from invasion. The study of animal territoriality has a longer history than the study of human territorial behavior.

Altman (1975) classifies our territories as primary, secondary, and public. A **primary territory** is one that evokes feelings of ownership that we control on a relatively permanent basis, and that is vital to our daily lives. For most of us, our primary territory would include our home, our dorm room, our place of employment, and our nation. **Secondary territories** are less important to us than primary territories, and control of them does not seem as essential to us; examples might be a study carrel at the library, our favorite table in the student cafeteria, or our favorite stair machine at the health center. **Public territories** are open to anyone in the community, and we generally make no attempt to control access to them—places such as public parks, public beaches, sidewalks, and stores. For people who are homeless and lack access to typical primary territories, however, public territories may serve as primary territories.

Systems perspective
Conflict perspective

Much of the literature on territoriality draws on the functionalist sociological tradition (discussed in Chapter 2), emphasizing the positive value of territorial behavior to provide order to the social world and a sense of security to individuals (Taylor, 1988). We know, however, that territorial behavior can also be the source of conflict, domination, and oppression.

Crowding has sometimes been used interchangeably with density, but environmental psychologists make important distinctions between these terms. **Density** is the ratio of persons per unit area of a space. Crowding is "the unpleasant experience of spatial restriction" (Gifford, 1987, p. 168). Crowding is not always correlated with density; the feeling of being crowded seems to be influenced by an interaction of personal, social, and cultural, as well as physical, factors.

Psychodynamic
perspective
Social constructionist
perspective

Irwin Altman (1975, p. 18) defines privacy as "selective control of access to the self or to one's group." This definition contains two important elements: Privacy involves control over information about oneself, as well as control over interactions with others. Some of us require more privacy than others, and some situations stimulate privacy needs more than other situations. Cheryl suspects that future visitors to her apartment will be disconcerted by the lack of privacy allowed for bathroom activities; not surprisingly, she makes no note of the lack of privacy for kitchen activities. It appears that people in different cultures use space differently to create privacy. Susan Kent (1991) theorizes that the use of partitions, such as walls or screens, to create private spaces increases as societies become more complex. She particularly notes the strong emphasis that European American culture places on partitioned space, both at home and at work (see Duvall-Early & Benedict, 1992). Have you given much thought to your need for private space? Do the clients at your field agency have private space?

Behavior Settings Theories

Social behavioral
perspective
Systems perspective

Would you expect to observe the same behaviors if you were observing Cheryl in different settings—for example, her parents' home, her new apartment, at work, or at a social event with friends? My guess is that you would not. A third major category of theories about the relationship between human behavior and the physical environment is **behavior settings theories.** According to these theories, consistent, uniform patterns of behavior occur in particular places, or **behavior settings**.

Behavior settings theory was developed by Roger Barker (1968), who was searching for the factors that influence different individuals to behave differently in the same environment. He and his colleagues studied human behavior in public settings, rather than in the laboratory where individual differences were usually studied. They unexpectedly noted that observations of different persons in the same setting, even when substantial time elapsed between the observations, were more similar than observations of the same person in different settings, even when there was only a short time between observations. For example, your behavior at a Phish concert is more similar to the behavior of other Phish heads at the concert than it is to your own behavior in the classroom.

Barker suggested that **programs**—consistent, prescribed patterns of behavior—develop and are maintained in many specific settings. You might argue that behavior settings theory is more about the social environment than the physical environment—that behavioral programs are socially constructed, developed by people in interaction, and not determined by the physical environment. As suggested earlier, however, Barker takes a transactional approach to person in environment (Minami & Tanaka, 1995; Wapner, 1995). In his view, "the behavior pattern and the milieu are dynamically inseparable" (Schoggen, 1989, p. 47). Behavioral programs are created conjointly by individuals and their inanimate surroundings, and behavior settings are distinctive in their physical-spatial features as well as their social rules. Rapoport (1990, p. 57) summarizes the relationships of the social and physical environments to behavior in these words: "*it is* *the social situation that influences people's behavior, but it is the physical environment that provides the cues* [emphasis in original]."

Behavior settings as conceptualized by Barker had a static quality, but Wicker (1987) has more recently written about the changing nature—the life histories—of behavior settings. In other words, behavior settings themselves are now seen as changing configurations of person and environment. Some settings disappear (have you been to a barn raising lately?), and some become radically altered. The high school prom that my daughter attended in 1993 was a different setting, with a very different behavioral program, from the high school prom that I attended in 1963.

Behavior settings theory has implications for social work assessment and intervention. It suggests that patterns of behavior are specific to a setting and, therefore, that we must assess settings as well as individuals when problematic behavior occurs. Cheryl was feeling depressed and suicidal at the beginning of the story, but we do not see behaviors that suggest she was feeling the same way at the end of the story. The behavioral setting may not be the only factor involved in this change, but it should be considered as one possible factor. Behavior settings theory also suggests that "the place in which we first master information helps recreate the state necessary to retrieve it" (Gallagher, 1993, p. 132). When we are assisting clients in skill development, we should pay particular attention to the discontinuities between the settings where the skills are being "learned" and the settings where those skills must be used.

Another key concept in behavior settings theory is the level of **staffing** (Barker, 1968; Wicker, 1979). Different behavior settings attract different numbers of participants, or staff. It is important to have a good fit between the number of participants and the behavioral program for the setting. Overstaffing occurs when there are too many participants for the behavioral program of a given setting; understaffing occurs when there are too few participants. Roger Barker and Paul Gump's (1964) study of the optimal high school size is a classic piece of research about optimal staffing for particular behavior settings. This research will be addressed later in the chapter, when we discuss the physical environment and the life course. The issue of appropriate staffing, in terms of number of participants, for particular behavioral programs in particular behavior settings has great relevance for the planning of social work programs.

The Natural Environment

Do you find that you feel refreshed from being in the natural environment—walking along the beach, hiking in the mountains, or even walking in your neighborhood? Research findings suggest that you may, and that you should consider the benefits of time spent in the **natural environment**—the portion of the environment influenced primarily by geological and nonhuman biological forces—for both you and your clients. Most of the research on the relationship between human behavior and the natural environment has been in the stimulation theory tradition—looking for ways in which aspects of the natural environment affect our thinking, feeling, social interaction, and health. In general, this research identifies a strong human preference for elements of the natural world and finds many positive outcomes of time spent in the natural environment (Kaplan & Kaplan, 1989). These benefits are summarized in Exhibit 7.3. The findings

- Engaging children's interest
- Stimulating children's imagination
- Stimulating activity
- Aiding recovery from mental fatigue
- Enhancing group cohesiveness and community cooperation
- Fostering serenity
- Fostering a sense of oneness or wholeness
- Fostering a sense of control
- Improving physical health
- Improving emotional state

are not surprising, given the distinctive place accorded to the natural environment in the cultural artifacts—music, art, literature—of all societies.

In a study of Israeli adults and children, Rachel Sebba (1991) found that almost all of the adults retrospectively identified an outdoor setting as the most significant place in their childhood. This finding held for both men and women, and for adults from different historical periods and different environmental and social backgrounds. Similarly, in a recent cross-cultural study of adults from Senegal, Ireland, and the United States, Newell (1997) found that 61 percent of the participants named a setting in the natural environment as their favorite place. Sebba also found features of the natural environment to be more effective than features of the built environment in engaging children's interest and stimulating their imaginations. Natural features also stimulated them to action, an outcome related to **activity**, as defined in Exhibit 7.1.

In recent years, practitioners in various disciplines have taken the age-old advice of poets, novelists, and philosophers that natural settings are good for body, mind, and spirit and have developed programs that center on activities in both wilderness and urban natural settings. Researchers who have studied the effects of such programs have found some positive gain and no evidence of negative effects (see Burton, 1981; Kaplan & Kaplan, 1989). Research studies on the impact of wilderness programs have reported two positive outcomes: recovery from mental fatigue with improved attention (Hartig, Mang, & Evans, 1991; Kaplan & Kaplan, 1989) and enhanced group cohesiveness (Ewert & Heywood, 1991). Kaplan and Kaplan's (1989) 10 years of research conducted for the U.S. Forest Service suggest strong spiritual benefits as well, with participants reporting serenity and a sense of oneness or wholeness as outcomes of their wilderness experiences (see the discussion of spirituality in Chapter 6). But it may not be necessary to travel to wilderness areas to benefit from activity in natural settings. Urban community gardening projects have been found to contribute to the development of community cooperation and to improved self-esteem among the participants (Lewis, 1972, 1979). Kaplan and Kaplan's research with individuals involved in both community gardening and backyard gardening indicates benefits that include a sense of tranquillity, sense of control, and improved physical health (Kaplan, 1983; Kaplan & Kaplan, 1987).

One does not have to be active in the natural environment to derive benefits from it. One study found that surgery patients with nature content in the views from their hospital windows recovered more quickly than did patients whose window views had no nature content (Ulrich, 1984). Two studies in prison settings found that inmates who had views of nature content from their cells sought health care less often than those without nature content in the views from their cells (Moore, 1981; West, 1986). In a psychiatric ward renovation project that included changes in or additions of paint, wallpaper, carpet, lighting, furniture, curtains, plants, and bathtubs, staff rated the addition of plants to be the most positive change (Devlin, 1992).

Three features of the natural environment have been found to be particularly influential on emotional states:

1. *Water.* A cross-cultural comparison of preferences for landscape elements found water to be the preferred element among both Korean and Western participants (Yang & Brown, 1992).

2. *Trees.* Sheets and Manzer (1991) found that when viewing line drawings and slides of urban streets with and without trees and shrubs, participants reported more positive feelings when viewing the tree-lined streets. They reported feeling friendlier, more cooperative, less sad, and less depressed. One recent study found that having well-maintained trees and grass increased the sense of safety of residents of a large inner-city housing project (Kuo, Bacaicoa, & Sullivan, 1998). Another study found that children in inner-city neighborhoods engage in more creative play in settings with trees than in settings without trees (Taylor, Wiley, Kuo, & Sullivan, 1998).

3. *Sunlight.* The relationship between sunlight and human behavior is curvilinear, with benefit coming from increasing amounts until a certain optimum point is reached, after which increasing amounts damage rather than benefit. Excessive sunlight can have negative impacts, such as glare and overheating, and inadequate sunlight has been identified as a contributor to depression, sometimes referred to as seasonal affective disorder (SAD), in some persons (Kaplan, Sadock, & Grebb, 1994). Boubekri, Hull, and Boyer (1991) found that sunlight penetration in indoor spaces was related to feelings of relaxation, with patches of sunlight as the optimum situation and both too little and too much penetration decreasing the feeling of relaxation.

Although the natural environment can be a positive force, it also has the potential for damaging mental, social, and physical well-being. The relationship between sunlight and human behavior provides a clue. The natural environment provides sensory stimulation in an uncontrolled strength, and the patterns of stimulation are quite unstable. Extremely stimulating natural events are known as natural disasters. The Federal Emergency Management Agency (1984, p. 1) includes the following natural events in its definition of natural disaster: "hurricane, tornado, storm, flood, high water, wind-driven water, tidal wave, tsunami, earthquake, volcanic eruption, landslide, mudslide, snowstorm, drought, fire, explosion, or other catastrophe." Lazarus and Cohen (1977) include these natural disasters in their discussion of cataclysmic events—a class of stressors with great force, sudden onset, excessive demands on human coping, and large scope. These events are considered to be almost universally stressful (Baum, 1991), and social workers often play an active role in services to communities that have experienced natural disasters.

The Built Environment

It is exactly this uncontrollable quality of the natural environment that humans try to overcome in constructing the **built environment**—the portion of the physical environment attributable solely to human effort. The built environment is intended to create comfort and controllability, but unfortunately, technological developments often have negative impacts as well. The toxic waste problem is but one example of the risks we have created but not yet learned to control. Social workers have called attention to the fact that the risks of environmental hazards are falling disproportionately on minority and low-socioeconomic communities (Rogge, 1993). This unequal burden is a central theme in the story of the Walker Community found in Chapter 11. Research on the relationship between human behavior and the built environment draws heavily on control theories as well as stimulation theories. Some researchers study stimulation exclusively, others study control exclusively, but most researchers study both—providing a good example of research that attempts to integrate ideas from different theoretical perspectives to achieve a more comprehensive understanding of changing person/environment configurations.

Institutional Design

The ideas of Humphry Osmond (1957, 1959, 1966) about the importance of architecture for the therapeutic functions of mental hospitals stimulated a line of inquiry in different institutional settings, including psychiatric hospitals, state schools for mentally retarded persons, college dormitories, and correctional facilitates. This work reflects both stimulation and control theories. These studies have had some impact on institutional design, and probably contributed to the deinstitutionalization movement in mental health and mental retardation services during the 1970s. Too often, however, what is known about therapeutic use of architecture (see Exhibit 7.4) gets lost in the sociopolitical processes by which design decisions are made. In other words, we know more than we use. The following discussion draws heavily on Paul Cherulnik's (1993) review of 13 of the best research projects on human behavior and the built environment.

Therapeutic Institutions. Osmond noted that mental hospital patients have disturbances of perception (hallucinations and delusions), mood, and thinking that cause them significant difficulties in social relationships. He proposed that the mental hospitals of his era (1950s and 1960s) were designed in such a way as to aggravate these difficulties, with spaces of massive size, large rooms, high ceilings, hard surfaces, and long corridors. Osmond thought that these massive spaces complicated visual and auditory discrimination and discouraged social interaction. He also noted patients' lack of privacy. They shared large sleeping rooms and large, open dayrooms; had no access to spaces where they could not be observed; and were allowed no personal items. According to Osmond, this lack of privacy damaged the patients' already fragile self-concepts. He described physical designs that discourage social interaction as **sociofugal spaces**. **Sociopetal spaces**, on the other hand, encourage social interaction; Osmond thought that these spaces would be characterized by small rooms and personalized, noninstitutionalized spaces. Weisman refers to this social interaction aspect of the physical environment as **sociality** (see the definition in Exhibit 7.1). Although there is much empirical support for the idea that sociopetal design features encourage social interaction, there is some evidence

EXHIBIT 7.4

Selected Research
Findings about the
Therapeutic Use of
Architecture

Therapeutic Design Features	Positive Behaviors
Tables with chairs instead of shoulder-to-shoulder and back-to-back seating. Large spaces broken into smaller spaces. Flowers and magazines placed on tables.	Increase in both brief and sustained interaction.
Special activity centers with partitions. Sleeping dormitories divided into two-bed rooms with table and chairs. Long hallways broken up. Sound baffles added to high ceilings. Improved lighting, bright colors, and large signs added.	Increase in social interaction. Decrease in passive and inactive behavior.
Painted walls replacing bars. Carpeted floors. Conventional furniture with fabric upholstery. Visually interesting public areas. Private rooms with outside windows. Solarium with exercise equipment.	Decrease in violent behavior in correctional facilities.
Open sleeping wards and dayroom turned into personal living spaces and a lounge. Places for personal belongings provided. Personalized decorations. Institutional furniture replaced with noninstitutional furniture. Rugs, lamps, and draperies added. Control over lighting.	Increase in social interaction. Decrease in stereotypical behavior. Increase in alert purposive behavior. Decrease in intrusive behaviors. Increase in use of personal space.
Suite-design rooms versus corridor-design rooms. Short corridors versus long corridors.	Less crowding stress. Less social withdrawal. Less learned helplessness.

that defensive people are more sociable in sociofugal spaces than in sociopetal spaces (Gifford & Gallagher, 1985).

Robert Sommer refined Osmond's ideas in his redesign of a sociofugal dayroom in a geriatric ward in which, despite its attractiveness, little social interaction occurred. He focused on the arrangement of the furniture. Chairs and couches were arranged shoulder-to-shoulder along the walls in rows facing each other at a distance too great for conversation; some chairs were clustered back-to-back. Sommer and Ross (1958) conducted a six-week experiment with a new arrangement of furniture to see if social interaction increased. The new, more sociopetal arrangement eliminated shoulder-to-shoulder and back-to-back seating, substituting tables with four chairs around them to encourage face-to-face interaction and to break up the large space into smaller spaces. Flowers and magazines were placed on the tables to encourage the residents to sit at them. The research indicated a substantial increase in both brief and sustained social interaction in the dayroom.

Osmond and Sommer were focusing on one specific type of behavior: social interaction. Other researchers have broadened the focus to include other behaviors. More than a decade after the Sommer and Ross experiment, a group of behaviorally oriented architects redesigned a locked ward for 50 long-term psychiatric patients at Cleveland State Hospital (Cherulnik, 1993). The researchers were interested in increasing the level of social interaction, but the primary behavioral target was the lack of purposeful activity. The redesign was intended to create both sociopetal spaces (to foster social interaction) and private spaces. To encourage social interaction and increase residents' options, activity spaces were created in the dayroom on raised platforms that were circular or semicircular, defined by partitions. To provide privacy, partitions were built to divide the sleeping dormitories into two-bed modules, which also included table and chairs. This redesign also broke up the long hallways. Sound baffles were added below the ceilings to reduce sound reflection and facilitate conversation. Lighting was improved, bright colors added, and large signs provided to assist in orientation to place. This aspect of the physical environment is known as **legibility** (see Exhibit 7.1). The researchers found that the overall incidence of social interaction doubled, and the incidence of passive or inactive behavior declined. Holahan and Saegert (1973) replicated these physical design elements, comparing a traditional with a redesigned psychiatric admissions ward in a large municipal hospital, and reported similar findings of increased social interaction and decreased passive or inactive behavior.

Correctional Settings.   Similar design elements also have been tested in correctional settings, with different goals: prevention of violence and brutalization among inmates, and safety of the professional staff. The physical designs include painted walls (replacing bars), carpeted floors, conventional furniture with fabric upholstery, visually interesting public areas, private rooms with outside windows, and solarium with exercise equipment. In spite of overcrowding in some of the experimental facilities, the redesign resulted in impressive reductions in violent behaviors (Wener, Frazier, & Farbstein, 1985). Despite these research findings, for sociopolitical reasons the results are not being used.

Institutions for Persons with Mental Retardation.   The **normalization principle**—which drove policy regarding programs for persons with mental retardation during the 1970s and 1980s, emphasizing the importance of a homelike physical environment (Wolfensberger, 1973)—is based on stimulation theory. One team of interdisciplinary researchers used a sophisticated experimental design to test whether certain behaviors of institutionalized persons with profound mental retardation and organic anomalies would be more positively influenced by increasing privacy and control (control theory) or by improving the homelike appearance of the ward (stimulation theory). The targeted behaviors were social withdrawal, stereotypical behavior such as rocking or repeated vocalizations, alert purposeful behavior such as alert observation of events, use of personal space, intrusion into others' space, and frequency of social interaction.

The researchers found positive changes in the targeted behaviors in both the homelike renovation and the renovation based on privacy and control, as compared to the targeted behaviors in the prerenovation traditional institutional environment. However, increased privacy and control had a greater positive impact on the targeted behaviors than did improved homelike appearance (Friedman, 1976). These findings are consistent with those of Cooper and Hasselkus (1992), who asked clients with physical disabilities about preferred aspects of the physical environment; the central theme of their responses was control. It is also consistent with the joy with which Cheryl embraced her "small, dark, roach-infested" first apartment.

This is not to say that physical attractiveness is not important to persons with mental retardation and physical disabilities. Remember that targeted behaviors also improved with homelike renovations. But it does suggest that control of the physical environment may well be a higher value to them.

College Dormitories.   Some of you have had the experience of moving from home to a college dormitory in recent years, and you may have wondered about some changes in your behavior at the time. Control theorists have speculated that the lack of private areas other than the student's room, large public bathrooms, and long corridors force students into more social interaction than they desire and lead to crowding stress, social withdrawal, and learned helplessness. (See Chapter 2 for a discussion of learned helplessness.) Experimental research does indeed provide evidence that suite-design rooms rather than corridor-design rooms, and short corridors rather than long corridors, in college dormitories result in less crowding stress, social withdrawal, and learned helplessness (Aiello, Baum, & Gormley, 1981; Baum & Davis, 1980; Baum & Valins, 1977).

Large Hospitals.   Have you had the experience of feeling lost and disoriented when visiting a family member in a large hospital, even when you were there the night before? Large, complex institutional buildings, such as large hospitals, offer examples of another way to improve human control over the physical environment: providing adequate and clear signs to help people find their way. During the planning of the new hospital complex at the University of Michigan in Ann Arbor, a team of researchers invited input from patients and visitors as well as from staff. Some of these studies had to do with the use of signs. The researchers discovered that patients and visitors often differed from staff in their recommendations about what kind of signage would be helpful (Carpman, Grant, & Simmons, 1984). Findings such as these remind us of the importance of getting consumer input into environmental designs.

Defensible Space and Crime Prevention

Applying the concept of territoriality to crime prevention, Oscar Newman (1972, 1980) developed his theory of **defensible space**. This theory suggests that residential crime and fear of crime can be decreased by means of certain design features that increase residents' sense of ter-

EXHIBIT 7.5

Design Features to
Create Defensible
Space

- Real and symbolic barriers, such as fences, walls, or shrubs, to divide the residential environment into smaller, more manageable sections
- Opportunities for surveillance of both interior spaces and exterior spaces by residents
- Opportunities for personalizing both interior and exterior spaces
- Proximity to safe or nonthreatening areas

Source: Based on Oscar Newman, 1972, 1980.

ritoriality and, consequently, their motivation to "watch out" for the neighborhood. The design features that Newman recommended are listed in Exhibit 7.5.

Much of the research about defensible space has been conducted in public low-income housing, and the findings from these settings provide strong support for the theory (Fowler, 1981; Fowler, McCalla, & Mangione, 1979; Newman, 1972; Perkins, Wandersman, Rich, & Taylor, 1993; Sampson, 1983). The findings suggest that design features help reduce crime and the fear of crime because criminals, as well as residents, perceive the redesigned spaces to be under greater control of the residents.

Research findings that have been used to challenge the defensible space theory have studied crime deterrence in public spaces, such as buses, telephone booths, or business districts, rather than in residential areas (Baldwin, 1975; Mayhew, Clarke, Hough, & Winchester, 1980; Sturman, 1980). This research cannot be interpreted as contradicting the defensible space theory, however, because Newman never suggested that public territories were defensible space. In fact, Newman looked for ways to carve up expansive public spaces near public housing, turning those spaces into primary and secondary territories (Altman, 1975) that residents would be more likely to view as defensible spaces.

Behavior Settings and Addictions

An emerging line of research suggests that behavior settings are an important element in substance addiction. For instance, Winifred Gallagher (1993) reports that large numbers of American soldiers who used heroin during the Vietnam conflict left the drug behind when they returned to an environment that they did not associate with it.

Social behavioral
perspective

Shepard Siegel's research (Siegel, 1991; Siegel, Hinson, Krank, & McCully, 1982) also supports the idea that behavior settings play an important role in substance addiction. Siegel found that when a person with a heroin addiction takes a customary dose of heroin in an environment where he or she does not usually take the drug, the reaction is much more intense, and an overdose may even occur. This consistent finding over time has led Siegel to suggest that **tolerance**—the ability to take increasing amounts of the drug without feeling increased effects—is embedded in the environment in which the drug is usually taken. He has also found that behavior settings stimulate craving, even when the person has been in recovery for some time. Siegel recommends that treatment include systematic exposure to cues from the behavior setting, with no reinforcement of drug ingestion, to provide environmental deconditioning. You may recognize that this approach to treatment comes from classical conditioning.

Siegel reports that "studies from all over the world show that after a year, most of those who don't relapse after drug treatment have relocated" (cited in Gallagher, 1993, p. 138). Maybe that is why many people with addictions—like William George, whom you will encounter in Chapter 8—attempt to shake their addictions by moving to a new environment.

Place Attachment

Have you ever been strongly attached to a specific place—a beloved home, a particular beach or mountain spot, a house of worship, even your university library? **Place attachment**—the process in which people and groups form bonds with places—is the subject of a growing literature (Low & Altman, 1992). Although place attachment is usually discussed in terms of emotional bonding, Low and Altman (1992, p. 5) emphasize the "interplay of affect and emotions, knowledge and beliefs, and behaviors and actions" that forges the people/place bond. Consider the role of behaviors and actions, laboring and sweating, in the attachment to the lost home described by a survivor of the 1972 Buffalo Creek flood:

> I have a new home right now, and I would say that it is a much nicer home than what I had before. But it is a house, it is not a home. Before, I had a home. And what I mean by that, I built the other home. I took a coal company house, I remodeled it, I did the work on it myself. I put many a drop of sweat and drove many a nail into it, and I labored and sweated and worried over it. And it was gone. I left home Saturday morning and I had a home. On Saturday evening I didn't have nothing. (quoted in Erikson, 1976, p. 175)

This example focuses on attachment to home, but researchers have looked at attachment to places of different scale. We will run into the concept of place attachment again in Chapter 11 when we discuss community as a dimension of environment.

In the context of place attachment, **place** is defined as a "space that has been given meaning through personal, group, or cultural processes" (Low & Altman, 1992, p. 5). The literature on place attachment emphasizes emotional bonding to environmental settings that are satisfying in terms of one or more of the aspects of physical environment/behavior relationships presented in Exhibit 7.1, with different researchers focusing on different aspects. Those who focus on sociality remind us that attachment to places may be based largely on our satisfying relationships with people in those places—once again reminding us of the inseparability of people and environments.

When a strong place attachment develops, Gifford (1987) suggests, "the meaning of place and the meaning of self begin to merge" (p. 62). When a particular place becomes an important part of our self identity, this merger of place and self is known as **place identity**. Place identity can develop where there is strong negative, as well as positive, place attachment, as a boy named Kareem observes:

> It's strange, but I really like when the lights go off in the movies because then I'm no longer a "homeless kid." I'm just a person watching the movie like everyone else. A lot of the children at the hotel believe that they are "hotel kids." They've been told by so many people

for so long that they are not important, that they live up to what is expected of them. It gets so some children have no dreams and live in a nightmare because they believe that they are "hotel kids." It's worse than being in jail. In jail you can see the bars and you know when you're getting out. In the hotel you can't see the bars because they're inside of you and you don't know when you're getting out. (quoted in Berck, 1992, p. 105)

Home and work settings are most likely to become merged with our sense of self (Altman, 1993). Place attachment can also play a strong role in group and cultural identity (Low & Altman, 1992), and cultures often designate both sacred and taboo places that arouse emotions suitable to such places (Gallagher, 1993).

Researchers have been particularly interested in what happens to people when a place of identity is lost. We should also consider the long-term consequences of early experiences, such as homelessness or frequent movement between foster homes, in which no stable place attachment forms, or that result in a negative place attachment. Probably the best-known research on place identity is Fried and Gleicher's (1961) study of people relocated as a result of urban redevelopment projects. Planners assumed that people would be pleased to be moved from old, physically rundown neighborhoods into new apartments, but Fried and Gleicher found that relocated residents often sat in their new apartments and grieved for their lost homes. William Yancey (1971) later suggested that planners had undervalued the informal networks that were embedded in the deteriorating neighborhoods. He also argued that the architectural designs of the new apartments—designs that had received high praise in architectural journals—provided no spaces for building new networks; the new apartments were sociofugal spaces, low in sociality. Yancey, therefore, reminds us that attachment to place is often intertwined with attachment to people. He also reminds us that professionals often differ from consumer groups in their ideas about what makes good environments. Social workers, as well as architects and urban planners, need continual reminders to maximize client input when planning services and programs.

Homelessness

In Chapter 8, you will encounter William George, who has been homeless for several years, living on the streets of Chicago and San Diego. Place attachment has become a difficult problem for him, made more difficult by the fact that some familiar places have come to trigger his craving for crack cocaine.

According to federal legislation, a person is considered homeless when he or she "lacks a fixed, regular, and adequate nighttime residence" or has a nighttime residence that is "a supervised publicly or privately operated shelter designed to provide temporary living accommodations, an institution that provides temporary residence for individuals intended to be institutionalized, or a public or private place not designed for, or ordinarily used as, a regular sleeping accommodation for human beings" (Stewart B. McKinney Act, 1994). The National Coalition for the Homeless (NCH) (1997b) points out that this definition does not apply as well in rural areas as it does in urban areas, because there are few shelters in rural areas. Many homeless rural people live in crowded situations with relatives, or in substandard housing.

Although it is difficult to count the number of people who are homeless, there is general agreement that homelessness has increased in the past 15–20 years. National data from a 1994 study indicate that 12 million adults in the United States have been homeless at some point in their lives (reported in NCH, 1997b). Slightly more than half (51%) of all homeless persons are adults between the ages of 31 and 50. Families with children make up approximately 40 percent of homeless persons, and single men account for another 45 percent. One recent study found that African Americans account for 57 percent of the homeless populations in cities, European Americans for 30 percent, Hispanic Americans for 10 percent, Native Americans for 2 percent, and Asian Americans for 1 percent. Homeless persons in rural areas are much more likely to be European Americans (NCH, 1997b).

Poverty and a shortage of affordable housing appear to be the primary factors involved in the rising rate of homelessness (NCH, 1997a). As the housing market tightens, some groups are more likely than others to become homeless at some point. Groups particularly vulnerable to homelessness include people who are unemployed or working in low-wage jobs, women and children who are the victims of domestic violence, veterans, persons with mental illness, and persons with substance abuse disorders (NCH, 1997b). Many people move in and out of homelessness but remain vulnerable to becoming homeless again even when they have homes.

Accessible Environments for Persons with Disabilities

Accessibility is one of the key concepts for the study of human behavior and the physical environment (see Exhibit 7.1). In recent years, we have been reminded that environments, particularly built environments, can be disabling because of their inaccessibility to many persons, including most people with disabilities. An emerging model of thinking about disability emphasizes that it is primarily a "problem in the relationship between the individual and the environment" (Law & Dunn, 1993, p. 2).

Conflict perspective

This way of thinking about disability was the impetus for legislation at all levels of government during the 1970s and 1980s, most notably two pieces of federal legislation (Gilson, 1996). The Rehabilitation Act of 1973 (Public Law 93-112) was the first federal act to recognize the need for civil rights protection for persons with disabilities. It required all organizations receiving federal assistance to have an affirmative action plan to ensure accessibility of employment to persons with disabilities. The Americans with Disabilities Act of 1990 (ADA) (Public Law 101-336) extended the civil rights of persons with disabilities to the private sector. It seeks to end discrimination against persons with disabilities and promote their full participation in society.

The five titles of the ADA seek to eliminate environmental barriers to the full participation of persons with disabilities. You will want to be aware of the legal rights of your clients with disabilities.

- **Title I** addresses discrimination in the workplace. It requires reasonable accommodations, including architectural modification, for disabled workers.
- **Title II** requires that all public services, programs, and facilities, including public transportation, be accessible to persons with disabilities.

- **Title III** requires all public accommodations and services operated by private organizations to be accessible to persons with disabilities. It specifically lists 12 categories of accommodations: hotels and places of lodging; restaurants; movies and theaters; auditoriums and places of public gathering; stores and banks; health care service providers, hospitals, and pharmacies; terminals for public transportation; museums and libraries; parks and zoos; schools; senior centers and social service centers; and places of recreation.

- **Title IV** requires all intrastate and interstate phone companies to develop telecommunication relay services and devices for persons with speech or hearing impairments, to allow them to communicate in a manner similar to persons without impairments.

- **Title V** covers technical guidelines for enforcing the ADA.

Under industrial capitalism, wages are the primary source of livelihood. People who cannot earn wages, therefore, tend to be poor. Research indeed indicates that 35 to 40 percent of persons living in persistent poverty in the United States live in households headed by a person with a disability (Ruggles, 1991). People with disabilities who lobbied for passage of the ADA argued that government was spending vast sums of money for what they called "dependency programs" but was failing to make the investments required to make environments accessible so that people with disabilities could become employed (Johnson, 1992).

Judy Bachelder and Claudia Hilton (1994) remind us of the high prevalence of disabilities among older persons, the fastest growing group in the United States. More accessible environments may be an important way to buffer the expected deleterious effects of a large elderly population. As the baby boomers age, they will benefit from the earlier activism of the disability community.

Exhibit 7.6 lists some of the elements of environmental design that improve accessibility for persons with disabilities. It is important to remember, however, that rapid developments in assistive technology are likely to alter current guidelines about what is optimal environmental design. For example, the minimum space requirements in the ADA's guidelines for wheelchairs are already too tight for the new styles of motorized wheelchairs.

The Physical Environment and Human Behavior across the Life Course

Developmental perspective

People have different physical environment needs at different ages, and may respond to features of the physical environment in different ways as they progress through the life course. Some of these differences have been discussed earlier in this chapter. Because the built environment has been designed, for the most part, to accommodate the needs and responses of adults, this section calls attention to some of the special needs and responses of children, adolescents, and elderly adults.

Children

In infancy and early childhood, home is the primary physical environment, but day-care centers constitute a major environment for increasing numbers of young children. As children grow older, neighborhood and school become important environments.

EXHIBIT 7.6

Elements of
Accessible
Environments
for Persons
with Disabilities

- Create some close-in parking spaces widened to 8 feet to accommodate unloading of wheelchairs (one accessible space for every 25 spaces).
- Create curb cuts or ramping for curbs, with 12 inches of slope for every inch of drop in the curb.
- Make ramps at least 3 feet wide to accommodate wheelchairs, and provide a 5-foot-by-5-foot square area at the top of ramps to entrances to allow space for door opening.
- Remove high-pile carpeting, low-density carpeting, and plush carpeting, at least in the path of travel. Put nonslip material on slippery floors.
- Avoid phone-in security systems in entrances (barriers for persons who are deaf).
- Make all doorways at least 32 inches wide (36 is better).
- Use automatic doors or doors that take no more than 5 pounds of force to open.
- Use door levers instead of doorknobs.
- Create aisles that are at least 3 feet wide (wider is better). Keep the path of travel clear.
- Connect different levels in buildings with ramps (for small level changes) or a wheelchair-accessible elevator.
- Place public phones no higher than 48 inches (35–42 is optimal).
- Place other things that need to be reached at this optimal height.
- Brightly light foyers and areas with directories to assist persons with low vision. Use 3-inch-high lettering in directories.
- Install braille signs about 5 feet off the ground.
- Make restroom stalls at least 3 feet deep by 4 feet wide (5 feet by 5 feet is optimal).
- Install toilets that are 17 to 19 inches in height.
- Hang restroom sinks with no vanity underneath, so that persons in wheelchairs can pull up to them.
- Use both visual and audible emergency warning systems.

Source: Based on Johnson, 1992.

Research indicates that the physical environment can have both positive and negative effects on child development. Thomas David and Carol Weinstein (1987) suggest that the physical environments of children should be designed to serve the five common functions of child development:

1. *Personal identity.* Children need "personalized furnishings and individual territories" (David & Weinstein, 1987, p. 8) to assist in the development of personal identity. Place identity is essential to the development of personal identity.

2. *Sense of competence.* A sense of competence is supported when children have physical spaces and furnishings of a size and scale that allow them to meet their personal needs with minimal assistance. Thus, storage areas, furniture, and fixtures should be at the appropriate height and of the appropriate size for children.

3. *Intellectual, social, and motor development.* Development of intellectual, social, and motor skills is supported by the opportunity to move, explore, and play with interesting materials. Environments that restrict movement inhibit development in all domains.

4. *Security and trust.* Familiar, comfortable, and safe physical environments support the development of security and trust.

5. *A balance of social interaction and privacy.* Physical environments should support social interaction, but also provide private spaces that allow children the opportunity to retreat from overstimulating situations. Crowding, clutter, and high noise levels have been found to have negative effects on child development. One study found that children who come from crowded homes and attend crowded day-care centers are more likely to exhibit withdrawal, aggression, competitiveness, and hyperactivity than children where crowding is present in neither or only one of these environments (Maxwell, 1996). Constant exposure to high noise levels has been found to have a negative effect on language development (Evans & Maxwell, 1997).

Adolescents

After the rapid physical growth of puberty, adolescents have outgrown the need for physical environments with reduced scale and size. They have not outgrown the need for personalized furnishings and individual territories, however. Research indicates that privacy needs increase in adolescence (Sinha et al., 1995). At the same time, with the increased emphasis on peer relationships, adolescents have a special need for safe gathering places and recreational opportunities.

Since the 1964 publication of Barker and Gump's *Big School, Small School: High School Size and Student Behavior,* considerable attention has been given to the question of optimal high school size. Gump (1987) suggests two reasons that high schools need to be larger than elementary schools. First, high schools provide more varied curricular offerings than elementary schools to assist students to sort out their interests and competencies, which requires a larger and more specialized faculty. Second, high schools offer a varied set of extracurricular activities to meet the need for safe gathering places and recreational opportunities, which requires sufficient numbers of students to "staff" each activity and sufficient numbers of faculty sponsors. There is some agreement that high schools of fewer than 500 students will result in "understaffing." On the other hand, as high schools grow larger, they lose some of the continuity and intimacy of small schools, and very large student populations result in "overstaffing," with meaningful opportunities for participation unavailable to many students.

Elderly Adults

The special needs of elderly adults in relation to the physical environment have not been studied as extensively as the special needs of children. There is general agreement, however, that home and neighborhood are the primary physical environments for elderly adults (Carp, 1987). Housing of elderly adults has become a major social policy issue.

Because there are more differences among elderly adults than among children and adolescents, it is difficult to make definitive statements about their needs in relation to the physical environment. To assist in assessing the needs of individual clients who are elderly, however, you may find it helpful to adapt the previous list of five ways that the physical environment supports child development:

1. *Personal identity.* As they attempt to hold onto personal identity in the midst of multiple losses, elderly adults will benefit from personalized furnishings and personal territories.

2. *Sense of competence.* Elderly adults are more likely to maintain a sense of competence when the demands of the physical environment match the capabilities of the person. Few modifications are needed for those elderly adults with no disabilities, but it may be necessary to intensify the level of sensory stimulation to accommodate losses in the sensory system. For those elderly adults with one or more disabilities, however, modifications such as the ones listed in Exhibit 7.6 may be appropriate. Researchers have found that only about 10 percent of elderly adults who need modifications in the home environment because of disabilities actually make those modifications (Gilderbloom & Markham, 1996).

3. *Intellectual, social, and motor skills.* Maintenance and development of intellectual, social, and motor skills will be supported by opportunities to read, think, reflect, explore, and work with interesting materials; by opportunities for social interaction; and by opportunities for movement.

4. *Security and trust.* Safe homes and neighborhoods are essential for a sense of security and trust.

5. *A balance of social interaction and privacy.* Home environments, private or institutional, should provide private spaces as well as opportunities for social interaction.

IMPLICATIONS FOR SOCIAL WORK PRACTICE

This discussion of the relationship between human behavior and the physical environment suggests several practice principles:

- Where appropriate, collaborate with design professionals to ensure that specific built environments are accessible, adaptable, and comfortable; provide adequate privacy and control; provide an optimal quality and intensity of stimulation; and facilitate social interaction.

- Assess the physical environment of your social service setting. Do clients find it accessible, legible, and comfortable? Do they find that it provides adequate privacy and control? Does it provide optimal quality and intensity of sensory stimulation? If it is a residential setting, does it promote social interaction?

- Routinely evaluate the physical environments of clients—particularly those environments where problem behaviors occur—for accessibility, legibility, comfort, privacy and control, and sensory stimulation. Check your evaluation against the clients' perceptions. If you have no opportunity to see these environments, have the clients evaluate them for you. Provide space on the intake form for assessing the physical environments of clients.

- Know the physical environments of the organizations to which you refer clients. Assist referral agencies and clients in planning how to overcome any existing environmental barriers.

- Be alert to the meanings that particular environments hold for clients.

- When assisting clients to learn new skills, pay attention to the discontinuities between the setting where the skills are learned and the settings where they will be used.

- When clients are entering new physical environments that may provide serious challenges, help them rehearse navigation of the new environment, with a site visit if possible.

- When designing social service programs, consider issues of optimal staffing, of both staff and clients, for particular behavior settings.

- When planning group activities, ensure the best possible fit between the spatial needs of the activity and the physical environment where the activity will occur.

- Keep the benefits of the natural environment in mind when planning both prevention and remediation programs. When possible, help clients gain access to elements of the natural environment, and where appropriate, help them plan activities in the natural environment.

- Assist clients to use cues from the physical environment (such as neighborhood landmarks, or carpet color in institutions) to simplify negotiation of that environment.

- Recognize that people have attachments to places as well as to people.

- Maximize opportunities for client input into design of their built environments.

- Become familiar with technology for adapting environments to make them more accessible.

- When planning services with clients, ensure the best possible fit between the client's sensory and mobility resources and limitations and the physical environments in which they are to live and interact.

- Recognize the special needs of children, adolescents, and elderly adults in relation to aspects of the built environment.

MAIN POINTS

1. To better understand the relationship between the physical environment and human behavior, social workers can draw on multidisciplinary research from the social sciences of psychology, sociology, geography, and anthropology, and from the design

disciplines of architecture, landscape architecture, interior design, and urban and regional planning.

2. Eleven key concepts for the study of the physical environment and human behavior are accessibility, activity, adaptability, comfort, control, crowding, legibility, meaning, privacy, sensory stimulation, and sociality.

3. Three broad categories of theories about human behavior and the physical environment are stimulation theories, control theories, and behavior settings theories. Stimulation theories focus on the physical environment as a source of sensory information, which is essential for human well-being. Control theories focus on how much control we have over our physical environments and the attempts we make to gain control. Behavior settings theories focus on consistent, uniform patterns of behavior that occur in particular places.

4. Researchers have found a strong human preference for elements of the natural environment, particularly water, trees, and sunlight.

5. Researchers have also found the positive outcomes of time spent in the natural environment to include recovery from mental fatigue, enhanced group development, sense of tranquillity, sense of control, and improved physical health.

6. Stimulation in the natural environment cannot be controlled. Extreme levels of stimulation produce natural disasters, which are highly stressful events.

7. Built environments may be sociofugal spaces, which discourage social interaction, or sociopetal spaces, which encourage social interaction.

8. Research indicates that design changes that increase comfort and control in the built environment lead to increased social interaction, increased purposefulness of behavior, and decreased aggression.

9. Professionals and clients may attach different meanings to the physical environment and develop different preferences for aspects of the physical environment.

10. There is some evidence that built environments can be designed to encourage a perception of control by both residents and criminals, thereby discouraging crime.

11. An emerging line of research suggests that behavior settings are an important element in substance addiction.

12. Place attachment is a process in which people and groups form bonds with places.

13. A recent recognition that physical environments can be disabling has led to legislation to protect the civil rights of persons with disabilities.

14. Children, adolescents, and elderly adults have special needs with respect to the built environment, particularly needs for control, privacy, and stimulation.

KEY TERMS

accessibility

activity

adaptability

behavior settings

behavior settings theories

boundary regulating mechanisms

built environment

comfort

control

control theories

crowding

defensible space

density

legibility

meaning

natural environment

normalization principle

personal space

place

place attachment

place identity

primary territory

privacy

program

public territory

secondary territory

sensory stimulation

sociality

sociofugal spaces

sociopetal spaces

staffing

stimulation theories

stimulus deprivation

stimulus overload

territoriality

Title I (ADA)

Title II (ADA)

Title III (ADA)

Title IV (ADA)

Title V (ADA)

tolerance

WORLD WIDE WEB RESOURCES

National Coalition for the Homeless

http://nch.ari.net/wwwhome.html

Official National Coalition for the Homeless site contains facts about homelessness, legislation
and policy, research, housing and poverty issues, and other Internet resources.

Americans with Disabilities Act Document Center

http://janweb.icdi.wvu.edu/kinder/

Maintained by Duncan Kinder through West Virginia University, site contains ADA statutes,
regulations, guidelines, technical sheets, and other assistance documents.

Eldercare Web: Residential Living options

http://www.elderweb.com/liveopt.htm

Very well-established site on the elderly, run by Karen Stevenson Brown, CPA, contains links for
housing for the elderly, options, what to look for in living options, safety issues, and much
more.

CHAPTER 8

Social Institutions and Social Structure

CASE STUDY ■ *William George of Small Town, Chicago, and San Diego*

Patterns of Social Life

Contemporary Trends in U.S. Social Institutions
>Trends in Family and Kinship
>Trends in Religion
>Trends in Government and Politics
>Trends in the Economy
>Trends in Education
>Trends in Social Welfare
>Trends in Health Care
>Trends in Mass Media

Social Structure and Social Inequality
>Trends in Social Inequality
>Theories of Social Inequality

■ **IMPLICATIONS FOR SOCIAL WORK PRACTICE**

■ **MAIN POINTS**

■ **KEY TERMS**

■ **WORLD WIDE WEB RESOURCES**

WILLIAM GEORGE OF SMALL TOWN, CHICAGO, AND SAN DIEGO

William George spent the first 10 years of his life in a small town in Indiana, the next 20 years in Chicago, and moved to San Diego 8 years ago to "start over." He has decided that life in San Diego is not that different from life in Chicago, except the winters are a lot kinder.

Many of William's childhood memories involve moving. William was the second of three children born to Harold and Wilma George. He remembers his first four years as being "pretty good." His dad made a fairly good living working as a security guard, and his parents were making plans to buy a small house and move out of the trailer park. Those plans were put to rest when Harold was shot and killed during a break-in at work. Wilma found it very hard to manage without Harold. There were few jobs in their small town for a woman without a high school education, and the jobs she could find were evening shifts. Child care was a constant problem, and money was always tight. The family was on and off welfare several times, and they finally moved into the public housing project. Wilma was admitted to the state hospital on two occasions to be treated for depression. Sometimes William and his siblings lived at home with their mother, sometimes with their maternal grandmother, and sometimes with their mother's younger sister, Ruby, and her family. William remembers these times with Aunt Ruby as the happiest times of his childhood.

When William was 10, his mother remarried, and the family moved to Chicago in search of better jobs. This marriage was turbulent from the beginning, and William remembers a small apartment that seemed to close in on a family that often had no working adult, a family where screaming and hitting were regular forms of communication. After living in a small town all his life, William found the streets of Chicago overwhelming. School was no refuge. With all the moving around, turbulence at home, violence in the neighborhood, going to school hungry, and perhaps an undiagnosed learning disability, William fell hopelessly behind. It seemed to him that his teachers gave up on him long before he gave up on himself. When he dropped out of school at age 16, he felt a great sense of relief to be free of the failure and humiliation that he had come to associate with school.

After he left school, William worked a variety of odd jobs until he was hired as a semiskilled laborer in a manufacturing plant. He was a good worker and held the same job until the company where he worked went out of business. He was 23 by this time, married, and the father of two young children. The job market was not good for a young man who had dropped out of high school. After a few weeks, William found a job in construction, but at less pay, and he felt ashamed that he was not able to provide a higher standard of living for his family. He had promised himself that his children would never

CASE STUDY

have to suffer the kind of financial setback that had so altered the course of his childhood. He became depressed and began to join some of his coworkers in a few beers after work, and later in experimentation with marijuana. The time and money involved in this after-work activity became a source of tension in his marriage.

William stayed at this job for about three years. Then he ran into an old friend who told him about a new job opportunity in another construction company. William followed up on this lead and was hired, with a nice pay increase. The new job eased the financial hardships at home, but the marital tensions persisted. After a few weeks, one of his new coworkers introduced him to crack cocaine, calling it the "best thing yet." William had never had such an intensely pleasant reaction to alcohol or marijuana, and soon he was buying crack whenever he could. At first, he had no trouble doing his job, but after a few months, he was getting into trouble for being late and for poor performance on the job. Tension with his wife increased, and she finally asked him to leave.

William went to live with his sister, but she asked him to leave after a few months, and he lost his job about the same time. He began to live in abandoned buildings with a group of men he met on the streets. Sometimes they found day labor work, and other times they begged and stole to stay alive. Whenever they had money, they bought crack. From time to time, William's sister or brother would let him move in with them, but it never worked for very long.

When William was 29, his Aunt Ruby, who now lived in San Diego, came to Chicago to visit. Distressed to learn about William's situation, she went to visit him in the abandoned building where he lived. Aunt Ruby convinced William to go into a detoxification program and moved him to San Diego to live with her when he completed the program.

Soon after moving to San Diego, William found a job in construction, and he was determined to "start over." Things went well for a while, but after a few months, his craving for crack was triggered when a coworker showed him a crack pipe he had brought to work. Soon William found his crack use getting out of control again, and before long he had lost his job and moved out of Aunt Ruby's apartment to avoid causing her more pain.

For the past few years, William has made his home in a series of abandoned buildings or "abandominiums," as he and his friends call them. He often works day labor jobs with one of the labor pools, arriving early in the morning, getting an assignment for the day, and being paid at the end of the day. Although the pay is low, the work unstable, and the supervisors harsh, he likes

CASE STUDY

to work this way, because he can get some control of his drug use by controlling how much money he has in his pocket at any time. He has developed
several chronic health problems, but receives no medical assistance. He talks
occasionally with the social worker at the homeless shelter and with the local
parish priest, particularly when he is worried about the health and safety of
other "street people." He has begun to let them know about the hold crack has
on him and about the despair behind his bantering. He is too ashamed to get
in touch with members of his family.

Patterns of Social Life

As you read this story, it is easy to focus on William and his behavior and lose sight of the environments in which his behavior has been transacted. Although you do not want to lose sight of
the personal dimensions of William's story, in this chapter you will be considering the broad patterns of social life that William has encountered.

A good way to begin is to imagine that you and 100 other people have made a space journey
to a new planet that has recently, thanks to technological breakthroughs, become inhabitable by
humans. You are committed to beginning a new society on this new frontier. How will you work
together to be successful in this endeavor? What will you need to do to ensure your survival? Sociologists and anthropologists have given much thought to how people work together to try to
ensure the survival of a society. They have identified two concepts—social institution and social
structure—as central to understanding those endeavors.

Social institution and social structure are among the more abstract concepts used by sociologists. Our understanding of these concepts is also complicated by the casual, everyday use of
the term *institution* to cover a variety of meanings. In this book, however, we will use David
Newman's (1995) definition of **social institutions** as "patterned ways of solving the problems
and meeting the requirements of a particular society" (p. 30). Andrew Van de Ven (1993) adds
that "they are solutions that consist of a set of rights and duties, an authority for enforcing them,
and some degree of adherence to collective norms of prudent reasonable behavior" (p. 142).
Rights and duties are organized into statuses and roles and the expected behaviors that accompany them. **Statuses** are specific social positions; roles, as suggested in Chapter 2, are the behaviors of persons occupying particular statuses. Sociologists have identified a set of interrelated
social institutions—such as family, religion, government, economy, education—with each institution organizing social relations in a particular sector of social life.

Social structure is the concept used to refer to this set of interrelated social institutions. Earl
Babbie (1994) suggests that in the broadest sense, social structure is another term for *society*, or
simply an acknowledgment that social life is patterned, not random. He further suggests that al-

Systems perspective

though we typically use the term *social structure* to imply a material entity, it is better thought of as a process—"a process of taking away individual freedom and structuring it for corporate action" (p. 13). In other words, **social structure** is a set of interrelated social institutions developed by human beings to impose constraints on human interaction for the purpose of the survival and well-being of the collectivity.

Sociological treatment of social institutions and social structure emphasizes the ways in which they persist and contribute to social stability. But often they persist in spite of unintended consequences and evidence that they are ineffective. For this reason, Van de Ven (1993) suggests that social institutions are imperfect solutions to past problems. Richard Scott (1995) reminds us that social institutions persist only when they are carried forward by individual actors and only when they are actively monitored. Robert Goodin (1996) suggests that it is accurate to think of social institutions as relatively stable, but they also change, and it is important to study how they change. He proposes that they change in three ways: by accident, by evolution, and by design. This view of social institutions and social structure, as relatively stable but also changing, is consistent with the transactional perspective of this book. This view seems justified given the extraordinary changes in several major social institutions since 1960, in societies around the world (Caplow, 1991; Caplow, Bahr, Modell, & Chadwick, 1991; Farley, 1996; Langlois, 1994; Oberschall, 1996; Zdravomyslova, 1996).

Sociologists commonly identify five interrelated social institutions: family and kinship, religion, government and politics, economy, and education. In addition, they have identified three other key social institutions in modern industrialized societies: social welfare, health care, and mass media (Newman, 1995; Popple & Leighninger, 1993). The discussion in this chapter will include all eight of these major social institutions. Exhibit 8.1 presents the eight social institutions and the major functions that they perform for society.

Contemporary Trends in U.S. Social Institutions

You have plans to become a social worker, so it is probably safe to assume that you have been at least a casual observer of trends in social institutions. As casual observers, we all keep abreast of trends by making personal observations, listening to stories of people in our social network, and consuming the output of the mass media. In our casual observations about trends in social life, we make comparisons between the contemporary social world as we understand it and some past social world as we understand it. This type of comparison provides many opportunities for error. We may view the contemporary world through a lens that is biased by age, gender, social status, religion, or political persuasion, and we may tend to romanticize the past. To avoid these errors, social workers must become professional, not casual, observers of trends in the social world. As planners and administrators, we must design and implement programs that are responsive to trends in social life. Those of us who engage clients directly, to ameliorate problems of living, must understand the changing social situations in which those problems have developed and are being maintained. The purpose of this chapter is to help you observe trends in a more professional way so that you can function more effectively as a social worker.

EXHIBIT 8.1
Key Social
Institutions and the
Functions They
Perform

Social Institution	Functions Performed
Family and kinship	Regulating procreation
	Conducting initial socialization
	Providing mutual support
Religion	Answering questions about meaning and purpose of life
	Socializing individuals
	Maintaining social control
	Providing mutual support
Government and politics	Making and enforcing societal rules
	Resolving internal and external conflicts
	Mobilizing collective resources to meet societal goals
Economy	Regulating production, distribution, and consumption of goods and services
Education	Passing along formal knowledge from one generation to next
	Socializing individuals
Social welfare	Promoting interdependence
	Dealing with issues of dependence
Health care	Promoting the general health
Mass media	Managing the flow of information, images, and ideas

Because 1960 is often seen as a turning point for contemporary social life (Caplow, 1991; Farley, 1996), we will focus for the most part on the trends in social institutions from 1960 to the present. These trends demonstrate the blessings as well as the unresolved problems of industrial capitalism. However, because the profession of social work developed in response to some of the particular problems created by industrial capitalism, we will give special attention to social problems related to the current stage of industrialization.

Unfortunately, by the time you read these words, even the most recent data presented will already be old. If you have not developed research skills already, this is a good time for you to learn to use your library and the Internet to find social data. Why not make a trip to the library or the information superhighway to see if you can update some of the trends described here? Are trends holding and projections materializing?

Trends in Family and Kinship

Although William George is currently estranged from his family, family and kinship relationships are a very important part of his unfolding story. Family and kinship is perhaps the most basic social institution, and in simple societies it fulfills many of the functions assigned to other social institutions in complex societies. Although the functions of family and kinship have been the subject of some controversy since 1960, modern societies generally agree that the **family and kinship institution** is primarily responsible for the regulation of procreation, for the initial socialization of new members of society, and for mutual support.

The family and kinship institution has experienced some extraordinary changes since 1960. These four changes, taken together, have had a far-reaching impact on human behavior:

1. *Medical advances and court rulings have made childbearing discretionary.* Around 1962, reliable oral contraceptives became generally available, followed shortly by widespread use of surgical sterilization (Caplow, 1991). Then, quite unexpectedly, the U.S. Supreme Court legalized abortion in 1973, in the famous *Roe* v. *Wade* case. The result was a sharp decline in fertility; the birthrate dropped by nearly half between 1960 and 1995 (see Exhibit 8.2). By 1988, close to two out of five married women and/or their husbands had been surgically sterilized. Data on abortion are incomplete, but Farley (1996) reports a ratio of 330 abortions to 1000 live births in the year following *Roe* v. *Wade*. This ratio peaked at 440

EXHIBIT 8.2

Birthrates for Married and Unmarried Women (Ages 15–44), and Percentage of Total Births to Unmarried Women, 1960 to 1993

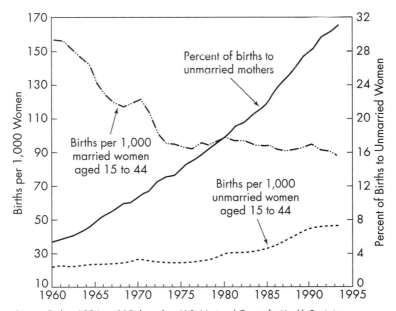

Source: Farley, 1996, p. 118; based on U.S. National Center for Health Statistics, 1995, *Vital Statistics of the United States: Vol. 1. Natality,* Tables 1-76, 1-77 and 1-78; 1995, *Monthly Vital Statistics Reports,* Vol. 44, No. 3 (supplement), Table 14.

abortions to 1000 live births in 1983, and stabilized at about 380 in 1992. Data indicate that the preponderance of abortions are performed on unmarried women, meaning that abortion reduces the illegitimacy rate more than the fertility rate (Caplow, 1991). One trend is particularly notable. Fertility is declining among two-parent families and increasing among single-parent families (Farley, 1996; Hogan & Lichter, 1995; Poston & Dan, 1996). As shown in Exhibit 8.2, birthrates among married women declined sharply between 1960 and 1980, whereas birthrates for unmarried women almost doubled between 1980 and 1996. These two trends taken together have resulted in a substantial increase in the percentage of babies born to unmarried women, rising to more than 32 percent in 1996 (National Center for Health Statistics, 1998). As a consequence, the child-rearing function in American society is shifting from the relatively prosperous two-parent family to the lower-income single-parent family. The majority of children still live in two-parent families, but the proportion is declining steadily, and fewer children now live in middle-income families (Farley, 1996).

2. *Unmarried cohabitation is no longer legally prohibited.* Farley (1996) suggests that cohabitation may have replaced marriage as the typical way to begin a live-in sexual relationship. Prior to the mid-1960s, unmarried cohabitation was discouraged by a combination of local laws and regulations, federal statutes, and unofficial regulation (Caplow, 1991) that made it impossible for unmarried couples to reserve a hotel room, buy a house, or rent an apartment. A federal statute prohibited the interstate transportation of females for immoral purposes, and sexually active adolescents were labeled as juvenile delinquents. Judicial rulings between 1965 and 1975 removed many of these legal prohibitions. The first ruling came from the U.S. Supreme Court in 1965 in the case of *Griswold* v. *Connecticut*. Acting on a previously unnoticed constitutional right to marital privacy, the court struck down a state law prohibiting the use of contraceptives. This ruling became the basis for extending the right to privacy to other relations between consenting adults. Unofficial regulators followed the lead. College administrators ceased their efforts to ensure chastity of unmarried students; hotelkeepers discontinued their policies of checking the marital status of cohabiting registrants; banks began to provide mortgage loans to unmarried cohabitants, including gay and lesbian couples; and social agencies extended benefits to unmarried mothers.

3. *No-fault divorce has become accessible.* The divorce rate in the United States has been gradually increasing since 1870, and it is currently much higher than the rates in other advanced industrial societies (Farley, 1996). Until 1966, divorce was granted to couples only when one party was at fault (Caplow, 1991). New York was the first state to develop a no-fault divorce law, and by 1985 all states had some form of no-fault divorce. Between 1965 and 1974, the divorce rate doubled, from 10 to 20 divorces per 1,000 married women per year (Caplow, 1991). It is estimated that more than one-half of marriages begun in the 1970s will end in divorce (Farley, 1996).

4. *Large numbers of mothers of young children have entered the paid labor force.* Although the increasing employment of married women is a long-term trend, the increase during the period 1960–1990 was spectacular, particularly for married women with children under 6. In 1960, 30 percent of married couples included wives in the paid labor force; by 1994, it was

61 percent (Farley, 1996). In 1960, 19 percent of married women with young children were in the labor force; by 1987, the figure had risen to 57 percent (Caplow, 1991). The rates are even higher for divorced and separated mothers. In 1987, 85 percent of divorced women with children between the ages of 6 and 17 were in the labor force, higher than the rate for married men (Caplow, 1991). This recent increase of married women in the labor force cuts across occupational levels.

Caplow (1991) notes two long-term trends in family relationships that are likely to continue: greater valuing of autonomy and self-direction, as opposed to obedience and conformity, in children; and equalization of power between men and women. The popular media have been attributing the "breakdown in the American family" to these trends. But contrary to popular opinion, available data indicate that changes in the family and kinship institution have not been accompanied by a decline in family relationships (Caplow, 1991). Consistently, approximately 70 percent of married persons in the United States report their marriage to be very happy, and only 2 percent report being very unhappily married. In fact, national surveys indicate that people are more satisfied with their family lives than with their friendships, hobbies, or work. Unlike William George, the great majority of families keep regular contact with households of kin and maintain regular and affectionate relationships with elder parents.

Nevertheless, social service programs serving families, children, and older adults need to be responsive to these changing trends. The confluence of declining family size, increasing numbers of single parents, and increasing numbers of women in the paid labor force calls for a reexamination, in particular, of our assumptions about family caregiving for dependent persons. Social workers should lead the way in discourse about social policies that can strengthen families and alleviate family stressors. These issues receive greater attention in Chapter 14.

Trends in Religion

In his despair, William George is beginning to use his contacts with the parish priest to find purpose and meaning in his life. The **religious institution** is the primary institution for answering these sorts of questions. It also serves important socialization, social control, and mutual support functions.

Alexis de Tocqueville (cited in Caplow, 1991, p. 66) was struck by the importance of religion in the United States 150 years ago, and available data suggest that he would find the situation unchanged if he returned today (Wald, 1997). International data indicate that Americans have much higher weekly attendance at religious services than Europeans; they spend more time in private devotions and more money on religious activities than residents of other advanced industrial countries.

Americans have greater confidence in organized religion than in most other U.S. social institutions, and churches receive a large share of philanthropic gifts. Those gifts are a major source of support for social services in the United States. For example, expenditures for welfare activities by Catholic Charities are second only to expenditures by the U.S. government (Wald, 1997). Ram Cnaan (1997) suggests that social workers need to become more aware of the role that religious congregations are playing in social service delivery in the contemporary era.

Church attendance and church membership have been relatively stable since 1960, as have survey responses to other measures of religiosity. Respondents in opinion surveys consistently report that religion is a major source of support in times of trouble (Caplow, 1991). It is important, therefore, that the social work assessment process include assessment of the role of religion in clients' lives.

At the same time, however, opinion poll data indicate an increase in the percentage of persons reporting no religious preferences, from 3 percent in 1957 to 11 percent in 1990 (U.S. Bureau of the Census, 1992, p. 58). It is not clear what these data mean. Roof's (1993) study of the "spiritual journeys of the baby boom generation" found this cohort to have intensely personal approaches to religion and to make frequent changes in religious allegiance. A statement of no preference may simply reflect this fluidity of allegiance and not a lack of religious belief. Roof's findings are consistent with the Middletown III study, which found that high school students indicated much more religious tolerance in 1977 than in 1924 (Caplow, Bahr, & Chadwick, 1983).

Historically, U.S. religious life has been dominated by the Judeo-Christian tradition. That continues to be the case, but since the passage of the Immigration Act of 1965, a growing minority of Buddhists, Muslims, and Hindus inhabit the United States (Wentz, 1998). Recent news stories have suggested that Islam is the fastest growing religion in the United States (Briggs, 1994). It is difficult to determine precise trends in religious preference because the U.S. Census Bureau is not allowed to inquire into matters of religion, and data must be drawn from a variety of sources that collect data at different time periods and use different definitions. Exhibit 8.3 shows trends in religious preference between 1957 and 1990, based on surveys conducted by The Gallup Organization, Inc. (reported in U.S. Bureau of the Census, 1992, p. 58). Religious diversity seems to be increasing, but at present the United States remains a predominantly Christian na-

EXHIBIT 8.3

Trends in Religious Preference, 1957–1990

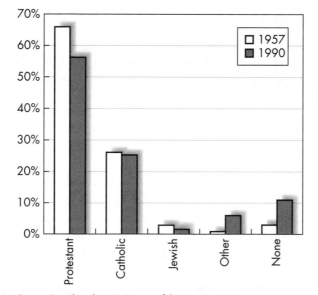

Source: Based on the U.S. Bureau of the Census, 1992, p. 58.

tion. In contrast, approximately one-third of the world's population is estimated to be Christian (U.S. Bureau of the Census, 1992, p. 60).

Christian denominations in the United States exhibit much diversity, and different scholars have classified Christian denominations in different ways. For example, Kenneth Wald (1997) distinguishes among Mainline Protestants, Evangelical Protestants, Black Protestants, and Roman Catholics. Wald suggests that Mainline Protestants put top priority on moral teachings about altruism and issues of social justice; Evangelical Protestants emphasize personal salvation and put high priority on issues of sexual morality. Exhibit 8.4 shows an estimated breakdown of religious preference in the United States about 1992, based on a composite of Wald's analysis of data from the American National Election Studies (Wald, 1997) and U.S. Census Bureau (1992, p. 58) analysis of data from The Gallup Organization, Inc. Trends between 1960 and 1990 show growth in the ranks of Evangelical Protestants and losses in the ranks of Mainline Protestants (Caplow, 1991).

In recent years, a host of controversial issues based in religious beliefs—abortion, homosexuality, pornography, assisted suicide—have stirred passions and dominated political agendas. These issues center on three controversies: controversies about the role of women in society, controversies about sexual expression, and controversies about the meaning of life and death. James Davison Hunter (1991, 1994) has used the phrase *culture wars* to describe the deep divisions among religious groups on these issues. Wald (1997) found that religious groups are not totally consistent across issues, however:

■ Jews and the Nonreligious put the highest value on abortion rights and women's rights; Evangelical Protestants and Black Protestants are the most opposed to both abortion rights and women's rights; Mainline Protestants and Catholics take an intermediate position on these issues.

EXHIBIT 8.4
Religious Preference, 1992

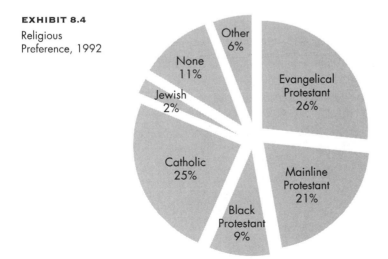

Sources: Based on U.S. Bureau of the Census, 1992, p. 58; Wald, 1997.

- Jews are the most supportive of nondiscrimination against gays and lesbians; Evangelical Protestants and Mainline Protestants are the least supportive; Catholics and the Nonreligious are in an intermediate position. Black Protestants are more favorably disposed to protect gays and lesbians from employment discrimination than to grant them other legal protections.

- Black Protestants are far more favorable toward government programs to assist African Americans than any other religious group. Mainline Protestants and Evangelical Protestants are the least supportive of these programs; Jews, the Nonreligious, and Catholics are in an intermediate position.

It should be noted that Catholics in the United States are more ethnically diverse than white Protestants, and different Catholic ethnic groups vary substantially in their religious beliefs. These differences may account for the moderate position of Catholics reported by Wald (Roof & McKinney, 1987).

Social workers should not assume that all persons of a religious group hold the same beliefs on social issues. But we must be aware of religious beliefs, both our own and those of clients, when working with controversial social issues.

Trends in Government and Politics

The **government and political institution** is responsible for how decisions get made and enforced for the society as a whole. It is expected to resolve both internal and external conflicts and mobilize collective resources to meet societal goals.

Rational choice perspective

Governments vary a great deal in the extent to which power is concentrated, and political scholars disagree about the degree of concentration of power in the United States (Newman, 1995). Crook, Pakulski, and Waters (1992) argue that political power is less concentrated in the United States than in either 20th-century communist countries or West European democracies. They describe the U.S. model as a **broker model** in which government mediates among competing interest groups rather than serving as an active manager. Interest groups have access to government through lobbying, litigation, and constitutional challenges.

Conflict perspective

Crook et al. do not see the government as neutral in its responses to interest groups, however. They suggest that the financial cost of political action is a serious constraint for many groups in the United States, and that the U.S. model has not worked well for groups with few economic resources. Recent trends in government and politics support their analysis.

Although changes in the political arena often appear to defy our attempts to find patterns, five trends since 1960 are worth noting:

1. *Federal authority has expanded.* Beginning in the 1960s, the federal government began to extend its authority into areas previously governed under state, local, and private auspices (Caplow, 1991), such as health care, education, sexuality, work environments, the arts, crime control, and treatment of persons with disabilities. This expansion of the federal role resulted in significant increases in the federal budget but not in the federal workforce, which has actually declined in relation to the national population (Caplow, 1991). This trend to-

ward expansion has been countered with recent serious efforts to diminish the role of the federal government (Dionne, 1996).

2. *The public has lost confidence in government and politics.* William George spent part of his childhood in a government-operated housing project, received public welfare assistance as a child, attended public schools, visited his mother in a state mental hospital, and received detoxification services from a state-funded program. He is quick to convey both his gratitude for and his disappointment in these government services. Available data indicate that Americans have less confidence in all of their social institutions than they did before 1960 (Caplow et al., 1991), but loss of confidence is most pronounced in relation to government. Lipset and Schneider (1983) noted growing antigovernment sentiment and increasing perception of governmental unresponsiveness throughout the 1960s and 1970s. According to more recent opinion polls, reports E. J. Dionne (1996), Americans have little confidence in what government *can* do, but at the same time they want government to do more and to do it more effectively. Social work reformers must pay attention to both messages, because social welfare programs have suffered from this loss of confidence in government. Loss of confidence in government appears to be an international trend, often interpreted as a symptom of globalization and the postmodern emphasis on diversity (Crook et al., 1992; Robertson, 1992). Whatever the cause, there are other signs of this waning confidence in government: a slow but steady decline in voting participation, a rapid expansion in the number of federal officials indicted and convicted of corruption since 1970, and the strong showing of a third-party presidential candidate in 1992 (Caplow, 1991; Dionne, 1996).

3. *Political campaigns have become increasingly commercialized.* Political campaigns, once run by amateurs, are now run by public relations professionals (Caplow, 1991; Dionne, 1996). Candidates are now "packaged" like any other product. Sophisticated political opinion polls provide up-to-the-minute information on voter behavior. Television commercials, consisting of 30-second "sound bite" messages, are widely used. Massive fund-raising drives are needed to pay for these expensive ways of campaigning. The cost of a presidential campaign increased tenfold between 1960 and 1988, and the average cost of running for Congress increased twentyfold during the same period (Caplow, 1991).

4. *Political action committees have been playing an increasing role.* **Political action committees (PACs)** are organizations formed to represent special interests in the electoral process. PACs exist all along the political continuum. They are permitted to collect funds from individuals and make much larger contributions than political parties and candidates are permitted to collect from individual contributors. Before campaign financing reform in 1974 prohibited large individual donations, there were a few hundred PACs; by 1993, there were close to 5,000 (Caplow, 1991; Makinson, 1993), including **Political Action for Candidate Election (PACE)** of the National Association of Social Workers (NASW). Newman (1995) cites evidence that PACs exert strong influence on the activities of elected officials.

5. *Diversity among political leaders has been increasing.* Although they are still underrepresented, racial and ethnic minorities and women have made gains in political leadership since 1960. Caplow (1991) reports that as of 1960, only a handful of African Americans

held elective office at all levels of government. The numbers increased to 1,474 in 1970; 4,963 in 1980; and 6,703 in 1988. After the 1996 elections, African Americans comprised 7 percent of the U.S. Congress (36 out of 535), compared to 11 percent of the U.S. population (League of Women Voters, 1997). Hispanic Americans have experienced a similar pattern of increasing participation, making up 3 percent of the U.S. Congress elected in 1996 and 7.6 percent of the electorate (League of Women Voters, 1997). The increase in female elected officials has not been as rapid. The number of women in Congress increased from 10 to 25 between 1960 and 1990. After the 1996 elections, women held 11 percent of the seats in the U.S. Congress, but comprised 51 percent of the voting-age population (League of Women Voters, 1997).

Michael Reisch (1997) reminds us that social work has been "at the mercy of political forces throughout its history" (p. 81). Suggesting that this is more the case today than ever before, he argues that social workers cannot afford to ignore processes and trends in the political arena. We must learn to use the government and political institution to promote social services that contribute to the well-being of individuals and communities. Given the trends in social inequality (discussed later in this chapter), it is particularly important that social workers monitor the impact of public policies on poverty and inequality.

Trends in the Economy

The **economic institution** has the primary responsibility for regulating the production, distribution, and consumption of goods and services. In a capitalistic market economy, as in the United States, what one consumes is dependent on how much one is paid for selling goods and services. Most people, if they are not self-employed, exchange labor for wages, which they then use for consumption. This labor for wages has come to be called **work**. The nature of work has been ever-changing since premodern times, but the rate of change has accelerated wildly since the beginning of the industrial revolution.

Chirot's (1994) historical analysis reveals a series of industrial cycles beginning in the late 1700s, each with its own dominant technology. The fifth industrial cycle began in the 1970s, with electronics as the dominant technology. Transitions between industrial cycles produce periods of instability in the economic institution, as some workers' skills become obsolete and other people take advantage of new opportunities.

Five recent trends affecting work have been identified as likely to continue into the 21st century (Farley, 1996; Noll & Langlois, 1994; Reskin & Padavic, 1994):

Conflict perspective

1. *The economic institution is undergoing fundamental change.* For several decades, the proportion of workers in the service sector has been increasing and the proportion in manufacturing has been decreasing. This trend is called **economic restructuring.** Experts expect that by 2005, only 13 percent of the labor force will work in manufacturing and 81 percent will be in jobs in the service sector (Reskin & Padavic, 1994). This shift is important because of the income inequalities in the service sector and because, overall, wages are lower in the service sector. The loss of manufacturing jobs has led to a decline in the average earnings of men, with the effect more severe for men of color. William George, who is a white man, suf-

fered a decline in income and self-esteem when his manufacturing plant closed. In many ways, he has never recovered from that loss, which triggered reminders of childhood losses.

2. *Many business organizations have been downsizing.* In the transition to the current industrial era, the U.S. economic institution faced difficulties resulting from the shift to electronic technology. Industries based on the older technology were caught with expensive investments in manufacturing capacity at a time when markets were shrinking and low-cost competition from other parts of the world was increasing. U.S. corporations responded by **downsizing** for greater efficiency. White-collar workers became almost as vulnerable to layoffs as blue-collar workers, as corporations flattened their organizational structure by eliminating managerial positions (Bernstein, 1997; Levy, 1995). Public opinion surveys have indicated a widespread sense of job insecurity and a decreasing sense of loyalty to employers. Workers who survive corporate downsizing sometimes "jump ship" because they are unhappy with the increased workload that produces greater efficiencies (Bernstein, 1997). Levy (1995) predicts that unemployment for semiskilled workers will be a longer-term trend than for white-collar workers.

3. *Employers are upgrading and deskilling many jobs.* The manufacturing sector of the labor force includes many semiskilled and skilled blue-collar jobs. The service sector, on the other hand, is sharply divided between highly paid technical positions and poorly paid clerical, cleaning, and maintenance jobs. Many of the poorly paid jobs are the result of **deskilling**, or downgrading, as new technologies make the jobs more routine. Some of the well-paid jobs are the result of **skill upgrading**, in which technological and economic change create the need for workers to have more advanced training or to take additional responsibility. Researchers disagree about whether there is more deskilling or skill upgrading in the service sector, but they agree that the net result is sharp increases in socioeconomic inequality (Levy, 1995; Sassen, 1994).

4. *The contingent workforce is growing.* **Contingent work** is "any job in which workers lack an explicit or implicit contract for long-term employment or one in which the minimum hours vary unsystematically" (Reskin & Padavic, 1994, p. 168). Contingent workers include part-time employees, temporary employees, and independent contractors. They lack job security and usually receive no fringe benefits. In 1988, contingent workers comprised 25–30 percent of the labor force. In 1992, two-thirds of new jobs in the private sector were temporary jobs (Reskin & Padavic, 1994). There is general agreement that job security will remain elusive in the current industrial cycle (Bernstein, 1997; Levy, 1995). The job market for semiskilled workers is expected to stay weak, and workers of all educational levels are expected to be highly mobile in the labor market (Levy, 1995).

Conflict perspective

5. *Labor force diversity is increasing.* Women, minorities, and immigrants make up a growing segment of the labor force. Some sociologists consider the increase in labor force participation of women to be the most important social change in the contemporary era (for example, Caplow, 1991). Between 1960 and 1992, the percentage of the labor force that was female increased from 32 percent to 46 percent, and experts predict that the participation rates of women and men will continue to converge (Reskin & Padavic, 1994). This trend has enormous implications for social service programs that have been built on the model of a

family with a female caregiver at home. The labor force patterns by race and ethnicity are more complicated. Projections for change between 1990 and 2005 show whites dropping from 78.6 percent of the labor force to 73 percent, blacks increasing from 10.7 percent to 11.6 percent, and Hispanic Americans growing from 7.7 percent to 11.1 percent (Reskin & Padavic, 1994). African Americans, Asian Americans, and members of other ethnic groups are expected to account for approximately 35 percent of new entrants to the labor force between 1992 and 2005 (U.S. Department of Labor, 1994/1995). For most of the 20th century, the proportion of black women in the labor force exceeded the proportion of white women, but in 1993, the figures reversed: 57.9 percent of white women were in the labor force compared to 57.1 percent of black women. For the same year, the labor force participation of white men was 76.3 percent compared to 69.1 percent for black men. Hispanic men were even more likely than white men to be in the labor force, for one of two reasons: they are concentrated in service and farm jobs, or they live in regions of the country where the job market is stronger (Reskin & Padavic, 1994). As illustrated in Exhibit 8.5, historically, white men have earned more than either men of color or white women, and men of every race and ethnicity have earned more than women of the same race or ethnicity. In the period from 1975 to 1990, women slowly reduced the earnings gap with white men, but black men and Hispanic men lost ground. Most analysts agree that this shift is due to economic restructuring, and Reskin and Padavic (1994) report that the narrowing gap between men and women is due more to decreased wages for men than to increased wages for women.

EXHIBIT 8.5

Median Incomes of Full-Time, Year-Round Workers as a Percentage of White Men's Incomes, by Sex, Race, and Ethnic Origin, 1955–1990

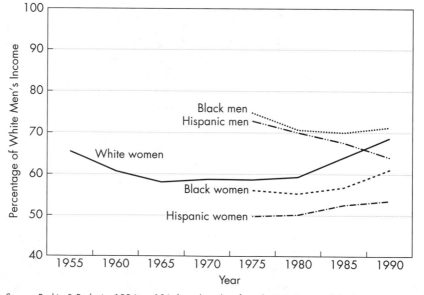

Source: Reskin & Padavic, 1994, p. 106; based on data from the U.S. Bureau of the Census, 1981, Table 67; U.S. Bureau of the Census, 1983, Tables 37 and 39; U.S. Bureau of the Census, 1988, Tables 27 and 29; U.S. Bureau of the Census, 1991, Table 24.

Social workers who participate in policy development must be informed about the serious challenges to job security in the contemporary era. Social workers are also called on to deal with many of the social problems arising out of these changes in the economic institution—problems such as inadequate resources for family caregiving, domestic violence, substance abuse, depression, and anxiety (Rose, 1997). Social workers attached to the workplace need to be skillful in influencing organizational policy and linking the work organization to the wider community, as well as in assessing specific worker situations.

Trends in Education

Conflict perspective

William George is a high school dropout in an era when educational attainment is becoming increasingly important in the labor market. The primary purpose of the **educational institution** is to pass along formal knowledge from one generation to the next—a function that was largely performed by the family, with some help from the church, until the 19th century. In the 20th century, the educational institution has become increasingly responsible for passing along values and behaviors to prepare students for roles as parents, citizens, workers, and consumers (Mare, 1995; Popple & Leighninger, 1993). The addition of these socializing functions has not been without controversy, however, and many people think that schools are now performing functions that would more appropriately be performed by family and religion. Perhaps unintentionally, schools have also become influential in determining who is economically successful and who is not, and thus in maintaining social inequality.

In the 20th century, average educational attainment has increased spectacularly in the United States (Caplow, 1991; Mare, 1995). At the beginning of the century, high school graduation was a privilege experienced only by an elite few, but over the next few decades high school education was extended to a majority of youth (Caplow et al., 1991). More recently, the percentage of adults with high school degrees has increased from 55 percent in 1970 to 81 percent in 1994. In the same period, the percentage of adults with college degrees has doubled, from 11 percent to 22 percent (Mare, 1995). From 1960 to 1975, the number of graduate degrees awarded in the United States increased almost fivefold, but the increase since 1975 has been much more gradual (Caplow, 1991).

Some educational inequalities have been reduced in the contemporary era, but others persist (Mare, 1995). In the 1980s, as elementary and secondary education became nearly universal, differences in educational attainment based on race and ethnicity almost disappeared at the elementary and secondary school levels. Today, however, race and ethnicity interact with income level to produce high dropout rates from secondary school, particularly among low-income students and Hispanic students (see Exhibit 8.6). Differences in access to and progress through a college education also persist. In the 1980s, women pulled ahead of men in the percentages continuing to college after high school, reached parity with men for college completion, and narrowed the substantial gap with men for receipt of graduate degrees.

Mare (1995) has studied the educational attainment of people born between 1940 and 1970, who make up the majority of the current labor force. As shown in Exhibit 8.7, he found racial and ethnic differences in completion of at least some postsecondary education. Mare emphasizes the immigration status of some ethnic groups because, as demonstrated here with His-

EXHIBIT 8.6

High School Dropout
Rate by Income and
Race/Ethnicity
(Ages 16–24), 1996

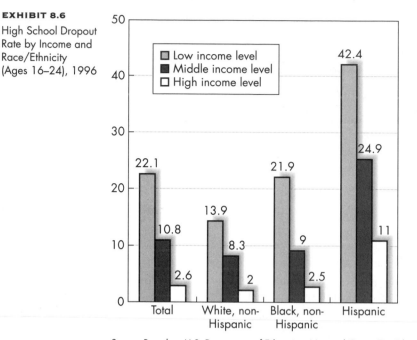

Source: Based on U.S. Department of Education, National Center For Educational Statistics, 1997.

panic Americans, foreign-born groups may have faced very different educational situations from native-born groups of the same ethnic heritage. He suggests that these racial and ethnic differences in school attainment will perpetuate economic inequalities related to race and ethnicity because the parents' attainment is a big factor in educational opportunities for the next generation. He reports that between 1980 and 1990, educational attainment probabilities grew substantially for Asian Americans and European Americans, but stayed the same for the other groups.

Conflict perspective
     Racial and ethnic differences in educational attainment have been exacerbated by trends in educational funding. In the 1980s, federal government support for elementary and secondary education was cut by about one-third, and state and local governments have needed to increase their support (Reich, 1992). The result has been growing disparities among states and among local school districts, as Jonathan Kozol so clearly chronicles in his book *Savage Inequalities: Children in America's Schools* (1991). In the deteriorating central cities, like the one where William George spent his teen years, poor and largely minority families, paying the higher tax rates common to urban areas, are sending their children to schools that are seriously substandard. Meanwhile, families in the wealthier suburbs, paying lower tax rates, have access to public schools with highly enriched programs. In 1997 data from Illinois, the average per pupil expenditure was $4,539 in the five most poorly funded high school districts in the state and $13,753 in the five best funded districts (IEA-NEA, 1997). The majority of the children in poorly funded school districts throughout the country are African American and Hispanic American. Even if they graduate from high school and continue into postsecondary education, they will not arrive at

EXHIBIT 8.7
Percentage of
Cohorts Born
1940–1970 with
Postsecondary
Schooling

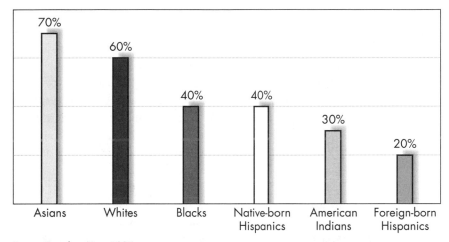

Source: Based on Mare, 1995.

college with equal preparation for success. They are further disadvantaged by the dramatic increases in tuition and fees that have been instituted over the past two decades (Caplow, 1991).

Studies in the 1980s reported that primary and secondary students in the United States were outperformed by students from most of the other advanced industrial countries, and the public school system came under attack throughout the 1980s and 1990s. In 1988, a subcommittee of the U.S. Congress formed to study the "Competitiveness and the Quality of the American Work Force" submitted a report titled *The Education Deficit* (Joint Economic Committee, 1989). The report concluded that the public school system was performing at the same level as it had 20 or 30 years earlier, but that this level was inadequate to the demands of the contemporary labor force. Levy (1995) suggests that, given the changes in the labor market, reforms are needed in the educational institution to provide better job skills for students who do not continue schooling beyond high school. Social workers should become active partners in efforts at educational reform, particularly in efforts that equalize educational opportunities.

Trends in Social Welfare

William George has a daily struggle to survive and feels despair about the manner in which he is performing the roles of father, partner, worker, and citizen. Where should he turn for help? As social workers, we are well aware of the network of social welfare agencies and programs that could help him. But others are not so aware, and there is thus some controversy about whether social welfare should be considered a social institution. It is included here because it meets Newman's definition of offering "patterned ways of solving problems and meeting the needs of a particular society."

Different writers have presented various definitions of the **social welfare institution,** but the definition provided by Philip Popple and Leslie Leighninger (1993) is particularly compatible with the definition of social institution used in this chapter: "Social welfare is the institution in modern industrial society that functions to promote interdependence and to deal with [issues] of dependence" (p. 36). Individuals are interdependent with institutions, as well as with other individuals, for survival and for satisfactory role performance. We depend on our doctors, day-care centers, families, friends, neighbors, and so on, and they depend on us. Sometimes, situations occur that increase our need for assistance or decrease the assistance available to us. For example, we may become sick or injured, lose our job, or take on a caregiving role for a new-born infant or a frail parent. In these situations, our ability to successfully fulfill role expectations is jeopardized—a situation that Popple and Leighninger refer to as dependence.

The social work profession and the social welfare institution developed when it became apparent that the existing institutions of family, religion, economy, and government were inadequate to the task of meeting dependency needs in a society that is organized as an industrialized market economy. At first, private service organizations were developed to meet dependency needs, but private organizations were soon followed by social welfare programs run by local governments. The social welfare institution grew dramatically after the federal government assumed social welfare responsibilities during the first administration of Franklin D. Roosevelt (1933–1937). Between 1929 and 1950, the combined state and federal expenditures for social welfare grew from just under $4 billion to nearly $24 billion (Popple & Leighninger, 1993). Since that time, the social welfare institution has grown enormously. A second wave of federal social welfare legislation was enacted from 1964 to 1966 under the administration of Lyndon Johnson, and by 1988 local, state, and federal governments spent more than $885 billion on social welfare programs (Caplow, 1991; Popple & Leighninger, 1993). In recent years, however, the social welfare institution has come under major attack, and concerted efforts have been made to reduce its size, or at least its government support.

The considerable controversy surrounding the social welfare institution involves complex attitudes. To help sort them out, Popple and Leighninger (1993) offer the following classification system:

Systems perspective

■ **Conservative perspective:** Social welfare is a backup system, not a social institution. In this view, families, usually the women in families, are responsible for providing personal care to dependent persons, such as children, frail elders, and people who are sick or disabled. It is assumed that the economic institution can be counted on to meet economic needs. When disruptions occur in either the family or the economy, religious institutions should provide aid to dependent persons. Only in the rare situations in which these core institutions cannot meet dependency needs do social welfare organizations have a role to play, and then they should provide assistance only on a temporary basis. Wilensky and Lebeaux (1958) refer to this view as a **residual approach** to social welfare.

Rational choice perspective

■ **Liberal perspective:** Social welfare is a frontline institution necessary to promote interdependence and deal with problems of dependence. In this view, modern societies are too complex, fragmented, and unstable for families, economic institutions, and religious institutions to cope with on their own. Although the risk factors and the patterns of dependence will continue to change with changes in other core institutions, people will continue to need the assistance of the social welfare institution. Wilensky and Lebeaux (1958) refer to this view as an **institutional approach** to social welfare.

Conflict perspective

■ **Radical perspective.** The social welfare institution is a deliberate attempt by persons in positions of power—typically referred to as the power elite—to placate and control less powerful members of society, thus preventing revolutionary attempts to redistribute power and material resources. This view is based on the influential work of Piven and Cloward (1971).

For much of the 20th century, the liberal perspective on social welfare has been dominant; it is this perspective that produced the expansion of the social welfare institution. In the past few years, however, the conservative perspective has prevailed. Dionne (1996) argues that current attempts to downsize the social welfare institution do not reflect a true liberal-to-conservative shift. Opinion poll data indicate that people *do* want government to be involved in an organized way to promote interdependence and deal with problems of dependence; they simply do not believe in the ability of government to do so effectively. Dionne suggests that this loss of confidence is realistic because the social welfare institution, like the government institution, has failed to keep pace with changes in the family and economic institutions. Each stage of industrialization brings its own possibilities and threats, and we have not yet built a good understanding of both the possibilities and the threats of the current era of industrialization.

Building this understanding is the current challenge for the social work profession, and perhaps this chapter will help you to think in new ways about how the social welfare institution and our profession can be effective. Dionne predicts that once we have a better understanding of the current stage, a new progressive era will begin. To be active partners in that new progressive era, social workers must clearly understand trends in the interrelated social institutions discussed in this chapter.

Trends in Health Care

Although sociologists do not usually identify health care as a social institution, Newman (1995) argues that it has become a major social institution in modern industrial societies. The **health care institution** is the primary institution for promoting the general health of a society.

Newman (1995) proposes that any society's health care institution, like its other institutions, is influenced by culture. He suggests that health care in the United States reflects the "aggressive 'can do' spirit" (p. 83) of the mainstream culture. Compared to European physicians, U.S. physicians recommend more routine examinations, prescribe more drugs, order more X rays and other diagnostic tests, and perform more surgery (Caplow, 1991; Newman, 1995). Psychiatrists in the United States often give a diagnosis of clinical depression for situations that British psychiatrists see as normal (Newman, 1995). Although alternative forms of health care have become more respectable in the United States in recent years, they are still considered more suspect in the United States than in European countries (Caplow, 1991). Coombs and Capper (1996) report that the rapid growth in **therapeutic medicine**—diagnosing and treating disease—has drained resources from the U.S. **public health system,** which focuses on disease prevention and health promotion.

Currently, the health care institution is in a state of flux. Health care in the United States has mainly been organized around two principles: **fee-for-service,** or paying for each visit to a health care provider, and **employment-based insurance,** or obtaining health insurance through one's employer (Gorin & Moniz, 1997). The problem is that this organization of the health care institution prohibits access to health care for some groups. In response to this concern, the U.S. Congress enacted Medicare and Medicaid in 1965 to provide government funding for health care for older adults, people with disabilities, and people living in poverty.

Since that time, the U.S. health care institution has grown and medical technology has advanced tremendously (Caplow et al., 1991). The costs of health care have thus increased dramatically. The percentage of GNP spent on health care increased from 4 percent in 1950 to 13 percent in 1993 (Caplow et al., 1991; Popple & Leighninger, 1993). Today, per capita expenditure on health care in the United States far exceeds that in other industrialized countries (Caplow, 1991; Caplow et al., 1991).

Efforts to contain the rapidly increasing costs of health care began in the 1970s. During the early 1990s, managed care plans, many of which operate on a for-profit basis, became popular. **Managed care** replaces fee-for-service with a system of **capitation,** in which health care organizations are paid according to the number of people in the system, not the number of services provided. By 1997, Gorin and Moniz (1997) report, two-thirds of insured workers were in managed care plans, and three-fourths of U.S. physicians worked in managed care networks.

Conflict perspective   Although the fee-for-service principle of health care delivery has been decimated, the principle of employment-based insurance has not been rejected. Levy (1995) proposes that obtaining health insurance through employers is poorly suited to the current industrial cycle, with its low job security and high workforce mobility. U.S. Census data indicate that 13.9 percent of the U.S. population was without health insurance in 1990; by 1996, this figure had increased to 15.6 percent (U.S. Bureau of the Census, 1998). Among poor persons, 30 percent are uninsured. Many are like William George, who has several chronic health problems but whose only source of health care is the hospital emergency room, because he lacks health insurance. Lacking the means to get good preventive care and to live healthfully, poor people are more likely than others to suffer from "trauma, infection, chronic disease, and malnutrition" (Newman, 1995, p. 349); they go to the hospital more often and have longer stays. Evans and Stoddart (1994) report that health status is closely linked to educational achievement, employment experiences, family support, and the physical environment. The early evidence suggests that people with chronic illnesses, poor people, and older adults may not fare well in a for-profit managed health care system (Gorin & Moniz, 1997).

The near future of health care delivery in the United States is uncertain. In 1994, Congress failed to pass a plan that included universal coverage. For-profit managed care subsequently became the dominant form of health care delivery. Growing public disillusionment with the quality of this form of health care is reflected in the popular media, evidenced by frequent newspaper cartoons and jabs in TV shows and movies (for example, the disparaging comment about an HMO in the 1997 movie *As Good as It Gets).*

Social workers must ensure that the voices of poor and other oppressed people are included in the public dialogue about health care reform. In the past, health care social work has been situated in hospitals, but managed care seeks to contain the use of hospitalization. Gorin and Moniz (1997, p. 159) are nonetheless optimistic about expanded roles for social workers in the health care institution—as health planners, counselors, educators, advocates, and health promotion experts—in such settings as public health departments, community-based clinics, health centers, and health networks.

Trends in Mass Media

In a democratic society with a capitalistic economy, the **mass media institution** is the primary institution for managing the flow of information, images, and ideas among all members of society. This view is controversial among media scholars (see Curran, 1996), but it cannot be denied that rapid advances in electronic communication technology since the 1950s have resulted in widespread access to multiple forms of mass communication, including newspapers, periodicals, books, radio, television, movies, videocassettes, audiocassettes, compact disks, telephones, fax machines, computer networks, and electronic mail. Electronic media now allow two-way communication, as well as one-way communication, and can store and manipulate vast amounts of information (Caplow, et al., 1991; Griswold, 1994).

In totalitarian societies, the flow of information, images, and ideas is controlled by the ruling class. In the United States, we have a long tradition of freedom of the press—a belief that the media must be free to serve as a public watchdog. Traditionally, the emphasis has been on the watchdog role in relation to the government and political institution. Exposure of the Watergate cover-up during the Nixon presidency is considered a high point in U.S. media history. However, the relationship between government and media is controversial, with some groups calling for more government censorship (for example, to limit children's access to pornography) and other groups calling for strict adherence to freedom of the press (Newman, 1995). Increasingly, however, the government and political institution feels pressured to compete with other "would-be opinion makers" (Blumler & Gurevitch, 1996, p. 127)—such as social movements and multinational corporations—for influence with the media. Chapter 12 discusses the important role of the mass media in the mobilization of social movements.

Conflict perspective

Recently, concern about media censorship has centered on censorship by the economic institution (Bagdikian, 1997; Curran, 1996; Newman, 1995). A mergers and acquisitions boom in the media institution during the past three decades has resulted in powerful media conglomerates, with ownership concentrated in the hands of a few individuals and corporations. Rupert Murdoch's News Corporation, for example, is a multinational corporation with global power (Curran, 1996). Increasingly, media organizations are owned by parent companies that do business in areas other than media, and Bagdikian (1997) presents evidence that media organizations sometimes refrain from critical investigation of the giant conglomerates that own them.

Social psychologists have been interested in the effects of the media on human behavior, focusing particularly on the effects of television, which has become the dominant form of mass media communication. In the United States, 98 percent of households have at least one television set (Caplow et al., 1991), and 66 percent of people regularly watch television while eating dinner (Watson, 1996). The average child in the United States watches 28 hours of television weekly and, over the course of a year, spends more time in front of the television than in school (Watson, 1996). Research on the effects of the media on human behavior is difficult to design, because it is difficult to isolate the effects of specific media forms in changing person/environment configurations and to capture the cumulative effect of multiple forms. Although the existing research thus contains many contradictions, media scholars agree on a few basic, consistent findings (Livingstone, 1996):

- The effect of the media on human behavior is small, when other factors are considered.
- The influence of TV on human behavior increases as time spent watching increases.
- Children and adolescents are more influenced by media presentations than adults.
- Some people are more affected by media presentations than others.

Social behavioral perspective

Although it is possible for the media to influence human behavior in both positive and negative ways, the research has focused, for the most part, on negative effects. Social workers and other professionals have been particularly concerned that television provides more models of antisocial than prosocial behavior. Feminists have been concerned about the influence of gender role stereotypes presented in the media (Ang & Hermes, 1996). Members of racial and ethnic minority groups, the disability community, and the gay and lesbian community have also been concerned about stereotypical media presentations of their groups (Croteau & Hoynes, 1997; Newman, 1995). William George has been heard to quip, "Yeah, I'm just like every other crackhead you see on TV." This remark not only indicates the pervasive influence of media images; it also exemplifies the media's tendency to negatively stereotype the poor and powerless. Mass media critics suggest that control of the media by political and economic elites results in control of cultural meanings to benefit elites and silence dissident views (Curran, 1996; Livingstone, 1996). The mass media have historically been controlled by white, middle- and upper-class men, who have presented their worldviews (Croteau & Hoynes, 1997) Croteau and Hoynes (1997) also provide evidence that mass media owners are interested in attracting affluent consumers and choose content with this aim in mind. Other media scholars, however, emphasize that media consumers are not passive recipients but active interpreters of the messages received, synthesizing messages from a variety of sources and thus keeping media images in perspective (Livingstone, 1996). Social workers can help by working collaboratively with other groups to influence media coverage of vulnerable populations and patterns of social inequality.

Social Structure and Social Inequality

The profession of social work has historically made a commitment to persons and groups who are disadvantaged in the distribution of resources by social institutions. That commitment has been reaffirmed in recent years by the major professional organizations. To carry out this commitment, we must have a way of understanding social inequality and its influence on human behavior. Throughout this chapter, I have presented information on how social inequality is created and maintained in eight interrelated major social institutions. This section summarizes recent trends in social inequality in the United States and discusses theories of inequality.

EXHIBIT 8.8

Ranking of Social
Inequality in
Ten Advanced
Industrial Countries

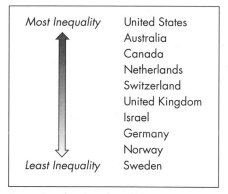

Most Inequality   United States
                    Australia
                    Canada
                    Netherlands
                    Switzerland
                    United Kingdom
                    Israel
                    Germany
                    Norway
Least Inequality Sweden

Source: Based on Smeeding, 1991.

Trends in Social Inequality

Social class is the term generally used by sociologists to describe "structures of inequality in modern societies" (Crompton, 1993, p. 21). In an analysis of trend data, Caplow et al. (1991) contend that "a high degree of economic inequality has characterized the United States from its beginning" (p. 185). Until recently, it was difficult to compare inequality in the United States to that in other advanced industrial countries because of a lack of comparable cross-national data on household income. But Smeeding (1991) has assembled a comprehensive data set for 10 advanced industrial countries that shows the United States to have the highest degree of inequality, as well as the highest rate of overall poverty. Exhibit 8.8 shows the ranking of the 10 countries studied, moving from the country with greatest inequality to the country with the least inequality.

In the period 1947–1973, income inequality in the United States declined slightly. Since 1974, however, income inequality has grown substantially (Larin & McNichol, 1997; Levy, 1995). A recent analysis of income trends in the United States found that, when adjusted for inflation, the average incomes of families in the lowest income group, the bottom fifth, fell by more than 20 percent; average incomes for families in the middle fifth fell by about 2 percent; and incomes for families in the top fifth increased by about 30 percent (Larin & McNichol, 1997). This long-term trend toward inequality has continued in recent years, a period of economic growth, for several reasons (Larin & McNichol, 1997; Levy, 1995):

- The value of the minimum wage decreased by 18 percent during this period.

- Government policies undermined the ability of labor unions to advocate for education and training.

- There were cutbacks in unemployment insurance (Larin & McNichol, 1997).

- Incomes of less-educated workers fell, and extremely high incomes grew (Levy, 1995). The gap in wages was particularly large among men.

- The number of high-income dual-earner couples, increased, as did the number of low-income single-parent families.

The distribution of wealth in the United States is far more uneven than the distribution of income (Caplow, 1991; Levy, 1995). A small number of individuals and households have financial assets in the billions, and a large number of individuals and households have negative net worth. These trends have been exacerbated by **regressive tax policies**—taking a higher proportion of lower incomes—at the federal and state level, which have become increasingly more regressive since the 1970s.

In the contemporary era, socioeconomic status is related to race and ethnicity, age, gender, parental status, and geographic location. In the 1960s and 1970s, African Americans made substantial progress in the labor market and narrowed the income gap with European Americans; in the 1970s, recent college graduates of both groups received approximately equal wages. Since the 1970s, however, the income gap between blacks and whites of similar age and education has widened again (Levy, 1995). Hispanic Americans do only slightly better than African Americans. Although the majority of households living below the poverty level are white—71 percent in 1960, 66 percent in 1990—black and Hispanic households are about three times as likely to be poor as white households (U.S. Bureau of the Census, 1992, p. 456).

This overrepresentation of African Americans and Hispanic Americans among the poor should not be taken to mean that all black and Hispanic families are poor. The representation of African Americans in the highest quintile for income tripled between 1949 and 1984 (Caplow et al., 1991). However, by 1990, African Americans and Hispanic Americans were still underrepresented in the highest income quintile, which included 21 percent of white households, 9 percent of black households, and 10 percent of Hispanic households (U.S. Bureau of the Census, 1992, p. 448). Although whites still outearn blacks, the current pattern of income inequality is similar among blacks and whites, with a recent tendency for slightly greater inequality of income among blacks. By 1987, within the African American community, the poorest quintile received less than 5 percent and the top quintile more than 48 percent of all income earned by African Americans (Caplow et al., 1991).

Over the past 50 years, vulnerability to poverty has shifted from older adults to children. Between 1949 and 1990, the proportion of the elderly population living in poverty decreased from nearly half to 12 percent (Caplow, 1991). In contrast, the proportion of children living in poverty rose from 15 percent in 1970 to 20 percent in 1990 (U.S. Bureau of the Census, 1992, p. 456). Among the elderly population, however, single persons—three out of four of whom are women—are still vulnerable to poverty, with 25 percent of unrelated older persons living in poverty in 1990, compared to 6 percent of older persons living in families (U.S. Bureau of the Census, 1992, p. 457). Among children, those living in single-parent, mother-only families are particularly vulnerable to poverty. In 1990, 61 percent of children living in mother-only families lived in poverty (U.S. Bureau of the Census, 1992, p. 457). William George is ashamed that his children fit this trend.

In the contemporary era, childbearing has become more discretionary than in previous eras, and fertility rates for married couples have dropped. In the advanced industrial state, unlike in the earlier agrarian state, children are an economic liability, and socioeconomic status is negatively affected by increasing family size. Smeeding's (1991) cross-national analysis found that the least represented group among the well-to-do, with the exceptions of single parents and single older persons, are two-parent families with a large number of children. In fact, data from the 10 advanced industrial countries studied by Smeeding indicate that more than half of all childless couples, on average, are well-to-do. Because of the collective interests at stake in the adequate socialization of the next generation of wage earners, some European countries have developed policies that provide incentives for having children (Caldwell, Stiehr, Modell, & Del Campo, 1994).

In 1970, poverty was primarily a rural problem. By 1990, poverty was much more of an urban problem, with 42 percent of poor people in the United States living in central cities. In 1990, almost one out of three central city children was poor (Levy, 1995). However, the geographic distribution of poor families varies with race and ethnicity. In 1990, approximately 80 percent of non-Hispanic white poor people lived in suburbs of large metropolitan areas, in smaller metropolitan areas, and in rural nonmetropolitan areas. The vast majority of black poor households, on the other hand, were in central cities. Poor black families are much more likely than poor white families to live in "concentrated poverty neighborhoods" (Frey, 1990), where social and economic isolation have severe consequences. Sassen (1994) suggests that the structure of jobs in the service economy is likely to lead to increasing economic polarization in central cities.

Theories of Social Inequality

Perhaps no question regarding the human condition has generated more intense and complex controversies and conflicts than the related issues of inequality and distributive justice. Unequal distribution of resources is probably as old as the human species and certainly has existed in all complex societies. Long before the discipline of sociology arose, thoughtful people constructed explanations and justifications for these inequalities (Crompton, 1993; Lenski, 1966). Although social class has been an important topic for sociology, by no means do sociologists agree about the role that social class plays in human behavior.

Historical Theories of Social Inequality. Early Hebrew prophets, writing about 800 B.C., denounced the rich and powerful members of society not only for their use of wealth and power but also for the means used in achieving them (see, for example, the second and third chapters of Micah). A very different view is found in the *Laws of Manu,* compiled by Hindu priests about 200 B.C., where social inequalities and caste systems are considered to be divinely ordained for the good of the world. Although both of these viewpoints have been present for recorded time, the view of inequality as the "natural order" or as divinely ordained has dominated in preindustrial societies, both past and present (Crompton, 1993; Lenski, 1966).

In the classical Greek period, Plato, in his effort to describe the ideal state, noted that people are born with innate differences in capabilities and suggested that a division of labor should be based on what each person is best fitted to do. He saw inequality as inevitable but proposed ways to alter the distribution of money, status, and power in pursuit of the collective "ideal state" and individual "good life." Plato regarded the family as the key support of institutionalized inequality because individuals are motivated to secure for family members, for whom they feel familial affection, any privileges that they have attained for themselves. He argued that the only way to ensure an egalitarian society was to take children from parents and have the state raise them. He demonstrated his distrust of power and privilege when he suggested that members of the ruling group should be prohibited from holding private property so that they would not be motivated by personal gain in the discharge of their duties (Plato, 1968). Aristotle, Plato's student, reacted against some of the radical positions of his teacher, asserting that "there are by nature free men and slaves, and that servitude is just and agreeable for the latter" (quoted in Dahrendorf, 1969, p. 18).

The Christian religious tradition has vacillated regarding the justice of inequality. Lenski's (1966) historical review suggests that leaders and scholars of the medieval Church saw inequality as a necessary prerequisite for the well-being of society. From the 12th century on, however, a succession of religious movements that criticized wealth and commended poverty flourished. This tradition influenced the development of the social work profession.

According to many scholars, the English revolution of 1648 signaled the demise of a philosophy of inequality as the natural order and the ascent of a philosophy of equality. The philosophy of social equality fostered two major revolutions, the American and the French, and a massive international political movement, socialism. Equality of political rights, and not of economic status, was the primary objective of the American and French revolutions. But Alexis de Tocqueville (1835/1945) argued that once the idea of equality caught hold, it was irresistible and created greater pressure for economic egalitarianism. Currently we face the paradox of pressure toward greater equality, as in the feminist and disability movements, along with the breakdown of socialist experiments.

Classical Sociological Theories of Social Inequality.   When social inequality was considered to be the "natural order" and divinely ordained, there was no need to search further for explanations of inequality. But as this traditional assumption gave way to a belief that human beings are born equal, persistent social inequalities required explanation and justification. Explanation of inequality and its relationship to human behavior became central questions for the emerging social and political sciences. Two classical theorists, Karl Marx (1818–1883) and Max Weber (1864–1920) have had lasting impact on the sociological analysis of social inequality. The following discussion of the theoretical perspectives of Marx and Weber draws heavily on the analysis by Rosemary Crompton (1993).

Marx was both a social theorist and a committed revolutionary. He was interested in explaining the social inequalities of industrial capitalism, but his interests went beyond explanation of inequality to promotion of a more just and equitable society. Marx emphasized the economic determinants of social class relationships and proposed that class lines are drawn according to roles in the capitalist production system. Although he did not propose a strict two-class system, he suggested a social class division based on a dichotomy of owners and controllers of production (bourgeoisie), on the one hand, and workers who must sell their labor to owners (proletariat), on the other. Marx saw the relationship between the classes to be based on exploitation and domination by the owners and controllers of production and alienation among the workers. He saw social class as a central variable in human behavior and a central force in human history and believed that **class consciousness**—not only the awareness of one's social class, but also hostility toward other classes—is what motivates people to transform society.

In contrast to Marx, who was a committed revolutionary, Weber argued for a value-free social science. Weber differed from Marx in other ways, as well. Marx saw a class division based on production roles (owners of production and workers); Weber saw a class division based on "life chances" in the marketplace. **Life chances** reflect the distribution of power within a community. Instead of Marx's dichotomous class system, Weber proposed that life chances fall on a continuum, and that the great variability found along the continuum reflects the multiple sources of power. Weber saw property, skills, and education as primary among these sources. Social class is an important variable in human behavior but not, as Marx believed, the primary variable. This difference in perspective on the causal importance of social class reflects the theorists' disagreement about the inevitability of class consciousness or class action. Marx saw class consciousness and communal action related to class as inevitable. Weber saw social class as a possible, but not inevitable; source of identity and communal action.

Systems perspective

Functionalism versus Conflict Theory. Attempts to determine the cause of persistent social inequalities have led to a debate among sociologists who embrace functional theories and sociologists who embrace conflict theories. Functional theories of social stratification present structural inequality (social classes) as necessary for society. According to this view, unequal rewards for different types of work guarantee that the most talented persons will work hard and produce technological innovation to benefit the whole society. The following quote from Kingsley Davis, a major functionalist theorist, presents the extreme functional position: "Social inequality is thus an unconsciously evolved device by which societies insure that the most important positions are conscientiously filled by the most qualified person" (Davis, 1949, p. 367). Functionalists assume a broad consensus about which positions deserve superior rewards, which maintains social stability. This theoretical perspective was dominant in American sociology during the 1940s and 1950s, but has faded in importance since then. It continues to be reflected, however, in the contemporary political institution.

Conflict perspective

Conflict theorists, on the other hand, emphasize the role of power, domination, and coercion in the maintenance of inequality (for example, Collins, 1971; Dahrendorf, 1959; Rex, 1961). According to this view, persons with superior wealth and income also hold superior social and political power and use that power to protect their privileged positions. Conflict theorists suggest that decisions about which positions should receive superior rewards are determined by persons with power, not by a broad consensus. Marx predicted that structural inequality would lead to tensions that ultimately produce a revolt by persons at the bottom of the hierarchical structure, and an overthrow of industrial capitalism. Many conflict theorists who do not share Marx's view of the inevitability of the overthrow of industrial capitalism nevertheless agree that inherent tensions related to structures of inequality lead to instability rather than consensus and stability. John Hagan is representative of these theorists. In his book *Crime and Disrepute* (1994), he presents evidence that high rates of street crime, which he considers a sign of social instability, are more common in societies with high levels of inequality.

Humanistic perspective

Structural Determinism versus Human Agency. Will knowledge of my social class position help you to predict my attitudes and behaviors? That question, which is highly relevant to social workers, has become a controversial one for contemporary social science. Social scientists who see human behavior as highly determined by one's position in the social class structure (**structural determinism**) are challenged by social scientists who emphasize the capacity of humans to create their own realities and who give central roles to human actors, not social structures **(human agency)**. Crompton (1993) suggests that this debate is related to several other debates that have fragmented contemporary sociology and have contributed to a general criticism that social class is no longer an important variable in determining a person's attitudes and behavior.

Remember that classical sociology took a very focused approach to the question of structural determinism. Both Marx and Weber asked only whether class consciousness is inevitable. Much of the debate about structural determinism has centered on this question, and not the more general question of how influential social class is on human behavior. Those who suggest that social class is no longer important in social life point out that contemporary social movements are centered around issues other than social class—issues such as the environment, world peace, gender, race, and morality. However, a wealth of contemporary social science research has reported social class as an important, though not singular, predictor of a range of attitudes and behaviors (Crompton, 1993). You will see these findings reflected throughout this book.

The debate about structural determinism is complicated by the lack of an agreed on classification system for social class. Most contemporary attempts to develop classification systems have been based on occupation (such as Dahrendorf, 1959), but this method has been criticized as too simplistic, giving rise to several problems:

- The inability to capture total wealth, which is not necessarily derived from occupation
- The question of where to locate women in occupational schemes based on the structure of "male" jobs
- The question of how to classify households with dual careers
- The question of how to capture impaired "life chances" based on racial discrimination
- The question of how to classify the many lower-level positions in the service sector

However, although occupational schemes are not comprehensive measures of social inequality, research indicates that occupation remains the single best measure of material advantage and disadvantage and is significantly associated with a range of attitudes and behavior (Crompton, 1993).

In recent years, a strong voice within sociology has argued that class is becoming increasingly irrelevant in advanced industrial states. According to this argument, stratification systems tend to converge in advanced industrial states because of the growth of more middle-class occupations in the service sector. As you may recall from the earlier discussion of trends in social inequality, current evidence points to further polarization rather than convergence. According to this line of argument, however, as the standard of living rises in these advanced industrial states and as basic needs become easier to meet, social class as measured by what you produce (occupation) becomes irrelevant, and **lifestyle** as measured by the products you consume (consumption) becomes most important. This argument is consistent with social science perspectives that argue for a cultural approach rather than a structural approach to understanding human behavior. Researchers have, in fact, found strong associations between occupational class and patterns of consumption (Crompton, 1993).

Social constructionist perspective

The discussion of the relationship between social structure and human behavior has often turned into a debate between structural determinists and cultural determinists, but attempts have been made in recent years to understand the mutual influences of structure, culture, and behavior. These attempts are consistent with the transactional perspective of this book, which suggests that both structure and culture are important and that they influence each other in dynamic transactions. Unequal material advantage is a social fact, but it is a fact about which people construct meanings—and the meanings that people construct will have some impact on future structures of material advantage. David Lockwood's (1966) analysis of the inseparable nature of structure and culture helps to explain the persistent findings of an association between social class and a range of attitudes and behaviors. According to Lockwood, individuals "visualise the . . . structure of their society from the vantage points of their own particular *milieu*, and their perceptions of the larger society will vary according to their experiences . . . in the smaller societies in which they live out their daily lives" (Lockwood, 1966, p. 249). Therefore, specific locations in the social structure will have some association with specific societal images or worldviews. This is not to say that social class alone determines worldview; a transactional perspective suggests that other factors, such as race, ethnicity, religion, gender, community, and family, mediate the effects of social class.

IMPLICATIONS FOR SOCIAL WORK PRACTICE

The trends in social institutions and social structure discussed in this chapter suggest several principles for social work practice. The practice principles have greatest relevance for social work planning and administration, but some are relevant for direct social work practice as well.

- Develop adequate information retrieval skills to keep abreast of trends in the interrelated social institutions, and the impact of these trends on human interdependence and dependence.

- Review social service programs serving children, older adults, and other dependent persons to ensure that they are responsive to changes in the family and kinship institution, as well as the economic institution.

- Be aware of the role that religious congregations play in social service delivery and the role that religion plays in the lives of clients.

- Monitor the impact of public policies on poverty and inequality.

- Learn to use political processes to promote social services that contribute to the well-being of individuals and communities.

- Be particularly aware of the impact of trends in the economic institution on client resources and functioning.

- When providing services in the workplace, become skillful in influencing organizational policy and linking the work organization to the wider community.

- Collaborate with other social workers and human service providers to advocate for greater equality of opportunity in the educational institution.

- Consider the extent to which contemporary social welfare programs, especially those with which you are personally involved, are "imperfect solutions to past problems" and how responsive they are to recent changes in the other major social institutions.

- Take the lead in public discourse about the fit between the current social welfare institution and trends in the other major social institutions.

- Work to ensure that the voices of poor and other oppressed people are included in public dialogue about health care reform.

- Collaborate with other social workers and human service providers to influence media coverage of vulnerable populations and patterns of social inequality.

MAIN POINTS

1. Social institutions are patterned ways of solving the problems and meeting the requirements of a particular society.

2. Social structure is a set of interrelated social institutions developed by human beings to impose constraints on human interaction for the purpose of the survival and well-being of the collectivity.

3. Social institutions are relatively stable but also changing. Most of the major U.S. social institutions have undergone extraordinary changes from 1960 to the present.

4. The family and kinship institution is primarily responsible for the regulation of procreation, for the initial socialization of new members of society, and for mutual support. Four important and far-reaching trends in the family and kinship institution have emerged in the contemporary era: childbearing became discretionary, unmarried cohabitation was no longer legally prohibited, no-fault divorce became accessible, and large numbers of mothers of young children entered the paid labor force.

5. The religious institution is the primary institution for answering questions about the meaning and purpose of life. Religion has remained very important in American life, but people's social attitudes and behavior differ based on religious affiliation.

6. The government and political institution is responsible for how decisions are made and enforced for the society as a whole. Five notable trends in the government and political institution from 1960 to the present are expansion of federal authority, loss of public confidence in government and politics, commercialization of political cam-

paigns, increasing role of political action committees, and increasing diversity among political leaders.

7. The economic institution has the primary responsibility for regulating the production, distribution, and consumption of goods and services. Five important recent trends in the labor market are expected to continue into the 21st century: economic restructuring, downsizing, upgrading and deskilling, increase in contingent workforce, and increasing diversity of workforce.

8. The primary purpose of the educational institution is to pass along formal knowledge from one generation to the next. Some educational inequalities have been reduced in the contemporary era, but others persist.

9. The purpose of the social welfare institution is to promote interdependence and deal with issues of dependence. Three perspectives on the social welfare institution are conservative, liberal, and radical.

10. The health care institution is the primary social institution for promoting the general health of a society. The health care institution has grown tremendously since 1960, but attempts to control runaway health care costs and to guarantee health care for all persons have been unsuccessful to date.

11. The mass media institution is the primary institution for managing the flow of information, images, and ideas in a democratic society.

12. Income inequality in the United States has increased sharply since 1980.

13. Sociologists have tried to answer two questions about the relationship between social class and human behavior: What is the cause of persistent social inequality? To what extent can human attitudes and behaviors be explained by social class position?

KEY TERMS

broker model
capitation
class consciousness
conservative perspective
contingent work
deskilling
downsizing
economic institution
economic restructuring
educational institution
employment-based insurance

family and kinship institution
fee-for-service
government and political institution
health care institution
human agency
institutional approach
liberal perspective
life chances
lifestyle
managed care
mass media institution

political action committees (PACs)
Political Action for Candidate Election (PACE)
public health system
radical perspective
regressive tax policies
religious institution
residual approach
skill upgrading

social class
social institution
social structure
social welfare institution
status
structural determinism
therapeutic medicine
work

WORLD WIDE WEB RESOURCES

Social Inequality and Classes
http://www.pscw.uva.nl/sociosite/TOPICS/Inequality.html
Site maintained by the University of Amsterdam Department of Sociology. Contains many links
to information on social inequalities, social stratification, classes, and poverty. Site is in English.

DSS Links
http://www.runet.edu/~lridener/DSS/race.html
Site written by Radford University Sociology professor Larry Ridener. Contains many links to information on racial inequality, gender inequality, age inequality, social class and poverty, social structure and social interaction, and politics.

Allyn & Bacon Sociology Links: Social Class and Poverty
http://www.abacon.com/sociology/soclinks/sclass.html
Site maintained by Allyn & Bacon Publishers. Contains links to sites on social class, poverty, homelessness, hunger, inequality, and welfare reform.

CHAPTER 9

Culture

Linwood Cousins, Western Michigan University

STAN AND TINA AT COMMUNITY HIGH SCHOOL

Community High School in Newark, New Jersey, has approximately 1300 students, the majority of whom are black (African American, Afro-Caribbean, and West African). Most of the students live in the community of Village Park, which has a total population of approximately 58,000 people, also predominantly black. Village Park has a distinct social history and identity as well as distinct physical boundaries that distinguish it from less prosperous communities and schools in Newark.

Village Park evolved from a middle- and working-class Jewish community that centered around its academic institutions, such as Community High. The school generated a national reputation for academic excellence as measured by the number of graduates who went on to become doctors, lawyers, scientists, professors, and the like. But after the Newark riots of the late 1960s, Jews and other whites started moving out. By the early 1970s, upwardly mobile middle- and working-class black families had become the majority in the community. The same process has occurred in other communities, but what's interesting about Village Park is that its black residents, like the Jewish residents who preceded them, continued to believe in the ethic of upward mobility through schooling at Community High.

Since the mid-1980s, however, Village Park and Community High have undergone another transformation. Slumps in the economy and ongoing patterns of racial discrimination in employment have reduced the income base of the community's families. Many families who were able to maintain a middle-class income moved to the suburbs as crime and economic blight encroached on the community. Increasingly, Village Park was taken over by renters and absentee landlords, along with the social problems—drug abuse, crime, school dropout—that accompany economically driven social despair.

Today the population profile of Newark presents an interesting ethnic mix: The city is simultaneously black and multiethnic. In 1993, the majority of Newark's residents were African American, but the city had a considerable population of other ethnic groups: Hispanics (Puerto Ricans, Colombians, Mexicans, Dominicans, and so on), Italians, Portuguese, Africans (from Nigeria, Sierra Leone, Liberia, Ghana, and other countries), Polish, and small groups of others. At the same time, the governing bodies of the city, the school system, and Community High in particular are predominantly composed of black people.

The intermingling of such history and traditions has had an interesting impact on the students at Community High. Like many urban high schools all over the nation, Community High has suffered disproportionate levels of dropout, low attendance, and violence. Yet a few parents, teachers, school staff, and

CASE STUDY

community officials have tried hard to rekindle the spirit of academic excellence and social competence that are parts of the school's tradition.

In this context, many of the students resist traditional definitions of academic success but value success nonetheless. Consider the behaviors of Stan and Tina, both students at Community High. Stan is the more troubled and more academically marginal of the two students. He is 17 years old, lives with his girlfriend who has recently had a baby, and has made a living selling drugs (which he is now trying to discontinue). Stan was arrested (and released) for selling drugs some time ago. He is also under questioning for the drug-related murder of his cousin because the police want him to identify the perpetrator. But Stan has considerable social prestige at school, and is academically successful when he attends school and is on focus. Stan's mother—who has hammered into his head the importance of education—is a clerical supervisor, his stepfather works in a meat factory, and his biological father sells drugs. Stan has three brothers, and his mother and biological father were never married.

Among his male and female peers, Stan is considered the epitome of urban maleness and style. Stan is an innovator. He mixes and matches the square-toe motorcycle boots normally associated with white bikers with the Tommy Hilfiger shirts and brand-name jeans commonly associated with urban, rap-oriented young people of color. At the same time, Stan is respected by teachers and administrators because he understands and observes the rules of conduct preferred in the classroom and because he can do his work at a level reflecting high intelligence. A couple of months ago, Stan visited Howard University in Washington, D.C., and was smitten by the idea that young black men and women were participating in university life. He says he will try very hard to go to that school after he graduates, but the odds are against him.

Tina is also 17 years old, but is more academically successful than Stan is. She ranks in the top 25 of her senior class and has been accepted into the premed program of a historically black university. Tina talks about the lower academic performance of some of her peers as something associated with being black. On the other hand, Tina also sees her successful academic performance, level of motivation, and assertive style of interacting in the classroom as part of being black.

Tina's father is an engineer, and her stepmother is a restaurant manager. Tina has never known her biological mother, and as an only child she was raised primarily by her father until about six years ago. They moved to Village Park from Brooklyn, New York, around that time. Tina's is the kind of family that is likely to leave Village Park not for the suburbs, but for a more productive and less hostile urban community. Tina has been raised in a community that, despite its ills, centers around black identity and culture. Like Stan, Tina is an innovator. She has been allowed to incorporate modes of language, demeanor, and clothing that are seen by some as decidedly mainstream in their origins. In fact, however, Tina mixes the aesthetics of black and mainstream white culture as well as the contemporary urban flavor that textures the lives of many youths today. Perhaps the results are most apparent in the way Tina mixes and matches hip-hop-influenced clothing, attitudes, and hairstyles with mainstream clothing styles, as well as the mannerisms associated with the norms and standards of professional occupations.

For Tina, to be black is to be both successful and touched by unsuccessful ways of living. Hence, anyone who would approach Tina as an ally of *the* system—defining the system in white terms—would meet with disappointment. They would discover that in Tina's view, and perhaps in Stan's, there is nothing generally wrong with black people and their behavior, but there is something wrong with black individuals who do things that are not in their own best interest, and consequently not in the best interest of the black community. Furthermore, Tina, Stan, and other students describe academic success and failure not just in terms of students' actions. They also criticize uninterested and complacent teachers and staff and schools that do not understand "how to educate black people," as another black senior at Community High forthrightly stated. (Based on an ethnographic study of culture, race, and class during the 1992–1993 academic year.)

The Challenge of Defining Culture

How should we as social workers interpret the features of Tina's and Stan's lives? Economics, race/ethnicity, traditions and customs, gender, political processes, psychology, academic processes, and a host of other factors are all involved. All of them—and more—can be considered elements of culture.

Social constructionist perspective

Just over 30 years ago, Peter Berger and Thomas Luckman made the following proposition: "Society is a human product. Society is an objective reality. Man is a social product" (Berger & Luckman, 1967, p. 61). If you replace "society" with "culture" you get the following: Culture is a human product, culture is an objective reality, and humankind is a cultural product. These restatements suggest the enormous span of human behavior we try to make intelligible through the concept of culture.

In this chapter you will learn how the concept of culture can help you unravel the puzzle of human diversity that is so dominant in public discussions today about a multicultural society. Culture can also help you understand changes in what people believe and value within families as well as the changes in society at large.

EXHIBIT 9.1
Categorical
Definitions of
Culture

Enumeration of Social Content

- That complex whole which includes knowledge, belief, art, morals, law, custom, and any other capabilities and habits acquired by humans as members of society; the sum total of human achievement.

Social Heritage/Tradition

- The learned repertory of thoughts and actions exhibited by members of a social group, independently of genetic heredity from one generation to the next.
- The sum total and organization of social heritages that have acquired social meaning because of racial temperament and the historical life of the group.

Rule or Way of Life

- The sum total of ways of doing and thinking, past and present, of a social group.
- The distinctive way of life of a group of people; their complete design for living.

Psychological and Social Adjustment and Learning

- The total equipment of technique—mechanical, mental, and moral—by use of which the people of a given period try to attain their ends.
- The sum total of the material and intellectual equipment whereby people satisfy their biological and social needs and adapt themselves to their environment.
- Learned modes of behavior that are socially transmitted from one generation to another within a particular society and that may be diffused from one society to another.

Ideas and Values

- An organized group of ideas, habits, and conditioned emotional responses shared by members of a society.
- Acquired or cultivated behavior and thought of individuals; the material and social values of any group of people.

Patterning and Symbols

- A system of interrelated and interdependent habit patterns of response.
- Organization of conventional understandings, manifest in act and artifact, that, persisting through tradition, characterizes a human group.
- Semiotics—those webs of public meaning that people have spun and by which they are suspended.
- A distinct order or class of phenomena—namely, those things and events that are dependent upon the exercise of a mental ability peculiar to the human species—that we have termed symboling; or material objects (such as tools, utensils, ornaments, amulets), acts, beliefs, and attitudes that function in contexts characterized by symboling.

Source: Adapted from Kroeber and Kluckhohn, 1952/1978, pp. 40–79.

Let me caution you, however. Defining culture can be a very arbitrary game. Alfred Kroeber and Clyde Kluckholn (1963, 1952/1978), two renowned anthropologists, have cataloged more than 100 definitions of culture (see Exhibit 9.1). Definitions and discussions of culture tend to reflect the theoretical perspectives and purposes of the definers.

Conflict perspective

Like other views of culture, the one I present here has its biases. In keeping with the emphasis in this book on power arrangements, it is my intent to present a view of culture that will expose not only social differences or human variation, but also the cultural bases of various forms of inequality. I am interested in the ways in which variations in human behavior have led to subjugation and have become the basis of, among others, racial, ethnic, economic, and gender oppression and inequality.

A Preliminary Definition of Culture

Culture as we have come to know it today is rooted in definitions based on behavioral and material inventions and accomplishments. The late-19th-century German intellectual tradition, for example, distinguished between peoples who had or did not have art, science, knowledge, and social refinement (Stocking, 1968). These aspects of culture were thought to free humans from the control of nature and give them control over nature. The word *culture* also derives from the Latin verb *colere*—to cultivate. Note that this sense of the concept is associated with tilling the soil and our agricultural origins (Wagner, 1981, p. 21)—another way of controlling nature.

But is culture simply the opposite of nature? According to Raymond Williams (1983, p. 87), "Culture is one of the two or three most complicated words in the English language"—partly because of culture's intricate historical development in several European languages, but more likely "because culture has come to be used for important concepts in several distinct intellectual disciplines and in several distinct and incompatible systems of thought." For example, early German intellectual traditions merged with English traditions to define culture as general processes of intellectual, spiritual, and aesthetic development. A modified version of this usage is found in the contemporary field of arts and humanities, which describes culture in terms of music, literature, painting, sculpture, and the like. By contrast, American tradition has produced the use of culture as we know it in contemporary social sciences to describe a particular way of life of a people, a period of time, or humanity in general. But even in this American tradition, anthropologists have used the concept to refer to the material production of a people while historians and cultural studies have used it to refer to symbolic systems such as language. Currently, these uses of the concept overlap considerably. Today, culture does not represent just inventions and accomplishments but also the all-pervasive milieu in which we live our lives.

Systems perspective
Pschodynamic perspective

A more useful definition for a transactional, multidimensional approach to human behavior sees culture as "a set of common understandings, manifest in act and artifact. It is in two places at once: inside somebody's head as understandings and in the external environments as act and artifact. If it isn't truly present in both spheres, it is only incomplete culture" (Bohannan, 1995, p. 47). **Culture,** in other words, includes both behavior (act) and the material outcomes of that behavior (artifact). It occurs within the constraints of nature, social conditions, and other realities of human existence. But at the same time, it is "inside our heads," or internal. Emotional and cognitive frames of reference—motivation, intention, and meaning—guide our actions. These processes influence how we express and understand our genetic and physiological endowments and propensities (Bohannan, 1995; D'Andrade, 1984/1995). Culture can also be understood less subjectively, if we focus on its external or public characteristics—behaviors, values, and affects that manifest our conscious and unconscious internal processes (Geertz, 1973; Rosaldo, 1989/

1993; Swidler, 1986). These public characteristics of culture transact within the context of structural constraints and institutional patterns discussed in Chapter 8.

It is through culture, consequently, that we construct and give meaning to material artifacts (such as art, shelter, transportation, or clothing). These meanings and artifacts are shaped and given a place in our belief systems, our ways of acting, our lifestyles, along with other things that we construct from the social and metaphysical world, such as religion, race and ethnicity, family and kinship, gender roles, and organizations and institutions.

Here's an example of how human beings construct meaning in a cultural context: Slaves of African descent were remarkable for interpreting their plight and quest for freedom in terms of their religious beliefs about the crucifixion and resurrection of Jesus Christ. This kind of Christian faith lives on today in the lives of some African Americans. You may encounter clients who believe that their social, economic, and psychological difficulties are the result of God's will rather than of the psychosocial causes we study and apply as social workers. To understand and apply culture thus means to include in our social work assessments people's propensity to construct various meanings about their circumstances. This cultural perspective will help you find more sustainable interpretations and solutions to issues you face as a social worker, especially when working with members of subjugated communities.

Although culture does encompass static artifacts, or the *content* of human existence—such as records of historical dates and events, names of famous people, places, traditions, customs, and things made from the world of physical matter—it is more. Culture is also about the *processes* of human behavior, change, and adaptation. These processes include the flexibility as well as the resistance of ethnic traditions, artistic tastes, and customs. Added to this equation is the context provided by the social, economic, and political circumstances in which a particular group of people may live at a particular moment in history (Bohannan, 1995). Think of how the traditions of immigrant families (for example, Italians, Irish, Polish, Japanese) have evolved over two or three generations in the United States. Some of these traditions have changed slowly and subtly—and some have changed dramatically—along with other changes in society at large.

We can also discuss culture as history. As history, however, culture is about more than dates, names, and records of events. Rather, it is an ongoing story about the connections among ideas, communities, peoples, nations, and social transformations within the constraints of the natural world (Roseberry, 1989). Think about the history of social work. It is more than mere dates and events. Think of the people involved, such as Mary Richmond—a leader in the early charity movement. Think about the philosophy and social practices she espoused in working with the disadvantaged people of her time. What do you know about her ethnic identity, socioeconomic status, gender, and living conditions and about the dominant thinking and political, social, and economic trends of her time? What do you know about what may have influenced her conception of social work and how those influences connect to the ideas and practices of contemporary social work? This line of thought reveals much more about American culture and the social work culture than dates alone would.

Like social work's history, historical processes in general are subject to a degree of strain, randomness, and unpredictability. We have not made history (nor the social work profession) just as we pleased, to paraphrase Marx (Ortner, 1984; Thompson, 1966). We are able to act more or less intentionally by enacting laws and customs that express our will as we carve out our social lives on a daily basis. However, due to human and natural processes, the results of our actions or the outcomes of our intentions frequently lead to unintentional and undesirable results. Consequently, we have wars, inventions, famines, diseases, and "ethnic cleansing." We also have racism and ethnocentrism, catastrophic school failure, poverty, and hunger, alongside a host of other human and natural disasters that, despite our intentions, change the way we live.

To sum up, culture includes multiple levels of traditions, values, and beliefs, as well as social and natural acts. These factors contain meaning, which can be conveyed in relations between people. In the process, however, meaning can be modified. The combined result is that culture engulfs and shapes the ever changing material and social lives of humans.

Culture so defined is therefore not limited to the elite. It affects all of us, including the students and staff at Community High School, as well as the social and academic process of schooling and education in which they participate. A cultural interpretation would reveal competition and strain. Many Village Park residents and Community High students have cultural frames of reference that give adversarial meanings to schooling and other forms of institutional participation. These individuals do not necessarily dismiss education, but they may see education as part of a system of mainstream institutions that have been oppressive and insensitive toward blacks. For example, when a teacher at Community High asks black students like Stan and Tina to stop talking out of turn in class, they hear more than an impartial and benign request. Of course, any adolescent student might resent being told to stop talking by an adult authority. But the nuances of the interpretation of that authoritative request by black students are likely to reflect their frames of reference as members of a community that perceives itself as subjugated.

The Evolution of Culture as a Concept

Ideas about culture have changed over time, in step with intellectual and political trends. Understanding these changes is integral to understanding current definitions of the concept. As you learned earlier, the concept of culture has a lengthy history. But for our purposes, we need go back no further than the Enlightenment and Romantic intellectual traditions. Exhibit 9.2 provides an overview of the evolution of culture as a concept since the 18th century.

The Enlightenment movement of the 18th century was concerned with, among other things, the universal application of a rational and scientific thought process. Enlightenment thinking also espoused the "psychic unity of humankind," promoting a search for similarities in human cultures that would demonstrate the universality of laws of behavior and reasoning.

One result of such thinking was the notion that cultures and civilizations could be ranked according to their developed logic, reason, and technology (or mastery and use of the physical environment). Africans, for example, were seen as less civilized than Europeans because their technology appeared less developed. It is this same schema that justifies interpreting the actions of Tina and Stan as less developed, less mature, and less rational than the actions of more mainstream students.

Another example is the issue of Ebonics, or Black or Nonstandard English, which played out in the Oakland, California, school system in 1997. Much research and public sentiment suggest that Ebonics is a nonlanguage, or at least an inferior and maladaptive language linked to the underdevelopment of black culture and the inferiority of black people as a whole (Morgan, 1994).

Time Period	Ideas and Human Processes
18th & 19th centuries: Enlightenment and Romanticism	Rankings of logic, reason, art, technology Culture seizing nature Psychic unity of humankind
19th & 20th centuries: Variation in human behavior and development	Cultural relativism Culture as patterns and structures Culture and personality Symbols as vehicles of culture
Contemporary understandings: Integration and synthesis of processes of human development and variation since 1950s	Cultural psychology (cognitive psychology and anthropology) Meaning, ecology, and culture Political and economic systems and culture Culture as private and public Physical environment, biology, and culture Ideology, history, common sense, tradition as cultural systems

These rankings of inferiority are based in part on the view that many African Americans are incompetent in their attempts to speak American Standard English and thus have some sort of cognitive and environmental deficiency (Morgan, 1994, p. 327). Such judgments emanate from perceptions of the assumed superiority of Western European and American cultural standards and values. It follows that since Black English is associated with black poverty, welfare, and illiteracy, it serves no culturally viable purpose as a means of communication and has no legitimacy or value as a cultural artifact of an entire ethnic and cultural group. Beyond the technical properties of language, however, linguistic anthropologists and others have documented the arbitrariness of the value of language in general, and the political, social, and cultural battles over Black English in particular (Baldwin, 1979; Baugh, 1987; Hoover, 1990; Kochman, 1981; Labov, 1982; Morgan, 1994). Put this way, it is no wonder that even when many African Americans speak and understand the value of American Standard English, they continue to speak Black English because of its currency in many black communities and commodities such as rap music and comedy. Language issues such as this, as well as bilingual education for persons who speak Spanish as a first language, can help you understand the cultural basis of your judgments whenever you are dealing with racial and ethnic minorities or other groups, such as the deaf community, that do not speak Standard English clearly and competently.

The other side of the coin is a Romantic orientation dating from the late 18th century. This orientation reflects the idea that all people and their cultures are *relatively* equal in value. The valuation of human culture and its outcomes extends beyond the measuring rod of reason, rationality, and logic; instead, differences in cultures reflect different frameworks of meaning and understanding, resulting in different designs for living (Benedict, 1946, 1934/1989). Unlike the Enlightenment approach, the Romantic orientation views different cultures as equal, rather than ranking them as inferior and superior (Shweder, 1984/1995, p. 28).

Such **cultural relativism** frames the core issues of contemporary multiculturalism. It would be inappropriate to ask which is superior, Islam or Christianity, black culture or white culture, African culture or European culture. They are coequal. As a social worker, you could contrast the academic performance and behavior of Community High students such as Tina and Stan with that of successful white students to identify differences between them. However, you would not rank the differences between them but would measure them against some mutually relevant standard, such as how well they enable students to succeed in their own communities. Thus, although from a mainstream perspective Stan's behavior may seem to doom him to failure, from the perspective of his peers he may be considered successful; he is popular at school, is likely to graduate, is moving away from the drug trade, and has a stable relationships with his girlfriend, baby, and other family members.

Despite the usefulness of Romanticism and cultural relativism, the premises of Enlightenment thinking are among several influences on our everyday understanding of culture. Consider recent public debates over crime, welfare, and other issues that associate chronic social problems with people's race/ethnicity and socioeconomic status. Some social scientists and the popular media frequently portray mainstream, Enlightenment-oriented values, attitudes, and morals in examining these issues (Murray, 1984; Murray & Herrnstein, 1994; Wilson, 1995).

One outcome of such thinking is **biological determinism**—the attempt to differentiate social behavior on the basis of biological and genetic endowment, or **phenotype**. One form of biological determinism is based on racial identity. A person's intellectual performance is associated with brown skin and other physical differences believed to be related to **race**. However, the relationship that ties phenotypical (racial) differences to differences in cognitive and intellectual capacities is unproven. There is no verifiable evidence that the composition and functioning of the brain differs between blacks and whites, Asians and Hispanics, or whatever so-called racial group you can identify and compare (Gould, 1981; Shaklin, 1994). Yet such false associations fit with many common notions about the differences between people and the natural, rank-order of civilization espoused by Enlightenment thinking.

Seemingly natural, ordained, and inevitable differences based on race reinforce the social tendency to think in terms of "we-ness" and "they-ness" (Ringer & Lawless, 1989). As a social work student, you can recognize the power and influence of such tendencies. As you move about your personal and professional life, pay attention to the images and thoughts you use to make sense of the economic, social, and behavioral difficulties of black people or other ethnic groups.

Culture and Variation in Human Behavior

Twentieth-century scholars of culture inherited both advances and limitations in thought from scholars of previous centuries. With these problems in mind, anthropologist Franz Boas encourages us to understand cultural differences as environmental differences interacting with the accidents of history. Boas said that by grasping the meaning of culture, we shall also be able to see how many of our lines of behavior that we believe to be founded deep in human nature are actually expressions of our culture and subject to modification with changing culture. Not all our standards are categorically determined by our quality as human beings, but may change with changing circumstances. It is our task to discover among all the varieties of human behavior those that are common to all humanity. (Boas, 1940/1948, p. 259)

Boas's ideas, along with those developed by others, have led to the following axioms (Kottak, 1994):

Social constructionist perspective

Social behavioral perspective

- Culture is learned through social interaction.

- A society may have customary practices, but not all members have the same knowledge of them or attach the same significance to them.

- Culture seizes nature.

- Culture is patterned; culture is symbolic; and culture is adaptive and maladaptive.

Why are these axioms important for social workers? Three things come to mind if we are going to work effectively and sensitively with people like Stan and Tina and communities like theirs, which vary from mainstream norms:

1. We must be able to understand how the beliefs, customs, traditions, values, and social institutions composing social behavior fit into the lives of our clients.

2. We must recognize that beliefs, customs, values, traditions, and social institutions vary in degrees of complexity from one society to another. People have a tendency to consider cultures other than their own as aberrations from a "universal" norm or standard that all people should meet. Two questions evolve from this point: Which norms and values are acceptable as universal, and based on what criteria? Are these universals adaptive or functional under all social, economic, political, and environmental conditions?

3. The final thing we must pay attention to is the development of emotional and cognitive frameworks as elements of society and culture. We must avoid the trap of confounding emotional and cognitive capacities with hierarchies of race and other ways of ranking humankind.

Cross-cultural studies of Native Americans, Samoans, Japanese, Europeans, and even Americans have examined the idea that each culture is whole and not merely an incomplete version of the standard or ideal culture. These studies have tested the universal applicability of Freud's psychosexual personality theory, ideas of national character, and ideas about social organization found in social trends and dominant lifestyles among Americans (Benedict, 1946, 1934/1989; Kroeber, 1917; Mead, 1935/1950, 1928/1961). For example, Margaret Mead studied male and female development of Americans in contrast to Samoans and other Pacific Islanders. She isolated cultural differences in child rearing, gender roles, and personality development. Ruth Benedict studied the role of national character and individual personality through an examination of the lives of Japanese. And Alfred Kroeber learned that changes in women's fashion in America are more than personal choice; they reflect cultural patterns.

While all of these studies have imperfections in methodology, theory, and interpretation, they still offer much insight to social workers about cultural and human variation within the United States. They point us toward regarding culture as patterns of behavior, as an influence on personality, and as a repository of symbols that have a more-or-less standard meaning for all members of the culture.

Culture as Patterns of Behavior.   Culture governs the behavior of individuals in a given society, structuring things like marriage and clothing styles. Traditional Japanese and Native American cultures, for example, are characterized by certain socially integrated individual behaviors. For example, in traditional or Native American cultures, one is expected to show deference to group interests and forgo individual interests. Public self-humiliation is expected for acts that are deemed inappropriate. In this sense, culture is the property of the social group (Goodenough, 1996).

Conflict perspective   **Ideology**—the dominant ideas within a culture about the way things are and should work—is also part of this equation. Problems of inequality and discrimination arise when ideological aspects of the social, economic, and political structures of society support the exploitation and subjugation of people based on race, ethnicity, gender, class, religion, and the like. Institutionalized racism or gender bias, for example, is the systematic incorporation of ideologies into the culture's structures in a way that directly and indirectly support subordination of one group of people. These subordinating elements are built into the everyday, taken-for-granted way the culture's members live their lives.

Viewing culture as structure and patterns helps us understand some human behavior, but it has been heavily criticized for ascribing too much behavior to external influences. In other words, behavior is also influenced by human agency or will. People are not helpless puppets, without motives, intentions, and the ability to think and improvise.

As social workers, we may at times be convinced that economic, social, and political structures are too strong for oppressed people to penetrate. Yet we are also likely to encounter individuals who have penetrated them to a degree. In other words, some people rise to success despite poverty, racism, gender oppression, and the like. While such penetration is encouraging, it can also be misleading. Not everyone can overcome structural barriers. For example, Tina may go to college and have a relatively successful life as a black woman. However, her success in penetrating the barriers of racism and other forms of oppression should not be used, as it often is, to discount the negative effects of oppression on other members of Tina's community.

Culture and Personality.   In a society, cultural processes interact with biological processes to shape the development of internal states of being, such as cognition, consciousness, perception, and feelings. These internal states are believed to organize experience, thereby influencing what we value and how we act in the world. In turn, our ways of acting in the world influence our cognition, consciousness, perceptions, and feelings.

Interestingly, the links between culture and personality were deduced from attempts to assimilate Native American children who were having problems in the standard American classroom. Anthropologists tried to understand why Native Americans were not participating successfully in school to the extent that other American children were. They found that Native

American children's perception of how they should participate in school—as in other enterprises within their culture—was community- or group-centered (Spindler, 1997). The European American approach they were being asked to adopt was individual-centered. Individual problem solving and achievement were antithetical to the norms these children had been raised to respect. This and other findings have been important to studies of other minority groups who have problems participating in schools and other social institutions.

Proponents of a culture-and-personality orientation focus on topics such as variations in child development, deviance, sexuality, and emotions within and across cultures. They seek to expose the cultural components of socialization and psychological selfhood, or how, as a matter of cultural processes, we become societies of social yet individual beings (Ortner, 1984; Shweder, 1991). Through cross-cultural comparisons, these anthropologists have demonstrated that Western culture is not universal and have exposed the **ethnocentrism** of Western ideals and theories regarding personality development (Mead, 1935/1950, 1928/1961, 1930/1968; Shweder & LeVine, 1984/1995; Whiting & Whiting, 1975).

As a result of the work of Mead and others, we have also been forced to understand cultural variations in sexual norms more broadly. For example, the sexual practices of adolescents reflect an interaction between biological propensities to mate and societal rules that dictate which sexual urges may be expressed and how. Sexual immorality or inappropriate sexual behavior is, therefore, culturally influenced rather than solely naturally derived and universal. We do not know what a natural expression of sexuality is because we cannot observe the behavior of people outside the influence of culture. Consequently, our sense of what adolescent sexual behaviors are right or wrong depends on our own family socialization, exposure to religious documents such as the Bible, and understanding of secular documents such as laws, regulations, and mental health diagnoses—as well as folk or everyday norms that integrate such information and other life experiences.

As social workers, we depend on the NASW Code of Ethics for professional guidance. But what is the source of the values and beliefs that guide our personal lives? And what happens when what we believe and value differs from our clients' beliefs and values? These questions raise the issue of how we form and act on meaning in our lives. This, perhaps more than anything we have discussed so far, is a cultural issue. Exhibit 9.3 demonstrates issues that arise as our personal social habits confront professional education about the principles, values, and ethics of social work.

Symbols in Culture.   Embedded in the issues just discussed is a question that social workers face all the time: Do we really know what's going on inside of people's heads—what they mean and intend? Examining people's actions can help us to explore this question by examining the ideas of scholars of both culture and cultural psychology to explain the role of cognition, symbols, and meaning (Bruner, 1990; D'Andrade, 1984/1995). By the 1960s, American scholars of culture (anthropologists, sociologists, psychologists, and linguists) were focusing chiefly on symbols, structure, and meaning as components of culture.

Briefly, symbols are vehicles of culture that shape perception, or the way a person sees, feels, and thinks about the world. A **symbol** is something, verbal or nonverbal, that comes to stand for something else. The letters *d-o-g* have come to stand for the animal we call *dog*; the large *M* and

EXHIBIT 9.3

Customary Social
Habits Interacting
with Social Work
Principles, Values,
and Ethics, on a
Continuum

What are your beliefs about the following interactions with clients and colleagues?

Continuum

Most Professional (Formal) .... *Least Professional (Informal)*

Greetings by handshake .... hugging .... kissing

Use of last name/title .... first name .... nickname
(Mr., Ms., Dr.)

Authority by credentials .... age, experience, ... religion/politics
(BSW, MSW, etc.)   gender, marital status

Sharing no personal .... pertinent information .... open-ended,
information   mutual sharing

Confidentiality .... sharing with professionals/ .... sharing with friends/
                                        family   community members

a golden arch stand for McDonald's restaurants or hamburgers; the American flag stands for our country, patriotism, and the like; water in baptism rites stands for something sacred and holy and moves a person from one state of being to another (D'Andrade, 1984/1995; Kottak, 1994). Conrad Kottak (1996) points out, "Water is not intrinsically holier than milk, blood or other liquids.... A natural thing has been arbitrarily associated with a particular meaning for Catholics" and other religious groups (p. 26). In short, symbols in culture participate in social action and communicate a host of feelings, thoughts, beliefs, and values that people employ to make sense of their daily lives (Ortner, 1973).

Race, ethnicity, and gender are symbols that can be thought of in this way as well. Pause for a moment and think about gender. Beyond biological differences, what comes to mind when you think of a girl or woman? What about a boy or man? How do the images, thoughts, and feelings you possess about gender influence how you interact with boys and girls, men and women? Gendered thinking undoubtedly influences your assessment of persons, even without actually meeting them.

How do symbols perform their cognitive function? How is it that we can sound out the combined letters *d-o-g* to produce the word *dog,* and the mental image of a dog, and the meanings associated with this animal in American culture (meanings and words for dogs differ across cultures) (D'Andrade, 1984/1995)? To answer these questions, scholars of language, linguistics, and cognitive psychology have focused on the internal wiring or programming of the brain, trying to understand how it stores, processes, and uses information. They have also focused on the cognitive structures and schemes, or frames of reference, that make communication or language semiotic. To be **semiotic** means to represent meaning through a system of discernible or understandable symbols and signs (Daniel, 1987; de Sassure, 1959/1966; Levi-Strauss, 1967, 1949/1969; Pierce, 1982; Sapir, 1949/1985).

Culture-as-symbol thinking has contributed to a broader understanding of culture and society. Clifford Geertz (1973) and others (see Ortner, 1984, for the key players) see culture and society as comprising social processes that can be interpreted through the **public symbols** that members of society use to communicate their common conceptions (Ortner, 1996, p. 129). Because the symbols are public, culture becomes something not singularly locked inside mental processes in people's heads. Symbols also become public through social action, which is expressed through symbols that communicate meaning.

The common conceptions of a culture include the members' value orientations as well as their **worldview**—a "picture of the way things in sheer actuality are, their concept of nature, of self, of society. It contains their most comprehensive ideas of order" (Geertz, 1973, p. 126). Finally, common conceptions include a people's **ethos**—the "tone, character, and quality of their life, its moral and aesthetic style and mood; it is the underlying attitude toward themselves and their world that life reflects" (Geertz, 1973, p. 126). Worldview is associated with the cognitive domain; ethos is associated more with the emotional or affective and stylistic dimensions of behavior (Ortner, 1984, p. 129).

As an example of the link between culture and symbols, Stan and Tina were described as innovators. Both restyled mainstream clothing to fit with their sense of meaning and with the values of their peers and their community. Additionally, in the classroom and with peers, Stan and Tina could switch between Standard English and Black English. The mode of language they used depended on the social and political message they wanted to convey to listeners. Thus, both were adept at using symbols such as clothing, language, and music to convey specific meanings in line with their worldview and ethos. An examination of Exhibit 9.4 will begin to expose the symbols that convey your worldview and ethos.

Because the symbols we use are arbitrary—they can mean one thing to you and something very different to others—conflict can easily arise. Jeans that are worn low on the hips by many black adolescents and young adults generally signify an ethos of hipness, toughness, and coolness, which is the style and mood for their generation. (Some of us who are professionals, or soon will be, have a similar need to fit in with the particular ethos and worldview that is important to us and to the people with whom we interact, and we are likely to choose an entirely different style of clothing.) The clothing, music, and language of black adolescents convey a different symbolic meaning to law enforcers, school officials, parents, and even social workers. In today's sociopolitical climate, these authority figures are likely to perceive the symbols as signs of drug and gang culture or as a form of social rebellion, decadence, or incivility.

Remember, in sum, that culture is both public and private. It has emotional and cognitive components, but these play out in public in our social actions. Symbols are a way of communicating private meaning through public or social action. Further, the actions by which Tina and Stan reappropriate black and mainstream styles can be largely understood in terms of their worldview (how they see the world) and ethos (how they feel about the world) in interaction with the world outside their community. Thus, in a cultural analysis, we cannot consider the public without the private, or worldview without ethos.

Social constructionist perspective

The idea that symbols express meaning within a culture is part of many recent models of practice in social work and psychology. Examples are the social constructionists, who focus on narratives and stories as emotional and behavioral correctives in clinical social work practice. These recent innovations are a new twist on an old insight: Reality is constructed through social and cultural relations.

EXHIBIT 9.4
Sociocultural
Creations

Ask yourself what judgments you make and meanings you attribute in the following areas:

Music:
Classical versus jazz
Rhythm and blues versus bluegrass
Celtic versus rock and roll

Food:
Hamburger versus eel
Ants versus hot dogs
Kangaroo tail versus squid
Pigs' feet versus horse

Household/Domestic Activities:
Parents and children sleeping in separate beds and/or separate rooms versus sleeping in the open

Sexual intercourse in private versus public

Bathing in private versus public

Breast feeding in private versus public

Families living, eating, sleeping in one large room versus separate rooms

Eating with fingers and hands versus forks, spoons, and knives

Arguments accompanying recent welfare reform legislation likewise reflect various meanings regarding poverty, single parenting, and work. During the 1960s, it was considered society's moral duty to combat poverty by assisting the poor. Today, poverty means or symbolizes laziness, the demise of family values, and other factors that shade into immorality. Thus, to help, now morally wrong, is to hurt.

A Contemporary, Holistic Application of Culture

Social workers can better account for the multidimensional nature of human behavior if they understand what culture is and how thinking about culture has evolved. But such understanding is not enough. For example, we might recognize that Tina's and Stan's ways of living are different from our own, but we are perhaps only saying that their lives are based on values, beliefs, and rationalizations that we don't fully understand. We could try to understand them, but it is all too easy to apply our own cultural frame of reference, which is based on our values, beliefs, and rationalizations. We are thus likely to learn more about ourselves than about these students. The most we can learn about the students by looking at them from our own frame of reference is how they compare to us. The comparison, however, is in our terms, not theirs. For example, we may well say that Stan is at greater than average risk of failing academically, but he might say that he is more successful than most at negotiating the oppressive school structure.

In the United States today, everybody seems to have some passing acquaintance with a wide variety of subcultures—urban street culture, gay culture, Amish culture, and so on—largely because of the images we all see on TV and in film. To a certain extent, then, these groups have moved from being "strange" to being "familiar." Yet our understanding of such groups, and of ourselves as Americans, remains suspect because the concepts of culture we have depended on for understanding are unidimensional. We have not understood the multidimensional cultural processes that govern the life of all groups in the United States.

Just what does a multidimensional approach to a culture analysis consist of, and what is it trying to explain? This is an important question for social workers. We need a multidimensional perspective of diversity and human behavior to ground our professional action.

A Practice Orientation

Thirty years ago, the problems of Village Park and Community High School would have been explained largely in terms of a **culture of poverty.** This theoretical orientation posited that black schools and communities faced poverty because of black people's own beliefs, values, traditions, and frames of reference. The mainstream culture's racism and discrimination were not considered to be factors. That black people were working in low-income jobs despite qualifications for better ones was not a factor. That major colleges and universities were denying admission to qualified black applicants was not a factor either. The list could go on. The culture-of-poverty orientation was used to argue both for and against publicly financed social programs. More insidiously, it was used to distinguish moral and immoral behavior or socially adaptive and maladaptive behavior. Interestingly, many people still attempt to explain issues such as welfare reform and the problems of inner cities using the same culture-of-poverty orientation that dominated similar debates many years ago.

Social constructionist perspective

Conflict perspective

Contemporary culture scholars (anthropologists, sociologists, psychologists, political scientists, social workers, economists) have also adopted some of the tenets of past theorizing. However, they have gone beyond it to shape what has come to be called a **practice orientation** (Berger & Luckman, 1967; Bourdieu, 1977; Giddens, 1979; Ortner, 1984, 1989, 1996; Sahlins, 1981). This theoretical orientation seeks to explain what people do as thinking, intentionally acting persons who face the impact of history and the restraints of structures that are embedded in our society and culture. It asks how social systems shape, guide, and direct people's values, beliefs, and behavior. It also asks how people, as human actors or agents, shape or perpetuate social systems. The underlying issues, in sum, are about understanding how, through culture, we construct meaning, intentionality, and public behavior, as well as systemic and cultural change, adaptation, and maintenance. The hope is to find a deeper understanding of racism, ethnicity, social class, and gender relations, among other sociocultural processes.

One example of the application of the practice orientation is to the issue of poverty. The practice orientation would not blame its prevalence and influence in Tina's and Stan's community solely on the failings of individuals. Rather, it would seek to identify structural factors, such as low-income jobs and racism, that serve as barriers to upward mobility. It would also seek to determine how poor African Americans perceive their conditions; how nonpoor, nonblack Americans perceive the conditions of poor African Americans; and how all of these perceptions shape the lives and influence the upward mobility of poor African Americans. At the same time, the practice orientation aims to understand how the perceptions and actions of nonpoor, nonblack Americans maintain structures of inequality in the institutions that define and offer educational and economic opportunities. Are poor African Americans as different in values, beliefs, and attitudes as other people think they are? Is there a "culture" of poverty, or do people in dire circumstances adapt their values and beliefs to the current demands of survival? These are matters of considerable importance and complexity.

Here's another example of the types of questions fruitfully addressed through the practice orientation. How have Stan's family and community influenced his behavior in general, and his response to racism and classism in school in particular? How have Stan's own responses contributed to his subordination as a black youth, thereby leaving certain oppressive structures in society unchanged? Likewise, how have the values and beliefs encoded through the rules and regulations in public schools like Community High served to perpetuate or reproduce various forms of structural or systemic subjugation? What is the role of the symbolic meaning of school and education—that schools are intrinsically good because they are largely about academic growth rather than sociocultural processes?

The same questions apply to social work. How have the values, beliefs, and practices of the profession helped to maintain the profession and society as they are? When we label a person or group as having a social problem or dysfunction, are we perpetuating or reproducing subjugation by creating social science–based categories of functioning among people? When we label people we have failed to help as resistant, unmotivated, and pathological, are we carelessly overlooking the ineffectiveness of our understanding and mode of intervention and instead blaming and reproducing the victim? These and other questions are important for all of us to ponder.

History, structure, and human agency are key aspects of a practice orientation. I have tried to demonstrate in this chapter how some life events reflect the intertwined influences of history, structure, and human agency. These kinds of interactions sometimes reflect social strain, and sometimes social solidarity. Sometimes they reflect a conflict between the objective and the subjective nature of cultural content—a conflict between what we do and what we believe. In any case, the relationship between human action and social systems is never simple in a political world (Ortner, 1984, 1989).

History.   History is made by people within the constraints of the system they are living in. Note that the definition of history is not solely a chain of events and experiences to which people simply react. Chains of events, dates, and the like, are important. However, to understand human diversity and to unearth sociocultural forms of oppression, exploitation, and subjugation, we must take into account the particular form that a society has at a particular moment, as explained by the diverse actions and motives of people as they make and transform the world in which they live (Ortner, 1989, p. 193).

Structure.   Structure implies the ordered forms and systems of human behavior existing in public life (for example, capitalism, kinship, public education). It also includes cognitive, emotional, and behavioral frameworks and dispositions that are embodied by and mapped onto who we are as people. Structure influences how we construct ourselves—that is, what we make of ourselves based on what things mean to us. We carry forth meanings, values, and beliefs through social, economic, and political practices in our everyday personal lives and the institutions in which we participate. We *reproduce* structures when we assume the rightness of our values, beliefs, and meaning and see no need to change them. The **hegemony,** or all-encompassing dominance, of structures in society makes change difficult.

Humanistic
perspective

Human Agency.   The hegemony of structure is incomplete, however, thanks to the force of human agency. People are not simply the pawns of history and structure; they are also active participants, capable of exercising will to shape their lives. Thus, racism, as structured into society, is not so completely dominant over Tina's and Stan's lives that they have no room for meaningful self-expression in their social and political lives.

The incomplete dominance of structure is represented by "slippages in reproduction, erosions in longstanding patterns, and moments of disorder and outright resistance"(Ortner, 1996, p. 17). Historically, such "slippages, erosions, disorder, and resistance" can be seen in slave revolts, race riots, and massive labor strikes, and even in changes in gender roles and relations. A more contemporary example is the way in which African American styles in rap music and clothes, favored by black teens like Tina and Stan, have risen in influence with white, middle-class young people. In fact, the general influence of African American music on the European American mainstream has been going on for many years.

Individuals and groups exercise agency in part by constructing culture. We invest the world with subjective order, meaning, and value, relying on our frame of mind or schema to consciously and unconsciously make choices and take action (Ortner, 1989, p. 18). We construct social and political identities and representations that serve as the basis of resistance and contestation. However, no individual or group is a fully free agent. We are heavily constrained by internalized cultural frameworks of emotion and cognition that operate as our conventional ways of thinking and feeling about the world, giving meaning to our existence and guiding our actions.

We are also constrained by external factors—material and social limits such as climate, disease, natural resources, and population size and growth (Ortner, 1989, p. 14). In these areas, however, we may be able to mediate, penetrate, or moderate such constraints through technology. Examples of technologies that modify facts of nature are medicines, agricultural breakthroughs, homes that shelter us from undesirable climatic conditions, transportation, and synthetic products that replace the use of wood in furniture and related items.

In sum, as human agents, we are "skilled and intense strategizers" (Ortner, 1996, p. 20). We are constantly stretching the process by which we live and define ourselves, all within the constraints of structures that can never wholly contain us. Human agency is a major source of hope and motivation for social workers who encounter people, organizations, and systems that seem unable to get beyond the personal and social restraints of daily life.

Practice (or Praxis)

Practice—or praxis—is the central organizing and unifying concept in the practice orientation. **Praxis**, simply put, is practical action within the context of history and structure. Think about Stan and his community again. Praxis explains how Stan's social activities, or actions, emerge from structure, reproduce structure, and yet participate in the transformation of structure, all in historical context. For example, Stan's participation in the illegal drug market contributes to the reproduction of economic and social vulnerability of young black males within his community. But because Stan has learned the connections among his illegal activities, the oppression of low-income black communities, and his own oppression as a black man, he has decided not only to stop his activity, but also to share his knowledge with other drug dealers so that they will reform themselves and their community. Anthropologist Philippe Bourgois describes a similar process in his ethnography *In Search of Respect: Selling Crack in El Barrio* (1995). In other words, praxis takes into account the impact of social and cultural factors on human beings. It also explains how we interpret and define such factors and, in some instances, transform them even while we are being transformed.

More important, praxis is political, in that it points out how certain aspects of human relations (such as race, ethnicity, gender) are negotiated and defined around authority, power, legitimacy, and so forth (Ortner, 1989, p. 195). Thought of in this way, life entails a "serious game" of struggle and contests that include some and exclude others. In life, some are imbued with power while others are not (Ortner, 1996, pp. 12–16). Social work is consumed by this serious game, which seems increasingly to define life in the United States and beyond.

Again, take schooling and Community High as an example. Community High has an organizational structure that is representative of specific social and cultural patterns and norms in society at large. These are expressed through rules and policies dictating what one should learn and how. Examine Stan and Tina's school situation. They are allowed to speak in class only when asked to do so by the teacher. A teacher's questions to Stan are to be answered only by him and not in consultation with his friends and classmates. (You might say he would be cheating if he asked his friends for help. If so, according to whom, and by what standard?) When Stan answers questions, he is not allowed to add his perception of the question's fairness or relevance. This may seem like a trivial matter, but when you observe its effects on generation after generation of students for whom such educational methods do not work, one has to raise questions.

Many Community High students perceive standard schooling processes as oppressive, irrelevant, and incompatible with their interests and the way they approach life and learning. Schooling is culturally incompatible for them. But when these students do not comply with or follow the school's standard processes in classrooms or elsewhere, their actions are interpreted as oppositional, defiant, pathological, and deviant.

Student actions like these can be called **cultural resistance** (Cousins, 1994; Giroux, 1983; Scott, 1985, 1990). In expressing their human agency, these students radically oppose interacting in school in the culturally prescribed ways, which are meaningless for them. Cultural resistance, when understood as more than a mere aberration or deviance, should influence schools and related institutions to reconsider the processes they use to deliver educational material or other services. Teachers should try new methods of teaching; administrators should search for more constructive disciplinary methods. To the extent that they do, students—and even the teachers and administrators—are actors transforming structures.

At the same time, however, many resistant students are themselves being transformed by the structures or educational processes they oppose. By participating in the dominant, mainstream, standardized structure of schooling, students are consciously and unconsciously learning the rules for "appropriate" social conduct in classrooms and elsewhere. They are learning the "proper" or conventional process of didactic exchange between teacher and student, as well as the system of individual merit by which achievement is measured in school and beyond.

Cultural Maintenance, Change, and Adaptation

Mainstream schooling systems and the lives of Tina and Stan provide a good example of how cultural structures or norms, values, patterns, and meanings are maintained, how they change, and how adaptation occurs. School systems are built on and operate by the norms, values, and beliefs preferred by those who have had the power to decide what is or is not an appropriate frame of reference by which to live. From the outside looking in, schools look like benign or innocent institutions, simply about academics and education. Yet which academic subjects are taught, how they are taught, and how they are to be learned involve an assertion of someone's values and beliefs, whether right or wrong, whether shared by many or few. These assertions are based in part on the interests of our capitalist economy and conventional political processes. Exhibit 9.5 lists some of the factors involved in the cultural construction of schooling.

Even in the face of evidence that the schools do not work for many of us, they persist. Such stubbornness makes schools complicit in the persistent poverty we have faced in this country; the systematic subjugation of girls and women; and the high dropout rates (though decreasing for some groups) and other current debacles of our educational system.

Common Sense, Tradition, and Custom.   Over the course of time, the ways in which schools do things have come to seem natural. They seem to fit with the common sense, traditions, and customs of most Americans.

Keep in mind, however, that **common sense** is a cultural system. It is what people come to believe everyone in a community or society should know and understand as a matter of ordinary, taken-for-granted social competence. It is based on a set of assumptions so unself-conscious as to seem natural, transparent, and an undeniable part of the structure of the world (Geertz, 1983; Swidler, 1986). For example, rain is wet, fire burns, and, as I hear more and more in the general population, as well as from many Community High students, "You can't make it without an education!"

EXHIBIT 9.5

Interactive
Sociocultural Factors
in the Construction
of Education and
Schooling for Tina
and Stan

Issue: Schools and education are social and cultural products.

Question: How is it that schools have come to share and be influenced by the following circumstances and interdependent domains of responsibility that influence one another, and extend beyond reading, writing, and arithmetic?

Political/Legal
Legislation, laws, and regulations regarding attendance and social behavior; the kind of educational content deemed appropriate; segregation/desegregation; school funding.

Family
Socialization regarding gender roles and relations; sex; discipline; health/hygiene/nutrition; recreation; emotional support and development.

Religion
Prayer; holidays; family and personal morality and ethics.

Social/Economic
Status, opportunities, and rewards associated with knowledge, grades, and credentials; individual versus collective achievement; appropriate versus inappropriate behavior/social skills; media, market, and popular cultural trends and factors.

Community
All the other domains, plus ethnic representation and attitudes; economic resources and stability; levels of crime.

Yet not everyone, especially oppressed and subjugated groups within a society, is likely to share these common schemes of meaning and understanding. Thus, common sense becomes self-serving for those who are in a position to determine what it is and who has it. We believe common sense tells us what actions are appropriate in school or in any number of other circumstances. But, as a part of culture, it is subject to historically defined standards of judgment related to maleness and femaleness, parenting, poverty, work, education, and mental and social (psychosocial) functioning, among other categories of social being. Thus, common sense helps make schools resistant to change.

We need to approach traditions and customs with the same caution we approach common sense. **Traditions** are cultural beliefs and practices so taken for granted that they seem inevitable parts of life (Swidler, 1986). **Customs** come into being and persist as solutions to problems of living (Goodenough, 1996, p. 294). Tradition is a process of handing down particular cultural beliefs and practices or customs. In particular, it is a process of ratifying particular beliefs and practices by connecting them to selected social, economic, and political practices until they are so taken for granted that they seem "natural" parts of life (Hobsbawm, 1983; Swidler, 1986; Williams, 1977). The actual beliefs and practices that are handed down, such as beliefs about marriage and raising children, are customs. Some traditions and customs are routine; others, such as special ceremonies, are extraordinary. They are not necessarily followed by everyone in the culture, but they seem ordained, and they stabilize the culture. They are in a sense collective memories of the group. They reflect what life objectively and subjectively means at a particular moment in time and are looked to as guides for the present and future.

Traditions and customs are selective, however, leaving out the experiences, memories, and voices of some group members while highlighting and including others. African American students generally do not experience schooling as reflecting their traditions and customs. Stan, Tina, and their peers often raise this point in their classes at Community High. And several residents of Village Park have been raising such issues for many years. To reflect Village Park's traditions and customs, Community High would have to place more value on Nonstandard English as students are learning Standard English. Literature and history classes would make salient connections between European traditions and customs and those of West Africans, Afro-Caribbeans, and contemporary African Americans. And processes for legitimating and including a student's family in schooling processes would include kinship bonds that are not based on blood ties or state foster-care systems.

Traditions and customs thus play a role in the strain that characterizes shifts from old patterns and styles of living to new ones in schools and elsewhere. To survive, traditions and customs have to bend without losing their essence. Nondominant ethnic, gender, religious, and other groups in the United States often have to bend if they are to share in economic and political power. In fact, the general survival of the traditions and customs of nondominant groups requires adaptability.

In sum, traditions and customs are parts of a process, most often changing ever so subtly and slowly but at times abruptly. In times of rapid change, customs and traditions come to be practiced in modes different from the ways a people or a group says is or always has been the case. The result is cultural change.

Assimilation and Accommodation.   In multicultural societies, the process of cultural change is usually characterized as either assimilation or accommodation. **Assimilation** is the process in which "the minority is incorporated into the dominant culture to the point that it no longer exists as a separate cultural unit" (Kottak, 1996, p. 271). Some people have argued that the root of the problems faced by African Americans is that they have not assimilated successfully. This argument is greatly oversimplified. First, to the extent that discrimination is based on skin color, assimilation is impossible. Second, some minorities have directly resisted giving up their ethnic identity.

Accommodation is more realistic, and in reality, more often the case in multicultural, multiethnic American society. **Accommodation** is the process of cultural change in which nondominant groups follow the norms, rules, and standards of the dominant culture only in specific circumstances. When the Punjabi Sikh children attend school in Stockton, California, they generally follow the rules of the school (Gibson, 1988). They do not, however, remove their head covering, socialize with peers in accord with American heterosexual standards and norms, or live by American cultural standards at home. Some of the Muslim students at Community High could be compared to the Punjabi. Black Muslim girls at Community High, for example, refuse to remove their head coverings or customary long gowns to attend school, even though the school asks them to do so.

Social workers who conduct a multidimensional cultural analysis can uncover the incompatibility in how groups of people interact in institutions; the political, social, and economic practices that undergird institutional norms and values; and the ways that both of these processes, if found to be harmful and maladaptive for some people, might be modified. Inequality emanating from the unequal power of individuals, groups, and institutions determines what meanings and actions we live by in school or elsewhere. Women, people of color, and poor people have historically not had a significant say in how—or whether—cultural change proceeds. But having a limited voice does not eliminate one's voice altogether. Consider the characteristic flavor of predominantly black schools and institutions, and institutions dominated by feminists, as well as nonwhite tastes in food, music, art, clothing, and the like. Again, social workers must comprehend and act in accord with such knowledge. If we accept dominant notions about the meaning of the actions of people of color and poor people and about the things that, consequently, should be done to them, we are likely to do nothing more than reproduce their subjugation.

Diversity

The *practice orientation* is a model for conceptualizing, organizing, and analyzing cultural processes that give a different meaning to things we take for granted. It is especially useful for interpreting variation in the social environment. Examples are race, ethnicity, social class, gender, and family—important symbols in the American psyche that summarize and elaborate a host of feelings, beliefs, thoughts, and values (Ortner, 1973). These key symbols are almost always about more than their overt or obvious meanings and intentions. They carry a legacy that stretches over centuries and continents, as is the case with Tina's and Stan's racial/ethnic identity.

Race.   Race is first and foremost a system of identity that has been constructed over many years through cultural, social, economic, and political relations. In the case of race, particular sociocultural meanings have been mapped onto biological aspects of human variation. Race has become a fundamental principle of social organization, even though it has no validity as a biological category (Omi & Winant, 1993; Shanklin, 1994). The physical characteristics (phenotypes) we associate with race are in fact variations resulting from human adaptation to different geographic environments over thousands of years. Although the phenotypes have been publicly categorized as European (white), African (black), Asian, Latino/Hispanic, and Native American, the physical attributes of each group have no intrinsic relationship to emotional, cognitive, or social capacities. **Racism** is the term for thinking and acting as if phenotype and these other capacities are related.

Depending on the social, economic, and political context, the meanings and uses of race shift. In one context, for example, being black or African American is an asset, while in another it is a deficit. Even among black students and communities, these meanings shift—as a result of the social, political, and economic advantages or disadvantages associated with a black racial identity at a particular moment in time. Consequently, race relations and identity issues in the 1960s were somewhat different than they are in the 1990s, because the social, economic, and political climates are very different.

Consider the issue of racial identity among Community High students. Today's black students experience less conflict among themselves about "acting white" than did the black students who attended Community High a decade ago (Fordham, 1996; Fordham & Ogbu, 1986; Ogbu, 1991). *Acting white* is the term used to identify behavior that fits with the norms of speech, demeanor, dress, and so on, that are preferred and valued by mainstream European American society. "White" norms are perceived to be at play in school activities such as doing homework, carrying books, and speaking in Standard English when answering questions in the classroom. Today, as a decade ago, black students who do "act white" are likely to receive more social, economic, and political acceptance within the larger society. They will also be accorded more privilege and prestige than those who act in accord with what is perceived as distinctly "black" behavior. These determinations are made by both blacks and nonblacks. Increasingly, however, the families of black students at Community High and the black community are allowing a greater range of flexibility regarding "black" behavior.

Stan and Tina offer examples of the current blurring of distinctions between behaviors that have historically been defined as black or white. Both students borrow from mainstream norms as they shape their ethnic identity. Stan reappropriates the mainstream meaning of Tommy Hilfiger shirts and biker boots. Tina can speak directly and assertively in class using mainstream Standard English, but her attitude and demeanor are perceived as distinctly black. Both of these students maintain an ethos and worldview seated in the experience of their black community, but at the same time, they are relatively accommodating toward mainstream standards. Such changes in meaning and practice are likely to continue in their community in predictable and unpredictable ways.

Ethnicity.   Ethnicity is often associated with static traditions, customs, and values that reflect a deep and enduring cultural identity and a desire to keep that identity intact. Ethnic identity has traditionally been asserted through preferences in food, clothing, language, religion, and the like. It is also often tied up with blood relations, geographic location, and nationality. Recent conflict between Bosnians and Serbs—a matter of nationality and land against a backdrop of religion—is a case in point. Recent conflicts in African countries such as Rwanda and Burundi provide further examples.

Ethnic identity is how ethnic groups define themselves and maintain meaning for living individually and collectively. In contemporary industrial societies, ethnic identity is part of a person's social identity, which includes occupational roles, gender roles, individual and family mobility, family rituals (regarding meals, for instance), and methods of solving family problems, to name a few. The meanings of a person's identity shift, however subtly and slowly, as a result of economic, social, and political processes interacting with individual beliefs and values. Ethnic people, consequently, do not end up practicing the exact particulars of what they espouse about their values, customs, traditions, and other things that make up ethnic identity.

Such a dilemma might be thought of as the difference between upholding the "spirit" of the law and the "letter" of the law. Ethnic groups in complex societies such as the United States often are better able to uphold the spirit rather than the letter of their values, customs, and beliefs. It is less a matter of truth or fact than one of process, change, and adaptation. When change and adaptation do not occur, ethnic culture may become a "trap," facilitate maladaptation, and leave a group economically, socially, and politically disenfranchised (Bohannan, 1995).

Social Class.   Social class, or **socioeconomic status (SES)**, is a dirty word among Americans. Americans generally believe that any class differences that may exist are of one's own making.

But class differences do exist, and they document another form of inequality, as well as imperfections in our capitalist economic system. Social class is a way of ascribing status, prestige, and power. It is based on education, income, and occupation. Each of these indices—how much education one has, how much money one makes or has, and what one does for a living—carries poignant meanings derived from subjective values and beliefs interacting with dominant customs, traditions, and notions of common sense. Social scientists do not fully know how or why, but the meanings associated with social class get condensed into our society's fascination with lifestyles.

The more common terms we use to categorize class status are upper, middle, working, and lower or underclass. These categories and their meanings become infused into identities such as race and ethnicity. Stan's and Tina's identities as blacks or African Americans automatically tend to reduce their social class status to the category of lower or underclass. The income, occupation, and education of Stan and Tina's families, however, would generally place them in the middle class.

A way to understand the power of class or socioeconomic status is to identify your family of origin's class status when you were living at home. Why was that status assigned? What did it mean in social terms? What do you think of when a person is referred to as lower class? What are your thoughts and beliefs about clients who are on welfare?

Gender.   Along with race, gender has been over the past 30 years, and remains today, one of the most contested concepts. Gender is what our culture symbolizes and means by maleness and femaleness. These terms are further defined through the prescribed roles of men and women, boys and girls, husbands and wives. The physical characteristics of male and female bodies, combined with their sexual and reproductive functions, carry strong symbolic meanings. Natural differences between males and females are perceived by many as an indisputable basis for assigning different gender roles.

Natural differences translate into inequitable power and opportunity for men and women, as seen in social, economic, and political arenas. In other words, natural differences translate into differences in rank, power, and prestige at home, at work, in churches, mosques, or synagogues, in school, and at play.

No doubt, meanings surrounding gender involve historical processes. Gender meanings are also the product of dominant structures reinforced by traditions, customs, and our dominant notions of common sense. A thorough understanding of gender is hindered without consideration of these factors. However, gender meanings are currently in flux in our society.

At Community High, for example, aggressive behavior by boys toward girls has generated a provocative response from girls. Girls have regendered some of their social practices by adopting the aggressive language and posturing of boys as a defense against the boys (Cousins & Mabrey, 1998). Many of Tina's female peers have abandoned ascribed characteristics such as passivity, weakness, and inactivity (lack of agency), which are part and parcel of the traditional meanings assigned to female gender roles (Ortner, 1996). One consequence, in school and beyond, is that these girls have been defined as unladylike and loud (Fordham, 1993). By contrast, the aggressiveness and loudness of boys have been defined as "boys being boys"—being who they naturally are and doing what they naturally do as males. In the domain of sexual activity, strong traditions and entrenched frames of reference among school staff and some students still render the girls as the polluted or promiscuous participants in sexual liaisons. Sexual activity only becomes a social problem for a boy if the boy gets a venereal disease or the girl gets pregnant. Underlying these gender relations are traditions and customs that have shaped how girls' and boys' bodies and activities are defined. Girls redefining themselves in response to environmental forces, however, is a good example of praxis.

Family. Family and kinship are key symbols in American life (Schneider, 1968; Stacey, 1990). Family may be defined as a set of relationships among two or more people to carry out various social and biological functions, such as support, nurturance, sexual mating, procreation, and child rearing. Family is also an ideological construct on which we impose ideas about intimacy, love, morality, and kinship connections and obligations. Issues of contemporary versus traditional family values, structure, and change can serve as one last example of how culture works as a process, as well as how cultural change and adaptation proceed.

We have been bombarded in recent years by scholarly and public dialogue about the demise of "family values." Many believe this demise leads to the destruction of family life and thereby society (Gallagher, 1996; Popenoe, 1996; Whitehead, 1997). Recent debates about family life and its role in the maintenance of society at large have been fueled by both research and the opinions of influential politicians. On one side is the argument that increases in single parenting, divorce, and out-of-wedlock births are a reflection and a source of moral malaise, misplaced or absent values, and consequently social instability and the demise of American society. Families of the past have been thrown up as the model for families of the present. On the other side are arguments attempting to counter the "hysteria" about family values. John Gillis (1996), in particular, notes that neither family change nor anxiety about such change is new. In fact, "diversity, instability, and discontinuity have been part of the European experience of family at least since the late Middle Ages, and continued into the new world" (Skolnick, 1997, p. 87).

At the heart of these debates is a process addressed differently by both sides: If we value family coherence in the form of a stable household consisting of mother, father, and children, why do we have such a high divorce rate, an increase in single parenting, and an increase in nontraditional types of relationships, suggesting almost the opposite? One side claims that recent trends reflect the absence of morals and virtue in our society; if we punish those who don't have morals and reward those who do, we can fix things. The other side argues that a host of medical and economic changes—including birth control and women working outside the home—have fueled social and cultural changes, in particular how women fit into the scheme of society and family life. Thus, while divorce is not desirable, neither is it as shameful and economically devastating for women as it has been in the past.

The process of family change and adaptation is complex. Much of it reflects the values we *want* our families to live by versus the values families actually *practice* in managing the psychological, social, biological, economic, and political facts of life. Skolnick (1997) describes this discrepancy as "the gap between the families we live with and the symbolic families we live by" (p. 86). Family life is structured by meanings, values, and beliefs that fit our desires and imaginations about what is right and appropriate. But family life is also constructed and lived in a world of competing and interacting meanings and material realities. People do not always do what they intend. They do construct and author their lives, so to speak, but they do so with a host of choices among very real constraints.

Stan and his parents intend for him to be successful in school and avoid criminal behavior. So far, however, Stan's life has not turned out the way he or his family wanted. Social workers who want to understand and assist families have to understand the processes that create these realities. They cannot be reduced solely to psychological, economic, or social factors outside of the cultural contexts that shape life: history, structure, human agency, common sense, traditions, customs, and the like. Added to this are the constantly changing social, economic, and political realities of life in our society.

The Meaning of Culture

Social workers must not limit themselves to understanding culture only in the terms provided by other academic, scholarly, and professional traditions. We must position ourselves to understand what culture means and how it works in our own terms and in a multidimensional context. Such an understanding of culture challenges simplistic psychological analyses of individual and collective human practices that claim to adequately explain child abuse/neglect, poverty, academic failure, parent/child problems, substance abuse, school dropout, and a host of other psychosocial and social policy issues. We want to know how our world and the world of our clients is constructed in all of its complexity. Even though such knowledge will inevitably remain incomplete due to the motion of life and the world of nature impinging on us, and we on it, we must try. Indeed, tools are available for just such an activity: a practice orientation and a multidimensional conceptualization of culture.

Ann Swidler's definition of culture summarizes what I have tried to express in this chapter. She sees culture as a "tool kit" of symbols, stories, rituals, and worldviews that people may use in varying configurations to solve different kinds of problems. Culture works by suggesting strategies of action or persistent ways of ordering or patterning action through time, rather than only shaping ultimate ends or values toward which action is directed (Swidler, 1986, p. 273; Rosaldo, 1989/1993).

In the case of Community High students like Stan and Tina, who they have become and how they perform depend on a complex maze of social and psychological processes embedded in American and African American cultures. The interaction of these processes contributes to Stan's and Tina's ethos and worldview. The extent to which these processes limit and restrain their overall academic and social success is an important question. Neither Stan nor Tina can live outside of the meaning of their blackness, or ethnicity, and gender in the strained social world they inhabit. Their individual human agency is a factor, however; it gives them latitude in how they interpret or act on such meanings. Tina has managed to transcend culturally insensitive school processes without giving up her ethnic identity. Stan is still finding his way. Still, their interpretations of life events could serve either as motivation or as a source of debilitating anxiety and despair. Their interpretations could also generate indignation and ethnic zealotry on the part of mainstream America. If they do, will Tina or Stan respond by becoming a race leader? Or will their interpretations result in a loss of self-worth and personal value, leading to a fatalistic dependence on drugs and alcohol to soften the reality of not being powerful and white?

Equally important, what will your interpretations be as a social worker encountering similar students? Will you have a grasp of the fact that people experience strain and contradictions between the meanings in their heads and the social, economic, and political realities of everyday public life?

By summarizing a contemporary paradox of family life, Arlene Skolnick offers us insight into a host of practice and policy issues for social work. Reiterating a point cited earlier, she says the problem is one in which "Americans have still not come to terms with the gap between the way we think our families ought to be and the complex, often messy realities of our lives" (Skolnick, 1997, p. 86). Insert *traditions, customs, values,* and so on, for the word *families,* and we have a succinct formulation of the simplicity and complexity of culture as a lived process in contemporary industrial societies.

IMPLICATIONS FOR SOCIAL WORK PRACTICE

I learned how the practice orientation works as an ethnographer at Community High, conducting research largely to describe the students' culture from their point of view as well as mine as a researcher. As a social worker, you may be doing ethnographic inquiry without knowing it. Here are a few principles you can follow:

- Recognize the categories of knowledge—social science theories and orientations, folk or common everyday theories and orientations—that you rely on to understand human behavior in the social environment. You, like everyone else in our culture, operate under the constraints of a multiplicity of customs, traditions, values, and beliefs.

- Embrace the traditions, customs, values, and behaviors of disparate groups identified by race, ethnicity, gender, nationality, and religion. Avoid approaching these groups in a cookbook, stereotyped, or one-size-fits-all fashion. To do so is to limit your understanding of people's lives and problems to a static notion of traditions, customs, and traits.

- Appreciate the tension between the force of structure and the resiliency and intentionality of human agency in complex societies such as ours. See the force of structure in unacceptable levels of poverty, low-wage labor, and social class divisions, as well as inequality based on race/ ethnicity and gender. But recognize the force of human agency every day as you see people penetrate and transcend their circumstances and participate in the transformation of their lives and society.

- Recognize the complexity of social existence. Attempt to understand both personal and social acts of making meaning, and realize how such acts give substance to and obscure our own lives as well as those of our clients.

- Consider understanding culture in terms of the practice orientation. It facilitates a "strengths" perspective and allows you to assess the simultaneous forces of history, structure, human agency, and the political context in which all of these forces work themselves out.

- Use the practice orientation to frame the actions of African Americans and other groups who resist being mainstream Americans. This perspective will help you see the creativity and hope, as well as the ugliness and pain, of their resistance.

MAIN POINTS

1. In contemporary society, culture refers to the ethos and worldview of a particular people, how they construct and employ meanings that guide their perceptions and behavior in multiple contexts.

2. Features of life such as ethnic customs, traditions, values, beliefs, and notions of common sense are not static entities, but neither are they changing very rapidly.

3. Under the influence of specific intellectual traditions of particular moments in history, the definition of culture has evolved. Today it helps us understand the diversity of human behavior in the context of the social and material worlds we inhabit.

4. Our understanding of others is always in terms of the understandings we have constructed both about ourselves and about how the world does and should operate. We can easily misunderstand others by using our own categories and rankings to order such realities.

5. Culture as a concept has grown from its use for ranking and categorizing traits, customs, habits, and traditions to its use for understanding the social principles, laws, rules, patterns, and regularities that govern human behavior at the level of structures and symbols.

6. Structures and symbols facilitate the creation and transmission of meaning both in our minds and through public behavior.

7. The categories of meaning we have created are cultural constructions that constrain us or free us as human agents in a world of social and material matter.

8. A practice orientation attempts to account for cultural processes by characterizing human action as a product of structure, a producer of structure, and a participant in the transformation of structure.

9. An understanding of praxis is necessary to grasp the increasing complexity of the construction and employment of meaning regarding identities, representations, illness and maladaptation, and the distribution of resources in a world based on political, social, and economic structures and processes.

KEY TERMS

accommodation

assimilation

biological determinism

common sense

cultural relativism

cultural resistance

culture

culture of poverty

customs

ethnic identity

ethnocentrism

ethos

hegemony

ideology

phenotype

practice orientation

praxis

public symbols

race

racism

semiotic

socioeconomic status (SES)

symbol

traditions

worldview

WORLD WIDE WEB RESOURCES

Diversity & Ethnic Studies: Virtual Community

http://www.public.iastate.edu/~savage/divweb2.htm

Maintained at Iowa State University. A collection of links to diversity-related Internet resources on topics such as African Americans, Native Americans, Asian Americans, U.S. Latinos, people with disabilities, lesbians, bisexuals and gays, and general multicultural links.

Multicultural Pavilion

http://curry.edschool.virginia.edu/go/multicultural/

Site maintained by Paul Gorski, a Ph.D. student at the University of Virginia. Contains resources, research, awareness activities, and links to multicultural topics.

Multiculturalism

http://multicultural.miningco.com/mbody.htm

Site developed by General Internet, Inc. Contains information, resources, bulletin boards, ethnic groups, and links to multicultural sites.

Formal Organizations

NEW LEADERSHIP AT BEACON CENTER

Beacon Center has a short but proud history of providing innovative services to persons who are homeless in the small midwestern city where it is located. It was established in 1980, thanks to one woman, Martha Green, and her relentless pursuit of a vision. While serving as executive director of the YWCA, Martha became increasingly concerned about the growing homeless population in the city. During the 1960s and early 1970s, she had worked in several positions in the city's antipoverty agency, and she was well known throughout the city for her uncompromising advocacy efforts for families living in poverty. She had supporters, and she had antagonists. Martha was also a skilled advocate and service planner, and she soon pulled together supporters for a new social service agency to address the special needs of homeless persons. A mix of private and public, federal and local, funds were secured, and Beacon Center (BC) opened with Martha Green as director, working with the assistance of one staff social worker. The agency grew steadily, and by 1990 it had a staff of 15, as well as several subcontracted programs.

Martha Green valued client input into program development and made sure that client voices were heard at all levels: at City Council meetings, in community discussions of program needs, in Center discussions of program needs and issues, in staff interviews, and at board meetings. She remained uncompromising in advocacy efforts, and she often angered city officials because she was unyielding in her demands for fair treatment of homeless persons. She advocated for their right to receive resources and services from other social service organizations, as well as for their right to congregate in public places. By the same token, she and the staff consistently reminded clients of their obligations as citizens and, gently but firmly, held them to those obligations. Clients were sometimes angered by this call for responsible behavior, but they appreciated the tireless advocacy of Martha Green and the staff. They also appreciated that they were kept fully informed about political issues that concerned them, as well as about actions taken by BC in relation to these issues.

Martha Green also had a vision regarding staff relationships. She was committed to collaborative work, to trusting frontline workers to make their own decisions, and to securing the participation of all staff on important policy decisions. Rules were kept to a minimum, and staff relationships were very personal. For example, a staff member needing to keep a medical appointment would make informal arrangements with another staff member to exchange an hour of service, with no need to "go through channels" or invoke formal sick leave. Martha believed in hiring the best-trained and most experienced staff for frontline positions and, over the years, hired and retained a highly skilled, committed core staff. She had high expectations of her staff, particularly in terms of their commitment to the rights of homeless persons, but she was also a nurturant administrator who was concerned about the personal well-being and professional development of each staff member. She established a climate of mutual respect where people could risk disagreeing. She spent some time every week working in each program area to ensure that she understood the agency's programs as they were experienced by clients and frontline staff. She kept staff fully informed about economic and political pressures faced by BC, and about her actions in regard to these issues. She regularly sought their input on these issues, and decisions were usually made by consensus. On occasion, however, around really sensitive issues—such as the choice between forgoing a salary increase or closing a program—she asked staff to vote by secret ballot to neutralize any potential power dynamics.

Martha had a vision, as well, about how a board of directors can facilitate a successful client-centered program. She saw the board as part of the BC system, just as staff and clients are part of the system. She worked hard to ensure that members chosen for the board shared the BC commitment to the rights of homeless persons, and she developed warm, personal relationships with them. She kept the board fully informed about issues facing BC, and she was successful in securing their support and active involvement in advocacy and resource development activities.

Over the years, BC became known as an innovative, client-centered service center, as well as a hardheaded advocacy organization. Staff and board members took pride in being part of what they considered to be a very special endeavor—one that also outstripped other social service organizations in its expertise, commitment, and compassion. Clients were not always satisfied with the services, but generally acknowledged among themselves that they were lucky to have the dedication of BC.

Reactions from the community were more mixed, however. The respect offered up was, in many circles, a grudging respect. Many city officials as well as staff of other social service organizations complained about the self-righteous attitudes and uncompromising posture of Martha Green and the staff at BC. These detractors acknowledged that the tactics of BC staff were successful in countering discrimination against homeless persons, but suggested that BC succeeded at much cost of goodwill. Although Martha Green believed in keeping staff, clients, and board members informed about the economic and political pressures faced by BC, she saw it as her job to carry the major responsibility for responding to, and absorbing, those pressures, to protect staff energy for serving clients.

CASE STUDY

Martha Green retired in 1995 and relocated with her husband to be closer to their children. An acting director was appointed at BC while a search for permanent director was underway. The acting director had worked several years at BC and shared much of Martha's administrative and service philosophy. She was not as good, however, at juggling the multiple demands of the position. Staff and clients felt a loss of support; board members lost some of their enthusiasm and confidence; and antagonists in the community saw an opportunity to mute some of BC's advocacy efforts. Staff maintained a strong commitment to the rights of homeless persons, but they lost some of their optimism about making a difference.

After eight months, Helen Blue, a former community college administrator, was hired as the new executive director. Helen was excited about this new professional challenge, but she had a somewhat different vision for BC. She was concerned about the alienation that had resulted, in some circles, from BC's hard-hitting advocacy stance, and she favored a more conciliatory approach. For example, after meeting with city officials, she assigned staff social workers the task of convincing clients to quit congregating in the city park near BC and to stay out of the business district during business hours. After meeting with directors of other social service organizations, she directed staff to be less demanding in their advocacy for clients.

Helen Blue was also concerned about the lack of rules and the "looseness" of attention to chain of command, and she began to institute new rules and procedures. Staff meetings and open community meetings with clients became presentations by Helen. Staff were no longer allowed to attend board meetings, and were not informed about what happened at them. Frontline staff often found their decisions overturned by Helen. When the first staff resignation came, Helen hired the replacement with no input from staff, clients, or board members.

On a recent visit to BC, a staff member was heard to say, "I don't want to leave this place; I still want to make a difference. But what was once a family to me has become a turbulent place to work. I miss the support, the sense of family, and the pride of being a special kind of place. We spend too much time finding ways to thwart Helen, and that is not why I became a social worker." On the same visit, a group of clients was overheard talking about BC. They agreed that there is no other place to turn, but all nodded agreement when one man suggested, "I knew what I could count on before, but now I can never be sure. It depends on who gets involved."

A Definition of Formal Organizations

You were probably born in a hospital. There is a good chance that you began to attend a house of worship at an early age. You may have enrolled in a child care-center by the age of 4. You have, by now, spent close to two decades in school. Along the way, you may have joined organizations such as Girl Scouts, Boy Scouts, YMCA, YWCA, or other athletic clubs. You may also have participated in programs offered by civic and social service organizations, as a member, recipient of services, or volunteer. You probably manage your finances with the assistance of a bank, and you meet your basic survival needs as well as fulfill your consumer wants through a variety of business organizations. Some of you are, or have been, members of sororities and fraternities, and some may be student members of the National Association of Social Workers (NASW). Most of you have been a paid employee of at least one formal organization, and many of you are currently enrolled in a field practicum in a social service organization like Beacon Center.

Formal organizations are pervasive in our lives. But what, exactly, is a formal organization? Bozeman's (1987, p. 6) definition of organization is consistent with my idea of what it is: A **formal organization** is a "formally structured and social collective established to attain goals by acquiring resources from the environment and directing those resources to activities perceived as relevant to the goals." This definition, like others found in the literature (for example, Blau & Scott, 1962; Etzioni, 1977; Katz & Kahn, 1978), has three key components: a collectivity of people, a highly formal structure, and the common purpose of working together to meet a goal or goals.

This definition leaves a lot of room for variation. Formal organizations differ in size, structure, culture, and goals. They also perform a variety of functions in contemporary society and influence human behavior in many ways. Exhibit 10.1 is a list of what contemporary organizations do. You can see that formal organizations are intricately woven into the fabric of life in contemporary society, that different organizations perform different societal functions, that formal organizations can be both functional and dysfunctional for society or for specific groups, and that some members of organizations benefit more than others from organizational goals and structure.

You might want to think about how well this list of functions of organizations describe Beacon Center, your School of Social Work, your field agency, and an organization where you have been an employee. Think, too, about how much formal organizations influence our behavior. They meet our needs, help us fulfill goals, and nurture our development. They also make stressful demands, thwart our goals, inhibit our holistic development, and constrain our behavior. The purpose for introducing theory and research about formal organizations in this chapter is twofold: (1) to help you understand the pervasive and multifaceted influence of formal organizations on human behavior, yours as well as that of the clients you serve; and (2) to assist you in understanding the organizations in which social workers practice.

Perspectives on Formal Organizations

At the current time, ways of thinking about organizations include such a variety of perspectives that Jeffrey Pfeffer (1982) has characterized the state of organization theory as "more of a weed patch than a well-tended garden" (p. 1). Likewise, the research on organizations and the related

EXHIBIT 10.1

The Functions
of Formal
Organizations

1. *Formal organizations are human facilitators.* Organizations help us get things done and meet our needs. Collective activities are often superior to individual efforts because of speed, accuracy, human connectedness, and other factors.

2. *Formal organizations organize society.* Every aspect of contemporary life is systematized and coordinated through formal organizations.

3. *Formal organizations are political institutions.* All organizations perform some type of political activity, whether it is personal politics, group politics, interorganizational politics, interest group politics, policy politics, or partisan politics. In addition, all organizations are involved in the promotion of the ideology of the political system in which they operate.

4. *Formal organizations are instruments of system maintenance and enhancement.* Organizations engage in activities that maintain or enhance the economic, political, and social systems in which they operate.

5. *Formal organizations are change agents.* Although organizations often resist change, they also play a role in societal reform and change.

6. *Formal organizations create culture and counterculture.* Organizations produce and promote the general cultural values of the popular culture as well as specific organizational cultural values that run counter to the popular culture. In this way, organizations may play a proactive role in the societies in which they operate.

7. *Formal organizations are tools of policy implementation.* Organizations provide some stability and predictability as they implement policy over time.

8. *Formal organizations are tools of development.* Organizations produce advancements in science, technology, and other aspects of human functioning. Some of these "advancements" improve the human condition, some aggravate it, and many provide both benefits and costs.

9. *Formal organizations are destructive forces.* The processes that organizations use to accomplish organizational goals may create environmental pollution or work conditions that are hazardous to the well-being of organizational members. The goals of the organization may be to develop products for waging war or products detrimental to the health of citizens.

10. *Formal organizations are instruments of repression and domination.* Organizations may be, and often are, instruments of control, domination, class rule, and exploitation.

11. *Formal organizations are alienators.* In many organizations, hierarchical structures with their arrangements of power generate inequality and alienation.

12. *Formal organizations are tension-management systems.* Organizations develop processes for managing the tensions between individual goals and organizational goals, among competing organizational goals, or among competing individual goals. Processes are also developed to manage class tensions related to inequalities in organizational structure.

13. *Formal organizations threaten individual rights.* Individual rights are limited, to varying degrees, by organizational roles, rules, and norms.

14. *Formal organizations form the administrative state of governance.* Webs of corporate organizations and government organizations create a highly centralized and concentrated social structure.

15. *Formal organizations are a forum for discourse.* Their members have multiple perspectives about goals, processes, and structures. Organizations, therefore, become sites for more or less democratic disagreement and negotiation, the active construction of meaning and purpose, and problem resolution.

Source: Based on Farazmand (1994); #15 from Fox and Miller (1995).

prescriptions for organizational administration reflect a "bewildering array of variables" (Pfeffer, 1982, p. 1). Nevertheless, four generalizations can be made about the abundant multi-disciplinary literature on formal organizations:

1. Early theories of organizations assumed that a rational organizational structure (bureau-cracy) would ensure the effective and efficient accomplishment of organizational goals, which were assumed to be clear and specific. Contemporary theories challenge the rationality of formal organizations, but the image of the modern organization as a rational instrument (machine) of efficiency and predictability has had a lasting influence on theories of organizations (Farazmand, 1994; Morgan, 1986).

2. Early theories focused on what happens inside organizations and ignored all aspects of their environments. In contrast, contemporary theories generally propose some sort of relationship between organization and environment (Hasenfeld, 1992).

3. Most organizational theory has been biased toward the interests of owners and managers rather than toward the interests of workers (Carter & Jackson, 1993; Farazmand, 1994). For this reason, you may struggle with the language in this chapter, finding it too mechanistic, aloof, and lacking in intimacy. In recent years, critical theorists have challenged this one-sided view of organizations and raised questions about domination and oppression in organizational life (Farazmand, 1994; Hearn & Parkin, 1993).

4. As Pfeffer (1997) has recently noted, organizational theory has paid little attention to the effects of the physical environment on organizational life. He recommends that the physical environment become a new direction for organizational theory and research—a recommendation consistent with the decision to include a chapter on the physical environment in this book.

Several people have attempted to organize the weed patch of organizational theory into a garden—to bring some order to the diversity of viewpoints without denying the complexity and multifaceted nature of contemporary formal organizations (for example, Dattalo, 1990; Hasenfeld, 1992; Morgan, 1986; Pfeffer, 1982). Here we use a classification system suggested by Ali Farazamand (1994, pp. 41–42) that includes four perspectives: instrumental rationality perspective, systems perspective, interpretive perspective, and critical perspective. No one of these perspectives accounts for all 15 functions of organizations listed in Exhibit 10.1, but taken together, they elaborate the multifaceted nature of organizations reflected in the 15 functions. Each perspective encompasses both classical and contemporary theories, and each has relevance for social work practice.

Instrumental Rationality Perspective

Rational choice perspective

When Helen Blue became the executive director at Beacon Center, she was concerned, among other things, about the lack of administrative formality, the lack of rules, and chain of command. She also wanted greater authority over planning and decision making. These concerns reflect the **instrumental rationality perspective,** which views the formal organization as a "goal-directed, purposefully designed machine" (Hasenfeld, 1992, p. 25). It assumes that organizations

EXHIBIT 10.2

The Instrumental
Rationality
Perspective
on Formal
Organizations

Major theme: The organization is a goal-directed, purposefully designed machine (closed system).	
Theory	**Central Idea**
The ideal-type bureaucracy (Weber)	Formal rationality—rules, regulations, and structures—are essential to goal accomplishment.
Scientific management (Taylor)	The most effective organizations maximize internal efficiency, the "one best way."
Human relations theory	Human relationships are central to organizational efficiency and effectiveness.
Decision theory	Organizational rationality has limits.

can be designed with structures and processes that maximize efficiency and effectiveness, concepts that are highly valued in this perspective. **Efficiency** is obtaining a high ratio of output to input, achieving the best outcome from the least investment of resources. **Effectiveness** is goal accomplishment. Exhibit 10.2 summarizes the central theories in this perspective.

The Ideal-Type Bureaucracy.   In the modern era, formal organization is often equated with bureaucracy (for example, Longres, 1995, p. 320). Indeed, Max Weber, the German sociologist who formulated a theory of bureaucracy at the turn of the century, saw bureaucracy and capitalism as inseparable (Weber, 1947). Weber proposed a **bureaucracy** as the most efficient form of organization for goal accomplishment. The characteristics of Weber's ideal-type bureaucracy are presented in Exhibit 10.3. Weber based the ideal-type bureaucracy on formal rationality, or the use of rules, regulations, and social structures to achieve the chosen ends (Ritzer, 1993).

Weber was enthusiastic about the advantages of the ideal-type bureaucracy over other ways of organizing for goal accomplishment, but he did not see bureaucracies as problem-free. He was concerned about the dehumanizing potential of bureaucracies—their potential to become an **iron cage of rationality** trapping people and denying many aspects of their humanity. Researchers have noted that the excessive use of rules and procedures often limits the efficiency and effectiveness of bureaucratic organizations.

In spite of the potential negative effects of bureaucracies, "it is safe to say that most organizations in the modern world are designed bureaucratically and seek maximum efficiency" (Farazmand, 1994, p. 9). This model applies to human service organizations, as well as organizations formed for other purposes (Hasenfeld, 1992). How closely do the social work organizations you have worked in fit the ideal-type bureaucracy? How much emphasis is put on efficiency? Helen Blue wants to move Beacon Center closer to the ideal-type bureaucracy than it was under Martha Green's leadership.

Scientific Management.   Another turn-of-the century approach to formal organizations has had lasting influence. Frederick W. Taylor's (1911) **scientific management**, sometimes referred

EXHIBIT 10.3

Characteristics of
Weber's Ideal-Type
Bureaucracy and
Taylor's Scientific
Management

Ideal-Type Bureaucracy
- Clear hierarchy and chain of command
- Clear division of labor based on specialized skills
- Formal rules of operation
- Formal and task-oriented communications
- Merit-based recruitment and advancement
- Keeping of files and records for administrative action

Scientific Management
- Time and motion studies to find the "one best way" to perform each organizational task
- Scientific selection and training of workers
- Training focused on performing tasks in the standardized "one best way"
- Close managerial monitoring of workers to ensure accurate implementation of task prescriptions and to provide appropriate rewards for compliance
- Managerial authority over planning and decision making, with no challenge from workers

to as Taylorism, was directed toward maximizing internal efficiency. The set of principles that Taylor developed to guide the design of organizations was widely adopted by both industry and government, first in the United States and then worldwide. These principles are listed in Exhibit 10.3, along with those of Weber's ideal-type bureaucracy.

In his provocative book *The McDonaldization of Society* (1993), George Ritzer proposes that McDonald's restaurant is a prototype organization, whose organizational style is "coming to dominate more and more sectors of American society as well as of the rest of the world" (p. 2). This new type of organization, which operates on the combined principles of bureaucratization and scientific management, has four key traits:

1. *Efficiency,* which is valued in a fast-paced society
2. *Quantification,* with an emphasis on saving time and money rather than on quality of product
3. *Predictability,* with the assurance that a Big Mac will be the same in San Francisco as in Washington, D.C., or Hong Kong
4. *Control,* with workers trained to do a limited number of things exactly as they are told to do them, and with maximum use of nonhuman technology

Ritzer gives many examples of the proliferation of the McDonald's model, including shopping malls; packaged tours; managed medical care; weight loss organizations; the "junk-food journalism" of *USA Today*; the use of machine-graded multiple-choice examinations; reliance on GPAs, PSATs, SATs, and GREs for evaluating educational accomplishment; franchised hotels; planned communities; and franchised child care-centers.

Principles of scientific management are frequently followed in social service organizations, and they are becoming more pervasive as managed care arrangements become more prominent in social service delivery. For example, these organizations undertake task and workload analyses to improve effectiveness and efficiency, and managers develop procedures, regulations, and decision trees to be implemented by direct service workers. Have you encountered any of these in your field setting? Although Helen Blue has initiated more procedures and regulations and believes in managerial authority over planning and decision making, she does not share scientific management's enthusiasm for "one best way" of delivering services.

Human Relations Theory.   **Human relations theory** introduced a new twist on maximizing organizational efficiency and effectiveness. The theory grew out of a series of studies conducted by Elton Mayo (1933) and associates at the Hawthorne plant of the Western Electric Company in the 1920s and 1930s. Seeking to improve the rationality of the organization, the researchers were studying the effects of working conditions, such as intensity of lighting, on productivity. As expected, the researchers found that productivity increased as the lighting intensity increased. To their surprise, however, productivity continued to increase even when they began to dim the lights in an attempt to confirm their findings. The researchers concluded that *technical rationality*—the development of rational structures, procedures, and processes—is not sufficient to ensure maximum productivity. *Social factors,* they concluded, are as important if not more important than technical factors in accomplishing organizational goals. They based this conclusion, which became the central proposition of a new theory, on their observation that productivity appeared to be related to worker morale and sense of social responsibility to the work group.

This interpretation of the research findings has been criticized on the basis of the **Hawthorne effect**—the tendency of experimental participants to perform in particular ways simply because they know they are being studied. In other words, critics have suggested that the participants in the study may have become more productive simply because they knew that their behavior was being studied.

Regardless of the validity of the initial findings, subsequent research led to the human relations theory of organizational management, which emphasized the heretofore unrecognized importance of human interaction in organizational efficiency and effectiveness. As the theory developed, it also proposed that democratic leadership is more effective than authoritarian management in securing worker cooperation.

The social workers at Beacon Center did indeed respond more cooperatively to Martha Green's democratic leadership than to Helen Blue's more authoritarian leadership. F. Ellen Netting, Peter M. Kettner, and Steven L. McMurtry (1993) have noted that the human relations approach is a favorite theory of organizations among social work students, who are after all fundamentally concerned with human interaction. In a similar vein, Hasenfeld (1992, p. 27) suggests that "the human relations approach is particularly important in the human services since it is assumed that the attitudes of the staff to their work situation and their coworkers will have direct consequences to how they relate to their clients."

Conflict perspective

It is important to note, however, that human relations theory is still in the instrumental rationality tradition. Like scientific management, it focuses on maximizing efficiency and effectiveness, and it endorses the interests of owners and managers. Managers must become leaders capable of securing the cooperation of workers, but they are still in control of the organization. Although the consideration of human interaction opens the possibility of nonrational factors in organizational life, human relations theorists still assume that, with "leadership skills," human interactions can be as rationally managed as structures and procedures. For this reason, Farazmand (1994, p. 13) refers to human relations theory as "twentieth century's most seductive managerial ideology."

Humanistic perspective

After losing ground during the 1950s, human relations theory was reinvigorated in the 1960s by **organizational humanism** and a subfield called organizational development. These theories suggest that organizations can maximize efficiency and effectiveness while also promoting individual happiness and well-being. Douglas McGregor (1960), for example, a proponent of organizational humanism, identified two opposing sets of assumptions from which managers view workers (summarized in Exhibit 10.4). McGregor suggested that **theory X** calls for directive management, but **theory Y** calls for greater democratization of decision making in organizations. In your work experiences, have you encountered either of these theories about workers? If so, how did you react as a worker?

Some research (for example, Herzberg, 1966) has supported the superiority of theory Y management over theory X management, but in one much-cited study, Morse and Lorsch (1970) found that the preferred management approach depends on the nature of the organizational task. Tasks that are predictable, repetitive, and technically precise are best accomplished with theory X management; tasks that are vague and diversified are best accomplished with theory Y management. Netting, Kettner, and McMurtry (1993) cite this study as evidence that social service organizations are often better suited to theory Y management, because social work tasks are "often loosely defined" (p. 134).

McGregor's work, like that of other organizational humanists, has a dual focus on individual well-being and organizational efficiency and effectiveness, but also assumes a fit between individual goals and organizational goals. Critical theorists, as you will see later, criticize the organizational humanists for their failure to recognize conflicting goals and power differentials within organizations. By focusing on individual well-being, however, organizational humanism serves as a bridge to the interpretive and critical perspectives. By focusing on the interdependencies of

EXHIBIT 10.4

Assumptions of Theory X and Theory Y

Assumptions of Theory X	**Assumptions of Theory Y**
Workers have an inherent dislike of work.	Workers see work as a natural activity.
Workers prefer to be told what to do.	Workers are self-directed when working on projects to which they are committed.
Workers respond to money as the primary motivator.	Workers seek responsibility when organizational goals are congruent with their needs. They have more creative contributions to make than organizations generally allow.

Source: Based on McGregor, 1960.

individuals and organizations, organizational humanism also serves as a bridge to the systems perspective.

Decision Making Theory. In the 1950s, organizational theorists in the instrumental rationality tradition began to write about the limits to organizational rationality. Herbert Simon (1957) presented a **decision making theory** of organizations, focusing on how the decisions of individuals in organizations affect the organization as a whole.

March and Simon (1958) argued that administrators cannot be perfectly rational in their decision making, because they face many constraints that limit their alternatives: incomplete information about alternatives for action, incomplete understanding of the consequences of those actions, and incapacity to explore more than a limited number of alternatives at a time. March and Simon used the term **bounded rationality** to describe this limited rationality of organizational actors. They also suggested that bounded rationality leads administrators and other organizational actors to **satisfice** rather than maximize when making decisions—to seek satisfactory rather than perfect solutions, and to discontinue the search for alternatives when a satisfactory solution is available. This is very similar to Gambrill's (1990) suggestion (see Chapter 2) that clinical social workers tend to discontinue their search for information prematurely.

Facilitated by developments in computer science, decision making theory has traveled in the direction of numerical data and quantification of information. Social service organizations, like other organizations, have developed sophisticated computer information systems to reduce the uncertainty of decision making. In child welfare, where reduction of uncertainty is a critical issue, researchers have developed computer-based models for different child welfare decision points, such as investigation decision, child removal decision, and reunification decision (Jaffe, 1979; Schuerman, Mullen, Stagner, & Johnson, 1989; Schwab, Bruce, & McRoy, 1985, 1986; Sicoly, 1989). These models are useful checklists for data to be collected by the social worker, but we do not yet know if they actually increase the safety of children because they have not yet been validated against follow-up data.

The decision making model emerged out of the instrumental rationality approach, but some versions also show kinship with both the systems and the interpretive perspectives. Decision making theory's attention to the constraints placed on organizational decision makers by a host of factors both internal and external to the organization is consistent with the systems perspective's emphasis on the interrelatedness of phenomena. The emphasis on nonrational elements in organizations, stronger in some versions of decision making theory than in others, is consistent with developments in the interpretive perspective. These similarities will become more apparent in the discussions that follow.

Systems Perspective

Systems perspective

Martha Green and Helen Blue had different styles of managing what happened inside Beacon Center, but they also had different styles of managing external pressures and resources. Martha focused on giving homeless persons a voice in efforts to secure political and economic resources for Beacon Center; Helen focused on conciliation with community and political leaders. In her own way, however, each was attentive to Beacon Center's relationship with its environment. In this respect, they negated one aspect of the instrumental rationality perspective, which views the organization as a closed system that can be controlled by careful attention to internal structure and processes. It is only what goes on inside the organization that matters; the external environment of the organization is irrelevant. During the 1950s and 1960s, this view of organizations was challenged by the systems perspective, which seems to inform the efforts of both Martha and Helen. All subsequent theorizing about organizations has been influenced by the systems perspective.

The **systems perspective** builds on the fundamental principle that the organization is in constant interaction with its multiple environments—social, political, economic, cultural, technological—and must be able to adapt to environmental change. Some systems theorists suggest mutual influence between organizations and their environments; other theorists see the influence as unidirectional, with organizational structure and processes being determined by the environment. A second important principle of the systems perspective is that organizations are composed of interrelated subsystems that must be integrated in order to achieve the organization's goals and meet environmental demands. Finally, in contrast to the instrumental rationality approach, the systems perspective holds that there are many different ways, rather than one best way, to reach the same ends. The idea that a system can attain its goals in a variety of ways is known as **equifinality**. Exhibit 10.5 summarizes the central ideas of three organizational theories in the systems perspective.

Contingency Theory. Paul R. Lawrence and Jay W. Lorsch (1967b) built **contingency theory** on the basic principle that there is no "one best way" to organize. That is not to say that all ways of organizing are equally suitable to a given organization at a given time. The best way to organize depends on both the task to be performed and the nature of the environments in which the organization operates. Regarding the task to be performed, a Morse and Lorsch (1970) study found that organizations in which tasks were vague and varied performed better when they were organized democratically and made maximum use of worker abilities. In contrast, organizations in which tasks were predictable and repetitive performed better when rigidly structured and coercively managed. Regarding the nature of the environment, a Lawrence and Lorsch study (1967a) found that scientific management works well when the organization operates in a stable

EXHIBIT 10.5

The Systems Perspective on Formal Organizations

Major theme: The organization is in constant interaction with multiple environments.	
Theory	**Central Idea**
Contingency theory	The best way to organize depends on tasks and environments.
Population-ecology theory	Only the "fittest" organizations survive; they are selected by the environment.
Resource-dependence and political economy models	The organization depends on the environment for political and economic resources.

environment, but that a democratic and flexible style of organization is more effective when operating in a turbulent and uncertain environment. As Helen Blue settles into her job as director of Beacon Center, she may find that the nature of her staff's duties points toward a more democratic structure.

Hasenfeld (1992) reports some support for contingency theory in research on human service organizations. He criticizes the theory, however, for its failure to consider power relations and the influence of political and economic interests on organizational processes. These issues are better addressed by the resource-dependence and political economy models.

Population-Ecology Theory.   Proponents of **population-ecology theory** take a "natural selection" view of organizations (Aldrich & Pfeffer, 1976; Hannan & Freeman, 1977). They criticize contingency theory for suggesting that organizations have the flexibility and power to adapt to their environments. Instead, the environment "selects" which organizations will survive and which will die. Population-ecology theory is based on Darwin's theory of evolution, in which only the "fittest" survive. In this view, organizations must respond to environmental changes by changing their form.

Population-ecology theory has been criticized for its deterministic view, which ignores the effects that organizations have on their environments. On the other hand, it has highlighted the tendency toward inertia that prevents organizations from changing in response to their changing environments. It is included here because it may have particular relevance to the social work profession in the midst of the rapid changes in major social institutions noted in Chapter 8. The profession of social work, developed to respond to social trends in one industrial era, must continually change to respond to its changing environments.

Resource-Dependence and Political Economy Models.   The resource-dependence model and the political economy model of organizations are closely related. The **resource-dependence model** is built on the basic premise that no organization can generate all of the necessary resources by itself and, therefore, all organizations must rely on resources from their environments. In contrast to the population-ecology theory, however, the resource-dependence model sees the organization as a very active participant in the organization/environment configuration, capable of influencing and changing the environment (Aldrich & Pfeffer, 1976; Pfeffer & Salancik, 1978). According to Aldrich and Pfeffer (1976, p. 83), managers must manage "their environments as well as their organizations, and the former activity may be as important, or even more important, than the latter."

The political economy model likewise focuses on the dependence of organizations on their environments for necessary resources and the impact of organization/environment interactions on the internal structure and processes of the organization (Wamsley & Zald, 1973). The **political economy model,** however, focuses more specifically, on two types of resources necessary to organizations: (1) political resources (legitimacy and power) and (2) economic resources. The greater the dependence of the organization on the environment for either of these types of resources, the greater the influence the environment will have on the organization. According to the political economy model, moreover, the internal interplay of political and economic interest also influences the methods by which work will be accomplished, as well as how decisions get made within the organization. Those units of an organization that play an important role in managing the organization's external economic and political environments command more internal power. Burton Gummer (1994) notes, in the current conservative political era, a growing tension between social service administrators, who are primarily responsible to politicians and funders, and line workers, who are primarily responsible to clients. Given these different responsibilities, Gummer (1997) suggests that the NASW code of ethics should give greater attention to administrative ethics.

Hasenfeld (1992) suggests that the political economy model is particularly potent for clarifying how social service organizations resolve such important issues as which clients to serve, which services to provide, how to organize service provision, and how to define staff and client roles. It is a fact of our lives that social service organizations are highly dependent on the external environment for both political and economic resources, but it is important to note that the political economy model recognizes clients as resources and as potential players in the political arena. Whether or not client groups support existing programs, social workers have an important role to play in facilitating their inclusion in the political process, a role that was a part of Martha Green's vision for Beacon Center. Are clients recognized as resources and potential players in the political arena in your field agency?

Interpretive Perspective

Social constructionist perspective

When Helen Blue became executive director at Beacon Center, she wanted to introduce more "rational order" and have fewer internal voices speaking about the kind of place the Center should be. It might be said that she found Martha Green's vision for Beacon Center to be too "interpretive." Theories of organizations within the **interpretive perspective** are quite diverse, but they all share one basic premise: Organizations are creations of human consciousness and reflect the worldviews of the creators; they are social constructions of reality.

The interpretive perspective rejects both the instrumental rationality and the systems perspectives. Contrary to instrumental rationality, the interpretive perspective focuses on processes rather than goals; emphasizes "disorganization, untidiness and flexibility" (Hassard, 1993, p. 3) rather than control and reason; and emphasizes a diversity of approaches rather than one right way. Contrary to the systems perspective, the interpretive perspective emphasizes human agency in creating organizations and challenges the constraining influence of external forces.

In addition to these basic premises, three propositions are common to the interpretive perspective:

1. Organizational survival is based more on "creative confusion" (Gergen, 1992) than on rational order.

2. Organizations are increasingly fragmented into multiple realities and should be studied through multiple voices rather than through the unitary voice of the manager (Linstead, 1993).

3. There is a need for new organizational structures that are more "decentralized, self-regulating, fluid, and flexible" (Thompson, 1993, p. 185). Policy networks, interagency task forces,

EXHIBIT 10.6
The Interpretive
Perspective
on Formal
Organizations

Major theme: The organization is a social construction of reality.	
Theory	**Central Idea**
Social action model (Silverman)	The organization is defined by individual actors.
Organizational culture model	Organizations are cultures with shared experiences and shared meanings.
Managing diversity model	Organizational systems and practices should maximize the potential advantages of diversity in organizational membership.
Discourse theory of public administration	Facilitating discourse about differences among the organization's members is the most effective way to achieve organizational goals.

and "adhocracies" are thought to be the prototype of the organization of the future (Fox & Miller, 1995).

Different interpretive theorists focus on different themes in relation to these basic premises. The four separate approaches summarized in Exhibit 10.6 will give you some sense of these differences.

Social Action Model.   One of the most influential contributions to the interpretive study of organizations is that of British sociologist David Silverman, presented in his 1971 book *The Theory of Organizations: A Sociological Framework*. Criticizing both instrumental rationality and systems perspectives, Silverman proposed an approach to organizations that emphasizes the active role of individual organizational actors in creating the organization—an approach known as **Silverman's social action model**. He proposed a set of questions, presented in Exhibit 10.7, to ask when studying a specific organization.

EXHIBIT 10.7
Silverman's
Questions for
Studying a Specific
Organization

1. Who are the principal actors in the organization?
2. What goals are the actors trying to achieve?
3. How are the different actors involved in the organization?
4. What strategies do they use to achieve their goals?
5. What are the consequences of their actions for each other and for the development of interactional patterns in the organization?

Source: Silverman, 1971.

In a more recent work, Silverman (1994) criticizes the singular emphasis of his earlier model on the "definitions of actors" (p. 3). He suggests that in reacting against deterministic theories of environmental constraints, he failed to acknowledge that "historical and structural factors are important in understanding activity in organizations" (p. 3). He further suggests that his portrayal of human behavior as free and undetermined failed to acknowledge the influence of cultural scripts and the tendency of humans to see their behavior as freer than it is. This self-critique is consistent with other recent criticisms of the limitations of the interpretive perspective (for example, Reed, 1993; Thompson, 1993).

Organizational Culture Model.   In contrast to Silverman's deemphasis of culture, Edgar Schein (1992) focuses on organizations as cultures with shared experiences that produce shared meanings, or interpretations. Organizations, therefore, exist as much in the heads of their members as in policies, rules, and procedures. The **organizational culture model** views organizations as ongoing, interactive processes of reality construction, involving many organizational actors. Organizational culture is made up of "slogans, evocative language, symbols, stories, myths, ceremonies, rituals, and patterns of tribal behavior" (Morgan, 1986, p. 133) but also of mundane, routine, day-to-day activities. For example, under Martha Green's leadership, the slogan "client input" was an important feature of the Beacon Center culture, buttressed by the day-to-day practice of soliciting client opinions. When we become new members of an organization, some aspects of its culture are immediately obvious. But other aspects are more difficult to decipher, causing us to feel uncomfortable and confused. For example, we may understand the cultural norms about dress and extended versus brief lunch hours after one day in the field practicum agency, but it may take us several weeks to decipher whether we are in a cooperative or competitive culture. There may be a clear slogan about commitment to clients, but it may take some time to decipher how that commitment is implemented, or whether it is.

Organizational culture is always evolving, and it is not always unitary. In many organizations, like Beacon Center under the administration of Helen Blue, competing beliefs and value systems produce subcultures. Given the evolution of organizational culture and rapid societal changes, it is not unusual to find a split between the "old guard" and the "new guard," or to find cultural divisions based on organizational function. For example, members of prevention units in community mental health centers may "speak a different language" than clinicians in the same agency. The result may be cultural fragmentation or cultural warfare.

According to the organizational culture approach, organizations choose their environments and interact with them based on their interpretive schemes. It could be said that when Martha Green was executive director, Beacon Center saw itself as more humane than, and therefore superior to, other organizations serving homeless persons. Founders, staff, and board members had certain definitions of other agencies and of their client group which they used to influence referring agencies, funding sources, and clientele. They clearly saw themselves as proactive, capable of influencing their environments. This behavior is consistent with the organizational culture premise that organizations, through their interpretive schemes, "often create the constraints, barriers, and situations that cause them problems" (Morgan, 1986, p. 137). Other agencies did feel a certain resentment toward the arrogance and self-righteousness of Beacon

Center under Martha Green's leadership. Under Helen Blue, on the other hand, clients and staff resented not being included in decisions.

Criticisms of the organizational culture approach are twofold (Morgan, 1986). One criticism is leveled at theorists who write about managing organizational culture. These theorists are sometimes criticized for being biased in favor of management and potentially exploitative of other employees. They are also criticized for overstating managers' potential to control culture, negating the role of multiple actors in the creation of shared meaning. The second criticism of the organizational culture approach is that it fails to take account of the fact that some members have more power than others to influence the construction of culture.

Managing Diversity Model.   In the 1990s, organizational theorists have developed an approach to organizational management called the **managing diversity model**. Given the trend toward greater diversity in the labor force, several social scientists (Cox, 1993; Thomas, 1991) have suggested that contemporary organizations cannot be successful unless they can learn to manage diverse populations.

Cox (1993, p. 11) defines managing diversity as "planning and implementing organizational systems and practices to manage people so that the potential advantages of diversity are maximized while its potential disadvantages are minimized." He continues, "I view the goal of managing diversity as maximizing the ability of all employees to contribute to organizational goals and to achieve their full potential unhindered by group identities such as gender, race, nationality, age, and departmental affiliation." Cox reviews the research relevant to management of diversity and comes to two conclusions: (1) Organizations that manage diversity effectively have an advantage in creativity, problem solving, and flexibility. (2) When diversity in the workforce is not effectively managed, communication problems and decision times increase, and member morale decreases. Cox cites research findings from the U.S. workforce that document higher turnover and absentee rates for women and for men of color than for white men. He suggests that the cause is organizational failure to effectively manage diversity. My personal experiences suggest that social service organizations are as liable as other types of organizations to fail in this way.

Cox (1993) suggests that effective management of diversity will not happen in many organizations without a more solid commitment. Management of diversity is still a young idea, and a long distance from the "one right way" of instrumental rationality, which has dominated modern thinking about organizations. Pioneering organizations in the United States have begun to develop specific "tools" to assist organizations to become more effective at managing diversity. Cox (1993) has summarized the relevant organizational objectives and the specific tools needed to accomplish those objectives (see Exhibit 10.8). How well would Cox say that your field agency is doing in managing diversity? Your school of social work?

Discourse Theory of Public Administration.   Charles Fox and Hugh Miller (1995) have proposed what they call a **discourse theory of public administration**. They argue that organizational theory has erred by exaggerating the rationality of human nature, by assuming that organizations are concrete entities, and by assuming consensus about organizational goals. Instead,

EXHIBIT 10.8
Strategies for
Effective
Management
of Diversity

Model Dimension	Tools
I. Culture *Objective:* Create climate in which members of all identity groups excel	1. Hire or promote people who embrace the new values 2. Reinforce values in rewards and appraisal 3. Educate and communicate
II. Pluralism *Objectives:* Create a two-way socialization process Ensure influence of minority culture perspectives on core organization norms and values	1. Managing/valuing diversity (MVD) training 2. New-member orientation programs 3. Language training 4. Diversity in key committees 5. Explicit treatment of diversity in mission statements 6. Identity-based advisory groups 7. Create flexibility in norm systems
III. Structural integration *Objective:* No correlation between culture group identity and job status	1. Diversity in key committees 2. Education program 3. Affirmative action programs 4. Targeted career development programs
IV. Integration in informal networks *Objective:* Eliminate barriers to entry and participation	1. Mentoring programs 2. Company-sponsored social events 3. Support groups
V. Institutional bias *Objective:* Eliminate bias ingrained in management systems	1. Culture audit 2. Survey feedback 3. Changes in manager performance evaluation and rewards 4. HR policy and benefits changes 5. Task forces
VI. Intergroup conflict *Objectives:* Minimize interpersonal conflict based on group identity Minimize backlash by dominant group members Promote intergroup understanding	1. Survey feedback 2. Conflict management training and conflict resolution techniques 3. MVD training 4. Core groups 5. EEO-related training

Source: Cox, 1993, p. 243.

they say, human behavior is more political than rational, organizations are social constructions created by a struggle over meanings, and differing meanings are reflected in disagreements and tensions about organizational goals. Speaking more specifically, they draw our attention to the widely held myth that in the United States we operate under a rational model of democracy, in which public policy and administration reflect the wishes of the people. They counter this myth with evidence that the public will is manipulated by the news media, political spin doctors, and special interest groups; that the majority of people do not vote or remain vigilant about public issues; and that the greatest influences on elected officials are lobbyists and special interest groups.

Fox and Miller (1995) suggest that the myth of a rational model of democracy has reinforced an inclination for public agencies to be organized, in large part, according to the principles of Taylor's scientific management and Weber's ideal-type bureaucracy. Fox and Miller argue instead for a new model of public policy and administration that can restore greater democracy to the political process. In their discourse model, public administrators would become midwives, using their skills and commitment to facilitate a more authentic public discourse among disparate groups about public issues. Midwife is a very different metaphor than scientific management. To be eligible to participate in the discourse, persons must be willing to speak sincerely; to take into consideration the "context of the problem, the lives of those affected, and the public interest" (Fox & Miller, 1995, p. 123); to maintain active engagement with the ongoing discourse; and to have a contribution, broadly defined, to make. Fox and Miller (1995) argue that authentic discourse cannot occur among people of unequal status; all participants in the discourse are equal citizens. This last point may have been what Martha Green had in mind when she tried to minimize power differences at Beacon Center.

Critical Perspective

Conflict perspective

Although it may appear that Martha Green administered Beacon Center from an interpretative perspective, it is probably more accurate to describe her worldview as a **critical perspective**. She tried to minimize the power differences in her organization, and when she asked her staff to vote on sensitive issues, she invoked the secret ballot to neutralize any possible power dynamics. Critical theorists share the interpretive perspective's bias about the role of human consciousness in human behavior, but critical theory undertakes, as its central concern, a critique of the status quo and a vision for change suggested by this critique. More specifically, critical theories of organizations focus on patterns of domination and oppression in organizations. This focus distinguishes the critical perspectives from the interpretive perspective, which ignores or negates issues of power and the possibility that persons in power positions can privilege their own versions of reality and marginalize other versions.

Morgan (1986) draws on the work of a diverse group of theorists and researchers to identify several ways in which organizations serve as "instruments of domination":

- Formal organizations create and continually reproduce patterns of social inequality through organizational hierarchies.

EXHIBIT 10.9
The Critical
Perspective
on Formal
Organizations

Major theme: Organizations are instruments of domination.	
Theory	**Central Idea**
Organizations as multiple oppressions	Organizations exclude and discriminate against multiple groups.
Nonhierarchical organizations	Organizations run by consensus, with few rules, and with informality are least likely to oppress employees.

- Employees are exposed to work conditions that are hazardous to their health and welfare—such as working with toxic materials or dangerous equipment—and work expectations that interfere with personal health maintenance and family life.

- Employees experience mental health problems caused by job insecurity in a downsizing and globalizing economy.

Exhibit 10.9 summarizes the two critical approaches to formal organizations discussed here: organizations as multiple oppressions and nonhierarchical organizations.

Organizations as Multiple Oppressions.　　Have you ever felt oppressed—voiceless, powerless, abused, manipulated, unappreciated—in any of the organizations of which you have been a member? Do you think that whole groups of people have felt oppressed in any of those organizations? In the contemporary era, the critical perspective has taken a more focused look at who is oppressed in organizations and the ways in which they are oppressed. This approach was influenced by feminist critiques, during the 1970s and 1980s, of the failure of traditional organizational theories to consider gender issues (Hearn & Parkin, 1993). Feminist critiques led to the recognition that other groups besides women had also been marginalized by formal organizations and by organizational theory.

Jeff Hearn and Wendy Parkin (1993) recommend viewing **organizations as multiple oppressions**—social constructions that exclude and discriminate against some categories of people. Oppression happens through a variety of processes, including "marginalization, domination and subordination, degradation, ignoring, harassment, invisibilizing, silencing, punishment, discipline and violence" (Hearn & Parkin, 1993, p. 153). These processes may also be directed at a variety of organizational actors, including "staff, members, employees, residents, patients and clients" (p. 153). Organizational domination can become compounded by multiple oppressions. Hearn and Parkin cite the example of a children's home where children were being sexually abused and female staff were dissuaded, by intimidation, from reporting the situation.

According to Hearn and Parkin, frequently oppressed groups include women, younger and older people, persons with disabilities, those of lower economic class, persons of color, and sexual minorities. These groups may be excluded from organizations; admitted only in subordinate roles as clients, patients, or students; or admitted but discriminated against within the organization. If groups that are excluded or otherwise oppressed form their own organizations, dominant groups construct a hierarchy of organizations that maintains the oppression, as when a black organization is viewed as inferior to similar white organizations.

Hearn and Parkin suggest that at the current time, the group most marginalized by formal organizations is persons with disabilities. They are often physically excluded from organizations by inaccessible environments, and they are further marginalized by a "prevailing ideology . . . of medicine and medication, with people's disabilities being seen as sickness or illness and able-bodied people being seen as able and well, rather [than] the environment being disabling" (Hearn & Parkin, 1993, pp. 157–158).

Critical theory, with its focus on domination and oppression, reminds us that mainstream organizational theory does not provide "organizational theory for the exploited" (Morgan, 1986, p. 316). Therefore, our understanding of organizations is incomplete and biased. If you have felt somewhat alienated in reading about the other theories in this chapter, you may be reacting to this bias. However, critical theory has been criticized for being ideological, giving priority to the voices of oppressed persons, just as Martha Green was criticised for giving too strong a voice to homeless persons. Critical theorists reply that their focus is no more ideological than is recognizing only the voices of the elite.

The critical perspective on organizations has special relevance to social workers. It helps us recognize the ways in which clients' struggles are related to oppressive structures and processes in the formal organizations with which they interact. We must be constantly vigilant about the multiple oppressions within the organizations in which we work and provide social services.

Nonhierarchical Organizations.   Helen Blue preferred a more hierarchical organizational structure than the one developed at Beacon Center under Martha Green's leadership. A constant theme in critical theory is that hierarchical organizational structures lead to alienation and internal class conflict. Critical theorists challenge the instrumental rationality argument that hierarchy is needed to maximize efficiency; they point out that in fact hierarchy is often inefficient but that it is maintained because it works well to protect the positions of persons in power. For example, the staff at Beacon Center wastes much time and energy trying to find ways to thwart Helen Blue's decisions.

Humanistic
perspective

The idea of the **nonhierarchical organization** is not new. Human relations theorists have recommended "participatory management," which involves lower-level employees in at least some decision making, for several decades. Historical evidence indicates that since the 1840s, experiments with nonhierarchical organizations have accompanied every wave of anti-modernist social movements in the United States (Rothschild-Whitt & Whitt, 1986). Recent feminist critiques of organizational theory have helped to stimulate renewed interest in nonhierarchical organizations. Nevertheless, such organizations constitute only a small portion of the population of formal organizations, and research on nonhierarchical organizations constitutes a very small part of the massive body of research on organizations (Iannello, 1992).

Exhibit 10.10 lists the traits of a model of nonhierarchical organization that Kathleen Iannello (1992) calls the consensual model. Based on their study of five nonhierarchical organizations, Rothschild-Whitt and Whitt (1986) summarized some of the special challenges, both

EXHIBIT 10.10
Traits of a
Consensual
Model of Formal
Organizations

- Authority vested in the membership rather than in an elite at the top of a hierarchy
- Decisions made only after issues have been widely discussed by the membership
- Rules kept to a minimum
- Personal, rather than formal, relationships among members
- Leadership based on election, with rotation of leadership positions
- No financial reward for leadership roles
- No winners and losers in decision making—decisions made based on unchallenged "prevailing sentiment" (consensus)

Source: Iannello, 1992.

internal and external, faced by consensual organizations. Internal challenges include increased time for decision making, increased emotional intensity due to the more personal style of relationships, and difficulty incorporating diversity. External challenges are the constraints of social, economic, and political environments that value and reward hierarchy. Almost a decade later, these same challenges were consistent themes in the stories about feminist organizations told by 25 authors and edited by Myra Marx Ferree and Patricia Yancey Martin (1995).

Based on her study of two successful feminist organizations, Iannello (1992) proposes that the internal challenges of the nonhierarchical organization can be addressed by what she calls a "modified consensual organization" model. Critical decisions continue to be made by the broad membership, but routine decisions are made by smaller groups; members are recognized by ability and expertise, but not by rank and position; there are clear goals, developed through a consensual process.

The two most prominent contemporary examples of organizations based on consensus are feminist organizations and Japanese firms. Both types of organizations typically feature a strong, shared ideology and culture, which should lead to relatively easy consensus. However, the available evidence suggests that feminist organizations in which membership crosses either ideological or cultural lines have not been successful in operating by consensus (Ferree & Martin, 1995; Iannello, 1992). Under Martha Green's administration, most decisions at Beacon Center were made by consensus, but Martha was sometimes criticized for building a staff with little ideological or cultural diversity.

Given the increasing diversity of the American workforce, management of difference and conflict can be expected to become an increasing challenge in organizational life. This is as true for social work organizations as for other organizations. To date, the literature on consensual organizations has failed to address the difficult challenges of diverse ideological and cultural perspectives among organizational members—issues that are the focus of the managing diversity model and the discourse theory. This is an area in which social work should take the lead.

Burnout: A Negative Organizational Outcome

It was suggested at the beginning of this chapter that formal organizations meet our needs, assist us to fulfill goals, and nurture our development—but that they also make stressful demands, thwart our goals, inhibit our holistic development, and constrain our behavior. Robert T. Golembiewski (1994, p. 211) uses more colorful language to talk about the negative effects of organizations, suggesting "a long history of commentary urges that organizational life bends people out of shape, and may even make them crazy." Indeed, some of the staff at Beacon Center have been heard to say, since Helen Blue took over, that they must leave the Center before they go crazy.

In the past two decades, researchers have attempted to answer the question "Is organizational membership hazardous to your health?" The answer, to date, is that organizational membership is *often* hazardous to health; and "burnout" is the identified hazard. There are many definitions of burnout, but I use a variation of the definition proposed by Cherniss (1980, p. 18): **Burnout** is a process in which a previously committed worker disengages from his or her work in response to stress and strain experienced in the job.

Burnout is most often studied using the Maslach Burnout Inventory (MBI) (Maslach & Jackson, 1981), which analyzes three domains: (1) emotional exhaustion, or a feeling of being near the "end of one's rope"; (2) depersonalization, or a strong tendency to distance oneself from others, thinking of them as things or objects; and (3) personal accomplishment, which refers to perceptions of doing well on a worthwhile project. Higher levels of emotional exhaustion and depersonalization and lower levels of personal accomplishment indicate burnout.

Golembiewski (1994) has built an eight-phase model of burnout based on these three domains, with depersonalization representing the least serious domain of burnout, personal accomplishment a more serious domain, and emotional exhaustion the most serious domain, occurring in late-phase burnout. Golembiewski and colleagues have completed extensive research, with a large number of both public-sector and business organizations, and found several indicators of well-being to be associated with the phases of burnout. With progression through the phases of burnout, research participants report less work satisfaction; lower self-esteem; greater physical symptoms; lower performance appraisals; and greater hostility, anxiety, and depression. Golembiewski (1994) found that approximately 45 percent of 16,476 participants from 55 organizations were in the last three phases of burnout, with high levels of emotional exhaustion, as indicated by their scores on the MBI. That is a high level of hazard, and suggests that social workers need to be attuned to symptoms of job-related burnout.

Several internal organizational features have been found to be associated with burnout, as Exhibit 10.11 shows. By these criteria, it would appear that staff burnout would be more likely under Helen Blue's administration than under Martha Green's administration. Unfortunately, the research on burnout has not considered the effects of the external environments of formal organizations. Helen's ability to forge better relationships with some external groups might mitigate some of the internal stressors.

It has also been suggested that social work is an occupation with above-average risk of burnout (Hasenfeld, 1983; Jayaratne & Chess, 1984; Pines & Kafry, 1978; Soderfeldt, Soderfeldt, & Warg, 1995). However, after reviewing the available (18) empirical studies of burnout in social

Features Associated with Low Burnout	Features Associated with High Burnout
High participation in work decisions	Low participation in work decisions
High job involvement	Low job involvement
High work satisfaction	Low work satisfaction
High sense of psychological community	Low sense of psychological community
High support from supervisor and coworkers	Low support from supervisor and coworkers
High trust in supervisor and coworkers	Low trust in supervisor and coworkers
High need satisfaction in job	Low need satisfaction in job
Low job tension	High job tension
High clarity about job requirements	Low clarity about job requirements
Group supervision	One-to-one supervision
High task orientation	Low task orientation
Low work pressure	High work pressure

Source: Golembiewski, 1994.

work, Soderfeldt et al. (1995) conclude that the available evidence, although methodologically weak, indicates that "social workers experience less burnout than comparable occupational groups" (p. 640). Still, they conclude, there is a need for sound methodological investigation of the prevalence and incidence of burnout in social work. To date, no social work researchers have used Golembiewski's stage model of burnout, but it seems to hold promise. We know that our work has many satisfactions as well as many stressors, but it would be interesting to discover which way the balance tilts and why.

Social Work and Formal Organizations

You have probably learned already that social work is a diverse profession; we use diverse methods to address a diversity of social problems—and we work in diverse types of organizations. We work in hospitals, outpatient health and mental health clinics, in-home programs, nursing homes and other residential programs, crisis shelters, prisons and jails, government social service agencies, private family and children's agencies, schools, the workplace, community centers, social movement organizations, research centers, planning organizations, and in private practice, among other places.

We can think about the differences among the organizations in which social workers are found in several ways. One is to divide them into host organizations, social work–oriented organizations, and human service organizations (Popple & Leighninger, 1993). In **host organizations**—such as schools, the workplace, correctional facilities, and hospitals—social service is not the primary purpose of the organization. Social workers in these settings work with other disciplines to meet organizational goals, and they often serve as mediators between clients and the organization. In contrast, **social work–oriented organizations** have social service delivery as their purpose and are staffed primarily by social workers. Family and children's agencies and government social service programs are examples of social work–oriented organizations. Social workers also work in **human service organizations,** whose staff come from a variety of disciplines but work in a coordinated fashion to provide an array of services. Community mental health centers and drug treatment programs are examples of human service organizations.

Another way to think about formal organizations in which social workers work has traditionally been to divide them into public and private organizations. **Public social service organizations** are those funded and administered by government; **private social service organizations** are privately funded and administered. This distinction made some sense in earlier eras, but it is not very useful in the contemporary era. Today, many public agencies contract programs out to private organizations, and many private organizations, like Beacon Center, receive public as well as private funding. The Social Security Act of 1935 ushered in an era of government dominance in both the funding and administering of social service programs, but for the past two decades, we have seen increasing **privatization** of social services, shifting the administration of programs back to private organizations (Netting & McMurtry, 1994; Kettner & Martin, 1994). This trend is based on a belief that privatization will lead to more efficient and effective service delivery. It has been estimated that approximately 50 percent of public social service dollars are contracted to private organizations (Kettner & Martin, 1994).

An increasingly important distinction among private service organizations is the distinction between *nonprofit* and *for-profit* organizations. Social workers have a long history with nonprofit organizations, but their involvement in for-profit organizations is more recent and has been increasing steadily since the 1970s (Popple & Leighninger, 1993).

Organizations in which social workers work have not been immune to the trends in the economic institution discussed in Chapter 8. Downsizing and the resulting "do more with less" climate have increased work-related stressors, and increasing economic inequality is producing stubborn social problems that must be addressed with shrinking resources. Social workers, like other workers, are increasingly involved in "contingent" labor situations—that is, in part-time, temporary, and contractual arrangements. More and more sectors of the social welfare system are using a managed care model, and searching for the "one best way." There is increasing evidence that social service organizations are favoring clients who can pay, or who qualify for payment by a third party, and failing to serve people who are poor or have the most challenging problems (Netting & McMurtry, 1994). The "information revolution" has raised new issues about protection of client confidentiality. Given these challenges, a solid grounding in organizational theory can be an important tool in the social work survival kit.

IMPLICATIONS FOR SOCIAL WORK PRACTICE

Several principles for social work action are recommended by this discussion of formal organizations:

- Be alert to the influence of formal organizations on the client's behavior. Be particularly alert to the ways in which the social service organization where you work, as well as other social service organizations to which you frequently refer clients, influence the client's behavior.

- Develop an understanding of the organizational goals of the social service organization where you work, and how the tasks that you perform are related to these goals.

- Develop an understanding of the shared meanings in the social service organization where you work, and of the processes by which those meanings are developed and maintained.

- Develop an understanding of the forces of inertia and other constraints on rational decision making in the social service organization where you work.

- Develop an understanding of the social, political, economic, cultural, and technological environments of the social service organization where you work.

- Develop an understanding of the sources of legitimacy, power, and economic resources for the social service organization where you work, and an understanding of how they influence internal decisions.

- Collaborate with colleagues at the social service organization where you work to understand and enhance the creative use of diversity.

- Collaborate with colleagues at the social service organization where you work to facilitate the inclusion of clients in the political process, internally as well as externally.

- Collaborate with colleagues at the social service organization where you work, and with other relevant parties, to facilitate a more authentic discourse about policy issues among disparate groups.

- Collaborate with colleagues at the social service organization where you work to develop an understanding of multiple oppressions within the organization.

- Be attuned to the symptoms of job-related burnout in yourself, your colleagues, and your clients.

MAIN POINTS

1. Formal organizations—collectivities of people, with a high degree of formality of structure, working together to meet a goal or goals—are important influences on human behavior.

2. Formal organizations help us in many ways; they also cause stress and strain in our lives.

3. Perspectives on formal organizations can be classified into four broad categories: instrumental rationality perspective, systems perspective, interpretive perspective, and critical perspective.

4. The instrumental rationality perspective assumes that organizations can be designed with structures and processes that maximize efficiency and effectiveness.

5. Theories in the instrumental rationality perspective include Weber's ideal-type bureaucracy, characterized by clear hierarchy and chain of command, a clear division of labor, formal rules of operation, formal communications, merit-based recruitment and advancement, and record keeping; Taylor's scientific management, which includes studies to find the "one best way" to perform all tasks, scientific selection and training of workers, close managerial monitoring of workers, and managerial authority; human relations theory, which suggests that social factors are as important as technical factors in goal accomplishment; and decision theory, which proposes limits to the rationality of organizational actors.

6. The systems perspective sees the formal organization in constant interaction with multiple environments, and composed of interrelated subsystems.

7. Examples of the systems perspective include contingency theory, which proposes that the best way to organize depends on the task to be performed and the nature of the organization's environments; population-ecology theory, which suggests that organizations must respond to environmental changes by changing their forms to survive; resource-dependence model, which suggests that organizations must rely on resources from their environments but that they can also influence their environments; and the political economy model, which suggests that organizations depend on their environments for both political and economic resources.

8. Both the interpretive and the critical perspectives emphasize human consciousness in creating organizations, but critical theories focus on patterns of domination and oppression in organizations, which interpretive theories ignore or negate.

9. The interpretive perspective includes Silverman's social action model, which emphasizes the role of individual organizational actors in creating the organization; the organizational culture model, which sees organizations as cultures with shared experiences, leading to shared meanings; the managing diversity approach, which calls attention to the need for contemporary organizations to manage diverse populations; and discourse theory, which suggests that public administrators must facilitate a more authentic public discourse about public issue among groups with differing views.

10. Two critical approaches are the organizations as multiple oppressions approach, which sees organizations as social constructions that exclude some categories of people and discriminate against other categories of people; and the nonhierarchical

organizations approach, which seeks to overcome the inefficiency of hierarchies maintained mostly to protect the positions of people in power.

11. Research in both public-sector and business organizations indicates that formal organizations may be hazardous to the health of their members. Burnout—whose symptoms include emotional exhaustion, depersonalization, and a lack of personal accomplishment—is the most identified hazard.

12. Social workers work in many diverse types of organizations.

KEY TERMS

bounded rationality
bureaucracy
burnout
contingency theory
critical perspective
decision making theory
discourse theory of public administration
effectiveness
efficiency
equifinality
formal organization
Hawthorne effect
host organizations
human relations theory
human service organizations
instrumental ratationality perspective
interpretive perspective
iron cage of rationality

managing diversity model
nonhierarchical organization
organizational culture model
organizational humanism
organizations as multiple oppressions
political economy model
population-ecology theory
private social service organizations
privatization
public social service organizations
resource-dependence model
satisfice
scientific management
Siverman's social action model
social work–oriented organizations
systems perspective
theory X
theory Y

WORLD WIDE WEB RESOURCES

Historical Background of Organizational Behavior
http://www.cba.nev.edu/~ewertheim/introd/history.hum#scimgt
Site maintained at Northeastern University. Contains a paper by Professor Edward Wertheim on Taylorism and scientific management, the human relations movement, theory x and y, and schools of thought in organizational behavior.

Chaos Theory in the Management of Organizations
http://ftp.ec.vanderbilt.edu/chaos/management/index/htm
Site maintained at Vanderbilt University. Contains paper on the application of chaos theory to
organizational management.

Communities

TWO STORIES OF COMMUNITY: JOYCE MILLER AND ANN AND EVAN MAXWELL

Joyce Miller has lived in Walker Community, a central-city neighborhood of a moderate-sized Midwestern city, for all of her 56 years. When Joyce was a child, Walker was a mix of low- and middle-income black families, but over the years, the middle-income families have moved away from the neighborhood. After her husband was killed in the Vietnam War, Joyce stayed in Walker to raise her three children. Now her children are grown with children of their own, and they also live in Walker.

Joyce has been saddened to watch the gradual deterioration of Walker Community. Much of the housing stock is now dilapidated. A physician and a dentist once ran their practices out of their homes in Walker, but they have both been dead for some time, and medical care has not been available in the neighborhood since their deaths. The building that once housed a textile factory, which was a source of employment for many people in the neighborhood, has been boarded up for almost 20 years. Joyce once worked there, but now she feels lucky to have a job as an account clerk in a large plant that is a 12-minute car ride, or a 20-minute bus ride, from her house. She has also helped many other Walker residents to get jobs at the plant. The only businesses operating in Walker at this time are a few laundromats, two convenience markets, and three liquor stores. Residents of Walker must leave the neighborhood to transact most of their business. The schools are overcrowded and in need of repairs, and Joyce is concerned because her grandchildren are not having an opportunity to become familiar with computers. The two churches in the neighborhood have been a source of support to many families, but their financial resources are never sufficient to meet the needs of the neighborhood.

A few years ago, Joyce became concerned that her grandchildren seemed to be getting caught up in the growing despair in Walker Community. It is not Joyce's style to sit idly by, and she began talking with anybody who was interested about the need to revitalize the Walker Community Association. It wasn't long before Joyce was elected president of the revitalized association. The association has taken on a variety of projects to strengthen the resources and relationships in Walker, and is currently involved in a fierce battle to block the development of a toxic waste site near the elementary school that Joyce's grandchildren attend.

Joyce is proud that the association is helping Walker to regain some of its sense of community. She recently began to meet with social work faculty at the nearby state university to explore the possibility of applying for grant funds to expand the association's efforts. Some association members have criticized her for attending these meetings, suggesting that the social work faculty will "take over" the association, imposing their own ideas rather than listening to community members.

Ironically, Joyce's request has stimulated a great deal of controversy among the social work faculty as well. No two faculty members can seem to agree on whether and how to get involved with Walker Community. They can't even agree on what a community is. One of the faculty members points out that communities in the late 20th century can be very different from our traditional perception. She relates a story told by Joel Garreau in *Edge City: Life on the New Frontier* (1991, pp. 275–278) about Ann and Evan Maxwell, a couple in Southern California.

They moved to Laguna Niguel in 1970, to live in the hills above the Pacific Coast. The daunting commute to Evan's journalism job in Los Angeles was offset by the striking natural beauty of Laguna Niguel. The Maxwells became successful coauthors of the Fiddler series of mystery books, and in 1984, Evan decided to leave his journalism job to devote his full energies to writing books. He found that leaving the newspaper was both liberating and unsettling. He cherished the new freedom, but was surprised to learn how much he had depended on the support of friends at work, and how much his sense of identity was tied up in the newspaper. Evan talks about leaving the newspaper as a loss of community.

The Maxwells also began to notice that they had lost all sense of community in Laguna Niguel, with the runaway growth and development that had transformed Southern California. They are planning to leave Laguna Niguel. They report that they have almost no contact with their neighbors, and Laguna Niguel does not seem like their community anymore. Instead, "their community includes writers in Seattle and Indiana, agents and editors in New York, a computer junk man in the Silicon Valley who buys and sells overstock equipment, and a refugee from the Massachusetts Route 128 computer realm who now reconditions covered wagons" (p. 277). Electronic technologies allow them to be in touch with these people on a weekly basis. The Maxwells are delighted that a sense of community can now be easily achieved across great distances.

Ironically, the Maxwells are thinking about moving to the Four Corners region of Colorado, a place of great natural beauty, but also a place that operates on old ideas about the connections between people and their geographically based communities.

The social work faculty agree, as do most people these days, that we are "in the midst of a major cultural revolution" (Griswold, 1994, p. 139) that is global in scope. And they agree that this cultural revolution, sparked by the explosive growth in electronic communication, is having far-reaching effects on human communities (Chirot, 1994; Crook, Pakulski, & Waters, 1992; Griswold, 1994; Harvey, 1989; Robertson, 1992; Smart, 1993). But juxtaposing the stories of the Maxwells and Joyce Miller raises five important questions:

1. Is there such thing as community in the late 20th century?
2. If so, how do we define community in this era?
3. Which is more relevant to social work, territorial community or relational community?
4. What is the current state of community theorizing and research?
5. What relationships should social workers have with communities?

These five questions will frame the discussion of the relationship between community and human behavior in this chapter.

Community in the Late 20th Century

Although the circumstances of their lives are very different, both Joyce Miller and the Maxwells appear to see themselves as members of a community. In contemporary times, however, we have heard much about "loss of community" and "search for community." Writing in the late 1980s, sociologist Larry Lyon (1987, p. xii) commented: "In the 1960s, I was taught that we had all lost our feelings of the psychological community. In the 1970s, I learned that the conflict built into capitalist societies was ripping apart what little territorial community remained. And now, in the 1980s, we 'know' that the psychological feelings of community still exist." The same can be said today. Indeed, the available evidence suggests that many communities—the Laguna Niguels as well as the Walkers—are stressed, but that communities, like individuals, often have greater resilience than was once thought (Guest & Lee, 1983; A. Hunter, 1974, 1978; Suttles, 1972; Varady, 1986).

A Revival of Interest in Community Practice

From the earliest history of social work in the United States, social workers have been interested in the health of communities and in the influence of community on individual behavior (Doherty, 1995; Hardcastle, Wenocur, & Powers, 1997). Social work's interest in community has ebbed and flowed, however, with more interest shown in some periods than in others. Stanley Wenocur and Steven Soifer (1997) suggest that there have been three peak periods of intense social work interest in community: the Progressive Era at the turn of the century, the Depression years of the 1930s, and the Civil Rights era of the 1960s. Contemporary critiques of social work accuse the profession of replacing its original focus on community with a preoccupation with personality problems of individuals (Specht & Courtney, 1994). The social work literature, however, reflects a recent revival of interest in community (for example, Fisher & Karger, 1997;

Hardcastle et al., 1997; "Revitalization," 1997). This renewed interest is fueled by growing divisions in our society and the deteriorating state of many central city neighborhoods, as well as by a resurgence of interest in community sociology and the development of the discipline of community psychology.

The signs of renewed interest are many. A new social work journal, *Journal of Community Practice*, began publication in 1994. *Families in Society: The Journal of Contemporary Human Services* devoted its March–April 1997 issue to "Community Development," and in September 1997, *Social Work,* the journal of the National Association of Social Workers, devoted a special issue to "Revitalization of Impoverished Communities." A list of the articles in these special issues, presented in Exhibit 11.1, provides a good snapshot of current approaches to community practice. In addition, several new social work textbooks on community practice were published in 1997 (Fisher & Karger, 1997; Hardcastle et al., 1997).

EXHIBIT 11.1
Contents of Special
Journal Issues on
Community Practice

Families in Society, **Vol. 78, no. 2 (March–April 1997): "Community Development"**

Building on the Strengths and Assets of Families and Communities

A 21st-Century Map for Healthy Communities and Families

Community-Centered Family Service

Families and Schools Together (FAST): Integrating Community Development with Clinical Strategies

From Parent Training to Community Building

Head Start and Social Work

From Child Development to Community Development: One Agency's Journey

Social Work, **Vol. 42, no. 5 (September 1997): "Revitalization of Impoverished Communities"**

The Revitalization of Impoverished Communities

Public Schools and the Revitalization of Impoverished Communities: School-Linked Family Resource Centers

Asset Building as a Community Revitalization Strategy

Implementing Comprehensive Community Development: Possibilities and Limitations

Role of Latina-Owned Beauty Parlors in a Latino Community

The Little Village Project: A Community Approach to the Gang Problem

Building Community: Principles for Social Work Practice in Housing Settings

Youths and Communities: Toward Comprehensive Strategies for Youth Development

Assessing the Impact of Community Violence on Children and Youth

Countering Urban Disinvestment through Community-Building Initiatives

Nonprofit Organizations and Innovation: A Model of Neighborhood-Based Collaboration to Prevent Child Maltreatment

Strengthening Neighborhoods by Developing Community Networks

Despite this renewed interest in community among social workers, Claudia Coulton (1995) notes that knowledge about community is not well developed in the social work literature. Coulton calls for social work research that addresses "how communities work and how their capacities can be built" (p. 438).

Social workers traditionally have turned to *community sociology* for theory and research on the topic. Although sociological interest in community never disappeared totally, it did decline during the 1950s and 1960s (Lyon, 1987, p. 13). Community theory and research were scant—almost nonexistent—during this period, and the community section was dropped from the annual meetings of the American Sociological Association (ASA) from 1957 to 1972. With a resurgence in interest, however, membership in this section, now renamed Community and Urban Sociology, reached 579 in 1997 (personal communication, ASA meeting, 1998).

Although the decline in academic interest in community sociology during the 1950s and 1960s probably had multiple causes, sociologists suggest that it was related in large part to the rising prominence of the concept of mass society (Lyon, 1987; Woolever, 1992). **Mass society** is standardized and homogenized—a society that has no ethnic, class, regional, or local variations in human behavior. Standardized public education, mass media, and residential mobility are cited as the primary mechanisms by which societies become standardized and homogenized. If mass society has no local or group-based variations in norms, values, and behavior, then community, which is local and group-based, loses its relevance to the study of human behavior.

Just as the rising prominence of the concept of mass society contributed to the eclipse of community theory and research, recognition of the limits of mass society as a way of understanding human behavior contributed to the revitalization of community sociology. Beginning in the late 1960s, it became apparent that even though some standardization and homogenization had occurred, mass society had not eradicated ethnic, class, regional, and local variations in human behavior. In the 1980s, a more balanced view of community developed within sociology, a view that recognizes the contributions that both community and mass society make to human behavior (Cuba & Hummon, 1993; Flanagan, 1993; Keane, 1991; Lyon, 1987; Woolever, 1992). In this view, some standardization is present, but local variations still occur. In recent years, scholars from several disciplines have suggested that conflict between communities of competing interests is a more serious problem than the decline of community (Bellah, Madsen, Sullivan, Swidler, & Tipton, 1985; Etzioni, 1993; J. D. Hunter, 1994; Newbrough & Chavis, 1986; Rawls, 1993). These scholars identify strong and hotly contested group-based variations in norms, values, and behavior.

Recent interest in community among social workers has been fueled not only by a resurgence of community sociology, but also by the development of the discipline of *community psychology*. During the 1960s, in the midst of concern about the ineffectiveness of existing psychotherapeutic methods, community was discovered—or rediscovered—by the community mental health movement. The field of community psychology developed and became Division 27 of the American Psychological Association (Heller, 1989). Like social workers, community psychologists have turned to the sociological literature for community theory and have as yet engaged in minimal theory building of their own (Heller, 1989; Hunter & Riger, 1986).

A Definition of Community

So if community exists, what is it? Joyce Miller and the Maxwells seem to agree that it is about interaction and common interests or concerns. To Joyce Miller, it is also about a shared geography. How do their definitions of community fit with the social science literature? Actually, the question "What is community?" has not been an easy one for social scientists. In fact, George Hillery's 1955 review of the classical as well as current sociological literature found 94 distinct definitions. Twenty years later, Seymour Sarason (1974) struggled to define the related concept "sense of community." Sarason concluded that even though "sense of community" is hard to define, "you know when you have it and when you don't" (p. 157).

How should we interpret the fuzziness of "community" and "sense of community"? The radical positivist view is that any concept with so many meanings is unscientific, and its potential utility is therefore highly suspect. But Larry Lyon (1987) suggests that the multiplicity of definitions of community is evidence that the concept is meaningful to scholars with diverse interests and perspectives. I would certainly agree that a concept such as community should not be discarded simply because it has been hard to define. Over the past two decades, sociologists have in fact worked to develop greater agreement about the meaning of the concept *community*, and community psychologists have been equally diligent about developing greater clarity for the concept *sense of community*. Both lines of inquiry are relevant to social work.

Sociological attempts to reach agreement on the definition of community have centered on Hillery's report that approximately three-fourths of the 94 definitions found in the sociological literature included the same three elements: geographic area, social interaction, and common ties (Hillery, 1955, p. 118). Joyce Miller's understanding of community seems very similar, but Ann and Evan Maxwell would probably question the first of these elements, geographic area.

Historically, community did have a geographic meaning in sociology. More recently, however, two different sociological meanings of community have developed: community as a geographic concept and community as an interactional concept (Gusfield, 1975). In this chapter, we will be discussing both meanings of community, because both appear to have relevance for human behavior in the contemporary era. In the future, it may make sense to develop different terms to cover the two concepts, but this discussion will use the following definition, a synthesis of the work of George Hillery (1955), Larry Lyon (1987), and Wendy Griswold (1994): **Community** is people bound either by geography or by network links (webs of communication), sharing common ties, and interacting with one another.

And what does Joyce Miller mean when she says that the Walker Community is regaining some of its sense of community? In 1974, Seymour Sarason proclaimed the enhancement of "sense of community" as the mission of community psychology. Other community psychologists quickly responded by drawing on the literatures on group cohesiveness and community sociology to develop a conceptual definition (McMillan, 1976, cited in McMillan & Chavis, 1986) and a 40-item Sense of Community Scale (Doolittle & MacDonald, 1978). For this chapter, I will use the definition set forth by McMillan and Chavis (1986, p. 9): **Sense of community** is "a feeling that members have of belonging, a feeling that members matter to one another and to the group, and a shared faith that members' needs will be met through their commitment to be

EXHIBIT 11.2

Essential Elements of
Community and
Sense of Community

> ### *Community* (from community sociology literature)
> ■ Linked by geography or webs of communication
>
> ■ Common ties
>
> ■ Interaction
>
> ### *Sense of Community* (from community psychology literature)
> ■ Membership
>
> ■ Influence
>
> ■ Integration and fulfillment of needs
>
> ■ Shared emotional connection

Sources: Based on George Hillery, 1955; Larry Lyon, 1987; Griswold, 1994; McMillan & Chavis, 1986.

together." These could well be the qualities that the Maxwells saw missing in Laguna Niguel, and Joyce Miller probably meant something very much like this when she referred to the improving sense of community in Walker.

McMillan and Chavis also identified four essential elements of sense of community, summarized in Exhibit 11.2 along with the three essential elements of community. Note that, taken together, the essential elements of sense of community sound similar to the "common ties" element of the definition of community.

Territorial Community and Relational Community

In telling the Maxwells' story, Garreau argues that community in the contemporary era is based on voluntary association (**relational community**), not on geography or territory (**territorial community**). Some examples of relational community are

■ The social work community

■ The gay and lesbian community

■ The disability community

■ The feminist community

■ The African American community

■ The Latino community

■ A faith community

■ A school of social work

■ A soccer league

■ *ruralswk@papa.uncp.edu* (Rural Social Work List Serve)

Remember that community does not exist unless all three elements of the definition (listed in Exhibit 11.2) are present: geographic or communication links, common ties, and interaction.

Although the Maxwells no longer feel a sense of connection to their neighbors, they get a personal sense of community from their electronic connections. It appears, however, that Ann and Evan will continue to search for territorial community, while at the same time staying strongly connected to their electronically based relational community. For Joyce Miller, her family, and her neighbors, however, the health of their territorial community is critically entertwined with their own personal well-being.

In premodern times, human groups depended, by necessity, on the territorial community to meet their human needs. But each development in communication and transportation technology has loosened that dependency somewhat. Electronic communications now connect people over distant spaces, with a high degree of both immediacy and intimacy. In the past week, I have enjoyed e-mail conversations with four students who commute some distance to school, my high school debate partner, an M.S.W. classmate in St. Louis, my daughter in New Zealand, my son in Philadelphia, my brother-in-law in Atlanta, my publisher in Los Angeles, and an old friend in Massachusetts. For many people, "local ties . . . form only a small portion of social connections, and the strongest sources of social support, at least for those who are mobile, may exist outside of the local neighborhood" (Hunter & Riger, 1986, p. 58). That is certainly the situation for Ann and Evan Maxwell, but it is much less true for Joyce Miller. What about for you? Are your strongest supports based on territorial or relational community?

Maybe it is just nostalgic longing, but Garreau's telling of the Maxwells' story suggests that when technology opens the possibilities for relational communities, it does not necessarily spell the death of territorial community. Griswold (1994, p. 150) proposes that "human beings may well learn to operate simultaneously in global, relational communities and in local, spatial ones." Perhaps that is what the Maxwells hope to do once they have relocated to Colorado. Griswold recognizes the possibility that the new technologies will simply allow us to develop and maintain a larger network of increasingly superficial relationships. But she also points out the possibility that the new capacity to be immediately and intimately connected across space could help us to develop more shared meanings and become more tolerant of our differences.

As social workers concerned about social justice, we must understand the multiple implications of inequality of access to the new technologies. These technologies open opportunities for relational community, and the multitude of resources provided by such communities. Skills in using the new technologies are also increasingly rewarded in the labor market. Unless access to these technologies is equalized, however, territorial community will remain central to the lives of some groups—most notably, young children and their caregivers, older adults, poor families, and many persons with disabilities, who have their own special technological needs. On the other hand, the new technologies may make it easier for some people with disabilities to gain access to relational community, even while inaccessible physical environments continue to block their access to territorial community.

Although both territorial and relational communities are relevant to social work, social work's commitment to social justice will require renewed emphasis on territorial community. That same commitment also requires social workers to work toward equalization of access to both territorial and relational community.

Theories of Community

Both social work and community psychology continue to turn to community sociology for theory. In a 1979 paper presented to the Community Section of the American Sociological Association, Roland Warren (1988) suggested that theorizing about community, like sociological theory in general, reflects a multiplicity of paradigms. He recommended that multiple theories be used, because each one explains particular aspects of community. Two decades later, it still seems wise for social workers to follow Warren's advice and use multiple theories for understanding multidimensional community (Flanagan, 1993). That approach is, of course, consistent with the multidimensional approach of this book.

Five perspectives on community seem particularly relevant for social work: (1) community as spatial arrangements, (2) community as ideal type, (3) community as social system, (4) community as contest, and (5) community as social bond. The first of these approaches, community as spatial arrangements, applies only to territorial communities, but the other four approaches can be applied equally well to both relational and territorial communities. Our discussion of the first four approaches to community draws heavily on the work of community sociologists Lyon (1987) and Flanagan (1993). Discussion of the fifth, community as social bond, draws on the work of community psychologists (such as McMillan & Chavis, 1986; Sarason, 1974) as well as communitarian philosophers (such as Bellah et al., 1985; Etzioni, 1993; Rousseau, 1991).

In combination, these five approaches to community should enable you to scan more widely for factors contributing to the problems of living among vulnerable populations, to recognize community resources, and to think more creatively about possible interventions. Using approaches that are not only varied but even discordant should assist you in thinking critically about human behavior and prepare you for the often ambiguous practice situations that you will encounter.

Community as Spatial Arrangements

Beginning with Robert Park's (1936) human ecology theory, a diverse group of sociological theorists have focused on community as spatial arrangements. Their interests have included city placement; population growth; land use patterns; the process of suburbanization; the development of "edge" cities – newly developed business districts of large scale located on the edge of major cities; and the relationships among central cities, suburbs, and edge cities. They are also interested in variations in human behavior related to the type of spatial community, such as rural area, small town, suburb, or central city. If we were to think about the Maxwells' community in terms of spatial arrangements, we would note the runaway exurban growth and development and the upper-middle-class status of the residents in Laguna Niguel. In Joyce Miller's case, we would note the central-city location, the concentration of poor families, the dilapidated housing stock, and the lack of professional services, business, and industry in Walker Community.

Social constructionist
perspective

Symbolic interactionists have studied how symbolic images of communities—the way people think about their communities—are related to spatial arrangements (Feldman, 1990; Hunter, 1974; Strauss, 1961; Suttles, 1972; Wilson & Baldassare, 1996). In a survey of a random sample of Denver employees, Feldman (1990) found that a large majority thought of themselves as either a "city person" or a "suburbanite." Participants largely agreed about the spatial attributes that distinguish cities from suburbs. In comparison to suburbs, they saw cities as having more heterogeneity of social and physical environment, less nature, poorer maintenance, and "more people, cars, noise, crime, stress, and concerns for safety" (Feldman, 1990, p. 200). Feldman found that, as a group, both city people and suburbanites report a preference for the type of spatial community in which they reside.

The multidisciplinary theory on human behavior and the physical environment, discussed in Chapter 7, has also been extended to the study of community as spatial arrangements (Cherulnik, 1993; Newman, 1972, 1981; Taylor, 1988). Specifically, social scientists have focused on elements of environmental design that encourage social interaction as well as those that encourage a sense of control and the motivation to "look out" for the neighborhood. They have identified such elements as large spaces broken into smaller spaces, personalized spaces, and spaces for both privacy and congregation. Wilson and Baldassare (1996), who studied the spatial arrangements in a suburban region, found that satisfaction with the amount of privacy from neighbors' houses was associated with an overall sense of community.

The human ecology perspective in sociology has also been influential, but it has made greater contributions to research methodology than to theory building. Factorial ecology uses statistical analysis to study the spatial patterning of dimensions of community. Such community studies have consistently found that five factors explain much of the variation in the structure, growth rates, and land use patterns of territorial communities in the United States: socioeconomic status, family structure, ethnicity, residential mobility, and population density (Lyon, 1987). These community factors have also been found to influence individual attitudes and behaviors, such as satisfaction with community, participation in community activities, delinquent behavior, and adolescent sexual activity (Adams, 1992; Brewster, Billy, & Grady, 1993; Figuera-McDonough, 1991; Sampson & Groves, 1989). This research also indicates that territorial community has effects, both positive and negative, on child development (Coulton, 1996).

Factorial ecology may have an increasing role to play in studies of territorial community because of the development of sophisticated computer-based **geographic information systems (GIS),** which can map the spatial distribution of a variety of social data (Medyckyj-Scott & Hearnshaw, 1993). Social work planners and administrators have begun to use GIS to develop a better understanding of the communities they serve. The social work faculty looking at Walker Community may want to use a GIS program to show how Walker compares to other neighborhoods in the same central city on such important variables as family structure, race and ethnicity, business and industrial development, employment, educational attainment, housing stock, public spaces, and health and welfare services. A GIS program could also be used to map the land use patterns in Laguna Niguel, and this information could be used to analyze whether there are particular aspects of the spatial arrangements that undermine sense of community.

Thinking about territorial communities as spatial arrangements can help social workers decide which territorial communities to target, for which problems, and with which methods. An interdisciplinary literature has recently focused on the compounding and interrelatedness of problems in deteriorating impoverished neighborhoods in central cities—neighborhoods like Joyce Miller's Walker Community. Philanthropic funders have responded with comprehensive community initiatives (CCIs) to fund multifaceted community-building programs that address the economic and physical conditions, as well as social and cultural issues, of these impoverished communities (Ewalt, 1997). These are the funding initiatives that Joyce Miller is discussing with the social work faculty. Typical elements of the comprehensive programs funded by these initiatives are economic and commercial development, education, employment, housing, leadership development, physical revitalization, social services, and support networks (Chaskin, Joseph, & Chipenda-Dansokho, 1997).

Community as Ideal Type

Spatial arrangements aside, both the Maxwells and Joyce Miller are concerned about commitment, identification, and relationships within their communities. This concern is at the heart of the oldest theory of community, Tonnies's (1887/1963) gemeinschaft and gesellschaft (translated as community and society). In **gemeinschaft** communities, relationships are personal and traditional; in **gesellschaft** communities, relationships are impersonal and contractual. The defining characteristics of gemeinschaft and gesellschaft communities are listed in Exhibit 11.3.

Tonnies shared the view of other early European sociologists, such as Weber and Durkheim, that modernization was leading us away from gemeinschaft and toward gesellschaft. We can find evidence of such movement in the stories of the Maxwells and Joyce Miller. Capitalism, urbanization, and industrialization have all been proposed as causes of the movement toward gesellschaft. Some theorists suggest that electronic technology is moving us into a third type of community—sometimes referred to as a post-gesellschaft, or postmodern, community—characterized by diversity and unpredictability (Lyon, 1987).

Tonnies saw gemeinschaft and gesellschaft as ideal types that will never exist in reality. However, they constitute a hypothetical dichotomy against which the real world can be compared. Although Tonnies's work is more than a century old, the gemeinschaft/gesellschaft dichotomy has proven to be a powerful analytical construct, and it continues to be used in community research. It is also reflected in later typological theories. For example, Cooley (1902/1964) proposes that the social world can be defined in terms of primary groups (intimate face-to-face groups to which we form attachments) and secondary groups (less intimate, more impersonal groups). MacIver (1931) makes a similar distinction between communal (personal) relations and associational (impersonal) relations, and Sorokin (1928) writes in terms of familistic (personal) rela-

EXHIBIT 11.3
Gemeinschaft and
Gesellschaft
Communities

Gemeinschaft	Gesellschaft
Strong identification with community	Little identification with community
Authority based on tradition	Authority based on laws and rationality
Relationships based on emotionalism	Relationships based on goal attainment and emotional neutrality
Others seen as whole persons	Others seen as role enactors

Source: Based on Lyons, 1987.

tionships versus contractual (formal and impersonal) relationships. Some theorists have envisioned more of a continuum than a dichotomy, such as Redfield's folk/urban continuum and Becker's sacred-secular continuum (Lyon, 1987). Most typology theorists believe that modern society is moving from one type to the other, but Becker (1957) is a little different. He suggests that modern society does not always move toward the secular but instead moves back and forth a great deal on the sacred/secular continuum. To Becker, the sacred is best characterized by reluctance to change (traditional authority in Tonnies's gemeinschaft), and the secular is best characterized by readiness to change (emotional neutrality in Tonnies's gesellschaft).

Empirical research supports the idea that territorial communities vary along the gemeinschaft/gesellschaft continuum (Cuba & Hummon, 1993; Hunter & Riger, 1986; Keane, 1991; McKinney & Loomis, 1958, cited in Lyon, 1987; Woolever, 1992). But causation appears to be much more complex than the theorists propose. A number of variables characterizing a community—including mobility patterns, age distribution, gender distribution, education, and family structure—have been found to predict placement along the gemeinschaft/gesellschaft continuum (Cuba & Hummon, 1993; Keane, 1991; Woolever, 1992). Although the findings are inconsistent, population size and density have not been found to be as powerful and consistent predictors of placement on the continuum as had been theorized (Booth, 1976; Choldin, 1978a, 1978b; Dohrenwend & Dohrenwend, 1974; Fischer, 1973a, 1973b, 1984; Freedman, 1975; Kasl & Harburg, 1975; Keane, 1991; Loo, 1974; Srole, 1972; Wilson, 1985; Woolever, 1992).

You may recall that the theorists suggest that communities are not actually ideal types but some mix of gemeinschaft and gesellschaft. For example, Ann and Evan Maxwell's electronic community was developed for doing business, but members of this community visit each other whenever they can, inquire about the health of family members, and send gifts and other acknowledgments of important family events. Joyce Miller felt that her community was drifting further from its gemeinschaft roots; neighbors seldom talked to each other and there was little sense of community. She has put considerable effort into improving relationships and community members' sense of identification with Walker Community. Researchers tend to focus, however, on either gemeinschaft or gesellschaft. Research to date has not captured the rich mix of gemeinschaft and gesellschaft relationships in communities and their interactive impact on human behavior. Social workers might benefit by recognizing both the gemeinschaft and gesellschaft qualities of the communities they serve.

Community as Social System

Systems perspective

A third way to think about communities is as social systems with cultures and patterns of interactions. The social systems perspective has been applied less rigorously to communities, however, than to families, small groups, and formal organizations. In part, the lack of clarity about community boundaries may be to blame. You may recall that boundary is an important concept in the social system perspective. We can usually be quite specific in describing who is a member, and who is not, when talking about families, small groups, and formal organizations. But, whether we are discussing territorial or relational communities, the boundaries of a community are not usually as straightforward.

EXHIBIT 11.4
Aspects of
Community Culture
and Community
Structure

Community Culture
- Pattern of meanings
- Enduring patterns of communication
- Symbols that guide thinking, feelings, and behaviors

Community Structure
- Pattern of interactions
- Institutions
- Economic factors
- Political factors

Source: Based on Griswold, 1994.

Social constructionist
perspective

The social systems perspective focuses on social interaction rather than on the physical aspects of community. Griswold (1994) suggests that social interaction in a community can be understood in two different ways: as culture and as structure. Exhibit 11.4 shows the differences between these two aspects of community. For thinking about community in terms of its culture, symbolic interaction theory is promising (for example, Snow & Anderson, 1993) because of its emphasis on the development of meaning through interaction. Ethnography is also particularly useful for studying community culture. The goal of ethnographic research is to understand the underlying rules and patterns of everyday life, in a particular location or among a particular group, from the "native point of view" (Spradley, 1979) rather than the researcher's point of view.

Community can also be studied in terms of its structure. Social network theory, which was introduced in Chapter 2, is proving to be a promising tool for studying patterns of relationships and their consequences for human behavior (Emirbayer & Goodwin, 1994; Wellman & Leighton, 1979). You may recall that social network theory was discussed with the rational choice perspective in Chapter 2. When it is used to understand the reciprocity of exchanges among members, it fits with a rational choice perspective. However, when it is used, as it is here, simply to understand patterns of relationships among community members, it fits with a systems perspective. Emirbayer and Goodwin (1994, p. 1448) define a **network** as "the set of social relations or social ties among a set of actors." The density of interactions and the strength of ties among members indicates the **social cohesion** of a community. **Strength of ties** is measured by the "frequency, duration, emotional intensity, reciprocal exchange" (p. 1448) of interactions among community members.

Roland Warren's (1978) work has been particularly useful in correcting the earlier singular focus on internal community networks to the exclusion of relationships with external systems. Warren differentiates between **horizontal linkage,** or interaction within the community, and **vertical linkage,** or interaction with systems outside the community. This distinction between horizontal and vertical linkage extends Tonnies's discussion of gemeinschaft and gesellschaft. Vertical linkage may produce some of the standardization expected in mass society, but horizontal linkage allows the local community to develop its own particular meanings for events in the external world. Network theory is particularly promising for its ability to integrate the study of both horizontal and vertical linkages, connecting the micro and macro worlds.

Warren's ideas provide conceptual tools for strengthening horizontal linkages, but they also warn social workers to avoid the naive view that all community problems can be solved by focusing exclusively on interactions within the community. Social workers will do well to remember that strong vertical, intercommunity linkages are also necessary for healthy community. Isolated communities with strong internal ties are likely to develop strong subcultures that provide a sense of identity for community members but may not provide the necessary tools for cross-cultural exchanges. Isolated communities need members who can serve as a bridge for key resources, such as employment opportunities. Joyce Miller, for example, has served as a bridge to employment for some residents of Walker Community. Her current attempts to use the nearby school of social work as a bridge to federal resources are viewed with suspicion by some members of her community, who fear that these efforts will undermine the interactions within the community, but Joyce recognizes that outside resources can also be used to strengthen her community.

The Maxwells, on the other hand, derive many personal and professional benefits from their electronic community, which links them vertically across geographies and cultures. But this community would be of little help to them if they were locked out of their house, had car trouble, or developed a medical emergency. For these situations, horizontal ties to a geographic community are important.

Community as Contest

Conflict perspective

Joyce Miller and the Walker Community Association have decided to do battle to prevent the development of a toxic waste site in their community. They have also discovered that they are facing adversaries with strong economic resources and with access to political power. To understand the relationship between contest and community, we can turn to the conflict perspective. Conflict theory's emphasis on dissension, power, and exploitation has been problematic for social workers and social scientists, however, because it is not seen as a tidy fit with the concept "sense of community."

More seriously, conflict theory brings the social work profession face to face with its divergent roles in society. Harry Specht (1994) writes about our historical mission to "help poor people, to improve community life, and to solve difficult social problems" (p. x). The operative CSWE Curriculum Policy Statement and the NASW Code of Ethics emphasize the role of social work in the promotion of social justice. Neo-Marxist theory suggests, however, that social services are increasingly used to smooth over problems and, consequently, allow dominant groups to maintain the status quo (Castells, 1977). Nudging social work away from such suspect activities, critical theory recommends that we take a strong stance against existing patterns of domination, and political economy theory points up for us the negative consequences for nonprivileged communities of interlocking economic and political structures (Agger, Goldrich, & Swanson, 1964; Logan & Molotch, 1987). These theories suggest that we cannot make significant improvements in the lives of persons in vulnerable communities without challenging existing patterns of domination. Conflict theorists have a point, and indeed the mission of social work is social reform, but, as Wenocur and Soifer (1997, p. 199) remind us, "the legitimacy and salaries of social workers depend heavily on governmental and philanthropic support." This dilemma of social reform versus professionalization is the subject of further discussion in Chapter 12.

Although social workers may envision a world with less conflict and competition, we must recognize that conflict, power, and exploitation are very much a part of contemporary life. In the late 20th century, community social workers must be aware of two important ways in which community can be a contest:

1. *Privileged groups seek to protect their privilege, and nonprivileged groups push for change.* This type of contest is consistent with a neo-Marxist approach. Joyce Miller and the Walker Community Association are involved in a contest of this type, as they challenge the assumption that low-income communities should absorb the risks associated with scientific and technological development. The struggle over accessible physical environments initiated by the disability community is another example of this type of contest. A final example is the contest between homeless persons and other community groups for valued space.

2. *Interest groups of relatively equal status compete to control resources or cultural symbols.* Two territorial communities, such as two adjacent suburbs, may compete for funds for housing, or two relational communities may struggle for the hearts and minds of society at large. It is possible that Ann and Evan Maxwell will find themselves embroiled in a conflict between pro-development and anti-development groups when they move to Colorado. The sometimes violent struggle between the pro-life and the pro-choice movements is an example of a contest to control cultural symbols about gender roles (J. D. Hunter, 1994). As James Davidson Hunter (1994), John Rawls (1993), and Amitai Etzioni (1993) suggest, we desperately need community-builders who can help us turn our "culture wars" into culture conversations—respectful conversations based on substance rather than power politics. Social work is well suited to play a leadership role in developing such respectful conversations. Fisher and Karger (1997) make a similar observation: "Increasingly, social workers are challenged to heal social fractures. Contemporary history suggests that modern societies fracture along various fault lines, including ethnic, religious, racial, tribal, and geographic lines. . . . The effort needed to arrest this phenomenon is herculean, and the more society unravels, the harder it becomes to reweave its diverse social threads" (p. 136). Social workers will have to become comfortable with conflict if we are to take leadership roles in healing these social fractures.

Recognizing community as contest raises several questions of values for social workers:

- Which communities will we strengthen?
- Which issues will we address?
- Where will we stand on the contests?
- When will we take sides, and when will we work for common ground?

A profession that makes a commitment to social justice needs a well-articulated theory of social justice to guide resolution of such questions. At the moment, we are, as Frederic Reamer (1993) suggests, deeply divided in our understanding of social justice, with the central point of tension being differences over the values of individualism versus communalism. A good place to begin articulating a theory of social justice for social work would be with active discussion of such recent contributions as the constitutional, or individual liberty, approach of John Rawls's *Political Liberalism* (1993)and the communitarian approach of Amitai Etzioni's *The Spirit of Community* (1993). Although these works differ in significant ways, both share a concern for unity in diversity, recognize the challenges of pluralism, and advocate for preservation of individual liberties while moving the pendulum away from radical individualism to greater emphasis on the "commons."

Community as Social Bond

In one notable attempt to move us away from radical individualism and toward greater emphasis on the "commons," Robert Bellah and his colleagues (1985) assert that most Americans speak in the **first language of individualism.** Our symbols and identities have been shaped by a language rich with words and concepts for expressing ideas of individual freedom, individual identity, personal mastery, and individual pathology. They also assert, however, that a **second language of community** lies dormant in us—a language of connectedness, unity, mutual responsibility, mutual aid, and shared identity. For example, when the Maxwells and Joyce Miller talk about sense of community, they are talking about the quality of the connections community members make with each other and the commitment they feel to each other. They are thinking about community as a social bond that unifies people. This language of community sounds very much like the gemeinschaft community posited by Tonnies.

Mary Rousseau (1991, p. vii) suggests that "in the 'second language' of community, persons are seen as innately connected to each other, naturally cooperative in pursuing a fulfillment dictated by the traits of our common human nature and dignity." In her philosophy of community, Rousseau proposes that community is a necessary good, a requirement for our well-being, essential to our humanity. It might be argued that the increased longevity of cancer patients who participate in support groups (Spiegel, Bloom, Kraemer, & Gottheil, 1989) and the finding of lower rates of violence in urban neighborhoods with a strong sense of community (Sampson, Raudenbush, & Earls, 1997) provide empirical support for Rousseau's assertion. Rousseau also suggests, however, that the language of community was largely lost during the process of industrialization, and that much about contemporary life mitigates against finding that voice.

It is this idea of community—the tie that binds, the social bond—to which we refer when we lament the loss of community or when we talk longingly about searching for community, strengthening community, or building sense of community. We may have retained more sense of community than is sometimes thought, but how do we reclaim more of the "second language" to improve the social bonds? Both social work and community psychology have discovered how hard it is to hold onto the language of community when the world in which they operate is so heavily steeped in the language of individualism, with its emphasis on autonomy and self-determination. Social work has struggled with the issue of communalism versus individualism for almost a century. Community psychology is a much younger field, but faces the same struggles. In his 1988 presidential address to the Community Psychology Division of the American Psychological Association, Kenneth Heller (1989) asked, "Where is the community in community psychology?" Speaking of the community psychology literature, Keller commented, "With some notable exceptions ... discussions of community theories are hard to find, and the study of individuals has been the single largest content category of articles published in community psychology journals" (p. 1).

Robert Wuthnow (1994) suggests that the small-group movement of the past two decades has been a quest for community in the midst of a rapidly changing world. Participants in his research project reported that they joined small groups because of a "desire for intimacy, support, sharing, and other forms of community involvement" (p. 52), which they were not finding in their neighborhoods and workplaces.

Community psychologists McMillan and Chavis (1986) turned to the literature on group cohesiveness to understand how to enhance the social bonds of community. As you may recall, they identified four essential elements in the definition of *sense of community*: (1) membership, (2) influence, (3) integration and fulfillment of needs, and (4) shared emotional connection. Note, however, that although sense of community is a concept in the tradition of the second language of community, even their discussion of its elements often reflects the first language of individualism.

1. *Membership* is based on boundaries, emotional safety, sense of belonging and identification, personal investment, and a common symbol system. Boundaries clarify who is in and who is out and protect against threat. Personal investment in a community is enhanced when we feel that we have worked for membership. Common symbols facilitate integration of the community, in part by intentionally creating social distance between members and nonmembers. However, communities built on exclusion, rather than inclusion, could be contributing to the fragmentation of social life (Fisher & Karger, 1997; Hardcastle et al., 1997).

2. *Influence* is bidirectional. On the one hand, "members are more attracted to a community in which they feel that they are influential" (McMillan & Chavis, 1986, p. 12). On the other hand, "cohesiveness is contingent on the group's ability to influence its members" (p. 11).

3. *Integration and fulfillment of needs* refers to individual reinforcement or reward for membership, but McMillan and Chavis conclude that "a strong community is able to fit people together so that people meet others' needs while they meet their own" (p. 13).

4. *Shared emotional connection* is enhanced when members are provided with "positive ways to interact, important events to share and ways to resolve them positively, opportunities to honor members, opportunities to invest in the community, and opportunities to experience a spiritual bond among members" (p. 14).

Before leaving this discussion of community as social bond, let us return to the idea of unity in diversity that was an element in the theories of John Rawls and Amitai Etzioni. This idea of **unity in diversity** has been used by social work scholars in a variety of ways to describe the goal of community social work practice (Fisher & Karger, 1997; Gutierrez, 1997). You may recall from Chapter 1 that the transactional approach of this book focuses on unity of persons and environments. You also may remember that a sense of unity with others was discussed, in Chapter 6, as an attribute of a spiritual experience. And you have read in this chapter that McMillan and Chavis (1986) suggest that experiencing "a spiritual bond among members" is one way to achieve a shared emotional connection.

Interestingly, *unity* is a word from the second language of community, and *diversity* is a word from the first language of individualism. Mixing the languages in this way can help to ensure that unity, or "the common good," is not simply code language for protecting the privileged position of dominant groups. Writing about a social work approach that she calls "multicultural community organizing," Lorraine Gutierrez (1997, p. 250) raises the question "How do we respect diversity and reduce inequality while working toward a common good?" Fisher and Karger (1997, p. 180) appear to answer that question when they propose that "the promotion of public activism and a vision of an inclusive and egalitarian public good are principles by which social work can be organized." They see social conflict as an essential component of the process of developing unity in diversity—"of course, it is inappropriate to tell those who do not have power or whose voices were not heard before, to be less divisive or aggressive in pursuit of their interests and voice" (p. 134)—but they also call for coalition building and healing of social fractures.

Social Workers and Communities

As suggested in Chapter 8, Western modernization, capitalism, industrialization, and urbanization have brought great costs as well as benefits. The profession of social work was developed as one force to minimize the costs—a communal force to correct for extremes of individualism (Falck, 1988). Wenocur and Soifer (1997, p. 199) note that "social work may be the only profession in the United States whose Code of Ethics enjoins us to promote the general welfare of society." In its efforts to promote the general social welfare, social work has always been involved with communities in some way. The nature of social work's relationships with communities has changed over time, however, and there are long-standing disagreements about appropriate roles for social workers in communities. These disagreements are evident in recent attempts to reconceptualize community practice for social work (Fisher & Karger, 1997; Hardcastle et al., 1997). Here we summarize the issues involved in four of these points of disagreement.

Community as Context for Practice versus Target of Practice

Social workers who view community as a context for practice focus on working with individuals and families, although they also recognize the ways in which communities provide opportunities and barriers for client behaviors and agency responses. In contrast, social workers who view community as a target of practice focus on enhancing the health of the community.

There seems to be a growing consensus that social work needs to recognize community as both context and target of practice (Fisher & Karger, 1997; Hardcastle et al., 1997; McDonald et al.,1997; Sviridoff & Ryan, 1997). Community agencies are working "to address the multiple needs of families" and at the same time to help in building "protective, caring, and connected communities" (McDonald, 1997, p. 115). For example, they are combining family therapy and parent education with community building to help children succeed at school (Feikema, Segalavich, & Jeffries, 1997; McDonald et al., 1997; Webster-Stratton, 1997).

Even with a combined community practice model, questions still arise about when to intervene with individuals and families and when to focus on larger collectivities and groups. Recent examples from the social work literature demonstrate this tension. Specht and Courtney (1994) call for putting the social back in social work with a "community-based system of social care" and elimination of the psychotherapeutic role. Carol Swenson (1994) has responded thoughtfully, with an appreciation for the communal values (the second language of community) articulated by Specht and Courtney. She disagrees, however, with the conclusion that the objectives of community building and psychotherapy are incompatible, recommending instead a continued dual focus on community and individual. She suggests "it will be difficult to 'help communities create good' if those communities are composed of large numbers of individuals who are alone and purposeless" (p. 198).

In the second language of community, the words "numbers of individuals who are alone and purposeless" suggest the need for strengthening the sense of community, at the collective community level, and would make a poor defense for psychotherapy. In the first language of individualism, however, problems of isolation and purposelessness can only be handled one-on-one, with professional helpers. I agree with Swenson that the psychotherapeutic role should not be eliminated from social work's repertoire, but I do think that social workers have come to rely too heavily on this role, and may be using it for problems for which it is neither efficient nor effective. I support Fisher and Karger's (1997) position that an integrated community practice should avoid an overreliance on one-to-one and family sessions, opting, where appropriate, for "collective and group formats" (p. 50).

Agency Orientation versus Social Action

Community social work practice has roots in a **social action model** of community organization, which was developed by leaders of the settlement house movement. This model of community practice is political in nature, emphasizing social reform and challenge of structural inequalities. Fisher and Karger (1997) report that by the 1930s, this social action model had been replaced by an **agency-based model,** which promoted social agencies and the services they provided. This model of community practice is nonpolitical and puts little or no emphasis on social change. It is based on the assumption that the best way to strengthen communities is to provide social services. Proponents of the agency-based model of community organizing often focus on coordination of services across agencies (Spergel & Grossman, 1997).

Saul Alinsky, founder of one of the best-known community organizing training centers, was critical of the agency-based model of community social work (Fisher & Karger, 1997). He did not think that social justice is ensured by providing social services. However, agency-based provision of social services, and interagency coordination of services, often does contribute to the well-being of communities. We need social workers who will advocate for the retention of threatened services, as well the development of new services. However, this type of community social work practice is not sufficient to meet the needs of communities or to fulfill social work's historical commitment to social justice. Thus, recent initiatives to revitalize impoverished neighborhoods have combined resource development with efforts to strengthen sense of community (Cohen & Phillips, 1997). Bringing community members together for the purposes of building or strengthening the sense of community and identifying community problems and community resources is known as **locality development,** or **social development**. I recommend an integrated approach to community social work practice that enhances community-based services, builds sense of community, and advocates for social reform.

Conflict Model of Practice versus Collaborative Model

Conflict perspective

Over the years, social work has taken different positions on the question of whether social workers should lean toward conflict or collaboration, ebbing and flowing in its "tradition of nagging the conscience of America" (Fisher & Karger, 1997, p. 188). In liberal times, social work has been more willing to embrace conflict approaches; in conservative times, more collaborative approaches have been preferred. In the early 1900s, social work reformers used social surveys to expose exploitive industries and disseminated the results widely in newspapers and magazines (Fisher & Karger, 1997). Today, however, Wenocur and Soifer (1997) note a trend away from "challenging the establishment" toward a model of "partnerships between local community groups, government officials, and corporate leaders" (p. 203).

Contemporary social trends call for a contemporary style of community practice that draws on both conflict and collaborative models. Community social workers need skills for exposing and challenging social injustice as well as for resolving conflict and building coalitions. The choice of tactics will depend on the specific person/environment configurations encountered.

Some person/environment configurations call for community social workers to elevate community conflict for the purpose of challenging exploitation and oppression. Throughout this book, we emphasize the need for social workers to take a critical perspective that recognizes power and oppression as important factors in the negotiation of social life. A critical perspective also calls for social workers to challenge existing patterns of domination and oppression. With the trend toward devolution of government responsibilities to the local level, the local territorial community becomes increasingly important to these efforts. Social work research can identify and expose local patterns of exploitation. Community social workers can use consciousness-raising tactics to help oppressed groups understand their situations. They can use a variety of advocacy skills to make appeals for the rights and needs of oppressed groups. Fisher and Karger (1997, p. 130) report that many contemporary social critics "see grassroots community organizations as potentially the most effective progressive balance to the elite domination."

Other person/environment configurations call for community social workers to resolve community conflicts. Fisher and Karger (1997) remind us that "public life is about difference, and about learning to create a society by interacting with others who have different opinions and experiences" (p. 26). Social work's professional organizations have taken a position that values diversity. I agree with that position and also suggest that social workers should value the conflict that accompanies diversity. Conflict is not always a bad thing, but communities often need help in negotiating their differences. Social workers can help to develop a civil discourse on controversial issues, a discourse that includes the voices of people who have previously been marginalized and excluded. Community social workers can use a variety of conflict resolution skills to help different community groups understand and respect each other's experiences and to engage in respectful and effective problem-solving activities. It remains to be seen whether cyber-communities, such as the one to which Ann and Evan Maxwell belong, will increase or decrease opportunities for discourse with those who are different from us.

There is considerable agreement among social work scholars that social workers should focus on helping to develop broad issues that can unite diverse groups in social reform efforts; two examples of such issues are health care and financial security in a global economy (Fisher & Karger, 1997; Gutierrez, 1997; Hardcastle et al., 1997; Wenocur & Soifer, 1997). Fisher and Karger

(1997) emphasize the need to build greater solidarity between poor and middle-class people. Wenocur and Soifer (1997) propose that regional coalitions will be necessary to develop viable solutions to the problems of impoverished central-city neighborhoods like Walker Community, and Gutierrez (1997) suggests the need to build coalitions across cultural groups.

Expert versus Partner in the Social Change Process

Joyce Miller has sought the funding expertise of the faculty at the nearby school of social work, but some members of the Walker Community Association fear that the social workers will impose their own definitions of the community's problems and their own ideas about solutions to those problems. Whether that happens will depend, in large part, on the model of community social work held by the social workers.

The **social planning model** of community social work is based on the premise that the complexities of modern social problems require expert planners schooled in a rational planning model. In this model, the community power structure is the author of social change efforts (Fisher & Karger, 1997). This approach is often referred to as a top-down approach to social change.

Locality development and other social action models of community social work take a different view: community practice should support and enhance the ability of community members to identify their own community's needs, assets, and solutions to problems (Lowe, 1997; Naperstek & Dooley, 1997). Social workers work in partnership with community members and groups, and remain open to learning from the community (Gutierrez, 1997). This approach is often known as a bottom-up approach to social change.

A social planning model is appropriate for problems requiring specialized technical knowledge. Community members are the experts, however, about community needs and community assets. They also have the capacity to be active partners in identifying solutions to community problems. The faculty at the school of social work near Walker Community have expertise about pursuing grant funding and using GIS systems to map community variables. They will need to work as partners with the Walker Community, however, to identify community needs, community resources, solutions to community problems, and barriers to change.

IMPLICATIONS FOR SOCIAL WORK PRACTICE

The preceding discussion of community has many implications for social work practice:

- Be informed about the communities you serve; learn about their readiness to change, their spatial arrangements (for territorial communities), their cultures, their patterns of internal and external relationships, their conflicts, and their sense of community.

- Avoid overreliance on individual and family sessions; make use of small- and large-group formats where appropriate.

- When working with individuals and families, assess their opportunities to be supported by and to make contributions to the community, and assess the limits imposed by their territorial and relational communities.

- Recognize the central role of territorial community in the lives of many young persons and their caregivers, older adults, and poor families.

- If you are a social work planner or administrator, become familiar with computer-based geographical information systems for mapping social data.

- Where appropriate, strengthen interaction within the community (horizontal linkages) to build sense of community and maximize use of internal resources.

- Where appropriate, strengthen intercommunity interactions (vertical linkages) to ensure adequate resources to meet community needs.

- Where appropriate, advocate for the retention of threatened social services, the coordination of existing services, and the development of new services.

- Where appropriate, collaborate with others to challenge exploitation and oppression in communities.

- Where appropriate, use consciousness-raising tactics to help oppressed groups understand their situations.

- Where appropriate, assist communities to negotiate differences and resolve conflicts.

- Where appropriate, assist in the development of coalitions to improve the resource base for community problem solving.

- Assess both community strengths and community problems.

- Involve community members in identification of community strengths and community problems, in goal setting, and in intervention activities.

- When working with impoverished communities, work with other individuals and organizations to develop comprehensive, multidimensional, integrated strategies.

MAIN POINTS

1. After several decades of declining interest, we are currently seeing a resurgence of interest in community.

2. Community consists of people bound either by geography or network links, sharing common ties, and interacting with one another.

3. Sense of community is based on belonging, being important to each other, and having mutual commitment.

4. Both relational communities, based on voluntary association, and territorial communities, based on geography, are relevant to social work.

5. The well-being of many oppressed groups continues to be intertwined with territorial communities.

6. Five approaches to community have relevance for contemporary social work: community as spatial arrangements, community as ideal type, community as social system, community as contest, and community as social bond.

7. Community as spatial arrangements focuses on how human behavior is related to spatial arrangements such as population growth, land use patterns, and relationships between central cities, suburbs, and edge cities.

8. Community as ideal type proposes a hypothetical dichotomy, based on Tonnies's gemeinschaft and gesellschaft, against which real communities can be evaluated.

9. Community as social system focuses on community as a field for social interaction, looking at both the culture and the structure of the community.

10. Study of the structure of communities has been enhanced by developments in social network theory, which has developed tools for looking at sets of social relations, interactions among actors, and the strength of ties among members.

11. When studying the structure of a community, it is important to study both interaction within the community (horizontal linkage) and interaction with other communities (vertical linkage).

12. Community as contest focuses on conflict, power, and exploitation in contemporary communities. It recognizes contests based on power differentials, as well as contests to control cultural symbols among groups of relatively equal status.

13. Community as social bond is concerned with sense of community, unity, mutual responsibility, mutual aid, and shared identity.

14. Long-standing disagreements about social work's relationships to communities center on four points of tension: community as context for practice versus target of practice; agency-based model versus social action model; conflict model versus collaborative model of practice; and social worker as expert versus partner in the social change process.

KEY TERMS

agency-based model

community

first language of individualism

gemeinschaft

geographic information systems (GIS)

gesellschaft

horizontal linkage

locality development

mass society

network

relational community

second language of community

sense of community

social action model

social cohesion

social development

social planning model

strength of ties

territorial community

unity in diversity

vertical linkage

WORLD WIDE WEB RESOURCES

Social Psychology Web Links

http://www.psych.nwu.edu/psych/people/faculty/roese/social/sweb.htm

Site maintained by Neal Roese, Sociology professor at Northwestern University. Contains information and resources on social psychology, journals, organizations, research, and links to other Internet sites.

Community Psychology Network

http://www.geocities.com/~mattcook/

An online guide to community psychology maintained by Matt Cook. Contains links to other Internet sites, resources, discussion lists, journals, social policy issues, and professional groups.

CHAPTER 12

Social Movements

MARY JO KAHN AND THE VIRGINIA BREAST CANCER FOUNDATION

Mary Jo Kahn's mother was diagnosed with breast cancer at the age of 39; she died when she was 47. Mary Jo was also diagnosed with breast cancer when she was 39, about the same time that her older sister's breast cancer was diagnosed. Mary Jo has two other sisters who have never been diagnosed with breast cancer but who have had prophylactic mastectomies to prevent breast cancer. Mary Jo is the mother of two adolescent daughters.

Mary Jo's mother did not have a job outside the home, and she had few opportunities to talk with other women about breast cancer. Breast cancer was a lonely disease for her. When Mary Jo was diagnosed, her situation was very different. She shared the experience of breast cancer with her older sister. She joined a Mastectomy Support Group at the cancer center where she received medical care. She was embedded in a network of women activists who had worked together for several years on a variety of women's issues. Mary Jo had many opportunities to talk with other women about breast cancer, and she was outraged to learn how common the disease was, and yet how very little research was being done.

In 1991, Mary Jo began to talk with other women from her Mastectomy Support Group about the need for activist efforts to increase funding for breast cancer research. With the help of friends and family members, they organized a statewide rally for Mother's Day, 1991. They were mentored in these efforts by California Breast Cancer Action, which had itself been mentored by an AIDS activist group in the organization of a successful Mother's Day rally in California the previous year. They were also supported by Mary Jo's network of women activists, who were pleased to embrace a women's issue that was potentially noncontroversial. "We will not die silently anymore" became a theme for their emerging breast cancer movement. For the 1991 Mother's Day rally, Mary Jo's daughters made banners that announced "Hold the line at 1 in 9," referring to the statistic that 1 in 9 women were expected to develop breast cancer at the time.

Soon after the Mother's Day rally, an organizational meeting was held at Mary Jo's house to explore the possibility of formalizing the emerging breast cancer activist movement in Virginia. Twenty people attended the meeting, and for their group they chose the name The Virginia Breast Cancer Foundation. The first public meeting of the foundation was held in July 1991. Later that year the National Breast Cancer Coalition was formed, and the Virginia Breast Cancer Foundation became a member of that coalition.

The first national activity of the emerging breast cancer movement was the "Do the Write Thing" letter writing campaign during the fall of 1991. People were encouraged to write letters calling for more funding for breast cancer research to members of Congress, and the President. The campaign organizers set a goal of 180,000 letters, in recognition of the 180,000 women who would be diagnosed with breast cancer in the United States in 1991. To the delight of the organizers, more than 700,000 letters were delivered to the President. In Virginia, the goal was 4,300 letters; foundation members took buses to Washington to deliver 24,000 letters. The 1992 federal budget, passed in November 1991, contained a $42 million increase for breast cancer research.

In February 1992, breast cancer activists organized a conference and invited breast cancer researchers to present the latest research findings. They asked the researchers how much money would be needed to adequately fund breast cancer research, and the researchers suggested a $300 million increase.

Mary Jo Kahn took on the job of organizing rallies across the country on Mother's Day 1992, and the movement was able to organize 32 rallies in 38 states—compared with the two rallies in two states in 1991. The activists then focused on developing networks of concerned persons. They used these networks to deliver legislative alerts in the summer of 1992 and to publicize their campaign for a $300 million increase in funds for breast cancer research. Once again, the activists were successful.

The original goal of the breast cancer activist movement was to increase funding for breast cancer research. Once the movement began to succeed with this goal, another goal emerged: to ensure that women with breast cancer would have a voice on the committees that made research funding decisions. At first, the federal agencies involved were suspicious, verbalizing their concern that women with cancer would make emotional rather than informed decisions. The activists pressed their goal, however, and the pairing of researchers and women with cancer to make research funding decisions proceeded smoothly.

There is little doubt that the breast cancer activists benefited from circumstances in the political institution at the time their movement was emerging. A gender gap in political elections had become a serious issue following Anita Hill's testimony in the Clarence Thomas confirmation hearings. Activist women's issues such as abortion had become highly contentious, and politicians across the political spectrum welcomed a noncontroversial women's issue in 1992. The campaign for a $300 million increase in breast cancer research funds was presented during George Bush's presidency, while he was running for reelection.

At the time of the campaign, congressional mandates prohibited new taxes or the shifting of monies from one federal department to another. The breast cancer activists analyzed the situation this way: to get more money, they had to find a pocket of federal money that politicians would be willing to reappropriate to breast cancer research. The Cold War had just ended with the massive changes in Eastern Europe, and there was general agreement that the Department of Defense (DOD) had more money than it needed. So, the activists asked for $300 million of the DOD budget. Even the DOD was not opposed to this request, because they were faced with the possibility of laying off a large number of military doctors. So, ironically, the breast cancer activists worked collaboratively with the DOD to develop directions for breast cancer research.

In June 1997, Mary Jo Kahn was recognized by President Bill Clinton for her activism on behalf of women with breast cancer. (Mary Jo Kahn, personal communication, August 19, 1997)

A Definition of Social Movements

What happens when a group of people, like these women concerned about breast cancer, think that certain arrangements are unjust and need to be changed? Sometimes they work together to try to bring about the desired changes. Anthony Oberschall (1992, p. 1) summarizes such collective efforts well: "Most of the time people pursue their goals or seek relief from hardship on their own, through individual effort.... Yet, on occasion, many people pool their efforts in collective actions to benefit a large category of persons jointly—women, the elderly, blacks, farmers—not just themselves and their families. They find it necessary to challenge and change routines and institutions that others remain attached to." These joint efforts are **social movements**—"large-scale, collective efforts to bring about or resist changes that bear on the lives of many" (Oberschall, 1992, p. 2).

Larry Ray (1993) suggests that we think of social movements as either offensive or defensive. **Offensive social movements** seek to "try out new ways of cooperating and living together" (Habermas, 1981/1987, p. 394). The breast cancer and the virtual communities movements are examples of offensive social movements. **Defensive social movements**, on the other hand, seek to defend traditional values and social arrangements. Promise Keepers and property rights movements are examples of defensive social movements. Both types of social movements are common in the United States and across the world today.

The tendency today is to define social movements broadly, to include collective efforts to improve not just society but also individuals' lives. Indeed, self-help groups seem to be much more popular these days than traditional mass movements like the civil rights movement. However, Alfred Katz (1993) has posed the question of whether self-help groups—including therapeutic groups, social advocacy/action groups, groups created to support alternative lifestyles, and groups providing havens via a 24-hour live-in situation—can be called social movements, given their emphasis on personal development and revitalization rather than social change. He concludes that the proliferation of self-help groups should be considered a social trend but not a social movement, because the varied self-help groups are not unified into a movement. Others have argued, however, that the trend toward self-help groups itself represents a social movement (Wuthnow, 1994). I agree and would also argue that specific self-help groups, such as AA and Promise Keepers, are also social movements. These groups and others like them are collective efforts to change ways of thinking about specific aspects of social life.

Social Movements and the History of Social Work

Like many of the world's religions, some nation states, labor unions, the YMCA/YWCA, and the Boy Scouts and Girl Scouts, the profession of social work is generally considered to have its origin in social movements (Marx & McAdam, 1994). More specifically, the social work profession developed out of the confluence of two social movements: the charity organization society movement and the settlement house movement (Popple & Leighninger, 1993). You have probably studied these social movements in some of your other courses, so they will not be discussed in great detail here. But as social workers, we should recognize how intertwined the history of social work is with social movements.

Both the charity organization society movement and the settlement house movement emerged out of concern during the late 1800s about the ill effects of industrialization, including urban overcrowding and economic instability among low-paid workers. Both social movements developed in England and were transplanted to the United States. But in the beginning, their orientations were very different.

The **charity organization society (COS) movement** developed because private charity organizations became overtaxed by the needs of poor people. Middle- and upper-class people were fearful that a coalition of unemployed people and low-paid workers would revolt and threaten the stability of established political and economic institutions. Leaders of the COS movement saw poverty as based in individual pathology and immorality and set the goal of coordinating the giving of charity to ensure that no duplication occurred. Volunteer "friendly visitors" were assigned to poor families to help them correct character flaws and develop strong moral fiber. Leaders of the COS movement believed in private, rather than public, charity. Service—the provision of efficient and effective service—was the primary agenda of the COS.

The **settlement house movement** was stimulated by the same social circumstances, but was based on very different values and goals. Whereas COS leaders focused on individual pathology, leaders of the settlement house movement focused on environmental hazards. They developed settlement houses in urban neighborhoods where "settlers" lived together as "good neighbors" to poor families and were actively involved in "research, service, and reform" (Popple & Leighninger, 1993, p. 61). The settlers supported labor activities, lobbied for safe and sanitary housing, provided space for local political groups, offered day care, and provided a variety of cultural and educational programs. They published the results of their research widely and used it to push for governmental reform. **Social reform**—the creation of more just social institutions—was the primary agenda of the settlement house movement.

Over time, workers from the two social movements began to interact at annual meetings of the National Conference of Charities and Corrections, and social work as an occupation took shape. With efforts to professionalize the occupation of social work and, later, to win acceptance for the public social welfare institution, the social reform agenda of the settlement house movement lost ground. Direct service became the focus—specifically, individual and family casework in health and welfare agencies, and social work with groups in the settlement houses and YMCA/YWCAs. This transition away from reform toward a service model is not an uncommon trajectory of social movements. However, three-quarters of a century later, social work continues to experience a tension between service and social reform.

Although social work emerged from social movements, it is now a profession, not a social movement. Some social workers work for social movements, however, and the social work profession struggles with its relationship to a variety of social movements. For example, Chapter 11 discussed the tensions in community social work around issues of social action. With the profession's emphasis on social justice, we should understand how social movements emerge and become successful. That is why this chapter on social movements is included.

Perspectives on Social Movements

Conflict perspective

Early social science literature on social movements was based on a relatively unified perspective, commonly called **strain theory**. According to strain theory, social movements develop in response to some form of strain in society, when people's efforts to cope with stress become collective efforts. Different versions of strain theory focus on different types of social strains, such as strain due to rapid social change, strain due to social inequality, strain due to social isolation and lack of community, and strain due to conflicts in cultural beliefs (Hall, 1995; Marx & McAdam, 1994). Discussion in earlier chapters has built a case that each of these types of strain exists in the United States today.

Recent social science theory and research have been critical of social strain theory, however. Critics argue that strain is always present to some degree in all societies, but social movements do not always appear in response, and their intensity does not vary systematically with the level of strain (Hall, 1995; Marx & McAdam, 1994; McAdam, McCarthy, & Zald, 1996). These critics suggest that social strain is a necessary but not sufficient condition to predict the development of a social movement. Any social movement theory must start, they insist, with the condition of social strain, but other theories are needed to understand why a particular social movement develops when it does, what form that movement takes, and how successful the movement is in accomplishing its goals. Without the sense of outrage felt by the breast cancer advocates, the Virginia Breast Cancer Foundation would not have developed, at least not its social reform mission. But the situation of women with breast cancer had not changed suddenly, so why did the social reform movement develop when it did?

Psychodynamic perspective

Instead of focusing on social strains, some social psychologists have looked for psychological factors or attitudes that might explain which individuals are likely to get involved in social movements. A variety of psychological characteristics have been investigated, including authoritarian personality, emotional conflicts with parents, alienation, aggression, and relative deprivation. Empirical investigations have found very little support for a relationship between psychological characteristics and social movement participation, however. Research also indicates that a great many people who never join social movements have similar attitudes about movement goals to those of active movement participants (Marx & McAdam, 1994).

Theory and research about social movements have flourished in the past two decades. Throughout the 1970s, social movement scholars in the United States and Europe worked independently of each other and developed different theories and different research emphases (McAdam et al., 1996). In the past 10 years, however, U.S. and European social movement scholars have begun to work together and to engage in comparative analysis of social movements across place and time. Originally, these collaborative efforts focused only on social movements in the United States and Western Europe. Since the momentous political events in Eastern Europe in the late 1980s, however, Eastern European social movements have received extensive and intensive investigation. The next likely development in social movements scholarship will be to extend comparative analysis beyond the United States and Europe to nonindustrialized countries (McAdam et al., 1996).

Three perspectives on social movements have emerged out of this lively interest. I will be referring to these perspectives as the political opportunities (PO) perspective, the mobilizing structures (MS) perspective, and the cultural framing (CF) perspective. There is growing agreement among social movement scholars that no one of these perspectives provides adequate tools for understanding social movements (Hall, 1995; McAdam et al., 1996; Marx & McAdam, 1994; Tarrow, 1994). Each perspective adds important dimensions to our understanding of social movements, however, and taken together they provide a relatively comprehensive theory of social movements. Social movement scholars recommend research that synthesizes concepts across the three perspectives. The recent social movement literature offers one of the best examples of contemporary attempts to integrate and synthesize multiple theoretical perspectives to give a more complete picture of social phenomena.

Political Opportunities Perspective

Mary Jo Kahn and other breast cancer advocates saw political opportunity in the gender gap within the U.S. electorate and in the end of the Cold War. They thought that these circumstances opened the possibility for successful attempts at social reform. These observations are in line with the **political opportunities (PO) perspective**, whose main ideas are summarized in Exhibit 12.1.

Conflict perspective

The PO perspective begins with the assumption that social institutions, particularly political and economic institutions, benefit the more powerful members of society, often called **elites**, and disadvantage many. The elites typically have routine access to institutionalized political channels, while disadvantaged groups are denied access. Power disparities make it very difficult for some groups to successfully challenge existing institutions, but the PO perspective suggests that institutions are not consistently invulnerable to challenge by groups with little power. Social movements can at times take advantage of institutional arrangements that are vulnerable to challenge. The breast cancer advocates were convinced that the lack of funding for breast cancer research was related to gender power arrangements, but they astounded even

EXHIBIT 12.1
Key Ideas of
the Political
Opportunities
Perspective

- Social movements emerge when political opportunities are open.
- Political systems differ from each other, and change over time, in their openness to social movements.
- A given political system is not equally open or closed to all challengers.
- Success of one social movement can open the political system to challenges from other social movements.
- A given political system's openness to social movements is influenced by international events.
- Opportunities for social movements open at times of instability in political alignments.
- Social movements often rely on elite allies.

themselves by setting in motion a process that secured Department of Defense funding for breast cancer research.

The political system itself may influence whether a social movement will emerge at a given time, as well as the form the movement will take. Tarrow (1994) identifies four influential dimensions of political systems: the relative openness or closure of the system; the stability of political alignments; the availability of elite allies; and divisions among elites. Social movement scholars have analyzed the ways in which changes in one or more of these dimensions make the political system either receptive or vulnerable to challenge. The discussion that follows presents the first three of Tarrow's dimensions, treating the fourth dimension as a subset of the second.

Openness of the Political System. It might seem reasonable to think that activists will undertake collective action when political systems are open and avoid such action when political systems are closed (see Chapter 2 if you are having trouble remembering what we mean when we talk about systems as open and closed). Peter Eisinger (1973) argues that the relationship of system openness or closure to social movement activity is not that simple, however. He proposes a curvilinear relationship: Neither full access nor its total absence encourages the greatest degree of collective action. Some resistance stimulates movement solidarity, but too much resistance makes collective action too costly for social movement participants (Freeman, 1995; Oberschall, 1992).

In a similar vein, Tarrow (1994) suggests that, in general, democratic states facilitate social movements and authoritarian states repress them. He notes, however, that because democratic states invite participation, even criticism, many challenging issues that might spark social movements are "processed" out of existence through electoral processes. In Tarrow's words, "the legitimization and institutionalization of collective action are often the most effective means of social control" (1994, p. 96). In other words, it is hard to mount a social movement if it seems that the political system is easily influenced without serious collective action. Democratic states do not treat all challenges in the same manner, however, and are capable of being quite repressive at times. Membership in the Communist Party was outlawed in the United States in the 1950s, and black nationalists were ruthlessly suppressed in the 1970s (Tarrow, 1996). On the other hand, the repression found in authoritarian states may serve to radicalize social movement leaders (della Porta, 1996). And, as was evident in Eastern Europe in the late 1980s, authoritarian states are not always effective in repressing challenges. Marx and McAdam (1994) suggest that relaxation of social control in a previously repressive political system often has the unintended consequence of fueling the fire of long-held grievances.

Three other propositions associated with the PO perspective about the relationship between social movement activities and the openness of political systems deserve note:

1. A given political system is not equally open or closed to all challengers at a given time; some social movements are favored over others. Piven and Cloward (1977) remind us that universal franchise does not mean equal access to the political system; wealth buys access not easily available to poor people's movements. Indeed, the success of the breast cancer advocates may be, in no small way, related to the middle-class status of the movement's organizers and to their ability to frame breast cancer as an issue that transcends social class.

2. The success of one social movement can open the political system to the challenge of other social movements. For example, successful legislative action by the black civil rights movement during the 1960s opened the way for other civil rights movements, particularly the women's movement, which benefited from the targeting of women in Title VII of the Civil Rights Act of 1964 (McAdam, 1996a). However, the successful movement may open the way for opponent movements, called **countermovements**, as well as for allied movements. The women's movement has been countered by a variety of antifeminist movements, including the Right to Life movement and a set of interrelated movements that focus on traditional gender roles for family life.

3. Since the 18th century, social movements have diffused rapidly across national boundaries, and the fate of national social movements has been influenced by international events. The black civil rights movement in the United States was influenced by international attention to the gap between our national image as champion of human rights and the racial discrimination that permeated our social institutions (McAdam, 1996a). The recent revolution in communication technology, coupled with the globalization of market systems, is expected to quicken the diffusion of collective action, as evidenced by events in Eastern Europe during the late 1980s (Tarrow, 1994).

Stability of Political Alignments. PO theorists agree that the routine transfer of political power from one group of incumbents to another, as when a different political party takes control of the U.S. presidency or Congress, opens opportunities for the development or reactivation of social movements (McAdam et al., 1996; Marx & McAdam, 1994; Tarrow, 1994, 1996). At such times, some social movements lose favor, and others gain opportunity. McAdam et al. (1996) note that social movements on the Left mobilized during the Kennedy and Johnson administrations, and social movements on the Right mobilized during the Reagan and Bush administrations and again when the Republicans took over Congress in 1994. Piven and Cloward (1977) found changes in political party strength to be related to increased social movement activity among poor people in both the 1930s and 1960s.

Disruption of political alliances also occurs at times other than political elections, for both partisan and nonpartisan reasons, and such disruptions produce conflicts and divisions among elites. When elites are divided, social movements can sometimes encourage some factions to take the role of "tribunes of the people" (Tarrow, 1994, p. 88) and support the goals of the movement. The breast cancer advocates were able to capitalize on the desire of politicians across the political spectrum to find a noncontroversial women's issue. Disruptions in political alliances also occur when different branches of the government—such as the executive branch and the legislative branch—are at odds with each other. Such conflict has been the case throughout the history of the breast cancer activist movement. New coalitions may be formed, and the uncertainty that ensues may encourage groups to make new or renewed attempts to challenge institutional arrangements, hoping to find new elite allies. The breast cancer advocates found such an opening in their collaborative efforts with the Department of Defense.

Oberschall (1996) points to the events in Eastern Europe in the late 1980s as representing another type of political opportunity—one that has received little attention by social movement scholars—the opportunity that opens when a political regime loses legitimacy with those it governs. Oberschall (1996) suggests that a political regime that has lost both legitimacy and effectiveness "is skating on very thin ice" (p. 98). As reported in Chapter 8, many political analysts suggest that the current era is marked by a reduced capacity of nations to govern and increasing cynicism on the part of citizens about the capacity of governments to govern. Some social movement scholars suggest that this sort of instability is contributing to the global spread of social movement activity (Oberschall, 1996).

Availability of Elite Allies. Participants in social movements often lack both power and resources for influencing the political process. But they may be assisted by influential allies who play a variety of supportive roles. Tarrow (1996) notes that influential allies may be "friends in court, guarantors against brutal repression, or acceptable negotiators" (p. 55). They may provide financial support, or they may provide name and face recognition that attracts media attention to the goals and activities of the movement. Research indicates a strong correlation between the presence of elite allies and social movement success (Gamson, 1990; Tarrow, 1994). The success of the breast cancer activists was aided by their ability to find allies across the political spectrum.

Social movement participants often have ambivalent relationships with their elite allies, however. On the one hand, powerful allies provide needed resources; on the other hand, they may limit or distort the goals of the movement (Kriesi, 1996). The relationship between participants in the disability movement and actor Christopher Reeve is a good example of the tension that can develop between movement participants and their elite allies. When Christopher Reeve was paralyzed following an equestrian accident, the media quickly assigned him the role of star speaker for the disability community. Many in the disability movement were offended. Reeve's personal agenda is a cure for spinal cord injuries, but the movement's emphasis is on personal assistance for persons with disabilities—on living with disability, not cure (S. Gilson, personal communication, July 25, 1996). People in the disability movement were concerned that the emphasis on cure would undermine their efforts to win public acceptance of their disabilities and to make their environments more accessible.

Mobilizing Structures Perspective

Mary Jo Kahn attributes much of the success of the breast cancer activists to their ability to build a strong movement out of existing networks of mastectomy support groups and women activists. They also benefited from the mentoring provided by AIDS activists. Ms. Kahn suggests, in a more general way, that the involvement of women in paid work, where they come in contact with other women, has facilitated the development of social movements involving women's issues. These views are consistent with the **mobilizing structures (MS) perspective**, which starts from this basic premise: Given their disadvantaged position in the political system, social movement leaders must seek out and mobilize the resources they need—people, money, information, ideas, and skills—in order to reduce the costs and increase the benefits of movement activities (Oberschall, 1992; Taylor, 1995). In the MS perspective, social movements have no influence without effective organization of various kinds of **mobilizing structures**—"those collective vehicles, informal as well as formal, through which people mobilize and engage in collective action" (McAdam et al., 1996, p. 3). Mobilizing structures are the collective building blocks of social movements. The main ideas of the MS perspective are summarized in Exhibit 12.2.

Informal and Formal Structures.   MS scholars agree that social movements typically do not start from scratch, but build on existing structures. They disagree, however, on the relative importance of informal versus formal structures. The MS perspective has two theoretical building blocks, one that emphasizes formal mobilizing structures and one that emphasizes informal mobilizing structures:

1. **Resource mobilization theory** focuses on the organization and coordination of movement activities through formal organizations called **social movement organizations (SMOs)** (Zald & McCarthy, 1987). Theorists in this tradition are particularly interested in **professional social movements,** staffed by leaders and activists who make a professional career out of reform causes (Oberschall, 1992, p. 30). The antipoverty movement of the 1960s and various public interest research groups (PIRGs) are examples of professional social movements. Some social movement scholars suggest that professional social movements are more common in the United States than in Europe (Oberschall, 1992; Tarrow, 1994).

EXHIBIT 12.2
Key Ideas of
the Mobilizing
Structures
Perspective

- Social movements must be able to mobilize various kinds of formal and informal networks.
- Resource mobilization theory focuses on the coordination of movement activities through social movement organizations (SMOs).
- The political process model focuses on mobilization of the movement through informal networks.
- Mobilizing structures have a strong influence on the life course of social movements.
- To survive, social movements must be able to attract new members and sustain the involvement of current members.

2. The **political process model** focuses on everyday ties among people, in grassroots settings, as the basic structures for the communication and social solidarity necessary for mobilization (McAdam et al., 1996; McCarthy, 1996; Tarrow, 1994). The focus is thus on naturally existing networks based in family, work, and neighborhood relationships. Tarrow (1994) suggests that social networks "endure longer and are more likely to produce an ongoing social movement when they are rooted in preexisting social ties, habits of collaboration and the zest for planning and carrying out collective action that comes from a common life" (p. 150). Tarrow (1994) adds that these natural networks are hard to repress and control because, in a democratic society, people have the right to congregate in their private homes and other informal settings.

Although resource mobilization theory and the political process model disagree about the relative merits of formal and informal structures, they do agree that the costs of mobilizing social movements are minimized by drawing on preexisting structures and networks (McCarthy, 1987; Ray, 1993). The breast cancer activists have now developed formal organizations, but their early efforts depended on their informal networks, feminist groups, and mastectomy support groups. This aspect of their experience seems to be quite common. Marx and McAdam (1994) suggest that during their early stages social movements are dependent on the "cohesive, ongoing, face-to-face groups" (McCarthy, 1987, p. 55) found in existing organizations and networks. And the literature identifies numerous examples: Black churches and black colleges played an important role in the American civil rights movement (McAdam, 1982; Morris, 1981, 1984). The student movements of the 1960s benefited from friendship networks among activists of the civil rights movement (Oberschall, 1992). The radical wing of the women's movement emerged out of informal friendship networks of women who had been active in the civil rights and New Left movements of the 1960s (Evans, 1980). Antiabortion and other New Right movements have benefited from strong ties and commitments found in Catholic and conservative Protestant churches (Oberschall, 1992; Ray, 1993).

In fact, several social movement scholars have noted the particularly "religious roots and character of many American movements" (McAdam et al., 1996, p. 18). They suggest that this link is not surprising given the higher rates of church affiliation and attendance in the United States than in other comparable Western democracies.

Developmental perspective

The Life Course of Social Movements.   The MS perspective asserts that mobilizing structures have a strong influence on the life course of a social movement, making time an important dimension. Marx and McAdam (1994, p. 72) capture the general agreement among MS theorists that "the vast majority of social movements die aborning [but] the successful ones can last for years or even decades." The typical pattern is as follows: At the outset, the movement is ill defined, and the various mobilizing structures are weakly organized (Kriesi, 1996; Marx & McAdam, 1994). Once the movement has been in existence for a while, it is likely to become "larger, less spontaneous, better organized" (Marx & McAdam, 1994, p. 95). The mature social movement is typically led by the SMOs that were developed in the course of mobilization. The Virginia Breast Cancer Foundation is currently in this situation, but, as you may recall, it was not always so.

Social movement scholars disagree about whether the increasing role of formal organizations as time passes is a good thing or a bad thing. Many suggest that movements cannot survive without becoming more organized and taking on many of the characteristics of the institutions they challenge (Freeman, 1995; Hall, 1995; Marx & McAdam, 1994; Oberschall, 1992; Tarrow, 1994). On the other hand, Piven and Cloward (1977) suggest that this tendency of social movements to become more organized and less spontaneous dooms social movements, particularly poor people's movements, to failure. In their view, organizations abandon the oppositional tactics that brought early success and fail to seize the window of opportunity created by the unrest those tactics generated. Tarrow (1994) suggests that one of the most important problems facing social movement organizers is to create mobilizing structures that are sufficiently strong to stand up to opponents, but also flexible enough to respond to changing circumstances.

Jo Freeman (1995, p. 403) asserts that there is "no such thing as a permanent social movement." She suggests that every movement, at some point, changes into something else, often into many other things, through three basic processes:

1. *Institutionalization.* Some movements become part of existing institutions or develop durable SMOs with stable income, staff, and routine operations. The profession of social work is an example of a social movement that became institutionalized.

2. *Encapsulation.* Some social movements, or at least some parts of them, lose their sense of mission and begin to direct their activities inward, to serve members, rather than outward, to promote or resist change. That has been the trajectory of some labor unions (Clemens, 1996). Frederic Reamer (1992) suggests that social work's history includes periods of encapsulation, when social workers became more concerned about "professional advancement and autonomy, status, and financial security" (p. 12) than about social justice and the public welfare. Reamer suggests, in fact, that encapsulation is the social work profession's current situation.

3. *Factionalization.* Still other movements fall apart, often disintegrating into contentious, competing factions (Voss, 1996). This was the trajectory of the U.S. student protest movements after the violence at the 1968 Democratic Party convention in Chicago (Tarrow, 1994).

It is too early to tell what the long-term trajectory of the breast cancer activist movement will be.

Problems of Movement Membership. To remain vital, social movements must be able to attract new recruits and sustain the morale and commitment of current participants. The recent successes of the breast cancer activist movement are contributing to a strong membership at the present time, but its continued success will depend on the leaders' ability to continue to attract new recruits and maintain the involvement of current members.

Social movement leaders must manage a variety of membership issues that can threaten or facilitate their success. Three membership issues are particularly important to the success of social movements:

1. **Free riders** are people who stand to benefit from a social movement but make no contributions to its efforts. Social movements must find ways to overcome the free rider tendency and convince people to join and contribute (Oberschall, 1992).

2. **Infiltrators** are people from external groups who make a conscious effort to get inside a social movement and destroy it from within, often by instigating factionalism. Social movement scholars cite evidence of past government infiltration of a variety of social movements, including the black civil rights movement and the 1960s student movement (Marx & McAdam, 1994; Oberschall, 1992).

3. The **radical flank** of a social movement consists of "extremists" within the movement. Research suggests that radical flanks can contribute to the success of a movement, because elites are often more willing to fund, and otherwise support, moderate groups within the movement when confronted by a radical alternative (McAdam et al., 1996). Mary Jo Kahn believes that the early successes of the breast cancer movement were due, in part, to the fact that the cry for breast cancer research looked moderate to political leaders in comparison to the more contentious feminist issues of abortion and sexual harassment. Alternatively, the radical flank may push moderates to become more radical, with the result that outcomes may be more radical than originally expected.

Cultural Framing Perspective

Social constructionist perspective

The **cultural framing (CF) perspective** asserts that a social movement can succeed only when participants develop shared understandings and definitions of the situation. These shared meanings develop through a transactional process of consciousness raising, which social movement scholars call cultural framing. **Cultural framing** involves "conscious strategic efforts by groups of people to fashion shared understandings of the world and of themselves that legitimate and motivate collective action" (McAdam et al., 1996, p. 6). Exhibit 12.3 summarizes the central ideas of the CF perspective.

Social movement leaders and participants engage in a delicate balancing act as they construct cultural frames. To legitimate collective action, cultural frames must impel people to feel aggrieved or outraged about some situation that they consider unjust; but to motivate people to engage in collective action, cultural frames must be optimistic about the possibilities for improving the situation. Consider the slogans developed by the breast cancer activists. Some dramatized the severity of their situation and the fairness of their cause: "We will not die silently

EXHIBIT 12.3
Key Ideas of the
Cultural Framing
Perspective

- Social movements must be able to develop shared understandings that legitimate and motivate collective action.
- Social movements actively participate in the naming of grievances and injustices.
- Social movement leaders must construct a perception that change is possible.
- Social movements must articulate goals.
- Social movements must identify and create tactical choices for accomplishing goals.
- Contests over cultural frames are common in social movements.
- Social movements must be able to create cultural frames to appeal to diverse audiences.

anymore," "Do the Write Thing." Mary Jo Kahn's daughters also prepared banners that would capture the attention, and inspire the optimism, of their youthful peers: "Hold the line at 1 in 9." Simultaneously, social movements want to draw heavily on existing cultural symbols so that the movement frame will be "culturally resonant to fire people's minds" (Tarrow, 1994, p. 33) while they add new frames to the cultural stock, thus sponsoring new ways of thinking about social conditions. Tarrow (1994) summarizes the challenge of this balancing act well: "how to put forward a set of unsettling demands for unconventional people in ways that will not make enemies out of potential allies" (p. 10). Unfortunately, research has provided movement leaders with little guidance in how to achieve such balance in their slogans and symbols.

Exhibit 12.4 presents some cultural frames provided by social movements in the United States during the past few decades. You may not be familiar with all of these cultural frames, and you might want to check with your classmates to see if, collectively, you can identify the social movement with which each of the frames is associated. How well do you think these cultural frames serve both to legitimate and to motivate collective action? How well do they draw on existing symbols while promoting new ways of thinking?

A further complication in the process of constructing frames is that frames attractive to one audience are likely to be rejected by other audiences. McAdam (1996b) summarizes the challenge of diverse audiences for social movement frames this way: social movement groups "must master the art of simultaneously playing to a variety of publics, threatening opponents, and pressuring the state, all the while appearing nonthreatening and sympathetic to the media and other publics" (p. 344). Activists desire media attention because that is the most effective way to reach wide audiences, but they also know that they cannot control the way the movement will be framed by the media. The media are attracted to dramatic, even violent, aspects of a movement, but these aspects are likely to be rejected by other audiences (Tarrow, 1994). Movement activists are particularly concerned about the impact of the media on their **conscience constituency**—people attracted to the movement because it appears just and worthy, not because they will benefit personally.

Social movement framing is never a matter of easy consensus building, and intense **framing contests** may arise among a variety of actors, particularly in the later stages. Representatives

EXHIBIT 12.4

Selected Cultural Frames Presented by Social Movements in the United States

Pro-life	**MAKE LOVE, NOT WAR**	**Deaf Now**	CIVIL RIGHTS	*12 Steps*	
The Color Lavender	**I May Be Disabled But I'm Not Dead Yet**		Pro Choice		
The Peace Sign	Stonewall	***We Shall Overcome***			
A woman's body is her own	Family Values	***Take Back the Night***			
Welfare Rights	Unborn Child	*Our Homes, Not Nursing Homes*	GAY RIGHTS		
Every Child a Wanted Child	Reverence for Life	Piss on Pity			
I Have a Dream	**Hell No, We Won't Go**	*Our Daughters and Our Sons*			
black power	*Do Not Speak For Me, Listen To Me*	**Disability Rights**			

of the political system and participants in countermovements influence framing through their own actions and public statements, and internal conflicts become more pronounced. Leaders and followers often have different frames for the movement (Marx & McAdam, 1994), and there are often splits between moderate and radical participants. It is not at all unusual for movements to put forth multiple frames, with different groups sponsoring different frames. For example, Carden (1978) found a lack of consensus among leaders of different feminist movement organizations, with reformists focusing on employment issues and radicals seeking a fundamental restructuring of gender roles. When a movement captures media attention, there is often an intense struggle over who speaks for the movement.

Although the CF perspective has generated little empirical research to date, CF theorists have begun to examine the role of cultural framing in social movements. They have found that it provides language, ideology, and symbols for understanding that a problem exists, for recognizing windows of opportunity, for establishing goals, and for identifying pathways for action.

Frames for Understanding That a Problem Exists.   Social movements are actively involved in the "naming" of grievances and injustices. They do so in part by drawing on existing cultural symbols, but they also underscore, accentuate, and enlarge current understanding of the seriousness of a situation. In essence, they call attention to contradictions between cultural ideals and cultural realities. For example, the American civil rights movement called attention to the contradiction between democracy and racial discrimination. When the breast cancer activists organized Mother's Day rallies, they called attention to the discrepancy between the high value placed on women's roles as mothers and the failure to protect the health and lives of women.

In the United States, movement frames are often articulated in terms of "rights"—civil rights, disability rights, gay rights, animal rights, children's rights. In Europe, where there is less emphasis on individual liberty, "rights" frames are far less common in social movements (Tarrow, 1994).

In the past decade, fundamentalist religious movements have sprung up in many countries, including the United States. These movements have used "morality" frames, focusing on good and evil rather than justice versus injustice. Marx and McAdam (1994) report that, compared to Europe, the United States has historically produced a "disproportionate number of religiously inspired political movements" (p. 38). Such movements as prohibition, abolition, anticommunism, and antiabortionism have all had religious roots. A contemporary religious frame that crosses national boundaries as well as liberal and conservative ideologies is "reverence for life," expressed in such disparate movements as the environmental, health, antiabortion, animal rights, and anti–capital punishment movements (Marx & McAdam, 1994).

Frames for Recognizing a Window of Opportunity.   Gamson and Meyer (1996) suggest that the perception of opportunity to change a troublesome situation is culturally framed to some extent. On occasion, it is easy to develop a shared frame that opportunity exists or does not exist, but most situations are more ambiguous. Social movement leaders must successfully construct a perception that change is possible, because an opportunity does not exist unless it is recognized. They typically attempt to overcome concerns about the dangers and futility of activism by focusing on the risks of inaction, communicating a sense of urgency, and emphasizing the openness of the moment. They are intent on "keeping hope alive" (Gamson & Meyer, 1996, p. 286).

Calibrating this type of frame is a difficult task. On the one hand, overstating an opportunity can be hazardous (Piven & Cloward, 1977). Voss (1996) suggests that without "fortifying myths," which allow participants to see defeats as mere setbacks, unrealistically high expectations can degenerate into pessimism about possibilities for change. On the other hand, Gamson and Meyer (1996) suggest that "movement activists systematically overestimate the degree of political opportunity and if they did not, they would not be doing their job wisely" (p. 285). Unrealistic perceptions about what is possible can actually make change more possible. A $300 million increase for breast cancer research seemed unrealistic to many women involved in the advocacy movement, but this goal was achieved.

Frames for Establishing Goals.   Once it has been established that both problem and opportunity exist, the question of social movement goals arises. Is change to be narrow or sweeping, reformist or revolutionary? Will the emphasis be on providing opportunities for individual self-expression or on changing the social order? Marx and McAdam (1994) suggest that U.S. social movements have generally set goals for "inclusion and reform rather than radical change" (p. 11). Parents, Families, and Friends of Lesbians and Gays (PFLAG, 1995) is a fairly typical example of a contemporary U.S. social movement that has struck a balance between goals of individual change and changes in the social order. Exhibit 12.5 demonstrates how PFLAG strikes this balance in its statement of goals.

Typically, goals are poorly articulated in the early stages of a movement but are clarified through ongoing negotiations about the desired changes. The breast cancer activists began with the goal of increasing funding for research but later added the goal of giving women with breast cancer a voice in research funding decisions. More recently, they have become involved in activism to ensure that genetic testing for breast cancer will not be used to deny health insurance (Mary Jo Kahn, personal communication, August 19, 1997). Manuals for social activism suggest that modest and winnable objectives in the early stages of a movement help to reinforce the possibility of change (Gamson & Meyer, 1996).

Frames for Identifying Pathways for Action.   Some of the most important framing efforts of a social movement involve tactical choices for accomplishing goals. Social movement scholars generally agree that each society has a supply of forms of collective action that are familiar to social movement participants as well as the elites whom they challenge (Oberschall, 1992;

EXHIBIT 12.5

Goals Statement of Parents, Families, and Friends of Lesbians and Gays (PFLAG)

> To cope with an adverse society, **PFLAG PROVIDES SUPPORT.** To enlighten a sometimes frightened and ill-informed public, **PFLAG EDUCATES AND INFORMS.** To combat discrimination and secure equal rights, **PFLAG ADVOCATES JUSTICE.**

Source: PFLAG, 1995.

EXHIBIT 12.6

Forms of Collective
Action

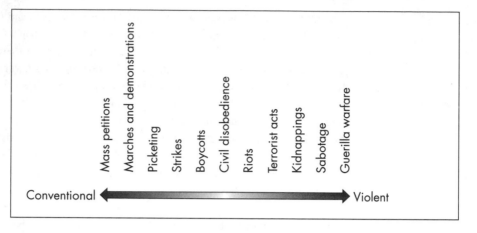

Tarrow, 1994). New forms are introduced from time to time, and spread quickly if they are successful. In the United States, marches on Washington have come to be standard fare in collective action, and activist groups exchange information on the logistics of organizing a march on Washington. On the other hand, the sit-down strike is no longer as common as it once was (Zald, 1996). The breast cancer activists have made extensive use of rallies and letter writing campaigns, and also have begun to make use of a relatively new tactic, organized road races. Tarrow (1994) suggests that contemporary social movements draw power from the large selection of forms of collective action currently in the cultural stock, and that many movements, notably the women's movement, have wisely used multiple forms of action.

Just as social movement goals fall on a continuum from reform to revolution, forms of collective action can be arranged along a continuum from conventional to violent, as shown in Exhibit 12.6. Nonviolent forms of collective action are the core of contemporary U.S. movements. Nonviolent disruption of routine activities is today considered the most powerful form of activism in the United States and in other Western democracies with relatively stable governments (McAdam, 1996b; Tarrow, 1994). The power of nonviolent disruption is that it creates uncertainty and some fear of violence, yet provides authorities in democratic societies with no valid argument for repression. Violent collective action, on the other hand, destroys public support for the movement. McAdam (1996b) suggests that Martin Luther King was ingenious in recognizing that the best path for the American civil rights movement was "successfully courting violence while restraining violence in his followers" (p. 349). Consequently, it was the police who lost public favor for their brutality, not the demonstrators.

Social Movement Outcomes

Because social movements are processes, not structures, they are not easy to research. Case study has been the predominant method of study, with recent emphasis on comparative case studies. Unfortunately, one researcher may declare a particular movement a failure while another researcher will see it as having succeeded. Different analyses may be based, in part, on different guidelines for success, but the researchers may also be evaluating the movement from different time perspectives. Tarrow (1994) suggests that "we need to look well past the end of a [movement] cycle to observe its effects" (p. 184). This is a reminder, again, of the importance of the time dimension in changing person/environment configurations.

Oberschall (1992) has observed that, like other human endeavors, social movements are neither completely successful nor completely unsuccessful. In general, however, the most successful social movements have outcomes that are far less radical than their proponents would like, and far more radical than their opponents would like. Social movements rarely produce the major redistribution of power that activists desire and movement goals specify. The women's movement has not achieved its goal of equality and nondiscrimination for women. The conservative Christian movement has not reached its goal of restoring traditional family and gender roles. And yet, one U.S. social movement scholar declares, "collective behavior and social movements have molded our contemporary institutions" (Oberschall, 1992, p. 2). Thus, the success of social movements can be measured not by their survival, but by the institutional changes they influence.

Sidney Tarrow, in his 1994 book *Power in Movement*, hypothesizes that the power of social movements is cumulative and can be appreciated only from a long-term historical perspective. Moreover, research on social movements documents a range of direct and indirect effects. Contemporary social movements have accomplished an impressive list of specific federal legislation, including the Civil Rights Act of 1964; Title IX, the federal law that prohibits gender-based discrimination in athletics or educational programs at institutions that receive federal funds; and the Americans with Disabilities Act of 1990. Considered by some scholars to be the most successful social movement in the United States since World War II, the black civil rights movement served as a model for organizing, opened opportunities, and provided hope for other aggrieved groups. Because of social movements, the political system has become more open and responsive to previously ignored groups, and voicing grievances has become an expected part of life in a democratic country. Many SMOs have become a stable part of the social environment, and activist-oriented networks outlast the movements that spawned them. Research indicates that although individual activists are often temporarily disillusioned at the end of a social movement, in the long term they are empowered and politicized by their participation (Tarrow, 1994).

Although the success of a given social movement depends on its unique configuration of political opportunities, mobilizing efforts, and cultural frames, social movement researchers agree on the factors that influence success or failure. Some of these factors are outside the control of the movement, but some of them can be successfully manipulated by movement leaders. The most obvious factor is the ability to attract a large number of participants. The most successful movements tap into existing networks and associations that have a shared culture, a strong sense of solidarity, and a common identity. These groups are the most likely to be willing to make sacrifices and remain committed over time, and to have the shared symbols to frame the movement (Oberschall, 1992; Tarrow, 1994). Religious movements, for example, benefit from long-lasting and widely cherished religious symbols (Oberschall, 1992). Other forces, however, can serve as serious threats to the success of a social movement. Internal conflicts and factionalism weaken the chances for success, as does a strong opponent. Initial successes may stimulate strong countermovements, or a backlash may develop in reaction to the radical flank of a movement.

The Future of Social Movements

Social movement scholars generally agree that social movements will continue to be a part of the social landscape in the foreseeable future (Oberschall, 1992; Marx & McAdam, 1994; Tarrow, 1994). In fact, some have predicted that we are entering an era of "movement societies," in which activist challenge and disruption of institutional arrangements will become a routine part of life (Marx & McAdam, 1994; Tarrow, 1994).

Acknowledging that social scientists are, in general, poor prognosticators, Marx and McAdam (1994, pp. 121–124) nevertheless venture six predictions about the future of social movements:

1. We are entering a period of heightened social movement activity.
2. Ideological conflicts will continue, exacerbated by the growing gap between rich and poor.
3. Social movements will take on an increasingly international character.
4. Race will continue to be a salient issue for protest activity in the United States.
5. In other parts of the world, ethnic nationalist movements will proliferate.
6. Social movements will continue to be based in existing groups or in established communities.

Marx and McAdam project four likely seedbeds for future social movements: churches and other religious institutions, colleges and universities, stable residential neighborhoods, and formal SMOs. They suggest that these are the mobilizing structures most likely to have the necessary resources, preexisting social ties, and shared understandings to mount effective reform movements.

Social Movements and Contemporary Social Work

Early in this chapter, I suggested that the professionalization of social work was accomplished by sacrificing the social reform fervor of its settlement house tradition. Social movement scholars have in fact found that it is difficult, if not impossible, to be both a profession and a reform movement (Freeman, 1995). The history of social work is a history of tension between the goal of professional service and the goal of social reform (Popple, 1992). This tension has been quite obvious in recent years. On the one hand, social workers and their professional organizations have devoted a lot of resources to obtaining licensure for clinical social workers and to securing private and public reimbursement for clinical social work services. On the other hand, recent revisions of documents by social work's leading professional organizations, the NASW Code of Ethics and CSWE's Curriculum Policy Statement, have added forceful language about the social justice goals of the profession.

Some social work scholars see a dual focus on professional service and social reform as achievable and even natural (Colcord & Mann, 1930; Lee, 1937; Schwartz, 1963); others see the two goals as incompatible (Lubove, 1966; Piven & Cloward, 1977). Philip Popple (1992) suggests that each generation of social workers must struggle anew with the tension between a conservative mandate from society for efficient service that manages problems of dependency and a liberal or radical mandate from the profession to promote social justice. He also suggests that social workers experience this tension differently in different political eras. In conservative political times, there is great disparity between the societal mandate for social workers to act as social control agents and the profession's social reform tradition. In such times, the social reform goal is not prominent. In liberal political times, however, there is less tension between the two goals, and social work's social reform goal is more visible. Popple's analysis is consistent with a tenet of the PO perspective on social movements: shifts in political alignments open or close opportunities for social movement activity.

Popple (1992) proposes that even though the social work profession's emphasis on social reform at any give time is influenced by political opportunities, the valuing of social justice is a permanent feature of social work in the United States. If this analysis is accurate, and I think it is, all social workers should be familiar with developments in social movement theory and research. At least four contemporary trends are increasing the need for social workers to understand how social movements develop and succeed:

1. Rapid changes in social institutions in the current industrial cycle are creating new social problems and patterns of social inequality that call for new solutions to social welfare problems.

2. As social movement scholars suggest (Marx & McAdam, 1994; Tarrow, 1994), we seem to be entering an era of heightened social movement activity, an era in which groups with long-standing grievances are framing those grievances—such as disabilities rights and gay rights—and organizing to seek reform in social institutions. We should be prepared for the possibility that their grievances will include shortcomings of the social welfare institution and the social work profession. Social workers were surprised to be considered part of the problem rather than part of the solution in the clients' rights movement of the 1960s, when clients of social service organizations identified ways in which their rights were being violated in the delivery of services (Hutchison, Dattalo, & Rodwell, 1994).

3. There is a trend toward the internationalization of social work, with exchanges among social workers across national boundaries occurring on several levels. To be good partners in this exchange, social workers in the United States will need to know about the political opportunities for social movements in other countries, and about the relative emphasis on professional service and social reform in the countries with which they have contact.

4. Social workers are increasingly involved in working with mutual aid groups that have the potential for activism. You will read more about this issue in Chapter 13.

Social workers practicing in SMOs known as social movement agencies or alternative social agencies are, of course, fundamentally concerned with developments in social movement scholarship. Cheryl Hyde (1992, p. 122) defines **social movement agencies** as "hybrid organizations in which the explicit pursuit of social change is accomplished through the delivery of services." These agencies attempt to change the world by providing revolutionary services that challenge or alter social institutions. Feminist health centers and emergency shelters for battered women are good examples of social movement agencies.

EXHIBIT 12.7
Attributes of
Alternative Social
Agencies

- Alternative social agencies are committed to social change.
- Alternative social agencies are committed to participatory democracy and the use of nonhierarchical governance structures.
- Alternative social agencies are organized to meet the needs of special populations that are not served by traditional social agencies.
- Alternative social agencies provide new or innovative types of services.
- The personnel at alternative social agencies are usually members of the target population or are ideologically committed to the target population. Volunteers provide many of the services.
- Alternative social agencies value smallness of size.
- Because they are not eligible for traditional sources of funding, alternative social agencies have a constant struggle for finances.

Source: Perlmutter, 1988.

Social movement agencies are also called **alternative social agencies**. Felice Perlmutter (1988) reports that a wide variety of alternative social agencies were developed in the 1970s and 1980s to meet needs that were not being addressed by traditional agencies in the social welfare institution. Perlmutter argues that social work is "an appropriate professional base" (p. 109) for leadership in alternative social agencies, but it is important for social workers to understand the special characteristics of alternative social agencies. The seven attributes that she identifies are listed in Figure 12.7. As you can see, social movement agencies are based on the critical perspective on formal organizations (Chapter 10), placing a high value on service to oppressed groups and on nonhierarchical forms of organization.

IMPLICATIONS FOR SOCIAL WORK PRACTICE

This discussion of social movements recommends several principles for social work activism:

- Become skillful in assessing political opportunities for social reform efforts.
- Become skillful in recognizing and mobilizing formal and informal networks for social reform activities.
- In conservative political eras, be vigilant about the temptation to encapsulate and lose sight of social work's social reform mission.
- Become skillful at attracting new recruits to social reform activities and sustaining the morale and commitment of current participants.

- Become skillful in managing internal movement conflicts and avoiding factionalism.
- Become skillful in developing cultural frames that legitimate and motivate collective action.
- Assist social workers in direct practice to assess the benefits and costs to clients of involvement in social movement activities.
- Assist social workers in the traditional social welfare institution to recognize the important role that reform social movements play in identifying new or previously unrecognized social injustices and social service needs.

MAIN POINTS

1. Social movements are formed when people feel that one or more social institutions are unjust and need to be changed.

2. Social movements are "large-scale, collective efforts to bring about or resist changes that bear on the lives of many" (Oberschall, 1992, p. 2).

3. The profession of social work has its origins in the confluence of two social movements: the charity organization society movement and the settlement house movement.

4. Three theoretical perspectives on social movements have emerged in the past two decades: the political opportunities perspective, the mobilizing structures perspective, and the cultural framing perspective. No one of these perspectives is sufficient for understanding social movements, but taken together, they provide a multidimensional understanding of social movements.

5. The political opportunities perspective suggests that social movements are influenced by three dimensions of political systems: the relative openness or closure of the system, the stability of political alignments (reflected, in part, in divisions among elites), and the availability of elite allies.

6. The mobilizing structures perspective suggests that social movements will have no influence unless they are able to effectively organize various kinds of formal and informal networks.

7. The cultural framing perspective focuses on the "efforts by groups of people to fashion shared understanding . . . that legitimate and motivate collective action" (McAdam et al., 1996, p. 6).

8. Social movements are neither completely successful nor completely unsuccessful.

9. Social movement scholars believe that we are entering a period of heightened social movement activity.

10. Four likely seedbeds for future social movements have been identified: churches and other religious institutions, colleges and universities, stable residential neighborhoods, and formal SMOs.

11. Contemporary social work, like historical social work, must manage a tension between professional services and social reform.

12. Social movement agencies, also known as alternative social agencies, attempt to change the world through revolutionary services.

KEY TERMS

alternative social agencies
charity organization society (COS)
   movement
conscience constituency
countermovement
cultural framing
cultural framing (CF) perspective
defensive social movement
elites
framing contests
free riders
infiltrators
mobilizing structures

mobilizing structures (MS) perspective
offensive social movement
political opportunities (PO) perspective
political process model
professional social movements
radical flank
resource mobilization theory
settlement house movement
social movement
social movement agencies
social movement organizations (SMOs)
social reform
strain theory

WORLD WIDE WEB RESOURCES

Empowerment Practice and Social Change
http://weber.u.washington.edu/~jamesher/herrick.htm
Site maintained and written by James Herrick, D.S.W., University of Washington. Contains a discussion of empowerment theory and its relationship to social change with a primary focus on individual enlightenment and emancipation.

Collective Behavior and Social Movements

http://www.ssc.wise.edu/~myers/cbsm/active.htm

Site maintained by David Myers, Assistant Professor of Sociology at Notre Dame University. Contains links to activism sites on the web, from African-American activist pages to the National Organization for Women.

Narratives of Possibility: Social Movements, Collective Stories, and the Dilemmas of Practice

http://webe1.u.washington.edu/~jamesher/kling.htm

Site maintained by James Herrick, D.S.W., University of Washington. Article on theories of social movements written by Joseph Kling, St. Lawrence University.

CHAPTER 13

Small Groups

Elizabeth P. Cramer, Virginia Commonwealth University

CASE STUDY ■ *Terry's Support Group*

Small Groups in Social Work
Therapy Groups
Mutual Aid Groups
Psychoeducational Groups
Self-Help Groups
Task Groups

Dimensions of Group Structure

Group Composition
Inclusion versus Exclusion
Heterogeneity versus Homogeneity
Cohesiveness

Basic Group Processes
Theories of Group Processes
Group Development
Group Dynamics

The Effects of Physical Environment on Group Processes
Material Aspects of the Physical Environment
Territoriality
Interperson Distance
Density and Crowding
Spatial Arrangements

■ **IMPLICATIONS FOR SOCIAL WORK PRACTICE**

■ **MAIN POINTS**

■ **KEY TERMS**

■ **WORLD WIDE WEB RESOURCES**

TERRY'S SUPPORT GROUP

As she drove to a meeting of her Wednesday night support group, Terry popped a Melissa Etheridge CD into the player. A year ago, she would have barely recognized the singer's name. Now, she listens to her tapes incessantly. But much more has changed in Terry's life these past several months. One year ago, she was married—to a man. Terry and Brad had an amiable two-year marriage, but Terry had felt a sense of loneliness and discomfort throughout their marriage. She loved Brad, but could not commit to him deep in her heart. She also felt an unhappiness beyond her marriage to Brad. Terry realized she had to discover what was contributing to her unhappiness. After some serious soul-searching, she joined a support group composed of women much like herself.

In sixth grade, Terry was inseparable from her best friend, Barb. Barb and Terry shared many of the preteen developmental stages together: starting menstruation, kissing boys for the first time, being picked on as the youngest children in the middle school, and wearing shirts that show your belly button. Barb loved Terry and Terry loved Barb in that very special way that best friends do.

One night when Terry was sleeping over at Barb's house, Barb suggested that they play the dating game. Terry had played the game before at a boy-girl party. The lights go out, and the boys and the girls pair up to plan a make-believe date. At Barb's house, when Terry protested because there were no boys to play the game with them, Barb suggested that they could switch off playing boys and girls. So Terry and Barb enacted the date themselves, including a long good-night kiss. That was the first and last time Barb and Terry played the dating game. They did not discuss this incident ever again.

Terry went through her preteen and adolescent years dating boys and imagining the kind of guy she might marry. In college, Terry had another sexual experience with a female. She had been at a party with some friends where heavy drinking occurred. The group of friends with whom she went to the party decided to spend the night at the home of the hostess instead of trying to drive home drunk. Bed space was sparse; therefore, beds needed to be shared. Terry and Patricia shared a twin-size bed in a private room. The two women crawled into bed and giggled about the fact that the two of them were sharing this tiny space. The giggling turned into tickling, and the tickling turned into kissing and touching. The next morning, Terry blamed this sexual experience on the alcohol.

After college, Terry worked as a loan officer in a bank. A few years into her job, at age 26, she met Brad. After several relationships with men, she was ready to discontinue the dating scene. Brad and Terry developed a close relationship quickly and were engaged within nine months of meeting each other.

CASE STUDY

Terry and Brad bought a house, combined their possessions, and began what they both thought would be the rest of their lives together. But that scenario didn't work out.

When Terry came to the women's coming-out support group for the first time, she was petrified. Beverly, a woman on Terry's softball team, promised she would meet Terry in the parking lot and they'd go together. Sure enough, Beverly was in the parking lot with a big smile and hug: "Hey, girl. You'll be all right." They walked to the front of the building, past the sign that read "Gay and Lesbian Community Center" (Terry was sure the sign must have been at least as big as a Ping-Pong table). Beverly rang the doorbell and gave Terry a reassuring look. An African American woman who looked to be in her 50s answered the door: "Hi, Beverly. Hello, Terry . . . I'm Doris. I'm so glad you could make it here tonight. Come on in."

What was so new that evening is now so familiar. Terry looks forward to seeing the faces of those faithful members who return each week; she sympathizes with the nervousness and shyness of the new members. "Temperature reading"—a review of group members' excitements, concerns, and hopes and wishes—begins each group session. Sometimes, temperature reading is short and superficial; other times, it goes on for nearly the whole meeting, with much disclosure, intensity, and sometimes crying. The facilitators, both lesbians, plan activities for each session, but are flexible enough to allow the members to control the flow of the session. They share a good deal about themselves and their own coming-out processes. Each of the group members' stories is unique. The group includes bisexual women and women questioning their sexual orientation, as Terry did when first attending the group.

One of the first people in the group to befriend Terry was Kathy, another woman who had been heterosexually married. Kathy approached Terry during social time, an informal gathering after the meeting to schmooze and have refreshments. Kathy shared that she too had questioned her sexual orientation during the time she was married. Kathy and Terry became friends outside of the group; in fact, much of Terry's current friendship network has grown out of the group. She often sees group members at gay and lesbian functions that she has begun to attend, such as the gay/lesbian theater company and the monthly women's potlucks. How different her circle of friends has become compared to when she and Brad were together and they socialized primarily with other white, childless, heterosexual couples.

Terry still feels like a "baby dyke" around her friends, most of whom have been out for much longer than she. She still has many questions about lesbian and gay culture, but she feels comfortable to ask them in the group. She has also found that she can help other women who are just beginning to come out by sharing her experiences. Sometimes she is embarrassed by the discussion in the group, however. For example, the facilitators keep an envelope marked "sex questions," where group members can anonymously submit questions about lesbian sex; the facilitators periodically read them to the group to open a discussion. The frankness of such discussions makes Terry's face turn red sometimes, but she's glad she has a place to find answers about these things. Terry also didn't realize some of the differences between the predominantly white lesbian community and the black lesbian community and has now learned from her friends about some of the issues faced by African American lesbians.

Terry is consistently amazed at the diversity within the group—women of different races, educational backgrounds, socioeconomic classes, disabilities, religions, and ages. Just last week, for example, seven women attended the group: three African Americans, two women who self-identify as bisexual, one who identifies herself as disabled, one woman who is Jewish, and two women younger than 21.

Tonight, as Terry pulls into the parking lot and gets out of the car, a woman pulls into the space next to her. Terry hasn't seen her before. The woman steps out of the car and looks around nervously. Terry walks over to her: "Hi, have you been to the group before?" "No." "C'mon, I'll walk in with you."

Small Groups in Social Work

Small groups play a significant role in our lives. Terry's support group is a type with special relevance to social work practice, but most of us also become involved in friendship groups, task groups at work, self-help groups, or sports teams, to name but a few other types.

In a mobile society, where family members may live in different parts of the country and community gathering places (such as a town hall) may be few, groups serve a useful function. They offer individuals an opportunity to meet others and work together to achieve mutual goals. Exhibit 13.1 shows how group members may benefit from belonging to a group. Specht and Courtney (1994) speculate that groups provide the social support, connection, and healing that various persons (such as clergy) or institutions (such as churches) did in the past. They note that groups "may be only one manifestation of a new communalism in which persons try to find a sense of purpose or meaning by identifying with a particular group" (p. 48). In the hustle and bustle of everyday lives, the warmth and sense of "realness" of a productive and healthy group is inviting.

EXHIBIT 13.1
Benefits of Small Groups

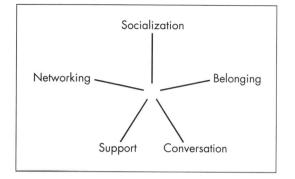

Small groups may be formally defined in a number of ways. A few scholarly definitions of small groups, along with examples from Terry's story, are displayed in Exhibit 13.2. Although these definitions differ, there is general agreement that small groups are more than a collection of individuals who may have similar traits or be in physical proximity. Persons who live on the same block may be in close proximity but have little social interaction and not perceive themselves as a group. Thus we may define a **small group** as a collection of individuals who interact with each other, perceive themselves as belonging to a group, are interdependent, join together to accomplish a goal or fulfill a need, and are influenced by a set of rules and norms (Johnson & Johnson, 1994).

A significant element of social work practice today is **group work,** which serves people's needs by bringing them together in small groups. Group work emerged in this country in the late 1800s/early 1900s as a social movement, rather than a social work method. Early group work took place within the settlement houses, YMCA/YWCA, Jewish community centers, and the Scouts. These groups focused primarily on recreation, social integration, immigration issues, character building, and social reform. We are now seeing a resurgence in recreation and social-skill-building groups, reminiscent of early group work. Social skills groups with elementary-age children (LeCroy, 1992), hoops groups with adolescent males (Pollio, 1995), and physical fitness groups for the elderly (Corey & Corey, 1992) are three examples.

By the 1930s/1940s, formal organizations were promoting group work. In 1935, the Group Work Section of the National Conference on Social Work emerged, and in 1937 the American Association for the Study of Group Work formed. The American Association of Group Workers, formed in 1946, later merged with other organizations to become the National Association of Social Workers (NASW).

During World War II, group work became popular in hospitals and other clinical settings, resulting in some tension between group workers and caseworkers. Following the war, the philosophy of group work shifted from a strengths to a more problem-focused orientation. Nevertheless, group workers continued to attempt to influence the social work profession as a whole. During the 1960s and 1970s, social work education focused on teaching group work, and some students even majored in "group work." But then group work content declined as social work education shifted its focus to individuals and families. Ironically, at the same time, joining

EXHIBIT 13.2
Definitions of Small
Groups

Author(s)	Definitions	Examples
Hare, Blumberg, Davies, & Kent (1994)	Two or more individuals who have shared values that help them maintain an overall pattern of activity, acquire or develop resources and skills to use in that activity, and conform to a set of norms that define roles in the activity, and who have enough cohesiveness and leadership to coordinate their resources and roles in order to accomplish their goals.	The coming-out group at the Gay and Lesbian Community Center shares such values as exploration and acknowledgment of sexual orientation, an overall pattern of activity (weekly meetings), resources and skills (Center space, two trained facilitators), norms or roles for the activity (structured group meetings, group guidelines), cohesiveness, and leadership (facilitators).
Johnson & Johnson (1994)	Two or more individuals who are each aware of membership in the group and of who else belongs to the group, who have a positive interdependence, and who develop and achieve mutual goals.	The friends Terry has developed through her association with the coming-out group are aware of themselves as a group of friends, are interdependent, and achieve goals of socialization and companionship through attending gay and lesbian functions together.
Shaw (1981)	Two or more individuals who through their interactions influence and are influenced by each other.	At the party Terry attended while in college, a group of friends were drinking and chose to stay overnight at the home of the hostess rather than drive after drinking.

groups became more common in the United States. The 1980s and 1990s saw the rise of mutual aid groups (Gitterman & Shulman, 1994), a popular type of social work group today.

Today, in a managed care era, groups are viewed as a financially prudent method of service delivery. Additionally, empirical studies have shown the effectiveness of groups in addressing a number of social and emotional problems, such as mental illness (Yalom, 1995). Group work content is coming back into the social work curriculum, and social work students are being exposed to group work through their field placements. Furthermore, graduating students have informed me that potential employers ask if they have had course content on group work.

A number of scholars have established classifications for groups encountered in social work. For instance, Corey and Corey (1992) describe six types of groups, and Zastrow (1997) identifies ten. This chapter will focus on five: therapy groups, mutual aid groups, psychoeducational groups, self-help groups, and task groups. As you read about them, however, remember that groups may not fall exclusively into one category; rather, they may share elements of several group types. For example, a group for parents and friends of seriously mentally ill persons may include psychoeducational material about the nature of mental illness and its impact on family members, provide mutual aid to its members through discussion of taboo areas, and offer a therapeutic component in the examination of family patterns and dynamics.

Therapy Groups

One common type of group is known as the **therapy group,** or psychotherapy group. Reid (1997, p. 6) defines group psychotherapy as "a form of psychotherapy that treats an individual simultaneously for emotional and behavioral disorders by emphasizing interaction and mutuality. Group psychotherapy is seen as using group treatment techniques to help individuals resolve emotional problems." An example of this type of group is a therapy group for adult incest survivors.

Therapy groups typically have fewer members and meet for a longer duration than self-help, psychoeducational, or mutual aid groups. Such a group may have six or fewer members, may be led by a person who considers her- or himself to be a "therapist," may meet weekly for a year or more, and may involve intrapsychic exploration of thoughts and emotions. Therapy groups do not necessarily meet for long periods, however. **Brief treatment models** are becoming increasingly popular in a managed care environment.

Mutual Aid Groups

In Terry's story, we witness many benefits of **mutual aid groups**:

- Sharing data: coming-out stories, events in the lesbian community

- Engaging in a dialectical process of discovery: theories about sexual orientation, insight into when one first felt one was not heterosexual

- Discussing taboo subjects: the "sex questions" envelope

- Realizing that one is not alone (all in the same boat): others who are not heterosexual and have had similar feelings regarding coming-out and disclosure

- Finding support: a place to be oneself in a homophobic society

- Making mutual demands: gentle challenges to internalized homophobia and unhealthy coping mechanisms, such as alcohol use or thoughts of suicide, that women may utilize as a way to live in two worlds

- Problem-solving: disclosure decisions for individuals and the larger issue of self-disclosure of a stigmatized identity

- Rehearsing new behaviors: role-playing of disclosure scenarios or confrontations with people who make homophobic jokes

- Finding strength in numbers: pride march

Gitterman and Shulman (1994, p. 14) have articulated a good summary of why mutual aid groups work:

> The group is an enterprise in mutual aid, an alliance of individuals who need each other, in varying degrees, to work on certain problems. The important fact is that this is a helping system in which the clients need each other as well as the worker. This need to use each other, to create not one but many helping relationships, is a vital ingredient of the group process and constitutes a common need over and above the specific tasks for which the group was formed.

In general, mutual aid groups are led by someone, either a professional or a trained individual, who identifies with the population that the group targets. For example, the two facilitators of the women's coming-out group self-identify as lesbians. In fact, some mutual aid groups form as an alternative to professionally led therapy groups. There is no requirement, however, that in order to be an effective leader one must have "been there." The groups may be time-limited (for example, a 10-week group for siblings of children with disabilities) or ongoing (such as a weekly support group for incarcerated males).

Mutual aid groups also have the potential for activism. A group of persons may meet initially to gain support and share concerns, but may transform some of their healing energy into social change efforts. For instance, mutual aid groups for battered women may attend a Take Back the Night march (to protest violence against women) as a group, and then courageously approach the microphone to speak about their own experiences of victimization and empowerment.

Psychoeducational Groups

Psychoeducational groups, in which social workers and other professionals share their expertise with group members, are becoming more common in the United States. Reid (1997) notes, "Helping professionals are frequently asked to provide information on topics such as divorce, schizophrenia, depression, human development, and child guidance" (p. 10). As he further explains, "The request is not for treatment per se but for knowledge and information. Citizens look to the particular agency with its staff of professionals and collective expertise for direction in the form of lectures, seminars, and study groups" (p. 10). The group could be a one-time workshop, or it could last several sessions.

A psychoeducational group is not a therapy group; the treatment of emotional and behavioral problems is not the primary function. However, psychoeducational groups can be therapeutic when members share feelings and concerns. An example would be a one-time group meeting for family and friends of persons in a drug rehabilitation center. The stated purpose may be to provide education about the recovery process to family members and friends, but during the session, group members may share feelings about their loved one's addiction and how it has affected their lives.

Self-Help Groups

In general, **self-help groups** are not professionally led, although a professional may serve in the role of consultant. An informal leader may emerge in a self-help group, or leadership may be rotated among the membership. Self-help groups are often used as a supplement to professional treatment. For example, someone who is receiving outpatient substance abuse treatment may be referred to Alcoholics Anonymous; someone in a family preservation program may be referred to Parents Anonymous. Self-help groups often have no limit on their life span and have rotating membership (people come and go from the group).

Corey and Corey (1987) summarize the benefits of self-help groups as follows:

Self-help groups serve a critical need for certain populations that is not met by professional mental-health workers. Such groups, composed of people with a common interest, provide a support system that helps reduce psychological stress and gives the members the incentive to begin changing their life. Self-help groups stress a common identity based on a common life situation to a far greater extent than do most other groups. The members share their experiences, learn from one another, offer suggestions for new members, and provide encouragement for people who sometimes see no hope for their future. (p. 13)

Self-help groups offer their members some of the social functions mentioned in the beginning of this chapter—a chance to meet others and have meaningful interactions, a place to feel as though one belongs and to give support to others. In short, self-help groups offer a social support system. As discussed in Chapter 5, social support has been shown to help people prevent and overcome disease and to maintain good psychological health (Wasserman & Danforth, 1988). Additionally, some persons believe that there is less stigma in attending a self-help group than a "treatment" or "therapy" group, the latter being more often associated with those who are seriously ill or have major problems in living.

As discussed in Chapter 12, another benefit of self-help groups is their potential for activism. In a popular support group manual used in domestic violence programs (Duluth Domestic Abuse Intervention Project, undated), one of the steps in the group process is titled "Options for Actions." These options include actions on the personal, institutional, and cultural levels. A vigil in honor of battered women killed by their assailants is an example of such an action. One study by Chesney and Chesler (1993) found that parents of children with cancer who were members of self-help groups were significantly more involved than other parents of such children in working to improve the medical system in which their children were involved.

Task Groups

Most persons have been involved in task groups, such as a committee at work or a task force in the community. In social work practice, task groups are often short-term and are formed to accomplish specific goals and objectives. An example would be a needs assessment committee formed at an agency to determine the problems and concerns of the population the agency serves. Although members of other types of groups may take on tasks (for example, researching a subject and presenting it to the group), the **task group** is created with the express purpose of achieving some specific task.

Task groups are used frequently among social workers involved in planning and administration roles, but are much less common in other social work roles. Task groups are often led by professionals who are appointed or elected to chair the task group. Leaders may be chosen because of their position in the agency or their expertise in the area.

Dimensions of Group Structure

Terry's coming-out group serves a variety of functions, with elements of mutual aid, therapy, psychoeducational, and self-help groups. But that one group cannot provide for all of Terry's needs. She also belongs to a group of friends with whom she attends social functions, a group of coworkers, and a softball team. Each group plays a unique part in Terry's life. For example, the softball team provides an outlet for competition and team-building; the work group offers a context for achievement and accomplishment. But all these groups are obviously structured quite differently. They can be categorized according to how they develop, how they determine membership, and how long they last.

The types of groups encountered in social work have typically been organized for a purpose. Such **formed groups** "are established through some outside influence, such as an agency, and are convened for a particular purpose" (Reid, 1997, p. 10). Examples of formed groups include not only therapy groups, mutual aid groups, psychoeducational groups, self-help groups, and task groups, but also such groups as college classes, PTAs, and choirs.

Natural groups, in contrast, "develop in a spontaneous manner on the basis of friendship, location, or some naturally occurring event. Without external initiative, the members simply come together" (Reid, 1997, p. 10). Peer groups, street gangs, and a group of patients who have befriended each other in a psychiatric hospital are examples of natural groups.

A **time-limited group** is one with a set time for termination; an **ongoing group** is open-ended. Both formed and natural groups may be time-limited or ongoing, short- or long-term. A formed group, for example, may last for a two-hour period (for example, a focus group) or for months or years (for example, Terry's coming-out group). A natural group may last a lifetime (a group of close friends from high school) or just through some event (tablemates at a workshop).

Finally, both natural and formed groups may be open, closed, or fluctuate between open and closed. **Open groups** permit the addition of new members throughout the group's life. In **closed groups**, the minimum and maximum size of the group is determined in advance, before the group begins or as it is being formed, and others are prohibited from joining once that limit is reached. A group can start off open and then become closed. An example would be a group of persons who have been attending a drop-in support group for women in abusive relationships who decide after a few months that they would like to close the group to do some more intensive work in group sessions. Alternatively, a closed group may open up, as when the number of members has decreased considerably and new members are needed to keep the group going.

These three dimensions of group structure interact in complex ways. The coming-out group that Terry attends, although it is a formed group, is open and ongoing. Attendance has ranged from 3 to 18 persons, and the group may continue indefinitely. An example of a closed natural group is an informal group of middle school girls who call themselves the "lunch bunch." The five girls eat lunch together every day and have let it be known among their peers that no others are welcome. An example of a time-limited closed group is a 12-week group for men and women who are going through a divorce. Interested persons must register prior to the group's beginning, and once the first session begins, no new members are permitted.

An example of an ongoing, open, formed group is a bereavement group that meets every Tuesday evening at the local hospital and allows any person who would like support to join the group on any Tuesday. Another example is a group that spontaneously meets at the basketball courts on Sunday afternoons to play ball. Whoever shows up can get into a game, with no predetermined limit to the number of people allowed to play.

Particular structures and types of groups may lend themselves to group work with certain populations. For example, mutual aid groups of a time-limited or ongoing nature are recommended when working with abused women (Duluth Domestic Abuse Intervention Project, undated); groups modeled along the stages of recovery are recommended when doing group work with persons who are addicted to alcohol or other drugs (Rugel, 1991). Funding and space limitations, lack of personnel, and the agency's philosophy of treatment (for example, brief versus long-term) may also influence the structure and type of group that an agency provides.

Group Composition

Another important element of small groups is their composition—the types of people who are members. Three issues regarding group composition are discussed in this section: inclusiveness/exclusiveness, heterogeneity/homogeneity, and cohesiveness.

Inclusion versus Exclusion

Terry's coming-out group is relatively inclusive. It is open to any woman who is lesbian, bisexual, or questioning her sexual identity. The members self-identify, and the facilitators do not have criteria for determining whether a person is lesbian, bisexual, or questioning. In contrast, the heterosexual couples with whom Terry formerly associated make up a relatively exclusive group. Very few new couples have joined the group over the years, and in fact Terry herself is excluded now that she is no longer part of a heterosexual couple.

Natural groups often have implicit or explicit rules about who gets to belong and who doesn't. Take the previous example of the "lunch bunch": the girls determined who would belong. Formed groups have rules of membership too. A sorority or fraternity establishes a process to select who will belong. A group for persons with serious mental illness includes those persons who define themselves as such. Space constraints and personnel issues may determine who gets to belong: the room may only hold eight people, only one social worker may be hired to facilitate the group. Task groups may be composed of those with the most relevant experience to contribute, those who have been appointed by a person in authority, or those who show the greatest interest in the task. Effective task groups often include members with a variety of resources for the task at hand.

Heterogeneity versus Homogeneity

The degree of heterogeneity/homogeneity of groups may vary along several dimensions, such as age, race, sexual orientation, gender, level of education, coping style, religion, socioeconomic status, disabilities, and problem areas or strengths. Usually groups are homogeneous on one or a few of these dimensions and heterogeneous on the rest. For example, Terry's group is homogeneous regarding gender and sexual orientation but quite heterogeneous on other dimensions, including race, age, socioeconomic status, disabilities, educational status, occupation, age at first awareness of sexual orientation, and amount of disclosure of sexual orientation to others.

Often heterogeneity/homogeneity is a matter of perception (Chau, 1990; Dufrene & Coleman, 1992). For example, in several studies of groups with African Americans, Davis (1984) found that European American members had a different perception from African American members regarding the racial balance of the group. If the group was in proportion to the population of African Americans in the geographic area, then the European American members perceived the group as balanced. If the group had equal numbers of white and black members, the black members viewed the group as balanced. The white members, however, perceived the group as imbalanced, because the number of African Americans exceeded the psychological threshold of European American members.

Which is better for group work, heterogeneous or homogeneous groups? Yalom (1995, p. 255) notes that heterogeneous groups are better for "long-term intensive interactional group therapy." Homogeneous groups, on the other hand, are better for "support or symptomatic relief over a brief period." Yalom goes on to state that homogeneous groups are "often effective for individuals with monosymptomatic complaints or for the noncompliant patient" (p. 255). Homogeneous groups tend to build cohesion more quickly, offer more immediate support to members, and have better attendance and less conflict. Yet Yalom does not recommend homogeneous groups for long-term psychotherapeutic work that involves personality change, because they tend to remain at superficial levels and don't challenge individuals' behavioral patterns and dynamics as much as heterogeneous groups. However, homogeneous groups based on such characteristics as race or sex may be an exception. Boyd-Franklin (1987) touts group therapy for black women, arguing that the homogeneous membership allows for more intensive exploration of common problems.

Even heterogeneous groups usually have a homogeneous factor: the purpose or common goal of the group. Differences among people may be overridden by the overall function of groups—a place for people to seek human connection, and in Wasserman and Danforth's (1988, p. 69) words, "a sustaining and healing sense of unification and belonging." I am reminded of a friend who spoke to me of her experiences attending a support group for family members who had lost their loved ones. As the only African American group member, she said she felt like a "fly in a milk carton," but her fellow group members were the only people she knew who truly understood her grief.

An interesting research finding is that the heterogeneity/homogeneity issue takes on less importance the briefer and more structured the group. Compositional issues are more significant in groups that are less structured and that focus on group interaction (Yalom, 1995). In Terry's group, the homogeneity of sexual orientation provides the safety and support to explore the heterogeneity of the group. In natural groups, heterogeneity or homogeneity may be affected by such variables as the location (some geographic areas are highly homogeneous), preferences of group members (people tend to form natural groups with those with whom they feel some connection), and social norms and values (acceptance or condemnation of mixed groups).

Cohesiveness

One important variable related to group composition is **group cohesiveness**—group identity, commitment, and sense of belonging. Yalom (1995) postulates that "cohesiveness in group therapy is the analogue of relationship in individual therapy" (p. 47). Groups with a "greater sense of solidarity, or 'we-ness,' value the group more highly, and will defend it against internal and external threats" (p. 48). Groups that are cohesive tend to have higher rates of attendance, participation, and mutual support.

Cohesiveness does not mean the absence of conflict or dislike among group members. Even a cohesive group may sometimes experience bickering, frustration, or alienation.

Some groups may develop rituals or habits to increase cohesiveness among members. For example, a gang member may receive a tattoo as an initiation rite, the group may name itself (the "lunch bunch"), a member who has been in the group for six months may receive a pin, or group members may be expected to call another member when they are having difficulty.

Basic Group Processes

To be effective, group workers need tools for understanding the group processes in which they participate. Group processes are those unique interactions among group members that result from being in a group together. The ways that people behave in groups and why are of interest to us because we spend much of our time in groups and groups have strong influence on our behaviors.

Theories of Group Processes

The fields of social psychology and sociology have been in the forefront of empirical research on group processes. Three of the major theories of group processes are discussed in this section: expectation states theory, status characteristics theory, and exchange theory. Each one helps us understand why and how certain members of a group develop and maintain more power than other members to influence the group's activities.

Rational choice perspective

Expectation States Theory.   Joan and Bob are both members of a task force formed in a housing project community to increase healthy social interactions among the children and beautify the grounds. Joan, a person who is known to be artistic, makes a suggestion that the group involve kids in painting murals on communal buildings and then hold a contest for the best mural. Bob, a person who is not known to be artistic, suggests that the group solicit volunteer contributions from local artists who would donate paintings and other artwork to display on the inside of buildings. **Expectation states theory** suggests that group members will be more willing to go along with Joan's idea than with Bob's because of Joan's greater perceived expertise in artistic matters.

Expectation states theory relies on the concept of **performance expectations**—predictions of how well an act will accomplish a group's task (Meeker, 1994). Group members may have high performance expectations (the act will help them successfully complete a task) or low performance expectations (the act will fail to help them complete the task), or mixed expectations.

Group members who have contributed successful suggestions for task accomplishment in the past tend to carry more power and prestige within the group. They are viewed as people "in the know" or people "who have good ideas." Thus, task force members expect Joan, as an artistic individual, to suggest an idea for beautifying the grounds that will be successful. On the other hand, they question the worthiness of Bob's suggestion because of his limited artistic talent. Joan has more power and prestige within the group on this particular subject than Bob.

In Terry's coming-out group, Beverly carries some influence. She has attended for quite a long time, and is one of the "core" members who come to the group consistently. As an influential member, she is expected to articulate and enforce the group's rules and to assist new members in acclimating to the group. Group members expect Beverly to share her insights about the coming-out process and perceive her as a knowledgeable person especially when discussing issues faced by African American lesbians.

In mutual aid groups, certain members may carry more influence than others because of the expectations others have about their contributions. Group members seem to listen to certain members who are expected to offer wise advice or who have the most experience with a certain problem. On the flip side, some group members are consistently ignored or carry little influence with other members. These may be persons who are considered suspect by the rest of the group or who are perceived as having less to offer than others.

Status Characteristics Theory.   In the coming-out group, Beverly is perceived as a knowledgeable person regarding coming out and the unique issues faced by African American lesbians. But in another setting, the color of Beverly's skin might negatively influence how she is perceived by other people. Stereotypes about African Americans may cause other people to question Beverly's interests, skills, or values. Such stereotypes are the key to **status characteristics theory,** in which the power and prestige of group members are correlated with their status.

Social constructionist perspective

A central concept in this theory is the **status characteristic**—an attribute considered potentially relevant to the group's task. "Status characteristics reflect cultural beliefs that may or may not be objectively true.... [I]t merely is assumed that if people believe something is true, they will act as if it were true, and thus it will tend to be true in its consequences" (Balkwell, 1994, pp. 124–135). For example, if people expect that someone using a wheelchair is incapable of playing basketball for a charity fund-raiser, then they will act as if a person using a wheelchair is unable to play basketball. They may disqualify that person from playing, thereby demoralizing the individual with the disability and preventing the person from contributing to the success of the fund-raiser.

Sometimes, status characteristics are not initially evident. Group members will then search for status differentials as the group interacts. As status characteristics become more obvious, the power and prestige order in the group is formed.

Gender is an influential status characteristic in our society, perhaps because it is so easily discerned. In mixed-gender groups, males have greater participation and influence than females (Balkwell, 1994; Garvin & Reed, 1983), and males or females with traditionally masculine personality traits are likely to exhibit more dominant behavior (Seibert & Gruenfeld, 1992). In same-sex groups, gender is not an initial status differential; instead, members develop expectations of each other based on other status characteristics, such as education, race, or experience. Regardless of gender, a person's perceived ability also affects performance expectations. Gender and specific task ability both influence the level of social persuasion. For example, a female may be perceived as incapable of handling a complex mechanical problem in a work group, but may be able to develop influence if she shows that she can accomplish the task successfully (Schneider & Cook, 1995).

One assumption of status characteristics theory is that people rely on their stereotypes in the absence of proof that those characteristics are irrelevant (Balkwell, 1994, p. 126). In our example of assumptions people may make about persons using wheelchairs, the burden of proof would be on the persons using wheelchairs to demonstrate that they could indeed play basketball, thus establishing the inapplicability of others' assumptions about the disability.

Rational choice perspective

Exchange Theory.   Sometimes in coming-out groups, those who have been "out" for the longest time have implicit power over those newly out, who are often termed "baby dyke." A "let me show you the ropes and tell you what this is about" attitude can be used to gain power and influence over another person and to create dependency: "you need me to help you understand what you are getting yourself into." But social power can also be used in a positive way in a coming-out group, as when those who have been in the lesbian community for a long time offer support and information to others with the intention of providing mutual aid. To understand power as a social commodity, we can look to exchange theory (Thibaut & Kelley, 1959), which assumes that human interactions can be understood in terms of rewards and costs.

According to exchange theory, social power is what determines who gets valued resources in groups and whether those resources are perceived as being distributed in a just manner. Conflicts within the group often revolve around power issues—those who want the power in the group, those who have power and don't want to give it up, and those who don't want others to have power over them.

Groups are particularly vulnerable to conflicts over power, because "social power resides in the structure of a social interaction situation" rather than being an innate quality of an individual. "Sometimes it [power] works within a relationship between two people, but often it works within the complex relationships among a set of three, four, or many more people. Different primary and secondary social networks, where variations occur in who interacts with whom, make up the social situations in which power emerges and produces effects in predictable ways" (Stolte, 1994, p. 173).

Power not only determines the distribution of group resources; it also influences people's expectations of others' abilities, even when the power results from structural conditions (such as luck) and not from innate personal ability (Lovaglia, 1995). Emotion also influences perceived power and influence, regardless of status. If a person has negative emotions toward a high-status person, the power of the high-status person will lessen (Lovaglia, 1995).

Power differences among group members can create status differences, but not necessarily. Group members may rate more highly the abilities and influences of high-power members, which may in turn influence expectations for high-power members, but negative feelings toward high-power members may mitigate their influence.

The exercise of social power often brings with it a concern about justice, fairness, and equality. Most of us would agree that power should not be exercised to the special benefit or detriment of some group members. However, justice is a relative rather than absolute term. Any two persons may have quite different ideas about what constitutes justice. For some, justice would be an equal distribution of resources; for others, justice would be an equitable (but not necessarily equal) distribution.

How persons evaluate the equity of a situation depends on such factors as cultural values, self-interest, the situation, the relationships among those affected, and personal characteristics (Hegtvedt, 1994). People tend to operate more from self-interest in impersonal conditions than when they have personal bonds with others. The status of the person for whom justice claims are being considered affects the definition of justice, the perception of injustice, and the resolution of injustices. In addition, what may be perceived as fair on an individual level may be perceived as unfair when viewed from a group perspective. For example, suppose a group member is in crisis and asks for extended time in the group. The other five group members agree to give the person an extra 10 minutes because of the crisis. This extension, however, requires each group member to give up two minutes of her/his floor time. Giving one individual an extra 10 minutes may not seem like much, but that one action has a cost for five other group members. And what if one group member decides that he/she has a pressing issue to discuss and does not want to give up the two minutes? How the group would resolve this dilemma relates to its spoken and unspoken guidelines for handling matters of justice within the group.

Group Development

To understand the unique nature of groups and why they are effective in helping people, we need to examine the ways groups develop. Two common ways of viewing group development are by the stages they pass through and by the processes that facilitate the work of a group. This section provides a brief overview of stage theories and models and then discusses an example of the analysis of processes that facilitate the work of groups: Yalom's therapeutic factors in group psychotherapy.

Developmental perspective

Stage Theories and Models. A variety of scholars have attempted to delineate the life cycle of small groups. But researchers who focus on the stages of group development have reached no consensus as to how many stages there are, the order in which they appear, or the nature of those stages. Exhibit 13.3 displays seven of the models commonly cited in social work literature to describe the development of groups. Note, however, that controlled experiments investigating group stages are rare. Most theories of group stages have been developed by observing patterns and changes in groups, usually after the group has disbanded. Because most of the stage theories have been based on studies of time-limited, closed groups, they may not even be applicable to open-ended or ongoing groups.

Most stage theorists agree, however, on some basic principles: Groups don't necessarily move through each stage in order; groups may revert to an earlier stage; stages are not distinct entities but may be a blend or combination; the group's development is influenced by the leader and the members; and groups do not need to reach the most advanced developmental stage in order to be effective (Reid, 1997).

EXHIBIT 13.3

Stage Models of Group Development

Life-Span Metaphor	Bales (1950)	Tuckman (1965)	Sarri and Galinsky (1967)	Harford (1971)	Garland, Jones, and Kolodny (1973)	Northen (1988)	Levine (1991)
Conception			Origin	Pregroup planning		Planning and intake	
Birth	Orientation	Forming	Formation	Convening	Preaffiliation	Orientation	Parallel relations Authority crisis
Childhood			Intermediate I	Group formulation			Inclusion
Adolescence	Evaluation	Storming Norming	Revision Intermediate II	Integration, disintegration and conflict, reintegration or reorganization, synthesis	Power and control Intimacy	Exploring and testing	Intimacy crisis
Adulthood (Maturity)	Decision making	Performing	Maturation	Group functioning and group maintenance	Differentiation	Problem solving	Mutuality
Death			Termination	Pretermination Termination	Separation	Termination	Separation crisis Termination

Source: Reid, 1997.

Processes: Therapeutic Factors. If stage theories are inadequate for explaining how groups develop, what are we to use instead? The chief alternative is process models, which identify what goes on in groups and how those processes affect group members and their interactions. The advantage of process analysis is that it focuses on the interactions among group members rather than creating a norm for stage development.

Psychodynamic
perspective
Social behavioral
perspective
Humanistic
perspective

A good example of a process model is the one developed by Irving Yalom, one of the best-known group psychotherapists. Yalom (1995) describes 11 factors that operate in therapeutic groups to shape their functioning. These factors are listed and defined in Exhibit 13.4.

Some of Yalom's therapeutic factors may operate to some extent in groups other than therapy groups. For example, universality and imparting of information are two of the mutual aid processes described earlier in this chapter.

Additionally, certain factors may be more significant at particular stages of group development than at others. One study of 12 time-limited outpatient psychotherapy groups found that the development of cohesion varied according to the stage (or phase) of psychotherapy. For ex-

EXHIBIT 13.4

Therapeutic Factors
Involved in Group
Development

Therapeutic Factor	Definition
Instillation of hope	Confidence and optimism in the ability of the group and individual members to resolve issues and grow.
Universality	Sense that others share similar problems and feelings and that one is not alone.
Imparting of information	Leader's and group members' sharing of information and guidance around problems and concerns.
Altruism	Benefits experienced when one realizes that one has helped another person.
Corrective recapitulation of primary family group	(Re)experience of relationship patterns like those in one's family of origin while learning different approaches to relationships.
Development of socializing techniques	Examination of patterns of interacting with others and acquisition of new social skills.
Imitative behavior	Observation of how other group members handle their problems and feelings and recognition of how those methods apply to one's own situation.
Interpersonal learning	Process of learning about oneself through interaction with others.
Group cohesiveness	Sense of belonging that group members have and sense of acceptance and support they feel in the group.
Catharsis	Sharing of deep and sometimes painful emotions with nonjudgmental acceptance from group members.
Existential factors	Search for meaning and purpose in one's life.

Source: Yalom, 1995.

ample, in the earliest stage of the group, members sharing issues about their lives outside the group built cohesion; however, too much focus on the therapist during this stage tended to be countercohesive (Budman, Soldz, Demby, Davis, & Merry, 1993). In Terry's coming-out group, several therapeutic factors are evident at different times. When group members feel they can trust each other, catharsis and interpersonal learning are likely. When new members attend the group, they often desire to experience an instillation of hope, universality, imparting of information, and development of socializing techniques.

Group Dynamics

The overall development of the group is overlaid with patterns of interactions that can be characterized as **group dynamics**—such issues as how leaders are appointed or emerge, which roles members take in groups, and how communication networks affect interactions in groups.

Formal and Informal Leadership. Formal leaders are appointed or elected to lead the group by virtue of such characteristics as their position in the agency or community and their interest or expertise in relation to the group's focus. Informal leaders may emerge in groups where no formal leader exists, or in ones where formal leaders are established. In the latter case, a group member may feel more comfortable in a helper or leader role than as a client in the group, thereby mimicking actions of the formal leader.

Both formal and informal group leaders have a binary focus: the individuals in the group and the group as a whole. **Task-oriented leaders** facilitate problem-solving within the context of the group; **process-oriented leaders** identify and manage group relationships (Reid, 1997; Yalom, 1995). Any given leader usually fluctuates from one role to the other, although people tend to be either more task-oriented or more process-oriented.

Natural groups may have formal or informal leaders. A friendly softball game at the diamond on a Saturday morning may evolve into a complex hierarchy of leaders and followers as various activities are negotiated—who is on what team, who bats first, how long the game will last, who will decide batting order, and so on—and such process issues as team morale and cohesiveness are promoted.

Leaders of formed groups also take on various roles, depending on the purpose and structure of the group. A facilitator for a group for children with ADHD is a formal leader who may provide structured activities, support, and guidance for the children. Similarly, the leader of a one-time debriefing group may provide support and information to rescue workers after a fire. Informal leaders of formed groups might include a person who evolves into a leadership role in a work group assigned to some project.

Systems perspective Groups often have coleaders, or one appointed leader and one or more group members who serve as self- or group-appointed coleaders. The coming-out group has two facilitators, both of whom are self-appointed leaders. Doris is a 52-year-old African American lesbian in a long-term relationship. Marie is a European American, 28, who came out during high school. Doris tends to be the more nurturing facilitator and has a degree in social work. Marie considers herself a lesbian/gay activist and works at a clinic for persons with HIV/AIDS. She is more task-oriented and does much of the record keeping and information sharing in the group.

Researchers have made a wide range of discoveries about the types of people who tend to become group leaders:

■ People who become leaders in groups are likely to have personality traits of dominance, friendliness, task orientation, persuasiveness, and intelligence.

■ First-born persons are likely to become task-oriented leaders; later-borns will likely be relationship-oriented leaders (Hare, Blumberg, Davies, & Kent, 1994).

■ Gender and race influence leadership (both who takes leadership and the perception of leaders by group members). According to Garvin and Reed (1983), status differences based on gender influence the behaviors of both male and female group members, including their reactions to male and female group leaders. Both males and females tend to respect male leadership more quickly and easily. Males in a female-led group tend to challenge the leader(s) and expect female leaders to be more nurturing than male leaders.

■ Communication content, more than gender, influences leadership emergence in task-oriented groups. One study found task-relevant communication to be the sole significant predictor of emerged leadership, with no significant gender differences in the production of task-relevant communication (Hawkins, 1995).

■ In general, leaders who are elected by members tend to be more favorably perceived than leaders who are self-appointed or appointed by others.

■ Informal leaders may emerge in groups where formal leaders are present. Reid (1997) refers to this role as the "assistant therapist," the person who "asks leading questions of other members, analyzes behavior, and is always ready with an interpretation" (p. 246).

Formal and Informal Roles.   In addition to formal and informal leadership roles within the group, group members serve a variety of other roles. Those roles serve a purpose for the group as a whole and simultaneously fulfill group members' personal needs (Reid, 1997, p. 245). Thus, a person's group role often mirrors roles in other arenas. For instance, the group clown is often a clown in other areas of life.

Systems perspective

Roles of group members may have both positive and negative aspects. The peacemaker, for example, may serve the group function of reducing conflict and anxiety within the group—but perhaps at the cost of suppressing efforts to work through or resolve conflict within the group. The clown or jester reduces anxiety and stress in the group by joking, but also enables the group to avoid a painful subject. The scapegoat may remind group members of parts of themselves that they deny or of which they are fearful. The rescuer, who jumps in to defend anyone who appears to be confronted in the group, may be uncomfortable with others' pain or with unfair attacks against the group scapegoat, but may also keep the group from sanctioning an unacceptable violation of group norms (Reid, 1997).

From a therapeutic perspective, Yalom (1995) has categorized several types of "problem members," whom he refers to as "problem patients": the monopolist, the silent member, the boring member, the help-rejecting complainer, the psychotic member, the characterologically difficult member, and the borderline member. Yalom observes that he has yet to encounter an unproblematic member; each member has some problems-in-living. Furthermore, the behavior of the "problem patient" does not exist in a vacuum; "that patient always abides in a dynamic equilibrium with a group that permits or encourages such behavior" (p. 370). The behaviors of the "problem members" are attempts to cope with underlying feelings. The monopolist, for instance, talks incessantly to handle anxiety and to avoid talking about "real" feelings.

Hare (1994, pp. 443–444) reminds us that role is only one element of social interaction: "The other variables include the biological systems of the actors, their personalities, the structure and process of the small groups and organizations that they belong to, and the society, culture, and environment in which these are embedded." In other words, role is only one part of the picture.

Roles are not necessarily fixed and rigid. Rather, as Salazar (1996) argues, "roles develop **Social constructionist** interactionally," through give and take within the group. Roles are also a social construction, a **perspective** "product of expectations (of self and others' expectation of self) and a mechanism for the production and reproduction of structure" (p. 500). This view of roles is consistent with the transactional approach of this book.

Communication Networks.   Groups function more effectively when the members are able to communicate easily and with competence. Group workers can set the tone for the communication in the group by being clear, direct, and compassionate in their own communication. The free flow of ideas among members enhances productivity, particularly in task groups.

Communication networks are the links among members—who talks to whom, how information is transmitted, whether communication between members is direct or uses a go-between. Sociograms may be used to depict the physical arrangement of these communication channels. Typically the formal leader occupies the central position in a communication network, like the hub at the center of spokes on a wheel (Shaw, 1981). However, an informal leader may take the role of information giver and controller.

Group members' satisfaction with a group tends to be higher in "web" networks, where information passes freely among all group members, than in centralized "wheel" networks. (Exhibit 13.5 diagrams these patterns.) Centralized networks are the more efficient configuration for task groups addressing simple problems. Decentralized networks are more effective if the group is attempting to solve more complex problems (Shaw, 1981).

EXHIBIT 13.5

Common
Communication
Patterns in Groups

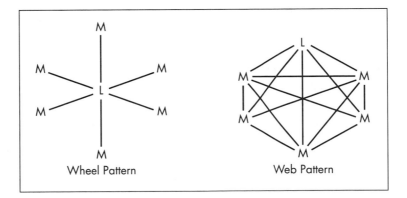

Wheel Pattern   Web Pattern

The Effects of Physical Environment on Group Processes

Besides the type and structure of groups, the physical environment also influences group interactions. The physical environment includes material aspects, territoriality, interperson distance, density and crowding, and spatial arrangements (Shaw, 1981). As you read this section, you might want to refer back to Chapter 7, which discusses the relationship between the physical environment and human behavior.

Material Aspects of the Physical Environment

The coming-out group is held at the Gay and Lesbian Community Center. The group meets in a room large enough for members to sit comfortably. The facilitators are able to control the temperature of the room. Occasionally, a Center volunteer will come into the building, and then the facilitators will shut the door to the group room to ensure privacy. No other group meets at the Center at the same time as the women's coming-out group. These are just a few elements of the material aspects of the physical environment. Material aspects include the structure and contents of the room (size, shape, furniture, arrangement of furniture), lighting, privacy, noise level, colors, and temperature of the space.

Shaw (1981) reviewed studies of the effects of material aspects on group functioning and found several variables that impact on members' perceptions and interactions. For example, in work groups, walls painted "cool blue" induced more women to complain of being cold with the temperature set at 75 degrees than when the color was changed to "warm yellows and restful greens" at the same temperature. A dimly lit room is perceived as more intimate. Unpredictable noise causes frustration and a lowering of productivity. Much of this research has been done in the workplace.

Studies have also shown that the attitudes of group members affect their experience of the material aspects of the environment. Persons are more tolerant of an unsatisfactory physical environment when they know that someone is concerned about their welfare and is trying to respond to their concerns about the physical environment—turning up the temperature in a cold room, rearranging furniture to facilitate member interaction, closing the door to the group room to reduce outside noise and increase privacy.

Territoriality

Each semester I notice how students "claim" a seat in the class. By the second or third week of the semester, they are referring to a particular chair as "my seat." An unspoken rule is that one does not sit in someone else's seat. Sitting in someone else's seat may be met with a gasp, glare, or a declaration: "Hey, you are in *my* seat!"

People have ways of marking their territory—a jacket thrown over a movie theater seat (this space is reserved) or graffiti on a wall of a subway. Groups also establish territories. For example, gangs who consider a certain part of town under their jurisdiction will defend that territory against rival gangs. Studies of territoriality have found that the permanence of the group's territoriality (how long the group has resided in a place and plans for future residence) influences the degree to which it will be defended (Shaw, 1981). The preferred size of territories may be influenced by such factors as group size, composition, gender (males typically claim more territory than females), and the relationship of members (strangers versus friends). People generally respect the space boundaries of groups. For example, if a group is talking in a hallway, most people will walk around the group rather than going in between the members, especially when the group members are conversing in an agitated manner (Shaw, 1981).

Interperson Distance

"Get out of my space." "Get out of my face." "Move back." These declarations are verbal attempts to establish a comfortable distance between oneself and others. Persons and groups establish norms about the appropriate distance between themselves and others. **Interperson distance,** as those norms are referred to, are influenced by such variables as age, sex, cultural background, relationship among the persons, the interaction situation, and status differences between persons. Interperson distance is the group version of the concept of personal space discussed in Chapter 7.

Studies on interperson distance have found that

- Strangers tend to maintain a greater interperson distance than friends.

- Females prefer closer interperson distances than males.

- Closer interperson distances are more acceptable in such settings as elevators and subways and with service providers like dentists than in situations where close physical proximity is not expected.

- Persons of higher status are more likely to invade the space boundaries of persons of lower status than vice versa (Shaw, 1981).

Norms for interperson distance have considerable influence on our perceptions and behavior. Terry believed that alcohol influenced her to alter her usual norms regarding the proper interperson distance between two females. Terry believed that she would not have shared a bed after a party unless she had been under the influence of alcohol. Considering this incident many years later and in the context of her emerging lesbian identity, Terry realizes that alcohol became the excuse for changing her usual preferences regarding personal space with a person of the same sex.

Researchers observing persons in different size rooms with various furniture arrangements have found that the size of a room and arrangement of chairs may also influence interperson distance. In a small room with tightly packed chairs, persons may experience the sense of not having enough personal space. Even in a large room, a large number of persons may also produce a feeling of discomfort (Shaw, 1981).

Density and Crowding

The coming-out group meets in a small room in the Center. When the attendance at a meeting is high, additional chairs need to be brought into the room, which makes the room seem even smaller. Population density—the number of people per unit of space—is correlated with the experience of crowding. The smaller the space and the greater the number of people in it, the more likely it is that one will feel crowded. The experience of crowding is influenced by other factors, however, such as gender, interperson distance, and the situation. For example, research on the connection between gender and crowding has discovered that women can accept greater stimulation before feeling crowded. All-male groups are more competitive (presumed to be a reaction to crowding) in smaller rooms than in larger rooms; this response may also be related to territoriality (Shaw, 1981).

The comfort group members feel with each other and each person's need for personal space also affect how crowded the room feels. Rooms can seem especially small when a topic with which one feels uncomfortable is being addressed. In that case, one may feel the need to "get outta here" no matter the size of the room.

Spatial Arrangements

Each semester, it seems, a student asks, "Why do all the black students sit together?" The response usually is, "Why do the white students sit together?" The answer to both questions is that people tend to sit near people with whom they are well acquainted. Seating arrangement has been shown to affect the communication pattern, the quality of interaction, and reaction to other members in groups (Shaw, 1981).

A circular formation for chairs tends to increase communication among group members and produce more positive ratings of self and others than a noncircular arrangement, because additional opportunities for eye contact increase member-to-member interaction. However, cultural values and norms may influence the level of one's comfort with circle arrangements and direct eye contact (Lum, 1992). For example, a greater degree of formality, as indicated by lecture-style rows, is generally preferred by Asian Americans, who view the worker/client relationship as formal. Direct eye contact may also be a sign of disrespect for some Asian American and Native American persons.

Persons tend to choose the seats in the room that reflect their perceived status. High-status individuals tend to select chairs at the head of a table or in a central position (Shaw, 1981). This phenomenon could be partially explained by status characteristics theory.

IMPLICATIONS FOR SOCIAL WORK PRACTICE

The overview of formed and natural groups in this chapter suggests a number of principles for social work assessment, intervention, and evaluation.

- In the assessment process with individuals or families, identify any natural or formed groups to which the person or family belongs. Ecomaps or sociograms may be used to identify such groups.

- In the assessment process with a potential group member, gather background information such as the motivation for joining the group, the expectations the person has of the leader and other group members, the strengths the person could offer the group, and previous experience with groups.

- In the assessment process, determine whether the group modality or another intervention modality would be most appropriate for the client.

- Develop and implement small groups when it is clear that a group would benefit the population that you serve. Determine what type(s) of groups would be most appropriate for that population. Consider groups for prevention when appropriate.

- Seek to build alliances with natural and self-help groups that reinforce or supplement the services that you are providing.

- Be aware of various groups in your community for referral and networking purposes.

- In the groups that you facilitate, pay careful attention to issues of group structure, development, composition, and dynamics.

- Assess the physical environment of groups. Be aware of how material aspects, territoriality, interperson distance, density and crowding, and spatial arrangements may influence the groups you intend to facilitate.

- Determine a method to evaluate the effectiveness of a group prior to its formation. Use the information from this evaluation to make needed changes in the group.

- Collaborate with colleagues from other disciplines to cofacilitate groups in interdisciplinary settings.

- Be aware of how managed care affects the use of groups as a practice modality.

MAIN POINTS

1. Small groups are typically defined as collections of individuals who interact with each other, perceive themselves as belonging to a group, are interdependent, join together to accomplish a goal or fulfill a need through joint association, and are influenced by a set of rules and norms.

2. Natural groups develop spontaneously on the basis of location, friendship, or some other naturally occurring event. Formed groups are convened for a particular purpose and are initiated by some outside influence, such as an organization.

3. Group work has had a long history in the social work profession and emerged in this country as a social movement rather than a social work method.

4. Types of social work groups include therapy, mutual aid, psychoeducational, self-help, and task groups. A group may be a combination of two or more types.

5. Groups may be open or closed, time-limited or ongoing. A group might begin as an open group, then decide later to close and not admit any more new members—or vice versa. Similarly, a group could begin with the intention of running for 12 weeks, but later decide to extend the group for a specific time period or indefinitely.

6. Three group composition issues that social workers should consider are inclusiveness or exclusiveness, heterogeneity or homogeneity, and cohesiveness.

7. Expectation states theory approaches the issue of basic group processes with the assumption that persons in a group will develop different levels of power and prestige based on the performance expectations that group members hold for each other. If a group holds high performance expectations for a particular member, then the group believes that person will likely be successful in some act.

8. Status characteristics theory postulates that group processes are deeply influenced by status characteristics, based on cultural beliefs about certain groups of people. Perceived status correlates with power and prestige and with performance expectations of persons in a group.

9. Power, influence, and dependence are all aspects of exchange theory, a third perspective on basic group processes. It assumes that through social interaction, persons exchange rewards and costs. The exercise of social power can garner more valued resources.

10. Issues of justice, fairness, and equality emerge among group members as valued resources are distributed. The group may also take on issues of justice, fairness, and equality in larger systems as part of the group's purpose.

11. Stage theories and models attempt to explain group development. Although scholars disagree about the exact stages that groups go through, they do generally agree that groups move through stages. Those stages may not occur in a specific order; groups may revert to an earlier stage; stages may be combined or blended; and groups can function productively even if they do not reach the most advanced developmental stage.

12. Yalom's 11 primary curative factors in psychotherapy groups are instillation of hope, universality, imparting of information, altruism, the corrective recapitulation of the primary family group, the development of socializing techniques, imitative behavior, interpersonal learning, group cohesiveness, catharsis, and existential factors.

13. Group dynamics are the patterns of interaction. They include formal and informal leadership, formal and informal roles of group members, and communication networks.

14. The physical environment in which groups meet includes the material aspects, such as the structure of the room, privacy, lighting, and noise level; territoriality, or the

ways groups mark what they consider to be theirs; interperson distance, or the norms groups or individuals in groups develop regarding the appropriate distance between themselves and others; density and crowding, which is affected by such variables as gender, interperson distance, and situation; and spatial arrangements, such as who sits with whom and how far away people sit from each other.

KEY TERMS

brief treatment model	open groups
closed groups	performance expectations
communication networks	process-oriented leader
expectation states theory	psychoeducational group
formed groups	self-help group
group cohesiveness	small groups
group dynamics	status characteristic
group work	status characteristics theory
interperson distance	task group
mutual aid group	task-oriented leader
natural groups	therapy group
ongoing groups	time-limited groups

WORLD WIDE WEB RESOURCES

American Self-Help Clearinghouse
http://www.cmhc.com/selfhelp/
Part of Mental Health Net, edited by Barbara White and Edward Madara. Contains links to a wide variety of online self-help groups from Adoption to Workaholics.

Association for the Advancement of Social Work with Groups (AASWG)
http://dominic.barry.edu/~kelly/aaswg/aaswg.html
Professional organization advocating in support of group work practice, education, research, and publication. Includes links to newsletters, discussion lists, bibliographies, chapter information, syllabi, social work links, and other group work links.

Association for Specialists in Group Work (ASGW)
http://psyctc.sghms.ac.uk/mirrors/aswg/index.html
A division of the American Counseling Association that promotes quality in group work training, practice, and research.

Group Psychotherapy
http://freud.tau.ac.il/~haimw/group2.html
Includes links to a discussion list, bibliography, journals, tapes, grants, and courses related to group psychotherapy.

Social Work Access Network (SWAN)
http://www.sc.edu/swan/newsgroups.html
Includes links to various newsgroups on Usenet, including those that are support-related.

Support-Group.Com
http://www.support-group.com
Provides Bulletin Boards and Online Chat as well as links to a variety of support groups for persons with health, personal, or relationship issues.

CHAPTER 14

Families

Nancy R. Vosler, Washington University, St. Louis

JUNIOR JONES'S COMPLEX FAMILY LIFE

Imagine that you are a school social worker at Fifth Street Elementary School in a large metropolitan city in the Midwest. Six-year-old Junior has been referred to you for hitting other children in his first-grade class, coming to school on several occasions wearing only a light jacket (walking through snow in January), and shouting expletives at his teacher when she reprimands him for his disruptive behavior.

In taking some family background information, you learn that Junior's mother, Angela Jones, age 25, has two younger children, Susan and Ken, who are twins age 3. Angela and her three children currently live in one side of a duplex owned by the mother of the twins' father, in an inner-city neighborhood that has experienced increasing drug activity and some drive-by shootings. The twins' father, John, sometimes stays with Angela, but more recently has been staying most of the time with his mother, Ruth, in the housing unit on the other side of the duplex. Junior's father, Roy, lives across town; he occasionally visits Junior and takes him for an "afternoon out"—to an amusement park or a sports event.

Angela is the youngest of four girls in her family of origin. Her father died in jail during a fight when Angela was 5. Her mother died after a long battle with cancer just before Junior's birth. Angela did not do well in school, began truanting sporadically in junior high school, was in juvenile detention for possession of marijuana, and spent nearly two years in a residential school when she was 14 and 15. Her mother was very ill during this time and believed that Angela's being in a residential setting was the "best plan" for her. Angela has not completed high school, but has worked briefly at several small retail stores. Following Junior's birth when she was 19, Angela began receiving AFDC, food stamps, and some housing assistance—except for brief periods when she was in a training program or was able to get a temporary job.

Angela and Roy, Junior's father, lived together for about six months just before and after Junior's birth. They met through a mutual friend, and had known each other for nearly a year when Angela became pregnant. Roy dropped out of school in the 11th grade, and off and on has done odd jobs such as car washing. He drinks heavily, and has done some experimenting with drugs. Not long after Junior was born, when Roy had been drinking most of one Saturday, he hit Angela, blackening her eye and face. She became frightened and moved, with Junior, into her sister Beth's apartment. Roy promised not to hurt her again; so about a week later, she moved back. However, within a few months, he was regularly threatening both her and the baby, and periodically he would become physically violent, throwing an object across the room and/or hitting Angela. Angela finally went to a shelter to get away, began a GED program, and there met John.

Angela notes that she and John "hit it off" immediately and began going out on a regular basis. She had left the shelter after an argument with a staff member, and again moved in with her sister Beth. When Beth's landlord threatened to evict Beth for having "too many people" in the apartment, Angela moved into an apartment with John, who at the time was working in construction and making a fairly good wage. She left Junior for several months with Beth and her two children, but after "getting settled" with John, she brought Junior to live with her and John.

John has an older sister in the armed forces. He dropped out of school in the 10th grade, but several years ago, at the urging of his mother, he completed his GED. John's parents are divorced. His father is on Social Security Disability and SSI, after an accident at work 10 years ago left him in a wheelchair; he periodically drinks heavily, and has in the past been violent toward John's mother. John's mother, Ruth, inherited from her parents a duplex in an inner-city neighborhood. She works nights for a small company that contracts to clean office buildings. In the past, she has supplemented her low-wage earnings with rent from the second housing unit in the duplex.

Nearly four years ago, when Angela found that she was pregnant with twins, John asked Ruth whether they (John, Angela, and Junior) could "rent" the duplex unit. At the time, a tenant had just moved out. Reluctantly, Ruth agreed; however, payment of rent has been sporadic, and conflict and shouting between Ruth and Angela have become much more frequent, especially recently. The birth and care of the twins, Susan and Ken, have been draining for Angela, and she has not even considered looking for work in the past three years. John's work has been sporadic as well, and he has been let go from several jobs for arguing with a boss or coworker. Conflict between John and Angela has also increased, and John is now living most of the time on his mother's side of the duplex, where he still has "his old room."

Angela, Junior, Susan, and Ken currently receive AFDC (TANF), food stamps, and Medicaid. Occasionally, Roy brings clothes or a toy for his son, Junior; but he is angry with the state for pursuing him for child support, saying that he makes so little already, he cannot afford to "pay the state" anything. John is also being pressured by the state to pay child support; however, both he and Angela clearly believe, like Roy, that any child support money collected (over $50 per month) goes to the state, not to his children.

CASE STUDY

Because Angela's housing and utilities have essentially been rent-free from Ruth for the past four years, Angela has been able to survive with some small assistance from her sister Beth and a food pantry in the neighborhood. However, buying clothes is always a problem, and Angela has been more and more stressed and frustrated. When Junior lost his winter coat recently at school, Angela cried in frustration and then, for several days, let him walk the two blocks to school with only his summer jacket "to teach him a lesson"—until her sister found out and gave Angela a hand-me-down winter coat for Junior from Beth's 8-year-old son.

Angela is angry with John for not supporting her or the children adequately. She is angry with Ruth for "making things worse" with her nagging about the rent. She is angry with Junior for "making trouble" for her at school. She is tired and depressed over feeling alone and overwhelmed with three very active children. She is also aware that the new welfare reform regulations require that she get a job and "go off" welfare within the next two years.

The neighborhood in which the Jones family lives has been declining over the past five to ten years. All of the factories in the adjacent industrial complex have closed their doors, leaving behind industrial waste and boarded-up buildings. A number of two-story apartment buildings in the area that were two-family dwellings have now been subdivided and converted into four-family apartment buildings. Several apartment fires in the surrounding streets over the past three years have resulted in abandoned and boarded-up buildings, which are sometimes broken into and used for drug dealing and other illegal activities. Gang graffiti has appeared on streets, sidewalks, and the sides of buildings. When gunfire is heard in the neighborhood, most residents go inside, close the door, and "hope for the best."

There is a small grocery store on the corner, across from the elementary school. The owner says that he is forced to charge very high prices because of constant thefts. The nearest chain grocery store is two miles away, and Angela would have to change buses going and returning if she used public transportation. Usually, at least once a week or so, she can get someone to drive her to the chain store and back—John, or Beth, or sometimes even Ruth—depending on whose car is operational at the time. When the twins were babies, and Ruth and Angela were on better terms, Angela could do laundry in Ruth's apartment. However, Angela now has to either wash by hand or walk a block and a half, with three children in tow, to the nearest laundromat. The local health center is a 10-minute bus ride away, and Angela notes that each time she has gone there, over the past four years, she and/or her children have been seen by a different doctor.

Angela blames John for not being able to "get and keep" a good job. However, she is also aware that "there aren't a lot of good jobs out there anymore." She has no idea what type of work she could do, once she is no longer eligible for "welfare." She is also very concerned about where she could get good-quality child care for the twins and after-school care for Junior—that is, if her employment is a "regular 9-to-5 job." She notes that Beth has been able to get a neighbor to watch out for her two children after school, so that Beth could take a six-month "nurse aide" training course. After completion of her training, Beth hopes to get a hospital job "with good wages and benefits" to help her raise her two children. The children's father, from whom Beth is now divorced, lives in a rural area more than three hours from the city and has not been paying child support on a regular basis. He lives in the same county as Beth's and Angela's two much older sisters, who, according to Angela, "have a lot of troubles of their own."

You are the only social worker at the elementary school and are new in your job. You want very much to help the 30 children who have been referred to you over the past few months, but with at least one new referral coming across your desk each week, you are unsure how best to proceed toward making a difference in your clients' lives. You do know that to craft a "plan for change" with Junior and his family, you will have to make some assumptions about who his family is and whether or not working with other family members besides Junior is necessary.

U.S. Families Today

Systems perspective

A definition of family may not be the most obvious place to start thinking about an approach to change for Junior. However, if you rely on the traditional definition of family—two biological parents, family ties based on "blood, adoption, or marriage" (Barker, 1987, p. 53)—you may not be able to correctly identify all those who make up Junior's support network. You may make more progress with the following definition of **family** adopted in 1981 by the National Association of Social Workers (NASW): "a grouping that consists of two or more individuals who define themselves as a family and who over time assume those obligations to one another that are generally considered an essential component of family systems" (NASW, 1982, p. 10). By this definition, certainly the current household consisting of Angela, Junior, Susan, and Ken is a family. In addition, John has perhaps been acting in a kind of stepparent role, and Junior also has contact with his biological father, Roy. Junior has lived with Beth and her family and so may consider them to be family as well. But the extent to which Ruth considers herself family for Junior is not at all clear. Understanding both patterns and problems in Junior's behavior requires sorting out relationships and boundaries—and consistent rule makers and authority figures—in his family life. Narrow definitions, labeling a family like Junior's as "broken" or "incomplete," constrict our ability to think creatively about families' strengths and potential options for change.

In some respects, Junior's family is quite normal by current standards. Several important demographic trends in family configurations have emerged over the past decades, as discussed in Chapter 8. One is the increase in the number of single-parent households. There are still many more single-mother than single-father families, but both types have been increasing—in terms of both numbers and percent of households (see, for example, Schwartz & Scott, 1994, p. 28; see also Johnson & Wahl, 1995). The long-term rise in divorce rates has paralleled the increase in single-parent households (Cherlin, 1992). Only recently have demographers also begun to pay attention to the rise in never-married single-parent households (Moore, 1995). An additional important trend is the high level of remarriage and the resulting stepfamilies, creating potentially very complex family relationships (Vosler & Proctor, 1991). Other trends affecting family relationships include increases in life spans with resulting care needs for elderly family members, increasing labor force participation by mothers with even very young children, and increasing racial, ethnic, and cultural diversity among the U.S. population as a whole (Johnson & Wahl, 1995; see also Vosler, 1996).

Recent empirical research has helped us understand some of the effects of these changes on families. Single parenthood is associated with poverty and concomitant family instability and risk (McLanahan & Sandefur, 1994; Vosler, 1996). Never-married parenting is also associated with prior economic—and resulting family—instability (Burton, 1995). These are interesting correlations, although causal relationships among poverty, family instability, divorce, never-married parenthood, and risk for negative child outcomes require further study (see Robertson & Vosler, 1997; Vosler & Robertson, 1998).

Changes in family structure, such as increases in single parenting, nonmarital childbearing, and stepfamilies, have occurred at the same time as significant shifts in the U.S. economy (also discussed in Chapter 8). These economic changes include more unequal wage distributions, with increasing concentrations at the top and the bottom and the "hollowing out" of middle levels, especially for men (Ryscavage, 1994); increasing numbers of families in which at least one adult is working full-time, yet not earning enough to bring the household above the U.S. poverty line (Vosler, 1996); and, as a result, the increasing necessity for families in the bottom half of the society to have at least two wage earners, often with both parents working full-time at low-wage jobs (Vosler, 1996). In addition, quality, affordable child care is not available for many families, and many working poor families have no health insurance, as companies have cut costs by shifting to part-time and temporary employees, for whom no or very few benefits are provided.

Theoretical Perspectives for Understanding Families

Besides an understanding of current social trends affecting families, a number of theoretical "lenses" are available to help you understand Junior's problematic behaviors, their connection to family functioning, and avenues for positive change. In this chapter, we will introduce and briefly discuss five theoretical perspectives: social behavioral perspective, family systems and family life cycle, the ABCX model of family stress and coping, the multilevel family practice model, and a strengths perspective.

Social Behavioral Perspective

Social behavioral
perspective

Family therapy often includes behavioral approaches, which stem from "behavior modification and social-learning traditions in psychology" (Walsh, 1993, p. 33). Social workers who approach family problems from this perspective examine communication and family rules, learned patterns of acceptable behaviors, and patterns of rewards for behaviors (who, what, how). Work with the family may involve coaching family members in communication skills, conflict management, and positive reinforcement of desired behaviors. Reid's (1985) "task-centered" approach to family problem-solving involves such in-session activities as "negotiating rules," practicing "positive exchange," and "modifying communication problems" (pp. 202–211), as well as assigning tasks to be carried out at home to reinforce and extend skills learned in the family session. Walsh (1993) summarizes, "Treatment problems and goals are specified in concrete and observable behavioral terms, with the aim of educating and guiding family members in a straightforward way to learn more effective modes of dealing with each other" (p. 34).

Using this approach for understanding Junior's problematic behaviors, the social worker might explore communication and behavioral rules between Junior and Angela, Junior and John, and Junior and Roy—as well as among Angela, Roy, Beth, John, and Ruth. It might also be useful to explore other social contexts from which Junior may be learning what are "acceptable" behavior patterns. For example, Junior spends many afternoons, evenings, and weekends playing in a vacant lot next door to his home, where children of various ages play (and often fight), largely without adult supervision or guidance toward positive activities. In this setting, he may be learning the aggressive behavior and disrespectful language that his teacher has noticed.

Using a behavioral approach, you would want to focus on what Junior has learned in the past—in various contexts—about the behaviors that are considered acceptable and rewarded or are considered unacceptable and punished. Are the behavioral rules in school very different from the explicit and implicit rules in the neighborhood and at home? Does he have to learn different rules for various contexts—for example, with Angela versus with Roy? Also, what roles do his current behaviors play in the rewards and punishments Junior receives both in school and at home? For example, is his "bad" behavior getting him needed attention from an overwhelmed and exhausted Angela? Does he consider negative attention better than no attention at all? Does Junior consider conflict that sometimes escalates into hitting a normal part of living—at home, in the neighborhood, and therefore at school? Do his outbursts at his teacher mirror exchanges he has heard and absorbed from watching conflict between family members (for example, Roy and Angela, John and Angela, Angela and Ruth)?

In short, analysis of the Jones family from a social behavioral perspective will direct your attention to Junior's learned behavior patterns in family and other contexts. The result, of course, will be that these behavioral patterns and interactions will be the likely focus of your efforts toward positive change.

Family Systems and Family Life Cycle Perspectives

Systems perspective

A behavioral approach tends to focus on the individual, or perhaps on dyadic interchanges. In contrast, a **family systems perspective** adds another "lens"—that of the family as a social system. As you might imagine, this approach "requires a shift from focusing on particular family members as individuals to attending to relationships and interactional patterns between and among the persons who make up the focal family unit" (Vosler, 1996, p. 14). Family members both affect and are affected by other family members; when change occurs for one, all are affected. In this view, families develop boundaries that delineate who is in the family at any given time. Among these members, families develop (sometimes explicitly, sometimes implicitly) organizational structures and roles for accomplishing tasks, commonly shared beliefs and rules, and verbal and nonverbal communication patterns. Necessary structures and roles include family provision ("breadwinners"), leadership and decision making, household maintenance and management, care of dependents, and child rearing (Vosler, 1996).

Developmental perspective

Carter and McGoldrick (1988b) expand the concept of "family system" to look at families over time, in what they call the **family life cycle**. They delineate six stages that most U.S. families seem to pass through: single young adults, new couples, families with young children, families with adolescents, families launching children and moving on, and families in later life (pp. 128–129). Each of these stages involves normative changes and challenging tasks, both for individual family members and for the family system as a whole. In this view, change is inevitable in families, and transitions offer opportunities for positive adaptation and growth. Carter and McGoldrick (1988b) caution, however, that this view may not fit many families in today's society, including divorced and remarried families.

Hartman and Laird (1983) apply both family systems and family life cycle perspectives in their "family-centered" model for social work practice. In the interdisciplinary field of marriage and family therapy, a number of specialized clinical models have been developed for working with families (see Walsh, 1993, p. 45). In all of these models, the focus for change is the family system itself, with the assumption that change in patterns between and among family members will address whatever problem first brought a family member to the attention of a social worker.

The family system and family life cycle perspectives have produced two important tools for assessment:

■ A multigenerational **genogram** (Carter & McGoldrick, 1988b) uses visual symbols to represent family members (circles for females, squares for males) and their relationships (marriage and birth lines) across generations. Exhibit 14.1 is an example of a genogram.

■ A **family time line** or chronology depicts key dates and events in the family's life over time (Satir, 1983; Vosler, 1996). A family time line can be used to locate both stressors and strengths. Exhibit 14.2 provides an example of a family time line.

Using this theoretical approach for addressing Junior and his problematic behaviors, you would focus on understanding the family system—the connections and interactional patterns among family members. From the genogram (Exhibit 14.1) and conversation with Angela, you might explore the possibility that this family has unclear boundaries. Is Roy in or out of the family system? Is John in, and if so, for whom? What is the family's understanding of his relationship

EXHIBIT 14.1
Jones Family Genogram

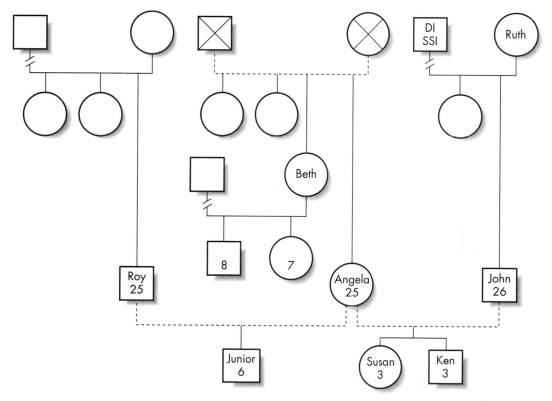

EXHIBIT 14.2
Jones Family Time Line

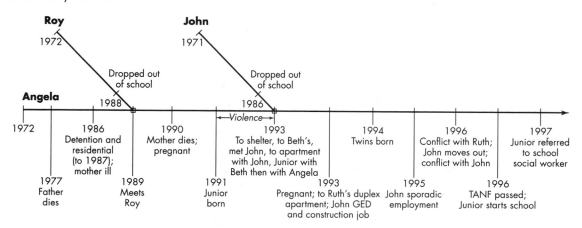

to Junior? Is Ruth in or out? What about Beth and her household? If family boundaries are unclear, Junior may be uncertain about who makes what decisions for him. Does Roy have parenting input or authority concerning Junior and his growth and development? Does Angela support—or subvert—Junior's relationship with Roy? Does John attempt to be a father to Junior? How does Junior view such efforts? Is either Ruth or Beth an additional parent for Junior? If so, how does he—and how does Angela—view their parenting efforts?

Organizational structures and roles in this family clearly entail a great deal of anxiety and frustration—even assuming that you and family members identify the primary family unit as Angela, Junior, Susan, and Ken, with John as parent to Susan and Ken and a kind of stepparent to Junior, and Beth, Ruth, and Roy in close but more auxiliary and supportive roles. Adequate and stable provision for basic family financial needs is an ongoing problem, creating escalating conflict within these multiple family relationships. Unable to manage successfully her multiple tasks and roles, Angela is becoming increasingly angry and frustrated. Attention to her depression is an immediate concern, but antidepressant medication alone is not likely to resolve her difficulties. Family beliefs that John alone should provide for the family financially, with Angela caring for home and children, may not be realistic, given his education and work history to date. Ruth's expectation that she will receive market-rate rent from John and Angela to supplement her low wages is probably unrealistic, at least at present, given their financial situation. Such conflicts over boundaries, roles, beliefs, and rules complicate communication and are likely making problem resolution almost impossible.

From a family life cycle perspective, "family with young children" is the current defining stage of Junior's family. This is normally a period of heavy child-rearing responsibilities, requiring time and energy for both physical and emotional care of quite dependent children. It is not surprising that the care of three active young children is draining for Angela, and letting her know that her experience in this regard is not unusual may provide some perspective on her feelings of being stretched to the limits of her endurance. There are also likely to be unresolved issues around Angela's breakup with Roy, which disrupted the normal development of their family. The "new couple" had moved very quickly into the next stage, being a family with a young child. The addition of a "new couple" relationship with John—and the addition of two more young children—has complicated relationships for all three of these parents (Angela, John, and Roy). During times of heavy child-rearing responsibilities, supportive relationships with adult friends can be very important for a primary caregiver such as Angela, but there is no indication that Angela has either time or energy for friendships outside of the extended family, or for self-care.

Thus, from the family systems and family life cycle perspectives, a primary area for clinical attention might be helping the family to create clear but permeable boundaries, including explicit arenas for family leadership and decision making. As noted previously, for example, discussion with family members could focus on clarifying Angela's role as the primary parent and authority for Junior, with others (John, as well as Beth, Ruth, and Roy) acting to support Angela's decisions and leadership. Additional areas for work might include developing positive communication and problem-solving patterns and delineating clear and age-appropriate rules for Junior's behavior and living situation—including adult time for him and each of his siblings individually and expectations for positive relationships with peers and teachers. This theoretical perspective assumes that work with both primary parenting adults—Angela and John—as well as supportive "kin" (Beth, Ruth, and hopefully Roy) will help the family move toward more consistent and positive interactional patterns, both for family living and for relationships with members of other social systems such as teachers and school personnel.

Often not addressed directly in this perspective, however, is the impact of constraints and changes in larger social systems. Any number of outside forces may subvert the positive new patterns that social workers and family members attempt to develop. For example, new welfare-to-work requirements for Angela are likely to leave her with less time and energy available to be a consistent parent for Junior and his siblings.

ABCX Model of Family Stress and Coping

Systems perspective
Social constructionist
perspective
Psychodynamic
perspective

The **ABCX model of family stress and coping** is based on work by Hill (1958) and was developed by McCubbin and his colleagues (McCubbin et al., 1980; McCubbin & Patterson, 1983). You have read about theories of individual stress and coping in Chapter 5; the ABCX model addresses family problems. It theorizes that to understand whether an event in the family system (A) becomes a crisis (X), we also need to understand both the family's resources (B) and the family's definitions (C) about the event.

Systems perspective

The ABCX model describes a "family transition process" following a stressor event. A period of disequilibrium is followed by three possible outcomes: (1) recovery to the family's previous level of functioning; (2) maladaptation, or permanent deterioration in the family's functioning; or (3) bonadaptation—improvement in the family's functioning over and above the previous level. Thus, under certain circumstances, a stressor event can actually be beneficial, if the family's coping process strengthens the family in the long term. They might, for instance, come together to deal with the crisis. One of the key influences on the long-term outcome is the level of resources available to the family both internally and from larger systems in which the family is embedded.

More recently, McCubbin and Patterson (1983) have conceptualized a *double* ABCX model, incorporating the concept of **stress pileup.** Over time, a series of crises may deplete the family's resources and expose the family to increasing risk of very negative outcomes (such as divorce, violence, or removal of children from the home). In this view, the balance of stressors and resources is an important consideration. Where there are significant numbers of stressors, there must also be a significant level of resources available to family members and the family as a whole.

McCubbin and Figley (1983) delineate two types of stressors. **Normative stressors** are the typical family life cycle transitions, such as the birth of a first child. **Nonnormative stressors** are potentially catastrophic events, such as natural disasters, drug abuse, unemployment, and family violence. These nonnormative events can quickly drain the family's resources and may leave family members feeling overwhelmed and exhausted. Lower-level but persistent stress—such as chronic illness or chronic poverty—can also result in stress pileup, resulting in instability within the family system and a sense of being out of control on the part of family members.

Two tools are especially useful for discovering patterns of stress, resources, and stress pileup:

EXHIBIT 14.3

Jones Family Ecomap

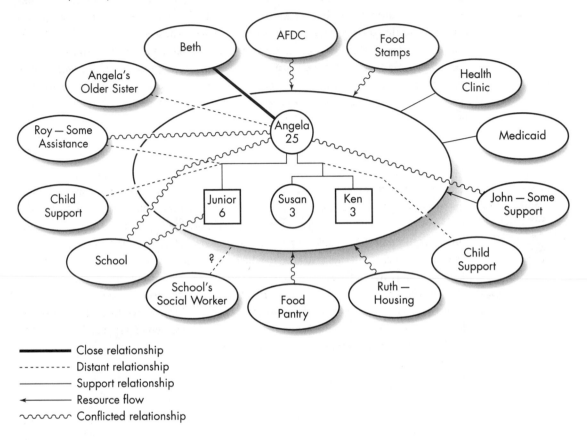

———— Close relationship
‑ ‑ ‑ ‑ ‑ ‑ ‑ Distant relationship
———— Support relationship
◄———— Resource flow
∿∿∿∿ Conflicted relationship

- An *ecomap* uses circles, lines, and arrows to show family relationships and the strength and directional flow of energy and resources to and from the family (Hartman & Laird, 1983; see also Vosler, 1996). Ecomaps help the social worker and the family to identify external sources of stress, conflict, and social support. Exhibit 14.3 is an example of an ecomap.

- A *family time line* helps to identify times in the family's life when events have "piled up." The social worker and the family can then begin to identify what resources have been tapped successfully in the past, as well as resource needs in the present. You can refer back to Exhibit 14.2 for an example of a family time line.

As you can see in the Jones family ecomap (Exhibit 14.3), Junior and his family are struggling with multiple stressors and currently have only a few resources to help them cope with the stress. Stress is coming primarily from relationships with Roy, John, Ruth, and Junior's school. The family is also stressed by inadequate income to meet necessary expenses. Not surprisingly, much of the interpersonal conflict revolves around financial needs and expectations, such as inadequate family and child support from Roy and John, and failure to pay rent as promised to Ruth.

Resources currently available to Angela and her family include Beth's emotional support and limited material support (such as the hand-me-down coat), as well as financial assistance from public sources (AFDC, food stamps, Medicaid) and the food pantry. Despite conflict between Angela and Ruth, Ruth has not yet evicted them and thus is providing substantial tangible support in the form of stable housing. Although Angela does not like—or feel good about—receiving public help in the form of AFDC, Food Stamps, Medicaid, and bags of groceries from the food pantry, these resources are providing her with much-needed assistance for the basic necessities of life. It is unclear whether the Jones family will consider you, the school social worker, as another stressor or as a resource for beginning to resolve some of the family's difficulties.

If the ecomap and the income and expense statement (the latter is discussed on page 420) are not enough to convince you, the Jones family time line (Exhibit 14.2) should alert you to the possibility of stress pileup for this family. Previous violence—especially between Roy and Angela—and its consequences may never have been dealt with. Although stable housing has been available to this family for the past three years, escalating conflict around John's unemployment, John and Angela's nonpayment of rent, and accumulating effects of chronic poverty (for example, no budgetary flexibility for a second winter coat for Junior) are likely to be affecting Angela's mental health, and therefore her ability to cope with the multitude of household tasks involved in raising three active and needy young children. Simply acknowledging the reality of stress pileup and lack of adequate resources may be a first important step in your establishing a positive relationship with this multiply stressed family.

Multilevel Family Practice Model

Systems perspective

The **multilevel family practice model** (Vosler, 1996) widens the social worker's theoretical framework to include the larger systems in which the family system is embedded—including the neighborhood, the local community, the state, the nation, and the current global socioeconomic system. Thus, the multilevel model is more broadly focused than the family systems perspective, acknowledging the economic, political, and cultural factors that affect which material resources are available to the family and how family members view their current situation and future challenges. This model recognizes, as suggested in Chapter 8, that the family institution is interrelated with other social institutions—religious, political, economic, educational, social welfare, health care, and mass media.

This model also incorporates a **developmental social construction view** (Vosler, 1996, p. 30), which alerts the social worker to the fact that current social institutions, along with their policies and programs (or lack of programs), have evolved over time and, therefore, can perhaps be modified. Consider, for example, recent changes in policies and programs designed to support low-income families. "Welfare reform" often assumes that jobs are available at wages that will enable the family provider ("breadwinner") to meet basic needs. That view is common among the political and economic elite, who have benefited recently from a booming economy and lower taxes. However, some state and local economies are doing better than others, and this assumption may be untenable for people living in areas of high unemployment or low prevailing wages or for people who lack the skills required in an information economy. Furthermore, basic support structures—such as affordable housing, quality child care, programs for after-school care and youth supervision, and affordable health insurance—may be beyond the means of substantial numbers of working poor families. Even when these supports are supposedly available in a state or even in a specific local community, they may not be truly accessible to a particular family who needs them because of lack of (or unreliable) transportation or because access requires substantial commitments of time and energy (such as travel outside the neighborhood where the family is currently living).

Social constructionist perspective

The picture for such families is grim, but it is not totally hopeless. The possibility exists that policymakers and the general public will observe the struggles of the working poor and once again institute policies to help them. However, change can occur only when social workers and other citizens become aware that current societal institutions are socially constructed and therefore, over time, can be modified or changed dramatically—for example, through social and economic development programs and policies. As a nation, the United States has substantially reduced poverty among the elderly population through the Social Security system; however, poverty among children continues to increase.

Several tools are available for assessment of multilevel family stressors and resources:

- **Monthly household income and expenses** can give the social worker and the family a quick look at current financial stress and resources (see Exhibit 14.4).

- The **family access to basic resources (FABR) chart** provides a more comprehensive look at potential supports and deficits by examining the family's access to a stable and adequate financial resource base (Vosler, 1990, 1996).

- A *home visit and neighborhood walk* provides the social worker with information about resources and stressors within the family's immediate environment.

- *Data mapping* examines the neighborhood's or community's patterns of poverty, housing, crime, basic and support services, and public transportation, providing a more comprehensive understanding of potential resources as well as gaps in services.

- *Agency context diagramming* represents visually a specific agency's links to other agencies and services.

These data sources can also provide information needed for effective program planning and policy changes at state, national, and even global levels.

Let's see how you could use these tools to develop a more accurate picture of the Jones family. Exhibit 14.4, the Jones family's monthly income and expenses, shows that income from AFDC and food stamps falls short of the family's basic living expenses by $60 per month—even though they currently have no expenses for rent and utilities. If Ruth forces Angela and her children out of their current housing, they will need at least an additional $400–500 monthly plus a deposit to pay for an apartment and utilities. Given the changes required by "welfare reform," Angela will be ineligible for Temporary Aid to Needy Families (TANF, which has now replaced AFDC at national and state levels) within two years. She will be expected to find a job that will enable her to be "self-sufficient." However, she will then have additional expenses of child care for the twins, after-school care for Junior, work expenses (including clothing and lunches for

EXHIBIT 14.4

Jones Family
Monthly Income
and Expenses

Income		Expenses	
Wages	$0	Rent	$0
Child Support	$0	Utilities	$0
AFDC	$350	Telephone	$25
Food Stamps	$340	Food and Household supplies (4–5 people)	($28/week) $602
Total	**$690**	Laundry	$23
		Clothes	$50
		School Supplies	$25
		Transportation (Bus/Car fare)	$25
		Total	**$750**

Income – Expenses = –$60

herself), transportation, and possibly medical insurance (if her employer does not pay the total premium as a work benefit). Angela's lack of education and work experience make it unlikely that she will be able to find a job at wage and benefit levels that will cover all of the family's basic needs. Thus, she will need to turn to Junior's father, Roy, and the twins' father, John, for child support payments. However, unless the two men have jobs that pay above the minimum wage, they may not be able to provide much in the way of stable financial support. Complicating the current picture is Ruth's limited income, which makes it important for her to receive at least some income from her "renters." On the plus side, once she is employed, Angela will be eligible for the Earned Income Tax Credit (EITC), which will provide very low-level—but needed—support.

Conflict perspective   A home visit and neighborhood walk would reveal additional stressors for Angela and her family, including a weekly walk with the children through their dangerous neighborhood to the crowded and rather run-down laundromat; high prices at the local convenience store; and the vacant lot next door—the only neighborhood "park"—where older youth and young adults "hang out" with unsupervised younger children. The nearest bus stop is two blocks away, and bus connections to other areas of the city involve transfers and long waits for the next bus. The Joneses' neighborhood has no banks, chain grocery stores, or major retail outlets. There is no equipment on the school playground, since school officials assess that "it would just get broken or stolen." Because of their uncertain income and inability to pay rent regularly, many families move into the neighborhood only to move out again six to nine months later. The school reports that at least 50 percent of the children entering in September will be gone by June, replaced by the same number of new faces—and often by increased numbers of students. Neighborhood residents as well as service providers are frustrated and angry, and at times seem despairing and hopeless.

Theoretically, a number of national, state, and local programs are available to this family. The JOBS program (for mothers) and Parents' Fair Share (PFS, for fathers) are designed to help parents move from welfare to work through education, job training, and work experience. Some child care is available through the Head Start program; however, there are long waiting lists for a child to be accepted into any of the programs (Early Start, Head Start, Even Start). Counseling, parent education, and support groups funded by the United Way and other nonprofit organizations are not currently available in Angela's immediate neighborhood, and their outreach efforts have not been particularly successful in recruiting low-income clients such as Angela, John, and Roy. The school board has been forced to eliminate funding for after-school activities such as tutoring and sports, because of budget deficits and city residents' abhorrence of tax increases. Over the past decade, higher-income families have moved to suburban areas in the surrounding counties, taking with them their tax dollars for schools, parks, playgrounds, and community activities.

The employment that Angela, John, and Roy—and even Ruth—have found over the past several years has for the most part consisted of low-wage jobs without benefits, and the work has often been only temporary or part-time. With unstable and inadequate income have come escalating family conflict and family instability. From the perspective of the adult members of this extended family, the future looks neither stable nor hopeful, and talking with the family about planning for positive change is likely to be very difficult.

Strengths Perspective

Humanistic perspective

The final "lens" for understanding and working with families to be discussed briefly here is the **strengths perspective**. This framework has developed primarily out of work with African American families (Boyd-Franklin, 1989; McAdoo, 1997) and with households headed by women (Miller, 1987). Often in the past, families that did not conform to the "traditional" model—two heterosexual parents with the male as the primary breadwinner and authority figure (Macklin, 1980)—were considered, by definition, to be deficient and potentially pathological. More recently, both researchers and practitioners have begun to document the strengths of nontraditional families and to advocate that social workers identify important stresses and strengths among their clients. Identifying strengths can change the social worker's view of where to begin and create a hopefulness about the future, so that the climate changes from one of despair over an overwhelming multiplicity of problems to an appreciation of how the family meets challenges to the best of its ability. Helping family members identify how they have coped creatively with adversity in the past may help them find hope for making changes in the present.

Although Angela, Junior, Susan, Ken, and John face many difficult stresses and resource deficits, they also—as individuals and as a family—have a number of strengths on which to build. John has completed a GED and has some work experience. Angela has begun work on her GED and has a small amount of work experience as well. In the past, Angela was able to end a violent relationship with Roy, moving herself and Junior to a safe environment. Angela has the support of her sister Beth, both emotionally and at times financially. John's mother Ruth has provided stable housing for this fragile family for nearly four years, and has continued to support John by allowing him to live at home when conflict escalates between him and Angela.

In spite of severe income deficits, Angela has been able to care reasonably well for her three children, combining public supports, help from the children's fathers, and periodic assistance from the neighborhood food pantry. When not overstressed by financial difficulties, John and Angela have a strong positive relationship. John states that he loves both the twins and Junior, and is committed to being a good father to all three. Roy also wants to be a good father to his son Junior, and states that he wants to work out a positive co-parenting relationship with Angela that will help Junior grow up healthy and strong—"so maybe he won't make some of the mistakes I've made in my life."

The school, as an institution in the neighborhood, may serve as a base for a team of professionals and local residents who work toward identifying neighborhood needs and funding resources for programs and services. You, as a school-based or neighborhood-based social worker, might spearhead the process of developing local education and training programs, local employment opportunities, counseling and parenting education services, child care, after-school care, youth services, economic development in the neighborhood, health care services, and opportunities for residents to meet around important issues and celebrate renewal of their neighborhood, their families, and their lives.

Issues of Diversity

As you can see from this review of theoretical perspectives, there is no one way to view families in order to work effectively with them toward positive change. The "correct" perspective is the one that best serves a particular family. The reality today is that a great deal of diversity exists among families, both in the United States and globally.

In the past, many of the clinical models for family practice were based on work with primarily middle-class and often two-biological-parent European American families. Family research in the 1960s and 1970s often relied on white middle-class families as subjects and respondents and then generalized findings for this specific population to "all families." In their 1980 article reviewing the family scholarship of the previous decade, Staples and Mirande (1980) called attention to this "cultural deviant" approach to family research, which relegated culturally different families with a variety of ethnic backgrounds—Asian, African American, Hispanic, and Native American—to the category of deviants. They advocated acknowledgment of "different, but functional, family forms" (Staples & Mirande, 1980, p. 159), which they called a **cultural variant approach**. In their view, "different" does not necessarily mean "deviant" or "deficient."

Others have advocated the cultural variant approach for understanding a wide variety of "different" family forms, including single-parent and remarried households, gay and lesbian families, foster families, families with one or more adopted children, extended family households, and couples without children. Walsh (1993) points out the need to examine our understanding of what is "normal" for these various family forms, because change efforts by practitioners are inevitably guided by what we consider to be "healthy" or "normal" patterns and behaviors.

A helpful guide to cultural diversity among a variety of families is McGoldrick, Giordano, and Pearce's book, *Ethnicity and Family Therapy* (1996; see also Mindel, Habenstein, & Wright,

1998), which discusses, for example, family differences in beliefs, rules, communication patterns, and organizational norms. Understanding differences as variations on themes rather than "deviations" or "deficiencies" is often a key component in working effectively with a family from an ethnic background different from your own.

Up-to-date family research is another important resource to help you understand specific stresses and resource needs among a variety of families. Empirical studies have demonstrated, for example, that children raised in a single-parent or remarried family can grow up physically, mentally, and psychologically healthy (Hetherington, Stanley-Hagan, & Anderson, 1989), but we also know that risks are involved with these family structures. Single-parent families are at risk for poverty and stress pileup (McLanahan & Sandefur, 1994), and remarried families tend to be complex and often must cope with a variety of internal stressors (Hetherington et al., 1989; Vosler & Proctor, 1991). Similarly, emerging bodies of empirically based literature are focusing on gay and lesbian families (Green & Bozett, 1991; Laird, 1993), families coping with serious illness and disability (Rolland, 1993), adolescent parents and nonmarital co-parenting (Vosler & Robertson, 1998), families in later life (Brubaker, 1991; Mancini & Blieszner, 1991), and grandparents serving as primary caregivers for grandchildren (Jendrek, 1993, 1994).

As we widen our understanding of "normal" to include diverse family forms and processes, we must not lose sight of the fact that certain behaviors and arrangements in families are neither normal nor healthy. Behaviors that must always be of grave concern to social workers include abuse and violence, sexual abuse, neglect, and prejudice and discrimination—whether based on racism, sexism, or other forms of exclusion such as sexual orientation, disability, age, class, religion, or ethnicity.

Finally, remember that different approaches help different families. A recent review has found that traditional family therapy, which focuses on family-level change alone, is not effective with "isolated, impoverished, single-parent families" (Proctor, Davis, & Vosler, 1995), especially in the United States. On the other hand, there is growing evidence that traditional family therapy, especially that based on the social behavioral and family systems perspectives, is effective with nonpoor families for such specific problems as marital discord, substance abuse, schizophrenia, psychosomatic disorders, and juvenile delinquency (Proctor et al., 1995). However, one overview of empirical evaluation studies found that evaluation "research of any sort has been conducted on only 35 of 150 (23 percent) possible method-problem combinations, and probable effectiveness has been shown on only 13 (9 percent) of the combinations" (Proctor et al., 1995, p. 947). Clearly, much more empirical research remains to be done in this area.

Elsewhere, a small study in Singapore, based on a multilevel family practice approach, found that making resources available in the neighborhood environment of low-income, highly stressed families—connected with a neighborhood-based family service agency, staffed by social work professionals trained in family systems practice—helped to create positive change for some families (Nair, Blake, & Vosler, 1997). In addition, Hopps, Pinderhughes, and Shankar (1995) describe effective community-based social work practice with a number of overwhelmed individuals and families in the United States today. However, further work is clearly needed in evaluating theories and models and in understanding the lives of impoverished families, particularly as poverty increases in the United States and as neighborhoods and local communities struggle with decreasing resources.

IMPLICATIONS FOR SOCIAL WORK PRACTICE

This discussion of families and family life, in the context of larger social systems, suggests several practice principles:

- Assess families from a variety of theoretical perspectives. Given recent economic shifts, be particularly aware of the impact of changes in larger systems on families' resources and functioning.

- Utilize appropriate family assessment tools, including the genogram, ecomap, time line, monthly income and expenses, FABR, home visit, neighborhood walk, data mapping, agency context diagramming, program evaluation, and policy analysis.

- Understand the neighborhood and local community of each of the families with which you work.

- Understand policies and changes at state and national levels, and how they affect both your own work and the lives of all families—particularly lower-income, stressed families.

- Collaborate with other social workers and human service providers in making needed changes at neighborhood, local, state, and national levels that will support families and enable your work with specific families to be effective.

- Where appropriate, encourage family members to become involved in neighborhood, local, state, and national efforts for positive change.

- As appropriate, work toward your agency's becoming involved in policy and advocacy work on behalf of families, including development of needed programs and services.

- Become involved in continuing efforts to develop up-to-date empirical knowledge about a variety of families, and the resources needed by families to grow strong and to raise healthy children.

MAIN POINTS

1. How we define *family* shapes our view of family membership and our approach in working with different types of families. A broad definition provides latitude for the social worker to explore with family members a variety of roles and connections.

2. Recent demographic trends among U.S. families include increases in single-parent and remarried households; growth of the elderly population; an increase in labor force participation among women, including mothers of very young children; and

increases in racial, ethnic, and cultural diversity among the U.S. population as a whole.

3. Research shows that poverty is associated with family instability, divorce, nonmarital childbearing, and risk for negative child outcomes.

4. Changes in the U.S. economy over the past several decades include a more unequal distribution of income and the loss of middle-income jobs, especially for men; increasing numbers of "working poor" families; and increasing necessity for families in the lower socioeconomic groups to have two full-time wage earners in order to meet basic needs.

5. Theoretical "lenses" for understanding families can be classified into five broad groupings: the social behavioral perspective, the family systems and family life cycle perspectives, the ABCX model of family stress and coping, multilevel family practice, and a strengths perspective.

6. The social behavioral perspective focuses on family communication, rules, and learning—including how family members positively and negatively exchange information and shape members' behaviors.

7. The family systems and family life cycle perspectives address family boundaries, organizational structures and roles, shared beliefs and rules, and communication patterns as these evolve and change over time. Family life cycle stages include single young adults, the couple, families with young children, families with adolescents, families launching children and moving on, and families in later life. Transitions from one stage to the next involve distinctive challenges and change, offering opportunities for new adaptations.

8. The ABCX model of family stress and coping directs our attention to both stressors and resources and the necessity for balancing them so the family can cope with change. Families inevitably encounter both normative and nonnormative stressors. Stress pileup can overwhelm even the strongest families. Stressor events can lead to deterioration in family functioning, but can also be opportunities for growth and positive change.

9. The multilevel family practice model widens the social worker's focus to include the larger systems in which the family is embedded, including the neighborhood, the local community, the state, the nation, and the global socioeconomic system. Economic changes at multiple levels affect families' ability to provide an adequate and stable financial base for family life. Resources and services in the neighborhood and local community are needed to support families in their important work of raising children.

10. A strengths perspective directs the attention of both worker and family members to supports and resources currently in place for the family, and to the family's successful coping efforts in past situations of adversity.

11. Work with families must take into consideration the diversity of families in today's society. The cultural variant approach values diversity and directs the social worker toward understanding the specific stresses and strengths experienced by families of diverse ethnic, racial, cultural, and religious backgrounds; single-parent households; remarried families; and families that vary from our traditional conceptions because of sexual orientation, age, disability, or foster or adoptive status.

12. Further research and knowledge building are necessary to understand how best to work with low-income families stressed by economic and social changes in larger systems. This work is an important challenge for all social work practitioners, researchers, and educators.

KEY TERMS

ABCX model of family stress and coping
cultural variant approach
developmental social construction view
family
family access to basic resources (FABR) chart
family life cycle
family systems perspective
family time line

genogram
monthly household income and expenses
multilevel family practice model
nonnormative stressors
normative stressors
strengths perspective
stress pileup

WORLD WIDE WEB RESOURCES

The Administration for Children and Families (ACF)
http://www.acf.dhhs.gov/
Government agency that is part of the Department of Health and Human Services. Site contains fact sheets about children and families, and information about ACF programs such as AFDC, child support enforcement, Head Start, and TANF

Council on Contemporary Families
http://www.slip.net/~ccf/
Nonprofit organization that promotes an inclusive view of families, including single parent and gay and lesbian families. Site contains information and research on families, along with links to other Internet resources.

Family Violence Awareness Page
http://www.famvi.com/
Site maintained by Gary Templeton. Contains facts and statistics about domestic violence, family violence and child abuse, local and national hotlines, and links to other Internet resources.

Margaret Ryan at Sacred Heart Center:
Social Work Practice in a
Multidimensional Environment

Margaret Ryan is executive director of Sacred Heart Center (SHC), a nonprofit multiservice community center founded in 1990 to serve an impoverished urban neighborhood. Margaret describes the services provided by SHC as "child-centered, family-focused, and neighborhood-based." They include:

- Programs for young children. Licensed day care, Head Start, and early childhood education (K–2).

- Programs for school-age children. After-school and summer programs, Boy and Girl Scouts, recreation programs (soccer, basketball, cheerleading, outdoor adventure, and social and cultural outings).

- Programs for adolescents. After-school and summer activities, job skills training, part-time employment placement, and academic support.

- Programs for families. Family literacy program (with child care provided); parenting skills training; parent support group; job readiness training; baby clothing, food, and equipment; emergency food and fuel assistance.

SHC also opens its facilities to community groups.

Margaret clearly sees the environment in which she works as multidimensional. In my conversation with her, I heard reference to physical environment, social institutions and social structure, culture, formal organizations, community, social movements, small groups, and families.

A drive around the neighborhood reveals empty lots where housing once stood, dilapidated buildings, five or six storefront churches, several small convenience stores, several laundromats, and, on the periphery, a grocery store that is a part of a chain developed specifically for central-city residents. There is one elementary school, but children must leave the neighborhood to attend middle and high school.

Margaret reports that she is constantly aware that her agency and the community it serves exist in an outdoor world that threatens—the mass media present frequent reminders that this neighborhood has the highest crime rate in the city. Margaret regularly makes decisions about how to keep people safe. She and the board of directors of SHC have perpetual discussions about whether to keep the Center's front door locked or unlocked. They continue to leave the door unlocked, because they think that this is an important symbol that signifies that they do not buy into the fear of the environment.

Margaret reports, however, that the violence in the neighborhood has a serious impact on families. Adults who use services at SHC talk about not "messing with people" as the one best way to stay safe. Margaret is concerned that this leads to social isolation. There is little interaction among neighbors, and gathering places are few. Children act the violence out, and the Center must respond with programs that address issues such as anger management and conflict resolution. Neighborhood children get few opportunities to play outside; they are kept inside because the outside is threatening. Recently, student volunteers from a prestigious private high school worked with students at SHC to organize a "Children's Walk Against Violence." Participants walked from SHC to city hall, and two participants spoke to the city council about their dream of a safe neighborhood.

The city has a redevelopment plan that includes demolishing all public housing units in the neighborhood. The replacement housing will be a mix of low- and middle-income housing, resulting in a diminished stock of low-income housing. Most of the families served by SHC currently live in public housing, and Margaret is concerned about their future.

SHC is affiliated with the Catholic diocese. This affiliation influences Margaret's work. She is sensitive to Catholic theology in her public statements, but she thinks that overall this affiliation is positive. It provides an umbrella that allows her to say and do a lot. She draws heavily on Catholic teachings about social justice and the preferential option for people who are poor. She thinks this makes it possible for her to talk more seriously about social work's social justice mission than she typically hears from other social workers. SHC does not evangelize, but Margaret is proud that the community center is based on the faith perspective of "walking with" people—for the long haul or as long as it takes. Staff acknowledge the spiritual dimension of the people they serve and draw on it as a resource in service provision, when appropriate.

SHC also works closely with the local Junior League, which has been generous with money and volunteer time to support SHC. Sometimes there is tension about agendas—as there could be about the housing redevelopment plan—but Margaret welcomes that tension. She thinks that social workers should become more comfortable negotiating such tensions—that we too often avoid collaborating with elite sponsors because we are not comfortable with difference in worldviews. In Margaret's view, if we don't actively engage the tensions, we lose opportunities to educate, build bridges, and heal wounds. She comments that she is willing to enter into dialogue with almost anybody—that she starts from the premise that people can agree about the end goal of improving life for families even when they don't agree about means to that end.

Margaret is an active member of an advocacy group that developed in response to "welfare reform" legislation passed over the past few years. Currently, this group is focusing on making sure that clients are fully informed of the appeals process in the social welfare system. They are planning to study child-care needs of women leaving welfare and to lobby for policies that put greater focus on training and education.

Margaret was recently appointed chair of the legislative committee of her state chapter of the National Association of Social Workers (NASW). She would like to see this organization put greater emphasis on social conditions and social justice issues—and less emphasis on advocating for the status of the profession.

Every Monday night for the past three years, Margaret has led a support group for parents who are trying to improve their parenting. About half of the group's 15 members have been ordered by the courts to attend these meetings because of child abuse or neglect.

Margaret and the staff at SHC are always looking for new ways to get families involved with the center's programs for children. Last year, they sponsored a raffle for a car. They celebrated the raffle drawing with a festive party at the Center. Arrangements were made for staff from the Children's Museum to be present with an inviting array of planned activities. Margaret emphasizes that the families who come to SHC really want things to be better for their children. The children represent hope for the future, and the motivation to try.

Something to Think About

Margaret Ryan gives a lot of thought to the multiple dimensions of environment in her work at Sacred Heart Center. The following questions will help you reflect on Margaret's work in this multidimensional environment and consider how you might work in similar situations:

- What evidence do you see that Margaret recognizes the influence of the physical environment on human behavior? Which social institutions seem influential in the life of the community served by Sacred Heart Center? What do you learn about the neighborhood culture and the culture of the Sacred Heart Center? What formal organizations are involved? What communities? Do you see any evidence of or possibilities for social movement activity? What types of small groups are evident? How does Sacred Heart Center work with families?

- Which dimensions of the environment seem most important to Margaret Ryan? If you were the director of Sacred Heart Center, which dimensions of the environment would seem most important to you? Where would you target your interventions? Why?

- Which perspectives on formal organizations seem to be reflected in Margaret Ryan's work? If you were director of Sacred Heart Center, what theoretical perspectives on formal organizations would seem useful to you? Why?

- If you were director of Sacred Heart Center, where would you stand on these issues: community as context for practice versus target of practice; agency orientation versus social action; conflict model of practice versus collaborative model; expert versus partner in the social change process?

WORKS CITED

Achterberg, J. (1985). *Imagery in healing: Shamanism and modern medicine.* Boston: Shambhala.

Adams, J., & Jacobsen, P. (1964). Effects of wage inequities on work quality. *Journal of Abnormal and Social Psychology, 69,* 19–25.

Adams, R. (1992). Is happiness a home in the suburbs? The influence of urban versus suburban neighborhoods on psychological health. *Journal of Community Psychology, 20,* 353–371.

Ader, R., Felten, D., & Cohen, N. (1990). Interactions between the brain and the immune system. *Annual Review of Pharmacology and Toxicology, 30,* 561–602.

Agger, R., Goldrich, D., & Swanson, B. (1964). *The rulers and the ruled: Political power and impotence in American communities.* New York: Wiley.

Aiello, J., Baum, A., & Gormley, F. (1981). Social determinants of residential crowding stress. *Personality and Social Psychology Bulletin, 7,* 643–649.

Akande, A. (1997). Determinants of personal space among South African students. *Journal of Psychology, 131,* 569–571.

Aldrich, H., & Pfeffer, J. (1976). Environments of organizations. In A. Inkeles, J. Coleman, & N. Smelser (Eds.), *Annual review of sociology* (Vol. 2, pp. 79–105). Palo Alto, CA: Annual Reviews.

Aldwin, C. (1994). *Stress, coping, and development.* New York: Guilford.

Allen-Meares, P., & Lane, B. A. (1987). Grounding social work practice in theory: Ecosystems. *Social Casework: The Journal of Contemporary Social Work, 68,* 517–521.

Altman, I. (1975). *The environment and social behavior: Privacy, personal space, territoriality and crowding.* Monterey, CA: Brooks/Cole.

Altman, I. (1993). Dialectics, physical environments, and personal relationships. *Communication Monographs, 60,* 26–34.

Altman, I., & Low, S. (Eds.). (1992). *Place attachment.* New York: Plenum.

Altman, I., & Rogoff, B. (1987). World views in psychology: Trait, interactional, organismic, and transactional perspectives. In D. Stokols & I. Altman (Eds.), *Handbook of environmental psychology, Vol. 1* (pp. 7–40). New York: Wiley.

Amato–von Hemert, K. (1994). Should social work education address religious issues? Yes! *Journal of Social Work Education, 36,* 7–11, 16–17.

American Heart Association. (1997a). *High blood pressure statistics.* [On-line]. Available: http://www.americanheart.org/Heart_and_Stroke_A_Z_Guide/hbps.html

American Heart Association. (1997b). *Statistics.* [On-line]. Available: http://www.americanheart.org/Heart_and_Stroke_A_Z_Guide/hbps.html

American Psychiatric Association. (1994). *Diagnostic and statistical manual of mental disorders* (4th ed.). Washington, DC: Author.

Americans with Disabilities Act of 1990 (Public Law 101-336). 104 Stat. 327.

Anderson, R., & Carter, I. (1974). *Human behavior in the social environment: A social systems approach.* Chicago: Aldine.

Anderson, R., & Carter, I. (1990). *Human behavior in the social environment: A social systems approach* (4th ed.). New York: de Gruyter.

Anderson, T. L. (1994). Drug abuse and identity: Linking micro and macro factors. *The Sociological Quarterly, 35,* 159–174.

Andrich, D., & Styles, I. (1994). Psychometric evidence of intellectual growth spurts in early adolescence. *Journal of Early Adolescence, 14,* 328–344.

Ang, I., & Hermes, J. (1996). Gender and/in media consumption. In J. Curran & M. Gurevitch (Eds.), *Mass media and society* (2nd ed.) (pp. 325–347). New York: Arnold.

Assagioli, R. (1965). *Psychosynthesis: A manual of principles and techniques.* New York: Viking Penguin.

Assagioli, R. (1973). *The act of will.* New York: Penguin.

Assagioli, R. (1989). Self-realization and psychological disturbances. In S. Grof & C. Grof (Eds.), *Spiritual emergency: When personal transformation becomes a crisis* (pp. 27–48). Los Angeles: Jeremy P. Tarcher.

Auslander, G., & Litwin, H. (1987). The parameters of network intervention: A social work application. *Social Service Review, 61,* 305–318.

Averill, J. (1980). A constructionist view of emotion. In R. Plutchik & H. Kellerman (Eds.), *Emotion theory, research, and experience: Vol. 1. Theories of emotion.* London: Academic Press.

Babbie, E. (1994). *What is society?* Thousand Oaks, CA: Pine Forge.

Bachelder, J., & Hilton, J. (1994). Implications of the Americans with Disabilities Act of 1990 for elderly persons. *American Journal of Occupational Therapy, 48*(1), 73–81.

Bagdikian, B. (1997). *The media monopoly* (5th ed.). Boston: Beacon Press.

Baldwin, J. (1975). Urban criminality and the "problem" estate. *Local Government Studies, 1,* 12–20.

Baldwin, J. (1979, July 29). If Black English isn't a language, then tell me, what is it? *New York Times.*

Balkwell, J. W. (1994). Status. In M. Foschi & E. J. Lawler (Eds.), *Group processes: Sociological analyses* (pp. 119–148). Chicago: Nelson-Hall.

Bandura, A. (1977a). Self-efficacy: Toward a unifying theory of behavioral change. *Psychological Review, 84,* 191–215.

Bandura, A. (1977b). *Social learning theory.* Englewood Cliffs, NJ: Prentice-Hall.

Bandura, A. (1986). *Social foundations of thought and action: A social cognitive theory.* Englewood Cliffs, NJ: Prentice-Hall.

Banyard, V. L., & Graham-Bermann, S. A. (1993). Can women cope? A gender analysis of theories of coping with stress. *Psychology of Women Quarterly, 17,* 303–318.

Barber, J. G. (1994). Alcohol addiction: Private trouble or social issue? *Social Service Review, 68,* 521–535.

Barker, R. (1968). *Ecological psychology: Concepts and methods for studying the environment of human behavior.* Stanford, CA: Stanford University Press.

Barker, R. L. (1987). *The social work dictionary.* Silver Spring, MD: National Association of Social Workers.

Barker, R., & Gump, P. (1964). *Big school, small school: High school size and student behavior.* Standford, CA: Stanford University Press.

Bates, R. (1950). *Interaction process analysis: A method for the study of small groups.* Reading, MA: Addison-Wesley.

Baugh, J. (1987). The situational dimension of linguistic power. *Language Arts, 64,* 234–240.

Baum, A. (1991). Toxins, technology, and natural disasters. In A. Monat & R. Lazarus (Eds.), *Stress and coping: An anthology* (pp. 97–139). New York: Columbia University Press.

Baum, A., & Davis, G. (1980). Reducing the stress of high-density living: An architectural intervention. *Journal of Personality and Social Psychology, 38,* 471–481.

Baum, A., & Valins, S. (1977). *Architecture and social behavior.* Hillsdale, NJ: Erlbaum.

Beck, A. T., & Weishaar, M. (1995). Cognitive therapy. In R. J. Corsini & D. Wedding (Eds.), *Current psychotherapies* (5th ed.) (pp. 229–261). Itasca, IL: Peacock.

Becker, G. (1981). *A treatise on the family.* Cambridge, MA: Harvard University Press.

Becker, H. (1957). Current sacred-secular theory and its development. In H. Becker & A. Boskoff (Eds.), *Modern sociological theory in continuity and change* (pp. 137–185). New York: Dryden Press.

Becvar, D., & Becvar, R. (1996). *Family therapy: A systemic integration* (3rd ed.). Boston: Allyn & Bacon.

Begun, A. L. (1993). Human behavior and the social environment: The vulnerability, risk, and resilience model. *Journal of Social Work Education, 29*(1), 26–35.

Bellah, R., Madsen, R., Sullivan, W., Swidler, A., & Tipton, S. (1985). *Habits of the heart: Individualism and commitment in American life.* Berkeley: University of California Press.

Benedict, R. (1946). *The chrysanthemum and the sword.* Boston: Houghton Mifflin.

Benedict, R. (1989). *Patterns of culture.* Boston: Houghton Mifflin. (Original work published 1934)

Bentley, K. J., & Walsh, J. (1996). *The social worker and psychotropic medication: Toward effective collaboration with mental health clients, families, and providers.* Pacific Grove, CA: Brooks/Cole.

Berck, J. (1992). *No place to be: Voices of homeless children.* Boston: Houghton Mifflin.

Berger, P., & Luckman, T. (1967). *The social construction of reality.* Garden City, NY: Doubleday.

Berkman, B., Millar, S., Holmes, W., & Bonander, E. (1991). Predicting elderly cardiac patients at risk for readmission. *Social Work in Health Care, 16*(1), 21–38.

Berlin, S. (1983). Cognitive-behavioral approaches. In A. Rosenblatt & Diana Waldfogel (Eds.), *Handbook of clinical social work* (pp. 1095–1119). San Francisco: Jossey-Bass.

Bernstein, P. (1997). *American work values: Their origin and development.* Albany: State University of New York Press.

Berzoff, J. (1989). From separation to connection: Shifts in understanding women's development. *Affilia, 4,* 45–58.

Besser, G. M., & Thorner, M. O. (1994). *Clinical endocrinology* (2nd ed.). London: Times Mirror International.

Blau, P. (1964). *Exchange and power in social life.* New York: Wiley.

Blau, P., & Scott, W. (1962). *Formal organizations.* San Francisco: Chandler.

Blood, R., & Wolfe, D. (1960). *Husbands and wives: The dynamics of married living.* New York: Free Press.

Bloom, M. (1984). *Configurations of human behavior: Life span development in social environments.* New York: Macmillan.

Bloom, M. (1990). *Introduction to the drama of social work.* Itasca, IL: Peacock.

Blumer, H. (1969). *Symbolic interactionism: Perspective and method.* Englewood Cliffs, NJ: Prentice-Hall.

Blumler, J., & Gurevitch. M. (1996). Media change and social change: Linkages and junctures. In J. Curran & M. Gurevitch (Eds.), *Mass media and society* (2nd ed.) (pp. 120–137). New York: Arnold.

Boas, F. (1948). *Race, language and culture.* New York: Free Press. (Original work published 1940)

Bohannan, P. (1995). *How culture works.* New York: Free Press.

Booth, A. (1976). *Urban crowding and its consequences.* New York: Praeger.

Boubekri, M., Hull, R., & Boyer, L. (1991). Impact of window size and sunlight penetration on office workers' mood and satisfaction. *Environment and Behavior, 23,* 474–493.

Bourdieu, P. (1977). *Outline of a theory of practice.* New York: Cambridge University Press.

Bourgois, P. (1995). *In search of respect: Selling crack in El Barrio.* New York: Cambridge University Press.

Boyd-Franklin, N. (1987). Group therapy for black women: A therapeutic support model. *American Journal of Orthopsychiatry, 57,* 394–401.

Boyd-Franklin, N. (1989). *Black families in therapy: A multisystems approach.* New York: Guilford.

Bozeman, B. (1987). *All organizations are public: Bridging public and private organizational theories.* San Francisco: Jossey-Bass.

Brende, J. O., & Goldsmith, R. (1991). Post-traumatic stress disorder in families. *Journal of Contemporary Psychotherapy, 21*(2), 115–124.

Breton, M. (1989). Liberation theology, group work, and the right of the poor and oppressed to participate in the life of the community. *Social Work with Groups, 12*(3), 5-18.

Brewster, K., Billy, J., & Grady, W. (1993). Social context and adolescent behavior: The impact of community on the transition to sexual activity. *Social Forces, 71,* 713–740.

Bricker-Jenkins, M., Hooyman, N. R., & Gottlieb, N. (Eds.). (1991). *Feminist social work practice in clinical settings.* Newbury Park, CA: Sage.

Briggs, E. (1994, May 27). Islam faith faces changes. *Richmond Times-Dispatch,* pp. A1, A14.

Bronfenbrenner, U. (1989). Ecological systems theory. *Annals of Child Development, 6,* 187–249.

Brubaker, T. H. (1991). Families in later life: A burgeoning research area. In A. Booth (Ed.), *Contemporary families: Looking forward, looking back* (pp. 226–248). Minneapolis: National Council on Family Relations.

Bruner, J. (1990). *Acts of meaning.* Cambridge, MA: Harvard University Press.

Budman, S. H., Soldz, S., Demby, A., Davis, M., & Merry, J. (1993). What is cohesiveness? An empirical examination. *Small Group Research, 24,* 199–216.

Burgess, R., & Nielsen, J. (1974). An experimental analysis of some structural determinants of equitable and inequitable exchange relationships. *American Sociological Review, 39,* 427–443.

Burrell, G., & Morgan, G. (1979). *Sociological paradigms and organizational analysis.* London: Heinemann.

Burt, M., & Katz, B. (1987). Dimensions of recovery from rape: Focus on growth outcomes. *Journal of Interpersonal Violence, 2,* 57–82.

Burt, R. (1983). *Corporate profits and cooperation: Networks of market constraints and directorate ties in the American economy.* New York: Academic Press.

Burton, C. A., & Richardson, R. C. (1996). Following in faith: The study of an African American caregiver. *Social Work and Christianity, 23*(2), 141–145.

Burton, L. (1981). *A critical analysis and review of the research on Outward Bound and related programs.* Unpublished doctoral dissertation, Rutgers University, New Brunswick, NJ.

Burton, L. M. (1995, September). Family structure and nonmarital fertility: Perspectives from ethnographic research. In U.S. Department of Health and Human Services (Public Health Service, Centers for Disease Control and Prevention, National Center for Health Statistics), *Report to Congress on out-of-wedlock childbearing* (pp. 147–165). Washington, DC: U.S. Government Printing Office (DHHS Pub. No. (PHS) 95-1257).

Caldwell, G., Stiehr, K., Modell, J., & Del Campo, S. (1994). Differing levels of low fertility. In S. Langlois (Ed.), *Convergence or divergence? Comparing recent social trends in industrial societies* (pp. 43–87). Buffalo: McGill–Queen's University Press.

Campbell, R. J. (1996). *Psychiatric dictionary* (7th ed.). New York: Oxford University Press.

Canda, E. R. (1988). Spirituality, religious diversity and social work practice. *Social Casework, 69*(4), 238–247.

Canda, E. R. (1990). An holistic approach to prayer for social work practice. *Social Thought, 16*(3), 3–13.

Canda, E. R. (1997a). Does religion and spirituality have a significant place in the core HBSE curriculum? Yes. In M. Bloom & W. C. Klein (Eds.), *Controversial issues in human behavior in the social environment* (pp. 172–177, 183–184). Boston: Allyn & Bacon.

Canda, E. R. (1997b). Spirituality. *Encyclopedia of social work: 1997 supplement* (19th ed.). Washington, DC: National Association of Social Workers Press.

Canda, E. R., & Chambers, D. (1994). Should spiritual principles guide social policy? Yes. In H. J. Karger & J. Midgley (Eds.), *Controversial issues in social policy* (pp. 64–69, 74–78). Boston: Allyn & Bacon.

Canda, E. R., & Phaobtong, T. (1992). Buddhism as a support system for Southeast Asian refugees. *Social Work, 37,* 61–67.

Cannon, W. B. (1924). *Bodily changes in pain, hunger, fear, and rage.* New York: Appleton.

Caplan, G. (1990). Loss, stress, and mental health. *Community Mental Health Journal, 26,* 27–48.

Caplow, T. (1991). *American social trends.* Fort Worth: Harcourt Brace Jovanovich.

Caplow, T., Bahr, H., & Chadwick, B. (1983). *All faithful people: Change and continuity in Middletown's religion.* Minneapolis: University of Minnesota Press.

Caplow, T., Bahr, H., Modell, J., & Chadwick, B. (1991). *Recent social trends in the United States, 1960–1990.* Buffalo: Campus Verlag/McGill–Queen's University Press.

Carden, M. (1978). The proliferation of a social movement: Ideology and individual incentives in the contemporary feminist movement. In L. Kriesberg (Ed.), *Research in social movements, conflicts and change Vol. 1,* (pp. 179–196). Greenwich, CT: JAI Press.

Carey, J. (Ed.). (1990). *Brain facts: A primer on the brain and nervous system*. Washington, DC: Society for Neuroscience.

Carp, F. (1987). Environment and aging. In D. Stokols & I. Altman (Eds.), *Handbook of environmental psychology* (pp. 329–360). New York: Wiley.

Carpenter, M. B. (1991). *Core text of neuroanatomy* (4th ed.). Baltimore: Williams & Wilkins.

Carpman, J., Grant, M., & Simmons, D. (1984). *No more mazes*. Ann Arbor: University of Michigan Hospitals, Office of the Replacement Hospital Program, Patient and Visitor Participation Project.

Carroll, M. (1998). Social work's conceptualization of spirituality. *Social Thought, 18*(2), 1–13.

Carter, B., & McGoldrick, M. (Eds.). (1988a). *The changing family life cycle* (2nd ed.). New York: Gardner.

Carter, B., & McGoldrick, M. (1988b). Overview: The changing family life cycle: A framework for family therapy. In B. Carter & M. McGoldrick (Eds.), *The changing family life cycle: A framework for family therapy* (2nd ed.) (pp. 3–28). New York: Gardner.

Carter, H., & Glick, P. (1976). *Marriage and divorce: A social and economic study*. Cambridge, MA: Harvard University Press.

Carter, M. V. (1984). Religion in Appalachian cultures: A brief outlook. *Religion: The Cutting Edge, 5*(1), 135–142.

Carter, P., & Jackson, N. (1993). Modernism, postmodernism and motivation, or why expectancy theory failed to come up to expectation. In J. Hassard & M. Parker (Eds.), *Postmodernism and organizations* (pp. 83–100). Newbury Park, CA: Sage.

Castells, M. (1977). *The urban question* (A. Sheridan, Trans.). London: Edward Arnold.

Chaskin, R., Joseph, M., & Chipenda-Dansokho, S. (1997). Implementing comprehensive community development: Possibilities and limitations. *Social Work, 42*, 435–444.

Chau, K. (1990). Social work with groups in multicultural contexts. *Group Work, 7(3)*, 8–21.

Cherlin, A. J. (1992). *Marriage, divorce, remarriage* (rev. ed.). Cambridge, MA: Harvard University Press.

Cherniss, C. (1980). *Staff burnout: Job stress in the human services*. Beverly Hills, CA: Sage.

Cherulnik, P. (1993). *Applications of environment-behavior research: Case studies and analysis*. Cambridge: Cambridge University Press.

Chesney, B. K., & Chesler, M. A. (1993). Activism through self-help group membership: Reported life changes of parents of children with cancer. *Small Group Research, 24*, 258–273.

Chestang, L. (1972). *Character development in a hostile environment* (Occasional Paper No. 3). University of Chicago, School of Social Service Administration, Chicago.

Chirot, D. (1994). *How societies change*. Thousand Oaks, CA: Pine Forge.

Choldin, H. (1978a). Social life and the physical environment. In D. Street & Associates (Eds.), *Handbook of contemporary urban life* (pp. 352–386). San Francisco: Jossey-Bass.

Choldin, H. (1978b). Urban density and pathology. *Annual Review of Sociology, 4*, 91–113.

Cingolani, J. (1984). Social conflict perspective on work with involuntary clients. *Social Work, 29*, 442–446.

Clark, J. (1994). Should social work education address religious issues? No! *Journal of Social Work Education, 36*, 11–16.

Clemens, E. (1996). Organizational form as frame: Collective identity and political strategy in the American labor movement, 1880–1920. In D. McAdam, J. McCarthy, & M. Zald (Eds.), *Comparative perspectives on social movements* (pp. 205–226). New York: Cambridge University Press.

Cnaan, R. (1997). Recognizing the role of religious congregations and denominations in social service provision. In M. Reisch & E. Gambrill (Eds.), *Social work in the 21st century* (pp. 271–284). Thousand Oaks, CA: Pine Forge.

Cohen, C., & Phillips, M. (1997). Building community: Principles for social work practice in housing settings. *Social Work, 42*, 471–481.

Cohen, D. (1989). Biological basis of schizophrenia: The evidence reconsidered. *Social Work, 34*, 255–257.

Cohen, P. (1968). *Modern social theory*. New York: Basic Books.

Cohen, S., & Wills, T. (1985). Stress, social support, and the buffering hypothesis. *Psychological Bulletin, 98*, 310–357.

Colcord, J., & Mann, R. (Eds.). (1930). *Mary E. Richmond, the long view: Papers and addresses*. New York: Russell Sage Foundation.

Coleman, J. (1990). *Foundations of social theory*. Cambridge, MA: Belknap Press of Harvard University Press.

Collins, A., & Pancoast, D. (1976). *Natural helping networks*. Washington, DC: National Association of Social Workers.

Collins, R. (1971). Functional and conflict theories of educational stratification. *American Sociological Review, 36*, 1002–1019.

Collins, R. (1981). On the micro-foundations of macro-sociology. *American Journal of Sociology, 86*, 984–1014.

Collins, R. (1988). *Theoretical sociology*. San Diego: Harcourt Brace Jovanovich.

Collins, R. (1990). Conflict thoery and the advance of macro-historical sociology. In G. Ritzer (Ed.), *Frontiers of social theory: The new syntheses* (pp. 68–87). New York: Columbia University Press.

Collins, R. (1994). *Four sociological traditions*. New York: Oxford University Press.

Colon, F. (1980). The family life cycle of the multiproblem poor family. In E. Carter & M. McGoldrick (Eds.), *Family life cycle* (pp. 343–381). New York: Gardner.

Commonwealth of Virginia. (1996, June 30). *Division of STD/HIV Surveillance Quarterly, 4*(2&3). Richmond, VA: Author.

Community development [Special issue]. (1997). *Families in Society, 78*(2).

Cook, K. (Ed.). (1987). *Social exchange theory.* Newbury Park, CA: Sage.

Cook, K., O'Brien, J., & Kollock, P. (1990). Exchange theory: A blueprint for structure and process. In G. Ritzer (Ed.), *Frontiers of social theory: The new syntheses* (pp. 158–181). New York: Columbia University Press.

Cooley, C. (1964). *Human nature and the social order.* New York: Scribner's. (Original work published 1902)

Coombs, D., & Capper, S. (1996). *Public health and mortality: Public health in the 1980s.* In D. Peck & J. Hollingsworth (Eds.), *Demographic and structural change: The effects of the 1980s on American society* (pp. 101–126). Westport, CT: Greenwood Press.

Cooper, B., & Hasselkus, B. (1992). Independent living and the physical environment: Aspects that matter to residents. *Canadian Journal of Occupational Therapy, 59*(1), 6–15.

Corey, M., & Corey, G. (1987). *Groups: Process and practice* (3rd ed.). Pacific Grove, CA: Brooks/Cole.

Corey, M., & Corey, G. (1992). *Groups: Process and practice* (4th ed.). Pacific Grove, CA: Brooks/Cole.

Coser, L. (1956). *The functions of conflict.* New York: Free Press.

Coser, L. (1975). Presidential address: Two methods in search of a substance. *American Sociological Review, 40,* 691–700.

Coulton, C. (1995). Riding the pendulum of the 1990s: Building a community context for social work research. *Social Work, 40,* 437–439.

Coulton, C. (1996). Effects of neighborhoods on families and children: Implications for services. In A. Kahn & S. Kamerman (Eds.), *Children and their families in big cities: Strategies for service reform* (pp. 87–120). New York: Columbia University, Cross-National Studies Research Program.

Cousins, L. (1994). *Community high: The complexity of race and class in a black urban high school* (Doctoral dissertation, University of Michigan, Ann Arbor, Michigan). University Microfilms International, Ann Arbor, Michigan.

Cousins, L., & Mabrey, T. (1998). Re-gendering social work practice and education: The case for African American girls. *Journal of Human Behavior in the Social Environment, 1*(2/3), 91–104.

Cowley, A. S. (1993). Transpersonal social work: A theory for the 1990s. *Social Work, 38,* 527–534.

Cowley, A. S. (1996). Transpersonal social work. In F. J. Turner (Ed.), *Social work treatment: Interlocking theoretical approaches* (4th ed.) (pp. 663–698). New York: Free Press.

Cowley, A. S., & Derezotes, D. (1994). Transpersonal psychology and social work education. *Journal of Social Work Education, 30,* 32–39.

Cox, T., Jr. (1993). *Cultural diversity in organizations: Theory, research, and practice.* San Francisco: Berrett-Koehler.

Crompton, R. (1993). *Class and stratification: An introduction to current debates.* Cambridge: Polity Press.

Crook, S., Pakulski, J., & Waters, M. (1992). *Postmodernization: Change in advanced society.* Newbury Park, CA: Sage.

Croteau, D., & Hoynes, W. (1997). *Media/society: Industries, images, and audiences.* Thousand Oaks, CA: Pine Forge.

Cuba, L., & Hummon, D. (1993). A place to call home: Identification with dwelling, community, and region. *The Sociological Quarterly, 34*(1), 111–131.

Curran, J. (1996). Mass media and democracy revisited. In J. Curran & M. Gurevitch (Eds.), *Mass media and society* (2nd ed.) (pp. 81–119). New York: Arnold.

Dahrendorf, R. (1959). *Class and class conflict in the industrial society.* London: Routledge.

Dahrendorf, R. (1969). On the origin of inequality among men. In A. Beteille (Ed.), *Social inequality* (pp. 16–44). Harmondsworth, Middlesex: Penguin.

D'Andrade, R. G. (1995). Cultural meaning systems. In R. Shweder & R. LeVine (Eds.), *Culture theory: Essays on mind, self, and emotion* (pp. 88–122). New York: Cambridge University Press. (Original work published 1984)

Daniel, E. V. (1987). *Fluid signs: Being a person the Tamil Way.* Berkeley: University of California Press.

Das, A., & Harries, B. (1996). Validating Fowler's theory of faith development with college students. *Psychological Reports, 78,* 675–679.

Dattalo, P. (1990). Teaching social work students to analyze and apply organizational theory. *Journal of Teaching in Social Work, 4*(2), 127–143.

David, T., & Weinstein, C. (1987). The built environment and children's development. In C. Weinstein & T. David (Eds.), *Spaces for children: The built environment and child development* (pp. 3–18). New York: Plenum.

Davis, K. (1949). *Human society.* New York: Macmillan.

Davis, L. (1984). Essential components of group work with black Americans. *Social Work with Groups, 7*(3), 97–109.

Davis, L. (1986). Role theory. In F. Turner (Ed.), *Social work treatment: Interlocking theoretical approaches* (3rd ed.) (pp. 541–563). New York: Free Press.

Delgado, M., & Humm-Delgado, D. (1982). Natural support systems: Sources of strength in Hispanic communities. *Social Work, 27,* 83–89.

Della Porta, D. (1996). Social movements and the state: Thoughts on the policing of protest. In D. McAdam, J. McCarthy, & M. Zald (Eds.), *Comparative perspectives on social movements* (pp. 62–92). New York: Cambridge University Press.

Derezotes, D. S. (1995). Spirituality and religiosity: Neglected factors in social work practice. *Arete, 20*(1), 1–15.

Derezotes, D. S., & Evans, K. E. (1995). Spirituality and religiosity in practice: In-depth interviews of social work practitioners. *Social Thought, 18*(1), 38–56.

de Sassure, F. (1966). *Course in general linguistics.* New York: McGraw-Hill. (Original work published in 1959)

de Tocqueville, A. (1945). *Democracy in America.* New York: Knopf. (Original work published 1835)

Devlin, A. (1992). Psychiatric ward renovation: Staff perception and patient behavior. *Environment and Behavior, 24,* 66–84.

Dewey, J., & Bentley, A. F. (1949). *Knowing and the known.* Boston: Beacon.

Dionne, E. J. (1996). *They only look dead: Why progressives will dominate the next political era.* New York: Simon & Schuster.

Doherty, W. (1995). Community considerations in psychotherapy. *The Responsive Community, 5*(1), 41–52.

Dohrenwend, B. P., & Dohrenwend, B. S. (1974). Psychiatric disorders in urban settings. In S. Arieti & G. Caplan (Eds.), *American handbook of psychiatry* (2nd ed.) (Vol. 2, pp. 427–447). New York: Basic Books.

Doolittle, R. J., & MacDonald, D. (1978). Communication and a sense of community in a metropolitan neighborhood: A factor analytic examination. *Communication Quarterly, 26,* 2–7.

Dudley, J. R., & Helfgott, C. (1990). Exploring a place for spirituality and religiosity in the social work curriculum. *Journal of Social Work Education, 26,* 287–294.

Dufrene, P. M., & Coleman, V. S. (1992). Counseling Native Americans: Guidelines for group process. *Journal of Specialists in Group Work, 17*(4), 229–234.

Duluth Domestic Abuse Intervention Project. (Undated). *In our best interest.* Support group manual available from the Duluth Domestic Abuse Intervention Project, 206 W. Fourth Street, Duluth, MN 55806.

Duvall, E. (1962). *Family development.* New York: Lippincott.

Duvall-Early, K., & Benedict, J. (1992). The relationship between privacy and different components of job satisfaction. *Environment and Behavior, 24,* 670–679.

Earle, A. M. (1987). *An outline of neuroanatomy.* Omaha: University of Nebraska Medical Center.

Eisinger, P. (1973). The conditions of protest behavior in American cities. *American Political Science Review, 67,* 11–28.

Ekeh, P. (1974). *Social exchange theory: The two traditions.* Cambridge, MA: Harvard University Press.

Ellsworth, P. C. (1991). Some implications of cognitive appraisal theories of emotion. In K. T. Strongman (Ed.), *International review of studies on emotions* (pp. 143–161). New York: Wiley.

Emerson, R. (1972a). Exchange theory: Part I. A psychological basis for social exchange. In J. Berger, M. Zelditch, Jr., & B. Anderson (Eds.), *Sociological theories in progress* (Vol. 2, pp. 38–57). Boston: Houghton Mifflin.

Emerson, R. (1972b). Exchange theory: Part II. Exchange relations and networks. In J. Berger, M. Zelditch, Jr., & B. Anderson (Eds.), *Sociological theories in progress* (Vol. 2, pp. 58–87). Boston: Houghton Mifflin.

Emirbayer, M., & Goodwin, J. (1994). Network analysis, culture, and the problem of agency. *American Journal of Sociology, 99,* 1411–1454.

Engel, G. (1977). The need for a new medical model: A challenge for biomedicine. *Science, 196,* 129-136.

Engels, F. (1970). *The origins of the family, private property and the state.* New York: International Publishers. (Original work published 1884)

Erikson, E. (1963). *Childhood and society* (2nd ed.). New York: Norton.

Erikson, E. (1968). *Identity: Youth and crisis.* New York: Norton.

Erikson, K. (1976). *Everything in its path: Destruction of community in the Buffalo Creek flood.* New York: Simon & Schuster.

Etzioni, A. (1977). *Modern organizations.* Englewood Cliffs, NJ: Prentice-Hall.

Etzioni, A. (1993). *The spirit of community.* New York: Crown.

Evans, G., & Howard, R. (1973). Personal space. *Psychological Bulletin, 80,* 334–344.

Evans, G., & Maxwell, L. (1997). Chronic noise exposure and reading deficits: The mediating effects of language acquisition. *Environment and Behavior, 29,* 638–656.

Evans, R., & Stoddart, G. (1994). Producing health, consuming health care. In P. Lee and C. Estes (Eds.), *The nation's health* (4th ed.) (pp. 6–13). Boston: Jones & Bartlett.

Evans, S. (1980). *Personal politics.* New York: Vintage.

Ewalt, P. (1997). The revitalization of impoverished communities. *Social Work, 42,* 413–414.

Ewert, A., & Heywood, J. (1991). Group development in the natural environment: Expectations, outcomes, and techniques. *Environment and Behavior, 23,* 529–615.

Falck, H. (1988). *Social work: The membership perspective.* New York: Springer.

Falicov, C., & Karrer, B. (1980). Cultural variations in the family life cycle: The Mexican American family. In E. Carter & M. McGoldrick (Eds.), *Family life cycle* (pp. 383–425). New York: Gardner.

Farazmand, A. (1994). Organization theory: An overview and appraisal. In A. Farazmand (Ed.), *Modern organizations: Administrative theory in contemporary society* (pp. 3–54). Westport, CT: Praeger.

Farley, R. (1996). *The American reality: Who we are, how we got here, where we are going.* New York: Russell Sage Foundation.

Farmer, R. J., & Pandurangi, A. K. (1997). Diversity in schizophrenia: Toward a richer biopsychosocial understanding for social work practice. *Health and Social Work, 22*(2), 109–116.

Farmer, R. J., Walsh, J., & Bentley, K. J. (1998). Schizophrenia. In B. A. Thyer & J. S. Wodarski (Eds.), *Handbook of empirical social work practice: Vol. 1. Mental disorders* (pp. 245–270). New York: Wiley.

Fauri, D. P. (1988). Applying historical themes of the profession in the foundation curriculum. *Journal of Teaching in Social Work, 2,* 17–31.

Federal Emergency Management Agency. (1984). *Program guide, disaster assistance programs.* Washington, DC: U.S. Government Printing Office.

Feikema, R., Segalavich, J., & Jeffries, S. (1997). From child development to community building: One agency's journey. *Families in Society, 78,* 185–195.

Feldman, R. (1990). Settlement-identity: Psychological bonds with home places in a mobile society. *Environment and Behavior, 22*(2), 183–229.

Ferree, M. M., & Martin, P. Y. (1995). *Feminist organizations: Harvest of the new women's movement.* Philadelphia: Temple University Press.

Figley, C. (1995). *Compassion: Coping with secondary traumatic stress disorder in those who treat the traumatized.* New York: Brunner/Mazel.

Figuera-McDonough, J. (1991). Community structure and delinquency: A typology. *Social Service Review, 65,* 68–91.

Fischer, C. (1973a). On urban alienations and anomic: Powerlessness and social isolation. *American Sociological Review, 38,* 311–326.

Fischer, C. (1973b). Urban malaise. *Social Forces, 52,* 221–235.

Fischer, C. (1984). *The urban experience* (2nd ed.). New York: Harcourt Brace Jovanovich.

Fisher, R., & Karger, H. (1997). *Social work and community in a private world.* New York: Longman.

Flanagan, L. M. (1996). The theory of self psychology. In J. Berzoff (Ed.), *Inside out and outside in: Psychodynamic clinical theory and practice in contemporary multicultural contexts* (pp. 173–198). Northvale, NJ: Jason Aronson.

Flanagan, W. (1993). *Contemporary urban sociology.* New York: Cambridge University Press.

Fontana, A. (1984). Introduction: Existential sociology and the self. In J. Kotarba & A. Fontana (Eds.), *The existential self in society* (pp. 3–17). Chicago: University of Chicago Press.

Ford, D., & Lerner, R. (1992). *Developmental systems theory: An integrative approach.* Newbury Park, CA: Sage.

Fordham, S. (1993). Those loud black girls: (Black) women, silence, and gender "passing" in the academy. *Anthropology and Education Quarterly, 2*(1), 3–32.

Fordham, S. (1996). *Blacked out: Dilemmas of race, identity, and success at Capital High.* Chicago: University of Chicago Press.

Fordham, S., & Ogbu, J. (1986). Black students' school success: Coping with the "Burden of 'Acting White.'" *Urban Review, 18*(3), 176–206.

Foss, L. (1994). The biomedical paradigm, psychoneuroimmunology, and the black four of hearts. *ADVANCES: The Journal of Mind-Body Health, 10*(1), 32–44.

Foucault, M. (1969). *The archaeology of knowledge and the discourse on language.* New York: Harper Colophon.

Fowler, F., Jr. (1981). Evaluating a complex crime control experiment. In L. Bickman (Ed.), *Applied social psychology annual* (Vol. 2, pp. 165–187). Beverly Hills, CA: Sage.

Fowler, J. F. (1980) Stage six and the kingdom of God. *Religious Education, 75,* 231–249.

Fowler, J. F. (1981). *Stages of faith: The psychology of human development and the quest for meaning.* San Francisco: Harper.

Fowler, J. F. (1996). *Faithful change: The personal and public challenges of postmodern life.* Nashville: Abindon Press.

Fowler, R., Jr., McCalla, M., & Mangione, T. (1979). *Reducing residential crime and fear: The Hartford neighborhood crime prevention program: Executive summary.* Washington, DC: National Institute of Law Enforcement and Criminal Justice.

Fox, C., & Miller, H. (1995). *Postmodern public administration: Toward discourse.* Thousand Oaks, CA.: Sage.

Frankl, V. E. (1988). *The will to meaning: Foundations and applications of logotherapy.* New York: Meridian.

Franklin, C. (1995). Expanding the vision of the social contructionist debates: Creating relevance for practitioners. *Families in Society, 76,* 395–407.

Franks, D. D. (1991). Mead's and Dewey's theory of emotion and contemporary constructionism. *Journal of Mental Imagery, 15*(1–2), 119–137.

Freedman, J. L. (1975). *Crowding and behavior.* New York: Viking.

Freeman, J. (1995). From seed to harvest: Transformations of feminist organizations and scholarship. In M. Ferree & P. Martin (Eds.), *Feminist organizations: Harvest of the new women's movement* (pp. 397–408). Philadelphia: Temple University Press.

Freud, S. (1978). *The interpretation of dreams* (A. A. Brill, Trans.). New York: Modern Library. (Original work published 1899)

Freud, S. (1928). *The future of an illusion.* London: Horace Liveright.

Freud, S. (1953). Three essays on the theory of sexuality. In J. Strachey (Ed. and Trans.), *The standard edition.* (Vol. 7, pp. 135–245). London: Hogarth Press. (Original work published 1905)

Frey, W. (1990). Metropolitan America: Beyond the transition. *Population Bulletin, 45*(2), 3–42.

Fried, M., & Gleicher, P. (1961). Some sources of satisfaction in an urban slum. *Journal of the American Institute of Planners, 27,* 305–315.

Friedman, A. (1976, September). On politics and design. *Contract,* pp. 6, 10, 12.

Fromm, E. (1941). *Escape from freedom.* New York: Avon.

Fromm, E., & Maccoby, M. (1970). *Social character in a Mexican village.* Englewood Cliffs, NJ: Prentice-Hall.

Fulmer, R. (1988). Lower-income and professional families: A comparison of structure and life cycle process. In E. Carter & M. McGoldrick (Eds.), *The changing family life cycle* (2nd ed.) (pp. 545–578). New York: Gardner.

Furushima, R. Y. (1983). Faith development in a cross cultural perspective. *Religious Education, 80,* 414–420.

Gallagher, M. (1996). *The abolition of marriage: How we destroy lasting love.* Washington, DC: Regnery.

Gallagher, W. (1993). *The power of place: How our surroundings shape our thoughts, emotions, and actions.* New York: Poseidon.

Gallup, G., & Castelli, J. (1989) *The people's religion: American faith in the 90's.* New York: Macmillan.

Galotti, K. M. (1989). Gender differences in self-reported moral reasoning: A review and new evidence. *Journal of Youth and Adolescence, 18,* 475–488.

Gambrill, E. (1987). Behavioral approach. In Anne Minahan (Ed.), *Encyclopedia of social work* (18th ed.) (Vol. 1, pp. 184–194). Silver Spring, MD: National Association of Social Workers.

Gambrill, E. (1990). *Critical thinking in clinical practice: Improving the accuracy of judgments and decisions about clients..* San Francisco: Jossey-Bass.

Gambrill, E. D. (1994). Concepts and methods of behavioral treatment. In D. K. Granvold (Ed.), *Cognitive and behavioral treatment: Methods and applications* (pp. 32–62). Pacific Grove, CA: Brooks/Cole.

Gamson, W. (1990). *The strategy of social protest.* Belmont, CA: Wadsworth.

Gamson, W., & Meyer, D. (1996). Framing political opportunity. In D. McAdam, J. McCarthy, & M. Zald (Eds.), *Comparative perspectives on social movements* (pp. 273–290). New York: Cambridge University Press.

Garbarino, J. (1976). A preliminary study of some ecological correlates of child abuse: The impact of socioeconomic stress on mothers. *Child Development, 47,* 178–185.

Garbarino, J. (1977). The human ecology of child maltreatment: A conceptual model for research. *Journal of Marriage and the Family, 39,* 721–735.

Garbarino, J., & Sherman, D. (1980). High-risk neighborhoods and high-risk families: The human ecology of child maltreatment. *Child Development, 51,* 188–198.

Garland, J., Jones, H., & Kolodny, R. (1973). A model for stages of development in social work groups. In S. Bernstein (Ed.). *Explorations in groupwork* (pp. 17–71). Boston: Milford Press.

Garreau, J. (1991). *Edge city: Life on the new frontier.* New York: Doubleday.

Garvin, C. D., & Reed, B. G. (1983). Gender issues in social group work: An overview. *Social Work with Groups, 6*(3/4), 5–18.

Gary, L E. (1995). African American men's perceptions of racial discrimination: A sociocultural analysis. *Social Work Research, 19,* 207–217.

Geertz, C. (1973). *The interpretation of cultures.* New York: Basic Books.

Geertz, C. (1983). Common sense as a cultural system. In *Local knowledge: Further essays in interpretive anthropology* (pp. 73–93). New York: Basic Books.

Gelberg, L., & Linn, L. S. (1988). Social and physical health of homeless adults previously treated for mental health problems. *Hospital and Community Psychiatry, 39,* 510–516.

Gelles, F. J. (1992). Poverty and violence toward children. *American Behavioral Scientist, 35,* 258–274.

George, L. (1993). Sociological perspectives on life transitions. *Annual Review of Sociology, 19,* 353–373.

Gergen, K. (1992). Organization theory in the postmodern era. In M. Reed & M. Hughes (Eds.), *Rethinking organization* (pp. 207–226). Newbury Park, CA: Sage.

Gergen, K. V., & Davis, K. R. (Eds.). (1985). *The social construction of the person.* New York: Springer-Verlag.

Germain, C. (1973). An ecological perspective in casework practice. *Social Casework: The Journal of Contemporary Social Work, 54,* 323–330.

Germain, C. (1978). Space: An ecological variable in social work practice. *Social Casework, 59,* 515–522.

Germain, C. (1981). The physical environment and social work practice. In A. Maluccio (Ed.), *Promoting competence in clients* (pp. 103–124). New York: Free Press.

Germain, C. (1994). Human behavior and the social environment. In R. Reamer (Ed.), *The foundations of social work knowledge* (pp. 88–121). New York: Columbia University Press.

Germain, C., & Gitterman, A. (1980). *The life model of social work practice.* New York: Columbia University Press.

Germain, C., & Gitterman, A. (1996). *The life model of social work practice: Advances in theory and practice* (2nd ed.). New York: Columbia University Press.

Gibson, M. (1988). *Accommodation without assimilation: Sikh immigrants in an American high school.* Ithaca, NY: Cornell University Press.

Giddens, A. (1979). *Central problems in social theory: Action, structure and contradiction in social analysis.* Cambridge: Cambridge University Press.

Gifford, R. (1987). *Environmental psychology: Principles and practice.* Boston: Allyn & Bacon.

Gifford, R., & Gallagher, T. (1985). Sociability: Personality, social context, and physical setting. *Journal of Personality and Social Psychology, 48,* 1015–1023.

Gilderbloom, J., & Markham, J. (1996). Housing modification needs of the disabled elderly: What really matters? *Environment and Behavior, 28,* 512–535.

Gilligan, C. (1982). *In a different voice.* Cambridge, MA: Harvard University Press.

Gillis, J. (1996). *A world of their own making: Myth, ritual, and the quest for family values.* New York: Basic Books.

Gilson, S. (1996). *The disability movement and federal legislation.* Unpublished manuscript, Richmond, VA.

Gilson, S. F. (1991). Attentional development during maturation as assessed with scalp endogenous potentials and related behavioral measures (Doctoral dissertation, University of Nebraska Medical Center, 1990). *UMI Dissertation Information Service,* 9201187.

Gilson, S. F., Tusler, A., & Gill, C. (1997). Ethnographic research in disability identity: Self-determination and community. *Journal of Vocational Rehabilitation, 9*(1), 7–17.

Giroux, H. (1983). *Theory and resistance in education: A pedagogy for the opposition.* New York: Bergin & Garvey.

Gitterman, A., & Shulman, L. (1994). *Mutual aid groups, vulnerable populations, and the life cycle.* (2nd ed.). New York: Columbia University Press.

Goldstein, E. (1984). *Ego psychology and social work practice.* New York: Free Press.

Goldstein, E. (1986). Ego psychology. In F. Turner (Ed.), *Social work treatment* (3rd ed.) (pp. 375–406). New York: Free Press.

Goldstein, E. (1995). *Ego psychology and social work practice* (2nd ed.). New York: Free Press.

Golembiewski, R. (1994). Is organizational membership bad for your health? Phases of burnout as covariants of mental and physical well-being. In A. Farazmand (Ed.), *Modern organizations: Administrative theory in contemporary society* (pp. 211–227). Westport, CT: Praeger.

Goodenough, W. (1996). Culture. In D. Levison & M. Ember (Eds.), *Encyclopedia of cultural anthropology* (Vol. 1, pp. 291–298). New York: Holt.

Goodin, R. (1996). Institutions and their design. In R. Goodin (Ed.), *The theory of institutional design* (pp. 1–53). New York: Cambridge University Press.

Gorin, S., & Moniz, C. (1997). Social work and health care in the 21st century. In M. Reisch & E. Gambrill (Eds.), *Social work in the 21st century* (pp. 152–162). Thousand Oaks, CA: Pine Forge.

Gottesman, I. I. (1991). *Schizophrenia genesis.* New York: Freeman.

Gould, S. (1981). *The mismeasure of man.* New York: Norton.

Gouldner, A. (1970). *The coming crisis of western sociology.* New York: Basic Books.

Gourgey, C. (1994). From weakness to strength: A spiritual response to disability. *Journal of Religion in Disability and Rehabilitation, 1*(1), 69–80.

Granvold, D. K. (1994). Concepts and methods of cognitive treatment. In D. K. Granvold (Ed.), *Cognitive and behavioral treatment: Methods and applications* (pp. 3–31). Pacific Grove, CA: Brooks/Cole.

Green, G. D., & Bozett, F. W. (1991). Lesbian mothers and gay fathers. In J. C. Gonsiorek & J. D. Weinrich (Eds.), *Homosexuality: Research implications for public policy* (pp. 197–214). Newbury Park, CA: Sage.

Greenberg, L. S. (1996). Allowing and accepting of emotional experience. In R. D. Kavanaugh, B. Zimmerberg, & S. Fein (Eds.), *Emotion: Interdisciplinary perspectives* (pp. 315–336). Mahwah, NJ: Lawrence Erlbaum.

Griswold, W. (1994). *Cultures and societies in a changing world.* Thousand Oaks, CA: Pine Forge.

Grof, S. (1988). *Adventures in self-discovery: Dimensions of consciousness and new perspectives in psychotherapy and inner exploration.* Albany: State University of New York.

Guest, A. M., & Lee, B. A. (1983). The social organization of local areas. *Urban Affairs Quarterly, 19,* 217–240.

Gummer, B. (1994). Can administrative controls and pressure for efficiency and effectiveness be balanced with the staff's demand for decentralization and participation? No. In M. Austin & J. Lowe (Eds.), *Controversial issues in communities and organizations* (pp. 260–264). Boston: Allyn & Bacon.

Gummer, B. (1997). Ethics and administrative practice: The politics of values and the value of politics. In M. Reisch & E. Gambrill (Eds.), *Social work in the 21st century* (pp. 350–356). Thousand Oaks, CA: Pine Forge.

Gump, P. (1987). School and classroom environments. In D. Stokols & I. Altman (Eds.), *Handbook of environmental psychology* (pp. 691–732). New York: Wiley.

Gusfield, J. R. (1975). *The community: A critical response.* New York: Harper Colophon.

Gutheil, I. (1991). The physical environment and quality of life in residential facilities for frail elders. *Adult Residential Care Journal, 5,* 131–145.

Gutheil, I. (1992). Considering the physical environment: An essential component of good practice. *Social Work, 37,* 391–396.

Gutierrez, L. (1997). Multicultural community organizing. In M. Reisch & E. Gambrill (Eds.), *Social work in the 21st century* (pp. 249–259). Thousand Oaks, CA: Pine Forge.

Habermas, J. (1984). *The theory of communicative action: Vol. 1, Reason and the rationalization of society.* Boston: Beacon Press.

Habermas, J. (1987). *The theory of communicative action: Vol. 2, Lifeworld and system: A critique of functionalist reason* (T. McCarthy, Trans.). Boston: Beacon Press. (Original work published 1981)

Hagan, J. (1994). *Crime and disrepute.* Thousand Oaks, CA: Pine Forge.

Hahn, H. (1993). The politics of physical differences: Disability and discrimination. In M. Nagler (Ed.), *Perspectives on disability* (2nd ed.) (pp. 37–42). Palo Alto, CA: Health Markets Research.

Hall, M. (1995). *Poor people's social movement organizations: The goal is to win.* Westport, CT: Praeger.

Hannan, M., & Freeman, J. (1977). The population ecology of organizations. *Amercian Journal of Sociology, 82,* 929–964.

Hannerz, U. (1992). *Cultural complexity: Studies in the social organization of meaning.* New York: Columbia University Press.

Hardcastle, D., Wenocur, S., & Powers, P. (1997). *Community practice: Theories and skills for social workers.* New York: Oxford University Press.

Hare, A. P. (1994). Types of roles in small groups: A bit of history and a current perspective. *Small Group Research, 25,* 433–448.

Hare, A. P., Blumberg, H. H., Davies, M. F., & Kent, M. V. (1994). *Small group research: A handbook.* Norwood, NJ: Ablex.

Hart, J. (1970). The development of client-centered therapy. In J. T. Hart & T. M. Tomlinson (Eds.), *New directions in client-centered therapy.* Boston: Houghton Mifflin.

Hartford, M. (1971). *Groups in social work.* New York: Columbia University Press.

Hartig, T., Mang, M., & Evans, G. (1991). Restorative effects of natural environment experiences. *Environment and Behavior, 23,* 3–26.

Hartman, A. (1970). To think about the unthinkable. *Social Casework: The Journal of Contemporary Social Work, 51,* 467–474.

Hartman, A. (1978). Diagrammatic assessment of family relationships. *Social Casework, 59,* 465–476.

Hartman, A. (1995). Diagrammatic assessment of family relationships. *Families in Society, 76,* 111–122.

Hartman, A., & Laird, J. (1983). *Family-centered social work practice.* New York: Free Press.

Harvey, D. (1989). *The condition of postmodernity.* Cambridge, MA: Basil Blackwell.

Hasenfeld, Y. (1983). *Human service organizations.* Englewood Cliffs, NJ: Prentice-Hall.

Hasenfeld, Y. (1992). Theoretical approaches to human service organizations. In Y. Hasenfeld (Ed.), *Human services as complex organizations* (pp. 24–44). Newbury Park, CA: Sage.

Hassard, J. (1993). Postmodernism and organizational analysis: An overview. In J. Hassard & M. Parker (Eds.), *Postmodernism and organizations* (pp. 1–23). Newbury Park, CA: Sage.

Hawkins, K. W. (1995). Effects of gender and communication content on leadership emergence in small task-oriented groups. *Small Group Research, 26,* 234–249.

Hayduk, L. (1983). Personal space: Where we now stand. *Psychological Bulletin, 94,* 293–335.

Hearn, G. (1958). *Theory building in social work.* Toronto: University of Toronto Press.

Hearn, G. (1969). *The general systems approach: Contributions toward an holistic conception of social work.* New York: Council on Social Work Education.

Hearn, J., & Parkin, W. (1993). Organizations, multiple oppressions and postmodernism. In J. Hassard & M. Parker (Eds.), *Postmodernism and organizations* (pp. 148–162). Newbury Park, CA: Sage.

Hegtvedt, K. A. (1994). Justice. In M. Foshci & E. J. Lawler (Eds.), *Group processes: Sociological analyses* (pp. 177–204). Chicago: Nelson-Hall.

Heller, K. (1989). The return to community. *American Journal of Community Psychology, 17*(1), 1–14.

Hendricks, G., & Weinhold, B. (1982). *Transpersonal approaches to counseling and psychotherapy.* Denver: Love.

Hepworth, D. H., Rooney, R. H., & Larsen, J. (1997). *Direct social work practice: Theory and skills* (5th ed.). Pacific Grove, CA: Brooks/Cole.

Herzberg, F. (1966). *Work and the nature of man.* Cleveland: World.

Hetherington, E. M., Stanley-Hagan, M., & Anderson, E. R. (1989). Marital transitions: A child's perspective. *American Psychologist, 44,* 303–312.

Hewitt, J. P. (1994). *Self and society: A symbolic interactionist social psychology* (6th ed.). Boston: Allyn and Bacon.

Hill, R. (1958). Generic features of families under stress. *Social Casework, 49,* 139–150.

Hillery, G. (1955). Definitions of community: Areas of agreement. *Rural Sociology, 20,* 111–123.

Hines, P. (1988). The family life cycle of poor black families. In E. Carter & M. McGoldrick (Eds.), *The changing family life cycle* (pp. 513–544). New York: Gardner.

Hiratuska, J. (1994, March). Mind-body wellness link probed: NIH forum cites value of low-cost psychosocial supports. *NASW News, 39*(3), 1.

Ho, M. K. (1992). *Minority children and adolescents in therapy.* Newbury Park, CA: Sage.

Hobfoll, S., Freedy, R., Lane, C., & Geller, P. (1990). Conservation of social resources: Social support resource theory. *Journal of Social and Personal Relationships, 7,* 465–478.

Hobsbawm, E. (1983). Introduction: Inventing tradition. In E. Hobsbawm & T. Ranger (Eds.), *The invention of tradition* (pp. 1–14). New York: Cambridge University Press.

Hogan, D., & Lichter, D. (1995). Children and youth: Living arrangements and welfare. In R. Farley (Ed.), *State of the union: America in the 1990s: Vol. 2. Social trends* (pp. 93–139). New York: Russell Sage Foundation.

Holahan, C., & Saegert, S. (1973). Behavioral and attitudinal effects of large-scale variation in the physical environment of psychiatric wards. *Journal of Abnormal Psychology, 82,* 454–462.

Holmberg, S. K., & Kane, C. F. (1995). Severe psychiatric disorder and physical health risks. *Clinical Nurse Specialist, 9,* 287–298.

Homans, G. (1958). Social behavior as exchange. American Journal of Sociology, 63, 597–606.

Hoover, M. (1990). A vindicationist perspective on the role of Ebonics (black language) and other aspects of ethnic studies in the university. *American Behavioral Science, 34,* 251–262.

Hopps, J. G., Pinderhughes, E., & Shankar, R. (1995). *The power to care: Clinical practice effectiveness with overwhelmed clients.* New York: Free Press.

Horn, L. J. (1991). Rehabilitation in brain disorders: 1. Basic sciences. *Archives of Physical Medicine and Rehabilitation, 72*(4–S), S317–319.

Horney, K. (1939). *New ways in psychoanalysis.* New York: Norton.

Horney, K. (1967). *Feminine psychology.* New York: Norton.

House, J. S., Landis, K. R., & Umberson, D. (1988). Social relationships and health. *Science, 241,* 540–545.

Hunter, A. (1974). *Symbolic communities.* Chicago: University of Chicago Press.

Hunter, A. (1978). Persistence of local sentiments in mass society. In D. Street (Ed.), *Handbook of contemporary urban life.* San Francisco: Jossey-Bass.

Hunter, A., & Riger, S. (1986). The meaning of community in community mental health. *Journal of Community Psychology, 14,* 55–71.

Hunter, J. D. (1991). *Culture wars: The struggle to define America.* New York: Basic Books.

Hunter, J. D. (1994). *Before the shooting begins: Searching for democracy in America's culture wars.* New York: Free Press.

Hutchison, E., Dattalo, P., & Rodwell, M. (1994). Reorganizing child protective services: Protecting children and providing family support. *Children and Youth Services Review, 16*(5–6), 319–338.

Hutton, M. S. (1994). How transpersonal psychotherapists differ from other practitioners: An empirical study. *Journal of Transpersonal Psychology, 26*(2), 139–174.

Hyde, C. (1992). The ideational system of social movement agencies: An examination of feminist health centers. In Y. Hasenfeld (Ed.), *Human services as complex organizations* (pp. 121–144). Newbury Park, CA: Sage.

Iannello, K. (1992). *Decisions without hierarchy: Feminist interventions in organization theory and practice.* New York: Routledge.

IEA-NEA. (1997). *IEA-NEA: School funding in Illinois: Supporting documents: Inequities* [On-line]. Available: http://ieanea.org/fundings/sd_inequity.html. Size 2K-4-Mar-97.

Imre, R. (1984). The nature of knowledge in social work. *Social Work, 29,* 41–45.

Jaffe, E. (1979). Computers in child placement planning. *Social Work, 24,* 380–385.

James, W. (1890). *Principles of psychology.* New York: Holt.

Jayaratne, S., & Chess, W. (1984). Job satisfaction, burnout, and turnover: A national study. *Social Work, 29,* 448–453.

Jendrek, M. P. (1993). Grandparents who parent their grandchildren: Effects on lifestyle. *Journal of Marriage and the Family, 55,* 609–621.

Jendrek, M. P. (1994). Grandparents who parent their grandchildren: Circumstances and decisions. *The Gerontologist, 34*(2), 206–216.

Johnson, D. W., & Johnson, F. P. (1994). *Joining together: Group theory and skills* (5th ed.). Boston: Allyn & Bacon.

Johnson, G. B., & Wahl, M. (1995). Families: Demographic shifts. In R. L. Edwards et al. (Eds.), *Encyclopedia of social work* (19th ed.) (Vol. 2, pp. 936–941). Washington, DC: NASW Press.

Johnson, H. C. (1989). Disruptive children: Biological factors in attention deficit and antisocial disorders. *Social Work, 34,* 137–144.

Johnson, H. C. (1996). Violence and biology: A review of the literature. *Families in Society 77,* 3–18.

Johnson, H. C., Atkins, S. P., Battle, S. F., Hernandez-Arata, L., Hesselbrock, M., Libassi, M. F., & Parish, M. S. (1990). Strengthening the "bio" in the biopsychosocial paradigm. *Journal of Social Work Education, 26,* 109–123.

Johnson, M. (Ed.) (1992). *People with disabilities explain it all for you.* Louisville, KY: Advocado Press.

Johnson, T. (1990). Empowerment as a Christian helping strategy: Bridging the chasm between client and institutional oppression. *Social Work and Christianity: An International Journal, 17*(2), 66–78.

Joint Economic Committee (1989). *The education deficit.* 100th Congress, 2nd Session, S. Prt. 100–139, December 14, 1988. Washington, DC: U.S. Government Printing Office.

Jordan, J. (1992). The relational self: A new perspective for understanding women's development. *Contemporary Psychotherapy Review, 7,* 56–71.

Joseph, M. V. (1987). The religious and spiritual aspects of clinical practice: A neglected dimension of social work. *Social Thought, 13*(1), 12–23.

Joseph, M. V. (1988). Religion and social work practice. *Social Casework, 69,* 443–452.

Jung, C. G. (1933). *Modern man in search of a soul.* New York: Harcourt, Brace & World.

Jung, C. G. (1959). *The archetypes and the collective unconscious.* Princeton, NJ: Princeton University Press.

Kahana, B. (1992). Late-life adaptation in the aftermath of extreme stress. In M. Wykel, E. Kahana, & J. Kowal (Eds.), *Stress and health among the elderly* (pp. 5–34). New York: Springer.

Kahneman, D., & Tversky, A. (1984). Choices, values, and frames. *American Psychologist, 39,* 341–350.

Kahneman, E., & Tversky, A. (1982). The psychology of preferences. *Scientific American, 246,* 160–173.

Kapit, W., Macey, R. I., & Meisami, E. (1987). *The physiology coloring book.* Cambridge, MA: Harper Collins.

Kaplan, H., & Sadock, B. (1998). *Synopsis of psychiatry* (8th ed.). Baltimore: Williams and Wilkins.

Kaplan, H., Sadock, B., & Grebb, J. A. (1994). *Synopsis of psychiatry* (7th ed.). Baltimore: Williams & Wilkins.

Kaplan, R. (1983). The role of nature in the urban context. In I. Altman & J. F. Wohlwill (Eds.), *Behavior and the natural environment* (pp. 127–161). New York: Plenum.

Kaplan, R., & Kaplan, S. (1987). The garden as restorative experience: A research odyssey. In M. Francis & R. T. Hester (Eds.), *The meanings of the garden: Conference proceedings.* Davis: University of California, Center for Design Research.

Kaplan, R., & Kaplan, S. (1989). *The experience of nature: A psychological perspective.* New York: Cambridge University Press.

Karls, J. M., & Wandrei, K. E. (Eds.). (1994). *Person-in-environment system: The PIE classification system for social functioning problems.* Washington, DC: National Association of Social Workers.

Kasl, S. V., & Harburg, E. (1975). Mental health and urban environment: Some doubts and second thoughts. *Journal of Health and Social Behavior, 16,* 268–282.

Katz, A. (1993). *Self-help in America: A social movement perspective.* New York: Twayne.

Katz, D., & Kahn, R. (1978). *The social psychology of organizations* (2nd ed.). New York: Wiley.

Keane, C. (1991). Socioenvironmental determinants of community formation. *Environment and Behavior, 23*(1), 27–46.

Keefe, T. (1996). Meditation and social work treatment. In F. J. Turner (Ed.), *Social work treatment: Interlocking theoretical approaches* (4th ed.) (pp. 434–460). New York: Free Press.

Kelley, H., & Thibaut, J. (1978). *Interpersonal relations: A theory of interdependence.* New York: Wiley.

Kennedy, S., Kiecolt-Glaser, J. K., & Glaser, R. (1988). Immunological consequences of acute and chronic stressors: Mediating role of interpersonal relationships. *British Journal of Medical Psychology, 61,* 77–85.

Kent, S. (1991). Partitioning space: Cross-cultural factors influencing domestic spatial segmentation. *Environment and Behavior, 23,* 438–473.

Kettner, P., & Martin, L. (1994). Will privatization destroy the traditional nonprofit human services sector? No. In M. Austin & J. Lowe (Eds.), *Controversial issues in communities and organizations* (pp. 166–171). Boston: Allyn & Bacon.

Keutzer, C. (1982). Physics and consciousness. *Journal of Humanistic Psychology, 22,* 74–90.

Kilbury, R., Bordieri, J., & Wong, H. (1996). Impact of physical disability and gender on personal space. *Journal of Rehabilitation, 62*(2), 59–61.

Kinkade, K. (1973). *A Walden Two experiment: The first five years of Twin Oaks Community.* New York: Morrow.

Kochman, T. (1981). *Black and white styles in conflict.* Chicago: University of Chicago Press.

Kohlberg, L. (1969). *Stages in the development of moral thought and action.* New York: Holt, Rinehart, & Winston.

Kottak, C. P. (1994). *Anthropology: The exploration of human diversity.* New York: McGraw-Hill.

Kottak, C. P. (1996). *Mirror for humanity: A concise introduction to cultural anthropology.* New York: McGraw-Hill.

Kozol, J. (1991). *Savage inequalities: Children in America's schools.* New York: Crown.

Kravetz, D. (1982). An overview of content on women for the social work curriculum. *Journal of Education for Social Work, 18*(2), 42–49.

Kriesi, H. (1996). The organizational structure of new social movements in a political context. In D. McAdam, J. McCarthy, & M. Zald (Eds.), *Comparative perspectives on social movements* (pp. 152–184). New York: Cambridge University Press.

Krill, D. (1986). Existential social work. In F. Turner (Ed.), *Social work treatment: Interlocking theoretical approaches* (pp. 181–217). New York: Free Press.

Krill, D. F. (1996). Existential social work. In F. J. Turner (Ed.), *Social work treatment* (4th ed.) (pp. 250–281). New York: Free Press.

Kroeber, A. (1917). The superorganic. *American Anthropologist, 19,* 163–213.

Kroeber, A., & Kluckhohn, C. (1963). *Culture: A critical review of concepts and definitions.* New York: Vintage.

Kroeber, A., & Kluckhohn, C. (1978). *Culture: A critical review of concepts and definitions.* Cambridge, MA: Peabody Museum. (Original work published 1952)

Kropf, N., & Greene, R. (1994). Erikson's eight stages of development: Different lenses. In R. Greene (Ed.), *Human behavior theory: A diversity framework* (pp. 75–114). New York: Aldine de Gruyter.

Kuo, F., Bacaicoa, M., & Sullivan, W. (1998). Transforming inner-city landscapes: Trees, sense of safety, and preference. *Environment and Behavior, 30,* 28–59.

Labov, W. (1982). Objectivity and commitment in linguistic science: The case of the Black English trial in Ann Arbor. *Language in Society, 11,* 165–210.

Laing, R. D. (1967). *The politics of experience.* New York: Ballantine.

Laing, R. D. (1969). *The politics of the family.* New York: Pantheon.

Laird, J. (1984). Sorcerers, shamans, and social workers: The use of ritual in social work practice. *Social Work, 29,* 123–128.

Laird, J. (1993). Lesbian and gay families. In F. Walsh (Ed.), *Normal family processes* (2nd ed.) (pp. 282–328). New York: Guilford.

Laird, J. (1994). Changing women's narratives: Taking back the discourse. In L. Davis (Ed.), *Building on women's strengths: A social work agenda for the twenty-first century* (pp. 179–210). New York: Haworth Press.

Lane, H. J. (1984). Self-differentiation in symbolic interactionism and psychoanalysis. *Social Work, 34,* 270–274.

Langer, E., Fiske, S., Taylor, S., & Chanowitz, B. (1976). Stigma, staring, and discomfort: A novel-stimulus hypothesis. *Journal of Experimental Social Psychology, 12,* 451–463.

Langlois, S. (1994). *Convergence or divergence? Comparing recent social trends in industrial societies.* Buffalo: McGill–Queen's University Press.

Lantz, J. E. (1996). Cognitive theory and social work practice. In F. J. Turner (Ed.), *Social work treatment* (4th ed.) (pp. 94–115). New York: Free Press.

Larin, K., & McNichol, E. (1997). *Pulling apart: A state-by-state analysis of income trends.* Washington, DC: Center on Budget and Policy Priorities.

Law, M., & Dunn, W. (1993). Perspectives on understanding and changing the environments of children with disabilities. *Physical and Occupational Therapy in Pediatrics, 13*(3), 1–18.

Lawrence, P. R., & Lorsch, J. W. (1967a). Differentiation and integration in complex organizations. *Administrative Science Quarterly, 12,* 1–47.

Lawrence, P. R., & Lorsch, J. W. (1967b). *Organization and environment.* Boston: Harvard University Graduate School of Business Administration.

Lazarus, R. S. (1980). Thoughts on the relations between cognition and emotion. *American Psychologist, 37,* 1019–1024.

Lazarus, R. S. (1993). Coping theory and research: Past, present, and future. *Psychosomatic Medicine, 55,* 234–247.

Lazarus, R. S., & Cohen, J. (1977). Environmental stress. In L. Altman & J. Wohlwill (Eds.), *Human behavior and the environment: Current theory and research* (Vol. 2: 89–127). New York: Plenum.

Lazarus, R. S., & Lazarus, B. N. (1994). *Passion and reason: Making sense of our emotions.* New York: Oxford University Press.

League of Women Voters. (1997). Diversity of representation. In *League of Women Voters Web Site* [On-line]. Available: http://www.lwv.org/~lwvus/report.html

LeCroy, C. W. (1992). *Case studies in social work practice.* Belmont, CA: Wadsworth.

Lee, P. (1937). *Social work as cause and function, and other papers.* New York: New York School of Social Work.

Leiby, J. (1977). Social welfare: History of basic ideas. In J. B. Turner (Ed.), *Encyclopedia of social work* (17th ed.) (pp. 1513–1518). Washington, DC: National Association of Social Workers.

Leiby, J. (1985). Moral foundations of social welfare and social work: A historical view. *Social Work, 30,* 323–330.

Lenski, G. (1966). *Power and privilege.* New York: McGraw-Hill.

Levi, M., Cook, K., O'Brien, J., & Faye, H. (1990). The limits of rationality. In K. Cook & M. Levi (Eds.), *The limits of rationality* (pp. 1–16). Chicago: University of Chicago Press.

Levin, J. D. (1992). *Theories of the self.* Washington, DC: Hemisphere.

Levine, B. (1991). *Group psychotherapy.* Prospect Heights, IL: Waveland Press.

Levine, S., Coe, C., & Wiener, S. G. (1989). Psychoneuroendocrinology of stress: A psychobiological perspective. In F. R. Brush & S. Levine (Eds.), *Psychoendocrinology* (pp. 341–377). New York: Academic Press.

Levinson, D. (1996). *The seasons of a woman's life.* New York: Knopf.

Levi-Strauss, C. (1967). *Structural anthropology.* New York: Doubleday.

Levi-Strauss, C. (1969). *The elementary structures of kinship.* Boston: Beacon Press. (Original work published 1949)

Levy, F. (1995). Incomes and income inequality. In R. Farley (Ed.), *State of the union: America in the 1990s: Vol. 1. Economic trends* (pp. 1–57). New York: Russell Sage Foundation.

Lewis, C. (1972). Public housing gardens: Landscapes for the soul. In *Landscape for living* (pp. 277–282). Washington, DC: U.S. Department of Agriculture.

Lewis, C. (1979). Healing in the urban environment: A person/plant viewpoint. *Journal of American Planning Association, 45,* 330–338.

Lifchez, R., & Davis, C. (1987). Living upstairs, leaving home, and at the Moscow Circus. In M. Saxton & F. Howe (Eds.), *With wings: An anthology of literature by and about women with disabilities.* New York: Feminist Press.

Lincoln, Y., & Guba, E. (1985). *Naturalistic inquiry.* Beverly Hills, CA: Sage.

Linstead, S. (1993). Deconstruction in the study of organizations. In J. Hassard & M. Parker (Eds.), *Postmodernism and organizations* (pp. 49–70). Newbury Park, CA: Sage.

Lipset, S., & Schneider, W. (1983). *The confidence gap: Business, labor, and government in the public mind.* New York: Free Press.

Littrell, J. (1996). How psychological states affect the immune system: Implications for interventions in the context of HIV. *Health and Social Work, 21,* 287–295.

Livingstone, S. (1996). On the continuing problem of media effects. In J. Curran & M. Gurevitch (Eds.), *Mass media and society* (2nd ed.) (pp. 305–324). New York: Arnold.

Lockwood, D. (1966). Sources of variation in working class images of society. *Sociological Review, 14,* 244–267.

Loewenberg, F. M. (1988). *Religion and social work practice in contemporary American society.* New York: Columbia University Press.

Logan, J., & Molotch, H. (1987). *Urban fortunes: The political economy of place.* Berkeley and Los Angeles: University of California Press.

Logan, S. L., Freeman, E. M., & McRoy, R. G. (1990*). Social work practice with black families: A culturally specific perspective.* New York: Longman.

Long, P. W. (1996). *Major depressive disorder: Treatment.* [Online]. Available: www.mentalhealth.com

Longres, J. (1995). *Human behavior in the social environment* (2nd ed.). Itasca, IL: Peacock.

Loo, C. (1974). *Crowding and human behavior.* New York: MSS Information Corporation.

Lovaglia, M. J. (1995). Power and status: Exchange, attribution, and expectation states. *Small Group Research, 26,* 400–426.

Low, S., & Altman, I. (1992). Place attachment: A conceptual inquiry. In I. Altman & S. Low (Eds.), *Place attachment* (pp. 1–12). New York: Plenum.

Lowe, J. I. (1997). A social-health model: A paradigm for social work in health care. In M. Reisch & E. Gambrill (Eds.), *Social work in the 21st century.* Thousand Oaks, CA: Pine Forge.

Lubove, R. (1966, May 23). Social work and the life of the poor. *The Nation,* 609–611.

Luepnitz, D. (1988). *The family interpreted: Feminist theory and clinical practice.* New York: Basic Books.

Lum, D. (1992). *Social work practice and people of color: A process-stage approach* (2nd ed.). Pacific Grove, CA: Brooks/Cole.

Lyon, L. (1987). *The community in urban society.* Philadelphia: Temple University Press.

MacIver, R. (1931). *Society: Its structure and changes.* New York: Ray Long and Richard R. Smith.

Macklin, E. D. (1980). Nontraditional family forms: A decade of research. In F. M. Berardo (Ed.), *Decade review: Family research 1970–1979* (pp. 175–192). Minneapolis: National Council on Family Relations. [Also published as a special issue of *Journal of Marriage and the Family,* 1980, 42(4)]

Mader, S. S. (1998). *Human biology* (5th ed.). Boston: McGraw-Hill.

Magai, C. (1996). Personality theory: Birth, death, and transfiguration. In R. D. Kavanaugh, B. Zimmerberg, & S. Fein (Eds.), *Emotion: Interdisciplinary perspectives* (pp. 171–202). Mahwah, NJ: Lawrence Erlbaum.

Maier, H. W. (1978). *Three theories of child development* (3rd ed.). New York: Harper and Row.

Maier, S., Watkins, L., & Fleshner, M. (1994). Psychoneuroimmunology: The interface between behavior, brain, and immunity. *American Psychologist, 49,* 1004–1017.

Makinson, L. (1993). *Open secrets: The encyclopedia of congressional money and politics.* Washington, DC: Congressional Quarterly.

Mancini, J. A., & Blieszner, R. (1991). Aging parents and adult children: Research themes in intergenerational relations. In A. Booth (Ed.), *Contemporary families: Looking forward, looking back* (pp. 249–264). Minneapolis: National Council on Family Relations.

Mann, M. (1986). *The sources of social power* (Vol. 1). New York: Cambridge University Press.

March, J., & Simon, H. (1958). *Organizations.* New York: Wiley.

Marcia, J. (1993). The ego identity status approach to ego identity. In J. E. Marcia, A. S. Waterman, D. R. Mattesson, S. L. Arcjer, & J. L. Orlofsky (Eds.), *Ego identity: A handbook for psychosocial research.* New York: Springer-Verlag.

Mare, R. (1995). Changes in educational attainment and school enrollment. In R. Farley (Ed.), *State of the union: America in the 1990s Vol. 1* (pp. 155–243). New York: Russell Sage Foundation.

Markowitz, M. (1997, September). *Protease inhibitors: A new family of drugs for the treatment of HIV infection: What they are, how they work, when to use them* (rev. ver. 4). [On-line]. Available: http://www.iapac.org/consumer/proinbk.html

Martin, P. Y., & O'Connor, G. G. (1989). *The social environment: Open systems applications.* New York: Longman.

Marty, M. (1980). Social service: Godly and godless. *Social Service Review, 54,* 463–481.

Marx, G., & McAdam, D. (1994). *Collective behavior and social movements: Process and structure.* Englewood Cliffs, NJ: Prentice-Hall.

Marx, K. (1967). *Capital: A critique of political economy* (S. Moore & E. Aveling, Trans.) (Vol. 1). New York: International Publishers. (Original work published 1887)

Maslach, C., & Jackson, S. (1981). *Maslach Burnout Inventory: Research edition.* Palo Alto, CA: Consulting Psychologists Press.

Maslow, A. (1962). *Toward a psychology of being.* New York: Van Nostrand.

Maslow, A. (1971). *Farther reaches of human nature.* New York: Viking.

Maxwell, L. (1996). Multiple effects of home and day care crowding. *Environment and Behavior, 28,* 494–511.

Mayhew, P., Clarke, R., Hough, J., & Winchester, S. (1980). Natural surveillance and vandalism to telephone kiosks. In R. Clarke & P. Mayhew (Eds.), *Designing out crime* (pp. 67–74). London: Her Majesty's Stationery Office.

Maynard, F. M. (1998, February 25). *The post-polio syndrome and re-rehabilitation.* [On-line]. Available: http://www.azstarnet.com/~rspear/rehab2.html

Mayo, E. (1933). *The human problems of an industrial civilization.* New York: Macmillan.

McAdam, D. (1982). *Political process and the development of black insurgency, 1930–1970.* Chicago: University of Chicago Press.

McAdam, D. (1996a). Conceptual origins, current problems, future directions. In D. McAdam, J. McCarthy, & M. Zald (Eds.), *Comparative perspectives on social movements* (pp. 23–40). New York: Cambridge University Press.

McAdam, D. (1996b). The framing function of movement tactics: Strategic dramaturgy in the American civil rights movement. In D. McAdam, J. McCarthy, & M. Zald (Eds.), *Comparative perspectives on social movements* (pp. 338–355). New York: Cambridge University Press.

McAdam, D., McCarthy, J., & Zald, M. (1996). Introduction: Opportunities, mobilizing structures, and framing processes: Toward a synthetic, comparative perspective on social movements. In D. McAdam, J. McCarthy, & M. Zald (Eds.), *Comparative perspectives on social movements* (pp. 1–20). New York: Cambridge University Press.

McAdoo, H. P. (Ed.). (1997). *Black families* (3rd ed.). Thousand Oaks, CA: Sage.

McCarthy, J. (1987). Pro-life and pro-choice mobilization: Infrastructure deficits and new technologies. In M. Zald & J. McCarthy (Eds.), *Social movements in an organizational society* (pp. 49–66). New Brunswick, NJ: Transaction.

McCarthy, J. (1996). Constraints and opportunities in adopting, adapting, and inventing. In D. McAdam, J. McCarthy, & M. Zald (Eds.), *Comparative perspectives on social movements: Political opportunities, mobilizing structures, and cultural framings* (pp. 141–151). New York: Cambridge University Press.

McCarthy, J., & Zald, M. (1977). Resource mobilization in social movements: A partial theory. *American Journal of Sociology, 82,* 1212–1239.

McCubbin, H. I., & Figley, C. R. (1983). *Stress and the family: Vol. 1: Coping with normative transitions.* New York: Brunner/Mazel.

McCubbin, H. I., Joy, C. B., Cauble, A. E., Comeau, J. K., Patterson, J. M., & Needle, R. H. (1980). Family stress and coping: A decade review. In F. M. Berardo (Ed.), *Decade review: Family research 1970–1979* (pp. 125–141). Minneapolis: National Council on Family Relations. [Also published as a special issue of *Journal of Marriage and the Family,* 1980, 42(4)]

McCubbin, H. I., & Patterson, J. M. (1983). The family stress process: The double ABCX model of adjustment and adaptation. In H. I. McCubbin, M. B. Sussman, & J. M. Patterson (Eds.), *Social stress and the family: Advances and developments in family stress theory and research* (pp. 7–37). New York: Haworth.

McDonald, L. (1997). Building on the strengths and assets of families and communities. *Families in Society, 78,* 115–116.

McDonald, L., Billingham, S., Conrad, T., Morgan, A., O, N.,

Payton, E. (1997). Families and Schools Together (FAST): Integrating community development with clinical strategies. *Families in Society, 78,* 140–155.

McGoldrick, M. (1988). Women and the family life cycle. In E. Carter & M. McGoldrick (Eds.), *The changing family life cycle* (pp. 31–68). New York: Gardner.

McGoldrick, M., Giordano, J., & Pearce, J. K. (Eds.). (1996). *Ethnicity and family therapy* (2nd ed.). New York: Guilford.

McGregor, D. (1960). *The human side of enterprise.* New York: McGraw-Hill.

McKinney, J., & Loomis, C. (1958). The typological tradition. In J. Roucek (Ed.), *Contemporary sociology.* New York: Philosophical Library.

McLanahan, S., & Sandefur, G. (1994). *Growing up with a single parent: What hurts, what helps.* Cambridge, MA: Harvard University Press.

McMillan, D. (1976). *Sense of community: An attempt at definition.* Unpublished manuscript, George Peabody College for Teachers, Nashville.

McMillan, D., & Chavis, D. (1986). Sense of community: A definition and theory. *Journal of Community Psychology, 14,* 6–23.

McWhirter, D., & Mattison, A. (1984). *The male couple: How relationships develop.* Englewood Cliffs, NJ: Prentice-Hall.

Mead, G. H. (1934). *Mind, self, and society.* Chicago: University of Chicago Press.

Mead, M. (1950). *Sex and temperament in three primitive societies.* New York: New American Library. (Original work published 1935)

Mead, M. (1961). *Coming of age in Samoa.* New York: Morrow Quill. (Original work published 1928)

Mead, M. (1968). *Growing up in New Guinea: A comparative study of primitive education.* New York: Dell. (Original work published 1930)

Mechanic, D. (1995). Sociological dimensions of illness behavior. *Social Science and Medicine, 41,* 1207–1216.

Medyckyj-Scott, D., & Hearnshaw, H. (Eds.). (1993). *Human factors in geographical information systems.* Boca Raton, FL: CRC Press.

Meeker, B. F. (1994). Performance evaluation. In M. Foshci & E. J. Lawler (Eds.), *Group processes: Sociological analyses* (pp. 95–117). Chicago: Nelson-Hall.

Meyer, C. (1976). *Social work practice* (2nd ed.). New York: Free Press.

Meyer, C. (Ed.). (1983). *Clinical social work in an eco-systems perspective.* New York: Columbia University Press.

Meyer, C. (1993). *Assessment in social work practice.* New York: Columbia University Press.

Middleton, P. (1989). Socialism, feminism and men. *Radical Philosophy, 53,* 8–19.

Mikulincer, M. (1994). *Human learned helplessness: A coping perspective.* New York: Plenum.

Miller, D. (1987). *Helping the strong: An exploration of the needs of families headed by women.* Silver Spring, MD: National Association of Social Workers.

Millison, M. B., & Dudley, J. R. (1990). The importance of spirituality in hospice work: A study of hospice professionals. *Hospice Journal, 6*(3), 63–78.

Minami, H., & Tanaka, K. (1995). Social and environmental psychology: Transaction between physical space and group-dynamic processes. *Environment and Behavior, 27,* 43–55.

Mindel, C. H., Habenstein, R. W., & Wright R., Jr. (Eds.). (1998). *Ethnic families in America: Patterns and variations* (4th ed.). Upper Saddle River, NJ: Prentice Hall.

Mischey, E. J. (1981). Faith, identity, and personality in late adolescence. *Character Potential: A Record of Research, 9*(4), 175–185.

Moberg, D. O. (1990). Spiritual maturity and wholeness in the later years. *Journal of Religious Gerontology, 7,* 5–24.

Monte, C. (1995). *Beneath the mask: An introduction to theories of personality* (5th ed.). Fort Worth, TX: Harcourt Brace Jovanovich.

Moore, E. (1981). A prison environment's effect on health care service demands. *Journal of Environmental Systems, 11,* 17–34.

Moore, K. A. (1995, September). Executive summary: Nonmarital childbearing in the United States. In U.S. Department of Health and Human Services (Public Health Service, Centers for Disease Control and Prevention, National Center for Health Statistics), *Report to Congress on out-of-wedlock childbearing* (pp. v–xxii). Washington, DC: U.S. Government Printing Office (DHHS Pub. No. (PHS) 95-1257).

Morell, C. (1996). Radicalizing recovery: Addiction, spirituality, and politics. *Social Work, 41,* 306–312.

Morgan, G. (1986). *Images of organization.* Newbury Park, CA: Sage.

Morgan, M. (1994). Theories and politics in African American English. *Annual Review of Anthropology, 23,* 325–345.

Morris, A. (1981). The black southern sit-in movement: An analysis of internal organization. *American Sociological Review, 46,* 744–767.

Morris, A. (1984). *The origins of the civil rights movement: Black communities organizing for change.* New York: Free Press.

Morse, J., & Lorsch, J. (1970). Beyond theory Y. *Harvard Business Review, 45,* 61–68.

Mortimer, J. T., & Simmons, R. G. (1978). Adult socialization. *Annual Review of Sociology, 4,* 421–454.

Moyers, B. (1993). *Healing and the mind.* New York: Doubleday.

Muff, J. (1996). Images of life on the verge of death: Dreams and drawings of people with AIDS. *Perspectives in Psychiatric Care, 32*(3), 10–21.

Murray, C. (1984). *Losing ground: American social policy, 1950–1980.* New York: Basic Books.

Murray, C., & Herrnstein, R. (1994). *The bell curve: Intelligence and class structure in American life.* New York: Free Press.

Musick, M. A. (1996). Religion and subjective health among black and white elders. *Journal of Health and Social Behavior, 37,* 221–237.

Nair, S., Blake, M. L., & Vosler, N. R. (1997). Multilevel social systems practice with low-income families in Singapore. *Families in Society, 78*(3), 291–298.

Nakhaima, J. M., & Dicks, B. H. (1995). Social work practice with religious families. *Families in Society, 76,* 360–368.

Naperstek, A., & Dooley, D. (1997). Countering urban disinvestment through community-building initiatives. *Social Work, 42,* 506–514.

Nathanson, I. G. (1995). Divorce and women's spirituality. *Journal of Divorce and Remarriage, 22,* 179–188.

National Association of Social Workers (1982). Changes in NASW family policy. *NASW News, 27*(2), 10.

National Center for Health Statistics. (1998). *Statistical rolodex—United States.* [On-Line]. Available: http://www.cdc.gov/nchswww/fastats/usa.htm

National Coalition of the Homeless. (1997a). *NCH fact sheet #2* [On-line]. Available: http://www2.ari.net/home/nch/numbers.html

National Coalition of the Homeless. (1997b). *NCH fact sheet #3* [On-line]. Available: http://www2.ari.net/home/nch/who.html

National Institute of Neurological Disorders and Stroke. (1997). *Post-polio syndrome: Fact sheet.* [On-line]. Available: www.ninds.hih.gov/healinfo/disorder/ppolio/ppolio

Nee, L. E. (1995). Effects of psychosocial interactions at a cellular level. *Social Work, 40,* 259–262.

Netting, F. E. (1984). Church-related agencies and social welfare. *Social Service Review, 58,* 404–420.

Netting, F. E., Kettner, P. M., & McMurtry, S. L. (1993). *Social work macro practice.* New York: Longman.

Netting, F. E., & McMurty, S. L. (1994). Will privatization destroy the traditional nonprofit human services sector? Yes. In M. Austin & J. Lowe (Eds.), *Controversial issues in communities and organizations* (pp. 158–164). Boston: Allyn & Bacon.

Neugarten, B. (1979). Time, age, and the life cycle. *American Journal of Psychiatry, 136,* 887–894.

Newbrough, J.R., & Chavis, D. M. (1986). Psychological sense of community: I, Foreword. *Journal of Community Psychology, 14,* 3–5.

Newell, P. (1997). A cross-cultural examination of favorite places. *Environment and Behavior, 29,* 495–514.

Newman, D. (1995). *Sociology: Exploring the architecture of everyday life.* Thousand Oaks, CA: Pine Forge.

Newman, O. (1972). *Defensible space.* New York: Macmillan.

Newman, O. (1980). *Community of interest.* Garden City, NY: Anchor/Doubleday.

Newman, O. (1981). *Community of interest*. New York: Doubleday.

Nicholson, B. L. (1997). The influence of pre-emigration and postemigration stressors on mental health: A study of Southeast Asian refugees. *Social Work Research, 21*, 19–31.

Niebuhr, R. (1932). *The contribution of religion to social work*. New York: Columbia University Press.

Noll, H., & Langlois, S. (1994). Employment and labour-market change: Toward two models of growth. In S. Langlois (Ed.), *Convergence or divergence? Comparing recent social trends in industrial societies* (pp. 89–113). Buffalo: McGill–Queen's University Press.

Northen, H. (1988). *Social work with groups* (3rd ed.). New York: Columbia University Press.

Novello, A. C. (1993). *Surgeon General's report to the American public on HIV infection and AIDS*. Rockville, MD: CDC National AIDS Clearinghouse.

O'Brien, P. J. (1992). Social work and spirituality: Clarifying the concept for practice. *Spirituality and Social Work Journal, 3*(1), 2–5.

Oberschall, A. (1992). *Social movements: Ideologies, interests, and identities*. New Brunswick, NJ: Transaction.

Oberschall, A. (1996). Opportunities and framing in the Eastern European revolts of 1989. In D. McAdam, J. McCarthy, & M. Zald (Eds.), *Comparative perspectives on social movements: Political opportunities, mobilizing structures, and cultural framings* (pp. 93–121). New York: Cambridge University Press.

Ogbu, J. (1991). Immigrant and involuntary minorities in comparative perspective. In M. Gibson & J. Ogbu (Eds.), *Minority status and schooling: A comparative study of immigrant and involuntary minorities*. New York: Garland.

Omi, M., & Winant, H. (1993). On the theoretical status of the concept of race. In C. McCarthy & W. Crichlow (Eds.), *Race, identity, and representation in education*. New York: Routledge.

Ortiz, L. P. A. (1991). Religious issues: The missing link in social work education. *Spirituality and Social Work Journal, 2*(2), 13–18.

Ortner, S. (1973). On key symbols. *American Anthropologist, 75*, 1338–1346.

Ortner, S. (1984). Theory in anthropology since the sixties. *Comparative Studies in History and Society, 26*(1), 126–166.

Ortner, S. (1989). *High religion: A cultural and political history of Sherpa Buddhism*. Princeton, NJ: Princeton University Press.

Ortner, S. (1996). *Making gender: The politics and erotics of culture*. Boston: Beacon Press.

Osmond, H. (1957). Function as the basis of psychiatric ward design. *Mental Hospitals, 8*, 23–29.

Osmond, H. (1959). The relationship between architect and psychiatrist. In C. Goshen (Ed.), *Psychiatric architecture* (pp. 16–20). Washington, DC: American Psychiatric Association.

Osmond, H. (1966). Some psychiatric aspects of design. In L. B. Holland (Ed.), *Who designs America?* Garden City, NY: Anchor.

Panksepp, J. (1991). Affective neuroscience: A conceptual framework for the neurobiological study of emotions. In K. T. Strongman (Ed.), *International review of studies on emotions* (pp. 59–99). New York: Wiley.

Papalia, D. E., & Olds, S. W. (1995). *Human development* (6th ed.). New York: McGraw-Hill.

Park, R. (1936). Human ecology. *American Journal of Sociology, 17*, 1–15.

Parsons, T. (1951). *The social system*. Glencoe, IL: Free Press.

Perkins, D., Wandersman, A., Rich, R., & Taylor, R. (1993). The physical environment of street crime: Defensible space, territoriality and incivilities. *Journal of Environmental Psychology, 13*(1), 29–49.

Perlmutter, F. (1988). Administering alternative social agencies: Educational implications. *Administration in Social Work, 12*(2), 109–118.

Pfeffer, J. (1982). *Organizations and organization theory*. Boston: Pitman.

Pfeffer, J. (1997). *New directions for organizational theory*. New York: Oxford University Press.

Pfeffer, J., & Salancik, G. (1978). *The external control of organizations: A resource dependence perspective*. New York: Harper & Row.

PFLAG. (1995). *Our daughters and sons: Questions and answers for parents of gay, lesbian and bisexual people*. Washington, DC: Author.

Pierce, C. (1982). *Writings of Charles S. Pierce: A chronological edition*. Bloomington: Indiana University Press.

Pincus, A., & Minahan, A. (1973). *Social work practice: Model and method*. Itasca, IL: Peacock.

Pines, A., & Kafry, D. (1978). Occupational tedium in the social services. *Social Work, 23*, 499–507.

Piven, F., & Cloward, R. (1971). *Regulating the poor: The functions of public welfare*. New York: Vintage Books.

Piven, F., & Cloward, R. (1977). *Poor people's movements: Why they succeed, how they fail*. New York: Pantheon.

Plato. (1968). *The republic* (A. Bloom, Trans.). New York: Basic Books.

Plutchik, R. (1991). Emotions and evolution. In K. T. Strongman (Ed.), *International review of studies on emotions* (pp. 37–58). New York: Wiley.

Pollio, D. E. (1995). Hoops group: Group work with young "street" men. *Social Work with Groups, 18*(2/3), 107–116.

Popenoe, D. (1996). *Life without father: Compelling new evidence that fatherhood and marriage are indispensable for the good of children and society*. New York: Martin Kessler Books.

Popple, P. (1992). Social work: Social function and moral purpose. In P. Reid & P. Popple (Eds.), *The moral purposes of social work: The character and intentions of a profession* (pp. 141–154). Chicago: Nelson-Hall.

Popple, P., & Leighninger, L. (1990). *Social work, social welfare, and American society.* Boston: Allyn & Bacon.

Popple, P., & Leighninger, L. (1993). *Social work, social welfare, and American society* (2nd ed.). Boston: Allyn & Bacon.

Poston, D., & Dan, H. (1996). Fertility trends in the United States. In D. Peck & J. Hollingsworth (Eds.), *Demographic and structural change: The effects of the 1980s on American society* (pp. 85–110). Westport, CT: Greenwood Press.

Prichard, D. (1996). *The primary and secondary impact of critical incident stress on police officers and domestic partners.* Unpublished doctoral dissertation, Virginia Commonwealth University, Richmond.

Procidano, M., & Heller, K. (1983). Measures of perceived social support from friends and family: Three validation studies. *American Journal of Community Psychology, 11,* 1–24.

Proctor, E. K., Davis, L. E., & Vosler, N. R. (1995). Families: Direct practice. In R. L. Edwards et al. (Eds.), *Encyclopedia of social work* (19th ed.) (Vol. 2, pp. 941–950). Washington, DC: NASW Press.

Rapoport, A. (1990). *Meaning of the built environment.* Tucson: University of Arizona Press.

Rawls, J. (1993). *Political liberalism.* New York: Columbia University Press.

Ray, L. (1993). *Rethinking critical theory: Emancipation in the age of global social movements.* Newbury Park, CA: Sage.

Reamer, F. (1992). Social work and the public good: Calling or career? In P. Reid & P. Popple (Eds.), *The moral purposes of social work: The character and intentions of a profession* (pp. 11–33). Chicago: Nelson-Hall.

Reamer, F. (1993). *The philosophical foundations of social work.* New York: Columbia University Press.

Reed, M. (1993). Organizations and modernity: Continuity and discontinuity in organization theory. In J. Hassard & M. Parker (Eds.), *Postmodernism and organizations* (pp. 163–182). Newbury Park, CA: Sage.

Rehabilitation Act of 1973 (Public Law 93-112). 87 Stat. 335.

Reich, R. (1992). *The work of nations.* New York: Vintage.

Reid, K. E. (1997). *Social work practice with groups: A clinical perspective* (2nd ed.). Pacific Grove, CA: Brooks/Cole.

Reid, W. J. (1985). *Family problem solving.* New York: Columbia University Press.

Reid, W., & Smith, A. (1989). *Research in social work* (2nd ed.). New York: Columbia University Press.

Reisch, M. (1997). The political context of social work. In M. Reisch & E. Gambrill (Eds.), *Social work in the 21st century* (pp. 80–92). Thousand Oaks, CA: Pine Forge Press.

Reskin, B., & Padavic, I. (1994). *Women and men at work.* Thousand Oaks, CA: Pine Forge.

Resnick, H., & Jaffee, B. (1982). The physical environment and social welfare. *Social Casework, 63,* 354–362.

Ressler, L. (1998). The relation between church and state: Issues in social work and the law. *Social Thought, 18*(2), 81–95.

Revitalization of impoverished communities [Special issue]. (1997). *Social Work, 42*(5).

Rex, J. (1961). *Key problems of sociological theory.* London: Routledge.

Richman, J. M., Rosenfeld, L. B., & Hardy, C. J. (1993). The social support survey: A validation study of a clinical measure of the social support process. *Research on Social Work Practice 3,* 288–311.

Richmond, M. (1901). Charitable cooperation. In *Proceedings of the National Conference of Charities and Corrections.* Boston: Elles.

Richmond, M. (1917). *Social diagnosis.* New York: Russell Sage.

Ringer, B., & Lawless, E. (1989). *Race-ethnicity and society.* New York: Routledge.

Ritzer, G. (1992). *Contemporary sociological theory* (3rd ed.). New York: McGraw-Hill.

Ritzer, G. (1993). *The McDonaldization of society.* Thousand Oaks, CA: Pine Forge.

Robbins, S. P., Chatterjee, P., & Canda, E. R. (1998). Transpersonal theory. *Contemporary human behavior theory: A critical perspective for social work* (pp. 353–393). Boston: Allyn & Bacon.

Robertson, J. G., & Vosler, N. R. (1997, July). *Nonmarital parents in St. Louis and Missouri: Report submitted to the Division of Family Services and the Division of Child Support Enforcement of the Missouri Department of Social Services.* St. Louis: Washington University School of Social Work.

Robertson, R. (1992). *Globalization: Social theory and global culture.* Newbury Park, CA: Sage.

Rodwell, M. (1987). Naturalistic inquiry: An alternative model for social work assessment. *Social Service Review, 61,* 231–246.

Rogers, C. (1951). *Client-centered therapy.* Boston: Houghton Mifflin.

Rogge, M. (1993). Social work, disenfranchised communities, and the natural environment: Field education opportunties. *Journal of Social Work Education, 29,* 111–120.

Rolland, J. S. (1993). Mastering family challenges in serious illness and disability. In F. Walsh (Ed.), *Normal family processes* (2nd ed.) (pp. 444–473). New York: Guilford.

Roof, W. (1993). *A generation of seekers: The spiritual journeys of the baby boom generation.* San Francisco: HarperCollins.

Roof, W., & McKinney, W. (1987). *American mainline religion: Its changing shape and future.* Rutgers, NJ: State University Press.

Rosaldo, R. (1993). *Culture and truth: The remaking of social analysis.* Boston: Beacon Press. (Original work published 1989)

Rose, N. (1997). The future economic landscape: Implications for social work practice and education. In M. Reisch & E.

Gambrill (Eds.), *Social work in the 21st century* (pp. 28–38). Thousand Oaks, CA: Pine Forge.

Roseberry, W. (1989). European history and the construction of anthropological subjects. In *Anthropologies and histories: Essays in culture, history, and political economy.* New Brunswick, NJ: Rutgers University Press.

Rosenzweig, M. R., & Leiman, A. L. (1982). *Physiological psychology.* Lexington, MA: Heath.

Rothschild-Whitt, J., & Whitt, J. (1986). *The cooperative workplace.* Cambridge: Cambridge University Press.

Rousseau, M. (1991). *Community: The tie that binds.* New York: University Press of America.

Rubin, A., & Babbie, E. (1993). *Research methods for social work* (2nd ed.). New York: Columbia University Press.

Rugel, R. P. (1991). Addictions treatment in groups: A review of therapeutic factors. *Small Group Research, 22,* 475–491.

Ruggles, P. (1991). Short- and long-term poverty in the United States: Measuring the American "underclass." In L. Osberg (Ed.), *Economic inequality and poverty: International perspectives* (pp. 157–192). Armonk, NY: Sharpe.

Russel, R. (1998). Spirituality and religion in graduate social work education. *Social Thought, 18*(2), 15–29.

Ryscavage, P. (1994). Gender-related shifts in the distribution of wages. *Monthly Labor Review, 117*(7), 3–15.

Safyer, A. W., & Spies-Karotkin, G. (1988). The biology of AIDS. *Health and Social Work, 13,* 251–258.

Sahlins, M. (1981). *Historical metaphors and mythical realities: Structure in the early history of the Sandwich Islands Kingdom.* Ann Arbor: University of Michigan Press.

Salazar, A. J. (1996). An analysis of the development and evolution of roles in the small group. *Small Group Research, 27,* 475–503.

Saleebey, D. (1985). In clinical social work practice, is the body politic? *Social Service Review, 59,* 578–592.

Saleebey, D. (1992). Biology's challenge to social work: Embodying the person-in-environment perspective. *Social Work, 37,* 112–118.

Saleebey, D. (1994). Culture, theory, and narrative: The intersection of meanings in practice. *Social Work, 39,* 351–359.

Sampson, F., Raudenbush, S., & Earls, F. (1997). Neighborhoods and violent crime: A multilevel study of collective efficacy. *Science, 277,* 918–924.

Sampson, R. (1983). Structural density and criminal victimization. *Criminology: An Interdisciplinary Journal, 21,* 276–293.

Sampson, R., & Groves, W. B. (1989). Community structure and crime: Testing social-disorganization theory. *American Journal of Sociology, 94,* 774–802.

Sapir, E. (1985). *Selected writings in language, culture, and personality.* Berkeley: University of California Press. (Original work published 1949)

Sarafino, E. P. (1990). *Health psychology: Biopsychosocial interactions.* New York: Wiley.

Sarason, S. (1974). *The psychological sense of community: Prospects for a community psychology.* San Francisco: Jossey-Bass.

Sarri, R., & Galinsky, M. (1967). A conceptual framework for group development. In R. Vinter (Ed.), *Readings in group-work practice* (pp. 72–94). Ann Arbor, MI: Campus Publisher.

Sassen, S. (1994). *Cities in a world economy.* Thousand Oaks, CA: Pine Forge.

Satir, V. (1983). *Conjoint family therapy* (3rd ed.). Palo Alto, CA: Science and Behavior Books.

Schacter, S., & Singer, J. E. (1962). Cognitive, social, and physiological determinants of emotional states. *Psychological Review, 69,* 379–399.

Schein, E. (1992). *Organizational culture and leadership* (2nd ed.). San Francisco: Jossey-Bass.

Schneider, D. (1968). *American kinship: A cultural account.* Englewood Cliffs, NJ: Prentice-Hall.

Schneider, J., & Cook, K. (1995). Status inconsistency and gender: Combining revisited. *Small Group Research, 26,* 372–399.

Schoggen, P. (1989). *Behavior settings.* Stanford, CA: Stanford University Press.

Schriver, J. (1995). *Human behavior and the social environment: Shifting paradigms in essential knowledge for social work practice.* Boston: Allyn & Bacon.

Schuerman, J., Mullen, E., Stagner, M., & Johnson, P. (1989). First generation expert systems in social welfare. *Computers in Human Servcies, 4*(1–2), 111–122.

Schutt, R. (1996). *Investigating the social world: The process and practice of research.* Thousand Oaks, CA: Pine Forge.

Schutz, A. (1967). *The phenomenology of the social world.* (G. Walsh & F. Lehnert, Trans.) Evanston, IL: Northwestern University Press. (Original work published 1932)

Schwab, A. J., Bruce, M. E., & McRoy, R. G. (1985). A statistical model of child placement decisions. *Social Work Research & Abstracts, 21*(2), 28–34.

Schwab, A. J., Bruce, M. E., & McRoy, R. G. (1986). Using computer technology in child placement decisions. *Social Casework, 67*(6), 359–368.

Schwartz, M. (1973). Sexism in the social work curriculum. *Journal of Social Work Education, 9*(3), 65–70.

Schwartz, M. A., & Scott, B. M. (1994). *Marriages and families: Diversity and change.* Englewood Cliffs, NJ: Prentice Hall.

Schwartz, W. (1963). Small group science and group work practice. *Social Work, 8,* 40–41.

Scott, J. (1985). *Weapons of the weak: Everyday forms of peasant resistance.* New Haven, CT: Yale University Press.

Scott, J. (1990). *Domination and the arts of resistance: Hidden transcripts.* New Haven, CT: Yale University Press.

Scott, R. (1995). *Institutions and organizations.* Thousand Oaks, CA: Sage.

Seabury, B. (1971). Arrangement of physical space in social work settings. *Social Work, 16,* 43–49.

Sebba, R. (1991). The landscapes of childhood: The reflection of childhood's environment in adult memories and in children's attitudes. *Environment and Behavior, 23,* 395–422.

Seibert, S., & Gruenfeld, L. (1992). Masculinity, femininity, and behavior in groups. *Small Group Research, 23,* 95–112.

Seligman, M. (1992). *Helplessness: On depression, development, and death.* New York: Freeman.

Selzer, M. E. (1995). Mechanisms of functional recovery in traumatic brain injury. *Journal of Neurologic Rehabilitation, 9,* 73–82.

Sermabeikian, P. (1994). Our clients, ourselves: The spiritual perspective and social work practice. *Social Work, 39,* 178–183.

Seyle, H. (1991). History and present status of the stress concept. In A. Monat & R. S. Lazarus (Eds.), *Stress and coping: An anthology* (3rd ed.) (pp. 21–35). New York: Columbia University Press.

Shanklin, E. (1994). *Anthropology and race.* Belmont, CA: Wadsworth.

Shaw, M. E. (1981). *Group dynamics: The psychology of small group behavior* (3rd ed.). New York: McGraw-Hill.

Sheets, V., & Manzer, C. (1991). Affect, cognition, and urban vegetation: Some effects of adding trees along city streets. *Environment and Behavior, 23,* 285–304.

Sheridan, M. J. (1995). Honoring angels in my path: Spiritually-sensitive group work with persons who are incarcerated. *Reflections: Narratives of Professional Helping, 1*(4), 5–16.

Sheridan, M. J., & Amato–von Hemert, K. (in press). The role of religion and spirituality in social work education and practice: A survey of student views and experiences. *Journal of Social Work Education.*

Sheridan, M. J., & Bullis, R. K. (1991). Practitioners' views on religion and spirituality: A qualitative study. *Spirituality and Social Work Journal, 2*(2), 2–10.

Sheridan, M. J., Bullis, R. K., Adcock, C. R., Berlin, S. D., & Miller, P. (1992). Practitioners' personal and professional attitudes and behavior toward religion and spirituality: Issues for education and practice. *Journal of Social Work Education, 28,* 190–203.

Sheridan, M. J., Wilmer, C., & Atcheson, L. (1994). Inclusion of content on religion and spirituality in the social work curricululm: A study of faculty views. *Journal of Social Work Education, 30,* 363–376.

Sherman, E., & Reid, W. (1994). *Qualitative research in social work.* New York: Columbia University Press.

Shweder, R. (1991). *Thinking through cultures: Expeditions in cultural psychology.* Cambridge, MA: Harvard University Press.

Shweder, R. (1995). Anthropology's Romantic rebellion against the Enlightenment, or there's more to thinking than reason and evidence. In R. Shweder & R. LeVine (Eds.), *Culture theory: Essays on mind, self, and emotion* (pp. 27–66). New York: Cambridge University Press. (Original work published 1984)

Shweder, R., & LeVine, R. (Eds.). (1995). *Culture theory: Essays on mind, self, and emotion.* New York: Cambridge University Press. (Original work published 1984)

Sicoly, F. (1989). Prediction and decision making in child welfare. *Computers in Human Services, 5*(3–4), 43–56.

Siegel, S. (1991). Feedforward processes in drug tolerance and dependence. In R. Lister & H. Weingartner (Eds.), *Perspectives on cognitive neuroscience* (pp. 405–416). New York: Oxford University Press.

Siegel, S., Hinson, R., Krank, M., & McCully, J. (1982). Heroin "overdose" death: Contribution of drug-associated environmental cues. *Science, 216,* 436–437.

Silverman, D. (1971). *The theory of organizations: A sociological framework.* New York: Basic Books.

Silverman, D. (1994). On throwing away ladders: Re-writing the theory of organizations. In J. Hassard & M. Parker (Eds.), *Towards a new theory of organizations* (pp. 1–23). New York: Routledge.

Simon, H. (1957). *Administrative behavior* (2nd ed.). New York: Macmillan.

Sinha, S., & Mukherjee, N. (1996). The effect of perceived cooperation on personal space requirements. *Journal of Social Psychology, 136,* 655–657.

Sinha, S., Nayyar, P., & Mukherjee, N. (1995). Perception of crowding among children and adolescents. *Journal of Social Psychology, 135,* 263–268.

Siporin, M. (1975). *Introduction to social work practice.* New York: Macmillan.

Siporin, M. (1985). Current social work perspectives on clinical practice. *Clinical Social Work Journal, 13,* 198–217.

Siporin, M. (1986). Contribution of religious values to social work and the law. *Social Thought, 12*(4), 35–50.

Skocpol, T. (1979). *States and social revolutions.* New York: Cambridge University Press.

Skolnick, A. (1997). Family values: The sequel. *The American Prospect, 32* (May–June), 86–94.

Slater, S. (1995). *The lesbian family life cycle.* New York: Free Press.

Smart, B. (1993). *Postmodernity.* New York: Routledge.

Smeeding, T. (1991). Cross-national comparisons of inequality and poverty. In L. Osberg (Ed.), *Economic inequality and poverty: International perspectives* (pp. 39–59). Armonk, NY: M. E. Sharpe.

Smith, E. D. (1995). Addressing the psychospiritual distress of death as reality: A transpersonal approach. *Social Work, 40,* 402–413.

Smith, E. D., & Gray, C. (1995). Integrating and transcending divorce: A transpersonal model. *Social Thought, 18*(1), 57–74.

Snow, D., & Anderson, L. (1993). *Down on their luck: A study of homeless street people.* Berkeley: University of California Press.

Soderfeldt, M., Soderfeldt, B., & Warg, L. (1995). Burnout in social work. *Social Work, 40,* 638–646.

Sommer, R. (1969). *Personal space: The behavioral basis of design.* Englewood Cliffs, NJ: Prentice-Hall.

Sommer, R., & Ross, H. (1958). Social interaction on a geriatrics ward. *International Journal of Social Psychiatry, 4,* 128–133.

Soria, R., Stapleton, J. M., Gilson, S. F., Sampson-Cone, A., Henningfield, J. E., & London, E. D. (1996). Subjective and cardiovascular effects of intravenous nicotine in smokers and non-smokers. *Psychopharmacology, 128,* 221–226.

Sorokin, P. (1928). *Contemporary sociological theories.* New York: Harper.

Specht, H. (1994). Preface. In H. Specht & M. Courtney, *How social work has abandoned its mission: Unfaithful angels* (pp. ix–xii). New York: Free Press.

Specht, H. (1986). Social support, social networks, social exchange, and social work practice. *Social Service Review, 60,* 218–240.

Specht, H., & Courtney, M. E. (1994). *Unfaithful angels: How social work has abandoned its mission.* New York: Free Press.

Spencer, S. (1961). What place has religion in social work education? *Social Service Review, 35,* 161–170.

Spergel, I., & Grossman, S. (1997). The Little Village Project: A community approach to the gang problem. *Social Work, 42,* 456–470.

Spiegel, D., Bloom, J., Kraemer, H., & Gotthcil, E. (1989). Effect of psychosocial treatment on survival of patients with metastatic breast cancer. *Lancet, 334,* 888–891.

Spindler, G. (Ed.). (1997). *Education and cultural processes: Anthropological approaches.* Prospect Heights, IL: Waveland Press.

Spradley, J. (1979). *The ethnographic interview.* New York: Holt, Rinehart, & Winston.

Srole, L. (1972). Urbanization and mental health: Some reformulations. *American Scientist, 60,* 576–583.

Stacey, J. (1990). *Brave new families: Stories of domestic upheaval in late twentieth century America.* New York: Basic Books.

Staples, R., & Mirande, A. (1980). Racial and cultural variations among American families: A dicennial review of the literature on minority families. In F. M. Berardo (Ed.), *Decade review: Family research 1970–1979* (pp. 157–173). Minneapolis: National Council on Family Relations. [Also published as a special issue of *Journal of Marriage and the Family,* 1980, *42*(4)]

Stein, H., & Cloward, R. (1958). *Social perspectives on behavior: A reader in social science for social work and related professions.* New York: Free Press.

Stephens, K., & Clark, D. (1987). A pilot study on the effect of vis-ible stigma on personal space. *Journal of Applied Rehabilitation Counseling, 18,* 52–54.

Stewart B. McKinney Act. (1994). U.S.C. 11301, et seq.

Stocking, G. W., Jr. (1968). *Race, culture, and evolution: Essays on the history of anthropology.* New York: Free Press.

Stolte, J. F. (1994). Power. In M. Foshci & E. J. Lawler (Eds.), *Group processes: Sociological analyses* (pp. 149–176). Chicago: Nelson-Hall.

Strauss, A. (1961). *Images of the American city.* New York: Free Press.

Streeter, C., & Gillespie, D. (1992). Social network analysis. *Journal of Social Service Research, 16,* 201–221.

Stuart, R. (1989). Social learning theory: A vanishing or expanding presence? *Psychology: A Journal of Human Behavior, 26,* 35–50.

Sturman, A. (1980). Damage on buses: The effects of supervision. In R. Clarke & P. Mayhew (Eds.), *Designing out crime* (pp. 31–38). London: Her Majesty's Stationery Office.

Subramanian, K., & Ell, K. O. (1989). Coping with a first heart attack: A group treatment model for low-income Anglo, Black, and Hispanic patients. *Social Work with Groups, 12*(4), 99–117.

Sue, D. W., & Sue, D. (1990). *Counseling the culturally different: Theory and practice* (2nd ed.). New York: Wiley.

Sullivan, P. (1994). Should spiritual principles guide social policy? No. In H. J. Karger & J. Midgley (Eds.), *Controversial issues in social policy* (pp. 69–74). Boston: Allyn & Bacon.

Sundstrom, E., Bell, P., Busby, P., & Asmus, C. (1996). Environmental psychology: 1989–1994. *Annual Review of Psychology, 47,* 485–513.

Suttles, G. D. (1972). *The social construction of communities.* Chicago: University of Chicago Press.

Sviridoff, M., & Ryan, W. (1997). Community-centered family service. *Families in Society, 78,* 128–139.

Swenson, C. (1994). Clinical practice and the decline of community. *Journal of Teaching in Social Work, 10,* 195–212.

Swenson, C. H., Fuller, S., & Clements, R. (1993). Stage of religious faith and reactions to terminal cancer. *Journal of Psychology and Theology, 21,* 238–245.

Swidler, A. (1986). Culture in action: Symbols and strategies. *American Sociological Review, 51,* 273–286.

Tarrow, S. (1994). *Power in movement: Social movements, collective action, and politics.* New York: Cambridge University Press.

Tarrow, S. (1996). States and opportunities: The political structuring of social movements. In D. McAdam, J. McCarthy, & M. Zald (Eds.), *Comparative perspectives on social movements* (pp. 41–61). New York: Cambridge University Press.

Taylor, A., Wiley, A., Kuo, F., & Sullivan, W. (1998). Growing up in the inner city: Green spaces as places to grow. *Environment and Behavior, 30,* 3–27.

Taylor, E. H. (1989). Schizophrenia: Fire in the brain. *Social Work, 34*: 258–261.

Taylor, F. W. (1911). *Principles of scientific management.* New York: Harper & Row.

Taylor, R. (1988). *Human territorial functioning: An empirical, evolutionary perspective on individual and small group territorial cognitions, behaviors, and consequences.* Cambridge: Cambridge University Press.

Taylor, V. (1995). Watching for vibes: Bringing emotions into the study of feminist organizations. In M. Ferree & P. Martin (Eds.), *Feminist organizations: Harvest of the new women's movement* (pp. 223–233). Philadelphia: Temple University Press.

Thibaut, J. W., & Kelley, H. H. (1959). *The social psychology of groups.* New York: Wiley.

Thoits, P. A. (1989). The sociology of emotions. *Annual Review of Sociology, 15,* 317–342.

Thomas, R., Jr. (1991). *Beyond race and gender: Unleashing the power of your total work force by managing diversity.* New York: AMACOM.

Thompson, E. P. (1966). *The making of the English working class.* New York: Vintage Press.

Thompson, P. (1993). Postmodernism: Fatal distraction. In J. Hassard & M. Parker (Eds.), *Postmodernism and organizations* (pp. 183–203). Newbury Park, CA: Sage.

Thomson, R. G. (Ed.). (1996). *Freakery: Cultural spectacles of the extraordinary body.* New York: New York University Press.

Thyer, B. (1991). Behavioral social work: It is not what you think. *Arete, 16,* 1–9.

Thyer, B. (1994). Social learning theory: Empirical applications to culturally diverse practice. In R. Greene (Ed.), *Human behavior theory: A diversity framework* (pp. 133–146). New York: Aldine de Gruyter.

Titone, A. M. (1991). Spirituality and psychotherapy in social work practice. *Spirituality and Social Work Communicator, 2*(1), 7–9.

Tonnies, F. (1963). *Community and society* (C. P. Loomis, Ed.). New York: Harper & Row. (Original work published 1887)

Tracy, E., & Whittaker, J. (1990). The social network map: Assessing social support in clinical practice. *Families in Society, 71,* 461–470.

Traub, S. H., & Little, C. B. (1994). *Theories of deviance* (4th ed.). Itasca, IL: Peacock.

Tuckman, B. (1965). Developmental sequence in small groups. *Psychological Bulletin, 63,* 384–399.

Turner, J. H. (1996). The evolution of emotions in humans: A Darwinian-Durkheimian analysis. *Journal for the Theory of Social Behavior, 26*(1), 1–33.

Turner, R. P., Lukoff, D., Barnhouse, R. T., & Lu, F. G. (1995). Religious or spiritual problem: A culturally sensitive diagnostic category in the DSM-IV. *Journal of Nervous and Mental Disease, 183,* 435–444.

Ulrich, R. (1984). View through a window may influence recovery from surgery. *Science, 224,* 420–421.

U.S. Bureau of the Census. (1992). *Statistical abstracts of the United States: 1992* (112th ed.). Washington, DC: Author.

U.S. Bureau of the Census. (1998). *USA Statistics in brief: Health, social welfare, government, employment* [On-Line]. Available: http://www.census.gov/statab/www/part3.html

U.S. Department of Education, National Center for Education Statistics. (1997). *Dropout rates in the United States, 1996* (NCES 98-250). Washington, DC: Author.

U.S. Department of Labor. (1994/1995). *Occupational outlook handbook.* Washington, DC: Author.

Van de Ven, A. (1993). The institutional theory of John R. Commons: A review and commentary. *Academy of Management Review, 18,* 129–152.

Varady, D. (1986). Neighborhood confidence: A critical factor in neighborhood revitalization. *Environment and Behavior, 18,* 480–501.

Vaux, A. (1988). *Social support: Theory, research, and intervention.* New York: Praeger.

Vaux, A. (1990). An ecological approach to understanding and facilitating social support. *Journal of Social and Personal Relationships, 7,* 507–518.

Villemagne, V. L., Phillips, R. L., Liu, X., Gilson, S. F., Dannals, R. F., Wong, D. F., Harris, P. J., Riff, M., Pert, C., Bridge, P., & London, E. D. (1996). Peptide T and glucose metabolism in AIDS dementia complex. *The Journal of Nuclear Medicine, 37,* 1177–1180.

Vosler, N. R. (1990). Assessing family access to basic resources: An essential component of social work practice. *Social Work, 35,* 434–441.

Vosler, N. R. (1996). *New approaches to family practice: Confronting economic stress.* Thousand Oaks, CA: Sage.

Vosler, N. R., & Proctor, E. K. (1991). Family structure and stressors in a child guidance clinic population. *Families in Society, 72,* 164–173.

Vosler, N. R., & Robertson, J. G. (1998). Nonmarital co-parenting: Knowledge building for practice. *Families in Society, 79*(4), 149–159.

Voss, K. (1996). The collapse of a social movement: The interplay of mobilizing structures, framing, and political opportunities in the Knights of Labor. In D. McAdams, J. McCarthy, & M. Zald (Eds.), *Comparative perspectives on social movements* (pp. 227–258). New York: Cambridge University Press.

Wachs, T. (1992). *The nature of nurture.* Newbury Park, CA: Sage.

Wagner, G., Serafini, J., Rabkin, J., Remien, R., & Williams, J. (1994). Integration of one's religion and homosexuality: A weapon against internalized homophobia? *Journal of Homosexuality, 26*(4), 91–110.

Wagner, R. (1981). *The invention of culture.* Chicago: University of Chicago Press.

Wald, K. (1997). *Religion and politics in the United States* (3rd ed.). Washington, DC: Congressional Quarterly.

Wallace, J. (1989). A biopsychosocial model of alcoholism. *Social Casework, 70,* 325–332.

Wallace, R., & Wolf, A. (1995). *Contemporary sociological theory: Continuing the classical tradition* (4th ed.). Englewood Cliffs, NJ: Prentice-Hall.

Wallerstein, I. (1974–1989). *The modern world system* (Vols. 1–3). New York: Academic Press.

Walsh, F. (1993). Conceptualization of normal family processes. In F. Walsh (Ed.), *Normal family processes* (2nd ed.) (pp. 3–69). New York: Guilford.

Walsh, J. (1995). The impact of schizophrenia on the client's religious beliefs: Implications for families. *Families in Society, 76,* 551–558.

Walsh, J. (1998). Psychopharmacological treatment of bipolar disorder. *Research on Social Work Practice, 8,* 406–425.

Walsh, J., & Connelly, P. R. (1996). Supportive behaviors in natural support networks of people with serious mental illness. *Health and Social Work, 21,* 296–303.

Walsh, S. L., Gilson, S. F., Jasinski, D. R., Stapleton, J. M., Phillips, R. L., Dannals, R. F., Schmidt, J., Preston, K. L., Grayson, R., Bigelow, G. E., Sullivan, J. T., Contoreggi, C., & London, E. D. (1994). Buprenorphine reduces cerebral glucose metabolism in polydrug abusers. *Neuropsychopharmacology, 10,* 157–170.

Wamsley, G., & Zald, M. (1973). *The political economy of public organizations.* Lexington, MA: Heath.

Wang, C. (1992). Culture, meaning and disability: Injury prevention campaigns and the production of stigma. *Social Science and Medicine, 35,* 1093–1102.

Wapner, S. (1995). Toward integration: Environmental psychology in relation to other subfields of psychology. *Environment and Behavior, 27,* 9–32.

Warren, R. (1978). *The community in America.* Chicago: Rand McNally.

Warren, R. (1988). Observations on the state of community theory. In R. Warren & L. Lyon, *New perspectives on the American community* (5th ed.) (pp. 84–86). Chicago: Dorsey.

Wasserman, H., & Danforth, H. E. (1988). *The human bond: Support groups and mutual aid.* New York: Springer.

Watson, G. (1996). The perils of television. In *Gray Watson's television page* [On-line]. Available: http://www.letters.com/~gray/television.html

Weber, M. (1947). *The theory of economic and social organization.* New York: Free Press.

Weber., M. (1958). *The Protestant ethic and the spirit of capitalism* (T. Parsons, Trans.). New York: Scribner's. (Original work published 1904–1905)

Webster-Stratton, C. (1997). From parent training to community building. *Families in Society, 78,* 156–171.

Weenolsen, P. (1988). *Transcendence of loss over the life span.* New York: Hemisphere.

Weick, A. (1986). The philosophical context of a health model of social work. *Social Casework, 67,* 551–559.

Weick, A. (1994). Overturning oppression: An analysis of emancipatory change. In L. Davis (Ed.), *Building on women's strengths: A social work agenda for the twenty-first century.* New York: Haworth Press.

Weiner, B. (1985). An attributional theory of achievement motivation and emotion. *Psychological Review, 92,* 548–573.

Weisman, D. (1997). Does religion and spirituality have a significant place in the core HBSE curriculum? No. In M. Bloom & W. C. Klein (Eds.), *Controversial issues in human behavior in the social environment* (pp. 177–183). Boston: Allyn & Bacon.

Weisman, G. (1981). Modeling environment-behavior systems: A brief note. *Journal of Man-Environment Relations, 1*(2), 32–41.

Weitz, R. (1996). *The sociology of health, illness, and health care: A critical approach.* Belmont, CA: Wadsworth.

Wellman, B., & Leighton, B. (1979). Networks, neighborhoods, and communities: Approaches to the study of the community question. *Urban Affairs Quarterly, 14,* 363–390.

Wener, R., Frazier, W., & Farbstein, J. (1985). Three generations of evaluation and design of correctional facilities. *Environment and Behavior, 17,* 71–95.

Wenocur, S., & Soifer, S. (1997). Prospects for community organization. In M. Reisch & E. Gambrill (Eds.), *Social work in the 21st century* (pp. 198–209). Thousand Oaks, CA: Pine Forge.

Wentz, R. (1998). *The culture of religious pluralism.* Boulder, CO: Westview Press.

Werner, C., Altman, I., & Oxley, D. (1985). Temporal aspects of homes: A transactional perspective. In I. Altman & C. Werner (Eds.), *Home environments* (pp. 1–32). New York: Plenum.

Wesley, C. (1975). The women's movement and psychotherapy. *Social Work, 20,* 120–124.

West, M. (1986). *Landscape views and stress responses in the prison environment.* Unpublished master's thesis, University of Washington, Seattle.

Wheeler, H. (Ed.). (1973). *Beyond the punitive society.* San Francisco, CA: Freeman.

Whitehead, B. (1997). *The divorce culture.* New York: Knopf.

Whiting, B., & Whiting, J. (1975). *Children of six cultures: Studies of childrearing.* Cambridge, MA: Harvard University Press.

Wicker, A. (1979). *An introduction to ecological psychology.* Monterey, CA: Brooks/Cole.

Wicker, A. (1987). Behavior settings reconsidered: Temporal stages, resources, internal dynamics, context. In D. Stokols &

I. Altman (Eds.), *Handbook of environmental psychology* (Vol. 1, pp. 613–654). New York: Wiley.

Wiener, L., Moss, H., Davidson, R., & Fair, C. (1992). Pediatrics: The emerging psychosocial challenges of the AIDS epidemic. *Child and Adolescent Social Work Journal, 9,* 381–407.

Wilber, K. (1977). *The spectrum of consciousness.* Wheaton, IL: Quest.

Wilber, K. (1995). *Sex, ecology, spirituality: The spirit of evolution.* Boston: Shambhala.

Wilber, K. (1996). *A brief history of everything.* Boston: Shambhala.

Wilber, K. (1997). *The eye of spirit: An integral vision for a world gone slightly mad.* Boston: Shambhala.

Wilber, K., Engler, J., & Brown, D. (1986). *Transformations of consciousness: Conventional and contemplative perspectives on development.* Boston: Shambhala.

Wilensky, H., & Lebeaux, C. (1958). *Industrial society and social welfare* (enlarged paperback ed.). New York: Russell Sage Foundation.

Willer, D. (1987). *Theory and the experimental investigation of social structures.* New York: Gordon and Breach.

Williams, R. (1977). *Marxism and literature.* Oxford: Oxford University Press.

Williams, R. (1983). *Key words: A vocabulary of culture and society* (rev. ed.). New York: Oxford University Press.

Wilson, G., & Baldassare, M. (1996). Overall "sense of community" in a suburban region: The effects of localism, privacy, and urbanization. *Environment and Behavior, 28*(1), 27–43.

Wilson, J. Q. (1995). *On character.* Washington, DC: AIE Press.

Wilson, T. C. (1985). Urbanism and tolerance: A test of some hypotheses drawn from Wirth and Stouffer. *American Sociological Review, 50,* 117–123.

Witkin, S., & Gottschalk, S. (1988). Alternative criteria for theory evaluation. *Social Service Review, 62,* 211–224.

Wittine, B. (1987, September/October). Beyond ego. *Yoga Journal,* pp. 51–57.

Wolfensberger, W. (1973). *The principle of normalization in human services.* Toronto: National Institute on Mental Retardation.

Wood, M., & Wardell, M. L. (1983). G. H. Mead's social behaviorism vs. the astructural basis of symbolic interactionism. *Symbolic Interaction, 6*(1), 85–96.

Woolever, C. (1992). A contextual approach to neighbourhood attachment. *Urban Studies, 29*(1), 99–116.

Wuthnow, R. (1994). *Sharing the journey: Support groups and America's new quest for community.* New York: Free Press.

Yalom, I. D. (1995). *The theory and practice of group psychotherapy* (4th ed.). New York: Basic Books.

Yancey, W. (1971). Architecture, interaction, and social control: The case of a large-scale public housing project. *Environment and Behavior, 2,* 3–21.

Yang, B., & Brown, J. (1992). A cross-cultural comparison of preferences for landscape styles and landscape elements. *Environment and Behavior, 24,* 471–507.

Yellow Bird, M. J. (1995). Spirituality in First Nations story telling: A Sahnish-Hidatsa approach to narrative. *Reflections: Narratives of Professional Helping, 1*(4), 65–72.

Zald, M. (1996). Culture, ideology, and strategic framing. In D. McAdams, J. McCarthy, & M. Zald (Eds.), *Comparative perspectives on social movements* (pp. 261–274). New York: Cambridge University Press.

Zald, M., & McCarthy, J. (1987). *Social movements in an organizational society.* New Brunswick, NJ: Transaction.

Zastrow, C. (1997). *Social work with groups: Using the class as a group leadership laboratory* (4th ed.). Chicago: Nelson-Hall.

Zdravomyslova, E. (1996). Opportunities and framing in the transition to democracy: The case of Russia. In D. McAdam, J. McCarthy, & M. Zald (Eds.), *Comparative perspectives on social movements* (pp. 122–137). New York: Cambridge University Press.

Zola, I. K. (1993). Self, identity and the naming question: Reflections on the language of disability. In M. Nagler (Ed.), *Perspectives on disability* (2nd ed.) (pp. 15–23). Palo Alto, CA: Health Markets Research.

Zuravin, S. J. (1986). Residential density and urban child maltreatment: An aggregate analysis. *Journal of Family Violence, 1,* 307–322.

Zuravin, S. J. (1989). The ecology of child abuse and neglect: Review of the literature and presentation of data. *Violence and Victims, 4,* 1010–1020.

Culture *(continued)*
  personality and, 276–277
  practice orientation and, 281–284
  praxis and, 284–285
  preliminary definition of, 270–272
  social work practice and, 293–294
Culture of poverty Oscar Lewis's (1959) description of a
  subculture among groups of poor people in Mexico City
  and San Juan, Puerto Rico. He suggested that these groups
  are marked by a distinctive set of values and beliefs that
  include marginality, fatalism, sensuality, spontaneity,
  impulsiveness, and aggression, 281
Customs Beliefs, values, and behaviors, such as marriage
  practices, child-rearing practices, dietary preferences, and
  attire, that are handed down across generations and
  become a part of a people's traditions, 286, 287
Cyclical time Time based on repetitive, recurring, or
  spiraling cycles of behavior, 22

D

Daily hassles Common occurrences that are taxing; used to
  measure stress, 135
David, Thomas, 224
Davis, Kingsley, 259
de Beauvoir, Simone, 58
Decision making theory A theory that sees organizational
  decision makers as constrained and limited in their
  capacity for rational decision making, 308
Defense mechanisms Unconscious, automatic responses
  that enable a person to minimize perceived threats or keep
  them out of awareness entirely, 139–140
Defensible space Newman's theory that certain physical
  design features can reduce crime and fear of crime in
  neighborhoods by enhancing residents' motivation to
  defend their territory, 218–219
Defensive social movement A social movement with the
  goal of defending traditional values and social arrangements, 356
Dendrite, 89
Density Ratio of persons per unit area of a space, 210–211
  group processes and, 401–402
Deskilling Decrease in the skill level needed for jobs in a
  particular labor sector, usually driven by new technologies,
  245
Determinism A belief that persons are passive products of
  their circumstances, external forces, and/or internal urges,
  26

Developmental perspective An approach that focuses on
  how human behavior changes and stays the same across
  stages of the life cycle, 53
  application of, 54–55
  central ideas of, 53
  criticisms of, 53–54
Developmental social construction view The belief that
  social patterns and institutions evolve from people's
  decisions over time, and that these social arrangements can
  therefore be modified and changed, 419
Deviance A negative labeling assigned when one's behavior
  is considered to be in violation of a prescribed social order
  by a majority of significant others, 150–151
Dewey, John, 49
Diabetes mellitus A disease of the endocrine system
  resulting from insulin deficiency or resistance to insulin's
  effects, 92
  effects of, 92–94
  prevalence of, 94
Diagnostic and Statistical Manual of Mental Disorders (DSM)
  (American Psychiatric Association), 124, 149, 153
Diastolic blood pressure The lowest arterial pressure,
  occurring when the ventricles of the heart are relaxing.
  Bottom reading of blood pressure, 99
Diathesis A vulnerability to stress and predisposition to
  disorder, 137
Dimension A feature that can be focused on separately but
  that cannot be understood without considering its
  embeddedness with other features, 17–18
Dimensions of Human Behavior: The Changing Life Course
  (Hutchison), 29, 37
Disabilities. *See* Individuals with disabilities
Discourse theory of public administration A model of
  public administration that emphasizes facilitating
  discourse about public issues among groups with different
  views, 312, 314, 316
Discrimination, 242
Diversity. *See also* Gender; *specific ethnic groups*
  among families, 423–424
  among political leaders, 243–244
  culture and, 288–292
  in labor force, 245–246
  multiple perspectives and, 37, 39
  unity in, 344–345
Divorce rate, 238, 412
Dopamine (DA) A neurotransmitter thought to play a role in
  influencing emotional behavior, cognition, and motor
  activity, 91

TO THE OWNER OF THIS BOOK

We invite your reactions to the book as well as your questions and sugestions for improving it. Send us a note via e-mail or write your comments below and mail them in the attached self-addressed envelope.

Elizabeth D. Hutchison
Virginia Commonwealth University
ehutch@atlas.vcu.edu